Critical Theory
A Reader

Critical Theory
A Reader

Edited and
introduced by
DOUGLAS TALLACK

HARVESTER
WHEATSHEAF

New York   London   Toronto   Sydney   Tokyo   Singapore

First published 1995 by
Harvester Wheatsheaf
Campus 400, Maylands Avenue
Hemel Hempstead
Hertfordshire, HP2 7EZ
A division of
Simon & Schuster International Group

Typeset in 10/12 pt Sabon by
Mathematical Composition Setters Ltd, Salisbury
Printed and bound in Great Britain by
Redwood Books, Trowbridge, Wiltshire

Library of Congress Cataloging in Publication Data

This information is available from the publisher.

British Library Cataloguing in Publication Data

A catalogue record for this book is available from
the British Library

ISBN 0-7450-1533-6

1 2 3 4 5   99 98 97 96 95

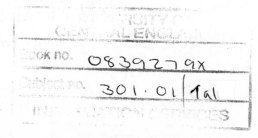

Contents

4: *Marxism*   265

5: *Post-Foundational Ethics and Politics*   355

Introduction:
Critical Theory:
Canonic Questions

Although there is no ideal moment to produce a Critical Theory *Reader*, the selection of texts can at least be informed by an estimate of the current intellectual situation. Critical Theory is patently no longer the up-and-coming field it was when the first post-New Criticism anthologies appeared in the early 1980s. In spite of damaging funding cuts and constraints, there has been a marked growth of theory and theory-related courses over the past fifteen years, with academic appointments (though not enough) to staff them. Indeed, as Perry Anderson and then Christopher Norris have observed, there is probably a relationship between hard political times and the flourishing of theory (see Anderson, 1979; Norris, 1990). But – less sceptically – publishers' lists convey the remarkable extent and high level of intellectual activity as well as the increasing interest in theory on the part of undergraduates and postgraduates, and beyond higher education as well. And, most revealingly, the minor genre of anti-theory polemics has taken a turn which suggests that it is the traditional disciplines or sections of those disciplines which feel embattled. In sum, Critical Theory is on the way to becoming established – so much so that its radical credentials are being challenged by a revived Cultural Studies, as well as by doubts that even a structuralist, post-structuralist, Marxist, psycho-analytic, feminist loop cannot contain current theorisations of, for example, gender and race. It sounds almost heretical to say so, but there is the basis for a canon in 'Critical Theory', itself now the most acceptable, if imprecise, generic name for a body of texts which reflects critically upon claims for disciplinary knowledge while occupying an (almost) indispensable position in a number of humanities and social science disciplines.

The first important publications of Roland Barthes, Jacques Derrida, Michel Foucault and Louis Althusser are now thirty to forty years old, while versions of Jacques Lacan's 'The Mirror Stage as Formative of the Function of the I' (Reading 2.10) date from the mid-1930s. And what gets called contemporary Western Marxism still relies in good part on the work of Benjamin and Adorno from the 1930s. Only an editor with a polemical agenda would omit these figures, or indeed – to hazard a guess – much more than a third of the theorists included in this

Reader. There are bound to be omissions, of course, though in some instances (Mikhail Bakhtin stands out) finding a manageable, mostly self-contained text was more of a deciding factor than any identifiable and consistent agenda. But this Introduction should not be given over to the usual assuaging of the editor's guilt at omissions, so it is important to draw a few conclusions from the texts which have been reprinted. To admit, and then seek to reflect, the authority of Theory, rather than to argue for it as earlier collections have needed to, can be a way of posing important questions instead of dodging them. This Introduction is kept deliberately short to allow for longer Introductions to each of the five Sections to follow, but there is space to broach a few questions. And since textbooks and anthologies are signs of their times, these questions probably have a relevance beyond the specific problems of selection and organisation which provoked them.

If many of the theorists select themselves, the choice of texts to represent them and the larger movements and schools can still allow important points to be made; as just two examples indicate. In the context of Section 1, the choice of a 'classic', such as Roland Barthes's 'Myth Today' (1957; Reading 1.1), demonstrates how difficult it is to separate structuralism from post-structuralism, and either of these categories from ideological analysis. The second issue, at least, remains live, and many of the most absorbing current debates are clarified by fully recognising the significance of structuralism. Its diagrammatics and oppositional grids now seem as dated as existentialist dilemmas and New Critical exegeses, but 'Myth Today' is a reminder of just how crucial structuralism has been to so much of what followed. The trajectory of Barthes's own career confirms the intimacy of the relationship between the early semiological ventures and the later pleasure in textuality, though, arguably, the political edge which is so apparent in the later sections of 'Myth Today' gets diffused in Barthes's work even as it has proved enormously influential in Cultural Studies and aspects of Marxist theory, where the arguments between structure and history are no less vital than they were for Sartre and Lévi-Strauss. The second example is Luce Irigaray's 'Why Define Sexed Rights?' (Reading 5.6). To include this 1988 interview, and not the more familiar 'This sex which is not one' or 'When our lips speak together' (both 1977), and to position Irigaray's work to one side of the expected feminist or psychoanalytic frameworks, is to question the categorising imperative in canon-formation, even as the status of Irigaray is rightly endorsed. But, more interestingly, 'Why Define Sexed Rights?' points to the important effect upon a leading theorist's work when she enters public debate more directly. One of the directions to be discerned in theoretical discourse is towards such engagement – either directly, as when Irigaray writes on AIDS, or Jacques Derrida comments on ethnic and nationalist disputes in post-communist Europe; or through a changing vocabulary in which ethics, the law and politics receive more prominence.

Acknowledging the (near) canonical status of Critical Theory can usefully spotlight some of its constituent elements, the widely recognised categories which are still the site of fiercer arguments than those which now attend Theory in general. These arguments are yet another reminder that the 1990s are one of those periods when categories and the metanarratives they generate seem to be especially vulnerable. But while the threat to Marxism (to take the obvious example) has historical causes which culminated in the collapse of communism, there is also a logic within post-1960s theory which should not be discounted as an explanatory cause of what is probably too loosely called postmodern dispersal and differentiation. One way to generalise about Critical Theory is to see it as a set of theoretical discourses variously predicated upon the following highly unstable tendencies and preoccupations: first, ground-breaking methodological advances, as in structuralism, which deliberately bracket hermeneutic questions because they are thought to rely too simplistically on traditional bases for knowledge, only for content-questions to return to haunt the whole project; second, deconstructive self-reflexivity; third, an increasingly immanent form of critique as the best option for inhabiting yet distancing oneself from a capitalism which is no longer thought to be definitively located; and, fourth, the substitution of power for truth as the primary focus for analysis. This anti-foundationalist, anti-essentialist logic in most contemporary theory makes 'Theory' a rather odd overall designation – but no less indispensable, as the work of Christopher Norris demonstrates (see especially Norris, 1985, 1990). His project, stretching back to a primer on deconstruction and coming through to his emergence as a theorist in his own right, is instructive precisely because of its consistent defence of Theory (Derrida, in particular, but also Paul de Man) in the service of philosophic rigour and truth. For Norris, there is an

> ambivalence about 'theory' as practised by post-structuralists, post-modernists and other fashionable figures on the current intellectual scene. That is to say, their 'radicalism' has now passed over into a species of disguised apologetics for the socio-political status quo, a persuasion that 'reality' is constituted through and through by the meanings, values or discourses that presently compose it, so that nothing could count as effective counter-argument, much less a critique of existing institutions on valid theoretical grounds. (Norris, 1990, pp. 3–4)

The explanatory value of some of the chief categories of Critical Theory are equally at stake. For substantive reasons, having to do with intellectual debts (one theorist to another) and the need for political cohesion (notably in the instance of feminism), it remains either necessary, or at least worthwhile, to retain the familiar organising concepts of structuralism, post-structuralism, psychoanalytic theory, feminism and Marxism. Nevertheless, the contents of each of the first four Sections of this collection strain the limits of categories or – more positively – extend their purview. It is illuminating, as well as disconcerting, when theorists cannot easily be contained by categories; for instance, the impossibility of understanding Althusser other than in the competing and overlapping contexts of structuralism, psycho-analytic theory and Marxism.

As a pedagogical tool, diagrams usually help the teacher rather than the students, but it may assist readers of this collection at least to mention that its ground-plan was a bewildering diagram of criss-cross, one-way and two-way solid and broken arrows, and therefore quite different from the ordered list of Contents. The respective pros and cons of section categories and permeable boundaries can be illustrated by taking the designation 'feminism', and considering how and why the feminist theorists in this collection could be differently located along a spectrum between concentration (in a single and much larger section which confirms commonality) and dissemination (for strategic, interventionist purposes). In a different, case-study-based collection, the politics of theory could be demonstrated *in situ*, as it were; here, the politics of theory may be mapped according to the respective allegiances to position and critique. The example of feminism is a salutary warning not to relegate categories to starting points or mere orthodoxies. Both can be spurs to action and can provide the framework for some of the most vital arguments, since these often occur where there is common ground. The Introductions to the five Sections of the book will deal with such arguments – for instance, between commonality based upon difference or upon sameness, or between those with degrees of allegiance to a linguistic model stemming from Saussure or an economic model deriving from Marx, and the extent to which these diverge.

Starting points for recent and current debates understood in a different sense – that is, as the foundational texts of Marx, Freud and Saussure, among others – pose a considerable problem for a collection such as this. Given the aim of reprinting examples of the latest theorising alongside canonic statements by the generation of Derrida and Foucault, seminal nineteenth- and early-twentieth-century texts have not been included, though some attempt is made to outline their importance in the Section Introductions. Another practical reason for restricting coverage is a forthcoming *Reader* in the same series devoted to the founding texts of Critical Theory. But there are intellectual reasons, too, most importantly that theorists create their own starting points: Althusser's Marx is different from Adorno's; Kate Millett's Freud and Philip Rieff's and Jacques Lacan's are barely recognisable as the same figure. This is probably the point to explain that, in an effort to move some of the discussions along, structuralism is underplayed in these Readings. I hope that this shortcoming is also partially compensated for by a lengthy Introduction which would otherwise seem out of proportion, though a further justification is that ideas do have a history – one of Michel Foucault's more polemical pronouncements notwithstanding – and structuralist and post-structuralist ideas consistently inform the other sections of this *Reader*.

Even at the macro-level of broad categories, it is hard to contain the centrifugal tendency in the most recent theorising, and so the luxury of a wild card has been claimed. The final Section, Section 5, on Post-Foundational Ethics and Politics, lays out one broad area of debate, which is neither immune from postmodern developments nor a mere symptom. The Section title does not imply what would be a silly assumption – that post-structuralists or Marxists, for instance, are not political or ethical – though one of the aims of the concluding part of this *Reader* is to return to Christopher Norris's theme and reflect upon the continuing effects of Derrida's work and the loss of old certainties within Western Marxism. Readings

5.4 and 5.5, by Jean-François Lyotard and Emmanuel Lévinas, indicate that there are other, very different, responses to the current crisis in theory from Norris's; while Richard Rorty's 'The Priority of Democracy to Philosophy' (1988; Reading 5.1) is an eloquent anti-crisis statement. The inclusion in Section 5 of pieces by Seyla Benhabib, Martha Nussbaum and Rorty, and the accompanying discussion of Hannah Arendt, also reinforce a claim implicit in the selection, elsewhere in this collection, of work by Philip Rieff (2.1), Kate Millett (2.3), Carol Gilligan (3.6), Heidi Hartmann (3.1) and Raymond Williams (4.4). That claim is for a less exclusively continental canon (or one heavily influenced by French and German theory) and for more recognition of Anglo-American (mostly American) engagements with common issues. This kind of *rapprochement* would have been frowned upon five or ten years ago, so sharply did much Critical Theory define itself against the Anglo-American tradition. A further consequence of achieving hard-won recognition is that theorists may feel more inclined to look again at figures like Rieff, Millett, Gilligan and also Herbert Marcuse (Reading 2.2) and Sebastiano Timpanaro (Reading 4.6), but also at Hannah Arendt, John Rawls, Alasdair MacIntyre, Erich Auerbach. ... If Section 5, in particular, of this *Reader* is any guide, it looks as though Critical Theory is reaching canonical status only for the controversies which have primarily defined it to be shifting ground. And there are other changes of orientation. To use Christopher Norris as an example again, it is interesting that he has recently changed his academic affiliation from a Department of English to a Department of Philosophy in the same institution, presumably because he feels that that is where the arguments are to be conducted. This is not to say that theoretical arguments do not physically take place in literature or English departments; rather, that the important breakthroughs have already been made there, even if there is still plenty of resistance, and that the crisis of 'English Studies' is no longer so pressing for most theorists. The final Section of this *Reader* suggests that some of the most important engagements could be with figures in political theory and, in the longer term, with policy studies.

One of the consequences, then, of the perceived authority of Critical Theory is that it has largely subsumed Literary Theory. Theorists with very literary-critical projects or training (J. Hillis Miller [1.6], Paul de Man [1.5], Gayatri Spivak [3.3], Naomi Schor [2.5], Raymond Williams [4.4] and Fredric Jameson [4.5] are examples from this collection) become part of larger enquiries into representation and history; some, it can be assumed, will therefore appear in their own right in the history of ideas in the late twentieth century. Therefore, one step which this *Reader* can take is to move on from the narrowly literary concerns which have dominated most collections since the impact of structuralism was felt. Many of the more literary-theoretical collections are still in print, so there is now no compelling reason to include extracts by the Russian Formalists, the Arnold–Eliot–New Critical line, and the Reader Response theorists. And there is no need to look for an explicit literary or aesthetic connection when deciding what to include from a theorist such as Michel Foucault (Reading 1.4). Students in 'English', just as much as those in the Social Sciences, are served better by an extract from *Power/Knowledge*, which identifies the conditions of knowledge in any regime of discourse, than by yet another reprinting of 'What is an author?'. Literary Theory and aesthetics more generally are undoubtedly among the most important sources of ideas and issues, and Herbert Marcuse (Reading 2.2), Julia Kristeva (Reading 1.3), Adorno (Reading 4.2), Derrida (Reading 1.2), and Paul de Man (Reading 1.5), in different ways, find in a carefully guarded formalism, and perhaps in aesthetics too, significant positions of distance and critique. But it does not follow that an attempt must be made to demonstrate the relevance of this or that theoretical position to the study of literature or, for that matter, any other distinct 'object' or even practice.

A related and probably more contentious step which this *Reader* can take is to make an unashamed case for ideas in a rather old-fashioned sense, and for the necessity for theoretical speculation as a vital stage in any kind of practice. Readers from different academic backgrounds *do* come together over ideas that transcend specific situations, and only some take their agreements and disagreements back to their own situations. Others find that theoretical speculation reveals different problems, obscured by situatedness. If all education is caught up with institutions, then Critical Theory is no exception, especially as it becomes more established. But this does not mean that the discussion of theoretical texts in an educational institution is not enlightening in the broadest sense – a concession which Foucault readily makes in Reading 1.4, but which those enamoured of domination theory and obsessed with only the positivistic elements in Enlightenment thinking tend to overlook. Theory can provoke reflection upon and intervention in existing disciplines (including literary studies or 'English'), but it can also assist in the formulation of broadly political/philosophical positions which operate beyond, as well as within, institutions. It can therefore usefully check as well as stimulate action until more is known and understood. If there is one Reading in this collection which illustrates this last point while also serving as an instance of the kind of old-fashioned discussion of ideas which Critical Theory can now afford to recognise, it is the chapter from Philip Rieff's *Freud: The mind of the moralist* (1959; Reading 2.1).

The preceding remarks suggest the potential for a rift between Critical Theory and Cultural Studies, with the editors of a recent collection entitled *Cultural Studies* claiming that 'Through the last two decades, when theory has sometimes seemed a decontextualized scene of philosophical speculation, cultural studies has regularly theorized in response to particular social, historical, and material conditions' (Grossberg *et al.*, 1992, p. 6). A Critical Theory *Reader* is not a contextualising exercise, however: indeed, no anthology can successfully be a sociology of knowledge, and even *Cultural Studies* tends towards theoretical speculation, since its texts must bear some transplanting if they are to have any commonality. There is a positive politics to commonality as well as to difference. A Critical Theory *Reader* can, though, encourage another kind of questioning of the autonomy implied in the word Theory: namely, that texts – theoretical texts as much as any other – interrelate; they are, in some formulations, inescapably intertextual, and sometimes explicitly so. Every editor hopes that some readers will go from cover to cover and, in the case of this collection, pick up the explicit interconnections, among them Habermas responding to Rorty, Kristeva to Derrida, Spivak to Cixous, and Miller to de Man. The last of these connections is the most revealing, because in this highly specialised (even precious) encounter between two literary critics are indications that literary deconstruction is more aware of its professionalised self-preoccupation. Perhaps the criticisms of Critical and Literary Theory from the Cultural Studies side are primarily about their 'establishment' feel, rather than about the ideas involved. If so, the impetus behind Cultural Studies, though not necessarily its situatedness, is a cue for theorists to expand the range of debates and ask some tough questions about the relationship between being 'critical' (through deconstruction or critique) and being constructive, possibly to the point when theorists who admit to the inadequacy of utopianism as a plan for the future (it continues as critique, of course), or accept the metaphorical status of determinate theories of history, have to contemplate the adjacent spheres of policy studies, political theory and ethical philosophy, and to resist the temptations to prejudge the respective claims of radicalism and reform.

To recognise a canonic aspect to Critical Theory is, finally, to be obliged to ask what else is going on in an increasingly central intellectual field which is itself defined by critiques and displacements of centrist positions, by an avant-gardist interest in the new, and by a commitment to the marginal and the excluded. The position of this mainstream *Reader* alongside two companion volumes (*Postmodernism*, edited by Thomas Docherty; and *Colonial Discourse and Post-Colonial Theory*, edited by Patrick Williams and Laura Chrisman) makes this last task even more urgent. Rather than meet the problem by including sections on such fields as post-colonialism and the latest twists in the postmodernist debate, or by subdividing existing categories, the impact of newer developments is reflected by choosing Readings which are, in many instances, already caught up in cross-boundary discussions, and by locating contentious texts in established categories: for example, Ernesto Laclau and Chantal Mouffe's postmodern rethinking of politics (Reading 4.1) and Trinh T. Minh-ha's essay on Third World difference (Reading 3.4). So quickly do -isms become established that the final Section of this *Reader* might also be regarded as adopting a critical position with reference to postmodernism.

No one could honestly claim to have expertise across a field which, for all its importance, is so difficult to define, whether substantively or by reference to what it is not. It would simply not have been possible to have put this *Reader* together without the experience, stretching back to 1980, of teaching, supervising and doing research in the School of Critical Theory at the University of Nottingham. With the exception of one specific acknowledgement in the final Section of the collection, it would be invidious to identify certain staff and students. I hope, however, that those who have helped me with particular suggestions, or 'over the years', will recognise their assistance. It will only confirm my high regard for them if they all think that they would have done the job better themselves.

1 □ Structuralism and Post-Structuralism

Introduction

Few texts can convey the crucial insights of structuralism while, at the same time, anticipating the reaction against it, loosely termed post-structuralism, *and* defending structuralism against the charge that it is simply a more scientific formalism and, as such, just as apolitical. Roland Barthes's 'Myth Today' (Reading 1.1) meets these requirements so successfully that it is hard to accept 1957 as the publication date for *Mythologies*, the book which collects a number of case studies of contemporary culture and rounds them off with such a stunning theoretical excursus.

In a *Reader* which seeks to update some of the theoretical debates of the past thirty-to-forty years, and in which all the Readings in Section 1 are departures from or, more accurately, departures from within structuralism, it is tempting to relegate the movement which so dominated intellectual life in the 1960s and 1970s to some kind of pre-history of what is now termed Critical Theory. It is as well, therefore, to devote extra space to structuralism and take a cue from Barthes who, early in 'Myth Today', defines the central concepts, 'signifier', 'signified' and 'sign', and summarises the vital contribution of Ferdinand de Saussure, while adding that 'semiology has not yet come into being' (Barthes, 1972b, p. 111). In *Elements of Semiology*, published in 1964, Barthes maintains that semiology can best prosecute its ambition to be a science of all signs by adopting the model of language, because linguistic signs have been more systematically examined than any other sign system. The particular system or discipline can then be investigated and its semiological functioning laid bare as never before, at the same time as a methodology is put in place which encourages interdisciplinary analysis, on the grounds that signification is what is common to different social and cultural activities. The tendency in Anglo-American intellectual life during the 1970s was to carry over structuralist advances primarily into literary theory because of literature's patently linguistic character (it was precisely this notion of a lowest common denominator which provoked predictable responses from many literary critics). Consequently, the indiscriminate quality of *Mythologies* needs to be emphasised. For all its claims to facilitate close, system-specific analysis, structuralism crossed boundaries as much as it established them. In the 1960s Saussure's model of language became paradigmatic for a number of important structuralist ventures which sought to analyse as systems of signs fashion, advertising, narrative and poetry, and whole cultures, as in Barthes's *Empire of Signs* (1970). Evidence of how wide-ranging was the structuralist endeavour may be found in Jacques Ehrmann's *Structuralism* (1970; first published as a special issue of *Yale French Studies* in 1966), a collection which rarely appears on reading lists now but was an interdisciplinary education to many readers.

In the *Course in General Linguistics* (first published in 1916), reconstructed posthumously from lectures delivered between 1907 and 1911, Saussure emerges as one of the great modern systematisers, adamant that any field of enquiry requires a synchronic rather than a diachronic or developmental analysis. Although the move towards synchronicity, if instituted as a theoretical principle rather than treated as a methodological manoeuvre, stored up problems for later theorists, who were persuaded by structuralism's insights but committed to historical/political projects, the benefits were none the less considerable, and can be appreciated in a few classics of structuralist analysis: Claude Lévi-Strauss's 'The structural study of myth' (1955); A.J. Greimas's *Sémantique structurale* (1966); Tzvetan Todorov's *The Fantastic: A structural approach to a literary genre* (1970); and Gérard Genette's *Narrative Discourse* (1972).

Hayden White's *Metahistory: The historical imagination in nineteenth-century Europe* (1973) is one of the most sophisticated American products of the structuralist revolution in thought. White pursues the disagreement between Lévi-Strauss and Jean-Paul Sartre over structure versus history by directing the linguistic and synchronic turn against historical explanation itself. He argues that the histories written by Michelet, Ranke, Tocqueville and Burckhardt are narrative emplotments rather than records of facts. As linguistic and structural entities, these histories can be distinguished by tropological preferences; Barthes is more forthright still in 'The discourse of history' (1967): 'the fact can only have a linguistic existence, as a term in a discourse, and yet it is exactly as if this existence were merely the "copy", purely and simply, of another existence situated in the extra-structural domain of the "real"' (Barthes, 1981, p. 17). Hence the polemical intent of Barthes's essay title, 'Myth Today', as a justification for his explanation of how it is that such cultural practices as wrestling matches, advertisements and menus signify each time they are enacted within a recognised system, which the proverbial visitor from Mars would have to learn 'today'.

The usual stopping place for theorists who have worked off Saussure's *Course* is this statement:

> in language there are only differences. Even more important: a difference generally implies positive terms between which the difference is set up; but in language there are only differences *without positive terms*. Whether we take the signified or the signifier, language has neither ideas nor sounds that existed before the linguistic system, but only conceptual and phonic differences that have issued from the system. The idea or phonic substance that a sign contains is of less importance than the other signs that surround it. (Saussure, 1974, p. 120)

Saussure's insight leads off in a number of directions. The idea of a differential relationship between signs is an affront to a literary criticism and an aesthetics in general deriving from Romanticism, because it is at the root of the claim that there is an arbitrary relationship between the signifier (phonic or graphic) and the signified (the mental concept). Structuralism, as it developed out of Saussure's work, contested the assumption that there is a natural meaning inherent in a sign, or at least in certain signs sometimes designated poetic signs. For an indication of the challenge which the notion of the arbitrary sign posed for the hope or assumption that words could be reattached to things and to an original design, and that inauthenticity in language could be checked, Saussure can be put against the American Romantic Henry David Thoreau. For Saussure, arbitrariness went all the way down to the individual letter, as Jonathan Culler explains in his Introduction to *Course in General Linguistics*: 'one may write *t* in numerous ways, so long as one preserves its differential value. There is no positive substance which defines it; the only requirement is that one keep it distinct from other letters with which it might be confused, such as *l, f, b, i, k*' (Saussure, 1974, p. xix). For Thoreau, however, writing about a thawing bank of sand in his book *Walden* (1854):

> No wonder that the earth expresses itself outwardly in leaves, it so labors with the idea inwardly. … The overhanging leaf sees here its prototype. *Internally*, whether in the globe or animal body, it is a moist thick *lobe*, a word especially applicable to the liver and lungs and the *leaves* of fat ('… *globus*, lobe, globe; also lap, flap, and many other words); *externally*, a dry thin *leaf*, even as the *f* and *v* are a pressed and dried *b*. The radicals of *lobe* are *lb*, the soft mass of the *b* (single-lobed or B, double-lobed), with the liquid *l* behind it pressing forward. (Thoreau, 1980, p. 204)

Saussurean structuralism instituted a gap between the world of signs and the world of objects or referents, though even to put it this way points to the tenacity of a referential model of signification (and to a hesitancy which post-structuralist thinkers exploited). The point, though, is that without a natural relationship between signifier and signified – to which Thoreau gives hyperbolic expression – the only way meaning can be explained is within the context of the system of language. It follows, then – and Saussure says as much in the statement above – that meanings, too (the sphere of the concept or signified), are relational. Before inspecting this conclusion, a second ramification of Saussure's diacritical model should be looked at.

By adopting a difference rather than reference model of language, Saussure – less dramatically than Darwin, Marx and Freud – undermines a consciousness-centred philosophy. To transfer attention from causal and originating explanations for meaning to structural explanations reveals that any sign is intelligible not by virtue of a self-conscious intender but through its differential relations with other signs in the linguistic system. The identity of an element in the linguistic system is arrived at negatively, according to how it differs from other elements in the system. This diacritical form of explanation provokes the radical idea that nothing is complete in itself. Secure limits and boundaries get transgressed: where does the self begin and end if, as Emile Benveniste insists in *Problems in General Linguistics* (1966), the personal pronoun 'I' cannot be defined outside the linguistic reality in which it manifests itself?

Not surprisingly, given the large-scale reaction against phenomenology and existentialism under way in France since the 1960s, certain pronouncements were trumpeted as the clarion call of the structuralist (and then post-structuralist) revolution. Barthes's expression 'the death of the author', or Derrida's 'the ends of man', were taken out of context and, in the furore, the valuable journeyman dimension of structuralism (particularly the work of Genette, Greimas and Todorov) received less credit than it deserved. More importantly, in context, the anti-humanism of the Saussurean model can be seen as potentially richer in intellectual content than transcendental views of the self because, arguably, it is not anti-humanist at all. Take, as an instance of the kind of statement which has been regularly misunderstood, Foucault's announcement in *The Order of Things* (1966):

> It is comforting, however, and a source of profound relief to think that man is only a recent invention, a figure not yet two centuries old, a new wrinkle in our knowledge, and that he will disappear again as soon as that knowledge has discovered a new frame. (Foucault, 1970, p. xxiii)

Foucault is setting aside the transcendental, even theological, self dating back to the late eighteenth century as precisely that – a historical concept which is no longer an adequate explanatory principle for the 'systems of regularities' which his archaeological approach reveals:

> If there is one approach that I do reject, however, it is that (one might call it, broadly speaking, the phenomenological approach) which gives absolute priority to the observing subject, which attributes a constituent role to an act, which places its own point of view at the origin of all historicity – which, in short, leads to a transcendental consciousness. It seems to me that the historical analysis of scientific discourse should, in the last resort, be subject, not to a theory of the knowing subject but rather to a theory of discursive practice. (Foucault, 1970, p. xiv)

The problem is not with the death of theological 'man' because – quite conceivably – that figure has impeded understanding of the human world, at least during the past century, when it has lagged behind intellectual and technological developments. The problem is with the lack in structuralism and some unguarded versions of post-structuralism, of a theory of agency and a way of talking about change over time. After all, looking at the workings of a modern society with a suitable scepticism about the more extreme formulations of the ideology of the sovereign self, of individualism, one can arrive at the quite sensible conclusion that the system is simply that which gives meaning to the individuals within it; it is the water that fish swim in. It is – in Foucault's terms when he writes about epistemes – that which allows sense to be made. And this, after all, is the key structuralist insight into intelligibility, though Foucault protests against any structuralist affiliations even as he memorably describes the conditions of knowledge without making reference to a transcendental knower. Once the relationship between structuralism and post-structuralism has been clarified, the question of agency and historical change calls for some further discussion, since it reappears in all the other Sections of this *Reader*.

In tension with Saussure's aim of marking out an area for study – in his case, the system of language – is the potential for instability in the notion of difference, which does not respect boundaries and undermines the self-sufficiency of any entity. It is this tension which partly explains the sense in which structuralism is inhabited by its supposed successor, post-structuralism. The chronology of the two movements also warns against any strict separation. Derrida's 'Structure, sign, and play in the discourse of the human sciences' was delivered as a conference paper in 1966 and reprinted in *Writing and Difference* in 1967, the year of publication for *Speech and Phenomena* and *Of Grammatology*, which contains his deconstruction of Saussure's theory of the sign. Foucault came to prominence with *The Order of Things*, published in the heyday of structuralism, while Jacques Lacan's route to a version of post-structuralism has its starting point in the 1930s controversies within the psychoanalytic profession. What is apparent, though, especially in Derrida and Foucault, is the way in which certain aspects of structuralism are accentuated to striking effect. First, Derrida – bearing in mind, of course, that his position is developed and refined in relation to other figures and movements besides Saussure and structuralism; notably, from the modern period, Hegel, Nietzsche, Freud, and Husserlian phenomenology. Derrida's relations with structuralism are particularly acute, however, because structuralism, far from advancing any kind of metaphysical simple (the self, reality, truth, God, history), seems to mark the break from such thinking. Yet the first sentence of 'Structure, sign, and play', the essay which brought Derrida wide attention, produces a tremor in the structuralist project:

> Perhaps something has occurred in the history of the concept of structure that could be called an 'event', if this loaded word did not entail a meaning which it is precisely the function of structural – or structuralist – thought to reduce or suspect. (Derrida, 1978, p. 278)

Derrida's hesitation over the word 'event' is a reminder that in his concern to complicate the concept of structure, he remains equally sceptical about the other side of the debate between structure and history, as is noticeable in the extract from 'Positions' (Reading 1.2). In 'Structure, sign, and play', however, his target is structure and the way in which the use of the concept by, presumably, structuralists has ruled out what he calls 'the structurality of structure', and what Roland Barthes rightly refers to as 'the structuralist activity'. In some respects, Derrida's alternative to the stability of 'structure' is unfortunate, since the notion of 'free play' is at odds with the carefulness of his reading of texts, and has also encouraged accusations of frivolity or – more damagingly in the long run – of an easy-going relativism. Derrida's more telling contribution is apparent elsewhere in the same essay:

> If totalization no longer has any meaning, it is not because the infiniteness of a field cannot be covered by a finite glance or a finite discourse, but because the nature of the field – that is, language and a finite language – excludes totalization. This field is in effect that of *play*, that is to say, a field of infinite substitutions only because it is finite,

that is to say, because instead of being an inexhaustible field, as in the classical hypothesis, instead of being too large, there is something missing from it: a center which arrests and founds the play of substitutions. One could say ... that this movement of play, permitted by the lack, or absence of a center or origin, is the movement of *supplementarity*. (Derrida, 1978, p. 289)

'Supplementarity' refers back to the differential relationship between signs in Saussure and the claim that no sign (and no entity, for that matter) is complete in itself but depends upon and, in turn, supports other signs. But 'field' recalls the attempt by Saussure and structuralist theorists to establish a field of analysis, whether it be language as a totality or a localised cultural myth. And it is this field which, Derrida points out, cannot be framed, because once the turn to language has been accepted, then what is being framed by language is language, with its logic of supplemental relations. The 'event' of structuralism is quite blatantly a linguistic event. It had been thought (and still was being thought when Derrida delivered his paper) that structuralism had introduced such a radical epistemological break with the shift to synchronic analysis and all that followed that this would permit the constitution of a scientific discourse. The episteme thereby inaugurated – the age of structuralism – would be epistemologically privileged, and so able to overlook all other sign systems. Foucault neatly isolates the problem which this ambition entails: 'The human sciences, when dealing with what is representation (in either conscious or unconscious form), will find themselves treating as their object what is in fact their condition of possibility' (Foucault, 1970, p. 364).

In his essay 'Differance', published in 1968, Derrida quotes Saussure on differences in language to confirm how dependent he is upon Saussure, and then adds:

The first consequence to be drawn from [Saussure's statement] is that the signified concept is never present in itself, in an adequate presence that would refer only to itself. Every concept is necessarily and essentially inscribed in a chain or a system, within which it refers to another and to other concepts, by the systematic play of differences. Such a play, then – differance – is no longer simply a concept, but the possibility of conceptuality, of the conceptual system and process in general. (Derrida, 1973, p. 140)

Respectful of Saussure's great contribution in bringing language to the fore rather than, say, the economic base in Marx, Derrida none the less seeks to explain why Saussure finds it necessary to set limits to his 'general' linguistics. He asks what it is that permits Saussure to carry out his descriptive work on language and, by extension, what permits the various structuralist analyses of sign systems. What has to be excluded for any system to appear complete, and therefore capable of being the model for other systems? Derrida demonstrates that Saussure's 'general' linguistics should more accurately be called a 'restricted' linguistics – two terms he foregrounds in an important essay from 1967, 'From restricted to general economy: a Hegelianism without reserve'. He concludes that Saussure's vital distinction between signifier and signified, and his insight into the arbitrariness of the sign, depend upon an initial exclusion of 'writing'. 'Writing' is understood in the common-sense meaning of not-spoken-but-written, but also as the worldly, the cultural, the historical, the institutional, the public; indeed, as the system of differences that each element in the system carries with it as a 'trace'.

Derrida shows that the analytic tools provided by linguistics are but another institutionalisation of metaphysics. In this connection, however, he insists that Saussure goes further, thereby revealing the powerful hold which a traditional metaphysics of reference and unity has upon any thinker. Having stressed arbitrariness and then outlawed symbolic writing, Saussure allows that there are some signs which are of a different order and which possess a 'natural bond between the sound and the sense': the sign as symbol, and as spoken not written. It is at this point that Derrida's deconstruction of Saussure – an anti-phenomenological thinker – intersects with his reading of Husserl, in whose work there is a decisive recourse to the supposed irreducibility of a moment of interior communication, or hearing oneself speak. Quite remarkably, then, Saussure appears in Derrida's reading as nostalgic for a pre-lapsarian fullness of meaning, embodied in a privileged sign, not so far from Coleridge, Wordsworth, Emerson, Thoreau and other Romantic theoreticians of language. Saussure resists his own insight and, in his exclusion of written language, resorts to melodramatic formulations, as Derrida observes:

> The contamination by writing, the fact or the threat of it, are denounced in the accents of the moralist or preacher by the linguist from Geneva. The tone counts; it is as if, at the moment when the modern science of the logos would come into its autonomy and its scientificity, it became necessary again to attack a heresy. (Derrida, 1976, p. 34)

Derrida's passing comparison with John Calvin is quite apt, since Calvinism and its institutionalised successor, Puritanism, both inaugurated modernity through their break with the assumed totality of the human and the divine, but then sought to repress the 'freedom' which their methodology for interpreting texts set loose.

In terms of Derrida's own project, his reading in *Of Grammatology* turns Saussure's 'difference' into 'differance'. Signs – which, Saussure argues, should be understood as part of a system – turn out to have a temporal dimension as well. Paul de Man – whose early essays parallel and even precede Derrida's work, but in the more specialised sphere of Romantic and Modernist literary theory – calls this 'the rhetoric of temporality' to suggest that signs not only differ from each other in their generation of meaning but also defer meaning (de Man, 1983, pp. 187–228). Derrida puts this nicely, almost in everyday terms:

> When we cannot take hold of or show the thing, let us say the present, the being-present, when the present does not present itself, then we signify, we go through the detour of signs. We take up or give signs; we make signs. The sign would thus be a deferred presence. Whether it is a question of verbal or written signs, monetary signs, electoral delegates, or political representatives, the movement of signs defers the moment of encountering the thing itself, the moment at which we could lay hold of it, consume or expend it, see it, have a present intuition of it. (Derrida, 1973, p. 138)

It is Saussure's insight still, but pursued according to a deconstructive logic which is capable of transforming the structuralist system into the familiar post-structuralist image of the labyrinth which closes and yet, through a *mise en abîme*, opens up Derrida's reading of Husserl in *Speech and Phenomena*:

> Everything has, no doubt, begun in the following way [he then quotes from Husserl's *Ideas I*]:
>
>> A name on being mentioned reminds us of the Dresden gallery. ... We wander through the rooms. ... A painting by Teniers ... represents a gallery of paintings. ... The paintings of this gallery would represent in their turn paintings, which on their part exhibited readable inscriptions and so forth.
>
> Certainly nothing has preceded this situation. Assuredly nothing will suspend it. It is not *comprehended*, as Husserl would want it, by intuitions or presentations. Of the broad daylight of presence, outside the gallery, no perception is given us or assuredly promised us. The gallery is the labyrinth which includes in itself its own exits. (Derrida, 1973, p. 104)

The broader point of Derrida's reading of Saussure's *Course in General Linguistics* is that no methodology is free from that for which it seeks to account. Even a systematic account of language such as Saussure initiates cannot generate a metalanguage adequate to itself, though it would be Derrida's claim that a scrupulous deconstructive reading can generate knowledge of that impossibility by working within and against the conceptual language of any enclosure. And so, in his close reading of Saussure, Derrida concludes that *even* Saussure overlooks language in the process of looking it over.

Before tracing the relationship between structuralist and post-structuralist tenets and practices in two other French theorists, Michel Foucault and Julia Kristeva, it may be helpful to comment on what may seem to be simply a literary parallel in the work of Paul de Man and J. Hillis Miller, but which introduces the cross-disciplinary notion of 'reading' and its ramifications. As already noted, de Man's early essays in many respects run alongside, and sometimes predate, Derrida's concentration upon the structure of the individual sign in *Speech and Phenomena* and the section on Saussure in *Of Grammatology*. In 'The intentional structure of the Romantic image' (1960) and 'The rhetoric of temporality' (1969), de Man's single-minded preoccupation is with the interpretive gap which opens up in the supposedly autonomous symbol or image which is the fulcrum of Romantic and Modernist aesthetics. In 'The rhetoric of temporality' this gap is explained through a skilful rewriting of literary history which reveals the persistence of allegorical, interpretive modes of thinking well into the period of Romanticism, which had, apparently, left such laboured modes behind. De Man conducts a similar argument against the dominance of organicist theory in the 1950s under the aegis of New Criticism, and in both essays he subjects the assumptions of periodisation to careful scrutiny. The essay on the New Criticism is reprinted in the first edition of *Blindness and Insight* (1971), and this coupling is an indispensable element in de Man's and also Miller's efforts to underpin canonical literary and theoretical texts by reading them agonistically, rather than dutifully. Thus, de Man maintains that in spite of a theoretical 'blindness' which keeps the New Critics wedded to the idea of a self-contained poetic form, it is the very stringency of their methods of close reading which leads to the insight that no totality is immune to the play of language or – in de Man's vocabulary – to the intentionality of rhetoric. Through his reading of Nietzsche in *Allegories of Reading*, published in 1979, de Man revitalises the nearly forgotten skills of rhetorical analysis, to such an extent that texts become a battleground of competing tropes.

In J. Hillis Miller's literary criticism there is a similar emphasis upon what language can do when it is freed from a metaphysics of form, authorial intention, narrative, theme, and periodisation. Miller, especially in the subdiscipline of criticism of fiction and narrative, consistently subjects traditional literary-critical preoccupations to the rigour of a battery of new close reading techniques to ask, for example, what a deconstructive literary history might be. What – to be more specific, still – remains of period and genre demarcations when a classic nineteenth-century realist novel like *Middlemarch* is read against the grain of its controlling assumptions that signs refer to things, and that narrative leads to conclusions which reinforce the accepted teleology of history? More generally, Miller's work is highly instructive for those who wish to identify the impact of a diacritical model of language in a theoretically informed literary criticism. The differences between Miller's first appraisals of his mentor, Georges Poulet (Miller, 1963, 1966) and his reappraisal after Derrida and de Man's work had become more widely known (Miller, 1970) serve to expose the shortcomings of a phenomenological criticism of identification, notably the assumption that language can bring about the unity of authorial intention and reader's perception.

The logic of Miller's detailed readings leads to the idea of text as labyrinth. In 'Ariadne's thread' (1976), reading becomes a retracing, which is yet a form of writing. The narrative which results bears an allegorical relationship to the 'original' narrative in the text to be read, constructing that original as it is dutifully followed. The temporal–spatial conundrums which Miller's readings throw up are akin to the logic which Derrida identifies in the movement of 'differance'. Nietzsche is also at the back of much of Miller's criticism, in particular the notion that in naming the truth (a definitive interpretation of a text or event or person) the play of metaphor is necessarily invoked and so the reader necessarily errs, meaning both to mistake and to err or wander as signs refer to signs. In Miller and de Man – as well as in Harold Bloom's *A Map of Misreading*, from the same period – there is an insistence on the necessity of misreading.

In retrospect, it would seem that many literary critics have been too easily enthralled by the ideas of close misreading and the text as an infinite web of signification – possibly because, in tandem, they offered a way of learning from structuralism while resisting its scientific aspirations. Deconstructive criticism, in a curious fashion, restored to literature its special quality, its inability to be closed down or limited. All the time that the New Critics, Romantic aesthetics and an old-fashioned authorial criticism remained the adversaries, literary deconstruction retained its radical, unsettling edge; but as the theoretical agenda changed, so the open text and the power to misread the text threw up new problems. In this connection, J. Hillis Miller's work is just as instructive at the 1990s end of the debate as it was when structuralism and post-structuralism so dramatically affected the idea of reading in the 1970s. If Miller's own reaction against phenomenology – almost a remaking of himself as a literary critic after a successful career working in and off phenomenological approaches – at first blunted his awareness of the implications of deconstruction when carried over into the field of literary theory and criticism (he was not alone in this!), his work since the mid-1980s reveals an acute self-consciousness of two old problems which deconstructive reading formulates in new ways: history and ethics.

In 'Defacing It: Hawthorne and History', a long essay published in 1991 which concentrates upon Hawthorne's 'The Minister's Black Veil', Miller faces up to the charge that deconstruction is a new New Criticism in its obsession with textual ambiguities – renamed aporias or moments of undecidability – and equally incapable of engaging with history and its claims to determine textual boundaries. De Man is forthright on this point:

> In literary studies, structures of meaning are frequently described in historical rather than in semiological or rhetorical terms. This is, in itself, a somewhat surprising occurrence, since the historical nature of literary discourse is by no means an *a priori* established fact, whereas all literature necessarily consists of linguistic and semantic elements. (de Man, 1979, p. 79)

Miller also takes the offensive, arguing that it is historical criticism which supposedly tries to respect the influence of historical factors in literary texts, but which actually neutralises history and renders it an inert theme in Hawthorne's explicitly historical short story: 'historical events ... become history when ... signs are read' (Miller, 1991, p. 114). Reading, for Miller, is an intervention which is caught up in 'the heterogeneity of a historical happening, its differentiation within itself, its contamination by an other than itself that is not outside in opposition to it but within' (Miller, 1991, p. 118). In the course of this argument, Miller derives support from de Man's assertion that

> the linguistics of literariness is a powerful and indispensable tool in the unmasking of ideological aberrations, as well as a determining factor in accounting for their occurrence. Those who reproach literary theory for being oblivious to social and historical (that is to say ideological) reality are merely stating their fear at having their own ideological mystifications exposed by the tool they are trying to discredit. They are, in short, very poor readers of Marx's *German Ideology*. (de Man, 1982, p. 11)

The extract reprinted from *The Ethics of Reading* (1987; Reading 1.6) could easily have appeared in Section 5, Post-Foundational Ethics and Politics, except that it is valuable to see Miller's concern with ethics as a reflection upon the route from the security of a structuralist enclosure, in which a limited, if innovative, agenda of explanatory expositions of contemporary culture kept larger questions at bay, to the release of interpretive energies in post-structuralism; but also to see this concern arising from a microscopic engagement with another close reader, Paul de Man. As Miller sees it, the question of ethics is not a matter of returning to the 'ethical content' of books. Ethics is *reading*. However, it is the power of deconstructive reading to construct a text which precipitates questions about its ethics, its limits, the restrictions it should acknowledge upon 'play'. The transgressing of limits which deconstruction enables, and which has provoked the objection that it is nihilistic, leads Miller to conclude that 'if the response [to a text] is not one of necessity, grounded in some "must", if it is a freedom to do what one likes, for example to make a literary text mean what one likes, then it is not ethical' (Miller, 1987a, p. 4). 'Reading', Miller announces, 'is extraordinarily hard work. It does not occur all that often' (p. 3); and when it does occur, it is more fundamental than the use of literature implied by a phrase such as 'the politics of interpretation' (p. 4): 'No doubt "reading" spreads out to involve institutional, historical, economic, and political "contexts", but it begins with the words on the page' and the reading situation. The echoes of the New Criticism and the scaling down of the wider context probably jar and smack of a retreat from a political agenda, though de Man does not see it this way:

> The ensuing foregrounding of material, phenomenal aspects of the signifier creates a strong illusion of aesthetic seduction at the very moment when the actual aesthetic function has been, at the very least, suspended. ... Literature involves the voiding, rather than the affirmation, of aesthetic categories. (de Man, 1982, p. 10)

Miller's essay on Paul de Man is part of a determined effort to identify 'the ethical moment' in any text, in which claims are made which cannot be avoided and leave the reader alone with her/his text. The timing of this essay is awkward, to say the least, because in 1987 the news broke of de Man's wartime collaborationist journalism (see de Man, 1988; Hamacher *et al.*, 1989). Miller's subsequent defence of de Man depends – rather lamely, it seems – upon a distinction between journalism and genuine writing, and the reading which each generates. During his contribution to the controversy, however, Miller makes the request that de Man's wartime essays be really 'read', together with his later work; and presumably, Miller would argue that in this encounter some insight into de Man's blindness in his journalism of fifty years ago may be obtained.

In the broader arena, away from professional literary-critical disputes, Miller demands attention through the modesty and literality of his case for reading. For reading and talking about reading is what theorists and students of theory do, and it is the basis for any broader applications they might advocate – political applications in particular. If there is a moment when reading, in Miller's sense of the word, should stop, and action take over, it is not a moment which should be unambiguously welcomed.

In a 1968 interview with Derrida, Julia Kristeva anticipates, through a series of questions on language, one of the directions of her own research, at least up to *Revolution in Poetic Language* (1974). There is a similarity between Derrida's identification of a radical disseminating force in the formality of a language system and Kristeva's understanding of the 'semiotic' dimension; indeed, far from being a neutral descriptive term, the 'semiotic', for Kristeva, is the dynamic and subversive quality in language, whereas semiology or structuralism is what one is left with if a purely spatial and synchronic view of language is adopted. Kristeva does not reinstate an evolutionary, developmental understanding of language; instead, she rethinks Lacan's account of the Imaginary and the Symbolic orders to posit a dynamic interplay between the semiotic and the symbolic, out of which comes the formation of the subject as a speaking subject. The semiotic and the symbolic are '*two modalities* of what is ... the same signifying process' (Kristeva, 1984, pp. 23–4) rather than self-contained positions within language. And these modalities are associated, respectively, with the pre-oedipal and oedipal stages.

But Kristeva's is no mere typology, though it does permit generic distinctions which have been of use to innovative literary critics interested in the (shifting) boundaries of narrative, poetry, theoretical discourse, and so forth. The importance of her work on language is most apparent in psychoanalysis and feminism. *Revolution*, which represents an important stage in Kristeva's assimilation and use of psychoanalysis, could as easily be a key source for the next Section of this *Reader*; while extracts from *About Chinese Women* or the essays 'Stabat mater' and 'Women's time' would be important – albeit difficult to categorise – additions to Section 3, Feminism. However, the extracts that have been reprinted (see Reading 1.3) show where Kristeva is coming from, and how she works through current research in linguistics to define her own terminology. Kristeva locates the source of resistance to the formalism of language and its rationalising order in what she calls – in a modification of Plato's term – the semiotic *chora*, 'a nonexpressive totality formed by the drives and their stases in a motility that is as full of movement as it is regulated' (Kristeva, 1984, p. 25). In effect, the repression of the marginal in language constructs the *chora* as the 'place' of negativity. With the entry of the subject into what Lacan calls the Symbolic Order the *chora* becomes an 'extremely provisional articulation' within language and, as such, disruptive and radical. This is an important reorientation of Lacanian thought in which the Symbolic Order carries the weight of the Law of the Father, and is the reason why Kristeva's semiotic should not be precisely equated with Lacan's Imaginary. Signification depends upon, rather than is annulled by, the attempted and partial repression of the *chora*, and so, too, does the identity of the subject. The *chora* remains a 'live' source of negativity or heterogeneity, recognisable, for instance, in the apparent disorder of modernist literature. Hence the importance of emphasising that the semiotic and the symbolic are not fixed positions or essences within language with which Kristeva can be categorically identified. It is interesting to observe Kristeva as a fairly neutral interviewer of Derrida (in one of the interviews reprinted in *Positions*) before turning to *Revolution in Poetic Language*, where she pointedly distinguishes the semiotic from the grammatological in his work, maintaining that the latter does not allow for either the energy of the semiotic or the production of the subject.

Kristeva picks up Mallarmé's 'The mystery in literature', and continues: 'Indifferent to language, enigmatic and feminine, this space underlying the written is rhythmic, unfettered, irreducible to its verbal translation' (Kristeva, 1984, p. 29). Yet it should not be assumed that for Kristeva, the semiotic and that which is *pre-* and also different, and therefore other, in any system is essentially and always feminine, and that she is therefore sympathetic to *écriture féminine*. The security of the pre-oedipal is available to baby boys and girls, though it is em-bodied in the mother – just as, in principle, the symbolic is not the patriarchal order, though in practice it is. Rather, the feminine is associated with the marginal and the suppressed in language, and gains its strength from this association, as in poetry; while the masculine is associated with the principle of order and rationality in the symbolic. But this is a product of how the relations within any system have become disposed, and it is here that the importance of Kristeva's approach through a broadly structuralist understanding of language is so important. The feminine and the masculine are modes of language, not modes of self, and the semiotic is therefore inseparable from the symbolic. *Revolution in Poetic Language* is, among other things, a promotion of the Modernist avant-garde of language – Mallarmé and James Joyce, for instance. Not surprisingly, because of this wider perspective and her vital theorising of the semiotic and symbolic dimensions of language – to constitute what she calls *signifiance* – the claims which can be made for language are so much greater here than within a structuralist paradigm. In Kristeva, there is an important – albeit familiar – claim that the marginal and the avant-garde can shake the foundations of the established power elite; and, by extension, that radical readings of texts can achieve similar ends. In less careful hands, an uncritical acceptance of movement or process might have difficulty distinguishing between the formal dynamic of change, even in commodity differentiation, and the radicality which Kristeva claims on behalf of the semiotic. And such a theoretical perspective might not give sufficient attention to the economic and institutional reasons which – for theorists like Jean-Paul Sartre, in *What is Literature?*, and Georg Lukács, in some of the essays in *Writer and Critic* – explain the distance from utilitarian language in Modernism.

Chris Weedon voices the dangers of this expanded view of language's revolutionary potential and the speaking subject:

In making femininity and masculinity universal aspects of language, rather than the particular constructs of specifically historically produced discourses, Kristeva's theory loses its political edge. Moreover, to equate the feminine with the irrational, even if the feminine no longer has anything to do with women, is either to concede rather a lot to masculinity or to privilege the irrational, neither of which is very helpful politically. (Weedon, 1987, pp. 89–90)

In fairness, the extract from *Revolution in Poetic Language* (Reading 1.3) and the book as a whole need to be read alongside Kristeva's efforts to give language a political, even an economic, context, though there is still a tendency in her work to make one revolution (that of the Modernist avant-garde) interchangeable with another (for example, the feminist revolution). And with language as the arena for revolution, the way is also open for a further step towards an anarchic subjectivism, the constant reorientating and realigning of positions in the semiotic modality which undermines the (more) fixed positions which exert control but can also provoke responses based upon common ground, whether of class, gender, region, or whatever.

And now to Michel Foucault, and how he relates to the categories of structuralism and post-structuralism. A different set of problems arise, and a different vocabulary must be learned, but there are certain similarities to the above accounts. Notwithstanding his annoyance at being called a structuralist, *The Order of Things* – where he protests his innocence – is still Foucault's most structuralist work, one in which he slices across a traditional history of ideas to identify and then investigate, in minute – if highly selective – detail, broad fields of knowledge. Yet Foucault's route out of a structuralist 'archaeology of knowledge' and into genealogical analysis is signalled in some of the methodological evasions of *The Order of Things*.

Just as Saussure chooses not to emphasise the developmental side of linguistics, so Foucault refuses to theorise the mechanism of change from one episteme to another. All we have are gnomic, even Romantic, observations – for instance, the one which concludes the Preface to *The Order of Things*, and announces a postmodern episteme:

> In attempting to uncover the deepest strata of Western culture, I am restoring to our silent and apparently immobile soil its rifts, its instability, its flaws; and it is the same ground that is once more stirring under our feet. (Foucault, 1970, p. xxiv)

An observation such as this cannot but draw attention to the position from which Foucault is able to propose and then carry out archaeological work. In the light of his own rhetoric, it is appropriate to ask where Foucault stands in relation to that which he describes. Either this is a non-question, because history moves as the plates of the earth's crust move, massively and under their own volition – in which case the 'death of man' must be taken much less historically than Foucault surely intends, and Foucault can be criticised for showing no interest in agency, or in asking the question: Why does knowledge so dispose itself in the classical or modern era? – or Foucault – like other structuralists – has posed the question of the self and agency, history and change, much more urgently than his serene methodology will allow, and an internal rethink is necessary; indeed, in Foucault, is under way even before the structuralist enterprise has run its course. The latter is a more productive tack to adopt, and by the end of *The Order of Things* Foucault, looking to

Nietzsche, is opening up his already ambitious project to deal with one of the recurring problems of modern thought: how to describe that of which one is a part:

> ... a philological critique, by means of a certain form of biologism, Nietzsche rediscovered the point at which man and God belong to one another, at which the death of the second is synonymous with the death of the first, and at which the promise of the superman signifies first and foremost the imminence of the death of man. In this Nietzsche, offering this future to us as both promise and task, marks the threshold beyond which contemporary philosophy can begin thinking again ... it is no longer possible to think in our day other than in the void left by man's disappearance. For this void does not create a deficiency; it does not constitute a lacuna that must be filled. It is nothing more, and nothing less, than the unfolding of a space in which it is once more possible to think. (Foucault, 1970, p. 342)

Interestingly, near the end of *Speech and Phenomena*, Derrida happens upon a similar image of movement: 'It remains, then, for us to *speak*, to make our voices *resonate* throughout the corridors in order to make up for [*suppléer*] the breakup of presence' (Derrida, 1973, p. 104).

In the interview with Alessandro Fontana and Pasquale Pasquino (Reading 1.4) Foucault reflects upon the limitations of *The Order of Things*, admitting that more attention to the 'internal regime of power' within a discourse is needed, and that he had been overly focused upon 'systematicity, theoretical form, or something like a paradigm'. It seems to have been Foucault's post-1968 reaction against the existing monolithic theories of power which, from Right or Left, totalised power that led him to micro-political analysis, 'the genealogy of relations of force, strategic developments, and tactics' within 'the fine meshes of power' in institutions, however local. It is in this change of perspective and acceptance that the structuralist model – any model, perhaps – could not effect an epistemological break which would ensure objectivity that Foucault offers a cautious account of agency and political resistance:

> What makes power hold good, what makes it accepted, is simply the fact that it doesn't only weigh on us a force that says no, but that it traverses and produces things, it induces pleasure, forms knowledge, produces discourse. (Foucault, 1980, p. 119)

Here also, however, is the nub of a problem which has made Foucault such an important point of reference in the kinds of debates covered in Section 5, for if Foucault escapes from totalising positions and the temptations of structuralism, he is then accused of failing to explain why wrongs should be righted. In Charles Taylor's view, Foucault is damaged by one of the influences which so liberates his thinking: 'a Nietzschean-derived stance of neutrality between the different historical systems of power' (Taylor, 1986, p. 79). The very success of Foucault's micro-analyses, and his preference for power over truth as a central concept, only underline the lack of the kind of synthesis which can be found in a book like C. Wright Mills' *The Power Elite* (1956), itself a response to an earlier period when totalising explanations went out of favour. For Mills, the local dimension of political action had certainly grown busier and more heterogeneous, but this was not the sphere where the big decisions of the modern world were made, and made on the basis of economics and class interest.

Finally, back to Roland Barthes. The direction he takes out of structuralism, through *S/Z* (1970) and *The Pleasure of the Text* (1973), needs less comment than does the political dimension of *Mythologies*. If Barthes's book is taken as a representative structuralist text, then it is clear that for all its supposed exclusion of the diachronic dimension, structuralism does not wall itself off from historical and political concerns; it rethinks them – or, at least, its methodological moves give the capacity for such rethinking. Barthes recognises that what Saussure did was not to cut us off from history but to discredit nineteenth-century assumptions about history as straightforwardly explanatory and neutral in its configuration of events. Barthes, following Saussure's project for a semiology, concentrates upon the way the sign moves from the arbitrary to the necessary, in the sense of what is necessary in a situation for communication to occur. The question which Barthes asks – but much structuralism, especially literary structuralism which had its own agenda, did not ask – is: Why is a structure constructed this way rather than that? This is a question which Foucault asks as genealogist rather than as archaeologist, and as power and knowledge are linked in his thinking. It is in this context that Barthes's casual remark that 'around 1954' he decided to combine Saussure and Brecht is so important in linking the laying-bare of a system's workings with a critique of that system's solidity, its seeming naturalness under certain circumstances.

However, in one of the less-discussed passages in 'Myth Today', Barthes leaves unresolved questions which would be asked only when structuralism, and then post-structuralism, had become more widely known, even institutionalised. Barthes accepts that in so far as what he is doing in *Mythologies* is a critique of ideology, not a neutral exposition, then it is specifically a critique of bourgeois myths. The matter of left-wing myths is not approached with Barthes's characteristic care, but becomes a justifiable target in certain strands of postmodern and liberal political theory in the 1980s and 1990s.

1.1 □ *Myth Today*

Roland Barthes

What is a myth, today? I shall give at the outset a first, very simple answer, which is perfectly consistent with etymology: *myth is a type of speech*.[1]

Myth is a type of speech

Of course, it is not *any* type: language needs special conditions in order to become myth: we shall see them in a minute. But what must be firmly established at the start is that myth is a system of communication, that it is a message. This allows one to perceive that myth cannot possibly be an object, a concept, or an idea; it is a mode of signification, a form. Later, we shall have to assign to this form historical limits, conditions of use, and reintroduce society into it: we must nevertheless first describe it as a form.

It can be seen that to purport to discriminate among mythical objects according to their substance would be entirely illusory: since myth is a type of speech, everything can be a myth provided it is conveyed by a discourse. Myth is not defined by the object of its message, but by the way in which it utters this message: there are formal limits to myth, there are no 'substantial' ones. Everything, then, can be a myth? Yes, I believe this, for the universe is infinitely fertile in suggestions. Every object in the world can pass from a closed, silent existence to an oral state, open to appropriation by society, for there is no law, whether natural or not, which forbids talking about things. A tree is a tree. Yes, of course. But a tree as expressed by Minou Drouet is no longer quite a tree, it is a tree which is decorated, adapted to a certain type of consumption, laden with literary self-indulgence, revolt, images, in short with a type of social *usage* which is added to pure matter.

Naturally, everything is not expressed at the same time: some objects become the prey of mythical speech for a while, then they disappear, others take their place and attain the status of myth. Are there objects which are *inevitably* a source of suggestiveness, as Baudelaire suggested about Woman? Certainly not: one can

From Barthes, R., *Mythologies*, trans. A. Lavers, Jonathan Cape, London, 1972, pp. 109–31.

conceive of very ancient myths, but there are no eternal ones; for it is human history which converts reality into speech, and it alone rules the life and the death of mythical language. Ancient or not, mythology can only have an historical foundation, for myth is a type of speech chosen by history: it cannot possibly evolve from the 'nature' of things.

Speech of this kind is a message. It is therefore by no means confined to oral speech. It can consist of modes of writing or of representations; not only written discourse, but also photography, cinema, reporting, sport, shows, publicity, all these can serve as a support to mythical speech. Myth can be defined neither by its object nor by its material, for any material can arbitrarily be endowed with meaning: the arrow which is brought in order to signify a challenge is also a kind of speech. True, as far as perception is concerned, writing and pictures, for instance, do not call upon the same type of consciousness; and even with pictures, one can use many kinds of reading: a diagram lends itself to signification more than a drawing, a copy more than an original, and a caricature more than a portrait. But this is the point: we are no longer dealing here with a theoretical mode of representation: we are dealing with *this* particular image, which is given for *this* particular signification. Mythical speech is made of a material which has *already* been worked on so as to make it suitable for communication: it is because all the materials of myth (whether pictorial or written) presuppose a signifying consciousness, that one can reason about them while discounting their substance. This substance is not unimportant: pictures, to be sure, are more imperative than writing, they impose meaning at one stroke, without analysing or diluting it. But this is no longer a constitutive difference. Pictures become a kind of writing as soon as they are meaningful: like writing, they call for a *lexis*.

We shall therefore take *language*, *discourse*, *speech*, etc., to mean any significant unit or synthesis, whether verbal or visual: a photograph will be a kind of speech for us in the same way as a newspaper article; even objects will become speech, if they mean something. This generic way of conceiving language is in fact justified by the very history of writing: long before the invention of our alphabet, objects like the Inca *quipu*, or drawings, as in pictographs, have been accepted as speech. This does not mean that one must treat mythical speech like language; myth in fact belongs to the province of a general science, coextensive with linguistics, which is *semiology*.

Myth as a semiological system

For mythology, since it is the study of a type of speech, is but one fragment of this vast science of signs which Saussure postulated some forty years ago under the name of *semiology*. Semiology has not yet come into being. But since Saussure himself, and sometimes independently of him, a whole section of contemporary research has constantly been referred to the problem of meaning: psychoanalysis, structuralism, eidetic psychology, some new types of literary criticism of which Bachelard has given the first examples, are no longer concerned with facts except inasmuch as they are endowed with significance. Now to postulate a signification is to have recourse to semiology. I do not mean that semiology could account for all these aspects of research equally well: they have different contents. But they have a common status: they are all sciences dealing with values. They are not content with meeting the facts: they define and explore them as tokens for something else.

Semiology is a science of forms, since it studies significations apart from their content. I should like to say one word about the necessity and the limits of such a formal science. The necessity is that which applies in the case of any exact language. Zhdanov made fun of Alexandrov the philosopher, who spoke of '*the spherical structure of our planet.*' '*It was thought until now*', Zhdanov said, '*that form alone could be spherical.*' Zhdanov was right: one cannot speak about structures in terms of forms, and vice versa. It may well be that on the plane of 'life', there is but a totality where structures and forms cannot be separated. But science has no use for the ineffable: it must speak about 'life' if it wants to transform it. Against a certain quixotism of synthesis, quite Platonic incidentally, all criticism must consent to the *ascesis*, to the artifice of analysis; and in analysis, it must match method and language. Less terrorized by the spectre of 'formalism', historical criticism might have been less sterile; it would have understood that the specific study of forms does not in any way contradict the necessary principles of totality and History. On the contrary: the more a system is specifically defined in its forms, the more amenable it is to historical criticism. To parody a well-known saying, I shall say that a little formalism turns one away from History, but that a lot brings one back to it. Is there a better example of total criticism than the description of saintliness, at once formal and historical, semiological and ideological, in Sartre's *Saint-Genêt*? The danger, on the contrary, is to consider forms as ambiguous objects, half-form and half-substance, to endow form with a substance of form, as was done, for instance, by Zhdanovian realism. Semiology, once its limits are settled, is not a metaphysical trap: it is a science among others, necessary but not sufficient. The important thing is to see that the unity of an explanation cannot be based on the amputation of one or other of its approaches, but, as Engels said, on the dialectical co-ordination of the particular sciences it makes use of. This is the case with mythology: it is a part both of semiology inasmuch as it is a formal science, and of ideology inasmuch as it is an historical science: it studies ideas-in-form.[2]

Let me therefore restate that any semiology postulates a relation between two terms, a signifier and a signified. This relation concerns objects which belong to different categories, and this is why it is not one of equality but one of equivalence. We must here be on our guard for despite common parlance which simply says that the signifier *expresses* the signified, we are dealing, in any semiological system, not with two, but with three different terms. For what we grasp is not at all one term after the other, but the correlation which unites them: there are, therefore, the signifier, the signified and the sign, which is the associative total of the first two terms. Take a bunch of roses: I use it to *signify* my passion. Do we have here, then, only a signifier and a signified, the roses and my passion? Not even that: to put it accurately, there are here only 'passionified' roses. But on the plane of analysis, we do have three terms; for these roses weighted with passion perfectly and correctly allow themselves to be decomposed into roses and passion: the former and the latter existed before uniting and forming this third object, which is the sign. It is as true to say that on the plane of experience I cannot dissociate the roses from the message they carry, as to say that on the plane of analysis I cannot confuse the roses as signifier and the roses as sign: the signifier is empty, the sign is full, it is a meaning. Or take a black pebble: I can make it signify in several ways, it is a mere signifier; but if I weigh it with a definite signified (a death sentence, for instance, in an anonymous vote), it will become a sign. Naturally, there are between the signifier, the signified and the sign, functional implications (such as that of the part to the whole) which are so close that to analyse them may seem futile; but we shall see in a moment that this distinction has a capital importance for the study of myth as semiological schema.

Naturally these three terms are purely formal, and different contents can be given to them. Here are a few examples: for Saussure, who worked on a particular but methodologically exemplary semiological system – the language or *langue* – the signified is the concept, the signifier is the acoustic image (which is mental) and the relation between concept and image is the sign (the word, for instance), which is a concrete entity.[3] For Freud, as is well known, the human psyche is a stratification of tokens or representatives. One term (I refrain from giving it any precedence) is constituted by the manifest meaning of behaviour, another, by its latent or real meaning (it is, for instance, the substratum of the dream); as for the third term, it is here also a correlation of the first two: it is the dream itself in its totality, the parapraxis (a mistake in speech or behaviour) or the neurosis, conceived as compromises, as economies effected thanks to the joining of a form (the first term) and an intentional function (the second term). We can see here how necessary it is to distinguish the sign from the signifier: a dream, to Freud, is no more its manifest datum than its latent content: it is the functional union of these two terms. In Sartrean criticism, finally (I shall keep to these three well-known examples), the signified is constituted by the original crisis in the subject (the separation from his mother for Baudelaire, the naming of the theft for Genêt); Literature as discourse forms the signifier; and the relation between crisis and discourse defines the work, which is a signification. Of course, this tri-dimensional pattern, however constant in its form, is actualized in different ways: one cannot therefore say too often that semiology can have its unity only at the level of forms, not contents; its field is limited, it knows only one operation: reading, or deciphering.

In myth, we find again the tri-dimensional pattern which I have just described: the signifier, the signified and the sign. But myth is a peculiar system, in that it is constructed from a semiological chain which existed before it: it is a *second-order semiological system*. That which is a sign (namely the associative total of a concept and an image) in the first system, becomes a mere signifier in the second. We must here recall that the materials of mythical speech (the language itself, photography, painting, posters, rituals, objects, etc.), however different at the start, are reduced to a pure signifying function as soon as they are caught by myth. Myth sees in them only the same raw material; their unity is that they all come down to the status of a mere language. Whether it deals with alphabetical or pictorial writing, myth wants to see in them only a sum of signs, a global sign, the final term of a first semiological chain. And it is precisely this final term which will become the first term of the greater system which it builds and of which it is only a part. Everything happens as if myth shifted the formal system of the first significations sideways. As this lateral shift is essential for the analysis of myth, I shall represent it in the following way, it being understood, of course, that the spatialization of the pattern is here only a metaphor:

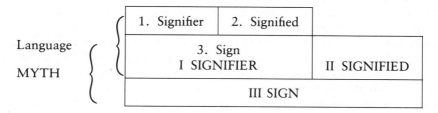

It can be seen that in myth there are two semiological systems, one of which is staggered in relation to the other: a linguistic system, the language (or the modes of representation which are assimilated to it), which I shall call the *language-object*, because it is the language which myth gets hold of in order to build its own system; and myth itself, which I shall call *metalanguage*, because it is a second language, *in which* one speaks about the first. When he reflects on a metalanguage, the semiologist no longer needs to ask himself questions about the composition of the language-object, he no longer has to take into account the details of the linguistic schema; he will only need to know its total term, or global sign, and only inasmuch as this term lends itself to myth. This is why the semiologist is entitled to treat in the same way writing and pictures: what he retains from them is the fact that they are both *signs*, that they both reach the threshold of myth endowed with the same signifying function, that they constitute, one just as much as the other, a language-object.

It is now time to give one or two examples of mythical speech. I shall borrow the first from an observation by Valéry.[4] I am a pupil in the second form in a French *lycée*. I open my Latin grammar, and I read a sentence, borrowed from Aesop or Phaedrus: *quia ego nominor leo*. I stop and think. There is something ambiguous about this statement: on the one hand, the words in it do have a simple meaning: *because my name is lion*. And on the other hand, the sentence is evidently there in order to signify something else to me. Inasmuch as it is addressed to me, a pupil in the second form, it tells me clearly: I am a grammatical example meant to illustrate the rule about the agreement of the predicate. I am even forced to realize that the sentence in no way *signifies* its meaning to me, that it tries very little to tell me something about the lion and what sort of name he has; its true and fundamental signification is to impose itself on me as the presence of a certain agreement of the predicate. I conclude that I am faced with a particular, greater, semiological system, since it is co-extensive with the language: there is, indeed, a signifier, but this signifier is itself formed by a sum of signs, it is in itself a first semiological system (*my name is lion*). Thereafter, the formal pattern is correctly unfolded: there is a signified (*I am a grammatical example*) and there is a global signification, which is none other than the correlation of the signifier and the signified; for neither the naming of the lion nor the grammatical example are given separately.

And here is now another example: I am at the barber's, and a copy of *Paris-Match* is offered to me. On the cover, a young Negro in a French uniform is saluting, with his eyes uplifted, probably fixed on a fold of the tricolour. All this is the *meaning* of the picture. But, whether naively or not, I see very well what it signifies to me: that France is a great Empire, that all her sons, without any colour discrimination, faithfully serve under her flag, and that there is no better answer to the detractors of an alleged colonialism than the zeal shown by this Negro in serving his so-called oppressors. I am therefore again faced with a greater semiological system: there is a signifier, itself already formed with a previous system (*a black soldier is giving the French salute*); there is a signified (it is here a purposeful mixture of Frenchness and militariness); finally, there is a presence of the signified through the signifier.

Before tackling the analysis of each term of the mythical system, one must agree on terminology. We now know that the signifier can be looked at, in myth, from two points of view: as the final term of the linguistic system, or as the first term of the mythical system. We therefore need two names. On the plane of language, that is, as the final term of the first system, I shall call the signifier: *meaning* (*my name is lion, a Negro is giving the French salute*); on the plane of myth, I shall call it: *form*. In the case of the signified, no ambiguity is possible: we shall retain the name *concept*. The third term is the correlation of the first two: in the linguistic system, it is the *sign*; but it is not possible to use this word again without ambiguity, since in myth (and this is the chief peculiarity of the latter), the signifier is already formed by the *signs* of the language. I shall call the third term of myth the *signification*. This word is here all the better justified since myth has in fact a double function: it points out and it notifies, it makes us understand something and it imposes it on us.

The form and the concept

The signifier of myth presents itself in an ambiguous way: it is at the same time meaning and form, full on one side and empty on the other. As meaning, the signifier already postulates a reading, I grasp it through my eyes, it has a sensory reality (unlike the linguistic signifier, which is purely mental), there is a richness in it: the naming of the lion, the Negro's salute are credible wholes, they have at their disposal a sufficient rationality. As a total of linguistic signs, the meaning of the myth has its own value, it belongs to a history, that of the lion or that of the Negro: in the meaning, a signification is already built, and could very well be self-sufficient if myth did not take hold of it and did not turn it suddenly into an empty, parasitical form. The meaning is *already* complete, it postulates a kind of knowledge, a past, a memory, a comparative order of facts, ideas, decisions.

When it becomes form, the meaning leaves its contingency behind; it empties itself, it becomes impoverished, history evaporates, only the letter remains. There here a paradoxical permutation in the reading operations, an abnormal regression from meaning to form, from the linguistic sign to the mythical signifier. If one encloses *quia ego nominor leo* in a purely linguistic system, the clause finds again there a fullness, a richness, a history: I am an animal, a lion, I live in a certain country, I have just been hunting, they would have me share my prey with a heifer, a cow and a goat; but being the stronger, I award myself all the shares for various reasons, the last of which is quite simply that *my name is lion*. But as the form of the myth, the clause hardly retains anything of this long story. The meaning contained a whole system of values: a history, a geography, a morality, a zoology, a Literature. The form has put all this richness at a distance: its newly acquired penury calls for a signification to fill it. The story of the lion must recede a great deal in order to make room for the grammatical example, one must put the biography of the Negro in parentheses if one wants to free the picture, and prepare it to receive its signified.

But the essential point in all this is that the form does not suppress the meaning, it only impoverishes it, it puts it at a distance, it holds it at one's disposal. One believes that the meaning is going to die, but it is a death with reprieve; the meaning loses its value, but keeps its life, from which the form of the myth will draw its nourishment. The meaning will be for the form like an instantaneous reserve of history, a tamed richness, which it is possible to call and dismiss in a sort of rapid alternation: the form must constantly be able to be rooted again in the meaning and to get there what nature it needs for its nutriment; above all, it must be able to hide there. It is this constant game of hide-and-seek between the meaning and the form which defines myth. The form of myth is not a symbol: the Negro who salutes is not the symbol of the French Empire: he has too much presence, he appears as a rich, fully experienced, spontaneous, innocent, *indisputable* image. But at the same time this presence is tamed, put at a distance, made almost transparent; it recedes a little, it becomes the accomplice of a concept which comes to it fully armed, French imperiality: once made use of, it becomes artificial.

Let us now look at the signified: this history which drains out of the form will be wholly absorbed by the concept. As for the latter, it is determined, it is at once historical and intentional; it is the motivation which causes the myth to be uttered. Grammatical exemplarity, French imperiality, are the very drives behind the myth. The concept reconstitutes a chain of causes and effects, motives and intentions. Unlike the form, the concept is in no way abstract: it is filled with a situation. Through the concept, it is a whole new history which is implanted in the myth. Into the naming of the lion, first drained of its contingency, the grammatical example will attract my whole existence: Time, which caused me to be born at a certain period when Latin grammar is taught; History, which sets me apart, through a whole mechanism of social segregation, from the children who do not learn Latin; paedagogic tradition, which caused this example to be chosen from Aesop or Phaedrus; my own linguistic habits, which see the agreement of the predicate as a fact worthy of notice and illustration. The same goes for the Negro-giving-the-salute: as form, its meaning is shallow, isolated, impoverished; as the concept of French imperiality, here it is again tied to the totality of the world: to the general History of France, to its colonial adventures, to its present difficulties. Truth to tell, what is invested in the concept is less reality than a certain knowledge of reality; in passing from the meaning to the form, the image loses some knowledge: the better to receive the knowledge in the concept. In actual fact, the knowledge contained in a mythical concept is confused, made of yielding, shapeless associations. One must firmly stress this open character of the concept; it is not at all an abstract, purified essence; it is a formless, unstable, nebulous condensation, whose unity and coherence are above all due to its function.

In this sense, we can say that the fundamental character of the mythical concept is to be *appropriated*: grammatical exemplarity very precisely concerns a given form of pupils, French imperiality must appeal to such and such group of readers and not another. The concept closely corresponds to a function, it is defined as a tendency. This cannot fail to recall the signified in another semiological system, Freudianism. In Freud, the second term of the system is the latent meaning (the content) of the dream, of the parapraxis, of the neurosis. Now Freud does remark that the second-order meaning of behaviour is its real meaning, that which is appropriate to a complete situation, including its deeper level; it is, just like the mythical concept, the very intention of behaviour.

A signified can have several signifiers: this is indeed the case in linguistics and psychoanalysis. It is also the case in the mythical concept: it has at its disposal an unlimited mass of signifiers: I can find a thousand Latin sentences to actualize for me the agreement of the predicate, I can find a thousand images which signify to me French imperiality. This means that *quantitively*, the concept is much poorer than the signifier, it often does nothing but re-present itself. Poverty and richness are in reverse proportion in the form and the concept: to the qualitative poverty of the form, which is the repository of a rarefied meaning, there corresponds the richness of the concept which is open to the whole of History; and to the quantitative abundance of the forms there corresponds a small number of concepts. This repetition of the concept through different forms is precious to the mythologist, it allows him to decipher the myth: it is the insistence of a kind of behaviour which reveals its intention. This confirms that there is no regular ratio between the volume of the signified and that of the signifier. In language, this ratio is proportionate, it hardly exceeds the word, or at least the concrete unit. In myth, on the contrary, the concept can spread over a very large expanse of signifier. For instance, a whole book may be the signifier of a single concept; and conversely, a minute form (a word, a gesture, even incidental, so long as it is noticed) can serve as signifier to a concept filled with a very rich history. Although unusual in language, this disproportion between signifier and signified is not specific to myth: in Freud, for instance, the parapraxis is a signifier whose thinness is out of proportion to the real meaning which it betrays.

As I said, there is no fixity in mythical concepts: they can come into being, alter, disintegrate, disappear completely. And it is precisely because they are historical that history can very easily suppress them. This instability forces the mythologist to use a terminology adapted to it, and about which I should now like to say a word, because it often is a cause for irony: I mean neologism The concept is a constituting element of myth: if I want to decipher myths, I must somehow be able to name concepts. The dictionary supplies me with a few: Goodness, Kindness, Wholeness, Humaneness, etc. But by definition, since it is the dictionary which gives them to me, these particular concepts are not historical. Now what I need most often is ephemeral concepts, in connection with limited contingencies: neologism is then inevitable. China is one thing, the idea which a French petit-bourgeois could have of it not so long ago is another: for this peculiar mixture of bells, rickshaws and opium-dens, no other word possible but *Sininess*.[5] Unlovely? One should at least get some consolation from the fact that conceptual neologisms are never arbitrary: they are built according to a highly sensible proportional rule.

The signification

In semiology, the third term is nothing but the association of the first two, as we saw. It is the only one which is allowed to be seen in a full and satisfactory way, the only one which is consumed in actual fact. I have called it: the signification. We can see that the signification is the myth itself, just as the Saussurean sign is the word (or more accurately the concrete unit). But before listing the characters of the signification, one must reflect a little on the way in which it is prepared, that is, on the modes of correlation of the mythical concept and the mythical form.

First we must note that in myth, the first two terms are perfectly manifest (unlike what happens in other semiological systems): one of them is not 'hidden' behind the other, they are both given *here* (and not one here and the other there). However paradoxical it may seem, *myth hides nothing*: its function is to distort, not to make disappear. There is no latency of the concept in relation to the form: there is no need of an unconscious in order to explain myth. Of course, one is dealing with two different types of manifestation: form has a literal, immediate presence; moreover, it is extended. This stems – this cannot be repeated too often – from the nature of the mythical signifier, which is already linguistic: since it is constituted by a meaning which is already outlined, it can appear only through a given substance (whereas in language, the signifier remains mental). In the case of oral myth, this extension is linear (*for my name is lion*); in that of visual myth, it is multidimensional (in the centre, the Negro's uniform, at the top, the blackness of his face, on the left, the military salute, etc.). The elements of the form therefore are related as to place and proximity: the mode of presence of the form is spatial. The concept, on the contrary, appears in global fashion, it is a kind of nebula, the condensation, more or less hazy, of a certain knowledge. Its elements are linked by associative relations: it is supported not by an extension but by a depth (although this metaphor is perhaps still too spatial): its mode of presence is memorial.

The relation which unites the concept of the myth to its meaning is essentially a relation of *deformation*. We find here again a certain formal analogy with a complex semiological system such as that of the various types of psychoanalysis. Just as for Freud the manifest meaning of behaviour is distorted by its latent meaning, in myth the meaning is distorted by the concept. Of course, this distortion is possible only because the form of the myth is already constituted by a linguistic meaning. In a simple system like the language, the signified cannot distort anything at all because the signifier, being empty, arbitrary, offers no resistance to it. But here, everything is different: the signifier has, so to speak, two aspects: one full, which is the meaning (the history of the lion, of the Negro soldier), one empty, which is the form (*for my name is lion*; *Negro-French-soldier-saluting-the-tricolour*). What the concept distorts is of course what is full, the meaning: the lion and the Negro are deprived of their history, changed into gestures. What Latin exemplarity distorts is the naming of the lion, in all its contingency; and what French imperiality obscures is also a primary language, a factual discourse which was telling me about the salute of a Negro in uniform. But this distortion is not an obliteration: the lion and the Negro remain here, the concept needs them; they are half-amputated, they are deprived of memory, not of existence: they are at once stubborn, silently rooted there, and garrulous, a speech wholly at the service of the concept. The concept, literally, deforms, but does not abolish the meaning; a word can perfectly render this contradiction: it alienates it.

What must always be remembered is that myth is a double system; there occurs in it a sort of ubiquity: its point of departure is constituted by the arrival of a meaning. To keep a spatial metaphor, the approximative character of which I have already stressed, I shall say that the signification of the myth is constituted by a sort of constantly moving turnstile which presents alternately the meaning of the signifier and its form, a language-object and a metalanguage, a purely signifying and a purely imagining consciousness. This alternation is, so to speak, gathered up in the concept, which uses it like an ambiguous signifier, at once intellective and imaginary, arbitrary and natural.

I do not wish to prejudge the moral implications of such a mechanism, but I shall not exceed the limits of an objective analysis if I point out that the ubiquity of the signifier in myth exactly reproduces the physique of the *alibi* (which is, as one realizes, a spatial term): in the alibi too, there is a place which is full and one which is empty, linked by a relation of negative identity ('I am not where you think I am; I am where you think I am not'). But the ordinary alibi (for the police, for instance) has an end; reality stops the turnstile revolving at a certain point. Myth is a *value*, truth is no guarantee for it; nothing prevents it from being a perpetual alibi: it is enough that its signifier has two sides for it always to have an 'elsewhere' at its disposal. The meaning is always there to *present* the form; the form is always there to *outdistance* the meaning. And there never is any contradiction, conflict, or split between the meaning and the form: they are never at the same place. In the same way, if I am in a car and I look at the scenery through the window, I can at will focus on the scenery or on the window-pane. At one moment I grasp the presence of the glass and the distance of the landscape; at another, on the contrary, the transparence of the glass and the depth of the landscape; but the result of this alternation is constant: the glass is at once present and empty to me, and the landscape unreal and full. The same thing occurs in the mythical signifier: its form is empty but present, its meaning absent but full. To wonder at this contradiction I must voluntarily interrupt this turnstile of form and meaning, I must focus on each separately, and apply to myth a static method of deciphering, in short, I must go against its own dynamics: to sum up, I must pass from the state of reader to that of mythologist.

And it is again this duplicity of the signifier which determines the characters of the signification. We now know that myth is a type of speech defined by its intention (*I am a grammatical example*) much more than by its literal sense (*my name is lion*); and that in spite of this, its intention is somehow frozen, purified, eternalized, *made absent* by this literal sense (*The French Empire? It's just a fact: look at this good Negro who salutes like one of our own boys*). This constituent ambiguity of mythical speech has two consequences for the signification, which henceforth appears both like a notification and like a statement of fact.

Myth has an imperative, buttonholing character: stemming from an historical concept, directly springing from contingency (a Latin class, a threatened Empire), it is *I* whom it has come to seek. It is turned towards me, I am subjected to its intentional force, it summons me to receive its expansive ambiguity. If, for instance, I take a walk in Spain, in the Basque country,[6] I may well notice in the houses an architectural unity, a common style, which leads me to acknowledge the Basque house as a definite ethnic product. However, I do not feel personally concerned, nor, so to speak, attacked by this unitary style: I see only too well that it was here before me, without me. It is a complex product which has its determinations at the level of a very wide history: it does not call out to me, it does not provoke me into naming it, except if I think of inserting it into a vast picture of rural habitat. But if I am in the Paris region and I catch a glimpse, at the end of the rue Gambetta or the rue Jean-Jaurès, of a natty white chalet with red tiles, dark brown half-timbering, an asymmetrical roof and a wattle-and-daub front, I feel as if I were personally receiving an imperious injunction to name this object a Basque chalet: or even better, to see it as the very essence of *basquity*. This is because the concept appears to me in all its appropriative nature: it comes and seeks me out in order to oblige me to acknowledge the body of intentions which have motivated it and arranged it there as the signal of an individual history, as a confidence and a complicity: it is a real call, which the owners of the chalet send out to me. And this call, in order to be more imperious, has agreed to all manner of impoverishments: all that justified the Basque house on the plane of technology – the barn, the outside stairs, the dove-cote, etc. – has been dropped; there remains only a brief order, not to be disputed. And the adhomination is so frank that I feel this chalet has just been created on the spot, *for me*, like a magical object springing up in my present life without any trace of the history which has caused it.

For this interpellant speech is at the same time a frozen speech: at the moment of reaching me, it suspends itself, turns away and assumes the look of a generality: it stiffens, it makes itself look neutral and innocent. The appropriation of the concept is suddenly driven away once more by the literalness of the meaning. This is a kind of *arrest*, in both the physical and the legal sense of the term: French imperiality condemns the saluting Negro to be nothing more than an instrumental signifier, the Negro suddenly hails me in the name of French imperiality; but at the same moment the Negro's salute thickens, becomes vitrified, freezes into an eternal reference meant to *establish* French imperiality. On the surface of language something has stopped moving: the use of the signification is here, hiding behind the fact, and conferring on it a notifying look; but at the same time, the fact paralyses the intention, gives it something like a malaise producing immobility: in order to make it innocent, it freezes it. This is because myth is speech *stolen and restored*. Only, speech which is restored is no longer quite that which was stolen: when it was brought back, it was not put exactly in its place. It is this brief act of larceny, this moment taken for a surreptitious faking, which gives mythical speech its benumbed look.

One last element of the signification remains to be examined: its motivation. We know that in a language, the sign is arbitrary: nothing compels the acoustic image *tree* 'naturally' to mean the concept *tree*: the sign, here, is unmotivated. Yet this arbitrariness has limits, which come from the associative relations of the word: the language can produce a whole fragment of the sign by analogy with other signs (for instance one says *aimable* in French, and not *amable*, by analogy with *aime*). The mythical signification, on the other hand, is never arbitrary; it is always in part motivated, and unavoidably contains some analogy. For Latin exemplarity to meet the naming of the lion, there must be an analogy, which is the agreement of the predicate; for French imperiality to get hold of the saluting Negro, there must be identity between the Negro's salute and that of the French soldier. Motivation is necessary to the very duplicity of myth: myth plays on the analogy between meaning and form, there is no myth without motivated form.[7] In order to grasp the power of motivation in myth, it is enough to reflect for a moment on an extreme case. I have here before me a collection of objects so lacking in order that I can find no *meaning* in it; it would seem that here, deprived of any previous meaning, the form could not root its analogy in anything, and that myth is impossible. But what the form can always give one to read is disorder itself: it can give a signification to the absurd, make the absurd itself a myth. This is what happens when common sense mythifies surrealism, for instance. Even the absence of motivation does not embarrass myth; for this absence will itself be sufficiently objectified to become legible: and finally, the absence of motivation will become a second-order motivation, and myth will be re-established.

Motivation is unavoidable. It is none the less very fragmentary. To start with, it is not 'natural': it is history which supplies its analogies to the form. Then, the analogy between the meaning and the concept is never anything but partial: the form drops many analogous features and keeps only a few: it keeps the sloping roof, the visible beams in the Basque chalet, it abandons the stairs, the barn, the weathered look, etc. One must even go further: a *complete* image would exclude myth, or at least would compel it to seize only its very completeness. This is just what happens in the case of bad painting, which is wholly based on the myth of what is 'filled out' and 'finished' (it is the opposite and symmetrical case of the myth of the absurd: here, the form mythifies an 'absence', there, a surplus). But in general myth prefers to work with poor, incomplete images, where the meaning is already relieved of its fat, and ready for a signification, such as caricatures, pastiches, symbols, etc. Finally, the motivation is chosen among other possible ones: I can very well give to French imperiality many other signifiers beside a Negro's salute: a French general pins a decoration on a one-armed Senegalese, a nun hands a cup of tea to a bed-ridden Arab, a white schoolmaster teaches attentive piccaninnies: the press undertakes every day to demonstrate that the store of mythical signifiers is inexhaustible.

The nature of the mythical signification can in fact be well conveyed by one particular simile: it is neither more nor less arbitrary than an ideograph. Myth is a pure ideographic system, where the forms are still motivated by the concept which they represent while not yet, by a long way, covering the sum of its possibilities for representation. And just as, historically, ideographs have gradually left the concept and have become associated with the sound, thus growing less and less motivated, the worn out state of a myth can be recognized by the arbitrariness of its signification: the whole of Molière is seen in a doctor's ruff.

Reading and deciphering myth

How is a myth received? We must here once more come back to the duplicity of its signifier, which is at once meaning and form. I can produce three different types of reading by focusing on the one, or the other, or both at the same time.[8]

1. If I focus on an empty signifier, I let the concept fill the form of the myth without ambiguity, and I find myself before a simple system, where the signification becomes literal again: the Negro who salutes is an *example* of French imperiality, he is a *symbol* for it. This type of focusing is, for instance, that of the producer of myths, of the journalist who starts with a concept and seeks a form for it.[9]

2. If I focus on a full signifier, in which I clearly distinguish the meaning and the form, and consequently the distortion which the one imposes on the other, I undo the signification of the myth, and I receive the latter as an imposture: the saluting Negro becomes the *alibi* of French imperiality. This type of focusing is that of the mythologist: he deciphers the myth, he understands a distortion.

3. Finally, if I focus on the mythical signifier as on an inextricable whole made of meaning and form, I receive an ambiguous signification: I respond to the constituting mechanism of myth, to its own dynamics, I become a reader of myths. The saluting Negro is no longer an example or a symbol, still less an alibi: he is the very *presence* of French imperiality.

The first two types of focusing are static, analytical; they destroy the myth, either by making its intention obvious, or by unmasking it: the former is cynical, the latter demystifying. The third type of focusing is dynamic, it consumes the myth according to the very ends built into its structure: the reader lives the myth as a story at once true and unreal.

If one wishes to connect a mythical schema to a general history, to explain how it corresponds to the interests of a definite society, in short, to pass from semiology to ideology, it is obviously at the level of the third type of focusing that one must place oneself: it is the reader of myths himself who must reveal their essential function. How does he receive this particular myth *today*? If he receives it in an innocent fashion, what is the point of proposing it to him? And if he reads it using his powers of reflection, like the mythologist, does it matter which alibi is presented? If the reader does not see French imperiality in the saluting Negro, it was not worth weighing the latter with it; and if he sees it, the myth is nothing more than a political proposition, honestly expressed. In one word, either the intention of the myth is too obscure to be efficacious, or it is too clear to be believed. In either case, where is the ambiguity?

This is but a false dilemma. Myth hides nothing and flaunts nothing: it distorts; myth is neither a lie nor a confession: it is an inflexion. Placed before the dilemma which I mentioned a moment ago, myth finds a third way out. Threatened with disappearance if it yields to either of the first two types of focusing, it gets out of this tight spot thanks to a compromise – it *is* this compromise. Entrusted with 'glossing over' an intentional concept, myth encounters nothing but betrayal in language, for language can only obliterate the concept if it hides it, or unmask it if it formulates it. The elaboration of a second-order semiological system will enable myth to escape this dilemma: driven to having either to unveil or to liquidate the concept, it will *naturalize* it.

We reach here the very principle of myth: it transforms history into nature. We now understand why, *in the eyes of the myth-consumer*, the intention, the adhomination of the concept can remain manifest without however appearing to have an interest in the matter: what causes mythical speech to be uttered is perfectly explicit, but it is immediately frozen into something natural; it is not read as a motive, but as a reason. If I read the Negro-saluting as symbol pure and simple of imperiality, I must renounce the reality of the picture, it discredits itself in my eyes when it becomes an instrument. Conversely, if I decipher the Negro's salute as an alibi of coloniality, I shatter the myth even more surely by the obviousness of its motivation. But for the myth-reader, the outcome is quite different: everything happens as if the picture *naturally* conjured up the concept, as if the signifier *gave a foundation* to the signified: the myth exists from the precise moment when French imperiality achieves the natural state: myth is speech justified *in excess*.

Here is a new example which will help understand clearly how the myth-reader is led to rationalize the signified by means of the signifier. We are in the month of July, I read a big headline in *France-Soir*: THE FALL IN PRICES: FIRST INDICATIONS. VEGETABLES: PRICE DROP BEGINS. Let us quickly sketch the semiological schema: the example being a sentence, the first system is purely linguistic. The signifier of the second system is composed here of a certain number of accidents, some lexical (the words: *first*, *begins*, *the* [fall]), some typographical (enormous headlines where the reader usually sees news of world importance). The signified or concept is what must be called by a barbarous but unavoidable neologism: *governmentality*, the Government presented by the national press as the Essence of efficacy. The signification of the myth follows clearly from this: fruit and vegetable prices are falling *because* the government has so decided. Now it so happens in this case (and this is on the whole fairly rare) that the newspaper itself has, two lines below, allowed one to see through the myth which it had just elaborated – whether this is due to self-assurance or honesty. It adds (in small type, it is true): 'The fall in prices is helped by the return of seasonal abundance.' This example is instructive for two reasons. Firstly it conspicuously shows that myth essentially aims at causing an immediate impression – it does not matter if one is later allowed to see through the myth, its action is assumed to be stronger than the rational explanations which may later belie it. This means that the reading of a myth is exhausted at one stroke. I cast a quick glance at my neighbour's *France-Soir*: I cull only a *meaning* there, but I read a true signification; I *receive* the presence of governmental action in the fall in fruit and vegetable prices. That is all, and that is enough. A more attentive reading of the myth will in no way increase its power or its ineffectiveness: a myth is at the same time imperfectible and unquestionable; time or knowledge will not make it better or worse.

Secondly, the naturalization of the concept, which I have just identified as the essential function of myth, is here exemplary. In a first (exclusively linguistic) system, causality would be, literally, natural: fruit and vegetable prices fall because they are in season. In the second (mythical) system, causality is artificial, false; but it creeps, so to speak, through the back door of Nature. This is why myth is experienced as innocent speech: not because its intentions are hidden – if they were hidden, they could not be efficacious – but because they are naturalized.

In fact, what allows the reader to consume myth innocently is that he does not see it as a semiological system but as an inductive one. Where there is only an equivalence, he sees a kind of causal process: the signifier and the signified have, in his eyes, a natural relationship. This confusion can be expressed otherwise: any semiological system is a system of values; now the myth-consumer takes the signification for a system of facts: myth is read as a factual system, whereas it is but a semiological system.

Notes

1. Innumerable other meanings of the word 'myth' can be cited against this. But I have tried to define things, not words.
2. The development of publicity, of a national press, of radio, of illustrated news, not to speak of the survival of a myriad rites of communication which rule social appearances makes the development of a semiological science more urgent than ever. In a single day, how many really non-signifying fields do we cross? Very few, sometimes none. Here I am, before the sea; it is true that it bears no message. But on the beach, what material for semiology! Flags, slogans, signals, sign-boards, clothes, suntan even, which are so many messages to me.
3. The notion of *word* is one of the most controversial in linguistics. I keep it here for the sake of simplicity.
4. *Tel Quel*, II, p. 191.
5. Or perhaps *Sinity*? Just as if Latin/latinity = Basque/x, x = Basquity.
6. I say 'in Spain' because, in France, petit-bourgeois advancement has caused a whole 'mythical' architecture of the Basque chalet to flourish.
7. From the point of view of ethics, what is disturbing in myth is precisely that its form is motivated. For if there is a 'health' of language, it is the arbitrariness of the sign which is its grounding. What is sickening in myth is its resort to a false nature, its superabundance of significant forms, as in these objects which decorate their usefulness with a natural appearance. The will to weigh the signification with the full guarantee of nature causes a kind of nausea: myth is too rich, and what is in excess is precisely its motivation. This nausea is like the one I feel before the arts which refuse to choose between *physis* and *anti-physis*, using the first as an ideal and the second as an economy. Ethically, there is a kind of baseness in hedging one's bets.
8. The freedom in choosing what one focuses on is a problem which does not belong to the province of semiology: it depends on the concrete situation of the subject.
9. We receive the naming of the lion as a pure *example* of Latin grammar because we are, *as grown-ups*, in a creative position in relation to it. I shall come back later to the value of the context in this mythical schema.

1.2 □ *Positions*

Jacques Derrida

Interview with
Jean-Louis Houdebine
and
Guy Scarpetta

[. . .]

Scarpetta: Perhaps we could come back to what you have said about history. I am thinking of the text in *Of Grammatology* in which you say: 'The word "history" doubtless has always been associated with the linear consecution of presence.' Can you conceive of the possibility of a concept of history that would escape this linear scheme? Can you see the possibility of what Sollers calls, for example, 'monumental history', that is, history conceived no longer as a linear scheme, but as a stratified, differentiated, contradictory practical series, that is, neither a monistic nor a historicist history?

Derrida: Of course. What we must be wary of, I repeat, is the *metaphysical* concept of history. This is the concept of history as the history of meaning, as we were just saying a moment ago: the history of meaning developing itself, producing itself, fulfilling itself. And doing so linearly, as you recall: in a straight or circular line. This is why, moreover, the 'closure of metaphysics' cannot have the form of a *line*, that is, the form in which philosophy recognizes it, in which philosophy recognizes itself. The closure of metaphysics, above all, is not a circle surrounding a homogeneous field, a field homogeneous with itself on its inside, whose outside then would be homogeneous also. The limit has the form of always different faults, of fissures whose mark or scar is borne by all the texts of philosophy.

The metaphysical character of the concept of history is not only linked to linearity, but to an entire *system* of implications (teleology, eschatology, elevating and interiorizing accumulation of meaning, a certain type of traditionality, a certain concept of continuity, of truth, etc.). Therefore it is not an accidental predicate

From Derrida, J., *Positions*, trans. A. Bass, University of Chicago Press, Chicago, 1981, pp. 56–67, 104–06.

which could be removed by a kind of local ablation, without a general displacement of the organization, without setting the entire system to work. It has happened that I have spoken very quickly of a 'metaphysical concept'. But I have never believed that there were *metaphysical* concepts *in and of themselves*. No concept is by itself,[1] and consequently in and of itself, metaphysical, outside all the textual work in which it is inscribed. This explains why, although I have formulated many reservations about the 'metaphysical' concept of history, I very *often* use the word 'history' in order to reinscribe its force[2] and in order to produce another concept or conceptual chain of 'history': in effect a 'monumental, stratified, contradictory' history; a history that also implies a new logic of *repetition* and the *trace*, for it is difficult to see how there could be history without it.

Nevertheless we must recognize that the concept of history, by the force of the system of predicates I just mentioned, can always be reappropriated by metaphysics. For example: we must first distinguish between history in general and the general concept of history. Althusser's entire, and necessary, critique of the 'Hegelian' concept of history and of the notion of an expressive totality, etc., aims at showing that there is not one single history, a general history, but rather histories *different* in their type, rhythm, mode of inscription – intervallic, differentiated histories. I have always subscribed to this, as to the concept of history that Sollers calls 'monumental'.[3]

[. . .]

That being said, the concept of history, no more than any other, cannot be subject to a simple and instantaneous mutation, the striking of a name from the vocabulary. We must elaborate a strategy of the textual work which at every instant borrows an old word from philosophy in order immediately to demarcate it. This is what I was alluding to just now in speaking of a double gesture or double stratification. We must first *overturn* the traditional concept of history, but at the same time mark the *interval*, take care that by virtue of the overturning, and by the simple fact of conceptualization, the interval not be *reappropriated*. Certainly a new conceptualization is to be produced, but it must take into account the fact that conceptualization itself, and by itself alone, can reintroduce what one wants to 'criticize'. This is why this work cannot be purely 'theoretical' or 'conceptual' or 'discursive', I mean cannot be the work of a discourse entirely regulated by essence, meaning, truth, consciousness, ideality, etc. What I call *text* is also that which 'practically' inscribes and overflows the limits of such a discourse. *There* is such a general text everywhere that (that is, everywhere) this discourse and its order (essence, sense, truth, meaning, consciousness, ideality, etc.) are *overflowed*, that is, everywhere that their authority is put back into the position of a *mark* in a chain that this authority intrinsically and illusorily believes it wishes to and does in fact, govern. This general text is not limited, of course, as will (or would) be quickly understood, to writings on the page. The writing of this text, moreover, has the exterior limit only of a certain *re-mark*. Writing on the page, and then 'literature', are determined types of this re-mark. They must be investigated in their specificity, and in a new way, if you will, in the specificity of their 'history', and in their articulation with the other 'historical' fields of the text in general.

This is why, briefly, I so often use the word 'history', but so often too with the quotation marks and precautions that may have led to the attribution to me of (I am going to abuse this expression, which will lead me to prefer another: 'good style') a 'rejection of history'.

[. . .]

Houdebine: [I]t seems to us that the itinerary of a deconstruction of logocentric discourse inevitably encounters the materialist text, which has long been the historical text repressed-suppressed by logocentric discourse (idealism, metaphysics, religion) taken as the discourse of a ruling ideology in its different historical forms. Do you agree with us about the necessity of marking out this encounter? And could you tell us why this necessity has been marked in your work, up to now, either in a marginal fashion (I am thinking most notably of several notes in '*La double séance*' which bear witness, moreover, to the necessity you felt at that time of strategically – and even politically – regulating the implications of your discourse), or in a lacunary fashion, as in the passage of '*La différance*' where you speak of putting into question 'the self-assured certitude of consciousness' and refer to Nietzsche and Freud, leaving in suspense (but this suspense itself is perfectly legible) any reference to Marx, and along with Marx to the text of dialectical materialism? But it is true that in Marx, as in Engels and Lenin, the putting into question of the self-certainty of consciousness is not 'based on the motif of *différance*', and that another general economy is at stake here (has been at stake for a long time), according to the conceptual series briefly enunciated just now, and to which we would have to add the Marxist concept of 'ideology'.

Derrida: Naturally, I cannot answer these questions in a word. Where to begin? In effect, there is what you call this 'encounter', which has seemed absolutely necessary to me for a long time. You can imagine that I have not been completely unconscious of it. That being said, I persist in believing that there is no theoretical or political benefit to be derived from precipitating contacts or articulations, as long as their conditions have not been rigorously elucidated. Eventually such precipitation will have the effect only of dogmatism, confusion, or opportunism. To impose this prudence upon oneself is to take seriously the difficulty, and also the heterogeneity, of the Marxist text, the decisive importance of its historical stakes.

Where to begin then? If one wished to schematize – but truly this is only a schema – what I have attempted can *also* be inscribed under the rubric of the 'critique of idealism'. Therefore it goes without saying that to the extent that dialectical materialism also operates this critique, it in no way incurs my reticence, nor have I ever formulated any on this subject.

Do me the credit of believing that the 'lacunae' to which you alluded are explicitly calculated to mark the sites of a theoretical elaboration which remains, *for me*, at least, *still to come*. And they are indeed lacunae, not objections; they have a specific and deliberate status, I even dare say a certain efficacity. When I say *for me*,

I understand this: the conjunction between the work I attempt – a limited work, but with its own field and framework, a work possible only in a historical, political, theoretical, etc., situation that is highly determined – and the entire text and conceptuality of Marxism cannot be *immediately given*. To believe so would be to erase the specificity of these fields and to limit their *effective* transformation. Now in both cases, shall we say, to proceed quickly, in question are 'fields' that inscribe the possibility and opening of their practical transformation. And when I say '*still to come*', I am still, and above all, thinking of the relationship of Marx to Hegel, and of the question we were speaking of just now (dialectics, difference, contradiction, etc.). Despite the immense work which already has been done in this domain, a decisive elaboration has not yet been accomplished, and for historical reasons which can be analyzed, precisely, only during the elaboration of this work.

In what I have begun to propose, I attempt to take into account certain recent acquisitions or determined incompletions in the orders of philosophy, semiology, linguistics, psychoanalysis, etc. ... Now, we cannot consider Marx's, Engels's or Lenin's texts as completely finished elaborations that are simply to be 'applied' to the current situation. In saying this, I am not advocating anything contrary to 'Marxism', I am convinced of it. These texts are not to be read according to a hermeneutical or exegetical method which would seek out a finished signified beneath a textual surface. Reading is transformational. I believe that this would be confirmed by certain of Althusser's propositions. But this transformation cannot be executed however one wishes. It requires protocols of reading. Why not say it bluntly: I have not yet found any that satisfy me.

No more than I have dealt with Saussure's text, or Freud's, or any other, as homogeneous volumes (the motif of homogeneity, the theological motif *par excellence*, is decidedly the one to be destroyed), I do not find the texts of Marx, Engels, or Lenin homogeneous critiques. In their relationship to Hegel, for example. And the manner in which they themselves reflected and formulated the differentiated or contradictory structure of their relationship to Hegel has not seemed to me, correctly or incorrectly, sufficient. Thus I will have to analyze what I consider a heterogeneity, conceptualizing both its necessity and the rules for deciphering it; and do so by taking into account the decisive progress simultaneously accomplished by Althusser and those following him. All this poses many questions, and today I could tell you nothing not already legible in the lacunae or notes to which you alluded, at least for anyone who wishes to pursue their consequences. Above all they refer to the general economy whose traits I attempted to outline based on a reading of Bataille.[4] It follows that if, and in the extent to which, *matter* in this general economy designates, as you said, radical alterity (I will specify: in relation to philosophical oppositions), then what I write can be considered 'materialist'.

As you may imagine, things are not so simple. It is not always in *the* materialist text (is there such a thing, *the* materialist text?) nor in *every* materialist text that the concept of matter has been defined as absolute exterior or radical heterogeneity. I am not even sure that there can be a 'concept' of an absolute exterior. If I have not very often used the word 'matter', it is not, as you know, because of some idealist or spiritualist kind of reservation. It is that in the logic of the phase of overturning this concept has been too often reinvested with 'logocentric' values, values associated with those of thing, reality, presence in general, sensible presence, for example, substantial plenitude, content, referent, etc. Realism or sensualism – 'empiricism' – are modifications of logocentrism. (I have often insisted on the fact that 'writing' or the 'text' are not reducible *either* to the sensible or visible presence of the graphic or the 'literal'.) In short, the signifier 'matter' appears to me problematical only at the moment when its reinscription cannot avoid making of it a new fundamental principle which, by means of theoretical regression, would be reconstituted into a 'transcendental signified'. It is not only idealism in the narrow sense that falls back upon the transcendental signified. It can always come to reassure a metaphysical materialism. It then becomes an ultimate referent, according to the classical logic implied by the value of referent, or it becomes an 'objective reality' absolutely 'anterior' to any work of the mark, the semantic content of a form of presence which guarantees the movement of the text in general from the outside. (I am not sure that Lenin's analysis, for example, does not always give in to this operation; and if it does so strategically, we must first reelaborate – in a transformational writing – the rules of this strategy. Then there would be no reservations to be made.) This is why I will not say that the concept of matter is in and of itself either metaphysical or nonmetaphysical. This depends upon the work to which it yields, and you know that I have unceasingly insisted, as concerns the nonideal exteriority of writing, the gram, the trace, the text, etc., upon the necessity of never separating them from *work*, a value itself to be rethought outside its Hegelian affiliation. What is announced here, as I tried to indicate in '*La double séance*' (double science, double sense, double scene), is again the operation of the double mark or the re-mark. The concept of matter must be marked twice (the others too): in the deconstructed field[5] – this is the phase of overturning – and in the deconstructing text, outside the oppositions in which it has been caught (matter/spirit, matter/ideality, matter/form, etc.). By means of the play of this interval between the two marks, one can operate both an overturning deconstruction and a positively displacing, transgressive, deconstruction.

Rigorously reinscribed in the general economy (Bataille)[6] and in the double writing of which we were just speaking, the insistence on matter as the absolute exterior of opposition, the materialist insistence (in contact with what 'materialism' has represented as a force of resistance in the history of philosophy) seems to me necessary. It is unequally necessary, varying with the sites, the strategic situations, the practical and theoretical points advanced. In a very *determined* field of the most current situation, it seems to me that the materialist insistence can function as a means of having the necessary generalization of the concept of text, its extension with no simple exterior limit (which also supposes the passage through metaphysical opposition), not wind up (under the influence of very precise interests, reactive forces determined to lead work astray into confusion), not wind up, then, as the definition of a new self-interiority, a new 'idealism', if you will, of the text. In effect, we must avoid having the indispensable critique of a certain naive relationship to the signified or the referent, to sense or meaning, remain fixed in a suspension, that is, a pure and simple suppression, of meaning or reference. I believe that I have taken precautions on this matter in the propositions that I have advanced. But it is true, and the proofs are not lacking, that this is never sufficient. What we need is to determine *otherwise*, according to a differential system, the *effects* of ideality, of signification, of meaning, and of reference. (We also would have to make room for a systematic analysis of the word 'effect' which is used so frequently today – not an insignificant fact – and for the new concept which it marks in still rather undecided fashion. The frequency of this usage multiplies by virtue of this active indetermination. A concept in the process of constituting itself first produces a kind of localizable effervescence in the work of nomination. This 'new' concept of *effect* borrows its characteristics from both the opposition cause/effect and from the opposition essence/appearance – *effect, reflect* – *without nevertheless being reduced to them*. It is this fringe of irreducibility that is to be analyzed.)

Of course we must redouble our prudence in reconsidering the problem of meaning and reference. The 'dialectics' of the same and the other, of outside and inside, of the homogeneous and the heterogeneous, are, as you know, among the most *contorted* ones.[7] The outside can always become again an 'object' in the polarity subject/object, or the reassuring reality of what is outside the text; and there is sometimes an 'inside' that is as troubling as the outside may be reassuring. This is not to be overlooked in the critique of interiority and subjectivity.[8] Here we are in an extremely complex logic. The improvised speech of an interview cannot substitute for the textual work.

Notes

Derrida's notes are indicated by his initials, J. D. The editor's notes of the original French edition are indicated by the abbreviation Ed. N. Translator's notes are indicated by the abbreviation T. N.

1. J. D. See '*La différance*', in *Marges de la Philosophie* (Paris: Les Editions de Minuit, 1972), p. 11.
2. J. D. An example: 'If the word "history" did not bear within itself the motif of a final repression of difference, one could say that only differences can be, from the outset and in all aspects, "historical". What is written as *différance* will indicate, then, the movement of play that "produces", in a way that is not simply an activity, these differences, these effects of difference. This does not mean that the *différance* which produces differences is before them, in a simple present that is itself unmodified, in-different. *Différance* is the nonfull, nonsimple "origin", the structured and differing origin of differences. The name "origin", therefore, is no longer suitable. ... Retaining at least the schema, if not the content of the demand formulated by Saussure, we will designate as *différance* the movement according to which language, or any other code, any system of reference in general, is constituted "historically" as a tissue of differences. "Is constituted", "is produced", "is created", "movement", "historically", etc., have to be understood beyond the metaphysical language in which they are caught, along with all their implications. We would have to show why the concepts of production, like those of constitution and of

history, from this point of view remain in complicity with what is in question here, but this would take us too far today – in the direction of the representation of the "circle" in which we appear to be enclosed – and I utilize them here, as I do many other concepts, only for strategic convenience and in order to undertake the deconstruction of their system at the point which is currently most decisive.' *Ibid.*, pp. 12–13. See also, for example, '*La double séance*', in *La dissémination* (Paris: Seuil, 1972), pp. 235–6. [. . .]

3. J. D. In my improvised response, I had forgotten that Scarpetta's question also named *historicism*. Of course, the critique of historicism in all its forms seems to me indispensable. What I first learned about this critique in Husserl (from *Philosophy as a Rigorous Science* to the *Origin of Geometry*: Hegel is always the target of this critique, whether directly or whether through Dilthey), who, to my knowledge, was the first to formulate it under this heading and from the point of view of theoretical and scientific (especially mathematical) rigor, seems valid to me in its argumentative framework, even if in the last analysis it is based on a historical teleology of truth. On this last question the issue is to be reopened. The issue would be: can one criticize historicism in the name of something other than *truth and science* (the value of universality, omnitemporality, the infinity of value, etc.), and what happens to science when the *metaphysical* value of *truth* has been put into question, etc.? How are the effects of science and of truth to be reinscribed? This brief reminder in order to mention that during the course of our interview Nietzsche's name was not pronounced. By chance? On what we are speaking about at this very moment, as on everything else, Nietzsche is for me, as you know, a very important reference. Finally, it goes without saying that in no case is it a question of a *discourse against truth* or against science. (This is impossible and absurd, as is every heated accusation on this subject.) And when one analyzes systematically the value of truth as *homoiosis* or *adequatio*, as the certitude of the *cogito* (Descartes, Husserl), or as a certitude opposed to truth in the horizon of absolute knowledge (*Phenomenology of the Mind*), or finally as *alētheia*, unveiling or presence (the Heideggerean repetition), it is not in order to return naively to a relativist or sceptical empiricism. (See, notably, *De la grammatologie* [Paris: Editions de Minuit, 1967], p. 232, and '*La différance*' in *Marges*, p. 7.) I repeat, then, leaving all their disseminating powers to the proposition and the form of the verb: *we must have* [*il faut*] truth. For those who mystify (themselves) to have it trippingly on the tongue. Such is the law. Paraphrasing Freud, speaking of the present/absent penis (but it is the same thing), we must recognize in truth 'the normal prototype of the fetish'. How can we do without it?

4. T. N. See 'From restricted to general economy: a Hegelianism without reserve', in *Writing and Difference*, trans. A. Bass (Chicago: University of Chicago Press, 1978).

5. J. D. To summarize that which marks it within the deconstructed field, again I will cite Nietzsche: 'Let us renounce the notions of "subject" and "object", and then the notion of "substance", and consequently all of its diverse modifications, for example, "matter", "spirit", and the other hypothetical beings, "eternity", and the "immutability of matter", etc. Thus we also get rid of materiality'. I also refer to his *Unzeitgemasse* ... , 2.

6. J. D. Here I permit myself to recall that the texts to which you have referred (particularly '*La double séance*', '*La dissémination*', '*La mythologie blanche*', but also '*La pharmacie de Platon*' and several others) are situated *explicitly* in relation to Bataille, and also explicitly propose a reading of Bataille.

7. J. D. On this subject, and notably on the paradoxes of dissymmetry and alterity, see for example 'Violence and metaphysics', in *Writing and Difference*.

8. J. D. Nor is the heterogeneity of 'matter' to be constituted as transcendence, whether the transcendence of the Law, the Great Exterior Object (constitutive and consoling severity of the paternal agency), or of the (appeasing and/or cruel) Element of the mother (see what Freud says about the well-known relationship mother/matter in the passage in which he makes evident that which *cannot be reduced* to the variation of *linguistic*, verbal signifiers.

See lecture 10 of the *Introductory Lectures on Psychoanalysis*, and also the end of 'Freud and the scene of writing' in *Writing and Difference*). This does not imply that matter has no necessary relationship to these agencies, but rather that the relationship is one of written concatenation, a play of substitution of differential marks that relate matter also to writing, to the remainder, to death, to the phallus, to excrement, to the infant, to semen, etc., or at least to everything in this that is not subject to the *relève*. And requires thus, that this relationship not be made either into a new essential determination of the Being of beings, the center of a new ontology, or into a new example of the *master-words*, which Marx, for example, definitively criticized in the *German Ideology*.

1.3 □ *From* Revolution in Poetic Language

Julia Kristeva

The Phenomenological Subject of Enunciation

We must specify, first and foremost, what we mean by the *signifying process* vis-à-vis general theories of meaning, theories of language, and theories of the subject.

Despite their variations, all modern linguistic theories consider language a strictly 'formal' object – one that involves syntax or mathematicization. Within this perspective, such theories generally accept the following notion of language. For Zellig Harris, language is defined by: (1) the arbitrary relation between signifier and signified, (2) the acceptance of the sign as a substitute for the extra-linguistic, (3) its discrete elements, and (4) its denumerable, or even finite, nature.[1] But with the development of Chomskyan generative grammar and the logico-semantic research that was articulated around and in response to it, problems arose that were generally believed to fall within the province of 'semantics' or even 'pragmatics', and raised the awkward question of the *extra-linguistic*. But language [*langage*] – modern linguistics' self-assigned object[2] – lacks a subject or tolerates one only as a *transcendental ego* (in Husserl's sense or in Benveniste's more specifically linguistic sense),[3] and defers any interrogation of its (always-already dialectical because trans-linguistic) 'externality'.

Two trends in current linguistic research do attend to this 'externality' in the belief that failure to elucidate it will hinder the development of linguistic theory itself. Although such a lacuna poses problems (which we will later specify) for 'formal' linguistics, it has always been a particular problem for semiotics, which is concerned with specifying the functioning of signifying practices such as art, poetry, and myth that are irreducible to the 'language' object.

From Kristeva, J., *Revolution in Poetic Language*, trans. M. Waller, Columbia University Press, New York, 1984, pp. 21–30, 140–46.

1. The first of these two trends addresses the question of the so-called 'arbitrary' relation between signifier and signified by examining signifying systems in which this relation is presented as 'motivated'. It seeks the principle of this motivation in the Freudian notion of the unconscious in so far as the theories of drives [*pulsions*] and primary processes (displacement and condensation) can connect 'empty signifiers' to psychosomatic functionings, or can at least link them in a sequence of metaphors and metonymies; though undecidable, such a sequence replaces 'arbitrariness' with 'articulation'. The discourse of analysands, language 'pathologies', and artistic, particularly poetic, systems are especially suited to such an exploration.[4] Formal linguistic relations are thus connected to an 'externality' in the psychosomatic realm, which is ultimately reduced to a fragmented substance [*substance morcelée*] (the body divided into erogenous zones) and articulated by the developing ego's connections to the three points of the family triangle. Such a linguistic theory, clearly indebted to the positions of the psychoanalytic school of London and Melanie Klein in particular, restores to formal linguistic relations the dimensions (instinctual drives) and operations (displacement, condensation, vocalic and intonational differentiation) that formalistic theory excludes. Yet for want of a dialectical notion of the *signifying process* as a whole, in which signifiance puts the subject in process/on trial [*en procès*], such considerations, no matter how astute, fail to take into account the syntactico-semantic functioning of language. Although they rehabilitate the notion of the fragmented body – pre-Oedipal but alway-already invested with semiosis – these linguistic theories fail to articulate its transitional link to the post-Oedipal subject and his always symbolic and/or syntactic language. (We shall return to this point.)

2. The second trend, more recent and widespread, introduces within theory's own formalism a 'layer' of *semiosis*, which had been strictly relegated to pragmatics and semantics. By positing a *subject of enunciation* (in the sense of Benveniste, Culioli, etc.), this theory places logical modal relations, relations of presupposition, and other relations between interlocutors within the speech act, in a very deep 'deep structure'. This *subject of enunciation*, which comes directly from Husserl and Benveniste (see n. 3), introduces, through categorial intuition, both *semantic fields* and *logical* – but also *intersubjective* – *relations*, which prove to be both intra- and trans-linguistic.[5]

[. . .]

To summarize briefly what we shall elucidate later, the two trends just mentioned designate *two modalities* of what is, for us, the same signifying process. We shall call the first *'the semiotic'* and the second *'the symbolic'*. These two modalities are inseparable within the *signifying process* that constitutes language, and the dialectic between them determines the type of discourse (narrative, metalanguage, theory, poetry, etc.) involved; in other words, so-called 'natural' language allows for different modes of articulation of the semiotic and the symbolic. On the other hand, there are nonverbal signifying systems that are constructed exclusively on the basis of the semiotic (music, for example). But, as we shall see, this exclusivity is relative,

precisely because of the necessary dialectic between the two modalities of the signifying process, which is constitutive of the subject. Because the subject is always *both* semiotic *and* symbolic, no signifying system he produces can be either 'exclusively' semiotic or 'exclusively' symbolic, and is instead necessarily marked by an indebtedness to both.

The Semiotic Chora Ordering the Drives

We understand the term 'semiotic' in its Greek sense: σημεῖον = distinctive mark, trace, index, precursory sign, proof, engraved or written sign, imprint, trace, figuration. This etymological reminder would be a mere archaeological embellishment (and an unconvincing one at that, since the term ultimately encompasses such disparate meanings), were it not for the fact that the preponderant etymological use of the word, the one that implies a *distinctiveness*, allows us to connect it to a precise modality in the signifying process. This modality is the one Freudian psychoanalysis points to in postulating not only the *facilitation* and the structuring *disposition* of drives, but also the so-called *primary processes* which displace and condense both energies and their inscription. Discrete quantities of energy move through the body of the subject who is not yet constituted as such and, in the course of his development, they are arranged according to the various constraints imposed on this body – always-already involved in a semiotic process – by family and social structures. In this way the drives, which are 'energy' charges as well as 'psychical' marks, articulate what we call a *chora*: a nonexpressive totality formed by the drives and their stases in a motility that is as full of movement as it is regulated.

We borrow the term *chora*[6] from Plato's *Timaeus* to denote an essentially mobile and extremely provisional articulation constituted by movements and their ephemeral stases. We differentiate this uncertain and indeterminate *articulation* from a *disposition* that already depends on representation, lends itself to phenomenological, spatial intuition, and gives rise to a geometry. Although our theoretical description of the *chora* is itself part of the discourse of representation that offers it as evidence, the *chora*, as rupture and articulations (rhythm), precedes evidence, verisimilitude, spatiality, and temporality. Our discourse – all discourse – moves with and against the *chora* in the sense that it simultaneously depends upon and refuses it. Although the *chora* can be designated and regulated, it can never be definitively posited: as a result, one can situate the *chora* and, if necessary, lend it a topology, but one can never give it axiomatic form.[7]

The *chora* is not yet a position that represents something for someone (i.e. it is not a sign); nor is it a *position* that represents someone for another position (i.e. it is not yet a signifier either); it is, however, generated in order to attain to this signifying position. Neither model nor copy, the *chora* precedes and underlies figuration and thus specularization, and is analogous only to vocal or kinetic rhythm. We must restore this motility's gestural and vocal play (to mention only the aspect relevant to language) on the level of the socialized body in order to remove motility from ontology and amorphousness[8] where Plato confines it in an apparent attempt to conceal it from Democritean rhythm. The theory of the subject proposed by the theory of the unconscious will allow us to read in this rhythmic space, which has no thesis and no position, the process by which significance is constituted. Plato himself leads us to such a process when he calls this receptacle or *chora* nourishing and maternal,[9] not yet unified in an ordered whole because deity is absent from it. Though deprived of unity, identity, or deity, the *chora* is nevertheless subject to a regulating process [*réglementation*], which is different from that of symbolic law but nevertheless effectuates discontinuities by temporarily articulating them and then starting over, again and again.

The *chora* is a modality of significance in which the linguistic sign is not yet articulated as the absence of an object and as the distinction between real and symbolic. We emphasize the regulated aspect of the *chora*: its vocal and gestural organization is subject to what we shall call an objective *ordering* [*ordonnancement*], which is dictated by natural or socio-historical constraints such as the biological difference between the sexes or family structure. We may therefore posit that social organization, always-already symbolic, imprints its constraint in a mediated form which organizes the *chora* not according to a *law* (a term we reserve for the symbolic) but through an *ordering*.[10] What is this mediation?

According to a number of psycholinguists, 'concrete operations' precede the acquisition of language, and organize preverbal semiotic space according to logical categories, which are thereby shown to precede or transcend language. From their research we shall retain not the principle of an operational state[11] but that of a preverbal functional state that governs the connections between the body (in the process of constituting itself as a body proper), objects, and the protagonists of family structure.[12] But we shall distinguish this functioning from symbolic operations that depend on language as a sign system – whether the language [*langue*] is vocalized or gestural (as with deaf-mutes). The kinetic functional stage of the *semiotic* precedes the establishment of the sign; it is not, therefore, cognitive in the sense of being assumed by a knowing, already constituted subject. The genesis of the *functions*[13] organizing the semiotic process can be accurately elucidated only within a theory of the subject that does not reduce the subject to one of understanding, but instead opens up within the subject this other scene of presymbolic functions. The Kleinian theory expanding upon Freud's positions on the drives will momentarily serve as a guide.

Drives involve pre-Oedipal semiotic functions and energy discharges that connect and orient the body to the mother. We must emphasize that 'drives' are always-already ambiguous, simultaneously assimilating and destructive; this dualism, which has been represented as a tetrad[14] or as a double helix, as in the configuration of the DNA and RNA molecule,[15] makes the semiotized body a place of permanent scission. The oral and anal drives, both of which are oriented and structured around the mother's body,[16] dominate this sensorimotor organization. The mother's body is therefore what mediates the symbolic law organizing social relations and becomes the ordering principle of the semiotic *chora*,[17] which is on the path of destruction, aggressivity, and death. For although drives have been described as disunited or contradictory structures, simultaneously 'positive' and 'negative', this doubling is said to generate a dominant 'destructive wave', that is drive's most characteristic trait: Freud notes that the most instinctual drive is the death drive.[18] In this way, the term 'drive' denotes waves of attack against stases, which are themselves constituted by the repetition of these charges; together, charges and stases lead to no identity (not even that of the 'body proper') that could be seen as a result of their functioning. This is to say that the semiotic *chora* is no more than the place where the subject is both generated and negated, the place where his unity succumbs before the process of charges and stases that produce him. We shall call this process of charges and stases a *negativity* to distinguish it from negation, which is the act of a judging subject [. . .]

Checked by the constraints of biological and social structures, the drive charge thus undergoes stases. Drive facilitation, temporarily arrested, marks *discontinuities* in what may be called the various material supports [*matériaux*] susceptible to semiotization: voice, gesture, colors. Phonic (later phonemic), kinetic, or chromatic units and differences are the marks of these stases in the drives. Connections or *functions* are thereby established between these discrete marks which are based on drives and articulated according to their resemblance or opposition, either by slippage or by condensation. Here we find the principles of metonymy and metaphor indissociable from the drive economy underlying them.

Although we recognize the vital role played by the processes of displacement and condensation in the organization of the semiotic, we must also add to these processes the relations (eventually representable as topological spaces) that connect the zones of the fragmented body to each other and also to 'external' 'objects' and 'subjects', which are not yet constituted as such. This type of relation makes it possible to specify the *semiotic* as a psychosomatic modality of the signifying process; in other words, not a symbolic modality but one articulating (in the largest sense of the word) a continuum: the connections between the (glottal and anal) sphincters in (rhythmic and intonational) vocal modulations, or those between the sphincters and family protagonists, for example.

All these various processes and relations, anterior to sign and syntax, have just been identified from a genetic perspective as previous and necessary to the acquisition of language, but not identical to language. Theory can 'situate' such processes and relations diachronically within the process of the constitution of the subject precisely because *they function synchronically within the signifying process of the subject himself*, i.e. the subject of *cogitatio*. Only in *dream* logic, however, have they attracted attention, and only in certain signifying practices, such as the *text*, do they dominate the signifying process.

It may be hypothesized that certain semiotic articulations are transmitted through the biological code or physiological 'memory' and thus form the inborn bases of the symbolic function. Indeed, one branch of generative linguistics asserts the principle of innate language universals. As it will become apparent in what follows, however, the *symbolic* – and therefore syntax and all linguistic categories – is a social effect of the relation to the other, established through the objective constraints of biological (including sexual) differences and concrete, historical family structures. Genetic programmings are necessarily semiotic: they include the primary processes such as displacement and condensation, absorption and repulsion, rejection and stasis, all of which function as innate preconditions, 'memorizable' by the species, for language acquisition.

Mallarmé calls attention to the semiotic rhythm within language when he speaks of 'The Mystery in Literature' ['Le Mystère dans les lettres']. Indifferent to language, enigmatic and feminine, this space underlying the written is rhythmic, unfettered, irreducible to its intelligible verbal translation; it is musical, anterior to judgment, but restrained by a single guarantee: syntax.

[. . .]

Our positing of the semiotic is obviously inseparable from a theory of the subject that takes into account the Freudian positing of the unconscious. We view the subject in language as decentering the transcendental ego, cutting through it, and opening it up to a dialectic in which its syntactic and categorical understanding is merely the liminary moment of the process, which is itself always acted upon by the relation to the other dominated by the death drive and its productive reiteration of the 'signifier'. We will be attempting to formulate the distinction between *semiotic* and *symbolic* within this perspective, which was introduced by Lacanian analysis, but also within the constraints of a practice – the *text* – which is only of secondary interest to psychoanalysis.

[. . .]

Non-Contradiction: Neutral Peace

Grammatology retains the essential features of a nonsubstantial, nonsemantic, and nonphenomenal device that might enable us to sort out the logocentric entanglement of substance, meaning, and phenomena, and indicate its exorbitant mobility. It is, in our view, the most radical of all the various procedures that have tried, after Hegel, to push dialectical negativity further and elsewhere. Difference, the trace, the gramme, writing [*écriture*], contain, retain, and harbor this dialectic in a way that, while avoiding totality, is nevertheless definite and very precise; 'a certain dialectic', writes Derrida, echoing Artaud:

> The present offers itself as such, appears, presents itself, opens the stage of time or the time of the stage only by harboring its own intestine difference, and only in the interior fold of its original repetition, in representation. In dialectics.

... For if one appropriately conceives the *horizon* of dialectics – outside a conventional Hegelianism – one understands, perhaps, that dialectics is the indefinite movement of finitude, of the unity of life and death, of difference, of original repetition, that is, of the origin of tragedy as the absence of a simple origin. In this sense, dialectics is tragedy, the only possible affirmation to be made against the philosophical or Christian idea of pure origin, against 'the spirit of beginning'.[19]

It is obvious that grammatology clears its way [*se fraye la route*] by attacking teleology and Hegelian semiology, and does so explicitly. What interests us here is the debt to Hegel that makes of 'arche-writing' 'the *movement* [emphasis added] of the *sign-function* linking a content to an expression, whether it be graphic or not', and not just a schema.[20]

Negativity is inscribed in arche-writing as a constitutive absence: the 'absence of the other', 'irreducible absence within the presence of the trace'; '*différance* is therefore the formation of form'.[21] As a result, we recognize in negativity the economy Derrida speaks of in 'Violence and Metaphysics', that of a 'strange dialogue between the Jew and the Greek, peace itself', which he finds in 'the form of the absolute, speculative logic of Hegel, the living logic which *reconciles* formal tautology and empirical heterology after having *thought* prophetic discourse in the preface to the *Phenomenology of Spirit*.'[22]

Clearly, the grammatological fabric's complex elaboration and its chronologically distended and topographically uneven strategy cannot be reduced to a homogeneous system. But from the texts on Husserl or Jabès onward, Derrida takes in [*recueille*] and reinvests Hegelian negativity in the phenomenological corpus in order to expose and question it. In the course of this operation, negativity has become positivized and drained of its potential for producing breaks. It holds itself back and appears as a delaying [*retardement*], it defers and thus becomes merely positive and affirmative, it inscribes and institutes through retention: 'The instituted trace cannot be thought without thinking the retention of difference within a structure of reference where difference appears *as such* and thus permits a certain liberty of variations among the full terms.' 'Without a retention in the minimal unit of temporal experience, without a trace retaining the other as other in the same, no difference would do its work and no meaning would appear.'[23]

Through this *ingathering* [*recueillement*], the trace absorbs and, in this sense, reduces – but not phenomenologically (thus we speak of *ingathering* and not of *reduction*) – the 'terms', 'dichotomies', and 'oppositions' that Hegelian negativity concatenates, reactivates, and generates. The trace that includes its effacement, and writing that inscribes only while under protection and by delaying[24] – both can be thought of as metaphors for a movement that retreats before the thetic but, sheltered by it, unfolds only within the stases of the semiotic *chora*. The trace thus expresses the preconditions and/or the (fetishistic, maternal) repressed element of logocentric reason and, in this sense, grammatology disturbs logic and its subject. In other words, grammatology denounces the economy of the symbolic function and opens up a space that the latter cannot subsume. But in its desire to bar the thetic and put (logically or chronologically) previous energy transfers in its place, the grammatological deluge of meaning gives up on the subject and must remain ignorant not only of his functioning as social practice, but also of his chances for experiencing *jouissance* or being put to death. Neutral in the face of all positions, theses, and structures, grammatology is, as a consequence, equally restrained when they break, burst, or rupture: demonstrating disinterestedness toward (symbolic and/or social) structure, grammatology remains silent when faced with its destruction or renewal.

Indeed, since *différance*[25] neutralizes productive negativity, it is conceived of as a *delay* [*retard*] that comes *before* a (pre)condition, a possibility, becoming and become, a movement preceding the sign, *logos*, the subject, *Being*, and located within every differentiated entity. It is the path of their becoming and, as such, is itself a *becoming*; its *Being* will be under erasure: 'It is thus the delay [*le retard*] which is in the beginning [*originaire*].' '*Différance*, the *pre-opening* [emphasis added] of the ontic-ontological difference ... and of all the differences which furrow Freudian conceptuality, such that they may be organized, and this is only an example, around the difference between 'pleasure' and 'reality', or may be derived from this difference.' 'Life must be thought of as trace *before* Being may be determined as presence.'[26] 'Without referring back to a "nature", the immotivation of the trace has always *become*. In fact, there is no unmotivated trace. ...' 'It is that starting from which a becoming-unmotivated of the sign, and with it all the ulterior positions between *physis* and its other, is possible.'[27] Or again, referring to the trace 'where the relationship with the other is marked', as a possibility always already oriented toward the sign, toward beings.[28] 'This formula, beside the fact that it is the questioning of metaphysics itself, describes the structure implied by the "arbitrariness of the sign", from the moment that one thinks of its possibility *short of* the derived opposition between nature and convention, symbol and sign, etc. These oppositions have meaning only *after the possibility of the trace*.'[29] Concealed in *Being* and all its variations, concealing the other within itself, and concealed from itself, the trace marks *anteriority* to every entity and thus to every position; it is the movement whose veiling produces metaphysics or, more accurately, metaphysics is a trace unknown to itself [*qui s'ignore*]. The grammatologist speaks to transcendence and unsettles it because he states its economy: 'The primordial difference of the absolute origin. ... That is perhaps what has always been said under the concept of "transcendental". ... Transcendence would be difference.'[30]

If in this way the trace dissolves every thesis – material, natural, social, substantial, and logical – in order to free itself from any dependence on the *Logos*, it can do so because it grasps the formation of the symbolic function preceding the mirror stage and believes it can remain there, even while aiming toward that stage. Grammatology would undoubtedly not acknowledge the pertinence of this psychoanalytic staging [*stadialité*], which depends on the categories and entities of beings. Yet to the extent (1) that the psychoanalytic discovery paves the way, in a certain sense, for grammatology itself, and (2) that grammatology designates an enclosure that is recognized as insurmountable, we may posit that the force of *writing* [*écriture*] lies precisely in its return to the space-time previous to the phallic stage – indeed previous even to the identifying or mirror stage – in order to grasp the becoming of the symbolic function as the drive's deferment [*différance*] faced with the absence of the object.

Although it begins by positing the heterogeneity in which *différance* operates, doesn't grammatology forget this heterogeneous element the moment it neglects the thetic? Doesn't it indefinitely delay this heterogeneous element, thus following its own systematic and philosophical movement of metalanguage or theory. Indeed grammatology seems to brush aside the drive 'residues' that are not included in the *différance* toward the sign, and which return, heterogeneous, to interrupt its contemplative retention and make language a practice of the subject in process/on trial. This instinctual heterogeneity – neither deferred nor delayed, not yet understood as a becoming-sign – is precisely that which *enters into contradiction with différance* and brings about leaps, intervals, abrupt changes, and breaks in its spacing [*espacement*]. Contradiction can only be the irruption of the heterogeneous which cuts short any *différance*. Indeed, without this heterogeneous element, ideational Hegelian contradiction, which is aimed toward the presence of Being and the subject, dissolves into differences.

But materialism and Freudian practice – to the extent that the latter is a materialist practice – show that it is impossible to gather up the heterogeneous element into *différance* without leaving any remainders. The return of the heterogeneous element in the movement of *différance* (symbolic retention, delayed becoming-sign-subject-Being), through perception and the unconscious (to use Freudian categories), brings about the revolution of *différance*: expenditure, semantico-syntactic anomaly, erotic excess, social protest, *jouissance*. This heterogeneity breaks through the barrier of repression and censorship that writing entails since, as the trace and its effacement, it is 'the original synthesis of primal *repression* and secondary repression, repression "itself"'.[31] The heterogeneous element is a threat to repression and tosses it aside. Does this mean that it breaks through 'primal' repression or repression 'itself'? Or does it mean that *différance* is instituted only out of the repression which the *heterogeneous element*, precisely, may pass through in the form of the 'residues of primary perceptions' or the 'exceptions' of nondeferred energy charges that can no longer be held in abeyance and are expended?[32]

The disturbance of *différance* calls into question the distinction between the 'pleasure principle' and the 'reality principle' and, with them, the very economy by which the symbolic is established. If this distinction is 'the original possibility, within life, of the detour, of deferral (*Aufschub*) and the original possibility of the economy of death',[33] then what thwarts it, and what takes the exact opposite course, far from setting up an economy of death, abruptly introduces death: this is none other than the 'principle' of *jouissance* as destruction, self-destruction, the return from 'reality' (always symbolico-logocentric) to 'matter'. Through the irruption of the nondeferred and impatient drive charge in *différance*, all the 'natural', 'cultural', 'physical', 'chemical', 'biological', and 'spiritual' heterogeneities are introduced in logic – heterogeneities that *différance* effaces but that Derrida recognizes as 'absolutely decisive', marked off by phenomenological reduction, and 'indispensable to all analyses of being-heard'.[34] Yet rejection no longer introduces them as phenomenological but instead as economic: as nonsymbolized material inside-outside, as mortal *jouissance* renewing the real, shutting down reality itself before including it in a new becoming of *différance*.

In this way sustained energetic force, substances, the world, and history, which the storing up of the negative in a deferred consumption had held back, are introduced into the semiotic device in the guise of phenomenal stases. This unleashing of the heterogeneous element as nonsymbolized and nonsymbolizable operates neither on the path of becoming-sign-subject-beings, nor in their neutralization, but in precipitating – as in a chemical reaction – the deferring stage [*la scène différante*] in the expenditure of the process of the subject and *signifiance*. A heterogeneous energy discharge, whose very principle is that of scission and division, enters into contradiction with what has been traced [*le tracé*], but produces only flashes, ruptures, and sudden displacements, which constitute preconditions for *new* symbolic productions in which the economy of *différance* will be able to find its place as well. But there is no guarantee that rejection will be able to maintain the scene of *différance*. Its expenditure could pierce and abolish it, and then all symbolic becoming would cease, thus opening the way to 'madness'. Similarly, without rejection, *différance* would be confined within a nonrenewable, nonproductive redundancy, a mere precious variant within the symbolic enclosure: contemplation adrift.

Both as a result of investigations such as these, and in rereading the theory of drives, one begins to suspect – even in psychoanalysis, where the notion has become so central that it seems incontrovertible since it revolves around the social, Stoic, and Cartesian subject – that *desire* cannot completely account for the mechanisms of the signifying process.[35] In technology and politics but also in art, areas have been found in which desire is exceeded by a 'movement' that surpasses the stases of desiring structuration and displaces the frameworks of intersubjective devices where phantasmatic identifications congeal. These discoveries move us closer to a notion that will prove to be essential in borderline functionings, which produce social and cultural innovations, but more importantly, this notion appears at the very foundation of the functioning of signifiance. To understand it, we must designate an event that occurs before and within the trajectory of Hegelian negativity, an event that lies between and beneath the psychoanalytic distinction between 'desire' and 'need', one that moves through and is inherent in biological and signifying development but links them together. We could call it *scission*, *separation*, or *rejection*: 'I am not dead, but I am separated.'[36]

Notes

1. See Zellig Harris, *Mathematical Structures of Language* (New York: Interscience Publishers, 1968). See also Maurice Gross and André Lentin, *Introduction to Formal*

Grammars, trans. M. Salkoff (Berlin: Springer-Verlag, 1970); M.-C. Barbault and J.-P. Desclés, *Transformations formelles et théories linguistiques*, Documents de linguistique quantitative, no. 11 (Paris: Dunod, 1972).

2. On this 'object' see *Langages* (December 1971), vol. 24, and, for a didactic, popularized account, see Julia Kristeva, *Le Langage cet inconnu* (Paris: Seuil, 1981).

3. Edmund Husserl, in *Ideas: General introduction to pure phenomenology*, trans. W. R. Boyce Gibson (London: Allen & Unwin, 1969), posits this subject as a subject of intuition, sure of this universally valid unity [of consciousness], a unity that is provided in *categories* itself, since transcendence is precisely the immanence of this 'Ego', which is an expansion of the Cartesian *cogito*. 'We shall consider conscious experiences', Husserl writes, '*in the concrete fullness and entirety* with which they figure in their concrete context – the *stream of experience* – and to which they are closely attached through their own proper essence. It then becomes evident that every experience in the stream which our reflexion can lay hold on has *its own essence open to intuition*, a "content" which can be considered in its *singularity in and for itself*. We shall be concerned to grasp this individual content of the *cogitatio* in its *pure* singularity, and to describe it in its general features, excluding everything which is not to be found in the *cogitatio* as it is in itself. We must likewise describe the *unity of consciousness* which is demanded *by the intrinsic nature of the cogitationes*, and so necessarily demanded that they could not be without this unity' (p. 116). From a similar perspective, Benveniste emphasizes language's dialogical character, as well as its role in Freud's discovery. Discussing the I/you polarity, he writes: 'This polarity does not mean either equality or symmetry: "ego" always has a position of transcendence with regard to *you*'. In Benveniste, 'Subjectivity in language', *Problems in General Linguistics*, Miami Linguistics Series, no. 8, trans. Mary Elizabeth Meek (Coral Gables, FL: University of Miami Press, 1971), p. 225. In Chomsky, the subject-bearer of syntactic synthesis is clearly shown to stem from the Cartesian *cogito*. See his *Cartesian Linguistics: A chapter in the history of rationalist thought* (New York: Harper & Row, 1966). Despite the difference between this Cartesian-Chomskyan subject and the transcendental ego outlined by Benveniste and others in a more clearly phenomenological sense, both these notions of the act of understanding (or the linguistic act) rest on a common metaphysical foundation: consciousness as a synthesizing unity and the sole guarantee of Being. Moreover, several scholars – without renouncing the Cartesian principles that governed the first syntactic descriptions – have recently pointed out that Husserlian phenomenology is a more explicit and more rigorously detailed basis for such description than the Cartesian method. See Roman Jakobson, who recalls Husserl's role in the establishment of modern linguistics, 'Linguistics in relation to other sciences', in *Selected Writings*, 2 vols (The Hague: Mouton, 1971), 2:655–96; and S.-Y. Kuroda, 'The categorical and the thetic judgment: evidence from Japanese syntax', *Foundations of Language* (November 1972), 9(2):153–85.

4. See the work of Ivan Fónagy, particularly 'Bases pulsionnelles de la phonation', *Revue Française de Psychanalyse* (January 1970), 34(1):101–36, and (July 1971), 35(4):543–91.

5. On the 'subject of enunciation', see Tzvetan Todorov, spec. ed., *Langages* (March 1970), vol. 17. Formulated in linguistics by Benveniste ('The correlations of tense in the French verb' and 'Subjectivity in language', in *Problems*, pp. 205–16 and 223–30), the notion is used by many linguists, notably Antoine Culioli, 'A propos d'opérations intervenant dans le traitement formel des langues naturelles', *Mathématiques et Sciences Humaines* (Summer 1971), 9(34):7–15; and Oswald Ducrot, 'Les Indéfinis et l'énonciation', *Langages* (March 1970), 5(17):91–111. Chomsky's 'extended standard theory' makes use of categorial intuition but does not refer to the subject of enunciation, even though the latter has been implicit in his theory ever since *Cartesian Linguistics* (1966); see his *Studies on Semantics in Generative Grammar*, Janua Linguarum, series minor, no. 107 (The Hague: Mouton, 1972).

6. The term 'chora' has recently been criticized for its ontological essence by Jacques Derrida, *Positions*, annotator and trans. Alan Bass (Chicago: University of Chicago Press, 1981), pp. 75 and 106, n. 39.

7. Plato emphasizes that the receptacle [ὑποδοχεῖον], which is also called space [χώρα] vis-à-vis reason, is necessary – but not divine since it is unstable, uncertain, ever changing and becoming; it is even unnameable, improbable, bastard: 'Space, which is everlasting, not admitting destruction; providing a situation for all things that come into being, but itself apprehended without the senses by a sort of bastard reasoning, and hardly an object of belief. This, indeed, is that which we look upon as in a dream and say that anything that is must needs be in some place and occupy some room ...' (*Timaeus*, trans. Francis M. Cornford, 52a–b). Is the receptacle a 'thing' or a mode of language? Plato's hesitation between the two gives the receptacle an even more uncertain status. It is one of the elements that antedate not only the *universe* but also *names* and even *syllables*: 'We speak ... positing them as original principles, elements (as it were, letters) of the universe; whereas one who has ever so little intelligence should not rank them in this analogy even so low as syllables', (*ibid.*, 48b). 'It is hard to say, with respect to any one of these, which we ought to call really water rather than fire, or indeed which we shall call by any given name rather than by all the names together or by each severally, so as to use language in a sound and trustworthy way. ... Since, then, in this way no one of these things ever makes its appearance as the *same* thing, which of them can we steadfastly affirm to be *this* – whatever it may be – and not something else, without blushing for ourselves? It cannot be done' (*ibid.*, 49b–d).

8. There is a fundamental ambiguity: on the one hand, the receptacle is mobile and even contradictory, without unity, separable and divisible: pre-syllable, pre-word. Yet, on the other hand, because this separability and divisibility antecede numbers and forms, the space or receptacle is called *amorphous*; thus its suggested rhythmicity will in a certain sense be erased, for how can one think an articulation of what is not yet singular but is nevertheless necessary? All we may say of it, then, to make it intelligible, is that it is amorphous but that it 'is of such and such a quality', not even an index or something in particular ('this' or 'that'). Once named, it immediately becomes a container that takes the place of infinitely repeatable separability. This amounts to saying that this repeated separability is 'ontologized' the moment a *name* or a *word* replaces it, making it intelligible: 'Are we talking idly whenever we say that there is such a thing as an intelligible Form of anything? Is this nothing more than a word?' (*ibid.*, 51c). Is the Platonic *chora* the 'nominability' of rhythm (of repeated separation)?

Why then borrow an ontologized term in order to designate an articulation that antecedes positing? First, the Platonic term makes explicit an insurmountable problem for discourse: once it has been named, that functioning, even if it is pre-symbolic, is brought back into a symbolic position. All discourse can do is differentiate, by means of a 'bastard reasoning', the receptacle from the motility, which, by contrast, is not posited as being 'a *certain* something' ['une *telle*']. Second, this motility is the precondition for symbolicity, heterogeneous to it, yet indispensable. Therefore what needs to be done is to try and differentiate, always through a 'bastard reasoning', the specific arrangements of this motility, without seeing them as recipients of accidental singularities, or a *Being* always posited in itself, or a projection of the *One*. Moreover, Plato invites us to differentiate in this fashion when he describes this motility, while gathering it into the receiving membrane: 'But because it was filled with powers that were neither alike nor evenly balanced, there was no equipoise in any region of it; but it was everywhere swayed unevenly and shaken by these things, and by its motion shook them in turn. And they, being thus moved, were perpetually being separated and carried in different directions; just as when things are shaken and winnowed by means of winnowing baskets and other instruments for cleaning corn ... it separated the most unlike kinds farthest apart from one another, and thrust the most alike closest together; whereby the different kinds came to have different regions, even before the ordered whole consisting of them came to be ... but were altogether in such a condition as we should expect for anything when deity is absent from it' (*ibid.*, 52d–53b). Indefinite 'conjunctions' and 'disjunctions' (functioning, devoid of Meaning), the *chora* is governed by a necessity that is not God's law.

9. The Platonic space or receptacle is a mother and wet nurse: 'Indeed we may fittingly compare the Recipient to a mother, the model to a father, and the nature that arises between them to their offspring' (*ibid*, 50d); 'Now the wet nurse of Becoming was made watery and fiery, received the characters of earth and air, and was qualified by all the other affections that go with these ...' (*ibid.*, 52d; translation modified).

10. 'Law', which derives etymologically from *lex*, necessarily implies the act of judgment whose role in safeguarding society was first developed by the Roman law courts. 'Ordering', on the other hand, is closer to the series 'rule', 'norm' (from the Greek γνώμων, meaning 'discerning' [adj.], 'carpenter's square' [noun]), etc., which implies a numerical or geometrical necessity. On normativity in linguistics, see Alain Rey, 'Usages, jugements et prescriptions linquistiques', *Langue Française* (December 1972), 16:5. But the temporary ordering of the *chora* is not yet even a *rule*: the arsenal of geometry is posterior to the *chora*'s motility; it fixes the *chora* in place and reduces it.

11. Operations are, rather, an act of the subject of understanding. [Hans G. Furth, in *Piaget and Knowledge: Theoretical foundations* (Englewood Cliffs, NJ: Prentice Hall, 1969), offers the following definition of 'concrete operations': 'Characteristic of the first stage of operational intelligence. A concrete operation implies underlying general systems or "groupings" such as classification, seriation, number. Its applicability is limited to objects considered as real (concrete)' (p. 260). – Trans.]

12. Piaget stresses that the roots of sensorimotor operations precede language and that the acquisition of thought is due to the symbolic function, which, for him, is a notion separate from that of language *per se*. See Jean Piaget, 'Language and symbolic operations', in *Piaget and Knowledge*, pp. 121–30.

13. By 'function' we mean a dependent variable determined each time the independent variables with which it is associated are determined. For our purposes, a function is what links stases within the process of semiotic facilitation.

14. Such a position has been formulated by Lipot Szondi, *Experimental Diagnostic of Drives*, trans. Gertrude Aull (New York: Grune & Stratton, 1952).

15. See James D. Watson, *The Double Helix: A personal account of the discovery of the structure of DNA* (London: Weidenfeld & Nicolson, 1968).

16. Throughout her writings, Melanie Klein emphasizes the 'pre-Oedipal' phase, i.e. a period of the subject's development that precedes the 'discovery' of castration and the positing of the superego, which itself is subject to (paternal) Law. The processes she describes for this phase correspond, *but on a genetic level*, to what we call the semiotic, as opposed to the symbolic, which underlies and conditions the semiotic. Significantly, these pre-Oedipal processes are organized through projection onto the mother's body, for girls as well as for boys: 'at this stage of development children of both sexes believe that it is the body of their mother which contains all that is desirable, especially their father's penis'. *The Psycho-analysis of Children*, trans. Alix Strachey (London: Hogarth Press, 1932), p. 269. Our own view of this stage is as follows: Without 'believing' or 'desiring' any 'object' whatsoever, the subject is in the process of constituting himself *vis-à-vis* a non-object. He is in the process of separating from this non-object so as to make that non-object 'one' and posit himself as 'other': the mother's body is the not-yet-one that the believing and desiring subject will imagine as a 'receptacle'.

17. As for what situates the mother in symbolic space, we find the phallus again (see Jacques Lacan, 'La Relation d'objet et les structures freudiennes', *Bulletin de Psychologie*, April 1957, pp. 426–30), represented by the mother's father, i.e. the subject's maternal grandfather (see Marie-Claire Boons, 'Le Meurtre du Père chez Freud', *L'Inconscient*, January–March 1968, 5:101–29).

18. Though disputed and inconsistent, the Freudian theory of drives is of interest here because of the predominance Freud gives to the death drive in both 'living matter' and the 'human being'. The death drive is transversal to identity and tends to disperse 'narcissisms' whose constitution ensures the link between structures and, by extension, life. But at the same time and conversely, narcissism and pleasure are only temporary positions from which the death drive blazes new paths [*se fraye de nouveaux passages*]. Narcissism and pleasure are therefore inveiglings and realizations of the death drive. The semiotic *chora*, converting drive discharges into stases, can be thought of both as a delaying of the death drive and as a possible realization of this drive, which tends to return to a homeostatic state. This hypothesis is consistent with the following remark: 'at the beginning of mental life', writes Freud, 'the struggle for pleasure was far more intense than later but not so unrestricted: it had to submit to frequent interruptions'. *Beyond the Pleasure Principle*, in *The Standard Edition of the Works of Sigmund Freud*, ed. James Strachey (London: Hogarth Press and the Institute of Psychoanalysis, 1953), 18:63.

19. Derrida, *Writing and Difference*, trans. Alan Bass (Chicago: University of Chicago Press, 1978), p. 248.

20. Derrida, *Of Grammatology*, trans. Gayatri Chakravorty Spivak (Baltimore, MD: Johns Hopkins University Press, 1976), p. 60.

21. *Ibid.*, pp. 47, translation modified, and 63. [For an explanation of the term '*différance*', see below, n. 25 – Trans.]

22. *Writing and Difference*, p. 153; translation modified.

23. *Of Grammatology*, pp. 46–7 and 62.

24. See 'Freud and the scene of writing', in *Writing and Difference*, pp. 196–231.

25. In his introduction to *Writing and Difference*, Alan Bass explains that Derrida's term, *différance*, 'combines in neither the active nor the passive voice the coincidence of meanings in the verb *différer*: to differ (in space) and to defer (to put off in time, to postpone presence). Thus, it does not function simply either as *différence* (difference) or as *différance* in the usual sense (deferral), and plays on both meanings at once', p. xvi – Trans.

26. *Writing and Difference*, pp. 203, 198 and 203; emphasis added.

27. *Of Grammatology*, pp. 47 and 48.

28. In their translation of Heidegger's *Being and Time*, Macquarrie and Robinson render *Sein* as 'Being' and *Seiendes* as 'entity' or 'entities'. In keeping with the standard French translations of the terms ('*être*' and '*étant*') and the practice of more recent translators, I have kept 'Being' but use 'beings' (lower case, plural) for the French *étant* (*Seiendes*). – Trans.

29. *Of Grammatology*, p. 47; emphasis added.

30. Derrida, *Edmund Husserl's 'Origin of Geometry': An introduction*, trans. John P. Leavey, Jr (Stony Brook, NY: Nicolas Hays, 1978), p. 153; translation modified.

31. *Writing and Difference*, p. 230; emphasis added; translation modified.

32. On the notion of expenditure, see Georges Bataille, *Oeuvres complètes* (Paris: Gallimard, 1970), 1:302–20: 2:147–58.

33. *Writing and Difference*, p. 198.

34. *Of Grammatology*, p. 63.

35. 'But culture is yet something else again: it implies a technological and political development which partly eludes desire', writes André Green, in 'La Projection: De

l'identification projective au projet', *Revue Française de Psychanalyse* (September–December 1971), 35(5–6):958.

36. Artaud, 'The new revelations of being', in *Selected Writings*, trans. Helen Weaver (New York: Farrar, Straus and Giroux, 1976), p. 414.

1.4 □ *Truth and Power*

Michel Foucault

Interviewers: Alessandro Fontana, Pasquale Pasquino

[. . .]

Q: [W]hat do you think today about this concept of discontinuity, on the basis of which you have been all too rapidly and readily labelled as a 'structuralist' historian?

A: This business about discontinuity has always rather bewildered me. In the new edition of the *Petit Larousse* it says: 'Foucault: a philosopher who founds his theory of history on discontinuity'. That leaves me flabbergasted. No doubt I didn't make myself sufficiently clear in *The Order of Things*, though I said a good deal there about this question. It seemed to me that in certain empirical forms of knowledge like biology, political economy, psychiatry, medicine, etc., the rhythm of transformation doesn't follow the smooth, continuist schemas of development which are normally accepted. The great biological image of a progressive maturation of science still underpins a good many historical analyses; it does not seem to me to be pertinent to history. In a science like medicine, for example, up to the end of the eighteenth century one has a certain type of discourse whose gradual transformation, within a period of twenty-five or thirty years, broke not only with the 'true' propositions which it had hitherto been possible to formulate but also, more profoundly, with the ways of speaking and seeing, the whole ensemble of practices which served as supports for medical knowledge. These are not simply new discoveries, there is a whole new 'regime' in discourse and forms of knowledge. And all this happens in the space of a few years. This is something which is undeniable, once one has looked at the texts with sufficient attention. My problem was not at all to say, '*Voilà*, long live discontinuity, we are in the discontinuous and a good thing too', but to pose the question, 'How is it that at certain moments and in certain orders of knowledge, there are these sudden take-offs, these hastenings of

From Foucault, M., *Power/Knowledge: Selected interviews and other writings*, *1972–1977*, trans. C. Gordon, L. Marshall, J. Mepham and K. Soper, ed. C. Gordon, Pantheon Books, New York, 1980, pp. 111–28, 130–33.

evolution, these transformations which fail to correspond to the calm, continuist image that is normally accredited?' But the important thing here is not that such changes can be rapid and extensive, or rather it is that this extent and rapidity are only the sign of something else: a modification in the rules of formation of statements which are accepted as scientifically true. Thus it is not a change of content (refutation of old errors, recovery of old truths), nor is it a change of theoretical form (renewal of a paradigm, modification of systematic ensembles). It is a question of what *governs* statements, and the way in which they *govern* each other so as to constitute a set of propositions which are scientifically acceptable, and hence capable of being verified or falsified by scientific procedures. In short, there is a problem of the regime, the politics of the scientific statement. At this level it's not so much a matter of knowing what external power imposes itself on science, as of what effects of power circulate among scientific statements, what constitutes, as it were, their internal regime of power, and how and why at certain moments that regime undergoes a global modification.

It was these different regimes that I tried to identify and describe in *The Order of Things*, all the while making it clear that I wasn't trying for the moment to explain them, and that it would be necessary to try and do this in a subsequent work. But what was lacking here was this problem of the 'discursive regime', of the effects of power peculiar to the play of statements. I confused this too much with systematicity, theoretical form, or something like a paradigm. This same central problem of power, which at that time I had not yet properly isolated, emerges in two very different aspects at the point of junction of *Madness and Civilisation* and *The Order of Things*.

Q: We need, then, to locate the notion of discontinuity in its proper context. And perhaps there is another concept which is both more difficult and more central to your thought, the concept of an event. For in relation to the event a whole generation was long trapped in an *impasse*, in that following the works of ethnologists, some of them great ethnologists, a dichotomy was established between structures (the *thinkable*) and the event considered as the site of the irrational, the unthinkable, that which doesn't and cannot enter into the mechanism and play of analysis, at least in the form which this took in structuralism.

[. . .]

Could you elaborate from our present standpoint on this renewal and reformulation of the concept of event?

A: One can agree that structuralism formed the most systematic effort to evacuate the concept of the event, not only from ethnology but from a whole series of other sciences and in the extreme case from history. In that sense, I don't see who could be more of an anti-structuralist than myself. But the important thing is to avoid trying to do for the event what was previously done with the concept of structure. It's not a matter of locating everything on one level, that of the event, but of realising that there are actually a whole order of levels of different types of events differing in amplitude, chronological breadth, and capacity to produce effects.

The problem is at once to distinguish among events, to differentiate the networks and levels to which they belong, and to reconstitute the lines along which they are connected and engender one another. From this follows a refusal of analyses couched in terms of the symbolic field or the domain of signifying structures, and a recourse to analyses in terms of the genealogy of relations of force, strategic developments, and tactics. Here I believe one's point of reference should not be to the great model of language [*langue*] and signs, but to that of war and battle. The history which bears and determines us has the form of a war rather than that of a language: relations of power, not relations of meaning. History has no 'meaning', though this is not to say that it is absurd or incoherent. On the contrary, it is intelligible and should be susceptible of analysis down to the smallest detail – but this in accordance with the intelligibility of struggles, of strategies and tactics. Neither the dialectic, as logic of contradictions, nor semiotics, as the structure of communication, can account for the intrinsic intelligibility of conflicts. 'Dialectic' is a way of evading the always open and hazardous reality of conflict by reducing it to a Hegelian skeleton, and 'semiology' is a way of avoiding its violent, bloody and lethal character by reducing it to the calm Platonic form of language and dialogue.

Q: In the context of this problem of discursivity, I think one can be confident in saying that you were the first person to pose the question of power regarding discourse, and that at a time when analyses in terms of the concept or object of the 'text', along with the accompanying methodology of semiology, structuralism, etc., were the prevailing fashion. Posing for discourse the question of power means basically to ask whom does discourse serve?

[. . .]

A: I don't think I was the first to pose the question. On the contrary, I'm struck by the difficulty I had in formulating it. When I think back now, I ask myself what else it was that I was talking about, in *Madness and Civilisation* or *The Birth of the Clinic*, but power? Yet I'm perfectly aware that I scarcely ever used the word and never had such a field of analyses at my disposal. I can say that this was an incapacity linked undoubtedly with the political situation we found ourselves in. It is hard to see where, either on the Right or the Left, this problem of power could then have been posed. On the Right, it was posed only in terms of constitution, sovereignty, etc., that is, in juridical terms; on the Marxist side, it was posed only in terms of the State apparatus. The way power was exercised – concretely and in detail – with its specificity, its techniques and tactics, was something that no one attempted to ascertain; they contented themselves with denouncing it in a polemical and global fashion as it existed among the 'others', in the adversary camp. Where Soviet socialist power was in question, its opponents called it totalitarianism; power in Western capitalism was denounced by the Marxists as class domination; but the mechanics of power in themselves were never analysed. This task could only begin after 1968, that is to say on the basis of daily struggles at grass-roots level, among those whose fight was located in the fine meshes of the web of power. This was where the concrete nature of power became visible, along with the prospect that these analyses of power would prove fruitful in accounting for all that had hitherto remained outside the field of political analysis. To put it very simply, psychiatric internment, the mental normalisation of individuals, and penal institutions have no doubt a fairly limited importance if one is only looking for their economic significance. On the other hand, they are undoubtedly essential to the general functioning of the wheels of power. So long as the posing of the question of power was kept subordinate to the economic instance and the system of interests which this served, there was a tendency to regard these problems as of small importance.

Q: So a certain kind of Marxism and a certain kind of phenomenology constituted an objective obstacle to the formulation of this problematic?

A: Yes, if you like, to the extent that it's true that, in our student days, people of my generation were brought up on these two forms of analysis, one in terms of the constituent subject, the other in terms of the economic in the last instance, ideology and the play of superstructures and infrastructures.

Q: Still within this methodological context, how would you situate the genealogical approach? As a questioning of the conditions of possibility, modalities and constitution of the 'objects' and domains you have successively analysed, what makes it necessary?

A: I wanted to see how these problems of constitution could be resolved within a historical framework, instead of referring them back to a constituent object (madness, criminality or whatever). But this historical contextualisation needed to be something more than the simple relativisation of the phenomenological subject. I don't believe the problem can be solved by historicising the subject as posited by the phenomenologists, fabricating a subject that evolves through the course of history. One has to dispense with the constituent subject, to get rid of the subject itself, that's to say, to arrive at an analysis which can account for the constitution of the subject within a historical framework. And this is what I would call genealogy, that is, a form of history which can account for the constitution of knowledges, discourses, domains of objects etc., without having to make reference to a subject which is either transcendental in relation to the field of events or runs in its empty sameness throughout the course of history.

Q: Marxist phenomenology and a certain kind of Marxism have clearly acted as a screen and an obstacle; there are two further concepts which continue today to act as a screen and an obstacle, ideology on the one hand and repression on the other.

[. . .]

A: The notion of ideology appears to me to be difficult to make use of, for three reasons. The first is that, like it or not, it always stands in virtual opposition to something else which is supposed to count as truth. Now I believe that the problem does not consist in drawing the line between that in a discourse which falls under the category of scientificity or truth, and that which comes under some other category, but in seeing historically how effects of truth are produced within discourses which in themselves are neither true nor false. The second drawback is that the concept of ideology refers, I think necessarily, to something of the order of a subject. Thirdly, ideology stands in a secondary position relative to something which functions as its infrastructure, as its material, economic determinant, etc. For these three reasons, I think that this is a notion that cannot be used without circumspection.

The notion of repression is a more insidious one, or at all events I myself have had much more trouble in freeing myself of it, in so far as it does indeed appear to correspond so well with a whole range of phenomena which belong among the effects of power. When I wrote *Madness and Civilisation*, I made at least an implicit use of this notion of repression. I think indeed that I was positing the existence of a sort of living, voluble and anxious madness which the mechanisms of power and psychiatry were supposed to have come to repress and reduce to silence. But it seems to me now that the notion of repression is quite inadequate for capturing what is precisely the productive aspect of power. In defining the effects of power as repression, one adopts a purely juridical conception of such power, one identifies power with a law which says no, power is taken above all as carrying the force of a prohibition. Now I believe that this is a wholly negative, narrow, skeletal conception of power, one which has been curiously widespread. If power were never anything but repressive, if it never did anything but to say no, do you really think one would be brought to obey it? What makes power hold good, what makes it accepted, is simply the fact that it doesn't only weigh on us as a force that says no, but that it traverses and produces things, it induces pleasure, forms knowledge, produces discourse. It needs to be considered as a productive network which runs through the whole social body, much more than as a negative instance whose function is repression. In *Discipline and Punish* what I wanted to show was how, from the seventeenth and eighteenth centuries onwards, there was a veritable technological take-off in the productivity of power. Not only did the monarchies of the Classical period develop great state apparatuses (the army, the police and fiscal administration), but above all there was established at this period what one might call a new 'economy' of power, that is to say, procedures which allowed the effects of power to circulate in a manner at once continuous, uninterrupted, adapted and 'individualised' throughout the entire social body. These new techniques are both much more efficient and much less wasteful (less costly economically, less risky in their results, less open to loopholes and resistances) than the techniques previously employed which were based on a mixture of more or less forced tolerances (from recognised privileges to endemic criminality) and costly ostentation (spectacular and discontinuous interventions of power, the most violent form of which was the 'exemplary', because exceptional, punishment).

Q: Repression is a concept used above all in relation to sexuality. It was held that bourgeois society represses sexuality, stifles sexual desire, and so forth. And when one considers, for example, the campaign launched against masturbation in the eighteenth century, or the medical discourse on homosexuality in the second half of the nineteenth century, or discourse on sexuality in general, one does seem to be faced with a discourse of repression. In reality, however, this discourse serves to make possible a whole series of interventions, tactical and positive interventions of surveillance, circulation, control, and so forth, which seem to have been intimately linked with techniques that give the appearance of repression, or are at least liable to be interpreted as such. I believe the crusade against masturbation is a typical example of this.

A: Certainly. It is customary to say that bourgeois society repressed infantile sexuality to the point where it refused even to speak of it or acknowledge its existence. It was necessary to wait until Freud for the discovery at last to be made that children have a sexuality. Now if you read all the books on pedagogy and child medicine – all the manuals for parents that were published in the eighteenth century – you find that children's sex is spoken of constantly and in every possible context. One might argue that the purpose of these discourses was precisely to prevent children from having a sexuality. But their *effect* was to din it into parents' heads that their children's sex constituted a fundamental problem in terms of their parental educational responsibilities, and to din it into children's heads that their relationship with their own body and their own sex was to be a fundamental problem as far as *they* were concerned; and this had the consequence of sexually exciting the bodies of children while at the same time fixing the parental gaze and vigilance on the peril of infantile sexuality. The result was a sexualising of the infantile body, a sexualising of the bodily relationship between parent and child, a sexualising of the familial domain. 'Sexuality' is far more of a positive product of power than power was ever repression of sexuality. I believe that it is precisely these positive mechanisms that need to be investigated, and here one must free oneself of the juridical schematism of all previous characterisations of the nature of power. Hence a historical problem arises, namely that of discovering why the West has insisted for so long on seeing the power it exercises as juridical and negative rather than as technical and positive.

[. . .]

To pose the problem [of power] in terms of the State means to continue posing it in terms of sovereign and sovereignty, that is to say, in terms of law. If one describes all these phenomena of power as dependent on the State apparatus, this means grasping them as essentially repressive: the Army as a power of death, police and justice as punitive instances, etc. I don't want to say that the State isn't important; what I want to say is that relations of power, and hence the analysis that must be made of them, necessarily extend beyond the limits of the State. In two senses: first of all because the State, for all the omnipotence of its apparatuses, is far from being able to occupy the whole field of actual power relations, and further because the State can only operate on the basis of other, already existing power relations. The State is superstructural in relation to a whole series of power networks that invest the body, sexuality, the family, kinship, knowledge, technology, and so forth. True, these networks stand in a conditioning–conditioned relationship to a kind of 'meta-power' which is structured essentially round a certain number of great prohibition functions; but this meta-power with its prohibitions can only take hold and secure its footing where it is rooted in a whole series of multiple and indefinite power relations that supply the necessary basis for the great negative forms of power. That is just what I was trying to make apparent in my book.

Q: Doesn't this open up the possibility of overcoming the dualism of political struggles that eternally feed on the opposition between the State on the one hand and Revolution on the other? Doesn't it indicate a wider field of conflicts than that of those where the adversary is the State?

A: I would say that the State consists in the codification of a whole number of power relations which render its functioning possible, and that Revolution is a different type of codification of the same relations. This implies that there are many different kinds of revolution, roughly speaking as many kinds as there are possible subversive recodifications of power relations, and further that one can perfectly well conceive of revolutions which leave essentially untouched the power relations which form the basis for the functioning of the State.

Q: You have said about power as an object of research that one has to invert Clausewitz's formula so as to arrive at the idea that politics is the continuation of war by other means. Does the military model seem to you, on the basis of your most recent researches, to be the best one for describing power; is war here simply a metaphorical model, or is it the literal, regular, everyday mode of operation of power?

A: This is the problem I now find myself confronting. As soon as one endeavours to detach power with its techniques and procedures from the form of law within which it has been theoretically confined up until now, one is driven to ask this basic question: isn't power simply a form of warlike domination? Shouldn't one therefore conceive all problems of power in terms of relations of war? Isn't power a sort of generalised war which assumes at particular moments the forms of peace and the State? Peace would then be a form of war, and the State a means of waging it.

A whole range of problems emerge here. Who wages war against whom? Is it between two classes, or more? Is it a war of all against all? What is the role of the army and military institutions in this civil society where permanent war is waged? What is the relevance of concepts of tactics and strategy for analysing structures and political processes? What is the essence and mode of transformation of power relations? All these questions need to be explored. In any case it's astonishing to see how easily and self-evidently people talk of warlike relations of power or of class struggle without ever making it clear whether some form of war is meant, and if so what form.

[. . .]

I believe one must keep in view the fact that along with all the fundamental technical inventions and discoveries of the seventeenth and eighteenth centuries, a new technology of the exercise of power also emerged which was probably even more important than the constitutional reforms and new forms of government established at the end of the eighteenth century. In the camp of the Left, one often hears people saying that power is that which abstracts, which negates the body, represses, suppresses, and so forth. I would say instead that what I find most striking about these new technologies of power introduced since the seventeenth and eighteenth centuries is their concrete and precise character, their grasp of a multiple and differentiated reality. In feudal societies power functioned essentially through signs and levies. Signs of loyalty to the feudal lords, rituals, ceremonies and so forth, and levies in the form of taxes, pillage, hunting, war, etc. In the seventeenth and eighteenth centuries a form of power comes into being that begins to exercise itself through social production and social service. It becomes a matter of obtaining productive service from individuals in their concrete lives. And in consequence, a real and effective 'incorporation' of power was necessary, in the sense that power had to be able to gain access to the bodies of individuals, to their acts, attitudes and modes of everyday behaviour. Hence the significance of methods like school discipline, which succeeded in making children's bodies the object of highly complex systems of manipulation and conditioning. But at the same time, these new techniques of power needed to grapple with the phenomena of population, in short to undertake the administration, control and direction of the accumulation of men (the economic system that promotes the accumulation of capital and the system of power that ordains the accumulation of men are, from the seventeenth century on, correlated and inseparable phenomena): hence there arise the problems of demography, public health, hygiene, housing conditions, longevity and fertility. And I believe that the political significance of the problem of sex is due to the fact that sex is located at the point of intersection of the discipline of the body and the control of the population.

Q: Finally, a question you have been asked before: the work you do, these preoccupations of yours, the results you arrive at, what use can one finally make of all this in everyday political struggles? You have spoken previously of local struggles as the specific site of confrontation with power, outside and beyond all such global, general instances as parties or classes. What does this imply about the role of intellectuals? If one isn't an 'organic' intellectual acting as the spokesman for a global organisation, if one doesn't purport to function as the bringer, the master of truth, what position is the intellectual to assume?

A: For a long period, the 'left' intellectual spoke and was acknowledged the right of speaking in the capacity of master of truth and justice.[1] He was heard, or purported to make himself heard, as the spokesman of the universal. To be an intellectual meant something like being the consciousness/conscience of us all. I think we have here an idea transposed from Marxism, from a faded Marxism indeed. Just as the proletariat, by the necessity of its historical situation, is the bearer of the universal (but its immediate, unreflected bearer, barely conscious of itself as such), so the intellectual, through his moral, theoretical and political choice, aspires to be the bearer of this universality in its conscious, elaborated form. The intellectual is thus taken as the clear, individual figure of a universality whose obscure, collective form is embodied in the proletariat.

Some years have now passed since the intellectual was called upon to play this role. A new mode of the 'connection between theory and practice' has been established. Intellectuals have got used to working, not in the modality of the 'universal', the 'exemplary', the 'just-and-true-for-all', but within specific sectors, at the precise points where their own conditions of life or work situate them (housing, the hospital, the asylum, the laboratory, the university, family and sexual relations). This has undoubtedly given them a much more immediate and concrete awareness of struggles. And they have met here with problems which are specific, 'non-universal', and often different from those of the proletariat or the masses. And yet I believe intellectuals have actually been drawn closer to the proletariat and the masses, for two reasons. Firstly, because it has been a question of real, material, everyday struggles, and secondly because they have often been confronted, albeit in a different form, by the same adversary as the proletariat, namely the multinational corporations, the judicial and police apparatuses, the property speculators, etc. This is what I would call the 'specific' intellectual as opposed to the 'universal' intellectual.

This new configuration has a further political significance. It makes it possible, if not to integrate, at least to rearticulate categories which were previously kept separate. The intellectual *par excellence* used to be the writer: as a universal consciousness, a free subject, he was counterposed to those intellectuals who were merely *competent instances* in the service of the State or Capital – technicians, magistrates, teachers. Since the time when each individual's specific activity began to serve as the basis for politicisation, the threshold of *writing*, as the sacralising mark of the intellectual, has disappeared. And it has become possible to develop lateral connections across different forms of knowledge and from one focus of politicisation to another. Magistrates and psychiatrists, doctors and social workers, laboratory technicians and sociologists have become able to participate, both within their own fields and through mutual exchange and support, in a global process of politicisation of intellectuals. This process explains how, even as the writer tends to disappear as a figurehead, the university and the academic emerge, if not as principal elements, at least as 'exchangers', privileged points of intersection. If the universities and education have become politically ultrasensitive areas, this is no doubt the reason why. And what is called the crisis of the universities should not be interpreted as a loss of power, but on the contrary as a multiplication and reinforcement of their power-effects as centres in a polymorphous ensemble of intellectuals who virtually all pass through and relate themselves to the academic system. The whole relentless theorisation of writing which we saw in the 1960s was doubtless only a swansong. Through it, the writer was fighting for the preservation of his political privilege; but the fact that it was precisely a matter of theory, that he needed scientific credentials, founded in linguistics, semiology, psychoanalysis, that this theory took its references from the direction of Saussure, or Chomsky, etc., and that it gave rise to such mediocre literary products, all this proves that the activity of the writer was no longer at the focus of things.

It seems to me that this figure of the 'specific' intellectual has emerged since the Second World War. Perhaps it was the atomic scientist (in a word, or rather a name: Oppenheimer) who acted as the point of transition between the universal and the specific intellectual. It's because he had a direct and localised relation to scientific knowledge and institutions that the atomic scientist could make his intervention;

but, since the nuclear threat affected the whole human race and the fate of the world, his discourse could at the same time be the discourse of the universal. Under the rubric of this protest, which concerned the entire world, the atomic expert brought into play his specific position in the order of knowledge. And for the first time, I think, the intellectual was hounded by political powers, no longer on account of a general discourse which he conducted, but because of the knowledge at his disposal: it was at this level that he constituted a political threat. I am only speaking here of Western intellectuals. What happened in the Soviet Union is analogous with this on a number of points, but different on many others. There is certainly a whole study that needs to be made of scientific dissidence in the West and the socialist countries since 1945.

[. . .]

It seems to me that we are now at a point where the function of the specific intellectual needs to be reconsidered. Reconsidered but not abandoned, despite the nostalgia of some for the great 'universal' intellectuals and the desire for a new philosophy, a new world-view. Suffice it to consider the important results which have been achieved in psychiatry: they prove that these local, specific struggles haven't been a mistake and haven't led to a dead end. One may even say that the role of the specific intellectual must become more and more important in proportion to the political responsibilities which he is obliged willy-nilly to accept, as a nuclear scientist, computer expert, pharmacologist, etc. It would be a dangerous error to discount him politically in his specific relation to a local form of power, either on the grounds that this is a specialist matter which doesn't concern the masses (which is doubly wrong: they are already aware of it, and in any case implicated in it), or that the specific intellectual serves the interests of State or Capital (which is true, but at the same time shows the strategic position he occupies), or, again, on the grounds that he propagates a scientific ideology (which isn't always true, and is anyway certainly a secondary matter compared with the fundamental point: the effects proper to true discourses).

The important thing here, I believe, is that truth isn't outside power, or lacking in power: contrary to a myth whose history and functions would repay further study, truth isn't the reward of free spirits, the child of protracted solitude, nor the privilege of those who have succeeded in liberating themselves. Truth is a thing of this world: it is produced only by virtue of multiple forms of constraint. And it induces regular effects of power. Each society has its regime of truth, its 'general politics' of truth: that is, the types of discourse which it accepts and makes function as true; the mechanisms and instances which enable one to distinguish true and false statements, the means by which each is sanctioned; the techniques and procedures accorded value in the acquisition of truth; the status of those who are charged with saying what counts as true.

In societies like ours, the 'political economy' of truth is characterised by five important traits. 'Truth' is centred on the form of scientific discourse and the institutions which produce it; it is subject to constant economic and political incitement (the demand for truth, as much for economic production as for political power); it is the object, under diverse forms, of immense diffusion and consumption (circulating through apparatuses of education and information whose extent is relatively broad in the social body, not withstanding certain strict limitations); it is produced and transmitted under the control, dominant if not exclusive, of a few great political and economic apparatuses (university, army, writing, media); lastly, it is the issue of a whole political debate and social confrontation ('ideological' struggles).

It seems to me that what must now be taken into account in the intellectual is not the 'bearer of universal values'. Rather, it's the person occupying a specific position – but whose specificity is linked, in a society like ours, to the general functioning of an apparatus of truth. In other words, the intellectual has a threefold specificity: that of his class position (whether as petty-bourgeois in the service of capitalism or 'organic' intellectual of the proletariat); that of his conditions of life and work, linked to his condition as an intellectual (his field of research, his place in a laboratory, the political and economic demands to which he submits or against which he rebels, in the university, the hospital, etc.); lastly, the specificity of the politics of truth in our societies. And it's with this last factor that his position can take on a general significance and that his local, specific struggle can have effects and implications which are not simply professional or sectoral. The intellectual can operate and struggle at the general level of that regime of truth which is so essential to the structure and functioning of our society. There is a battle 'for truth', or at least 'around truth' – it being understood once again that by truth I do not mean 'the ensemble of truths which are to be discovered and accepted', but rather 'the ensemble of rules according to which the true and the false are separated and specific effects of power attached to the true', it being understood also that it's not a matter of a battle 'on behalf' of the truth, but of a battle about the status of truth and the economic and political role it plays. It is necessary to think of the political problems of intellectuals not in terms of 'science' and 'ideology', but in terms of 'truth' and 'power'. And thus the question of the professionalisation of intellectuals and the division between intellectual and manual labour can be envisaged in a new way.

All this must seem very confused and uncertain. Uncertain indeed, and what I am saying here is above all to be taken as a hypothesis. In order for it to be a little less confused, however, I would like to put forward a few 'propositions' – not firm assertions, but simply suggestions to be further tested and evaluated.

'Truth' is to be understood as a system of ordered procedures for the production, regulation, distribution, circulation and operation of statements.

'Truth' is linked in a circular relation with systems of power which produce and sustain it, and to effects of power which it induces and which extend it. A 'regime' of truth.

This regime is not merely ideological or superstructural; it was a condition of the formation and development of capitalism. And it's this same regime which, subject to certain modifications, operates in the socialist countries (I leave open here the question of China, about which I know little).

The essential political problem for the intellectual is not to criticise the ideological contents supposedly linked to science, or to ensure that his own scientific practice is accompanied by a correct ideology, but that of ascertaining the possibility of constituting a new politics of truth. The problem is not changing people's consciousnesses — or what's in their heads — but the political, economic, institutional regime of the production of truth.

It's not a matter of emancipating truth from every system of power (which would be a chimera, for truth is already power) but of detaching the power of truth from the forms of hegemony, social, economic and cultural, within which it operates at the present time.

The political question, to sum up, is not error, illusion, alienated consciousness or ideology; it is truth itself. Hence the importance of Nietzsche.

Note

1. Foucault's response to this final question was given in writing.

1.5 □ *The Resistance to Theory*

Paul de Man

[. . .]

[W]e know that there has been, over the last fifteen to twenty years, a strong interest in something called literary theory and that, in the United States, this interest has at times coincided with the importation and reception of foreign, mostly but not always continental influences. We also know that this wave of interest now seems to be receding as some satiation or disappointment sets in after the initial enthusiasm. Such an ebb and flow is natural enough, but it remains interesting, in this case, because it makes the depth of the resistance to literary theory so manifest. It is a recurrent strategy of any anxiety to defuse what it considers threatening by magnification or minimization, by attributing to it claims to power of which it is bound to fall short.

[. . .]

What is it that is being threatened by the approaches to literature that developed during the sixties and that now, under a variety of designations, make up the ill-defined and somewhat chaotic field of literary theory? These approaches cannot be simply equated with any particular method or country. Structuralism was not the only trend to dominate the stage, not even in France, and structuralism as well as semiology are inseparable from prior tendencies in the Slavic domain. In Germany, the main impulses have come from other directions, from the Frankfurt School and more orthodox Marxists, from post-Husserlian phenomenology and post-Heideggerian hermeneutics, with only minor inroads made by structural analysis. All these trends have had their share of influence in the United States, in more or less productive combinations with nationally rooted concerns. Only a nationally or personally competitive view of history would wish to hierarchize such hard-to-label movements. The possibility of doing literary theory, which is by no means to be

From de Man, P., 'The resistance to theory', *Yale French Studies*, 63 (1982), pp. 5, 7–13, 15, 17–20.

taken for granted, has itself become a consciously reflected-upon question, and those who have progressed furthest in this question are the most controversial but also the best sources of information. This certainly includes several of the names loosely connected with structuralism, broadly enough defined to include Saussure, Jakobson and Barthes as well as Greimas and Althusser, that is to say, so broadly defined as to be no longer of use as a meaningful historical term.

Literary theory can be said to come into being when the approach to literary texts is no longer based on non-linguistic, that is to say historical and aesthetic, considerations or, to put it somewhat less crudely, when the object of discussion is no longer the meaning or the value but the modalities of production and of reception of meaning and of value prior to their establishment – the implication being that this establishment is problematic enough to require an autonomous discipline of critical investigation to consider its possibility and its status. Literary history, even when considered at the furthest remove from the platitudes of positivistic historicism, is still the history of an understanding of which the possibility is taken for granted. The question of the relationship between aesthetics and meaning is more complex, since aesthetics apparently has to do with the *effect* of meaning rather than with its content *per se*. But aesthetics is in fact, ever since its development just before and with Kant, a phenomenalism of a process of meaning and understanding, and it may be naive in that it postulates (as its name indicates) a phenomenology of art and of literature which may well be what is at issue. Aesthetics is part of a universal system of philosophy rather than a specific theory. In the nineteenth-century philosophical tradition, Nietzsche's challenge of the system erected by Kant, Hegel and their successors is a version of the general question of philosophy. Nietzsche's critique of metaphysics includes, or starts out from, the aesthetic, and the same could be argued for Heidegger. The invocation of prestigious philosophical names does not intimate that the present-day development of literary theory is a by-product of larger philosophical speculations. In some rare cases, a direct link may exist between philosophy and literary theory. More frequently, however, contemporary literary theory is a relatively autonomous version of questions that also surface, in a different context, in philosophy, though not necessarily in a clearer and more rigorous form. Philosophy, in England as well as on the Continent, is less free from traditional patterns than it sometimes pretends to believe and the prominent, though never dominant, place of aesthetics among the main components of the system is a constitutive part of this system. It is therefore not surprising that contemporary literary theory came into being from outside philosophy and sometimes in conscious rebellion against the weight of its tradition. Literary theory may now well have become a legitimate concern of philosophy but it cannot be assimilated to it, either factually or theoretically. It contains a necessarily pragmatic moment that certainly weakens it as theory but that adds a subversive element of unpredictability and makes it something of a wild card in the serious game of the theoretical disciplines.

The advent of theory, the break that is now so often being deplored and that sets it aside from literary history and from literary criticism, occurs with the introduction of linguistic terminology in the metalanguage about literature. By linguistic terminology is meant a terminology that designates reference prior to designating the referent and takes into account, in the consideration of the world, the referential function of language or, to be somewhat more specific, that considers reference as a function of language and not necessarily as an intuition. Intuition implies perception, consciousness, experience, and leads at once into the world of logic and of understanding with all its correlatives, among which aesthetics occupies a prominent place. The assumption that there can be a science of language which is not necessarily a logic leads to the development of a terminology which is not necessarily aesthetic. Contemporary literary theory comes into its own in such events as the application of Saussurian linguistics to literary texts.

The affinity between structural linguistics and literary texts is not as obvious as, with the hindsight of history, it now may seem. Peirce, Saussure, Sapir and Bloomfield were not originally concerned with literature at all but with the scientific foundations of linguistics. But the interest of philologists such as Roman Jakobson or literary critics such as Roland Barthes in semiology reveals the natural attraction of literature to a theory of linguistic signs. By considering language as a system of signs and of signification rather than an established pattern of meanings, one displaces or even suspends the traditional barriers between literary and presumably non-literary uses of language and liberates the corpus from the secular weight of textual canonization. The results of the encounter between semiology and literature went considerably further than those of many other theoretical models – philological, psychological or classically epistemological – which writers on literature in quest of such models had tried out before. The responsiveness of literary texts to semiotic analysis is visible in that, whereas other approaches were unable to reach beyond observations that could be paraphrased or translated in terms of common knowledge, these analyses revealed patterns that could only be described in terms of their own, specifically linguistic, aspects. The linguistics of semiology and of literature apparently have something in common that only their shared perspective can detect and that pertains distinctively to them. The definition of this something, often referred to as literariness, has become the object of literary theory.

Literariness, however, is often misunderstood in a way that has provoked much of the confusion which dominates today's polemics. It is frequently assumed, for instance, that literariness is another word for or another mode of, aesthetic response. The use, in conjunction with literariness, of such terms as style and stylistics, form or even 'poetry' (as in 'the poetry of grammar'), all of which carry strong aesthetic connotations, helps to foster this confusion, even among those who first put the term in circulation. Roland Barthes, for example, in an essay properly and revealingly dedicated to Roman Jakobson, speaks eloquently of the writer's quest for a perfect coincidence of the phonic properties of a word with its signifying function:

We would also wish to insist on the Cratylism of the name (and of the sign) in Proust. ... Proust sees the relationship between signifier and signified as motivated, the one copying the other and representing in its material form the signified essence of the thing (and not the thing itself). ... This realism (in the scholastic sense of the word), which conceives of names as the 'copy' of the ideas, has taken, in Proust, a radical form. But one may well ask whether it is not more or less consciously present in all writing and whether it is possible to be a writer without some sort of belief in the natural relationship between names and essences. The poetic function, in the widest sense of the word, would thus be defined by a Cratylian awareness of the sign, and the writer would be the conveyor of this secular myth which wants language to imitate the idea and which, contrary to the teachings of linguistic science, thinks of signs as motivated signs.[1]

To the extent that Cratylism assumes a convergence of the phenomenal aspects of language, as sound, with its signifying function as referent, it is an aesthetically oriented conception; one could, in fact, without distortion, consider aesthetic theory, including its most systematic formulation in Hegel, as the complete unfolding of the model of which the Cratylian conception of language is a version. Hegel's somewhat cryptic reference to Plato, in the *Aesthetics*, may well be interpreted in this sense. Barthes and Jakobson often seem to invite a purely aesthetic reading, yet there is a part of their statement that moves in the opposite direction. For the convergence of sound and meaning celebrated by Barthes in Proust and, as Gérard Genette has decisively shown,[2] later dismantled by Proust himself as a seductive temptation to mystified minds, is also considered here to be a mere *effect* which language can perfectly well achieve, but which bears no substantial relationship, by analogy or by ontologically grounded imitation, to anything beyond that particular effect. It is a rhetorical rather than an aesthetic function of language, an identifiable trope (paranomasis) that operates on the level of the signifier and contains no responsible pronouncement on the nature of the world – despite its powerful potential to create the opposite illusion. The phenomenality of the signifier, as sound, is unquestionably involved in the correspondence between the name and the thing named, but the link, the relationship between word and thing is not phenomenal but conventional.

This gives the language considerable freedom from referential restraint, but it makes it epistemologically highly suspect and volatile, since its use can no longer be said to be determined by considerations of truth and falsehood, good and evil, beauty and ugliness, or pleasure and pain. Whenever this autonomous potential of language can be revealed by analysis, we are dealing with literariness and, in fact, with literature as the place where this negative knowledge about the reliability of linguistic utterance is made available. The ensuing foregrounding of material, phenomenal aspects of the signifier creates a strong illusion of aesthetic seduction at the very moment when the actual aesthetic function has been, at the very least, suspended. It is inevitable that semiology or similarly oriented methods be considered formalistic, in the sense of being aesthetically rather than semantically valorized, but the inevitability of such an interpretation does not make it less aberrant. Literature involves the voiding, rather than the affirmation, of aesthetic categories. One of the consequences of this is that, whereas we have traditionally been accustomed to reading literature by analogy with the plastic arts and with music, we now have to recognize the necessity of a non-perceptual, linguistic moment in painting and in music, and learn to *read* pictures rather than to *imagine* meaning.

If literariness is not an aesthetic quality, it is also not primarily mimetic. Mimesis becomes one trope among others, language choosing to imitate a non-verbal entity just as paranomasis 'imitates' a sound without any claim to identity (or reflection on difference) between the verbal and non-verbal elements. The most misleading representation of literariness, and also the most recurrent objection to contemporary literary theory, considers it as pure verbalism, as a denial of the reality principle in the name of absolute fictions, and for reasons that are said to be ethically and politically shameful. The attack reflects the anxiety of the aggressors rather than the guilt of the accused. By allowing for the necessity of a non-phenomenal linguistics, one frees the discourse on literature from naive oppositions between fiction and reality, which are themselves an offspring of an uncritically mimetic conception of art. In a genuine semiology as well as in other linguistically oriented theories, the referential function of language is not being denied – far from it; what is in question is its authority as a model for natural or phenomenal cognition. Literature is fiction not because it somehow refuses to acknowledge 'reality', but because it is not *a priori* certain that language functions according to principles which are those, or which are *like* those, of the phenomenal world. It is therefore not *a priori* certain that literature is a reliable source of information about anything but its own language.

It would be unfortunate, for example, to confuse the materiality of the signifier with the materiality of what it signifies. This may seem obvious enough on the level of light and sound, but it is less so with regard to the more general phenomenality of space, time or especially of the self: no one in his right mind will try to grow grapes by the luminosity of the word 'day', but it is very difficult not to conceive the pattern of one's past and future existence as in accordance with temporal and spatial schemes that belong to fictional narratives and not to the world. This does not mean that fictional narratives are not part of the world and of reality; their impact upon the world may well be all too strong for comfort. What we call ideology is precisely the confusion of linguistic with natural reality, of reference with phenomenalism. It follows that, more than any other mode of inquiry, including economics, the linguistics of literariness is a powerful and indispensable tool in the unmasking of ideological aberrations, as well as a determining factor in accounting for their occurrence. Those who reproach literary theory for being oblivious to social and historical (that is to say, ideological) reality are merely stating their fear at having their own ideological mystifications exposed by the tool they are trying to discredit. They are, in short, very poor readers of Marx's *German Ideology*.

In these all too summary evocations of arguments that have been much more extensively and convincingly made by others, we begin to perceive some of the answers to the initial question: what is it about literary theory that is so threatening that it provokes such strong resistances and attacks? It upsets rooted ideologies by revealing the mechanics of their workings; it goes against a powerful philosophical tradition of which aesthetics is a prominent part; it upsets the established canon of literary works and blurs the borderlines between literary and non-literary discourse. By implication, it may also reveal the links between ideologies and philosophy. All this is ample enough reason for suspicion, but not a satisfying answer to the question. For it makes the tension between contemporary literary theory and the tradition of literary studies appear as a mere historical conflict between two modes of thought that happen to hold the stage at the same time. If the conflict is merely historical, in the literal sense, it is of limited theoretical interest, a passing squall in the intellectual weather of the world. As a matter of fact, the arguments in favor of the legitimacy of literary theory are so compelling that it seems useless to concern oneself with the conflict at all. Certainly, none of the objections to theory, presented again and again, always misinformed or based on crude misunderstandings of such terms as mimesis, fiction, reality, ideology, reference and, for that matter, relevance, can be said to be of genuine rhetorical interest.

It may well be, however, that the development of literary theory is itself overdetermined by complications inherent in its very project and unsettling with regard to its status as a scientific discipline. Resistance may be a built-in constituent of its discourse, in a manner that would be inconceivable in the natural sciences and unmentionable in the social sciences. It may well be, in other words, that the polemical opposition, the systematic non-understanding and misrepresentation, the unsubstantial but eternally recurrent objections, are the displaced symptoms of a resistance inherent in the theoretical enterprise itself. To claim that this would be a sufficient reason not to envisage doing literary theory would be like rejecting anatomy because it has failed to cure mortality. The real debate of literary theory is not with its polemical opponents but rather with its own methodological assumptions and possibilities. Rather than asking why literary theory is threatening, we should perhaps ask why it has such difficulty going about its business and why it lapses so readily either into the language of self-justification and self-defense or else into the overcompensation of a progammatically euphoric utopianism. Such insecurity about its own project calls for self-analysis, if one is to understand the frustrations that attend upon its practitioners, even when they seem to dwell in serene methodological self-assurance. And if these difficulties are indeed an integral part of the problem, then they will have to be, to some extent, ahistorical in the temporal sense of the term. The way in which they are encountered on the present local literary scene as a resistance to the introduction of linguistic terminology in aesthetic and historical discourse about literature is only one particular version of a question that cannot be reduced to a specific historical situation and called modern, postmodern, post-classical or romantic (not even in Hegel's sense of the term), although its compulsive way of forcing itself upon us in the guise of a system of historical periodization is certainly part of its problematic nature. Such difficulties can be read in the text of literary theory at all times, at whatever historical moment one wishes to select. One of the main achievements of the present theoretical trends is to have restored some awareness of this fact. Classical, medieval and Renaissance literary theory is now often being read in a way that knows enough about what it is doing not to wish to call itself 'modern'.

We return, then, to the original question in an attempt to broaden the discussion enough to inscribe the polemics inside the question rather than having them determine it. The resistance to theory is a resistance to the use of language about language. It is therefore a resistance to language itself or to the possibility that language contains factors or functions that cannot be reduced to intuition. But we seem to assume all too readily that, when we refer to something called 'language', we know what it is we are talking about, although there is probably no word to be found in the language that is as overdetermined, self-evasive, disfigured and disfiguring as 'language'.

[. . .]

The uncertain relationship between grammar and rhetoric (as opposed to that between grammar and logic) is apparent, in the history of the *trivium*, in the uncertain status of figures of speech or tropes, a component of language that straddles the disputed borderlines between the two areas. Tropes used to be part of the study of grammar but were also considered to be the semantic agent of the specific function (or effect) that rhetoric performs as persuasion as well as meaning. Tropes, unlike grammar, pertain primordially to language. They are text-producing functions that are not necessarily patterned on a non-verbal entity, whereas grammar is by definition capable of extra-linguistic generalization. The latent tension between rhetoric and grammar precipitates out in the problem of reading, the process that necessarily partakes of both. It turns out that the resistance to theory is in fact a resistance to reading, a resistance that is perhaps at its most effective, in contemporary studies, in the methodologies that call themselves theories of reading but nevertheless avoid the function they claim as their object.

What is meant when we assert that the study of literary texts is necessarily dependent on an act of reading, or when we claim that this act is being systematically avoided? Certainly more than the tautology that one has to have read at least some parts, however small, of a text (or read some part, however small, of a text about this text) in order to be able to make a statement about it. Common as it may be, criticism by hearsay is only rarely held up as exemplary. To stress the by no means self-evident necessity of reading implies at least two things. First of all, it implies that literature is not a transparent message in which it can be taken for granted that the distinction between the message and the means of communication is clearly established. Second, and more problematically, it implies that the grammatical decoding of a text leaves a residue of indetermination that has to be, but cannot be, resolved by grammatical means, however extensively conceived.

[. . .]

This undoing of theory, this disturbance of the stable cognitive field that extends from grammar to logic to a general science of man and of the phenomenal world, can in its turn be made into a theoretical project of rhetorical analysis that will reveal the inadequacy of grammatical models of non-reading. Rhetoric, by its actively negative relationship to grammar and to logic, certainly undoes the claims of the *trivium* (and by extension, of language) to be an epistemologically stable construct. The resistance to theory is a resistance to the rhetorical or tropological dimension of language, a dimension which is perhaps more explicitly in the foreground in literature (broadly conceived) than in other verbal manifestations or – to be somewhat less vague – which can be revealed in any verbal event when it is read textually. Since grammar as well as figuration is an integral part of reading, it follows that reading will be a negative process in which the grammatical cognition is undone, at all times, by its rhetorical displacement. The model of the *trivium* contains within itself the pseudo-dialectic of its own undoing and its history tells the story of this dialectic.

This conclusion allows for a somewhat more systematic description of the contemporary theoretical scene. This scene is dominated by an increased stress on reading as a theoretical problem or, as it is sometimes erroneously phrased, by an increased stress on the reception rather than on the production of texts. It is in this area that the most fruitful exchanges have come about between writers and journals of various countries and that the most interesting dialogue has developed between literary theory and other disciplines, in the arts as well as in linguistics, philosophy and the social sciences. A straightforward *report* on the present state of literary theory in the United States would have to stress the emphasis on reading, a direction which is already present, moreover, in the New Critical tradition of the forties and the fifties. The methods are now more technical, but the contemporary interest in a poetics of literature is clearly linked, traditionally enough, to the problems of reading. And since the models that are being used certainly are no longer *simply* intentional and centered on an identifiable self, nor *simply* hermeneutic in the postulation of a single originary, pre-figural and absolute text, it would appear that this concentration on reading would lead to the rediscovery of the theoretical difficulties associated with rhetoric. This is indeed the case, to some extent; but not quite. Perhaps the most instructive aspect of contemporary theory is the refinement of the techniques by which the threat inherent in rhetorical analysis is being avoided at the very moment when the efficacy of these techniques has progressed so far that the rhetorical obstacles to understanding can no longer be mistranslated in thematic and phenomenal commonplaces. The resistance to theory which, as we saw, is a resistance to reading, appears in its most rigorous and theoretically elaborated form among the theoreticians of reading who dominate the contemporary theoretical scene.

It would be a relatively easy, though lengthy, process to show that this is so for theoreticians of reading who, like Greimas or, on a more refined level, Riffaterre or, in a very different mode, H. R. Jauss or Wolfgang Iser – all of whom have a definite, though sometimes occult, influence on literary theory in this country – are committed to the use of grammatical models or, in the case of *Rezeptionsaesthetik*, to traditional hermeneutic models that do not allow for the problematization of the phenomenalism of reading and therefore remain uncritically confined within a theory of literature rooted in aesthetics. Such an argument would be easy to make because, once a reader has become aware of the rhetorical dimensions of a text, he will not be amiss in finding textual instances that are irreducible to grammar or to historically determined meaning, provided only he is willing to acknowledge what he is bound to notice. The problem quickly becomes the more baffling one of having to account for the shared reluctance to acknowledge the obvious. But the argument would be lengthy because it has to involve a textual analysis that cannot avoid being somewhat elaborate; one can succinctly suggest the grammatical indetermination of a title such as *The Fall of Hyperion*, but to confront such an undecideable enigma with the critical reception and reading of Keats's text requires some space.

The demonstration is less easy (though perhaps less ponderous) in the case of theoreticians of reading whose avoidance of rhetoric takes another turn. We have witnessed, in recent years, a strong interest in certain elements in language whose function is not only not dependent on any form of phenomenalism but on any form of cognition as well, and which thus excludes, or postpones, the consideration of tropes, ideologies, etc., from a reading that would be primarily performative. In some cases, a link is reintroduced between performance, grammar, logic, and stable referential meaning, and the resulting theories (as in the case of Ohman) are not in essence distinct from those of avowed grammarians or semioticians. But the most astute practitioners of a speech act theory of reading avoid this relapse and rightly insist on the necessity to keep the actual performance of speech acts, which is conventional rather than cognitive, separate from its causes and effects – to keep, in their terminology, the illocutionary force separate from its perlocutionary function. Rhetoric, understood as persuasion, is forcefully banished (like Coriolanus) from the performative moment and exiled in the affective area of perlocution. Stanley Fish, in a masterful essay, convincingly makes this point.[3] What awakens one's suspicion about this conclusion is that it relegates persuasion, which is indeed inseparable from rhetoric, to a purely affective and intentional realm and makes no allowance for modes of persuasion which are no less rhetorical and no less at work in literary texts, but which are of the order of persuasion by *proof* rather than persuasion by seduction. Thus to empty rhetoric of its epistemological impact is possible only because its tropological, figural functions are being bypassed. It is as if, to return for a moment to the model of the *trivium*, rhetoric could be isolated from the generality that grammar and logic have in common and considered as a mere correlative of an illocutionary power. The equation of rhetoric with psychology rather than with epistemology opens up dreary prospects of pragmatic banality, all the drearier if compared to the brilliance of the performative analysis. Speech act theories of reading in fact repeat, in a much more effective way, the grammatization of the *trivium* at the expense of rhetoric. For the characterization of the performative as sheer convention reduces it in effect to a grammatical code among others. The relationship between trope and performance is actually closer but more disruptive than what is here being proposed. Nor is this relationship properly captured by reference to a supposedly 'creative' aspect of performance, a notion with which Fish rightly takes issue. The performative power of language can be called positional, which differs considerably from conventional as well as from 'creatively' (or, in the technical sense, intentionally) constitutive. Speech act oriented theories of reading read only to the extent that they prepare the way for the rhetorical reading they avoid.

But the same is still true even if a 'truly' rhetorical reading that would stay clear of any undue phenomenalization or of any undue grammatical or performative codification of the text could be conceived – something which is not necessarily impossible and for which the aims and methods of literary theory should certainly strive. Such a reading would indeed appear as the methodical undoing of the grammatical construct and, in its systematic disarticulation of the *trivium*, will be theoretically sound as well as effective. Technically correct rhetorical readings may be boring, monotonous, predictable and unpleasant, but they are irrefutable. They are also totalizing (and potentially totalitarian), for since the structures and functions they expose do not lead to the knowledge of an entity (such as language) but are an unreliable process of knowledge production that prevents all entities, including linguistic entities, from coming into discourse as such, they are indeed universals, consistently defective models of language's impossibility to be a model language. They are, always in theory, the most elastic theoretical and dialectical model to end all models, and they can rightly claim to contain within their own defective selves all the other defective models of reading-avoidance, referential, semiological, grammatical, performative, logical, or whatever. They are theory and not theory at the same time, the universal theory of the impossibility of theory. To the extent, however, that they are theory, that is to say teachable, generalizable and highly responsive to systematization, rhetorical readings, like the other kinds, still avoid and resist the reading they advocate. Nothing can overcome the resistance to theory, since theory *is* itself this resistance. The loftier the aims and the better the methods of literary theory, the less possible it becomes. Yet literary theory is not in danger of going under; it cannot help but flourish, and the more it is resisted, the more it flourishes, since the language it speaks is the language of self-resistance. What remains impossible to decide is whether this flourishing is a triumph or a fall.

Notes

1. Gérard Genette, 'Proust et les noms', in *To Honor Roman Jakobson* (The Hague, 1967) part I, pp. 157 ff.
2. 'Proust et le langage indirect', in *Figures II* (Paris, 1969).
3. Stanley Fish, 'How to do things with Austin and Searle: Speech Act Theory and Literary Criticism', *MLN* 91 (1976), pp. 983–1025. See especially p. 1008.

1.6 □ *Reading Unreadability: de Man*

J. Hillis Miller

Allegories are always ethical, the term ethical designating the structural interference of two distinct value systems. In this sense, ethics has nothing to do with the will (thwarted or free) of a subject, nor *a fortiori*, with a relationship between subjects. The ethical category is imperative (i.e. a category rather than a value) to the extent that it is linguistic and not subjective. Morality is a version of the same language aporia that gave rise to such concepts as 'man' or 'love' or 'self', and not the cause or the consequence of such concepts. The passage to an ethical tonality does not result from a transcendental imperative but is the referential (and therefore unreliable) version of a linguistic confusion. Ethics (or, one should say, ethicity) is a discursive mode among others.

(PAUL DE MAN)[1]

Every construction, every system – that is, every text – has within itself the ignorance of its own exterior as the rupture of its coherence which it cannot account for.

(HANS-JOST FREY)[2]

This chapter attempts to 'read' the passage I have cited from *Allegories of Reading* (in defiance of Paul de Man's assertion that a critical text, as soon as it is taken as a text, is as 'unreadable' as any other text). What de Man means by 'unreadable', something far different from widespread notions that it has to do with the 'indeterminacy' of the meaning of the text, will be one of my concerns. My choice of the question of 'ethics' in de Man is meant to further my investigation of what it might mean to speak of an 'ethics of reading' through the reading of an example

From Miller, J. H., *The Ethics of Reading: Kant, de Man, Eliot, Trollope, James, Benjamin*, Columbia University Press, New York, 1987, pp. 41–7, 49–54, 58–9, 131–2.

drawn from literary criticism or 'theory', after the example from philosophy and before the properly 'literary' ones from Trollope, Eliot, and James. My choice is also intended to confront frequent charges that de Man's work is 'nihilistic', undermines the value of all humanistic study, reduces the work of interpretation to the free play of arbitrary imposition of meaning, finds in each text only what it went there to look for, and so on. What de Man actually says is so far from all this that it is a kind of puzzle to figure out how such ideas about his work have got around and pass current as valid intellectual coinage. Perhaps such ideas are just that, clichés passed from hand to hand by those who have never bothered to read de Man's work, no easy task, as I began by admitting.

[. . .]

By 'the ethics of reading' [. . .] I mean that aspect of the act of reading in which there is a response to the text that is both necessitated, in the sense that it is a response to an irresistible demand, and free, in the sense that I must take responsibility for my response and for the further effects, 'interpersonal', institutional, social, political, or historical, of my act of reading, for example as that act takes the form of teaching or of published commentary on a given text. What happens when I read *must* happen, but I must acknowledge it as *my* act of reading, though just what the 'I' is or becomes in this transaction is another question. To say that there is a properly ethical dimension to the act of reading sounds odd, as I have said. It would seem that the act of reading as such must have little to do with ethics, even though the text read may make thematic statements which have ethical import, which is not at all the same thing. Reading itself would seem to be epistemological, cognitive, a matter of 'getting the text right', respecting it in that sense, not a matter involving moral obligation.

Even less would Paul de Man's particular 'theory' of reading seem likely to have an ethical dimension. Epistemological categories, categories of truth and falsehood, enlightenment and delusion, insight and blindness, seem to control the admirable rigor of his essays. The category of ethics or, as he says, 'ethicity', does, however, somewhat surprisingly, appear at crucial moments in de Man's essays, for example in 'my' passage. The category of ethicity is one version of that insistence on a necessary referential, pragmatic function of language which distinguishes de Man's work from certain forms of structuralism or semiotics. It also gives the lie to those who claim 'deconstruction' asserts the 'free play' of language in the void, abstracted from all practical, social, or political effect. Of de Man one can say what he himself says of Rousseau: 'his radical critique of referential meaning never implied that the referential function of language could in any way be avoided, bracketed, or reduced to being just one contingent linguistic property among others, as is postulated, for example, in contemporary semiology which, like all post-Kantian formalisms, could not exist without this postulate' (AR, 207). Ethicity is for de Man associated with the categories of politics and history, though these three modes of what he calls 'materiality' are not the same. My goal here is to account for the presence of the word 'ethics' in de Man's vocabulary, and to present thereby a salient example within contemporary literary theory of an ethics of reading.

'Ethicity', like other forms of reference to the extra-linguistic by way of the linguistic, occurs for de Man not at the beginning, as a basis for language, and not at the end, as a final triumphant return to reality validating language, but in the midst of an intricate sequence, the sequentiality of which is of course only a fiction, a convenience for thinking as a narrative what in fact always occurs in the tangle of an 'all at once' mixing tropological, allegorical, referential, ethical, political, and historical dimensions. The passage I began by citing and propose in this chapter to try to 'read' follows in *Allegories of Reading* on the page after one of de Man's most succinct formulations of his paradigmatic model for the narrative pattern into which all texts fall:

> The paradigm for all texts consists of a figure (or a system of figures) and its deconstruction. But since this model cannot be closed off by a final reading, it engenders, in its turn, a supplementary figural superposition which narrates the unreadability of the prior narration. As distinguished from primary deconstructive narratives centered on figures and ultimately always on metaphor, we can call such narratives to the second (or the third) degree *allegories*. (AR, 205)

This formulation is by no means immediately transparent in meaning. I have elsewhere attempted to read it in detail.[3] What is most important here is the fact that the ethical moment, for de Man, occurs toward the end of this intricate sequence, as primary evidence of a text's inability to read itself, to benefit from its own wisdom. First comes the assertion of an unjustified and aberrant metaphor, then the 'deconstruction' of that metaphor, the revelation of its aberrancy, then the 'allegory', that is, the expression in a veiled form of the impossibility of reading that revelation of aberrancy. One form that repetition of the first error takes is the mode of referentiality that de Man calls 'ethicity.'

The first feature of the ethical for de Man, then, is that it is an aspect not of the first narrative of metaphorical denomination nor of the second narrative of the deconstruction of that aberrant act of denomination, but of the 'third' narrative of the failure to read which de Man calls 'allegory'. Says de Man: 'Allegories are always ethical.' The ethical, or what de Man calls, somewhat barbarously, 'ethicity', is not a primary category, but a secondary or in fact tertiary one. 'Ethicity' is necessary and it is not derivative from anything but the laws of language that are all-determining or all-engendering for de Man, but the ethical does not come first. It intervenes, necessarily intervenes, but it occurs at a 'later stage' in a sequence which begins with epistemological error, the error born of aberrant metaphorical naming. One must remember, however, that the sequential unfolding of 'earlier' and 'later' that makes all texts, in de Man's use of the term, 'narratives' is the fictional temporalization of what in fact are simultaneous linguistic operations: aberrant metaphorical naming, the deconstruction of that act of nomination, the allegory of the unreadability of those 'first' two linguistic acts, and so on. Of that allegory of the impossibility of reading 'ethicity' is a necessary dimension, since all allegories are ethical. In this sense ethicity is as first as any other linguistic act. It is unconditionally necessary.

But what does it mean to say that 'allegories are always ethical'? It is clear that the main target of de Man's attack here is Kant's ethical theory. To put this another way, the passage about ethics simultaneously rejects Kant and bends Kantian language to another purpose. In order to make an open space for his own ethical theory, de Man has simultaneously to reject the Kantian theory and appropriate its language to his own uses: 'The ethical category is imperative (i.e. a category rather than a value) to the extent that it is linguistic and not subjective.' In order to argue that ethicity is the product of a purely linguistic necessity de Man has to reject the notion that it has to do with subjectivity, or with freedom as a feature of selfhood, or with interpersonal relations, or with a categorical imperative coming from some transcendental source, whether from subjectivity in the form of the transcendental imagination or from some extrahuman transcendence. 'Ethics', says de Man, 'has nothing to do with the will (thwarted or free) of a subject, nor *a fortiori*, with a relationship between subjects.' And: 'The passage to an ethical tonality does not result from a transcendental imperative.'

Well, if ethics has nothing to do with any of the things it has traditionally been thought to be concerned with, with what then does it have to do? The answer is that ethical judgment and command is a necessary feature of human language. We cannot help making judgments of right and wrong, commanding others to act according to those judgments, condemning them for not doing so, responding ourselves to an ethical demand that will not be the less categorical and imperative for not coming from some transcendent extra-linguistic 'law'.

With the ground cleared of the chief alternative theories of ethics, especially the Kantian one, de Man can assert his own purely linguistic theory. What, in his case, does this mean, and how could an ethical judgment or command founded exclusively on language have the authority necessary in ethics, the 'I *must* do this; I *cannot do otherwise*, and I *ought* not to do otherwise'? The answer is that ethical judgment and command is a necessary part of that narrative of the impossibility of reading that de Man calls allegory. But what, exactly, does *this* mean? The failure to read, the reader will remember, takes the form of a further, secondary or tertiary, narrative superimposed on the first deconstructive narrative. This supplementary narrative shows indirectly, in the form of a story, someone committing again the 'same' linguistic error that the deconstructive narrative has lucidly identified and denounced. Only someone who can *read*, that is, who can interpret the allegory, which seems to say one thing but in fact says something else, will be able to see that what is really being narrated is the failure to read. But that act of reading will no doubt commit another version of the same error of the failure to read, and then again, in a perpetual fugacity of final clarity.

[. . .]

The formulation that 'allegories are always ethical' is therefore completed by a crucial definitional phrase: 'the term ethical designating the structural interference of two distinct value systems' (AR, 206). If the reader steps back for a moment from the context of de Man's intricate argumentation he or she will probably agree with me that this is an exceedingly odd definition of the term ethical: 'the structural interference of two distinct value systems'! For de Man the categories of truth and falsehood can never be reconciled with the categories of right and wrong, and yet both are values, in the sense of making an unconditional demand for their preservation. Surely one should want to dwell within the truth, and surely one should want to do what is right, but according to de Man it is impossible to respond simultaneously to those two demands. A statement can be true but not right or right but not true, but not both true and right at once.

Why is this? The answer is given in the four sentences that complete the paragraph I have been trying to read:

> The ethical category is imperative (i.e. a category rather than a value) to the extent that it is linguistic and not subjective. Morality is a version of the same language aporia that gave rise to such concepts as 'man' or 'love' or 'self', and not the cause or the consequence of such concepts. The passage to an ethical tonality does not result from a transcendental imperative but is the referential (and therefore unreliable) version of a linguistic confusion. Ethics (or, one should say, ethicity) is a discursive mode among others. (AR, 206)

For de Man, as for Kant, the fulfillment of an ethical demand must be necessary. It must be something I *have* to do, regardless of other competing demands. It is in this sense that it is a category rather than a value. A value is a matter of more or less, of differential comparisons according to some measuring yardstick. A categorical obligation is absolute and unconditional. We must do it, whatever the cost. In de Man's case, however, the necessity is linguistic rather than subjective or the effect of a transcendental law. It is a necessity to be in error or at the least confused, as always happens when I attempt to make language referential, and I *must* attempt to make it referential. I cannot do otherwise. In the case of ethics it is a necessity to make judgments, commands, promises about right and wrong which have no verifiable basis in anything outside language. It is in this sense that ethics (or ethicity) is a discursive mode among others. That is, ethics is not just a form of language, but a running or sequential mode of language, in short a story. Ethics is a form of allegory, one form of those apparently referential stories we tell to ourselves and to those around us.

[. . .]

> Understanding is not a version of one single and universal Truth that would exist as an essence, a hypostasis. The truth of a text is a much more empirical and literal event. What makes a reading more or less true is simply the predictability, the necessity of its occurrence, regardless of the reader or of the author's wishes. 'Es ereignet sich aber das Wahre' (not *die Wahrheit*) says Hölderlin, which can be freely translated, 'What is true is what is bound to take place.' And, in the case of the reading of a text, what takes place is a necessary understanding. What matrics the truth of such an understanding

is not some abstract universal but the fact that it has to occur regardless of other considerations. It depends, in other words, on the rigor of the reading as argument. Reading is an argument (which is not necessarily the same as a polemic) because it has to go against the grain of what one would want to happen in the name of what has to happen; this is the same as saying that an understanding is an epistemological event prior to being an ethical or aesthetic value. This does not mean that there can be a true reading, but that no reading is conceivable in which the question of its truth or falsehood is not primarily involved.

It would therefore be naive to make a reading depend on considerations, ethical or aesthetic, that are in fact correlatives of the understanding the reading is able to achieve. Naive, because it is not a matter of choice to omit or to accentuate by paraphrase certain elements in a text at the expense of others. We don't have this choice, since the text imposes its own understanding and shapes the reader's evasions. The more one censors, the more one reveals what is being effaced. A paraphrase is always what we called an analytical reading, that is, it is always susceptible of being made to point out consistently what it was trying to conceal.[4]

This luminous passage is one of the most important formulations de Man made about the ethics of reading and its relation to the epistemological dimension of reading. The understanding of a text is prior to its affirmation as an ethical value, but both are necessary. Both are bound to take place, even though they take place against the grain of the reader's or the author's wishes. 'Take place' is de Man's translation of Hölderlin's 'ereignet sich', in the lines from the late hymn, 'Mnemosyne', that he cites, wresting them from their context. It is a context, by the way, that is extremely enigmatic and that might take years of study and commentary to begin to 'understand', even though, if de Man is right, the first reading of Hölderlin's poem would cause its understanding to take place as a kind of foreknowledge. A reading 'takes place' as an event in the real world. *Ereignis* is the German word for event. Martin Heidegger has singled out this word in various places for commentary and analysis in relation, precisely, to that notion of *topos* or place. Each event takes place in a place which its occurrence as event makes into a place, as opposed to a vacant space with no meaning or coordinates. The same thing may be said of each act of reading. It takes place as an event in a certain spot and turns that spot in a certain sense into a sacred place, that is, into a place which is inaugural. Reading too turns empty space into a locus where something unique and unforeseen has occurred, has entered into the human world, and where it will have such effects as it will have. An act of reading, moreover, takes place, as something which is bound to happen as it does happen, to a certain person in a certain psychological, interpersonal, historical, political, and institutional situation, for example to a teacher or to a student in a certain university, or to a reader in a public library who happens to have taken the book down from the shelf.

Readings that 'take place' in this way are 'true' in the special sense of being true to an implacable law of language, that is, the law of the failure to read, not truth of correspondence to some transcendent and universal Truth with a capital T. Though de Man's formulation here is in terms of the necessary 'truth' of each reading, and though what he says makes it sound as if reading is a game in which we cannot lose, since we are bound to get it right, however limited we are as readers or however much our presuppositions about what the text is going to mean may seem to foredoom us to get it wrong, the careful reader of de Man, the reader for example of the passage which has been my main focus, will know that what is bound to take place in each act of reading is another exemplification of the law of unreadability. The failure to read takes place inexorably within the text itself. The reader must reenact this failure in his or her own reading. Getting it right always means being forced to reenact once more the necessity of getting it wrong. Each reader must repeat the error the text denounces and then commits again. By a strange but entirely cogent reversal which disqualifies the binary opposition between true and false, what de Man calls 'true' (not truth) here is the unavoidable exigency to be true to the obligation to lie, in the special sense de Man gives to lying. It is lying in the sense that one necessary moment in any act of reading is the referential turn which draws ethical conclusions, makes ethical judgments and prescriptions. These are unwarranted but they *must* follow the reading of the text. Both that understanding and the lie of unwarranted ethical affirmations are *bound* to take place, since both are inscribed within the text as its own failure to read itself. The reader in his act of reading must be true to that pattern.

The fact that the relation between ethical statements and the knowledge language gives is always potentially aberrant in no way means that ethical judgments do not work, do not sustain society, are not good in their effects. Ethical judgment, or 'ethicity' in general, works in fact in the same precarious way as the social contract in de Man's description of it. Its working is always threatened by its own lack of ground. It is sustained only by the fact that a group of people can be got to act as if it had a ground, that is, as if there were absolute justice in rewarding people for certain actions, punishing them for others. 'Finally,' says de Man:

> the *contractual* pattern of civil government can only be understood against the background of this permanent threat. The social contract is by no means the expression of a transcendental law: it is a complex and purely defensive verbal strategy by means of which the literal world is given some of the consistency of fiction, an intricate set of feints and ruses by means of which the moment is temporarily delayed when fictional seductions will no longer be able to resist transformation into literal acts. The conceptual language of the social contract resembles the subtle interplay between figural and referential discourse in a novel. (AR, 159)

[. . .]

Since 'Reading', for de Man, includes not just reading as such, certainly not just the act of reading works of literature, but sensation, perception, and therefore every human act whatsoever, in this case my apparently limited topic of the ethical dimension of reading would include the necessary but forever potentially aberrant referentiality of what he calls 'ethicity' in human life generally. For de Man the ethical is one (necessary and necessarily potentially aberrant) act of language among others, taking language in the inclusive sense which he gives it in 'Allegory of Reading (*Profession de foi*)'. Kant's concluding formulation in the *Grundlegung* would therefore in de Man's case have to be reformulated in a way that measures the difference, the great gulf, between them. De Man might have said: 'And so we do not indeed comprehend the practical unconditional necessity of the moral imperative, nor do we even comprehend its incomprehensibility, since the moral imperative itself, along with the human reason which strives to comprehend the incomprehensibility of its necessity, are both aspects of language, and it is impossible to use language as a tool with which to comprehend its own limitations.'

It is impossible to get outside the limits of language by means of language. Everything we reach that seems outside language, for example sensation and perception, turns out to be more language. To live is to read, or rather to commit again and again the failure to read which is the human lot. We are hard at work trying to fulfill the impossible task of reading from the moment we are born until the moment we die. We struggle to read from the moment we wake in the morning until the moment we fall asleep at night, and what are our dreams but more lessons in the pain of the impossibility of reading, or rather in the pain of having no way whatsoever of knowing whether or not we may have in our discursive wanderings and aberrancies stumbled by accident on the right reading? Far from being 'indeterminate' or 'nihilistic', however, or a matter of wanton free play or arbitrary choice, each reading is, strictly speaking, ethical, in the sense that it *has* to take place, by an implacable necessity, as the response to a categorical demand, and in the sense that the reader *must* take responsibility for it and for its consequences in the personal, social, and political worlds. Reading is one act among others, part, as Henry James says writing itself is, of the conduct of life, however unpredictable and surprising each act of reading may be, since the reader can never know beforehand what it is in this particular case of reading that is bound to take place. Such is the rigor of Paul de Man's affirmation of an ethics of reading. It imposes on the reader the 'impossible' task of reading unreadability, but that does not by any means mean that reading, even 'good' reading, cannot take place and does not have a necessary ethical dimension.

Notes

1. *Allegories of Reading* (New Haven, CT and London: Yale University Press, 1979), p. 206; henceforth AR.
2. 'Undecidability', trans. Robert Livingston, in *The Lesson of Paul de Man, Yale French Studies* (1985), 69:132.
3. In '"Reading" Part of a Paragraph of *Allegories of Reading*', forthcoming in *Reading Paul de Man Reading*, a volume of essays on de Man edited by Lindsay Waters.
4. Paul de Man, 'Foreword' to Carol Jacobs, *The Dissimulating Harmony* (Baltimore, MD and London: Johns Hopkins University Press, 1978), p. xi.

2 □ *Psychoanalytic Theory*

Introduction

There ought to be more of a dialogue between the first three Readings in this Section and the rest, but the effect of Jacques Lacan's work has been to create a powerful intellectual tradition within psychoanalytic theory which is less and less interested in positions which do not foreground the kind of theorisation of language represented in Section 1 of this *Reader*.

Philip Rieff's understanding of language in a therapeutic context is that it *does* represent (forbidden topics), but in a highly mediated manner, and that – *contra* Marx as well as post-structuralism – 'language ... is the essential medium of consciousness, and therefore the essential means of liberation' (Rieff, 1979, p. 335). Apart from this slightly dated but stubbornly persistent view of language, Rieff is also valuable – particularly when read alongside most of the texts reprinted in this book – precisely because he is a generaliser; that is to say, he wants to follow Freud and talk about the human condition, a theory of mind and 'modern man', and is unfashionably disinclined to qualify his categories. As the editor of Freud's *Collected Papers*, however, he is not a generaliser in the sense of eschewing detailed exposition.

Freud: The Mind of the Moralist (1959) has an established place in the secondary literature on Freud, but the consistent development of Rieff's subsequent work through *The Triumph of the Therapeutic* (1966) to *Fellow Teachers* (1973) has consolidated his position as a leading neo-conservative thinker, alongside such writers as Alasdair MacIntyre in *After Virtue* (1981). In *Freud* he has an angle upon the current concern with modernity and postmodernity – though he does not use the latter term – and upon ethics. Freud is a central element in Rieff's own position because he is an inescapable part of what it means to be modern: to be bereft of the consolations of the past and the future and, accordingly, thrown back upon the self and a preoccupation with it: quite a salutary read in a time when a slack understanding of much contemporary theory denigrates the importance of the self. Rieff's neo-conservatism is not apparent in any crass or polemical sense but in the acceptance of limits which are constructed not by dominant traditions of thought (Rieff seems to approve of Freud's lack of a religious temperament) but out of the internalisation of a tension within secular society between past and present; guilt and innocence; desire and repression; difference and sameness; and 'fantastic realities' and 'reasonable appearances' (Rieff, 1979, p. xii). Liberation, in Rieff's interpretation of Freud, is 'modest but nonetheless significant', and confined to 'the therapeutic hour' (Rieff, 1979, pp. 331, 332) and the patient's subsequent private reflection upon this break with the rationalised, compartmentalised world so memorably described by Max Weber in *The Protestant Ethic and the Spirit of Capitalism*. Therapy is to be measured against the necessity for control, authority, and the exercise of reticence. No relief should be sought in 'theological' utopias, such as Rieff sees Marx as entertaining and encouraging, but memory can help to resist the discontinuities which much contemporary theory embraces so positively.

The burden of life can only be shifted, not removed, but since it is a 'heavy burden of knowingness about life', a place is at least reserved for reason: 'Reason cannot save us, nothing can; but reason can mitigate the cruelty of living, or give sufficient reasons for not living' (Rieff, 1979, pp. xviii, xii). At a time when the Enlightenment project is under attack for its legacy of cruel unreason, Rieff's is an interesting and unusual defence, not least because near the end of Reading 2.1, he explores the narcissism which, he believes, is an unfortunate by-product of Freudian self-preoccupation in a period when the older culture of limits – what Weber calls the work ethic and Freud calls the reality principle – is waning. Rieff's historical and sociological account of the culture of therapy gestures towards certain aspects of postmodernism. The excess of candour which is a by-product of social modernism (and which, soon after Rieff's book appeared, took a quantum leap during the cultural rebellions of the sixties), combined with the self-preoccupation stimulated, directly and indirectly, by Freudian self-preoccupation to produce an 'emergent democracy of the sick' in which 'everyone can to some extent play doctor to others, and none is allowed the temerity to claim that he can definitively cure or be cured' (Rieff, 1979, p. 355). Although in some respects they are a cause of this state of affairs, Freud, as he appears in Rieff's book, and Freudian reason are none the less an alternative to modern 'psychological man' intent upon 'talking his way into a moral void', 'every sense of limit challenged' (Rieff, 1979, pp. xxiv, xxii). Rieff finds in Freud this maxim (in Rieff's words): 'each freedom at every moment depends upon the one thing forbidden to it, so all true visions take their direction from the turning of a blind eye' (Rieff, 1979, p. xxiv). The register is different – indeed, almost everything is different – but Rieff seems to be where certain post-structuralists find themselves: looking for limits, for a non-theological 'must', to set against their own insights into a post-foundational world.

On the questions of liberation and the need to return the patient to the world of limits and reticence, Rieff's Freud differs sharply from the Freud who dominates Herbert Marcuse's *Eros and Civilization* (1955; Reading 2.2). However, both Rieff and Marcuse endorse the importance which Freud placed on memory, though for Marcuse memory has a utopian potential rarely voiced during the 1950s. It is still a startling measure of the conformity of the postwar years in the United States that Marx is never mentioned in *Eros and Civilization*, even though the book attempts to bring Marx and Freud together by historicising one of the poles of Freudian theory, the reality principle. Marcuse wants to take the reality principle beyond the sphere of personal development, in which an infant is made aware of the restraints upon the desire for pleasure and thereby fitted for society; and – by rereading Freud's late work, *Civilization and its Discontents* (1930), through the lens of his basic model of the mind – to ask whether the benefits of subjugation to an ethic of work, order and progress have been worth the suffering. The apparently universal reality principle becomes, in Marcuse's rereading, a 'performance principle', representative of only a particular phase of Western society. Max Weber – also missing in name – is implicitly introduced to highlight the extent of technical and rational domination in what Marcuse would later call the 'one dimensional' society and Theodore Roszak would popularise as 'the technocracy' in his 1969 book *The Making of a Counter-Culture*. Marcuse returns to Freud's own theory to insist that the relationship between pleasure and reality principles is not fixed. The reality principle should be renamed the scarcity principle to describe 'a specific historical organization of human existence' under conditions of economic need which can be altered 'to create the preconditions for the gradual abolition of repression' (Marcuse, 1966, p. 5). A link with Marxian economics could be made, but Marcuse sticks with Freud's acknowledgement that the phase of pleasure does not wholly give way to reality but 'continues to exist in civilization itself' (p. 15) and can be reactivated through memory. Moreover, the struggle is repeated in each individual, a point which Marcuse underlines to suggest the potential for revolution even in an advanced Western society in which affluence or the promise of affluence affects class structure. The repressed can return even if, as Marcuse admits in later chapters of the book, it seems at present to find its outlet primarily in phantasy and aesthetics; on the latter point, he finds plenty of support in Frankfurt School thinking in general and Theodor Adorno's work on Modernism in particular.

Although Rieff's Freud does not talk about economic scarcity as such (Rieff believes it trivialises Freud to read his economic metaphors literally), *Eros and Civilization* is misunderstood if it is also read too literally. It needs to be read as a utopian text which aims to rescue the constituent utopian element in classical Marxism by linking it with 'the tabooed aspirations of humanity' in Freud, 'the claim for a state where freedom and necessity coincide' (Marcuse, 1966, p. 18). Through remembering a past state, a future can be imagined. Moreover, the criticisms of impracticality and lack of realism which are invariably levelled at *Eros and Civilization* are themselves vulnerable to Marcuse's critique of realism. This critique joins a broader assault on the Enlightenment project in Frankfurt School texts from Adorno and Max Horkheimer's *Dialectic of Enlightenment* (1944) through to Marcuse's *One Dimensional Man* (1964), and identifies the impulse towards practicality and realism as themselves part of the reality principle and therefore dependent upon, but failing to acknowledge, their other, the pleasure principle. However, the pessimistic strand in Frankfurt School thinking reasserts itself in the 'Political Preface' which Marcuse added to *Eros and Civilization* in 1966, in which the repressive tolerance of Western society, its 'democratic introjection' (Marcuse, 1966, p. xv), undermines the desire for liberation in a supposedly free society. Marxism is introduced explicitly in the 'Political Preface', but has to be understood and defended in an international context: 'Historical backwardness may again become the historical chance of turning the wheel of progress to another direction' (Marcuse, 1966, p. xvii).

Where Philip Rieff includes a straightforward account of Freud's misogyny but does not fully incorporate it into the case he makes on Freud's behalf, Marcuse's anticipation of the sexual revolution of the 1960s lacks any specific awareness of the political and social organisation of sex. A historicised Freud is reread to promote 'polymorphous sexuality' rather than genital intercourse, and to reveal that repression is surplus to what a society needs to progress, and is therefore a political rather than merely a psychological issue. But the context of this rebellion is the world of work: 'Libido would be released and would overflow the institutionalized limits within which it is kept by the reality principle' (Marcuse, 1966, p. 200). Male–female relations and their institutionalisation are therefore not directly addressed, even as the body is 'resexualized'. In contrast to Marcuse, Kate Millett (Reading 2.3) finds in Freud's work an intellectual underpinning for an exploitative sexual politics which outweighs Freud's radical critique of Victorian repressiveness. In *Sexual Politics*, published in 1969, Millett explains female discontents (such as those detailed in one of the other modern classics of the second women's movement, Betty Friedan's *The Feminine Mystique* [1963]) in terms of patriarchy, while Freud explains the situation of women through a basic, anatomical lack. 'Penis envy' produces the strong, if not uniform, tendencies towards masochism, narcissism and passivity which Freud observed in his case studies of women. Women are defined in negative terms (what is missing). The corollary is that male sexual aggression is given theoretical support, and becomes part of the life-force.

Millett historicises Freud, but quite differently from Marcuse. For Millett, Freud's reasoning derives from the social conditions of his time, but lacks a clear awareness of the specificity of those conditions. Consequently, the psychic damage he noticed in his female patients is rarely traced to the social ills of the time, as it is in the feminist literature of the late nineteenth and early twentieth century. Where Charlotte Perkins Gilman's short story 'The Yellow Wallpaper' (1892) and her theoretical text *Women and Economics* (1898) locate the cause of women's malaise in the subtle as well as obvious exercise of male power, Freud returns to physiology and to the family romance which it generates, in which the young female, on recognising that the lack of a penis is not peculiar to herself, transfers the responsibility to her mother and to her sex, before seeking to define herself with reference to her father, who – representing the male – will provide her with a penis in the form of a baby, a 'penis-child'. An assertion of female sexuality is similarly blocked, as in this statement from Freud's 'Some psychical consequences of the anatomical distinctions between the sexes' (quoted by Millett): 'the elimination of the clitoral sexuality is a necessary pre-condition for the development of femininity' (Millett, 1971, pp. 185–6).

Although Millett's literary criticism is not a primary concern here, her nearly exclusive attention to texts by male writers makes it difficult to appreciate how women can resist the patriarchal appropriation of the family romance. Thus, *Sexual Politics* could be used to situate a text such as Gilman's 'The Yellow Wallpaper' within the exercise of patriarchal power, but Millett's work does not illuminate the ways in which the author, narrator and narrator-as-character in Gilman's story exploit the few linguistic and mostly private resources that remain open. Undoubtedly, Millett's readings of D. H. Lawrence, Henry Miller, Norman Mailer and Jean Genêt reveal the existence of a shockingly blatant language of aggression and submission in apparently self-conscious texts; but these readings also point to shortcomings in Millett's theoretical approach in general. Whether Lawrence, Miller, Mailer and Genêt are realists or not, Millett reads them as though a social context can be straightforwardly extracted from their texts. In *Psychoanalysis and Feminism*, Juliet Mitchell classifies Millett's theoretical position on Freud as that of 'social realism', and argues that in her efforts to focus attention upon the sociology, rather than the physiology, of Freudianism, and to foreground gender rather than sex as the key term, Millett effectively denies the psychological reality of the unconscious, and so underplays the importance of sexuality: 'It is not what Freud says about women and femininity that is the real stake in the battle, but the very objects of psychoanalysis themselves, sexuality and the unconscious, that offend' (Mitchell, 1975, p. 352).

Alternatives to Millett's – but also Rieff's and Marcuse's – interpretation of Freud can be found in a number of different strands of psychoanalytic theory, but Jacques Lacan's (see Reading 2.4) reading of Freud through structuralist and post-structuralist theories of language has addressed the above problems most effectively, and has proved to be particularly provoking for feminism's engagement with psychoanalysis, as the discussion of Kristeva in the Introduction to Section 1 indicates. Lacan takes off from the very uncertainties, ambiguities and endless revisions in Freud's work (especially as these bear upon the question of human identity) which Millett cuts through, but he builds these into a systematic account of the unconscious. The unconscious emerges not just in slips of the tongue or jokes but when language consistently fails to meet desire (desire for the object represented in language, including the subject, the 'I'). Here, Lacan comes particularly close to developments in linguistics: Saussure, but also Roman Jakobson's distinction between metaphor and metonymy, which Lacan prefers to Freud's condensation and displacement, respectively. Any articulation of identity drags with it, in Derrida's sense, the traces of the system of which any element is a part.

However, Lacan, unlike Saussure, has a story to tell, and Reading 2.4 is an important episode in it. In the phase which Lacan calls the Imaginary, the subject has no sense of identity. At some point within this pre-oedipal, undifferentiated realm under the rule of the pleasure principle, the infant, in Lacan's telling, receives a coherent mirror-image which masks the lack of co-ordination in the infant. Once it is recognised, this illusory image sets in motion an economy of desire which outlasts the Imaginary as a discrete phase and in which the subject is caught in an alienated relationship with its image, out of which an ego is (mis)constructed. Given that Lacan's reading of Freud is being loosely set against other readings, the terminology of id, ego and superego is perhaps inaccurate, since Lacan gives more attention than do Rieff, Millett and Marcuse to Freud's earlier model of pre-conscious, unconscious and conscious phases. Nevertheless, the important point is that it is the entry into language – into what Lacan calls the Symbolic Order – which fully links the subject with desire, predicated upon a lack. It is this lack which might be seen as the unconscious, suggesting, therefore, that the unconscious is formed as consciousness is formed, and does not pre-exist consciousness as a biological entity. The symbolic brings a differentiated, rather than an imaginary, concept of identity. In the kind of statement which could have been quoted in the Introduction to Section 1, Lacan both explains, and almost succeeds in giving a formal, linguistic embodiment to, the situatedness of the subject in language: 'I am not wherever I am the plaything of my thought; I think of what I am where I do not think to think' (Lacan, 1977, p. 166).

Lacan follows Freud in associating the Symbolic Order with the rule of the father because it is the father's prohibition which inaugurates it by intervening in the mother–infant relationship. More generally, this stage is comparable with Freud's reality principle and with social life. However, in the Symbolic – and this is where Lacan's terminology is important – it is not the penis which rules but its signifier, the phallus. Power in positioning subjects is exercised through discourse, which – potentially, at least – becomes the arena for any resistance to subject positioning. Since male and female are instances of such positions, it follows that sexual difference arises out of division, and is not pre-given. In this connection, Freud himself figures differently from the way he appears in Kate Millett's very influential interpretation. In a 1933 essay, 'Femininity', Freud remarks that: 'psychoanalysis does not try to describe what a woman is – that would be a task it could scarcely perform – but sets about enquiring how she comes into being' (Freud, 1964, p. 116). The 'lack' which, in Millett's reading, is seen by Freud as an actual, physical lack, is, in Lacan's rereading, a lack that is built into language which, by its very presence, signifies the absence of the object. In its first manifestation on entering the Symbolic Order, the lack is the absence of the mother's body.

Jacqueline Rose claims that 'the history of psychoanalysis can in many ways be seen entirely in terms of its engagement with [the] question of feminine sexuality' (Mitchell and Rose, 1982, p. 28). The debate centres on the Symbolic: the need to inhabit and claim the Symbolic where social relations are established and, with them, power relations. Not to do so can result in psychosis. Juliet Mitchell, who collaborates with Rose on *Feminine Sexuality: Jacques Lacan and the 'école freudienne'* (1982), advances this argument and it is expanded by Rose, who points out that while Lacan cannot escape phallocentrism, his account of the dominance exercised by the phallus is situated firmly in language. She therefore warns against recourse to the pre-linguistic and pre-historical. Mitchell and Rose maintain that Freud and Lacan can be made use of by feminism rather than, as in Millett's account of Freud, summarily dismissed, but it is not clear why Lacan – and certainly why feminists – should concede so much to the father, even if it is a symbolic father and a symbolic phallus. To do so largely requires that a feminist response come from the margins – the margins of language in Kristeva, for example. The important element in Lacan's account of the Symbolic is the intervention of the father, yet this seems to be a consequence of social arrangements which have no ultimate authority. It is just that women are assumed to be the rearers of infants.

Lacan's linguistic understanding of the unconscious is important in Kristeva but also in Hélène Cixous and, especially, Luce Irigaray. An extract from Irigaray appears in Section 5 (Reading 5.6) but her most anthologised essay, the title essay in *This Sex Which Is Not One* (1977), ought to be mentioned here because it offers a number of possible responses to Freud and Lacan (depending how the essay is interpreted in the context of her other work). Irigaray turns away from the visual priority of Freudianism: what can be seen is the penis, so women are the unseen and, more than this, the unrepresentable in the Symbolic Order. To follow this logic is to return to the theories of penis envy and female castration, and to accept that pleasure is necessarily visual – an argument which, not surprisingly, has been advanced and contested in film theory (see Mulvey, 1989). Irigaray rejects the priority and uniformity of the look and, in 'This sex which is not one' she puts the case for touch as a vital sense, and for the doubleness (at least) of female sexual pleasure:

> Woman takes pleasure more from touching than from looking, and her entry into a dominant scopic economy signifies, again, her consignment to passivity: she is to be the beautiful object of contemplation. (Irigaray, 1985a, p. 26)

And:

> As for woman, she touches herself in and of herself without any need for mediation, and before there is any way to distinguish activity from passivity. Woman 'touches herself' all the time, and moreover no one can forbid her to do so, for her genitals are formed of two lips in continuous contact. Thus, within herself, she is already two – but not divisible into one(s) – that caress each other. (Irigaray, 1985a, p. 24)

The issue of clitoral and/or vaginal pleasure is the principal aspect of a psychoanalytic feminist theory of reading explored by Naomi Schor (Reading 2.5). Apart from Schor's specific argument, the clarity of which makes summary redundant, this Reading highlights two concerns that are already becoming apparent in this anthology. The first is the necessity for interdisciplinarity even as any essay is situated in a discipline or tradition of thought. Schor notes, in particular, that in order to read a literary text (for its representation of psychoanalytic feminist themes) the theoretical point of view must itself be interrogated – that is, read. And the second is that theory must – paradoxically – be grounded so that it does not float free in the manner of structuralism: 'the most pervasive and insidious form of idealism in our time'. Yet to ground feminist theory is to lay claim to the very ground on which is marked women's oppression: the body. Schor's response is a textual materialism, deriving from Derrida but aware of the uneasy relationship between feminism and deconstruction discussed by Gayatri Spivak in Reading 3.3 below. Schor puts it this way:

> the uses of deconstruction for feminism are not limited to the still timely inversion of the paradigm of sexual difference, they consist also in the homologous inversion of

what I would call the paradigm of significance: essential/accessory. In other words, these essays [including the one reprinted below] are written in the space opened up by the valorization of woman *and* the detail deconstruction entails. This is not to say that I believe that woman as writer or reader possesses an inborn affinity for details, an essentialist argument I regard as dangerous for the elaboration of both a feminist poetics and aesthetics. What I do believe is that a pronounced attention to details has traditionally been connoted as feminine and hence devalorized. And, further, that it is in textual details either overlooked or misprized by male critics that something crucial about woman's stake in representation is to be found. (Schor, 1985, p. x)

Naomi Schor's homologous relationship between body and text is a reminder that Irigaray has been criticised for placing too much authority in the body, and thereby falling into a biological essentialism. However, to take just one other line, Irigaray can be understood – and even her most forthright essay, 'This sex which is not one', can be understood – as promoting a struggle within the Symbolic. In 'The gesture in psychoanalysis', for instance, she concentrates upon the Symbolic to argue that symbolisation of psychoanalytic 'events' is itself very selective in its construction of gender differences and orders of priority. Her more recent work – of which Reading 5.6 is an example – pursues this more social line on a vital psychoanalytic debate.

Lacanian psychoanalytic theory and Lacan's autocratic style have generated schisms and offshoots. Gilles Deleuze and Félix Guattari's *Anti-Oedipus: Capitalism and schizophrenia*, first published in 1972 (see Reading 2.6), is a direct reaction against Lacan, and especially against his theorisation of desire. Guattari attended Lacan's seminars in the 1950s and 1960s, and underwent analysis with Lacan in the 1960s, but the experiences of 1968 provoked him, in conjunction with Deleuze, to develop a more politicised theory of the unconscious which they term schizoanalysis. *Anti-Oedipus* revisits many of the concepts touched on above and examined in greater detail in the Readings below, but with the intention of exposing Freudian and Lacanian psychoanalysis's fixation upon the Oedipus complex as part of society's structure of repression. Psychoanalysis is an 'institution' of power. It is through the family romance, within a capitalist society, that desire is controlled and directed into the sphere of commodification. The Oedipus complex accentuates the importance but also the relative powerlessness of the subject, thereby fitting an individual for a similar role under capitalism. Where Herbert Marcuse connects Freud's reality principle with the Protestant ethic, Deleuze and Guattari take account of the forms of control exercised in a consumer society. Specifically, they contest Lacan's understanding of desire as emanating from lack and argue, instead, for desire as productive rather than produced. Schizoanalysis seeks to liberate desire, which Deleuze and Guattari characterise as incapable of being finally reduced to any one principle or limited to any individual. With Lacan's Symbolic Order in mind, they describe desire as pre-existing the entry into language, but also as surviving it to become a social phenomenon in which bodily and semiotic flows are not to be distinguished. Desire is positive but, if released, issues not into a unified self (perhaps one difference between the Anglo-American and French counterculture) but into multiplicities. Guattari's Marxism has its centre not in the usual orthodoxies but in the weight he gives to group subjectivities, fluid but none the less significant associations, quite different from both the subject-based preoccupations of Freudian psychoanalysis, as Philip Rieff describes them, and the monolithic preoccupation with state power that marked the French Communist Party of the 1960s. As a critique of where power lies, there are similarities with Foucault's recognition that power is dispersed; but where all three theorists work off Nietzsche, only Deleuze and Guattari fully exploit the anarchic potential of a will to power. *Anti-Oedipus* comes out of 1968 and its aftermath, but in some ways that immediate context obscures the theoretical project of the book by associating it with an anti-intellectual counterculture.

2.1 □ *The Emergence of Psychological Man*

Philip Rieff

The important thing is not to be cured but to live with one's ailments.

ABBÉ GALIANI TO MADAME D'ÉPINAY

In a distinctively intimate way, psychoanalysis defends the private man against the demands made by both culture and instinct. Freud begins where G. E. Moore leaves off in the famous last chapter of *Principia Ethica* that declares personal affections and artistic pleasures the only true goods[1] in our experience. The private man needs to know how to defend his affections, for the most personal are the most easily spoiled. Psychoanalytic pedagogy is intended for the student weak in the understanding of the limited possibilities in life. Freud belongs, therefore, among those great teachers who have taken everyone as their potential subject. Seen in psychoanalytic depth, no man knows himself so well that he cannot learn something of fundamental importance from this novel enterprise in re-education. Freud speaks for the modern individual, elaborating his sense of separateness from the world and from even the most beloved objects in it. Such careful and detailed concentration on the self as Freud encourages may more often produce pedants of the inner life than virtuosi of the outer one. Yet, in default of other cures, egotism suits the age, and Freud's is only one of the most successful, and certainly the most subtle, of contemporary ideologies of self-salvation.

Calculation, Newman said, has never made a hero; but calculation can make the unheroic healthier. The essentially secular aim of the Freudian spiritual guidance is to wean away the ego from either a heroic or a compliant attitude to the community. Here Freud differed not only from the physicians of established faiths – Catholic or other – but also from the propagandists of secular faiths, those socialists and other radicals still essentially engaged in absorbing the individual into the

From Rieff, P., *Freud: The mind of the moralist*, 3rd edition, University of Chicago Press, Chicago, 1979, pp. 329–32, 334–5, 339–45, 353–7, 423–4.

community. He was not impressed by the clerical strategy of confirming faith by strengthening the individual's identification with the community. Whatever flush of interior health rises on first being received back into any community of belief after the sickness of alienation is quite temporary, Freud held. The old faiths have themselves produced the sickness they still seek to cure. The psychoanalytic physician cannot therefore direct the patient to seek relief by joining 'the catholic, protestant, or socialist community'. What is needed is to free men from their sick communities. To emancipate man's 'I' from the communal 'we' is 'spiritual guidance' in the best sense Freud could give to the words.[2]

Yet he also treated the neurotic as a social dilemma, as one unable to relate himself effectively to the established community. The prevailing image of psychoanalysis as reintegrating the neurotic, making him again a constructive member of society, must be studied very closely, for this does not signify that the patient gives his assent to the demands society makes upon his instinctual life; on the contrary, the successful patient has learned to withdraw from the painful tension of assent and dissent in his relation to society by relating himself more affirmatively to his depths. His newly acquired health entails a self-concern that takes precedence over social concern and encourages an attitude of ironic insight on the part of the self toward all that is not self. Thus the psychoanalyzed man is inwardly alienated even if he is often outwardly reconciled, for he is no longer defined essentially by his social relations. Psychoanalysis as a science carries an authentic alienating implication, from the breaking of the bondages of the past (advocated on the therapeutic level) to the critical appraisal of moral and religious beliefs (on the level of theory). Freud found contemptible Dostoevski's religious and political conservatism, despite his admiration for the writer's insights and experiences in the depths.* His own insights into the depths did not lead him to advocate a return to them, nor to new justifications for authoritarian codes of conduct. Rather, a less ambivalent freedom from authority is perhaps the more important motif of his doctrine, one in which authority is all the more secure.

This variety of belief in freedom makes itself felt most strongly in Freud's denial that psychoanalysis does criticize society or that it has any 'concern whatsoever with ... judgments of value'. Psychoanalysis neither needs nor desires 'to create a *Weltanschauung* of its own'. As a branch of science, subscribing to the scientific view of the world, psychoanalysis intends to be no doctrine but only a method: 'the intellectual manipulation of carefully verified observations' and the denial that any knowledge can be obtained from 'intuition or inspiration'.[3] Here the rational

---

* Freud notes that 'after the most violent struggles to reconcile the instinctual demands of the individual with the claims of the community', Dostoevski 'landed in the retrograde position of submission both to temporal and spiritual authority, of veneration both for the Tsar and for the God of the Christians, and of a narrow Russian nationalism – a position which lesser minds have reached with smaller effort'. Indeed the point of Freud's essay on Dostoevski, from which I am quoting, is not to examine Dostoevski's artistic endowment but to find out why he changed positions – why he 'threw away the chance of becoming a teacher and liberator of humanity and made himself one with their gaolers' (*Coll. Papers* V, 223). Thus, subtly, Dostoevski is identified with the position of the Grand Inquisitor.

method – working upon the irritational unconscious, which Freud conceived of as undercutting the 'proud superstructure of the mind'[4] – itself bespeaks a pre-eminent value. It is only just, when speaking of Freud, to speak of the humanism of his science. For after all his affirmations of the irrational, he reserves a possibility for rationality and freedom in science – understanding – itself, particularly in the method of treatment he devised: the creation of representative thought-art which, when interpreted, eases the patient's obsessions. On the one hand, then, Freud does advocate a rational reconciliation to social and cultural authority, granting that authority itself will under criticism become more reasonable; on the other hand, Freudianism supplies through its therapeutic stratagems and theoretical insights the means for a modest but none the less significant liberation.

I

Freud's emancipative intent first expressed itself in his method of treatment. By waiving the restrictions of conventional logic and prudery, the therapeutic hour provides the patient with a model refreshment. It puts an end to decorum, providing a private time in which anything may be said – indeed, in which the patient is encouraged to say everything. The analytic meeting is designed as an oasis in the desert of reticence in which the patient lives; it is much like those artificial ruins thoughtfully placed in eighteenth-century English formal gardens for the pleasure of those who wished to wander imaginatively from the beaten path.

[. . .]

[A] quality of the Freudian liberation is the interest taken in emotional recollection itself. Freud sees the therapy as withdrawing the patient from the world of 'hard reality', with which he has been unable to cope – though this withdrawal is only temporary, and its purpose is to return him more realistically equipped to that very reality. During this period of therapeutic withdrawal, however, Freud sanctions all the tabooed language and the shady topics which are conventionally proscribed. Memory, daydream, fantasy are what the patient is to deal in. He has total freedom to recall. The patient tries to recapture his childhood and the nightlife of dreams and sexuality; it is chiefly this material which is analyzed, according to the emancipative dialectic, just because it is not freely discussed in the ordinary daytime world.

Memory has a peculiar and central place in Freudian theory. It is constraining, since by remembering our bondages to the past we appreciate their enormity; but it is also, Freud believed, liberating, since by remembering we understand the terrors and pleasures of the past and move toward mastering them. The tabooed thoughts are accredited, raised to the status of momentous and decisive causes, by Freud's theory of personality, not only because they are explained as part of an inexorable sequence of development, but because the patient's attention is focused on them. In therapeutic explanation the taboos dominant since childhood tend to be weakened.

Even though the aims and activities of childhood have to be suppressed, superseded by 'reality', a science which so values the importance of these things is plainly a liberating one.

This helps explain Freud's special interest in dreams, which he interpreted as contemporaneous fragments of the superseded child life. Dreams themselves, as Freud saw, have an ambiguously emancipative role. They indicate a kind of freedom, because they take place when there is a 'slackening in the strength of the resistance'.[5] He imagined sleep as the de-individualized play time of the instincts, when we cast off the burden of being individuals and vent our gross infantile wishes and anxieties in dreams. In sleep all persons become for that brief respite ciphers of identical emotions, differentiated only secondarily by constitution and traumatic accent. On the other hand, dreams are a kind of betrayal, too, because the analyst (representing the outer world) uses them to pry out the patient's secrets. On the whole, however, Freud conceded that the dream was a sanctuary for the free play of the psyche. We cannot be held responsible, Freud argues, for the thoughts expressed in our dream life.[6] Night thoughts are not our own, in the moral proprietary sense, but belong to that other self which summons us thereby to account for our day lives.

Talk is therapeutic in itself. By talking about the instincts, Freud says, we do not cause the instinctual demand to disappear – this 'is impossible and not even desirable' – but we do accomplish a 'taming' of the instinct'.[7] Through talking about sexuality, we can control it, so that the healthy man can choose to express his sexual appetite and yet not be irrationally driven by it. Self-mastery being a function of self-consciousness, by making sexual desires conscious, says Freud, we gain mastery over them to a degree no system of repression can possibly equal.[8] Talk – language – is the essential medium of consciousness, and therefore the essential means of liberation.[*]

[. . .]

II

[. . .]

There are good reasons why sexuality is for Freud the one really profound subject matter, the demands of the instincts the most fundamental demands. A science that recognizes the instincts is a basic science, examining not this social system or that but the system of civilization as a formed thing in itself. Freud has made the greatest single contribution to the understanding of civilization – not merely to the understanding of our own. The incomparable significance of sexual life is that,

---

[*] Compare Marx: 'All forms and products of consciousness cannot be dissolved by mental criticism, by resolution into "self-consciousness" or transformation into "apparitions", "spectres", "fancies", etc., but only by the practical overthrow of the actual social relations which gave rise to this idealistic humbug' (*German Ideology* [New York, 1947], pp. 28–9).

'while art, religion, and the social order originated in part in a contribution from the sexual instinct',[9] civilization is also permanently opposed by sexuality. 'Woe, if the sexual instincts should be set loose! The throne [of civilization] would be overturned and the [ultimate] ruler trampled under foot'.[10] Yet, even in his cautious approach to sexuality as a scientific subject, Freud advanced the long-established assault on the repressions.

Sexuality has shown, for Freud and related figures of his century, a revolutionary potential somewhat diminished by the newer permissiveness in manners and speech which has followed Freud – and owes greatly to him. The idea of a sexual revolution is not new. In the late eighteenth and early nineteenth centuries, sexuality became the subject of the most advanced art and politics. The critical philosophy of industrial civilization, first put forth by Fourier and the Saint-Simonians, and after them in the literature of the 'young Germans', based itself on a deliberately anti-Christian eroticism. The sexual rebellion that was linked with socialism, before the conservative Karl Marx broke the connection on the pejorative word 'utopian', was closer to being genuinely revolutionary – i.e. a revolt from below – than we now can grasp, accustomed as we are by Marxism and its counterfeits to revolutions run by reason – i.e. from above. The goal of the sexual revolution was never a harmonious, classless society, but rather happier individuals freed from a false reverence for the general advantage of society. The great writers on sex, from de Sade to Lawrence, were less interested in society than in the individual, pressing in varying degrees for the freedom of the individual against the burdens of social morality.*

[. . .]

Yet Freud has none of the enthusiasm that characterizes the antinomian temper. Civilization, because of its discontents, was the basic problem of his psychological science. The cry for liberty did come from the instinctual depths, but Freud heard it with the cautious attention of a physician attending an eminent but dangerous patient. Sexuality for him is a force that permanently prevents any utopian transforming of the social order. Freud held no hope of transforming civilization. On the contrary, the great utopian possibility – in so far as he held to any – is whether repressive civilization can permanently tame the instincts. He took the traditional position of assuming a conflict between man's animal and spiritual nature – the spiritual being a residual quality in the transforming process of repressive civilization.

Freud found that the sexual scarcity characteristic of all civilizations (embodied in such institutions as monogamy) concentrated a certain surplus aggressiveness in

---

* For de Sade and Lawrence sexuality itself provides a utopian possibility. They assert masculine sexuality as the basis of a revolution against the prevailing feminine social order – this especially militates against political radicalism, since sex becomes an alternative to politics. Thus a new generation of Freudian-trained conservatives is rising in America. The doctrine of the revolutionary possibilities of sex is the positive side of the psychoanalytic reduction of the political radical to a special case of the neurotic.

the unconscious. A freer sexuality – a juster distribution of libido, the fundamental wealth of civilization – would lower the cost of civilization itself. Such an increase of sexual rations might go far toward resolving the nervousness of modern civilized behavior. But thus to widen the range of gratification, to relocate the problem of desire in the historical variety of 'objects', fails to resolve the psychological problem. Man creates his own scarcity; the aesthetic mechanics of satisfaction themselves make gratification chimerical. Any notion that Freud's doctrine of scarce satisfaction in some way reflects the economic doctrine of scarcity representative of the best social thought in his era is to render trivial Freud's point. His use of a quasi-economic metaphor to discuss sexuality gives no warrant for treating the insight frozen into this metaphor as dated. Nature still seeks a state of balance. Freud's is a theory of the equilibrium toward which the emotional life tends after every disturbance. Sexuality is subject no less completely to Freud's first law of the emotions than any other element of human existence. Only one way lies open to escape the dissatisfactions inherent in every satisfaction, and that is to grow equable. When the inner life is not easily disturbed it has achieved what is to Freud as nearly ideal a condition as he can imagine. There is something Oriental in the Freudian ethic. The 'Nirvana principle' crops up, now and again, in his later writings, intimating what is entailed in mastering the balances of nature.

Short of Nirvana, if sexuality could conceivably cease to trouble man, his destructive instincts would trouble him more. His dualism allowed Freud to maintain simultaneously a psychological version of the classical liberal and radical rationalist dream, that once civilization had reached a certain level of technological productivity (read 'reality adequacy') and 'consumption' (read 'satisfactions') the miseries of its earlier stages would drop away, and a psychological version of the equally powerful religious idea – with the redemption fantasy stripped to a minimum faith in reason. In the therapeutic encounter, reason and unreason unite to create a third force capable of mediating between the clashing instincts. But the instincts cannot be taught to abide each other; their fusion creates tension and the possibility of abrupt reversals. Besides, were aggression merely a response to the frustration of some sexual or social need, it could be resolved, or at least ameliorated, by a specifically social reform of the conditions of frustration. But an aggression that is built in, due to the presence of a 'death instinct',[*] cannot be entirely manipulated, let alone abolished. According to this view, civilization can never resolve its nervousness, for the principle of ambivalence, more than that of integration, characterizes human nature and society. Happiness can never be achieved by the panaceas of social permissiveness or sexual plenitude. Order can never be achieved by social suppression or moral rigor. We are not unhappy because we are frustrated, Freud implies; we are frustrated because we are, first of all, unhappy combinations of conflicting desires. Civilization can, at best, reach a balance of discontents.

---

[*] There is a significant parallel in Freud's idea, advanced in the *Three Essays*, of a primal repression prior to social inhibitions, which is set off by the instinctual process itself.

Here is no Swinburnian romance of free sexuality versus the moral law. Rather, Freud takes the romance out of sexuality, for romance is dependent upon taking the repressions for granted, in fact on their remaining entirely unconscious, so that they may be broken only at the price of guilt. The Freudian attitude, on the other hand, no longer takes them for granted, and therefore can no longer take sexuality as a static ideal, even against the present crippling incapacities of our erotic lives. Freud might seem to be suggesting an expansive erotic ideal. But any future sensual permissiveness is rendered suspect by what he asserts about the expansive erotic life of the past. Freud not only feared that sexual freedom might entail undesirable sacrifices in culture; he thought it itself a transient accomplishment. Love is not a final solution for Freud, but a therapeutic one. He acknowledged that the establishment of a repressive code (such as Christianity) might under certain circumstances (as during the satiety of pagan culture) prove beneficent, like an artificially induced scarcity which revives consumption after a long period of overproduction.[11] Therefore he was confident only of his analysis of our crippled condition, never of his prognosis. As a psychologist of fulfillment, Freud predicts disappointment: he sees the social value of repression, the complex nature of satisfaction. It is only in the therapeutic context – which is, after all, not life – that he rejects repression.

Freud was not hopeful; nor was he nostalgic. Retrospectively, he treasured no pagan or primitive past. He looked forward to no radically different future. Pagan antiquity had encouraged too much sensual pride and demonstrated the erotic illusion no less fully than Christianity, by encouraging spiritual pride, had demonstrated the ascetic illusion. Freud disdained permissiveness as much as asceticism; both falsely resolved the essential dualism in human experience, that very dualism between mind and flesh that produces the misery of the human condition. What man suffers from finally is no more the supremacy of spirit over flesh than of flesh over spirit; it is the dualism that hurts. Freud's own attitude toward a variety of historical dualisms, including Christianity, was always respectful, for he considered that they were but versions of a more fundamental dualism in the nature of man and in the cosmos. For this reason he never seriously entertained any utopian aspiration. Indeed, his own theory 'had always been strictly dualistic and had at no time failed to recognize, alongside the sexual instincts, others to which it ascribed force enough to suppress the sexual instincts'.[12] This dualism Freud described as between 'sexuality' and the 'ego instincts'; later he distinguished two polar instincts, love and death. *

---

* Freud thought that his version of these polar forces, which he called *Eros* and *Thanatos* and nominated as the 'primal instincts', had restored the cosmology of Empedocles ('Analysis Terminable and Interminable', *Coll. Papers* V, 347–50). But what he ascribes to Empedocles is common property of the whole school of transitional thinkers passing out of the mythic stage into philosophy – Anaximander, Empedocles, Heraclitus, Parmenides, and finally Plato. Actually, among these neo-mythic cosmologies, Freud's version more resembles Anaximander's than it does that of Empedocles. (I follow here the account of Cornford in *From Religion to Philosophy*, p. 65.) 'Anaximander was more purely rational than many of his successors. In later systems – notably in those of Parmenides and Empedocles – mythical associations and implications [of the love–hate, attraction–repulsion polarity] which [Anaximander] has expurgated, emerge again. In particular, we can discern that the prototype of all opposition or contrariety is the contrariety of sex'. As late as Plato's *Timaeus*, a sexual character still clings to the great contrarieties, Form (father) and Matter (mother).

Whatever the terminology, it is important to see that – unlike the Christian or rationalist consciousness – Freud denies any permanent healing of the 'derangement of communal life', of the struggle between individual interest and the economy of social demands, of the antagonism between binding and destructive forces in individual and group life. The most one can win against the eternal dualisms is a rational knowledge of their effects upon one's own life.

Perhaps it might be more accurate to see depth psychology not as an emancipation of sex but as an enfranchisement. Freud recognized that in fact the silent vote of the psychic world never had been silent. He is the Bentham of the unenfranchised unconscious; what he brought into the realm of legitimacy, he also brought to responsibility. If one cannot educate the ruled, then one must educate the rulers. This very aim, to educate the ruling ego, is a sure mark of Freud's classical liberalism. By enfranchising the uneducable populace of sexuality, Freud seeks to bring it into responsible relations with the ruling power. To the liberal political tradition, with its belief that the 'two nations' could be brought together, Freud offered a supporting parallel in psychological and moral theory, for he desired, as far as possible, to bring the instinctual unconscious into the rational community. For this new art of compromise a new kind of specialist is needed, one who can take a destiny apart and put it back together again in a slightly more endurable shape.

[. . .]

[Section III omitted]

IV

On the cultural significance of the neurotic character, Freud is entirely explicit. Neurotics are rebels out of weakness rather than strength; they witness to the inadequacies of cultural restraint. But they are unsuccessful rebels, for they pay too high a price for their revolt, and ultimately fail, turning their aggressions against themselves. Instead of being repressed and turned inward as the neurotic is, the normal personality is active and outgoing. Expedient normal attitudes lead to some active achievement in the outer world. The brisk managerial ego of the normal personality devotes itself to aggression against the environment, to the practical use of objects; it does not fixate upon them. As Freud put it elsewhere: neurotic anxiety comes from a libido which has 'found no employment'; therefore, the dream, like work, has a 'moralizing purpose'.[13] Again, the economic metaphor discloses Freud's ideal of health as well: a fully employed libido.

In a brilliant passage Freud describes the normal attitude toward reality as one combining the best features of neurotic and psychotic attitudes:

> Neurosis does not deny the existence of reality, it merely tries to ignore it; psychosis denies it and tries to substitute something else for it. A reaction which combines features of both these is the one we call normal or 'healthy'; it denies reality as little as neurosis, but then, like a psychosis, is concerned with effecting a change in it.[14]

Thus the neurotic character is the unsuccessful protestant of the emotional life; in him inwardness becomes incapacity. The normal character continues to protest, Freud implies, but is 'not content ... with establishing the alternation within itself'.[15] Thus, in Freud's conception of the normal man, there is a certain echo of the Romantic idea of genius – the ideal man who attains to the self-expression that other men, intimidated by convention, weakly forgo.

As the passage just quoted suggests, Freud did not draw a sharp line between the concepts of normal and neurotic. His dictum that 'we are all somewhat hysterical',[16] that the difference between so-called normality and neurosis is only a matter of degree,[17] is one of the key statements in his writings. Its meaning is threefold.

First, it declassifies human society, creating an essential democracy within the human condition. Even the Greek tragedy – the most aristocratic context – was leveled out by Freud; the unique crime of the tragic hero becomes an intention in every heart, and in the most ordinary of plots, the history of every family. Misfortune is not an exceptional possibility, occasioned by rare circumstances or monstrous characters, but is the lot of every person, something he has to pass through in his journey from infancy to old age. The aristocratic bias of the 'heroic' myth is replaced, in Freud, by the democratic bias of the 'scientific' myth: Oedipus *Rex* becomes Oedipus Complex, which all men live through. It is because of the suppressed tragedies of everyday life that men respond so fully to the more explicit tragedies on the stage. But this does not mean that Freud proposed a genuinely tragic view of life; he was much too realistic for that. Ordinary men compromise with their instinctual longings and become neurotic; the tragic hero, because he suffers and dies, must be presumed to have carried out his wishes in a way forbidden to most men.[18]

Secondly, to say that all men are neurotic means to imply an injunction to tolerance. At least Freud's discovery that the commonplace is saturated with the abnormal, the pathological – that psychopathology no longer deals with the exception but with the ordinary man – does something to alter established habits of moral judgment. It lightens the heavier burdens of guilt and responsibility, for many offenses can be made to appear smaller if perceived in sufficient depth.

Third, and more important, this conception of neurosis reveals the essentially ethical nature of Freud's idea of normality. Normality is not a statistical conception, for the majority is no longer normal. Normality is an ethical ideal, pitted against the actual abnormal. By another name, normality is the negative ideal of 'overcoming' – whatever it is that ought to be overcome. Being essentially negative, normality is an ever-retreating ideal. An attitude of stoic calm is required for its pursuit. No one catches the normal; everyone must act as if it can be caught. Nor can the psychological man forget himself in pursuit of the normal, for his normality consists of a certain kind of self-awareness. Not least of all, the analysts themselves, Freud thought, needed to return to analysis every few years to renew their knowledge of themselves.

The psychological ideal of normality has a rather unheroic aspect. Think of a whole society dominated by psychotherapeutic ideals. Considered not from the individual's but from a sociological point of view, psychoanalysis is an expression of a popular tyranny such as not even de Tocqueville adequately imagined. Ideally, the democratic tyranny which is the typical social form of our era will not have a hierarchy of confessors and confessants. Rather, [. . .] everyone must aspire to be a confessor. This is the meaning of the psychoanalytic re-education Freud speaks of. In the emergent democracy of the sick, everyone can to some extent play doctor to others, and none is allowed the temerity to claim that he can definitively cure or be cured. The hospital is succeeding the church and the parliament as the archetypal institution of Western culture.

What has caused this tyranny of psychology, legitimating self-concern as the highest science? In part, no doubt, it is the individual's failure to find anything else to affirm except the self. Having lost faith in the world, knowing himself too well to treat himself as an object of faith, modern man cannot be self-confident; this, in a negative way, justifies his science of self-concern. Though the world is indifferent to him, the lonely ego may here and there win something from it. For the rectitude and energetic naivety of the man who was the ideal type during the middle-class, Protestant phase of American culture, we have substituted the character traits of husbanded energy and finessed self-consciousness. The Frank Merriwell of a psychological culture will not, like the moral athlete of Protestant culture, turn his reveries into realities. Rather, he will be mindful to keep realities from turning into reveries.

V

In this age, in which technics is invading and conquering the last enemy – man's inner life, the psyche itself – a suitable new character type has arrived on the scene: the psychological man. Three character ideals have successively dominated Western civilization: first, the ideal of the political man, formed and handed down to us from classical antiquity; second, the ideal of the religious man, formed and handed down to us from Judaism through Christianity, and dominant in the civilization of authority that preceded the Enlightenment; third, the ideal of the economic man, the very model of our liberal civilization, formed and handed down to us in the Enlightenment. This last has turned out to be a transitional type, with the shortest life-expectancy of all; out of his tenure has emerged the psychological man of the twentieth century, a child not of nature but of technology. He is not the pagan ideal, political man, for he is not committed to the public life. He is most unlike the religious man. We will recognize in the case history of psychological man the nervous habits of his father, economic man: he is anti-heroic, shrewd, carefully counting his satisfactions and dissatisfactions, studying unprofitable commitments as the sins most to be avoided. From this immediate ancestor, psychological man has constituted his own careful economy of the inner life.

The psychological man lives neither by the ideal of might nor by the ideal of right which confused his ancestors, political man and religious man. Psychological man lives by the ideal of insight – practical, experimental insight leading to the mastery of his own personality. The psychological man has withdrawn into a world always at war, where the ego is an armed force capable of achieving armistices but not peace. The prophetic egoist of Western politics and Protestant Christianity who, through the model with which he provided us, also laid down the lines along which the world was to be transformed, has been replaced by the sage, intent upon the conquest of his inner life, and, at most, like Freud, laying down the lines along which those that follow him can salvage something of their own. Turning away from the Occidental ideal of action leading toward the salvation of others besides ourselves, the psychological man has espoused the Oriental ideal of salvation through self-contemplative manipulation. Ironically, this is happening just at the historic moment when the Orient, whose westernmost outpost is Russia, has adopted the Occidental ideal of saving activity in the world. The West has attempted many successive transformations of the enemy, the world. It now chooses to move against its last enemy, the self, in an attempt to conquer it and assimilate it to the world as it is. For it is from the self that the troublesome, world-rejecting ideal of the religious man came forth.

Freudianism closes off the long-established quarrel of Western man with his own spirit. It marks the archaism of the classical legacy of political man, for the new man must live beyond reason – reason having proved no adequate guide to his safe conduct through the meaningless experience of life. It marks the repudiation of the Christian legacy of the religious man, for the new man is taught to live a little beyond conscience – conscience having proved no adequate guide to his safe conduct through life, and furthermore to have added absurd burdens of meaning to the experience of life. Finally, psychoanalysis marks the exhaustion of the liberal legacy represented historically in economic man, for now men must live with the knowledge that their dreams are by function optimistic and cannot be fulfilled. Aware at last that he is chronically ill, psychological man may nevertheless end the ancient quest of his predecessors for a healing doctrine. His experience with the latest one, Freud's, may finally teach him that every cure must expose him to new illness.

Notes

1. G. E. Moore, *Principia Ethica* (Cambridge: Cambridge University Press, 1903), Ch. 6.
2. 'Postscript to a discussion on lay analysis', *Collected Papers* (London: Hogarth, 1950), V, 211–12.
3. *New Introductory Lectures*, pp. 232, 202–3.
4. 'Psychoanalysis and religious origins', *Coll. Papers* V, 94.
5. *Delusion and Dream*, p. 86.
6. See 'Moral responsibility for the content of dreams' (1925), *Coll. Papers* V, 154–7.
7. 'Analysis terminable and interminable', *Coll. Papers* V, 326.
8. '*Psychoanalysis*', in James Strachey, ed., *The Standard Edition of the Complete Psychological Works of Sigmund Freud*, 24 vols (London: Hogarth, 1953–73); henceforth SE, XVIII, 252.

9. 'The resistances to psychoanalysis', *Coll. Papers* V, 169.
10. *Ibid.*, p. 170.
11. Cf. *Three Essays*, SE VII, 149 fn., on the difference between the love life of antiquity and our own.
12. 'The resistance to psychoanalysis', *Coll. Papers* V, 169.
13. *The Interpretation of Dreams*, SE IV, 244.
14. 'The loss of reality in neurosis and psychosis', *Coll. Papers* II, 279
15. *Ibid.*, pp. 279–80.
16. *Three Essays*, SE VII, 171: Freud cites Moebius, who said 'with justice that we are all to some extent hysterics'.
17. Cf. 'Analysis terminable and interminable', *Coll. Papers* V, 337: 'Every normal person is only approximately normal: his ego resembles that of the psychotic in one point or another, in a greater or lesser degree. ...'
18. Cf. *Totem and Taboo*, SE XIII, 156.

2.2 □ *From* Eros and Civilization: A philosophical inquiry into Freud

Herbert Marcuse

Introduction

Sigmund Freud's proposition that civilization is based on the permanent subjugation of the human instincts has been taken for granted. His question whether the suffering thereby inflicted upon individuals has been worth the benefits of culture has not been taken too seriously – the less so since Freud himself considered the process to be inevitable and irreversible. Free gratification of man's instinctual needs is incompatible with civilized society: renunciation and delay in satisfaction are the prerequisites of progress. 'Happiness', said Freud, 'is no cultural value.' Happiness must be subordinated to the discipline of work as full-time occupation, to the discipline of monogamic reproduction, to the established system of law and order. The methodical sacrifice of libido, its rigidly enforced deflection to socially useful activities and expressions, *is* culture.

The sacrifice has paid off well: in the technically advanced areas of civilization, the conquest of nature is practically complete, and more needs of a greater number of people are fulfilled than ever before. Neither the mechanization and standardization of life, nor the mental impoverishment, nor the growing destructiveness of present-day progress provides sufficient ground for questioning the 'principle' which has governed the progress of Western civilization. The continual increase of productivity makes constantly more realistic the promise of an even better life for all.

From Marcuse, H., *Eros and Civilization: A philosophical inquiry into Freud*, with a new preface by the Author, Beacon Press, Boston, MA, 1966, pp. 3–8, 11–19.

However, intensified progress seems to be bound up with intensified unfreedom. Throughout the world of industrial civilization, the domination of man by man is growing in scope and efficiency. Nor does this trend appear as an incidental, transitory regression on the road to progress. Concentration camps, mass exterminations, world wars, and atom bombs are no 'relapse into barbarism', but the unrepressed implementation of the achievements of modern science, technology, and domination. And the most effective subjugation and destruction of man by man takes place at the height of civilization, when the material and intellectual attainments of mankind seem to allow the creation of a truly free world.

These negative aspects of present-day culture may well indicate the obsolescence of established institutions and the emergence of new forms of civilization: repressiveness is perhaps the more vigorously maintained the more unnecessary it becomes. If it must indeed belong to the essence of civilization as such, then Freud's question as to the price of civilization would be meaningless – for there would be no alternative.

But Freud's own theory provides reasons for rejecting his identification of civilization with repression. On the ground of his own theoretical achievements, the discussion of the problem must be reopened. Does the interrelation between freedom and repression, productivity and destruction, domination and progress, really constitute the principle of civilization? Or does this interrelation result only from a specific historical organization of human existence? In Freudian terms, is the conflict between pleasure principle and reality principle irreconcilable to such a degree that it necessitates the repressive transformation of man's instinctual structure? Or does it allow the concept of a non-repressive civilization, based on a fundamentally different experience of being, a fundamentally different relation between man and nature, and fundamentally different existential relations?

The notion of a non-repressive civilization will be discussed not as an abstract and utopian speculation. We believe that the discussion is justified on two concrete and realistic grounds: first, Freud's theoretical conception itself seems to refute his consistent denial of the historical possibility of a non-repressive civilization, and, second, the very achievements of repressive civilization seem to create the preconditions for the gradual abolition of repression. To elucidate these grounds, we shall try to reinterpret Freud's theoretical conception in terms of its own sociohistorical content.

This procedure implies opposition to the revisionist Neo-Freudian schools. In contrast to the revisionists, I believe that Freud's theory is in its very substance 'sociological',[1] and that no new cultural or sociological orientation is needed to reveal this substance. Freud's 'biologism' is social theory in a depth dimension that has been consistently flattened out by the Neo-Freudian schools. In shifting the emphasis from the unconscious to the conscious, from the biological to the cultural factors, they cut off the roots of society in the instincts and instead take society at the level on which it confronts the individual as his ready-made 'environment', without questioning its origin and legitimacy. The Neo-Freudian analysis of this environment thus succumbs to the mystification of societal relations, and their critique moves only within the firmly sanctioned and well-protected sphere of established institutions. Consequently, the Neo-Freudian critique remains in a strict sense ideological: it has no conceptual basis outside the established system; most of its critical ideas and values are those provided by the system. Idealistic morality and religion celebrate their happy resurrection: the fact that they are embellished with the vocabulary of the very psychology that originally refuted their claim ill conceals their identity with officially desired and advertised attitudes. Moreover, we believe that the most concrete insights into the historical structure of civilization are contained precisely in the concepts that the revisionists reject. Almost the entire Freudian metapsychology, his late theory of the instincts, his reconstruction of the pre-history of mankind belong to these concepts. Freud himself treated them as mere working hypotheses, helpful in elucidating certain obscurities, in establishing tentative links between theoretically unconnected insights – always open to correction, and to be discarded if they no longer facilitated the progress of psycho-analytic theory and practice. In the post-Freudian development of psychoanalysis, this metapsychology has been almost entirely eliminated. As psychoanalysis has become socially and scientifically respectable, it has freed itself from compromising speculations. Compromising they were, indeed, in more than one sense: not only did they transcend the realm of clinical observation and therapeutic usefulness, but also they interpreted man in terms far more offensive to social taboos than Freud's earlier 'pan-sexualism' – terms that revealed the explosive basis of civilization. The subsequent discussion will try to apply the tabooed insights of psychoanalysis (tabooed even in psychoanalysis itself) to an interpretation of the basic trends of civilization.

The purpose of this essay is to contribute to the *philosophy* of psychoanalysis – not to psychoanalysis itself. It moves exclusively in the field of theory, and it keeps outside the technical discipline which psychoanalysis has become. Freud developed a theory of man, a 'psycho-logy' in the strict sense. With this theory, Freud placed himself in the great tradition of philosophy and under philosophical criteria. Our concern is not with a corrected or improved interpretation of Freudian concepts but with their philosophical and sociological implications. Freud conscientiously distinguished his philosophy from his science; the Neo-Freudians have denied most of the former. On therapeutic grounds, such a denial may be perfectly justified. However, no therapeutic argument should hamper the development of a theoretical construction which aims, not at curing individual sickness, but at diagnosing the general disorder.

[. . .]

The Hidden Trend in Psychoanalysis

The concept of man that emerges from Freudian theory is the most irrefutable indictment of Western civilization – and at the same time the most unshakable defense of this civilization. According to Freud, the history of man is the history of his repression. Culture constrains not only his societal but also his biological existence, not only parts of the human being but his instinctual structure itself. However, such constraint is the very precondition of progress. Left free to pursue their natural objectives, the basic instincts of man would be incompatible with all lasting association and preservation: they would destroy even where they unite. The uncontrolled Eros is just as fatal as his deadly counterpart, the death instinct. Their destructive force derives from the fact that they strive for a gratification which culture cannot grant: gratification as such and as an end in itself, at any moment. The instincts must therefore be deflected from their goal, inhibited in their aim. Civilization begins when the primary objective – namely, integral satisfaction of needs – is effectively renounced.

The vicissitudes of the instincts are the vicissitudes of the mental apparatus in civilization. The animal drives become human instincts under the influence of the external reality. Their original 'location' in the organism and their basic direction remain the same, but their objectives and their manifestations are subject to change. All psychoanalytic concepts (sublimation, identification, projection, repression, introjection) connote the mutability of the instincts. But the reality which shapes the instincts as well as their needs and satisfaction is a sociohistorical world. The animal man becomes a human being only through a fundamental transformation of his nature, affecting not only the instinctual aims but also the instinctual 'values' – that is, the principles that govern the attainment of the aims. The change in the governing value system may be tentatively defined as follows:

from:	*to*:
immediate satisfaction	delayed satisfaction
pleasure	restraint of pleasure
joy (play)	toil (work)
receptiveness	productiveness
absence of repression	security

Freud described this change as the transformation of the *pleasure principle* into the *reality principle*. The interpretation of the 'mental apparatus' in terms of these two principles is basic to Freud's theory and remains so in spite of all modifications of the dualistic conception. It corresponds largely (but not entirely) to the distinction between unconscious and conscious processes. The individual exists, as it were, in two different dimensions, characterized by different mental processes and principles. The difference between these two dimensions is a genetic-historical as well as a structural one: the unconscious, ruled by the pleasure principle, comprises 'the older, primary processes, the residues of a phase of development in which they were the only kind of mental processes'. They strive for nothing but for 'gaining pleasure; from any operation which might arouse unpleasantness ("pain") mental activity draws back'.[2] But the unrestrained pleasure principle comes into conflict with the natural and human environment. The individual comes to the traumatic realization that full and painless gratification of his needs is impossible. And after this experience of disappointment, a new principle of mental functioning gains ascendancy. The reality principle supersedes the pleasure principle: man learns to give up momentary, uncertain, and destructive pleasure for delayed, restrained, but 'assured' pleasure.[3] Because of this lasting gain through renunciation and restraint, according to Freud, the reality principle 'safeguards' rather than 'dethrones', 'modifies' rather than denies, the pleasure principle.

However, the psychoanalytic interpretation reveals that the reality principle enforces a change not only in the form and timing of pleasure but in its very substance. The adjustment of pleasure to the reality principle implies the subjugation and diversion of the destructive force of instinctual gratification, of its incompatibility with the established societal norms and relations, and, by that token, implies the transubstantiation of pleasure itself.

With the establishment of the reality principle, the human being which, under the pleasure principle, has been hardly more than a bundle of animal drives, has become an organized ego. It strives for 'what is useful' and what can be obtained without damage to itself and to its vital environment. Under the reality principle, the human being develops the function of *reason*: it learns to 'test' the reality, to distinguish between good and bad, true and false, useful and harmful. Man acquires the faculties of attention, memory, and judgment. He becomes a conscious, thinking *subject*, geared to a rationality which is imposed upon him from outside. Only one mode of thought-activity is 'split off' from the new organization of the mental apparatus and remains free from the rule of the reality principle: *phantasy* is 'protected from cultural alterations' and stays committed to the pleasure principle. Otherwise, the mental apparatus is effectively subordinated to the reality principle. The function of 'motor discharge', which, under the supremacy of the pleasure principle, had 'served to unburden the mental apparatus of accretions of stimuli', is now employed in the 'appropriate alteration of reality': it is converted into *action*.[4]

The scope of man's desires and the instrumentalities for their gratification are thus immeasurably increased, and his ability to alter reality consciously in accordance with 'what is useful' seems to promise a gradual removal of extraneous barriers to his gratification. However, neither his desires nor his alteration of reality are henceforth his own: they are now 'organized' by his society. And this 'organization' represses and transubstantiates his original instinctual needs. If absence from repression is the archetype of freedom, then civilization is the struggle against this freedom.

The replacement of the pleasure principle by the reality principle is the great traumatic event in the development of man – in the development of the genus (phylogenesis) as well as of the individual (ontogenesis). According to Freud, this event is not unique but recurs throughout the history of mankind and of every individual. Phylogenetically, it occurs first in the *primal horde*, when the *primal father* monopolizes power and pleasure and enforces renunciation on the part of the sons. Ontogenetically, it occurs during the period of early childhood, and submission to the reality principle is enforced by the parents and other educators.

But, both on the generic and on the individual level, submission is continuously reproduced. The rule of the primal father is followed, after the first rebellion, by the rule of the sons, and the brother clan develops into institutionalized social and political domination. The reality principle materializes in a system of institutions. And the individual, growing up within such a system, learns the requirements of the reality principle as those of law and order, and transmits them to the next generation.

The fact that the reality principle has to be re-established continually in the development of man indicates that its triumph over the pleasure principle is never complete and never secure. In the Freudian conception, civilization does not once and for all terminate a 'state of nature'. What civilization masters and represses – the claim of the pleasure principle – continues to exist in civilization itself. The unconscious retains the objectives of the defeated pleasure principle. Turned back by the external reality or even unable to reach it, the full force of the pleasure principle not only survives in the unconscious but also affects in manifold ways the very reality which has superseded the pleasure principle. *The return of the repressed* makes up the tabooed and subterranean history of civilization. And the exploration of this history reveals not only the secret of the individual but also that of civilization. Freud's individual psychology is in its very essence social psychology. Repression is a historical phenomenon. The effective subjugation of the instincts to repressive controls is imposed not by nature but by man The primal father, as the archetype of domination, initiates the chain reaction of enslavement, rebellion, and reinforced domination which marks the history of civilization. But ever since the first, prehistoric restoration of domination following the first rebellion, repression from without has been supported by repression from within: the unfree individual introjects his masters and their commands into his own mental apparatus. The struggle against freedom reproduces itself in the psyche of man, as the self-repression of the repressed individual, and his self-repression in turn sustains his masters and their institutions. It is this mental dynamic which Freud unfolds as the dynamic of civilization.

According to Freud, the repressive modification of the instincts under the reality principle is enforced and sustained by the 'eternal primordial struggle for existence, ... persisting to the present day'. Scarcity [*Lebensnot*, Ananke] teaches men that they cannot freely gratify their instinctual impulses, that they cannot live under the pleasure principle. Society's motive in enforcing the decisive modification of the instinctual structure is thus 'economic; since it has not means enough to support life for its members without work on their part, it must see to it that the number of these members is restricted and their energies directed away from sexual activities on to their work'.[5]

This conception is as old as civilization and has always provided the most effective rationalization for repression. To a considerable extent, Freud's theory partakes of this rationalization: Freud considers the 'primordial struggle for existence' as 'eternal' and therefore believes that the pleasure principle and the reality principle are 'eternally' antagonistic. The notion that a non-repressive civilization is impossible is a cornerstone of Freudian theory. However, his theory contains elements that break through this rationalization; they shatter the predominant tradition of Western thought and even suggest its reversal. His work is characterized by an uncompromising insistence on showing up the repressive content of the highest values and achievements of culture. In so far as he does this, he denies the equation of reason with repression on which the ideology of culture is built. Freud's metapsychology is an ever-renewed attempt to uncover, and to question, the terrible necessity of the inner connection between civilization and barbarism, progress and suffering, freedom and unhappiness — a connection which reveals itself ultimately as that between Eros and Thanatos. Freud questions culture not from a romanticist or utopian point of view, but on the ground of the suffering and misery which its implementation involves. Cultural freedom thus appears in the light of unfreedom, and cultural progress in the light of constraint. Culture is not thereby refuted: unfreedom and constraint are the price that must be paid.

But as Freud exposes their scope and their depth, he upholds the tabooed aspirations of humanity: the claim for a state where freedom and necessity coincide. Whatever liberty exists in the realm of the developed consciousness, and in the world it has created, is only derivative, compromised freedom, gained at the expense of the full satisfaction of needs. And in so far as the full satisfaction of needs is happiness, freedom in civilization is essentially antagonistic to happiness: it involves the repressive modification (*sublimation*) of happiness. Conversely, the unconscious, the deepest and oldest layer of the mental personality, *is* the drive for integral gratification, which is absence of want and repression. As such it is the immediate identity of necessity and freedom. According to Freud's conception the equation of freedom and happiness tabooed by the conscious is upheld by the unconscious. Its truth, although repelled by consciousness, continues to haunt the mind; it preserves the memory of past stages of individual development at which integral gratification is obtained. And the past continues to claim the future: it generates the wish that the paradise be re-created on the basis of the achievements of civilization.

If memory moves into the center of psychoanalysis as a decisive mode of *cognition*, this is far more than a therapeutic device; the therapeutic role of memory derives from the *truth value* of memory. Its truth value lies in the specific function of memory to preserve promises and potentialities which are betrayed and even outlawed by the mature, civilized individual, but which had once been fulfilled in his dim past and which are never entirely forgotten. The reality principle restrains the cognitive function of memory — its commitment to the past experience of happiness which spurns the desire for its conscious re-creation. The psychoanalytic liberation of memory explodes the rationality of the repressed individual. As cognition gives way to re-cognition, the forbidden images and impulses of childhood begin to tell the truth that reason denies. Regression assumes a progressive function. The rediscovered past yields critical standards which are tabooed by the present. Moreover, the restoration of memory is accompanied by the restoration of the cognitive content of phantasy. Psychoanalytic theory removes these mental faculties from the noncommittal sphere of daydreaming and fiction and recaptures their strict truths. The weight of these discoveries must eventually shatter the framework in which they were made and confined. The liberation of the past does not end in its reconciliation with the present. Against the self-imposed restraint of the discoverer, the orientation on the past tends toward an orientation on the future. The *recherche du temps perdu* becomes the vehicle of future liberation.[6]

Notes

1. For a discussion of the sociological character of psychoanalytic concepts, see Heinz Hartmann, 'The application of psychoanalytic concepts to social science', *Psychoanalytic Quarterly*, vol. XIX, no. 3 (1950); Clyde Kluckhohn, *Mirror for Man* (New York: McGraw-Hill, 1949); and Heinz Hartmann, Ernst Kris, and Rudolph M. Lowenstein, 'Some psychoanalytic comments on "Culture and Personality"', in *Psychoanalysis and Culture: Essays in Honor of Géza Róheim* (New York: International Universities Press, 1951).
2. 'Formulations regarding the two principles in mental functioning', in *Collected Papers* (London: Hogarth, 1950), IV, 14. Quotations are used by permission of the publisher.
3. *Ibid.*, p. 18.
4. *Ibid.*, p. 16.
5. *A General Introduction to Psychoanalysis* (New York: Garden City Publishing Co., 1943), p. 273.
6. Ernest G. Schachtel's paper 'On memory and childhood amnesia' gives the only adequate psychoanalytic interpretation of the function of memory at the individual as well as societal level. The paper is entirely focused on the explosive force of memory, and its control and 'conventionalization' by society. It is, in my view, one of the few real contributions to the philosophy of psychoanalysis. Schachtel's paper is in *A Study of Interpersonal Relations*, ed. Patrick Mullahy (New York: Hermitage Press, 1950), pp. 3–49.

2.3 □ *Freud and the Influence of Psychoanalytic Thought*

Kate Millett

[. . .]

In reconsidering Freud's theories on women we must ask ourselves not only what conclusions he drew from the evidence at hand but also upon what assumptions he drew them. Freud did not accept his patients' symptoms as evidence of a justified dissatisfaction with the limiting circumstances imposed on them by society, but as symptomatic of an independent and universal feminine tendency.[1] He named this tendency 'penis envy', traced its origin to childhood experience and based his theory of the psychology of women upon it, aligning what he took to be the three corollaries of feminine psychology, passivity, masochism, and narcissism, so that each was dependent upon, or related to, penis envy.

As the Freudian understanding of female personality is based upon the idea of penis envy, it requires an elaborate, and often repetitious, exposition.[2] Beginning with the theory of penis envy, the definition of the female is negative − what she is is the result of the fact that she is not a male and 'lacks' a penis. Freud assumed that the female's discovery of her sex is, in and of itself, a catastrophe of such vast proportions that it haunts a woman all through life and accounts for most aspects of her temperament. His entire psychology of women, from which all modern psychology and psychoanalysis derives heavily, is built upon an original tragic experience − born female. Purportedly, Freud is here only relaying the information supplied by women themselves, the patients who furnished his clinical data, the basis of his later generalities about all women. It was in this way, Freud believed,

From Millett, K. (1971) *Sexual Politics*, Avon, New York, pp. 179–85.

he had been permitted to see how women accepted the idea that to be born female is to be born 'castrated':

> As we learn from psycho-analytic work, women regard themselves as wronged from infancy, as undeservedly cut short and set back; and the embitterment of so many daughters against their mothers derives, in the last analysis, from the reproach against her of having brought them into the world as women instead of as men.[3]

Assuming that this were true, the crucial question, manifestly, is to ask why this might be so. Either maleness is indeed an *inherently* superior phenomenon, in which case its 'betterness' could be empirically proved and demonstrated, or the female missapprehends and reasons erroneously that she is inferior. And again, one must ask why. What forces in her experience, her society and socialization have led her to see herself as an inferior being? The answer would seem to lie in the conditions of patriarchal society and the inferior position of women within this society. But Freud did not choose to pursue such a line of reasoning, preferring instead an etiology of childhood experience based upon the biological fact of anatomical differences.

While it is supremely unfortunate that Freud should prefer to bypass the more likely social hypothesis to concentrate upon the distortions of infantile subjectivity, his analysis might yet have made considerable sense were he sufficiently objective to acknowledge that woman is born female in a masculine-dominated culture which is bent upon extending its values even to anatomy and is therefore capable of investing biological phenomena with symbolic force. In much the same manner we perceive that the traumatizing circumstance of being born black in a white racist society invests skin color with symbolic value while telling us nothing about racial traits as such.

In dismissing the wider cultural context of feminine dissatisfaction and isolating it in early childhood experience, Freud again ignored the social context of childhood by locating a literal feminine 'castration' complex in the child's discovery of the anatomical differentiation between the sexes. Freud believed he had found the key to feminine experience – in that moment when girls discover they are 'castrated' – a 'momentous discovery which little girls are destined to make'.

> They notice the penis of a brother or playmate, strikingly visible and of large proportions, at once recognize it as the superior counterpart of their own small and inconspicuous organ, and from that time forward fall a victim to envy for the penis.[4]

There are several unexplained assumptions here: why is the girl instantly struck by the proposition that bigger is better? Might she just as easily, reasoning from the naivety of childish narcissism, imagine the penis is an excrescence and take her own body as norm? Boys clearly do, as Freud makes clear, and in doing so respond to sexual enlightenment not with the reflection that their own bodies are peculiar, but, far otherwise, with a 'horror of the multilated creature or triumphant contempt for her'.[5] Secondly, the superiority of this 'superior counterpart', which the girl is said to 'recognize at once' in the penis, is assumed to relate to the autoerotic satisfactions of childhood; but here again the child's experience provides no support for such an assumption.

Much of Freudian theory rests upon this moment of discovery and one is struck how, in the case of the female, to recapitulate the peculiar drama of penis envy is to rehearse again the fable of the Fall, a Fall that is Eve's alone.[6] As children, male and female first inhabit a paradisiacal playground where roles are interchangeable, active and passive, masculine and feminine. Until the awesome lapsarian moment when the female discovers her inferiority, her castration, we are asked to believe that she had assumed her clitoris a penis. One wonders why. Freud believes it is because she masturbated with it, and he assumes that she will conclude that what is best for such purposes must be a penis.[7] Freud insists upon calling the period of clitoral autoeroticism 'phallic' in girls.

Moreover, the revelation which Freud imagined would poison female life is probably, in more cases, a glimpse of a male playmate urinating or having a bath. It is never explained how the girl child makes the logical jump from the sight of bathing or urination to knowledge that the boy masturbates with this novel article. Even should her first sight of the penis occur in masturbatory games, Freud's supposition that she could judge this foreign item to be more conducive to autoerotic pleasure than her own clitoris (she having no possible experience of penile autoeroticism as males have none of clitoral) such an assumption is groundless. Yet Freud believed that female autoeroticism declines as a result of enlightenment, finding in this 'yet another surprising effect of penis-envy, or of the discovery of the inferiority of the clitoris.[8] Here, as is so often the case, one cannot separate Freud's account of how a child reasons from how Freud himself reasons, and his own language, invariably pejorative, tends to confuse the issue irremediably. Indeed, since he has no objective proof of any consequence to offer in support of his notion of penis envy or of a female castration complex,[9] one is struck by how thoroughly the subjectivity in which all these events are cast tends to be Freud's own, or that of a strong masculine bias, even of a rather gross male-supremacist bias.[10]

This habitual masculine bias of Freud's own terms and diction, and the attitude it implies, is increased and further emphasized by his followers: Deutsch refers to the clitoris as an 'inadequate substitute' for the penis; Karl Abraham refers to a 'poverty in external genitals' in the female, and all conclude that even bearing children can be but a poor substitute for a constitutional inadequacy.[11] As Klein observes in her critique of Freud, it is a curious hypothesis that one half of humanity should have biological reasons to feel at a disadvantage for not having what the other half possess (but not vice versa).[12] It is especially curious to imagine that half the race should attribute their clear and obvious social-status inferiority to the crudest biological reasons when so many more promising social factors are involved.

It would seem that Freud has managed by this highly unlikely hypothesis to assume that young females negate the validity, and even, to some extent, the existence, of female sexual characteristics altogether. Surely the first thing all children must notice is that mother has breasts, while father has none. What is possibly the rather impressive effect of childbirth on young minds is here overlooked, together with the girl's knowledge not only of her clitoris, but of her vagina as well.

In formulating the theory of penis envy, Freud not only neglected the possibility of a social explanation for feminine dissatisfaction but precluded it by postulating a literal jealousy of the organ whereby the male is distinguished. As it would appear absurd to charge adult women with these values, the child, and a drastic experience situated far back in childhood, are invoked. Nearly the entirety of feminine development, adjusted or maladjusted, is now to be seen in terms of the cataclysmic moment of discovered castration.

So far, Freud has merely pursued a line of reasoning he attributes, rightly or wrongly, to the subjectivity of female youth. Right or wrong, his account purports to be little more than description of what girls erroneously believe. But there is prescription as well in the Freudian account. For while the discovery of her castration is purported to be a universal experience in the female, her response to this fate is the criterion by which her health, her maturity and her future are determined through a rather elaborate series of stages:

> After a woman has become aware of the wound to her narcissism, she develops, like a scar, a sense of inferiority. When she has passed beyond her first attempt at explaining her lack of a penis as being a punishment personal to herself and has realized that that sexual character is a universal one, she begins to share the contempt felt by men for a sex which is the lesser in so important a respect.[13]

The female first blames her mother, 'who sent her into the world so insufficiently equipped' and who is 'almost always held responsible for her lack of a penis'.[14] Again, Freud's own language makes no distinction here between fact and feminine fantasy. It is not enough the girl reject her own sex, however; if she is to mature, she must redirect her self positively toward a masculine object. This is designated as the beginning of the Oedipal stage in the female. We are told that the girl now gives up the hope of impregnating her mother, an ambition Freud attributes to her. (One wonders how youth has discovered conception, an elaborate and subtle process which children do not discover by themselves, and not all primitive adults can fathom.) The girl is said to assume her female parent has mutilated her as a judgment on her general unworthiness, or possibly for the crime of masturbation, and now turns her anxious attention to her father.[15]

At this stage of her childhood the little girl at first expects her father to prove magnanimous and award her a penis. Later, disappointed in this hope, she learns to content herself with the aspiration of bearing his baby. The baby is given out as a curious item; it is actually a penis, not a baby at all: 'the girl's libido slips into position by means — there is really no other way to put it — of the equation "penis-child"'.[16] Although she will never relinquish some hope of acquiring a penis ('we ought to recognize this wish for a penis as being *par excellence* a feminine one')[17] a baby is as close to a penis as the girl shall get. The new penis wish is metamorphosed into a baby, a quaint feminine-coated penis, which has the added merit of being a respectable ambition. (It is interesting that Freud should imagine the young female's fears center about castration rather than rape – a phenomenon which girls are in fact, and with reason, in dread of, since it happens to them and castration does not.) Girls, he informs us, now relinquish some of their anxiety over their castration, but never cease to envy and resent penises,[18] and so while 'impotent' they remain in the world a constant hazard to the well-provided male. There are overtones here of a faintly capitalist antagonism between the haves and the have nots. This seems to account for the considerable fear of women inherent in Freudian ideology and the force of an accusation of penis envy when leveled at mature women.

The Freudian 'family romance', domestic psychodrama more horrific than a soap opera, continues. The archetypal girl is now flung into the Oedipal stage of desire for her father, having been persuaded of the total inadequacy of her clitoris, and therefore of her sex and her self. The boy, meanwhile, is so aghast by the implications of sexual enlightenment that he at first represses the information. Later, he can absorb it only by accompanying the discovery of sexual differentiation with an overpowering contempt for the female. It is difficult to understand how, setting aside the social context, as Freud's theory does so firmly, a boy could ever become this convinced of the superiority of the penis. Yet Freud assures us that 'as a result of the discovery of women's lack of a penis they [females] are debased in value for girls just as they are for boys and later perhaps for men'.[19]

Conflict with the father warns the boy that the castration catastrophe might occur to him as well. He grows wary for his own emblem and surrenders his sexual desires for his mother out of fear.[20] Freud's exegesis of the neurotic excitements of nuclear family life might constitute, in itself, considerable evidence of the damaging effects of this institution, since through the parents, it presents to the very young a set of primary sexual objects who are a pair of adults, with whom intercourse would be incestuous were it even physically possible.

While Freud strongly prescribes that all lingering hopes of acquiring a penis be abandoned and sublimated in maternity, what he recommends is merely a displacement, since even maternal desires rest upon the last vestige of penile aspiration. For, as she continues to mature, we are told, the female never gives up the hope of a penis, now always properly equated with a baby. Thus men grow to love women, or better yet, their idea of women, whereas women grow to love babies.[21] It is said that the female doggedly continues her sad phallic quest in childbirth, never outgrowing her Oedipal circumstance of wanting a penis by having a baby. 'Her happiness is great if later on this wish for a baby finds fulfilment in reality, and quite especially so if the baby is a little boy who brings the longed-for penis with him'.[22] Freudian logic has succeeded in converting childbirth, an impressive female accomplishment, and the only function its rationale permits her, into nothing more than a hunt for a male organ. It somehow becomes the male prerogative even to give birth, as babies are but surrogate penises. The female is bested at the only function Freudian theory recommends for her, reproduction. Furthermore, her libido is actually said to be too small to qualify her as a constructive agent here, since Freud repeatedly states she has less sexual drive than the male. Woman is thus granted very little validity even within her limited existence and second-rate biological equipment: were she to deliver an entire orphanage of progeny, they would only be so many dildoes.

Notes

1. Here Freud's procedure was very different from the liberal and humane attitude he adopted toward patients suffering from sexual inhibition.
2. See especially 'Femininity'. After making use of such patently invidious terms as 'the boy's far superior equipment' (p. 126), 'her inferior clitoris' (p. 127), 'genital deficiency' (p. 132), and 'original sexual inferiority' (p. 132), Freud proposes to his audience that penis envy is the foundation of his whole theory of female psychology, warning them that should they demur before his hypothesis, they would sabotage the entire construct: 'If you reject the idea as fantastic and regard my belief in the influence of lack of a penis on the configuration of femininity as an idée fixe, I am of course defenceless' (p. 132). My critique of Freud's notions of women is indebted to an unpublished summary by Frances Kamm.
3. Freud, 'Some character types met with in psycho-analytic work' (1916), in *Collected Papers of Sigmund Freud*, ed. Joan Riviere (New York: Basic Books, 1959), vol. IV, p. 323.
4. Freud, 'Some psychical consequences of the anatomical distinctions between the sexes' (1925), *Collected Papers*, vol. V, p. 190.
5. *Ibid.*, p. 191.
6. Not only has Adam grace within his loins to assure him he belongs to a superior species, but even his later fears of castration which come to him after a glimpse of the 'mutilated creature' causes him to repress his Oedipal desires (out of fear of a castrating father's revenge) and in the process develop the strong superego which Freud believes accounts for what he took to be the male's inevitable and transcendent moral and cultural superiority.
7. Because she feels free, equal, and active then, Freud says 'the little girl is a little man'. 'Femininity', p. 118. So strong is Freud's masculine bias here that it has obliterated linguistic integrity: the autoerotic state might as well, in both cases, be called 'clitoral' for all the light shed by these terms. Freud's usage is predicated on the belief that masturbation is the active pursuit of pleasure, and activity masculine *per se*: 'We are entitled to keep to our view that in the phallic phase of girls the clitoris is the leading erotogenic zone'. *Ibid.*
8. 'Some psychical consequences of the anatomical distinctions between the sexes', p. 193.
9. The entirety of Freud's clinical data always consists of his analysis of patients and his own self-analysis. In the case of penis envy he has remarkably little evidence from patients and his description of masculine contempt and feminine grief upon the discovery of sexual differences are extraordinarily autobiographical. Little Hans (Freud's own grandson), a five-year-old boy with an obsessive concern for his 'widdler', furnishes the rest of the masculine data. Though an admirable topic of precise clinical research, it was and is, remarkably difficult for Freud, or anyone else, to make generalizations about how

children first come to sexual knowledge, family and cultural patterns being so diverse, further complicated by the host of variable factors within individual experience, such as the number, age, and sex of siblings, the strength and consistency of the nakedness taboo, etc.

10. Ernest Jones aptly described Freud's attitude here as 'phallocentric'. There is something behind Freud's assumptions reminiscent of the ancient misogynist postulate that females are but incomplete or imperfect males – e.g. deformed humans, the male being accepted as the norm – a view shared by Augustine, Aquinas, etc.

11. Karl Abraham, 'Manifestations of the female castration complex', *International Journal of Psycho-Analysis*, vol. 3, March 1922.

12. Klein, pp. 83–4.

13. 'Some psychical consequences of the anatomical distinctions between the sexes', p. 192.

14. *Ibid.*, p. 193.

15. The description of female psychological development is from Freud's *Three Contributions to the Theory of Sex*, 'Femininity', 'Some psychical consequences of the anatomical distinctions between the sexes', and 'Female sexuality'.

16. 'Some psychical consequences of the anatomical distinctions between the sexes', p. 195.

17. 'Femininity', p. 128.

18. See 'Female sexuality' (1931), *Collected Works*, vol. V, pp. 252–72.

19. 'Femininity', p. 127.

20. 'Some psychical consequences of the anatomical distinctions between the sexes' and elsewhere in connection with the Oedipus complex in males.

21. 'Femininity', p. 134.

22. *Ibid.*, p. 128.

2.4 □ *The Mirror Stage as Formative of the Function of the I as Revealed in Psychoanalytic Experience*

Delivered at the 16th International Congress of
Psychoanalysis, Zürich, July 17, 1949

Jacques Lacan

The conception of the mirror stage that I introduced at our last congress, thirteen years ago, has since become more or less established in the practice of the French group. However, I think it worthwhile to bring it again to your attention, especially today, for the light it sheds on the formation of the *I* as we experience it in psychoanalysis. It is an experience that leads us to oppose any philosophy directly issuing from the *Cogito*.

Some of you may recall that this conception originated in a feature of human behaviour illuminated by a fact of comparative psychology. The child, at an age when he is for a time, however short, outdone by the chimpanzee in instrumental intelligence, can nevertheless already recognize as such his own image in a mirror. This recognition is indicated in the illuminative mimicry of the *Aha-Erlebnis*, which Köhler sees as the expression of situational apperception, an essential stage of the act of intelligence.

This act, far from exhausting itself, as in the case of the monkey, once the image has been mastered and found empty, immediately rebounds in the case of the child

From Lacan, J., *Écrits: A selection*, trans. A. Sheridan, Tavistock, London, 1977, pp. 1–7.

in a series of gestures in which he experiences in play the relation between the movements assumed in the image and the reflected environment, and between this virtual complex and the reality it reduplicates – the child's own body, and the persons and things, around him.

This event can take place, as we have known since Baldwin, from the age of six months, and its repetition has often made me reflect upon the startling spectacle of the infant in front of the mirror. Unable as yet to walk, or even to stand up, and held tightly as he is by some support, human or artificial (what, in France, we call a 'trotte-bébé'), he nevertheless overcomes, in a flutter of jubilant activity, the obstructions of his support and, fixing his attitude in a slightly leaning-forward position, in order to hold it in his gaze, brings back an instantaneous aspect of the image.

For me, this activity retains the meaning I have given it up to the age of eighteen months. This meaning discloses a libidinal dynamism, which has hitherto remained problematic, as well as an ontological structure of the human world that accords with my reflections on paranoiac knowledge.

We have only to understand the mirror stage *as an identification*, in the full sense that analysis gives to the term: namely, the transformation that takes place in the subject when he assumes an image – whose predestination to this phase-effect is sufficiently indicated by the use, in analytic theory, of the ancient term *imago*.

This jubilant assumption of his specular image by the child at the *infans* stage, still sunk in his motor incapacity and nursling dependence, would seem to exhibit in an exemplary situation the symbolic matrix in which the *I* is precipitated in a primordial form, before it is objectified in the dialectic of identification with the other, and before language restores to it, in the universal, its function as subject.

This form would have to be called the Ideal-I,[1] if we wished to incorporate it into our usual register, in the sense that it will also be the source of secondary identifications, under which term I would place the functions of libidinal normalization. But the important point is that this form situates the agency of the ego, before its social determination, in a fictional direction, which will always remain irreducible for the individual alone, or rather, which will only rejoin the coming-into-being [*le devenir*] of the subject asymptotically, whatever the success of the dialectical syntheses by which he must resolve as *I* his discordance with his own reality.

The fact is that the total form of the body by which the subject anticipates in a mirage the maturation of his power is given to him only as *Gestalt*, that is to say, in an exteriority in which this form is certainly more constituent than constituted, but in which it appears to him above all in a contrasting size [*un relief de stature*] that fixes it and in a symmetry that inverts it, in contrast with the turbulent movements that the subject feels are animating him. Thus, this *Gestalt* – whose pregnancy should be regarded as bound up with the species, though its motor style remains scarcely recognizable – by these two aspects of its appearance, symbolizes the mental permanence of the *I*, at the same time as it prefigures its alienating destination; it is still pregnant with the correspondences that unite the *I* with the statue in which man projects himself, with the phantoms that dominate him, or with the automaton in which, in an ambiguous relation, the world of his own making tends to find completion.

Indeed, for the *imagos* – whose veiled faces it is our privilege to see in outline in our daily experience and in the penumbra of symbolic efficacity[2] – the mirror-image would seem to be the threshold of the visible world, if we go by the mirror disposition that the *imago of one's own body* presents in hallucinations or dreams, whether it concerns its individual features, or even its infirmities, or its object-projections; or if we observe the role of the mirror apparatus in the appearances of the *double*, in which psychical realities, however heterogeneous, are manifested.

That a *Gestalt* should be capable of formative effects in the organism is attested by a piece of biological experimentation that is itself so alien to the idea of psychical causality that it cannot bring itself to formulate its results in these terms. It nevertheless recognizes that it is a necessary condition for the maturation of the gonad of the female pigeon that it should see another member of its species, of either sex; so sufficient in itself is this condition that the desired effect may be obtained merely by placing the individual within reach of the field of reflection of a mirror. Similarly, in the case of the migratory locust, the transition within a generation from the solitary to the gregarious form can be obtained by exposing the individual, at a certain stage, to the exclusively visual action of a similar image, provided it is animated by movements of a style sufficiently close to that characteristic of the species. Such facts are inscribed in an order of homeomorphic identification that would itself fall within the larger question of the meaning of beauty as both formative and erogenic.

But the facts of mimicry are no less instructive when conceived as cases of heteromorphic identification, inasmuch as they raise the problem of the signification of space for the living organism – psychological concepts hardly seem less appropriate for shedding light on these matters than ridiculous attempts to reduce them to the supposedly supreme law of adaptation. We have only to recall how Roger Caillois (who was then very young, and still fresh from his breach with the sociological school in which he was trained) illuminated the subject by using the term '*legendary psychasthenia*' to classify morphological mimicry as an obsession with space in its derealizing effect.

I have myself shown in the social dialectic that structures human knowledge as paranoiac[3] why human knowledge has greater autonomy than animal knowledge in relation to the field of force of desire, but also why human knowledge is determined in that 'little reality' [*ce peu de réalité*], which the Surrealists, in their restless way, saw as its limitation. These reflections lead me to recognize in the spatial captation manifested in the mirror stage, even before the social dialectic, the effect in man of an organic insufficiency in his natural reality – in so far as any meaning can be given to the word 'nature'.

I am led, therefore, to regard the function of the mirror stage as a particular case of the function of the *imago*, which is to establish a relation between the organism and its reality – or, as they say, between the *Innenwelt* and the *Umwelt*.

In man, however, this relation to nature is altered by a certain dehiscence at the heart of the organism, a primordial Discord betrayed by the signs of uneasiness and motor unco-ordination of the neonatal months. The objective notion of the anatomical incompleteness of the pyramidal system and likewise the presence of certain humoral residues of the maternal organism confirm the view I have formulated as the fact of a real *specific prematurity of birth* in man.

It is worth noting, incidentally, that this is a fact recognized as such by embryologists, by the term *foetalization*, which determines the prevalence of the so-called superior apparatus of the neurax, and especially of the cortex, which psychosurgical operations lead us to regard as the intraorganic mirror.

This development is experienced as a temporal dialectic that decisively projects the formation of the individual into history. The *mirror stage* is a drama whose internal thrust is precipitated from insufficiency to anticipation – and which manufactures for the subject, caught up in the lure of spatial identification, the succession of phantasies that extends from a fragmented body-image to a form of its totality that I shall call orthopaedic – and, lastly, to the assumption of the armour of an alienating identity, which will mark with its rigid structure the subject's entire mental development. Thus, to break out of the circle of the *Innenwelt* into the *Umwelt* generates the inexhaustible quadrature of the ego's verifications.

This fragmented body – which term I have also introduced into our system of theoretical references – usually manifests itself in dreams when the movement of the analysis encounters a certain level of aggressive disintegration in the individual. It then appears in the form of disjointed limbs, or of those organs represented in exoscopy, growing wings and taking up arms for intestinal persecutions – the very same that the visionary Hieronymus Bosch has fixed, for all time, in painting, in their ascent from the fifteenth century to the imaginary zenith of modern man. But this form is even tangibly revealed at the organic level, in the lines of 'fragilization' that define the anatomy of phantasy, as exhibited in the schizoid and spasmodic symptoms of hysteria.

Correlatively, the formation of the *I* is symbolized in dreams by a fortress, or a stadium – its inner arena and enclosure, surrounded by marshes and rubbish-tips, dividing it into two opposed fields of contest where the subject flounders in quest of the lofty, remote inner castle whose form (sometimes juxtaposed in the same scenario) symbolizes the id in a quite startling way. Similarly, on the mental plane, we find realized the structures of fortified works, the metaphor of which arises spontaneously, as if issuing from the symptoms themselves, to designate the mechanisms of obsessional neurosis – inversion, isolation, reduplication, cancellation and displacement.

But if we were to build on these subjective givens alone – however little we free them from the condition of experience that makes us see them as partaking of the nature of a linguistic technique – our theoretical attempts would remain exposed to the charge of projecting themselves into the unthinkable of an absolute subject. This is why I have sought in the present hypothesis, grounded in a conjunction of objective data, the guiding grid for a *method of symbolic reduction*.

It establishes in the *defences of the ego* a genetic order, in accordance with the wish formulated by Miss Anna Freud, in the first part of her great work, and situates (as against a frequently expressed prejudice) hysterical repression and its returns at a more archaic stage than obsessional inversion and its isolating processes, and the latter in turn as preliminary to paranoic alienation, which dates from the deflection of the specular *I* into the social *I*.

This moment in which the mirror stage comes to an end inaugurates, by the identification with the *imago* of the counterpart and the drama of primordial jealousy (so well brought out by the school of Charlotte Bühler in the phenomenon of infantile *transitivism*), the dialectic that will henceforth link the *I* to socially elaborated situations.

It is this moment that decisively tips the whole of human knowledge into mediatization through the desire of the other, constitutes its objects in an abstract equivalence by the co-operation of others, and turns the *I* into that apparatus for which every instinctual thrust constitutes a danger, even though it should correspond to a natural maturation – the very normalization of this maturation being henceforth dependent, in man, on a cultural mediation as exemplified, in the case of the sexual object, by the Oedipus complex.

In the light of this conception, the term primary narcissism, by which analytic doctrine designates the libidinal investment characteristic of that moment, reveals in those who invented it the most profound awareness of semantic latencies. But it also throws light on the dynamic opposition between this libido and the sexual libido, which the first analysts tried to define when they invoked destructive and, indeed, death instincts, in order to explain the evident connection between the narcissistic libido and the alienating function of the *I*, the aggressivity it releases in any relation to the other, even in a relation involving the most Samaritan of aid.

In fact, they were encountering that existential negativity whose reality is so vigorously proclaimed by the contemporary philosophy of being and nothingness.

But unfortunately that philosophy grasps negativity only within the limits of a self-sufficiency of consciousness, which, as one of its premises, links to the *méconnaissances* that constitute the ego, the illusion of autonomy to which it entrusts itself. This flight of fancy, for all that it draws, to an unusual extent, on borrowings from psychoanalytic experience, culminates in the pretension of providing an existential psychoanalysis.

At the culmination of the historical effort of a society to refuse to recognize that it has any function other than the utilitarian one, and in the anxiety of the individual confronting the 'concentrational'[4] form of the social bond that seems to arise to crown this effort, existentialism must be judged by the explanations it gives of the subjective impasses that have indeed resulted from it; a freedom that is never more authentic than when it is within the walls of a prison; a demand for commitment, expressing the impotence of a pure consciousness to master any situation; a voyeuristic–sadistic idealization of the sexual relation; a personality that realizes itself only in suicide; a consciousness of the other that can be satisfied only by Hegelian murder.

These propositions are opposed by all our experience, in so far as it teaches us not to regard the ego as centred on the *perception–consciousness system*, or as organized by the 'reality principle' – a principle that is the expression of a scientific prejudice most hostile to the dialectic of knowledge. Our experience shows that we should start instead from the *function of méconnaissance* that characterizes the ego in all its structures, so markedly articulated by Miss Anna Freud. For, if the *Verneinung* represents the patent form of that function, its effects will, for the most part, remain latent, so long as they are not illuminated by some light reflected on to the level of fatality, which is where the id manifests itself.

We can thus understand the inertia characteristic of the formations of the *I*, and find there the most extensive definition of neurosis – just as the captation of the subject by the situation gives us the most general formula for madness, not only the madness that lies behind the walls of asylums, but also the madness that deafens the world with its sound and fury.

The sufferings of neurosis and psychosis are for us a schooling in the passions of the soul, just as the beam of the psychoanalytic scales, when we calculate the tilt of its threat to entire communities, provides us with an indication of the deadening of the passions in society.

At this junction of nature and culture, so persistently examined by modern anthropology, psychoanalysis alone recognizes this knot of imaginary servitude that love must always undo again, or sever.

For such a task, we place no trust in altruistic feeling, we who lay bare the aggressivity that underlies the activity of the philanthropist, the idealist, the pedagogue, and even the reformer.

In the recourse of subject to subject that we preserve, psychoanalysis may accompany the patient to the ecstatic limit of the '*Thou art that*', in which is revealed to him the cipher of his mortal destiny, but it is not in our mere power as practitioners to bring him to that point where the real journey begins.

Notes

1. Throughout this article I leave in its peculiarity the translation I have adopted for Freud's *Ideal-Ich* [i.e. 'je-idéal'], without further comment, other than to say that I have not maintained it since.
2. Cf. Claude Lévi-Strauss, *Structural Anthropology*, Chapter X.
3. Cf. 'Aggressivity in psychoanalysis', p. 8 and *Écrits*, p. 180.
4. '*Concentrationnaire*', an adjective coined after World War II (this article was written in 1949) to describe the life of the concentration camp. In the hands of certain writers it became, by extension, applicable to many aspects of 'modern' life [Trans.].

2.5 □ *Female Paranoia: the case for psychoanalytic feminist criticism*

Naomi Schor

One can speak in general terms of the 'schizoid', but not of 'the paranoid' in *general*. Paranoia is always masculine or feminine. ...

(PHILIPPE SOLLERS)

As a substitute for penis envy, identification with the clitoris: neatest expression of inferiority, source of all inhibitions. At the same time [in Case X] disavowal of the discovery that other women too are without a penis.

(SIGMUND FREUD)

Even if, under the impact of recent developments in France, a growing number of American feminists have ceased to view Freud as one of womankind's prime enemies and psychoanalysis as a movement to be relegated to the junk heap of history, the theoretical foundations of psychoanalytic feminist literary criticism remain extremely shaky. I would ascribe this theoretical instability to a rather simple but far-reaching situation: those theoreticians who have contributed to articulating psychoanalysis and feminism are not necessarily or primarily interested in literary criticism (Mitchell, Dinnerstein, Irigaray); conversely, those who have contributed to articulating psychoanalysis and literature are not necessarily or primarily feminists (Felman). This leaves those who are attempting to read texts in a psychoanalytic perspective and with a feminist consciousness in something of a

From Schor, N., *Breaking the Chain: Women, theory, and French realist fiction*, Columbia University Press, New York, 1985, pp. 149–62, 182–4.

theoretical vacuum, straddling two approaches: on the one hand, a psychoanalytic feminist *thematics*, centering on the oedipal relationships (mother–daughter and, less frequently, father–daughter) as they are represented in works of literature; on the other, a psychoanalytic feminist *hermeneutics*, involving close readings of nonliterary texts, essentially those of Freud, Lacan, *et al.*, using the techniques of literary analysis (Irigaray, Cixous, Gallop). In what follows I shall attempt – in an admittedly, indeed deliberately sketchy fashion – to outline a new feminist thematics grounded in feminist hermeneutics. In other words: basing myself on a respectful but, literally, perverse reading of one of Freud's minor essays on femininity, I shall propose a psychoanalytic feminist hermeneutics which turns to account the specific contribution of women to contemporary theory, that is, their militant materialism. Finally, I shall illustrate my approach through a reading of Poe's *The Mystery of Marie Roget*. My progress from Freud to Poe is, of course, not innocent: it is, as we shall see, a return to the scene of the crime.

Female Paranoia

(Female) Paranoia as (Female) Theory

At first glance Freud's essay 'A case of paranoia running counter to the psychoanalytic theory of the disease' may seem like a particularly unpromising Freudian text to enlist in the elaboration of a theoretical model for feminist psychoanalytic criticism, for it bears blatant witness to precisely that aspect of Freud's writings which has most angered his feminist critics: the unexamined priority and primacy of the male paradigm. As we soon discover, this contradictory case [*eines ... widersprechenden Falles*] is a case of female paranoia which seems at first to call seriously into question the universal validity of the theory of paranoia derived from the analysis of a male paranoiac (Schreber). Freud, however, goes to great lengths to demonstrate that despite its apparent irregularity, when subjected to rigorous psychoanalytic investigation, even this contrary case conforms to the masculine model. This reduction of the atypical female exception to the prototypical masculine rule is a gesture of 'normalization' too familiar to Freud's feminist readers to be belabored here. What needs to be stressed is the fact that not only does this perplexing case, as we shall soon see, appear to threaten a dogma central to Freud's theory of paranoia – namely that the persecutor is, in fact, the object of a repressed homosexual desire – but that, in so doing, it threatens theory itself. By bringing the seemingly aberrant case of female paranoia under the sway of psychoanalytic theory, Freud is seeking to make the world safe for that theory which has, as he repeatedly states, deep affinities with paranoia. Thus, at the end of his analysis of the Schreber case, Freud writes: 'It remains for the future to decide whether there is more delusion in my theory than I should like to admit, or whether there is more truth in Schreber's delusion than other people care to believe';[1] similarly, in his late article 'Construction in analysis', he remarks: 'The delusions of patients appear to me to be the equivalents of the constructions which we build up in the course of analytic treatment – attempts at explanation and cure.'[2] But it is Freud's oft-cited comparison of paranoiacs and philosophers – 'the delusions of paranoiacs have an unpalatable external similarity and internal kinship to the systems of our philosophers'[3] – which has led many of his French readers to simply equate paranoia and theory, thereby minimizing – as Freud invites us to do – the differences between socially acceptable and deviant forms of system-building.

Female Paranoia vs. Male Paranoia

What is, then, at stake in Freud's text is the accuracy of his diagnosis: is there in fact such a clinical category as female paranoia? In other words: the urgent question posed by this case is not so much: does female paranoia corroborate the psychoanalytic theory of the disease, rather: can females theorize, albeit in the caricatural mode of the mad? Does the homology between male and female paranoia include the prestigious intellectual (hyper-)activity associated with the male model? This may strike some readers as a rhetorical question, since the very writing and publication of this theoretical text attests to my belief in women's ability to theorize; nevertheless, it must be raised. For while most authors dealing with the subject seem to agree that there are female paranoiacs – indeed, Phyllis Chesler lists paranoia among the 'female diseases'[4] – at least one prominent Freudian has suggested that the typical form of female paranoia is decidedly less systematic and elaborate than the typical male form of the disease:

> The usual persecutory paranoia, with its elaborate ideation, its excessive intellectuality, and its occurrence in individuals with a high power of sublimation, is essentially a highly organized and masculine psychosis, and is, as a matter of fact, much more common in men than in women. ... I should like at this point to make a possible differentiation between two of the types of true paranoia, the jealous and the persecutory. The latter, as we have seen, is an elaborate psychosis of an essentially masculine nature, and is the commonest form of paranoia in men. The jealous form, on the other hand, is par excellence the paranoia of women. ... In contradistinction to the philosophic, systematizing persecutory paranoia, the delusional jealousy is both feminine and rudimentary and, as it were, closer to the normal and the neurotic.[5]

These remarks are drawn from an essay entitled 'The analysis of a case of paranoia' (1929), which Freud cites in 'Female sexuality' (1931); its author is Ruth Mack Brunswick, Freud's favorite female disciple in his later years. Though this essay was written some fourteen years after the Freud essay under discussion, and has no direct bearing on it, it cannot go unmentioned, for it indicates the tremendous difficulties and dangers inherent in defining a specifically female form of paranoia, that is, as I will maintain throughout, of theory.

The Case for Psychoanalytic Feminist Criticism

At the outset Freud's case history is cast in the traditional narrative mode – 'Some years ago ...'[6] – but this innocuous opening is almost immediately belied by the unfolding of a complicated twice-told tale. In the course of their first meeting, the patient presents her case to Freud, indeed the entire text turns on a pun on the word case, *Fall*, which means both legal and medical case: the patient belongs to that class of paranoiacs known as *quérulants*, and she is referred to Freud not by another doctor, but by a lawyer. The facts of her *case*, as she recounts them during her first interview with Freud, are as follows: a fellow worker in the office where she had worked for years – the patient is a 'singularly attractive and handsome' (p. 151) thirty-year-old woman – had become interested in her and had invited her up to his place. Although she had never been interested in men and lived quietly with her old mother, and although her suitor could not offer marriage, the young woman agreed to visit his place in the daytime. There, as they were embracing, 'she was suddenly frightened by a noise, a kind of knock or tick' (*ibid.*). The young man assured her that the sound came from a small clock on a nearby writing desk. As she was leaving the house she met two men on the stairs. 'One of the strangers was carrying something which was wrapped up and looked rather like a box' (p. 152). On arriving home the young woman decided that this box-like object was a camera and that the sound she had heard was that of a shutter clicking. She thereupon became convinced that her lover had been trying to blackmail her and began to pursue him with her reproaches. Finally she went to consult the lawyer, who brought her to Freud.

For Freud the question posed by the patient's narrative is: does she *have* a case or *is* she a case? What prevents Freud from making up his mind is the fact that contrary to the psychoanalytic theory of paranoia, the persecutor – that is, the young man – is not of the same sex as the victim: 'there was no sign of the influence of a woman, no trace of a struggle against a homosexual attachment' (p. 153). Confronted with this difficulty, rather than conclude that his theory needed to be revised or that the patient did indeed have a legitimate case, Freud hypothesized that if the case did not fit the theory, then perhaps the case history was incomplete. He asks for and is granted a second interview with the young woman, who thereupon produces Narrative II, in which she reveals that she had visited the young man not once but twice. The insistent doubling in this text – there are the double frame of reference, the lawyer and the analyst, the two strangers, the double delusion – is hardly accidental, as doubling is a characteristic feature of paranoia, the persecutor always being in some sense the victim's double, if only as a projection effect. Now what is significant about the disparity between Narrative I and Narrative II is not so much the fact that there are two visits as the fact that something crucial occurred in the interval separating the two encounters. The doubling of the visit opens up another time frame, precisely the one during which the missing event took place: the day after the uneventful first rendezvous, the young woman saw her would-be lover talking to her supervisor, an elderly woman whom she describes as having white hair and looking like her mother. When she saw the two in conversation, she became convinced that they were speaking of her visit, further, that the elderly supervisor and the young man were lovers. She confronted her suitor with these suspicions, but he was so successful in allaying them that she consented to a second meeting. The conflation of the supervisor and the mother provided Freud with the information he needed to confirm his theory; beneath the male persecutor stood a female persecutor and one resembling the victim's mother: 'The *original* persecutor ... is here again not a man but a woman' (p. 155). Indeed the daughter's homosexual bond with her mother makes it difficult, not to say impossible, for her to enjoy a satisfactory heterosexual relationship.

Having successfully surmounted the principal difficulty posed by this perplexing case, Freud proceeds in the second half of the paper to turn his attention to what turns out to be by far the most striking and enigmatic aspect of the case, the nature of the sound heard by the patient. This part of the text can itself be divided into two parts: in the first, Freud seeks to demonstrate that there was nothing accidental about the noise; rather than triggering the delusion, the delusion latched on to the noise, because noise is an intrinsic component of the primal scene: 'The accidental noise is merely a stimulus which activates the typical phantasy of eavesdropping, itself a component of the parental complex' (p. 157). And, according to Freud, what we have here is a reenactment of the primal scene, with the patient coming to occupy the mother's place.[7]

But Freud does not stop there: in the second part of his discussion of the troublesome noise, in a dramatic though not atypical change of venue, he offers a hypothesis which renders the entire discussion of the order of events academic: 'I might go still further in the analysis of this apparently real "accident". I do not believe that the clock ever ticked or that any noise was to be heard at all. The woman's situation justified a sensation of throbbing [*Klopfen*] in the clitoris. This was what she subsequently projected as a perception of an external object' (pp. 158–9).

Female Psychoanalytic Theory is a Materialism

If we take Freud's patient as a paradigmatic female paranoiac and her delusion as an exemplary case of female theorizing, then the implications of Freud's audacious and quite possibly mad hypothesis must be articulated and examined in some detail. The first of these implications can be stated quite simply: female theorizing is grounded in the body. Indeed it may well be that female theorizing involves at least as much asserting the body's inscription in language as demonstrating the female body's exclusion from language, a more widely held view. As Guy Rosolato notes in his analysis of the Freud text: 'We must take another look at Freud's previously cited case, in order to emphasize *the very important part the body plays in it.* Freud views the projection as emanating only from the corporeal excitation and from nothing else. His construction presupposes it.'[8]

The question then becomes: is there any evidence to support my hypothesis that female psychoanalytically based and oriented theory is, by definition, a materialism riveted to the body, its throbbing, its pulsations, its rhythms? My question is here a rhetorical one, because by its very phrasing it contains its own affirmative answer: by linking up throbbing with the larger semantic field of rhythm, I am alluding to the critical vocabulary of the major French female theoretician of the past decade, Julia Kristeva. I am alluding in particular to her insistent valorization of what she terms the *semiotic* – in contradistinction to the *symbolic* – and which she defines as follows:

> It is chronologically anterior and synchronically transversal to the sign, syntax, denotation, and signification. Made up of facilitations and their traces, it is a provisional articulation, a non-expressive rhythm. Plato (*Thaetetus*) speaks of a chora, anterior to the One, maternal, having borrowed the term from Democritus' and Leucippes' 'rhythm'. ... The semiotic is a distinctive, non-expressive articulation; neither amorphous substance nor meaningful numbering. We imagine it in the cries, the vocalizing, the gestures of infants; it functions, in fact, in adult discourse as rhythm, prosody, plays on words, the non-sense of sense, laughter.[9]

Now although the semiotic is, in Kristeva's words, 'connoted' as maternal and coextensive with the pre-Oedipal, to take it for the specificity of women's writing [*écriture féminine*] would constitute a gross misunderstanding of Kristeva's theory. As she demonstrates repeatedly throughout both *Révolution dans le langage poétique* and *Polylogue*, semiotic breaks in and primacy over the symbolic characterize the avant-garde texts of such writers as Mallarmé, Lautréamont, and Artaud. This is not to say that the feminine does not enjoy a privileged relationship with the semiotic, for it does, but only in nonartistic, nontextual forms: for Kristeva, pregnancy and childbirth have been historically, in our culture, the female equivalent of (avant-garde) art:

> The speaker reaches this limit, this requisite of sociality, only by virtue of a particular, discursive practice called 'art'. A woman also attains it (and in our society, *especially*) through the strange form of split symbolization (threshold of language and instinctual drives, of the 'symbolic' and the 'semiotic') of which giving birth consists.[10]

What Kristeva elaborates, then, is not a theory about the female imagination (or imaginary); rather – and therein lies her unique contribution to feminist theory – a specifically female theory, one which must be seen as a response and an alternative to the most pervasive and insidious form of idealism in our time: structuralism. In the face of a powerful ideology of scientific neutrality, of an eerily disembodied, neutered linguistics, Kristeva proclaims the indelible imprint of the body on or in language, and in so doing, associates the practice of a feminist psychoanalytic criticism with a return to Freud potentially more radical than Lacan's. Whatever Kristeva's own misgivings about paranoia – she generally equates it with male homosexuality and 'logical unity',[11] though in her more recent writings she has stressed the part played by the repression and recuperation of female paranoia in the history of religion[12] – her own writings offer an impressive and precious confirmation of the connection between female paranoia and the body dramatized by Freud's patient.

The Vaginal vs. the Clitoral

Let us now return to Freud's text. As I noted above, Freud's startling hypothesis – the noise allegedly heard by the patient was nothing but a projection of the throbbing of her clitoris – is rich in implications; we have examined, however briefly, one of these implications – female theory is grounded in the body. Now, what of the others? The second is both more obvious and more problematic than the first: it is that female theory is clitoral. The distinction between body and clitoris is not, I would emphasize, merely a heuristic device enlisted to facilitate my discussion of Freud's text; it is fundamental to my understanding of that text and to the privilege I accord it in the elaboration of my own theory. As Rosolato remarks: 'The faintly perceived clitoral excitation remains isolated, enigmatic in its suspension, *separate*.'[13]

With the clitoris we enter the realm of speculation, for no *evidence* (leaving behind the scopic economy so inimical to women) can be marshaled in support of my provocative extrapolation from Freud's unconfirmed interpretation of the patient's delusion – a sort of paranoia in the third power – with its distinctly clinical overtones. In the absence of a Masters and Johnson type of study of text pleasure, how can one hope to distinguish between the 'vaginal' and the 'clitoral' schools of feminist theory? And what is to be gained by adopting this distinction? Before venturing into this truly 'dark continent', I would like to take two steps backward, to situate my enquiry, and thereby to mitigate – if I can – its outrageousness. The notion that there might be something like an erotics of theory flows naturally from Roland Barthes's notion of 'the pleasure of the text': thus, to some extent, the vaginal/clitoral paradigm may be said to be modeled on Barthes's pleasure/jouissance opposition. Now both Kristeva and Irigaray confidently and repeatedly assert that female theory is intimately bound up with *jouissance*, that is, with the most intense form of sexual pleasure. In one of the rare passages where Kristeva comments explicitly on the specific vocation of female theoreticians, she writes:

> It is perhaps not indifferent that it is left up to a woman subject to maintain here – and elsewhere – this frustrating discourse of heterogeneity. Since everyone knows that it is impossible to know what a woman wants, since she wants a master, she comes to represent that which is negative within the homogeneity of the community: 'the eternal irony of the tribe'. She is able to ironize communal homonymy because: 'in her vocation as an individual and in her pleasure, her interest is centered on the universal and remains alien to the particularity of desire'. Psychoanalysis would say that this means that she is bound up with *jouissance* (the 'universal' – the impossible) which she

distinguishes from the body ('particularity', the locus of 'desire' and 'pleasure'), all the while knowing that there is no *jouissance* other than that of the body ('particularity'). In other words, her knowledge is the knowledge of *jouissance* ('centered on the universal'), beyond the pleasure principle (the pleasure of the body, be it perverse).[14]

The question then becomes: does *jouissance* designate female orgasm in general, clitoral as well as vaginal, or rather strictly the vaginal, which has, at least since Freud, been held to be the specifically female form of orgasm. In *Des Chinoises*, Kristeva clearly locates the mother's *jouissance* in the vagina; as for Irigaray, in Carolyn Greenstein Burke's words, her 'fable of the generation of meaning' is 'vaginal'.[15] It would appear then, on the basis of this all too brief survey, that there is little or nothing in contemporary French feminist psychoanalytic theory to support my contention that female theory is clitoral; indeed, what little work has been done in this area (or zone) tends to valorize the vagina (or, as we have seen earlier, the womb). Prominent as it is, the 'throbbing clitoris' in Freud's text remains enigmatic and isolated.

Or does it? Perhaps we have arrived at this impasse because we have adopted the wrong approach. In order to proceed, we must retrace our steps and rephrase our question: which is not what is the locus of *jouissance* – for it seems quite clear that implicitly *jouissance* is vaginal – but rather why recent French feminist psycho-analytic theory has tended to valorize the vagina and what are the consequences of this valorization. To these questions I would answer as follows: the valorization of the vagina is for all practical purposes bound up with a theory of production of avant-garde feminist texts, the examples of the so-called *écriture féminine*. It goes hand in hand with a preoccupation with the ineffable, the unnamable, for as Eugénie Lemoine-Luccioni writes: 'It is to the extent that she experiences *jouissance*, that she is silent. There are no words to say *jouissance*.'[16] The dangers of this valorization of the vaginal mode of production are graphically illustrated by Lacan's evocation of Saint Theresa as represented by Bernini: 'you have only to go and look at Bernini's statue in Rome to understand immediately that she's coming, there is no doubt about it. And what is her *jouissance*, her *coming* from? It is clear that the essential testimony of the mystics is that they are experiencing it but know nothing about it.'[17] Finally, the vaginal theoreticians are always running the risk of seeing their writings recuperated by metaphysical thinkers like Lacan.

Now, obviously, to valorize the clitoris is also a risky enterprise; the paranoiac model is as fraught with pitfalls as the hysterical model which underlies the vaginal school of female theory. There is first and foremost the Freudian assimilation of the clitoral and the phallic (see epigraph *supra*) to be contended with: if French feminists – in contradistinction to American feminists and sexologists – have tended to valorize the vaginal form of *jouissance*, it is at least in part to lay claim to their difference, turning Freud's normative view of female sexuality into a positivity. There is further the argument that by emphasizing the clitoris one remains locked into male dichotomies: why *oppose* the clitoral and the vaginal, instead of stressing their complementarity?

To answer these important questions we must begin by considering the place of the clitoris in contemporary theory, for, however surprising this may sound to some, the clitoris lies at the heart or the center of an important polemic between Jacques Lacan and Jacques Derrida. It may be recalled that in his righting of Lacan's wrong reading of Poe's *The Purloined Letter*, Derrida points out that one of the most telling traces of Lacan's great and unacknowledged debt to Marie Bonaparte's psycho-biographical analysis of that particular text involves an unmistakable allusion to a note in Bonaparte, regarding Baudelaire's mistranslation of the line describing the exact location of the purloined letter which, writes Poe, hangs 'from a little brass knob just beneath the middle of the mantelpiece'. First Bonaparte, then Lacan:

> Baudelaire translates: '*suspendu ... à un petit bouton de cuivre au-dessus de la cheminée*'. The imprecision of Baudelaire's translation, as far as this sentence is concerned, is obvious: in particular, 'beneath' is translated by 'au-dessus' ('above'), which is completely wrong.

> Look! Between the cheeks of the fireplace, there's the object already in reach of a hand the ravager has but to extend. ... The question of deciding whether he seizes it above the mantel piece as Baudelaire translates, or beneath it, as in the original text, may be abandoned without harm to the inferences of those whose profession is grilling [*aux inférences de la cuisine*].[18]

Derrida's response is that, on the contrary, the question of the correct translation is of the essence, because '*on* the mantelpiece, the letter could not have been "between the cheeks of the fireplace", "between the legs of the fireplace"'[19] as Lacan states. Is Lacan's presumed rivalry with Bonaparte a sufficient explanation of his cavalier dismissal of a question of decisive importance for his thesis? I think not. Finally, as Derrida almost inadvertently suggests, what is significant is not so much what Lacan steals from Bonaparte, as what he misses altogether. And that is the meaning she attributes to the little brass knob in a brief allusion which, notes Derrida, 'the Seminar does not echo' and which reads: 'We have here, in fact, what is almost an anatomical chart, from which not even the clitoris (or brass knob) is omitted.'[20]

What bearing does this polemic have on our inquiry? Simply this: it demonstrates that the clitoris is coextensive with the detail. The clitoral school of feminist criticism might then well be identified by its practice of a hermeneutics focused on the detail, which is to say on those details of the female anatomy generally ignored by male critics and which significantly influence our reading of the texts in which they appear.[21] A particularly apt (but by no means unique) example of the kind of detail I am referring to is to be found in the least commented upon of the three tales that make up Poe's Dupin trilogy, *The Mystery of Marie Roget*, a tale of rape and murder which, not coincidentally I would argue, also contains Poe's most explicit theory of the detail, as indicated by its last sentence: 'It may be sufficient here to say that it forms one of the infinite series of mistakes which arise in the path of Reason through her propensity for seeking truth in *detail*.[22] Which is, of course, exactly what Dupin does, emphasizing in the process two aspects of the detail:

1. its prominence: Thus Dupin remarks in a sentence which could easily be superimposed on the conclusion quoted *supra*: 'I have therefore observed that it is by prominences above the plane of the ordinary, that reason feels her way, if at all, in her search for the true' (p. 180);
2. its marginality: 'experience has shown, and a true philosophy will always show, that a vast, perhaps the larger, portion of truth arises from the seemingly irrelevant'. In keeping with this principle, Dupin informs the narrator, he will, 'discard the interior points of the tragedy, and concentrate our attention on the outskirts' (p. 191).

This last word should be taken quite literally for, as Dupin goes on to demonstrate, the solution of the mystery of Marie Roget involves precisely drawing the correct inferences from the peculiar state of her *outer skirts*: 'The dress was much torn and otherwise disordered. In the outer garment, a slip, about a foot wide, had been torn off. It was wound three times around the waist, and secured by a sort of hitch in the back' (p. 174). This detail is repeated several times in the course of the narrative, but it is only when Dupin offers his reconstruction of the events that this detail is raised to textual (as well as referential) prominence by a combination of repetition and italicization:

> My inference is this. The solitary murderer, having borne the corpse for some distance … by means of the bandage *hitched* around its middle, found the weight, in this mode of procedure, too much for his strength. He resolved to drag the burden. … With this object in view, it became necessary to attach something like a rope to one of the extremities. It could be best attached about the neck, where the head would prevent its slipping off. And now the murderer bethought him, unquestionably, of the bandage about the loins. He would have used this, but for its volution about the corpse, the *hitch* which embarrassed it, and the reflection that it had not been 'torn off' from the garment. It was easier to tear a new slip from the petticoat. He tore it, made it fast about the neck, and so *dragged* his victim to the brink of the river. (p. 202)

For Dupin, the hitch (as well as the knot around the neck) serve as incontrovertible proof of the singularity of Marie's assassin: a gang would surely not have resorted to such a clumsy contrivance to transport a body. For the reader, the hitch appears as a kind of marker, a signal, in a word: a detail jutting out above the plane surface of the text, providing the would-be interpreter or literary detective with a 'handle' on the text. Now this detail is quite conspicuously bound up, as it were, with the female anatomy, for as a curious slippage in the text indicates, the hitch surrounds not so much the waist, as the 'loins' of the victim; indeed, the word 'rape' never appears in the text, rather we find such ambiguous expressions as 'brutal violence' (p. 174) or 'appalling outrage' (p. 179). In this tale whose invariant might well be said to be *translation*,[23] the hitch serves, in the end, not so much as a means of moving the corpse from one place to another, as it does as a *displacement* of the sexual crime. The hitch designates the locus of violence, while at the same time the use of the word 'bandage' attests to a wish to cover up and bind the wound. It is, in degraded form, the veil that male authors are forever drawing over the female sexual organs, thereby creating mysteries. The real mystery of Marie Roget lies hidden beneath the multiple circumvolutions of the text; the hitch is, to parody Freud, the navel of the tale.

In conclusion, I would suggest that if the rhetorical figure of vaginal theory is metonymy – as Irigaray would have it – or metaphor – as Kristeva would argue – the figure of clitoral theory is synecdoche, the detail-figure. It is, I would suggest further, no accident that Lacan, in his rewriting of Roman Jakobson's essay on 'Two types of language and two types of aphasic disturbance', should not only entirely do away with synecdoche (subordinated to metonymy in Jakobson's essay) but, more important, offer, as a privileged example of metonymy, a syntagm – 'Thirty sails' – which has since antiquity served to illustrate synecdoche.[24] Clearly in Lacan's binary structural linguistics, with its emphasis on the perfect symmetry of metaphor and metonymy, there is no room for this third trope, just as in his rewriting of Bonaparte's analysis of Poe, there is no room for the knob-clitoris. Let us now praise synecdoche!

Notes

An early version of this text was presented at a discussion session organized by Carolyn Greenstein Burke at the 1979 MLA; subsequently, a revised version appeared in the Special Feminist Issue of *Yale French Studies* (1981), no. 62, entitled 'French texts/American contexts', edited by the Dartmouth Feminist Collective, whose sound editorial recommendations are gratefully acknowledged.

1. Sigmund Freud, *The Standard Edition of the Complete Psychological Works*, ed. James Strachey and trans. James Strachey *et al.*, 24 vols (London: Hogarth, 1953–74); henceforth *S.E.* 12: 79.
2. Freud, *S.E.* 23: 268.
3. Freud, *S.E.* 17: 261.
4. Phyllis Chesler, *Women and Madness* [New York: Avon Books, 1973], pp. 42–3, 50.
5. Ruth Mack Brunswick, 'The analysis of a case of paranoia (delusion of jealousy)' [*Journal of Nervous and Mental Diseases* (1929), 70], p. 170.
6. Freud, *Collected Papers*, [Joan Rivière, tr. London: Hogarth Press, 1933] 2: 150. All future references will be included in the body of the text.
7. For an illuminating Lacanian reading of this text and this scene in particular, see Guy Rosolato, 'Paranoia et Scène Primitive', in *Essais sur le symbolique* [Paris: Gallimard, 1969], pp. 199–241.
8. *Ibid.*, p. 233. All translations mine except where otherwise noted.
9. Julia Kristeva, *Polylogue* (Paris: Seuil, 1977), p. 14. I wish to thank Alice Jardine for sharing with me her expertise in translating Kristeva's texts.
10. Kristeva, *Desire in Language: A semiotic approach to literature and art* [Leon Roudiez, ed.; Leon Roudiez, Tom Gora and Alice Jardine, trs., New York: Columbia University Press, 1980], p. 240.
11. Kristeva, *Polylogue*, p. 79.
12. See Kristeva, 'Féminité et écriture. En réponse à deux questions sur *Polylogue*', especially p. 500; and 'Héréthique de l'amour', in particular pp. 45–6.

13. Rosolato, p. 223.
14. Kristeva, *Polylogue*, p. 269; the quotations are from Hegel's *Phenomenology of Spirit*.
15. See, for example, in Kristeva, *About Chinese Women* [Anita Barrows, tr., New York: Urizen Books, 1977], p. 30; Carolyn Greenstein Burke, 'Report from Paris: women's writing and women's movement' [*Signs* (Summer, 1978)], p. 852, no. 18.
16. Eugénie Lemoine-Luccioni, *Partage des femmes* [Paris, Seuil, 1976], p. 101.
17. *Feminine Sexuality: Jacques Lacan and the école freudienne* [Jacqueline Rose, tr., New York: Norton, 1982], p. 147. On the preceding page Lacan makes it quite clear that he is concerned exclusively with vaginal *jouissance*: 'Petty considerations about clitoral orgasm or the *jouissance* designated as best one can, the other one precisely, which I am trying to get you to along the path of logic, since, to date, there is no other' (pp. 145–6).
18. Bonaparte and Lacan as quoted by Jacques Derrida in 'The purveyor of truth' [Willis Domingo *et al.* trs, *Yale French Studies* (1975)], p. 68.
19. Derrida, p. 69.
20. *Ibid.* Bonaparte's attention to the detail of the knob-clitoris should be read in the light of the amazing pages she devotes to the clitoris in her book *Female Sexuality*. Basing herself on the three developmental paths Freud charts for women, Bonaparte divides women into three categories: the *acceptative* (normal, vaginal women), the *renunciatory* (Virginal), and the *claimant* (homosexual and/or clitoridal). In the section entitled 'Evolutionary Perspectives', she focuses on strategies the 'clitoridals' resort to in their adaptation to the environment, in particular a bizarre surgical procedure, the so-called Halban-Narjani operation, which involves repositioning the clitoris closer to the urethral passage. According to Bonaparte's biographer, Celia Bertin, Narjani was the pseudonym Bonaparte adopted to write about female frigidity and to promote the therapeutic virtues of Halban's operation. In despair over her own persistent frigidity, in 1927, 'she let Halban sever her external clitoris from its position and move it closer to the opening of the vagina. She always referred to the procedure by the code name "Narjani", her pseudonym. The operation, performed in the presence of Ruth Mack under local anesthesia, took only twenty-two minutes.' *Marie Bonaparte: A life* [New York: Harcourt Brace Jovanovich, 1982], p. 170. Despite Freud's disapproval of her resort to surgery, Bonaparte had herself operated on by Halban twice more, first in 1930 and then again in 1931, to no avail.
21. Any attempt to link attention to all manner of details to a specifically feminist hermeneutics is bound to fail, for attention to details is characteristic of the post-Freudian textual approaches of Foucault, Barthes, and Derrida, to name only the most spectacular self-styled contemporary *detailists*. For another example of the kind of clitoral reading I am proposing here, see my complementary text: 'Female fetishism: the case of George Sand' (*Poetics Today*, forthcoming), where I focus on the detail of bizarre wounds inflicted on the female body in several of Sand's novels. The related question of the link between detailism and femininity is taken up more fully in my genealogy of the detail as aesthetic category, 'Sublime details: from Reynolds to Barthes'.
22. Edgar Allan Poe, *The Complete Tales and Poems* [New York: Random House, 1938], p. 222. All subsequent references will be included in the text.
23. The entire tale takes the form of a transposition of the facts of an actual crime which took place in New York City into a Parisian setting, and is made up for a large part of purported translations of French newspaper articles into English. Because this tale involves a de-naturalization, followed by a re-naturalization of American texts via a fictive Parisian setting, it is emblematic of the trans-Atlantic shuttle Franco-American scholars are perpetually engaged in.
24. Cf. Roman Jakobson's essay in *Fundamentals of Language* [The Hague: Mouton, 1956], and Jacques Lacan, 'The agency of the letter in the unconscious or reason since Freud', *Écrits* [Paris: Seuil, 1966], in particular pp. 156–7.

2.6 □ *Psychoanalysis and Capitalism*

Gilles Deleuze and Félix Guattari

The schizoanalytic argument is simple: desire is a machine, a synthesis of machines, a machinic arrangement – desiring-machines. The order of desire is the order of *production*; all production is at once desiring-production and social production. We therefore reproach psychoanalysis for having stifled this order of production, for having shunted it into *representation*. Far from showing the boldness of psychoanalysis, this idea of unconscious representation marks from the outset its bankruptcy or its abnegation: an unconscious that no longer produces, but is content to *believe*. The unconscious believes in Oedipus, it believes in castration, in the law. It is doubtless true that the psychoanalyst would be the first to say that, everything considered, belief is not an act of the unconscious; it is always the preconscious that believes. Shouldn't it even be said that it is the psychoanalyst who believes – the psychoanalyst in each of us? Would belief then be an effect on the conscious material that the unconscious representation exerts from a distance? But inversely, who or what reduced the unconscious to this state of representation, if not first of all a system of beliefs put in the place of productions? In reality, social production becomes alienated in allegedly autonomous beliefs at the same time that desiring-production becomes enticed into allegedly unconscious representations. And as we have seen, it is the same agency – the family – that performs this double operation, distorting and disfiguring social desiring-production, leading it into an impasse.

Thus the link between *representation-belief* and the family is not accidental; it is of the essence of representation to be a familial representation. But production is not thereby suppressed, it continues to rumble, to throb beneath the representative agency [*instance représentative*] that suffocates it, and that it in return can make resonate to the breaking point. Thus in order to keep an effective grip on the zones of production, representation must inflate itself with all the power of myth and

From Deleuze, G. and Guattari, F., *Anti-Oedipus: Capitalism and schizophrenia*, trans. R. Hurley, M. Seem and H. R. Lane, Athlone Press, London, 1984, pp. 296–316, 320–2, 393–4.

tragedy, it must give a *mythic and tragic presentation* of the family – and a familial presentation of myth and tragedy. Yet aren't myth and tragedy, too, productions – forms of production? Certainly not; they are production only when brought into connection with real social production, real desiring-production. Otherwise they are ideological forms, which have taken the place of the units of production. *Who believes in all this* – Oedipus, castration, etc.? The Greeks? Then the Greeks did not produce in the same way they believed? The Hellenists? Do the Hellenists believe that the Greeks produced according to their beliefs? This is true at least of the nineteenth-century Hellenists, about whom Engels said: you'd think they really believed in all that – in myth, in tragedy. Is it the unconscious that represents itself through Oedipus and castration? Or is it the psychoanalyst – the psychoanalyst in us all, who represents the unconscious in this way? For never has Engels's remark regained so much meaning: you'd think the psychoanalysts really believed in all this – in myth, in tragedy. (They go on believing, whereas the Hellenists have long since stopped.)

   The Schreber case again applies: Schreber's father invented and fabricated astonishing little machines, sadistico-paranoiac machines – for example head straps with a metallic shank and leather bands, for restrictive use on children, for making them straighten up and behave.* These machines play no role whatever in the Freudian analysis. Perhaps it would have been more difficult to crush the entire sociopolitical content of Schreber's delirium if these desiring-machines of the father had been taken into account, as well as their obvious participation in a pedagogical social machine in general. For the real question is this: of course the father acts on the child's unconscious – but does he act as a head of a family in an expressive familial transmission, or rather as the agent of a machine, in a machinic information or communication? Schreber's desiring-machines communicate with those of his father; but it is in this very way that they are from early childhood the libidinal investment of a social field. *In this field the father has a role only as an agent of production and antiproduction.* Freud, on the contrary, chooses the first path: it is not the father who indicates the action of machines, but just the opposite; thereafter there is no longer even any reason for considering machines, whether as desiring-machines or as social machines. In return, the father will be inflated with all the 'forces of myth and religion' and with phylogenesis, so as to ensure that the little familial representation has the appearance of being coextensive with the field of delirium. The production couple – the desiring-machines and the social field – gives way to a representative couple of an entirely different nature: family-myth. Once again, have you ever seen a child at play: how he already populates the technical social machines with his own desiring-machines, O sexuality – while the father or

---

* W. G. Niederland discovered and reproduced Schreber's father's machines: see especially 'Schreber, father and son', *Psychoanalytic Quarterly*, vol. 28 (1959), pp. 151–69. Quite similar instruments of pedagogical torture are to be found in the Contesse de Ségur: thus 'the good behavior belt', with an iron plate for the back and an iron rod to hold the chin in place' (*Comédies et proverbes, On ne prend pas les mouches*).

mother remains in the background, from whom the child borrows parts and gears according to his need, and who are there as agents of transmission, reception, and interception: kindly agents of production or suspicious agents of antiproduction.

Why was mythic and tragic representation accorded such a senseless privilege? Why were expressive forms and a whole *theater* installed there where there were fields, workshops, factories, units of production? The psychoanalyst parks his circus in the dumbfounded unconscious, a real P. T. Barnum in the fields and in the factory. That is what Miller,[1] and already Lawrence, have to say against psychoanalysis (the living are not believers, the seers do not believe in myth and tragedy)

[. . .]

Oedipus (or Hamlet) led to the point of autocritique; the expressive forms – myth and tragedy – denounced as conscious beliefs or illusions, nothing more than ideas; the necessity of a scouring of the unconscious, schizoanalysis as a curettage of the unconscious; the matrical fissure in opposition to the line of castration; the splendid affirmation of the orphan- and producer-unconscious; the exaltation of the process as a schizophrenic process of deterritorialization that must produce a new earth; and even the functioning of the desiring-machines against tragedy, against 'the fatal drama of the personality', against 'the inevitable confusion between mask and actor'.

[. . .]

Michel Foucault has convincingly shown what break [*coupure*] introduced the irruption of production into the world of representation. Production can be that of labor or that of desire, it can be social or desiring, it calls forth forces that no longer permit themselves to be contained in representation, and it calls forth flows and breaks that break through representation, traversing it through and through: 'an immense expanse of shade' extended beneath the level of representation.[2] And this collapse or sinking of the classical world of representation is assigned a date by Foucault: the end of the eighteenth and the beginning of the nineteenth century. So it seems that the situation is far more complex than we made it out to be, since psychoanalysis participates to the highest degree in this discovery of the units of production, which subjugate all possible representations rather than being subordinated to them. Just as Ricardo founds political or social economy by discovering quantitative labor as the principle of every representable value, Freud founds desiring-economy by discovering the quantitative libido as the principle of every representation of the objects and aims of desire. Freud discovers the subjective nature or abstract essence of desire just as Ricardo discovers the subjective nature or abstract essence of labor, beyond all representations that would bind it to objects, to aims, or even to particular sources. Freud is thus the first to disengage desire itself [*le désir tout court*], as Ricardo disengages labor itself [*le travail tout court*], and thereby the sphere of production that effectively eclipses representation. And subjective abstract desire, like subjective abstract labor, is inseparable from a movement of deterritorialization that discovers the interplay of machines and their agents underneath all the specific determinations that still linked desire or labor to a given person, to a given object in the framework of representation.

Desiring-production and machines, psychic apparatuses and machines of desire, desiring-machines and the assembling of an analytic machine suited to decode them: the domain of free syntheses where everything is possible; partial connections, included disjunctions, nomadic conjunctions, polyvocal flows and chains, trans-ductive* breaks; the relation of desiring-machines as formations of the unconscious with the molar formations that they constitute statistically in organized crowds; and the apparatus of social and psychic repression resulting from these formations – such is the composition of the analytic field. And this subrepresentative field will continue to survive and work, even through Oedipus, even through myth and tragedy, which nevertheless mark the reconciliation of psychoanalysis with representation. The fact remains that a conflict cuts across the whole of psychoanalysis, the conflict between mythic and tragic familial representation and social and desiring-production. For myth and tragedy are systems of symbolic representations that still refer desire to determinate exterior conditions as well as to particular objective codes – the body of the Earth, the despotic body – and that in this way confound the discovery of the abstract or subjective essence. It has been remarked in this context that each time Freud brings to the fore the study of the psychic apparatuses, the social and desiring-machines, the mechanisms of the drives, and the institutional mechanisms, his interest in myth and tragedy tends to diminish, while at the same time he denounces in Jung, then in Rank, the re-establishment of an exterior representation of the essence of desire as an objective desire, alienated in myth or tragedy. †

How can this very complex ambivalence of psychoanalysis be explained? Several different things must be distinguished. In the first place, symbolic representation indeed grasps the essence of desire, but by referring it to large 'objectities' [objectités] ‡ as to the specific elements that determine its objects, aims, and sources. It is in this way that myth ascribes desire to the element of the earth as a full body, and to the territorial code that distributes prescriptions and prohibitions. Likewise tragedy ascribes desire to the full body of the despot and to the corresponding

---

* For a definition of transduction with respect to production and representation, see 'Interview/Félix Guattari', Diacritics: a review of contemporary criticism, Fall 1974, p. 39: 'Signs work as much as matter. Matter expresses as much as signs. ... Transduction is the idea that, in essence, something is conducted, something happens between chains of semiotic expression, and material chains'. [Translators' note.]

† Didier Anzieu distinguishes between two periods in particular: 1906–1920, which 'constitutes the great period of mythological works in the history of psychoanalysis'; then a period of relative discredit, as Freud turns toward the problems of the second topography [Translators' note: the id, ego, and superego], and the relationships between desire and institutions and takes less and less of an interest in a systematic exploration of myths ('Freud et la mythologie', Incidences de la psychanalyse, no. 1 [1970], pp. 126–9).

‡ objectités: This term corresponds to the German Objektität. The following definition appears in Vocabulaire technique et critique de la philosophie (Paris: Presses Universitaires de France, 1968): 'the form in which the thing-in-itself, the real, appears as an object'. [Translators' note.]

imperial code. Consequently, the understanding of symbolic representations may consist in a systematic phenomenology of these elements and objectities (as in the old Hellenists or even Jung); or else these representations may be understood by historical study that assigns them to their real and objective social conditions (as with recent Hellenists). Viewed in the latter fashion, representation implies a certain lag, and expresses less a stable element than the conditioned passage from one element to another: mythic representation does not express the element of the earth, but rather the conditions under which this element fades before the despotic element; and tragic representation does not express the despotic element properly speaking, but the conditions under which – in fifth-century Greece, for example – this element diminishes in favor of the new order of the city-state.[3] It is obvious that neither one of these ways of treating myth or tragedy is suited to the psychoanalytic approach. The psychoanalytic method is quite different: rather than referring symbolic representation to determinate objectities and to objective social conditions, psychoanalysis refers them to the subjective and universal essence of desire as libido. Thus the operation of *decoding* in psychoanalysis can no longer signify what it signifies in the sciences of man; the discovery of the secret of such and such a code. Psychoanalysis must undo the codes so as to attain the quantitative and qualitative flows of libido that traverse dreams, fantasies, and pathological formations as well as myth, tragedy, and the social formations. Psychoanalytic interpretation does not consist in competing with codes, adding a code to the codes already recognized, but in decoding in an absolute way, in eliciting something that is uncodable by virtue of its polymorphism and its polyvocity.* It appears, then, that the interest psychoanalysis has in myth (or in tragedy) is an essentially critical interest, since the specificity of myth, understood objectively, must melt under the rays of the subjective libido: it is indeed the world of representation that crumbles, or tends to crumble.

It follows that, in the second place, the link between psychoanalysis and capitalism is no less profound than that between political economy and capitalism. This discovery of the decoded and deterritorialized flows is the same as that which takes place for political economy and in social production, in the form of subjective abstract labor, and for psychoanalysis and in desiring-production, in the form of subjective abstract libido. As Marx says, in capitalism the essence becomes subjective – *the activity of production in general* – and abstract labor becomes something real from which all the preceding social formations can be reinterpreted from the point of view of a generalized decoding or a generalized process of

---

* It cannot be said, therefore, that psychoanalysis adds a code – a psychological one – to the social codes through which histories and mythologists explain myths. Freud pointed this out apropos dreams: it is not a question of a deciphering process according to a code. In this regard, see Jacques Derrida's comments in *L'écriture et la différence* (Paris: editions du Seuil, 1967), pp. 310 ff.: 'It is doubtless true that [dream writing] works with a mass of elements codified in the course of an individual or collective history. But in its operations, its lexicon, and its syntax, a purely idiomatic residue remains irreducible, that must carry the whole weight of the interpretation, in the communication among unconsciouses. The dreamer invents his own grammar.'

deterritorialization: 'The simplest abstraction, then, which modern economics places at the head of its discussions, and which expresses an immeasurably ancient relation valid in all forms of society, nevertheless achieves practical truth as an abstraction only as a category of the most modern society.' This is also the case for desire as abstract libido and as subjective essence. Not that a simple parallelism should be drawn between capitalist social production and desiring-production, or between the flows of money-capital and the shit-flows of desire. The relationship is much closer: desiring-machines are in social machines and nowhere else, so that the conjunction of the decoded flows in the capitalist machine tends to liberate the free figures of a universal subjective libido. In short, the discovery of an activity of production *in general and without distinction*, as it appears in capitalism, is the identical discovery of *both* political economy *and* psychoanalysis, beyond the determinate systems of representation.

Obviously this does not mean that the capitalist being, or the being in capitalism, desires to work or that he works according to his desire. But the identity of desire and labor is not a myth, it is rather the active utopia *par excellence* that designates the capitalist limit to be overcome through desiring-production. But why, precisely, is desiring-production situated at the always counteracted limit of capitalism? Why, at the same time as it discovers the subjective essence of desire and labor – a common essence, inasmuch as it is the activity of production in general – is capitalism continually realienating this essence, and without interruption, in a repressive machine that divides the essence in two, and maintains it divided – abstract labor on the one hand, abstract desire on the other: political economy *and* psychoanalysis, political economy *and* libidinal economy? Here we are able to appreciate the full extent to which psychoanalysis belongs to capitalism. For as we have seen, capitalism indeed has as its limit the decoded flows of desiring-production, but it never stops repelling them by binding them in an axiomatic that takes the place of the codes. Capitalism is inseparable from the movement of deterritorialization, but this movement is exorcised through factitious and artificial reterritorializations. Capitalism is constructed on the ruins of the territorial and the despotic, the mythic and the tragic representations, but it re-establishes them in its own service and in another form, as images of capital.

Marx summarizes the entire matter by saying that the subjective abstract essence is discovered by capitalism only to be put in chains all over again, to be subjugated and alienated – no longer, it is true, in an exterior and independent element as objectity, but in the element, itself subjective, of private property: 'What was previously being external to oneself – man's externalization in the thing – has merely become the act of externalizing – the process of alienating.' It is, in fact, the form of private property that conditions the conjunction of the decoded flows, which is to say their axiomatization in a system where the flows of the means of production, as the property of the capitalists, is directly related to the flow of so-called free labor, as the 'property' of the workers (so that the State restrictions on the substance or the content of private property do not at all affect this form). It is also the form of private property that constitutes the center of the factitious reterritorializations of capitalism. And finally, it is this form that produces the images filling the capitalist field of immanence, 'the' capitalist, 'the' worker, etc. In other terms, capitalism indeed implies the collapse of the great objective determinate representations, for the benefit of production as the universal interior essence, but it does not thereby escape the world of representation. It merely performs a vast conversion of this world, by attributing to it the new form of an infinite subjective representation. *

We seem to be straying from the main concern of psychoanalysis, yet never have we been so close. For here again, as we have seen previously, it is in the interiority of its movement that capitalism requires and institutes not only a social axiomatic, but an application of this axiomatic to the privatized family. Representation would never be able to ensure its own conversion without this application that furrows deep into it, cleaves it, and forces it back upon itself. Thus subjective abstract Labor as represented in private property has, as its correlate, subjective abstract Desire as represented in the privatized family. Psychoanalysis undertakes the analysis of this second term, as political economy analyzes the first. Psychoanalysis is the technique of application, for which political economy is the axiomatic. In a word, psychoanalysis disengages the second pole in the very movement of capitalism, which substitutes the infinite subjective representation for the large determinate objective representations. It is in fact essential that the limit of the decoded flows of desiring-production be doubly exorcised, doubly displaced, once by the position of immanent limits that capitalism does not cease to reproduce on an ever expanding scale, and again by the marking out of an interior limit that reduces this social reproduction to restricted familial reproduction.

Consequently, the ambiguity of psychoanalysis in relation to myth or tragedy has the following explanation: psychoanalysis undoes them as objective representations, and discovers in them the figures of a subjective universal libido; but it reanimates them, and promotes them as subjective representations that extend the mythic and tragic contents to infinity. Psychoanalysis does treat myth and tragedy, but it treats them *as* the dreams and the fantasies of private man, *Homo familia* – and in fact dream and fantasy are to myth and tragedy as private property is to public property. What acts in myth and tragedy at the level of objective elements is therefore reappropriated and raised to a higher level by psychoanalysis, but as an unconscious dimension of subjective representation (myth as humanity's *dream*). What acts as an objective and public element – the Earth, the Despot – is now taken up again, but as the expression of a subjective and private reterritorialization: Oedipus is the fallen despot – banished, deterritorialized – but a reterritorialization is engineered, using the Oedipus complex conceived of as the daddy-mommy-me of today's everyman. Psychoanalysis and the Oedipus complex gather up all beliefs, all that has ever been believed by humanity, but only in order to raise it to the condition of a

---

* Michel Foucault shows that 'the human sciences' found their principle in production and were constituted on the collapse of representation, but that they immediately re-establish a new type of representation, as unconscious representation (*The Order of Things* [see note 2], pp. 352–67).

denial that preserves belief without believing in it (it's only a dream: the strictest piety today asks for nothing more). Whence this double impression, that psychoanalysis is opposed to mythology no less than to mythologists, but at the same time extends myth and tragedy to the dimensions of the subjective universal: if Oedipus himself 'has no complex', the Oedipus complex has no Oedipus, just as narcissism has no Narcissus.* Such is the ambivalence that traverses psychoanalysis, and that extends beyond the specific problem of myth and tragedy: with one hand psychoanalysis undoes the system of objective representations (myth, tragedy) for the benefit of the subjective essence conceived as desiring-production, while with the other hand it reverses this production in a system of subjective representations (dream and fantasy, with myth and tragedy posited as their developments or projections). Images, nothing but images. What is left in the end is an intimate familial theater, the theater of private man, which is no longer either desiring-production or objective representation. The unconscious as a stage. A whole theater put in the place of production, a theater that disfigures this production even more than could tragedy and myth when reduced to their meager ancient resources.

Myth, tragedy, dream, and fantasy – and myth and tragedy reinterpreted in terms of dream and fantasy – are the representative series that psychoanalysis substitutes for the line of production: social and desiring-production. A theater series, instead of a production series. But why in fact does representation, having become subjective representation, assume this theatrical form ('There is a mysterious tie between psychoanalysis and the theater')? We are familiar with the eminently modern reply of certain recent authors: the theater elicits the finite structure of the infinite subjective representation. What is meant by 'elicit' is very complex, since the structure can never present more than its own absence, or represent something not represented in the representation: but it is claimed that the theater's privilege is that of staging this metaphoric and metonymic causality that marks both the presence and the absence of the structures in its effects. While André Green expresses reservations about the adequacy of the structure, he does so only in the name of a theater necessary for the actualization of this structure, playing the role of revealer, a place by which the structure becomes visible.† In her fine analysis of the phenomenon of belief, Octave Mannoni likewise uses the theater model to show how the denial of belief in fact implies a transformation of belief, under the effect

---

* Didier Anzieu, 'Freud et la mythologie', pp. 124, 128: 'Freud grants myth no specificity. This is one of the points that have most seriously encumbered the subsequent relations between psychoanalysts and anthropologists. ... Freud undertakes a veritable leveling. ... The article 'On Narcissism: An Introduction', which constitutes an important step toward the revision of the theory of the drives, contains no allusion to the myth of Narcissus'.

† André Green goes very far in the analysis of the representation–theater–structure–unconscious relations: *Un oeil en trop* (Paris: Éditions de Minuit, 1969), Prologue (especially p. 43, concerning 'the representation of the nonrepresented in representation'). However, the criticism that Green makes of the structure is not conducted in the name of production, but in the name of representation, and invokes the necessity for extra-structural factors that must do nothing more than reveal the structure, and reveal it as Oedipal.

of a structure that the theater embodies or places on stage.[4] We should understand that representation, when it ceases to be objective, when it becomes subjective infinite – that is to say, imaginary – effectively loses all consistency, unless it is supported by a structure that determines the place and the functions of the subject of representation, as well as the objects represented as images, and the formal relations between them all. 'Symbolic' thus no longer designates the relation of representation to an objectity as an element; it designates the ultimate elements of subjective representation, pure signifiers, pure nonrepresented representatives whence the subjects, the objects, and their relationships all derive. In this way the structure designates the unconscious of subjective representation. The series of this representation now presents itself: (imaginary) infinite subjective representation–theatrical representation–structural representation. And precisely because the theater is thought to stage the latent structure, as well as to embody its elements and relations, it is in a position to reveal the universality of this structure, even in the objective representations that it salvages and reinterprets in terms of hidden representatives, their migrations and variable relations. All former beliefs are gathered up and revived in the name of a structure of the unconscious: we are still pious. Everywhere, the great game of the symbolic signifier that is embodied in the signifieds of the Imaginary – Oedipus as a universal metaphor.

Why the theater? How bizarre, this theatrical and pasteboard unconscious: the theater taken as the model of production. Even in Louis Althusser we are witness to the following operation: the discovery of social production as 'machine' or 'machinery', irreducible to the world of objective representation [*Vorstellung*]; but immediately the reduction of the machine to structure, the identification of production with a structural and theatrical representation [*Darstellung*].[5] Now the same is true of both desiring-production and social production: every time that production, rather than being apprehended in its originality, in its reality, becomes *reduced* [*rabattue*] in this manner to a representational space, it can no longer have value except by its own absence, and it appears as a lack within this space. In search of the structure in psychoanalysis, Moustafa Safouan is able to present it as a 'contribution to a theory of lack'. It is in the structure that the fusion of desire with the impossible is performed, with lack defined as castration. From the structure there arises the most austere song in honor of castration – yes, yes, we enter the order of desire through the gates of castration – once desiring-production has spread out in the space of a representation that allows it to go on living only as an absence and a lack unto itself. For a *structural unity* is imposed on the desiring-machines that joins them together in a molar aggregate; the partial objects are referred to a totality that can appear only as that which the partial objects lack, and as that which is lacking unto itself while being lacking in them (the Great Signifier 'symbolizable by the inherency of a -1 in the ensemble of signifiers'). Just how far will one go in the development of a lack of lack traversing the structure? Such is the structural operation: it distributes lack in the molar aggregate. The limit of desiring-production – the borderline separating the molar aggregates and their molecular elements the objective representations and the machines of desire – is now completely displaced. The limit now passes only within the molar aggregate itself, inasmuch as the latter is furrowed by the line of castration. The formal operations of the structure are those of extrapolation, application, and biunivocalization, which reduce the social aggregate of departure to a familial aggregate of destination, with the familial relation becoming 'metaphorical for all the others' and hindering the molecular productive elements from following their own line of escape.

When André Green looks for the reasons that establish the affinity of psycho-analysis with the theatrical and structural representation it makes visible, he offers two that are especially striking: the theater raises the familial relation to the condition of a universal metaphoric structural relation, whence the imaginary place and interplay of persons derives; and inversely, the theater forces the play and the working of machines into the wings, behind a limit that has become impassable (exactly as in fantasy the machines are there, but *behind the wall*). In short, the displaced limit no longer passes between objective representation and desiring-production, but between the two poles of subjective representation, as infinite imaginary representation, and as finite structural representation. Thereafter it is possible to oppose these two aspects to each other, the imaginary variations that tend toward the night of the indeterminate or the nondifferentiated, and the symbolic invariant that traces the path of the differentiations: the same thing is found all over, following a rule of inverse relation, or double bind. All of production is conducted into the double impasse of subjective representation. Oedipus can always be consigned to the Imaginary, but no matter, it will be encountered again, stronger and more whole, more lacking and triumphant by the very fact that it is lacking, it will be encountered again in its entirety in symbolic castration. And it's a sure thing that structure affords us no means for escaping familialism; on the contrary, it adds another turn, it attributes a universal metaphoric value to the family at the very moment it has lost its objective literal values. Psychoanalysis makes its ambition clear: to relieve the waning family, to replace the broken-down familial bed with the psychoanalyst's couch, to make it so that the 'analytic situation' is *incestuous in its essence*, so that it is its own proof or voucher, on a par with Reality.[6]

In the final analysis that is indeed what is at issue, as Octave Mannoni shows: how can belief continue after repudiation, how can we continue to be pious? We have repudiated and lost all our beliefs that proceeded by way of objective representations. The earth is dead, the desert is growing: the old father is dead, the territorial father, and the son too, the despot Oedipus. We are alone with our bad conscience and our boredom, our life where nothing happens; nothing left but images that revolve within the infinite subjective representation. We will muster all our strength so as to believe in these images, from the depths of a structure that governs our relationships with them and our identifications as so many effects of a symbolic signifier. The 'good identification'. We are all Archie Bunker at the theater, shouting out before Oedipus: there's my kind of guy, there's my kind of guy! Everything, the myth of the earth, the tragedy of the despot, is taken up again as shadows projected on a stage. The great territorialities have fallen into ruin, but the structure proceeds with all the subjective and private reterritorializations. What a perverse operation psychoanalysis is, where this neoidealism, this rehabilitated cult of castration, this ideology of lack culminates: *the anthropomorphic representation of sex*! In truth, they don't know what they are doing, nor what mechanism of repression they are fostering, for their intentions are often progressive. But no one today can enter an analyst's consulting room without at least being aware that everything has been *played out* in advance: Oedipus and castration, the Imaginary and the Symbolic, the great lesson of the inadequacy of being or of dispossession. Psychoanalysis as a gadget, Oedipus as a reterritorialization, a retimbering of modern man on the 'rock' of castration.

The path marked out by Lacan led in a completely different direction. He is not content to turn, like the analytic squirrel, inside the wheel of the Imaginary and the Symbolic; he refuses to be caught up in the Oedipal Imaginary and the oedipalizing structure, the imaginary identity of persons and the structural unity of machines, everywhere knocking against the impasses of a molar representation that the family closes round itself. What is the use of going from the imaginary dual order to the symbolic third (or fourth), if the latter is biunivocalizing whereas the first is biunivocalized? As partial objects the desiring-machines undergo two totalizations, one when the socius confers on them a structural unity under a symbolic signifier acting as absence and lack in an aggregate of departure, the other when the family imposes on them a personal unity with imaginary signifieds that distribute, that 'vacuolize' lack in an aggregate of destination: a double abduction of the orphan machines, inasmuch as the structure applies its articulation to them, inasmuch as the parents lay their fingers on them. To trace back from images to the structure would have little significance and would not rescue us from representation, *if the structure did not have a reverse side* that is like the real production of desire.

This reverse side is the 'real inorganization' of the molecular elements: partial objects that enter into indirect syntheses or interactions, since they are not partial [*partiels*] in the sense of extensive parts, but rather partial ['*partiaux*'] * like the intensities under which a unit of matter always fills space in varying degrees (the eye, the mouth, the anus as degrees of matter); pure positive multiplicities where everything is possible, without exclusiveness or negation, syntheses operating without a plan, where the connections are transverse, the disjunctions included, the conjunctions polyvocal, indifferent to their underlying support, since this matter that serves them precisely as a support receives no specificity from any structural or personal unity, but appears as the body without organs that fills the space each time an intensity fills it; signs of desire that compose a signifying chain but that are not

---

* *partiel:* partial, incomplete; *partial* (pl. *partiaux*): partial, biased, as biased judge. We have chosen to translate *objets partiels* throughout as 'partial objects' rather than as 'part-objects' (as in Melanie Klein), in anticipation of this point in the book where Deleuze and Guattari shift from Klein's concept of the partial objects as 'part of', hence as an incomplete part of a lost unity or totality (molar), toward a concept of the partial objects as biased, evaluating intensities that know no lack and are capable of selecting organs (molecular). (*Translators' note.*)

themselves signifying, and do not answer to the rules of a linguistic game of chess, but instead to the lottery drawings that sometimes cause a word to be chosen, sometimes a design, sometimes a thing or a piece of a thing, depending on one another only by the order of the random drawings, and holding together only by the absence of a link (nonlocalizable connections), having no other statutory condition than that of being dispersed elements of desiring-machines that are themselves dispersed.* It is this entire reverse side of the structure that Lacan discovers, with the 'o' as machine, and the 'O' as nonhuman sex: schizophrenizing the analytic field, instead of oedipalizing the psychotic field.

Everything hinges on the way in which the structure is elicited from the machines, according to planes of consistency or of structuration, and lines of selection that correspond to the large statistical aggregates or molar formations, and that determine the links and reduce production to representation – *that* is where the disjunctions become exclusive (and the connections global, and the conjunctions, biunivocal), at the same time that the support gains a specificity under a structural unity, and the signs themselves become signifying under the action of a despotic symbol that totalizes them in the name of its own absence or withdrawal. Yes, in fact, there the production of desire can be *represented* only in terms of an extrapolated sign that joins together all the elements of production in a constellation of which it is not itself a part. There the absence of a tie necessarily appears as an absence, and no longer as a positive force. There desire is necessarily referred to a missing term, whose very essence is to be lacking. The signs of desire, being nonsignifying, become signifying in representation only in terms of a signifier of absence or lack. The structure is formed and appears only in terms of the symbolic term defined as a lack. The great Other as the nonhuman sex gives way, in representation, to a signifier of the great Other as an always missing term, the all-too-human sex, the phallus of molar castration.†

---

* Lacan, *Écrits* (see Note 7), pp. 657–9. Serge Leclaire has made a profound attempt to define within this perspective the reverse side of the structure as the 'pure being of desire' ['La réalité du désir'] in *Sexualité humaine* (Paris: Aubier, 1970), pp. 242–9. In desire he sees a multiplicity of prepersonal singularities or indifferent elements that are defined precisely by the absence of a link. But this absence of a link – and of a meaning – is positive, 'it constitutes the specific force of coherence of this constellation'. Of course, meaning and link can always be re-established, if only by inserting fragments assumed to be forgotten: this is even the very function of Oedipus. But *'if the analysis again discovers the link between two elements, this is a sign that they are not the ultimate, irreducible terms of the unconscious'*. It will be noticed here that Leclaire uses the exact criterion of real distinction in Spinoza and Leibniz: the ultimate elements (the infinite attributes) are attributable to God, because they do not depend on one another and do not tolerate any relation of opposition or contradiction among themselves. The absence of all direct links guarantees their common participation in the divine substance. Likewise for the partial objects and the body without organs: the body without organs is substance itself, and the partial objects, the ultimate attributes or elements of substance.

† Lacan, *Écrits* (see Note 7), p. 819: 'For want of this signifier, all the others would represent nothing'. Serge Leclaire shots how the structure is organized around a missing term, or rather a signifier of lack: "It is the elective signifier of the absence of a link, the phallus, that we find again in the unique privilege of its relation to the essence of lack – an emblem of difference *par excellence* – the irreducible difference, the difference between the sexes. ... If man can talk, this is because at one point in the language system there is a guarantor of the irreducibility of lack: the phallic signifier' ('La réalité du désir', p. 251). How strange all this is!

Here too Lacan's approach appears in all its complexity; for it is certain that he does not enclose the unconscious in an Oedipal structure. He shows on the contrary that Oedipus is imaginary, nothing but an image, a myth; that this or these images are produced by an oedipalizing structure; that this structure acts only in so far as it reproduces the element of castration, which itself is not imaginary but symbolic. There we have the three major planes of structuration, which correspond to the molar aggregates: Oedipus as the imaginary reterritorialization of private man, produced under the structural conditions of capitalism, inasmuch as capitalism reproduces and revives the archaism of the imperial symbol or the vanished despot. All three are necessary – precisely in order to lead Oedipus to the point of its self-critique. The task undertaken by Lacan is to lead Oedipus to such a point. (Likewise, Elisabeth Roudinesco has clearly seen that, in Lacan, the hypothesis of an unconscious-as-language does not closet the unconscious in a linguistic structure, but leads linguistics to the point of its autocritique, by showing how the structural organization of signifiers still depends on a despotic Great Signifier acting as an archaism.)[7]

What is this point of self-criticism? It is the point where the structure, beyond the images that fill it and the Symbolic that conditions it within representation, reveals its reverse side as a positive principle of nonconsistency that dissolves it: where desire is shifted into the order of production, related to its molecular elements, and where it lacks nothing because it is defined as *the natural and sensuous objective being*, at the same time as the Real is defined as *the objective being of desire*. For the unconscious of schizoanalysis is unaware of persons, aggregates, and laws, and of images, structures, and symbols. It is an orphan, just as it is an anarchist and an atheist. It is not an orphan in the sense that the father's name would designate an absence, but in the sense that the unconscious reproduces itself wherever the names of history designate present intensities ('the sea of proper names'). The unconscious is not figurative, since its *figural* is abstract, the figure-schiz. It is not structural, nor is it symbolic, for its reality is that of the Real in its very production, in its very inorganization. It is not representative, but solely machinic, and productive.

Destroy, destroy. The task of schizoanalysis goes by way of destruction – a whole scouring of the unconscious, a complete curettage. Destroy Oedipus, the illusion of the ego, the puppet of the superego, guilt, the law, castration. It is not a matter of pious destructions, such as those performed by psychoanalysis under the benevolent neutral eye of the analyst. For these are Hegel-style destructions, ways of conserving. How is it that the celebrated neutrality, and what psychoanalysis calls – dares to call – the disappearance or the dissolution of the Oedipus complex, do not make us burst into laughter? We are told that Oedipus is indispensable, that it is the source of every possible differentiation, and that it saves us from the terrible nondifferentiated mother. But this terrible mother, the sphinx, is herself part of Oedipus; her nondifferentiation is merely the reverse of the exclusive differentiations created by Oedipus, she is herself created by Oedipus: Oedipus necessarily operates in the form of this double impasse. We are told that Oedipus in its turn must be overcome, and that this is achieved through castration, latency, desexualization, and sublimation. But what is castration if not still Oedipus, to the *n*th power, now symbolic, and therefore all the more virulent? And what is latency, this pure fable, if not the silence imposed on desiring-machines so that Oedipus can develop, be fortified in us, so that it can accumulate its poisonous sperm and gain the time necessary for propagating itself, and for passing on to our future children? And what is the elimination of castration anxiety in its turn – desexualization and sublimation – if not divine acceptance of, and infinite resignation to, bad conscience, which consists for the woman of 'the appeased wish for a penis ... destined to be converted into a wish for a baby and for a husband', and for the man in assuming his passive attitude and in '[subjecting] himself to a father substitute'[8]

We are all the more 'extricated' from Oedipus as we become a living example, an advertisement, a theorem in action, so as to attract our children to Oedipus: we have evolved in Oedipus, we have been structured in Oedipus, and under the neutral and benevolent eye of the substitute, we have learned the song of castration, the lack-of-being-that-is-life; 'yes it is through castration/that we gain access/to Deeeeesire'. What one calls the disappearance of Oedipus is Oedipus become an idea. Only the idea can inject the venom. Oedipus has to become an idea so that it sprouts each time a new set of arms and legs, lips and mustache: 'In tracing back the "memory deaths" your ego becomes a sort of mineral theorem which constantly proves the futility of living.'[9] We have been triangulated in Oedipus, and will triangulate in it in turn. From the family to the couple, from the couple to the family. In actuality, the benevolent neutrality of the analyst is very limited: it ceases the instant one stops responding daddy-mommy. It ceases the instant one introduces a little desiring-machine – the tape-recorder – into the analyst's office; it ceases as soon as a flow is made to circulate that does not let itself be stopped by Oedipus, the mark of the triangle (they tell you you have a libido that is too viscous, or too liquid, contraindications for analysis).

When Fromm denounces the existence of a psychoanalytic bureaucracy, he still doesn't go far enough, because he doesn't see what the stamp of this bureaucracy is, and that an appeal to the pre-Oedipal is not enough to escape this stamp: the pre-Oedipal, like the post-Oedipal, is still a way of bringing all of desiring-production – the anOedipal – back to Oedipus. When Reich denounces the way in which psychoanalysis joins forces with social repression, he still doesn't go far enough, because he doesn't see that the tie linking psychoanalysis with capitalism is not merely ideological, that it is infinitely closer, infinitely tighter; and that psychoanalysis depends directly on an economic mechanism (whence its relations with money) through which the decoded flows of desire, as taken up in the axiomatic of capitalism, must necessarily be reduced to a familial field where the application of this axiomatic is carried out: Oedipus as the last word of capitalist consumption – sucking away at daddy-mommy, being blocked and triangulated on the couch; 'So it's ...' Psychoanalysis, no less than the bureaucratic or military apparatus, is a mechanism for the absorption of surplus value, nor is this true from the outside, extrinsically; rather, its very form and its finality are marked by this social function. It is not the pervert, nor even the autistic person, who escapes psychoanalysis; the whole of psychoanalysis is an immense perversion, a drug, a radical break with reality, starting with the reality of desire; it is a narcissism, a monstrous autism: the characteristic autism and the intrinsic perversion of the machine of capital. At its most autistic, psychoanalysis is no longer measured against any reality, it no longer opens to any outside, but becomes itself the test of reality and the guarantor of its own test: reality as the lack to which the inside and the outside, departure and arrival, are reduced. Psychoanalysis *index sui*, with no other *reference* than itself or 'the analytic situation'.

Psychoanalysis states clearly that unconscious representation can never be apprehended independently of the deformations, disguises, or displacements it undergoes. Unconscious representation therefore comprises essentially, by virtue of its own *law*, a represented that is displaced in relation to an agency in a constant state of displacement. But from this, two unwarranted conclusions are drawn: that this agency can be discovered by way of the displaced represented; and this, precisely because this agency itself belongs to representation, as a nonrepresented representative, or as a lack 'that juts out into the overfull [*trop-plein*] of a representation'. This results from the fact that displacement refers to very different movements: at times, the movement through which desiring-production is continually overcoming the limit, becoming deterritorialized, causing its flows to escape, going beyond the threshold of representation; at times, on the contrary, the movement through which the limit itself is displaced, and now passes to the interior of the representation that performs the artificial reterritorializations of desire. If the displacing agency can be concluded from the displaced, this is only true in the second sense, where molar representation is organized around a representative that displaces the represented. But this is certainly not true in the first sense, where the molecular elements are continually passing through the links in the chain. We have seen in this perspective how the law of representation perverted the productive forces of the unconscious, and induced in its very structure a false image that caught desire in its trap (the impossibility of concluding from the prohibition as to what is actually prohibited). Yes, Oedipus is indeed the displaced represented; yes, castration is indeed the representative, the displacing agency [*le déplaçant*], the signifier – but none of that constitutes an unconscious material, nor does any of it concern the productions of the unconscious. Oedipus, castration, the signifier, etc., exist at the crossroads of two operations of capture: one where repressive social production becomes replaced by beliefs, the other where repressed desiring-production finds itself replaced by representations. To be sure, it is not psychoanalysis that makes us believe: Oedipus and castration are demanded, then demanded again, and these demands come from elsewhere and from deeper down. But psychoanalysis did find the following means, and fills the following function: causing beliefs to survive even after repudiation; causing those who no longer believe in anything to continue believing; reconstituting a private territory for them, a private *Urstaat*, a private capital (dreams as capital, said Freud).

That is why, inversely, schizoanalysis must devote itself with all its strength to the necessary destructions. Destroying beliefs and representations, theatrical scenes.

And when engaged in this task no activity will be too malevolent. Causing Oedipus and castration to explode, brutally intervening each time the subject strikes up the song of myth or intones tragic lines, carrying him back *to the factory*. As Charlus says, 'A lot we care about your grandmother, you little shit!' Oedipus and castration are no more than reactional formations, resistances, blockages, and armorings whose destruction can't come fast enough. Reich intuits a fundamental principle of schizoanalysis when he says that the destruction of resistances must not wait upon the discovery of the material.[10] But the reason for this is even more radical than he thought: there is no unconscious material, so that schizoanalysis has nothing to interpret. There are only resistances, and then machines desiring-machines. Oedipus is a resistance; if we have been able to speak of the intrinsically perverted nature of psychoanalysis, this is due to the fact that perversion in general is the artificial reterritorialization of the flows of desire, whose machines on the contrary are indices of deterritorialized production. The psychoanalyst reterritorializes on the couch, in the representation of Oedipus and castration. Schizoanalysis on the contrary must disengage the deterritorialized flows of desire, in the molecular elements of desiring-production. We should again call to mind the practical rule laid down by Leclaire, following Lacan, the rule of the right to non-sense as well as to the absence of a link: you will not have reached the ultimate and irreducible terms of the unconscious so long as you find or restore a link between two elements. (But how then can one see in this extreme dispersion – machines dispersed in every machine – nothing more than a pure 'fiction' that must give way to Reality defined as a lack, with Oedipus and castration back at a gallop, at the same time that one reduces the absence of a link to a 'signifier' of absence charged with representing the absence, with linking this absence itself, and with moving us back and forth from one pole of displacement to the other? One falls back into the molar hole while claiming to unmask the real.)

What complicates everything is that there is indeed a necessity for desiring-production to be induced from representation, to be discovered through its lines of escape. But this is true in a way altogether different from what psychoanalysis believes it to be. The decoded flows of desire form the free energy (libido) of the desiring-machines. The desiring-machines take form and train their sights along a tangent of deterritorialization that traverses the representative spheres, and that runs along the body without organs. Leaving, escaping, but while causing more escapes. The desiring-machines themselves are the flows-schizzes or the breaks-flows that break and flow at the same time on the body without organs: not the gaping wound represented in castration, but the myriad little connections, disjunctions, and conjunctions by which every machine produces a flow in relation to another that breaks it, and breaks a flow that another produces. But how would these decoded and deterritorialized flows of desiring-production keep from being reduced to some representative territoriality, how would they keep from forming for themselves yet another such territory, even if on the body without organs as the indifferent support for a last representation? Even those who are best at 'leaving', those who make leaving into something as natural as being born or dying, those who set out in search of nonhuman sex – Lawrence, Miller – stake out a far-off territoriality that still forms an anthropomorphic and phallic representation: the Orient, Mexico, or Peru. Even the schizo's stroll or voyage does not effect great deterritorializations without borrowing from territorial circuits: the tottering walk of Molloy and his bicycle preserves the mother's room as the vestige of a goal; the vacillating spirals of *The Unnamable* keep the familial tower as an uncertain center where it continues to turn while treading its own underfoot; the infinite series of juxtaposed and unlocalized parks in *Watt* still contains a reference to Mr Knott's house, the only one capable of 'pushing the soul out-of-doors', but also of summoning it back to its place. We are all little dogs, we need circuits, and we need to be taken for walks. Even those best able to disconnect, to unplug themselves, enter into connections of desiring-machines that re-form little earths. Even Gisela Pankow's great deterritorialized subjects are led to discover the image of a family castle under the roots of the uprooted tree that crosses through their body without organs.[11]

Previously we distinguished two poles of delirium, one as the molecular schizophrenic line of escape, and the other as the paranoiac molar investment. But the perverted pole is equally opposed to the schizophrenic pole, just as the reconstitution of territorialities is opposed to the movement of deterritorialization. And if perversion in the narrowest sense of the word performs a certain very specific type of reterritorialization within the artifice, perversion in the broad sense comprises all the types of reterritorializations, not merely artificial, but also exotic, archaic, residual, private, etc.: thus Oedipus and psychoanalysis as perversion. Even Raymond Roussel's schizophrenic machines turn into perverse machines in a theater representing Africa. In short, there is no deterritorialization of the flows of schizophrenic desire that is not accompanied by global or local reterritorializations, reterritorializations that always reconstitute shores of representation. What is more, the force and the obstinacy of a deterritorialization can only be evaluated through the types of reterritorialization that represent it; the one is the reverse side of the other. Our loves are complexes of deterritorialization and reterritorialization. What we love is always a certain mulatto – male or female. The movement of deterritorialization can never be grasped in itself, one can only grasp its indices in relation to the territorial representations. Take the example of dreams: yes, dreams are Oedipal, and this comes as no surprise, since dreams are a perverse reterritorialization in relation to the deterritorialization of sleep and nightmares. But *why return to dreams*, why turn them into the royal road of desire and the unconscious, when they are in fact the manifestation of a superego, a superpowerful and superarchaized ego (the *Urszene* of the *Urstaat*)? Yet at the heart of dreams themselves – as with fantasy and delirium – machines function as indices of deterritorialization. In dreams there are always machines endowed with the strange property of passing from hand to hand, of escaping and causing circulations, of carrying and being carried away. The airplane of parental coitus, the father's car, the grandmother's sewing machine, the little brother's bicycle, all objects of flight and theft, stealing and stealing away – the machine is always infernal in the family dream. The machine introduces breaks and flows that prevent the dream from being reconfined in its scene and systematized within its representation. It makes the most of an irreducible factor of non-sense, which will develop elsewhere and from without, in the conjunctions of the real as such. Psychoanalysis, with its Oedipal stubbornness, has only a dim understanding of this; for one reterritorializes on persons and surroundings, but one deterritorializes on machines. Is it Schreber's father who acts through machines, or on the contrary is it the machines themselves that function through the father? *Psychoanalysis settles on the imaginary and structural representatives of reterritorialization, while schizoanalysis follows the mechanic indices of deterritorialization.* The opposition still holds between the neurotic on the couch – as an ultimate and sterile land, the last exhausted colony – and the schizo out for a walk in a deterritorialized circuit.

[. . .]

The only thing that can save us from these impasses is an effective politicization of psychiatry. And doubtless, with R.D. Laing and David Cooper antipsychiatry went very far in this direction. But it seems to us that they still conceive of this politicization in terms of the structure and the event, rather than the process itself. Furthermore, they localize social and mental alienation on a single line, and tend to consider them as identical by showing how the familial agent extends the one into the other.* Between the two, however, the relationship is rather that of an *included disjunction.* This is because the decoding and the deterritorialization of flows define the very process of capitalism – that is, its essence, its tendency, and its external limit. But we know that the process is continually interrupted, or the tendency counteracted, or the limit displaced, by subjective reterritorializations and representations that operate as much at the level of capital as a subject (the axiomatic), as at the level of the persons serving as capital's agents (application of the axiomatic). But we seek in vain to assign social alienation and mental alienation to one side or the other, as long as we establish a relation of exclusion between the two. The deterritorialization of flows in general effectively merges with mental alienation, inasmuch as it *includes* the reterritorializations that permit it to subsist only as the state of a particular flow, a flow of madness that is defined thus because it is charged with representing whatever escapes the axiomatics and the applications of reterritorialization in other flows. Inversely, one can find the form of social alienation in action in all the reterritorializations of capitalism, inasmuch as they keep the flows from escaping the system, and maintain labor in the axiomatic framework of property, and desire in the applied framework of the family; but this social alienation includes in its turn mental alienation, which finds itself represented or reterritorialized in neurosis, perversion, and psychosis (the mental illnesses).

---

* David Cooper, 'Aliénation mentale et aliénation sociale', *Recherches*, December 1968, pp. 48–9: 'Social alienation comes for the most part to overlap the diverse forms of mental alienation. ... Those admitted into a psychiatric hospital are admitted not so much because they are sick, as because they are protesting in a more or less adequate way against the social order. The social system in which they are caught thereby comes to reinforce the damages wrought by the familial system in which they grew up. This autonomy that they seek to affirm with regard to a microsociety acts as an indicator of a massive alienation performed by society as a whole'.

A true politics of psychiatry, or antipsychiatry, would consist therefore in the following praxis: (1) undoing all the reterritorializations that transform madness into mental illness; (2) liberating the schizoid movement of deterritorialization in all the flows, in such a way that this characteristic can no longer qualify a particular residue as a flow of madness, but affects just as well the flows of labor and desire, of production, knowledge, and creation in their most profound tendency. Here, madness would no longer exist as madness, not because it would have been transformed into 'mental illness', but on the contrary because it would receive the support of all the other flows, including science and art – once it is said that madness is called madness and appears as such only because it is deprived of this support, and finds itself reduced to testifying all alone for deterritorialization as a universal process. It is merely its unwarranted privilege, a privilege beyond its capacities, that renders it mad. In this perspective Foucault announced an age when madness would disappear, not because it would be lodged within the controlled space of mental illness ('great tepid aquariums'), but on the contrary because the exterior limit designated by madness would be overcome by means of other flows escaping control on all sides, and carrying us along.*

It should therefore be said that one can never go far enough in the direction of deterritorialization: you haven't seen anything yet – an irreversible process. And when we consider what there is of a profoundly artificial nature in the perverted reterritorializations, but also in the psychotic reterritorializations of the hospital, or even the familial neurotic reterritorializations, we cry out, 'More perversion! More artifice!' – to a point where the earth becomes so artificial that the movement of deterritorialization creates of necessity and by itself a new earth. Psychoanalysis is especially satisfying in this regard: its entire perverted practice of the cure consists in transforming familial neurosis into artificial neurosis (of transference), and in exalting the couch, a little island with its commander, the psychoanalyst, as an autonomous territoriality of the ultimate artifice. A little additional effort is enough to overturn everything, and to lead us finally toward other far-off places. The schizoanalytic flick of the finger, which restarts the movement, links up again with the tendency, and pushes the simulacra to a point where they cease being artificial images to become indices of the new world. That is what the completion of the process is: not a promised and a pre-existing land, but a world created in the process of its tendency, its coming undone, its deterritorialization. The movement of the theater of cruelty; for it is the only theater of production, there where the flows cross the threshold of deterritorialization and produce the new land – not at all a hope, but a simple 'finding', a 'finished design', where the person who escapes causes other escapes, and marks out the land while deterritorializing himself. An active point of escape where the revolutionary machine, the artistic machine, the scientific machine, and the (schizo) analytic machine become parts and pieces of one another.

---

* Michel Foucault, 'La folie, l'absence d'oeuvre', *La Table ronde*, May 1964: 'Everything that we experience today in the mode of the *limit*, or of strangeness, or of the unbearable, will have joined again with the serenity of the positive'.

Notes

1. Henry Miller, *Hamlet* (Puerto Rico: Carrefour, 1939), vol. 1, pp. 124–9.
2. Michel Foucault, *The Order of Things* (New York: Random House, 1970), pp. 208–11 (on the opposition between desire or desiring-production and representation); pp. 253–6 (on the opposition between social production and representation, in Adam Smith and especially Ricardo).
3. On myth as the expression of the organization of a despotic power that represses the Earth, see Jean-Pierre Vernant, *Les origines de la pensée grecque* (Paris: Presses Universitaires de France, 1962), pp. 109–16; and on tragedy as the expression of an organization of the city-state that represses in its turn the fallen despot, Vernant, 'Oedipe sans complexe', *Raison présente*, August 1967.
4. Octave Mannoni *Clefs pour l'imaginaire ou l'autre scène* (Paris: Éditions du Seuil, 1969), Chs 1 and 7.
5. Louis Althusser and Etienne Balibar, *Reading Capital*, trans. Ben Brewster (New York: Pantheon, 1970).
6. Serge Leclaire, *Démasquer le réel* (Paris: Éditions du Seuil, 1971), pp. 28–31.
7. Elisabeth Roudinesco, 'L'action d'une métaphore', *La Pensée*, February 1972. See in Jacques Lacan, *Écrits* (Paris: Éditions du Seuil), p. 821, the way in which Lacan raises the idea of a 'signifier of the lack of this symbol' above the 'zero symbol', taken in its linguistic sense.
8. Sigmund Freud, 'Analysis terminable and interminable', *Standard Edition*, vol. 23, pp. 251–2.
9. Miller, *Hamlet*, pp. 124–5.
10. Wilhelm Reich, *The Function of the Orgasm*, trans. Vincent R. Carfagno (New York: Simon & Schuster, 1973), pp. 167–8. See also Wilhelm Reich, *Character Analysis* (New York: Simon & Schuster, 1974).
11. Gisela Pankow, *L'homme et sa psychose* (Paris: Aubier, 1969), pp. 68–72. And on the role of the house: 'La dynamique de l'espace et le temps vécu', *Critique*, February 1972.

3 □ *Feminism*

Introduction

Probably more than in any other field of theory, feminists have forwarded their projects methodologically through collaboration and argument. Reading 3.1 by Heidi Hartmann is typical in this respect. She establishes a position by working off, with and against other positions within socialist feminism and Marxism. Similarly, the locating of texts by Kristeva (Reading 1.3), Schor (Reading 2.5), Millett (Reading 2.3), Mouffe (Reading 4.7), Irigaray (Reading 5.6), and Benhabib (Reading 5.3) in other Sections at least illustrates the necessity for feminists to intervene in areas such as structuralism and post-structuralism, psychoanalytic theory, Marxism and postmodernism. Nevertheless, the case for a separate section on feminism is, if anything, stronger than for any other body of texts, and may even be analogous to claims which can be made on behalf of Critical Theory *vis-à-vis* the more context-specific, historically located activity of Cultural Studies. Even in this century, there are plenty of examples of periods when women were highly visible in social and political life at local and even national level, but feminism was unable to achieve much explanatory purchase, unable to become Theory (see Tallack, 1987). Although this Section cannot survey the current state of feminism, the role of feminism as Theory is an underlying concern, as is the basis of feminism as position in its intersections with other theoretical positions represented in this *Reader*. In addition to the relations with Marxism examined by Hartmann, the preceding Sections confirm – if confirmation is needed – that feminism has been significantly involved in the arguments of post-structuralism and psychoanalytic theory. It is also apparent from the Readings that a feminism of difference – meaning both the exploration and celebration of varying degrees of separatism from the larger society, or from projects whose assumptions are implicitly defined by men, as well as the claims made by women of colour – has questioned the tenets and ways of thinking associated with earlier feminists – Betty Friedan, Kate Millett, Shulamith Firestone and, to a lesser extent, Simone de Beauvoir.

The Reading from *Sexual Politics* (2.3) is a trenchant critique of Freud (too easily overlooked in the context of language-based readings of Freud), but does not do any justice to Kate Millett's formulation of patriarchy:

the relationship between the sexes is indeed a political one which involves the general control of one collectivity, defined by birth, over another collectivity, also defined by birth. Groups who rule by birthright are fast disappearing, yet there remains one ancient and universal scheme for the domination of one birth group by another – the scheme that prevails in the area of sex. ... [It is] sturdier than any form of segregation, and more rigorous than class stratification, more uniform, certainly more enduring. (Millett, 1971, pp. 24, 25)

While this is not an original theoretical insight, the distinction between sex and gender which Millett goes on to articulate gives the theoretical impetus to prise the cause of women away from arguments anchored in biology. However, there have been objections to Millett's apparently transhistorical definition of patriarchy. It is true, as Simone de Beauvoir observes in *The Second Sex*, that women have not been produced by history, as the traditional classes have, and that patriarchy persists; yet its configuration, and therefore its meaning, have changed. Moreover, class in the traditional sense does not disappear as a concept within either the male or the female sphere. Most importantly for feminism, patriarchy is not so all-encompassing that women have been unable to criticise and oppose it. The historical dimension of patriarchy – within which the gender- but not sex-defined woman must function in Millett's analysis – has been examined with particular care when Marxism and feminism have been in dialogue or in dispute, as Hartmann's account demonstrates.

In another of the classics of feminism, *The Dialectic of Sex* (1970) Shulamith Firestone finds the materialist basis for patriarchy which Millett's theory undoubtedly requires in a very particular interpretation of Friedrich Engels's account of the exploitation of female reproductive labour by men:

> Historical materialism is that view of the course of history which seeks the ultimate cause and the great moving power of all historical events in the dialectic of sex: the division of society into two distinct biological classes for procreative reproduction, and the struggles of these classes one with another; in the changes in the modes of marriage, reproduction and childcare. (Firestone, 1970, p. 20)

And later, in equally familiar language: 'the sexual-reproductive organization of society always furnishes the real basis, starting from which we alone can work out the ultimate explanation of the whole superstructure of economic, juridical and political institutions as well as the religious, philosophical and other ideas of a given period' (Firestone, 1970, p. 21). But this is to overlook the determining role of economic conditions and to substitute biology, with the result that only by technologically solving the realities of reproduction can any kind of dialectic of liberation be envisaged.

A more thoroughgoing historicisation of patriarchy than Firestone's needs, in the first instance, to move closer to Marx and Engels's broader definition of materialism, understood as a relationship to economic development leading to the formation of, and struggle between, classes. In Juliet Mitchell's *Woman's Estate*, Marx and Engels are followed up to a point; that is to say, economic determinants are accepted for the larger society and, in part, to explain women's position. However, Mitchell maintains that whatever progress is made towards economic equality, the family still functions ideologically – whereupon she introduces the psychodrama of the family romance, discussed in the Introduction to Section 2. To some degree, this is the different kind of approach – less materialist than psychoanalytic and ideological – which is required to explain why women occupy the subordinate positions. But Heidi Hartmann's charge is that male–female relations do have a material basis, though one which is slighted by Marxism's emphasis upon the link between social relations and capital. Marxism gives too little attention to women's exploitation as labourers in the home as well as in paid work, a problem which has hardly disappeared when socialism or communism has become dominant. At the crossover points, when women enter the paid labour force, Marxism's 'reserve army' theory is invaluable, but once they are removed from the labour market (as at the end of both World Wars) women slip out of focus, and the questions Why is the domestic sphere women's? and At what points are the interests of capital at odds with the interests of its male workers *vis-à-vis* 'their' women? are not answered. According to Hartmann:

> the categories of Marxist analysis ... do not explain why particular people fill particular places. They give no clues about why *women* are subordinate to *men* inside and outside the family and why it is not the other way around. *Marxist categories, like capital itself, are sex-blind.* (Hartmann, 1981, pp. 10–11)

Much of the work broadly classified as socialist feminism has come out of an Anglo-American tradition. Michèle Barrett, Sheila Rowbotham, Lydia Sargent, Iris Young and Zillah Eisenstein, as well as Mitchell and Hartmann, come to mind. However, in the absence of a Reading by her, it is especially important to comment on the contribution of Christine Delphy. Her work in a largely French intellectual tradition allows for a more direct comparison between post-structuralist and psychoanalytic feminism and socialist feminism. In the essays collected in 1984 as *Close to Home: A materialist analysis of women's oppression*, Delphy goes back to Marx and Engels – not to identify occasional instances of feminist awareness, but to borrow and re-use concepts which, in the account of capitalist relations, describe relations between men and women, primarily within the institution of marriage and the family: the appropriation of the woman's (unpaid) labour and the accompanying modes of domestic production; and the organisation of sexuality. Delphy's work should therefore be distinguished from arguments which situate the family wholly in the context of capitalism. Her distinct preference for economic relations between men and women as the cause of patriarchy, rather than the rule of the father (family business rather than family romance), puts her at odds with psychoanalytic feminists, while her rejection of biological explanations as reductive puts her at odds with theorists of difference who have celebrated the female world:

> One of the axioms if not the fundamental axiom of my approach is that women and men are *social* groups. I start from the incontestable fact that they are socially named, socially differentiated, and socially pertinent and I seek to understand these social practices ... it is women and men that interest me, not females and males. (Delphy, 1984; p. 24)

Delphy's work reveals a different dimension to French feminism in which economically grounded power relations, not the body, take priority.

Monique Wittig (see Reading 3.5) started the journal *Questions féministes* in 1977 with Christine Delphy (and Simone de Beauvoir), and they share many specific views – for instance that, in Wittig's words, 'there is no "feminine" writing'; as well as a similar constructionist objection to naturalising explanations: namely that when difference is discussed – particularly within the psychoanalytic context favoured by Irigaray and Cixous – this is liable to reinforce hierarchies. Wittig sets out the constructionist position with no qualifications:

> A materialist feminist approach shows that what we take for the cause or origin of oppression is in fact only the *mark* imposed by the oppressor ... what we believe to be a physical and direct perception is only a sophisticated and mythic construction, an 'imaginary formation' which reinterprets physical features ... through the network of relationships in which they are perceived. (They are seen *black*, therefore they *are* black; they are seen as *women*, therefore they *are* women. But before being *seen* that way, they had first to be *made* that way.) (Wittig, 1992, pp. 11–12)

Difference is a social construct, produced by the heterosexual regime of 'the straight mind'. Psychoanalytic theory is attacked as taking 'for granted that what founds society, any society, is heterosexuality' (Wittig, 1992, p. 24). Hence the importance, in Wittig's writings, of the lesbian who, for the straight mind, is not a woman at all: 'lesbians are not women' is the startling conclusion to 'The Straight Mind', meaning that they are not dependent upon men, this being the heterosexual definition of women. The lesbian, therefore, is proof of the social constructionist positions: 'a lesbian *has* to be something else, a not-woman, a not-man, a product of society, not a product of nature, for there is no nature in society' (Wittig, 1992, p. 13). To see the full importance – and some of the difficulties – of Wittig's position: her work may be compared and contrasted with Adrienne Rich's definition of lesbianism as part of a continuum of 'woman-identified experience'. In this sense, for Rich, 'all women are lesbians', a proposal which depends for its political efficacy upon the expansion of 'the erotic choice' to be a lesbian into 'conscious woman-identification' (Rich, 1980a, p. 659). Oddly, Wittig has to be definitive about 'the lesbian' in order to reveal the essentialism of other concepts. In *Essentially Speaking*, Diana Fuss's acute consideration of the contradictions in Wittig leads her to conclude that:

> As a materialist, Wittig states unequivocally that nothing exists prior to or outside matter, yet, as an anti-essentialist, she also suggests that the body is not matter – at least not in any pure or natural sense – but rather is a pure social construction. Obviously what we need to say here, as Wittig does, is that matter is itself socially constructed. But one can talk about the body as matter, it seems to me, without presuming that matter has an essence. Most anti-essentialists, however, are hesitant to discuss the body at all for fear of sounding essentializing. This caution leads Wittig, in the end, to elide the material body almost completely, and she achieves this lacuna

by effecting a nearly imperceptible slippage from the formulation 'the body *is* not matter' to the position 'the body *does* not matter': *it matters not.* (Fuss, 1989, p. 50)

With the help of Adrienne Rich's distinction between 'the body' and 'my body', Fuss goes on to maintain that to talk about the body seems more essentialist but is actually an abstraction; whereas to talk about one's own body is less totalising and essentialist, more specific and local and variable – but more material. It makes – as Fuss puts it – the body matter, and it gives a position from which to speak (see Fuss, 1989, pp. 52–3).

Hélène Cixous (see Reading 3.2) is the target of many of Wittig's and Delphy's criticisms. In part, this has to do with the intellectual context which informs Cixous's work and which only occasionally, and then in a rather unproductive way, abuts materialist, socialist feminism. For instance, Cixous's challenge to binary thinking in 'Sorties' (1975; see Cixous and Clément, 1986) is an important part of the internal revolution against structuralism. Cixous, like Derrida, argues that oppositions, and especially the opposition between male and female, are never in equilibrium but always denote the exertion of power, one term over the other. And, along with Kristeva (at least from *Revolution in Poetic Language* onwards) and Irigaray, Cixous draws heavily on Lacan. However, it is still the larger project of women's liberation from patriarchy which guides Cixous's involvement with other theoretical positions.

For all that 'différence' is a helpful notion for Cixous, her understanding and use of language is finally different from Derrida's. While both acknowledge the hierarchies of binary pairings, Derrida unsettles them – albeit temporarily – by reading against the dominant structures of any system, whereas Cixous wishes to release the potential in the secondary term. Her aim is partially realisable through what has come to be generalised as *écriture féminine*. This is a concept more to be enacted than to be defined, lest a rational(ising) discourse take over and reinstate the priority of one term in an opposition ('Head' over 'Emotions', 'Intelligible' over 'Sensitive', for instance). Cixous's own writing slips between genres, most commonly poetic prose and philosophical categorising (which she handles easily when required). Faced by objections that she is essentialising a category, she replies that she has been misread within a philosophical mode of expression. It is a version of the heresy of paraphrase with which poetic knowledge has often been defended. Even so, alongside Derrida, Cixous does seem to give free rein to what she sees as a female economy of writing which seeks to separate one term in any opposition from the other, whereas Derrida insists that the implication of one with the other is the real challenge to metaphysical thinking. A woman 'physically materializes what she's thinking; she signifies it with her body. In a certain way she *inscribes* what she's saying, because she doesn't deny her drives the intractable and impassioned part they have in speaking' (Cixous, 1981, p. 251). Feminine sexuality and feminine writing are heterogeneous, varied. But it is when Cixous is compared with Lacan that the full significance of speaking the body becomes apparent, because she favours the pre-Oedipal Imaginary and its symbiotic relationship with the mother over Lacan's orientation towards the Symbolic. To speak the body, for Cixous, is to articulate a different way of being from that under the Symbolic Order. 'Then,' she remarks, 'all the stories would have to be told differently, the future would be incalculable, the historical forces would, will, change hands, bodies; another thinking as yet not thinkable will transform the functioning of all society' (Cixous, 1981, p. 93).

In 'French feminism in an international frame', published in 1981 and included in *In Other Worlds*, Gayatri Spivak (see Reading 3.3) wonders about the value of feminist and avant-gardist theory more generally when they are brought up against other cultures. Accordingly, she offers a detailed critique of Kristeva's *About Chinese Women*, while Cixous's work is picked out for particular criticism because of the coincidence between the desire to liberate a feminine voice and avant-garde literary practice. In a contrasting register – oddly, one which is closer to Cixous's – Trinh T. Minh-ha (Reading 3.4) moves between theory and speculation to pursue Spivak's critique, regretting, in passing, the discrimination levelled against women of colour by white, First/Second World feminists. Dual systems analysis, which measures the relative explanatory power of the concepts of class and gender, is shown to be largely blind to race, ethnicity and nation. Trinh draws upon the advice of Audre Lorde (see Lorde, 1984) and Barbara Smith (see Hull, Scott and Smith, 1982), among others working on Afro-American feminism, to argue that 'difference' and 'authenticity' too easily become 'division' in academic discourse, and that difference needs to be reconceptualised by feminism in a cross-cultural perspective. She also points out the drawbacks – notably for women who are at least doubly disadvantaged – in opting for Kristeva's '"negative" feminist practice which continuously reminds us that "woman cannot be" or that we can no more speak about "woman" than "man"' (Trinh, 1989, pp. 103–4). The necessity for political action and a 'politics of location' (Adrienne Rich's phrase) also sharpens Spivak's perspective upon negativity and positivity. One of the consequences of her critical survey of French feminism, with its post-structuralist orientation, is that she feels obliged to define her relationship to Derridean deconstruction, acknowledging that there are limits to the negativity of deconstuction and its ability to remain undecided and in free play and, in response, delineating its 'positive' potential in a more explicitly political and historical context than she finds in much theory.

Post-structuralism, techno-feminism, the theorisation of difference from within feminism, and writing the body are all aspects of a reaction to 1970s feminism. The final reaction, represented by Carol Gilligan's work (Reading 3.6), is similar in a very broad sense to *écriture féminine*, inasmuch as it is woman-centred, but firmly in an Anglo-American context – and this, perhaps, makes all the difference. To accept as the standard of liberation the achievement of an androgynous state undermines the basis upon which women had come together and, effectively, denies women's experience. A further dimension of this change of tack, away from constructivism, is that women's experience and values can be seen as an indication of what could ensue if the demands of the women's movement were met and a male-dominated society were reformed or overturned. For instance, Adrienne Rich's

Of Woman Born, published in 1976, instigates a series of enquiries into the relationship between feminism and motherhood, a topic which Firestone's *Dialectic of Sex* had seemed to legislate against from within radical feminism. Rich's solution is to distinguish between the experience of mothering and how motherhood as an institution serves to maintain male power over women. The destruction of the institution of motherhood – and Rich recognises the need for alternative socioeconomic institutions that would free women – would be followed by almost unthought-of benefits for women, similar to those described by Irigaray and, more intangibly, by Cixous:

> I am really asking whether women cannot begin, at last, *to think through the body*, to connect what has been so cruelly disorganized – our great mental capacities, hardly used; our highly developed tactile sense; our genius for close observation; our complicated, pain-enduring, multi-pleasured physicality. (Rich, 1976, p. 284)

Although Carol Gilligan is also intent upon defending the particularity of women, her account of women's conception of morality takes society, rather than a separate woman-centred existence, as the larger context. To this extent, at least, she may be compared with Dorothy Dinnerstein and Nancy Chodorow who, in different ways, propose that the reform of society – and, within it, female–male relations – is best served by dual parenting. Dinnerstein (in *The Mermaid and the Minotaur* [1976]) and Chodorow (in *The Reproduction of Mothering* [1978]) go in search of explanations for why women and men are different, and find their answers in the pre-oedipal stage and women's monopoly of mothering, while male gender identity is thought to be formed out of separation and autonomy. Not unexpectedly, their work has fed into and stimulated the kinds of essentialist/non-essentialist discussions which have marked much of the theory summarised so far. Gilligan, however, concentrates upon the downgrading and even exclusion of women's moral views and ways of reasoning. Her own situation, as a student of psychologist Lawrence Kohlberg being taught to follow Kohlberg's six stages of human development, illustrates the way in which male views of morality-as-justice are taken as synonymous with the human response. Society is the poorer, Gilligan proposes. *In a Different Voice* (1982) is based on a case study of a group of twenty-nine women explaining their decision to have or not have an abortion. That her sample was sufficiently varied in age, ethnicity, class, and marital status suggests that, notwithstanding her reluctance to make such a claim, the version of the moral self emerging from the case study is a distinctively gendered one. Her case-study approach also lends itself to the conclusion that circumstances are crucial in how women reach a moral decision, while men abstract from the situation and focus on rights. This, though, has led to the retort that the ethics of care associated with women is a consequence of circumstances: women cope with and survive a patriarchal society by the process of reasoning which Gilligan describes.

Gilligan, Chodorow and Dinnerstein provide helpful comparisons and contrasts with the textualist and materialist feminisms which have been so influential over the past fifteen years. However – looking ahead to the final Section of this *Reader* – Gilligan's work seems to be having a delayed impact upon communicative ethics. For Seyla Benhabib (Reading 5.3), a contributor to this issue in her own right, Gilligan's research into the reversibility of perspectives in women's reasoning (or, to be more circumspect, in the reasoning of the women whom Gilligan studied) offers an antidote to the communicative rationality which Jürgen Habermas has promoted to deal with the down side of post-foundational theory. Gilligan deals with particularities rather than the generalities of her mentor, Lawrence Kohlberg, and has a concept of the other which is vital to any communicative ethics. It would be in the spirit of Gilligan's work, but also of Diana Fuss's important attempt to clarify the drawbacks of anti-essentialism (the drawbacks of essentialism are already well known), that the localised and ideologically inflected findings in *In a Different Voice* be subject to a process of translation, redescription and negotiation. Even the limited task of placing a theoretical text in a context (here, feminism), and then reflecting upon the validity of that decision, bears upon that process and upon feminism. With her own project in mind in *Situating the Self* (1992), Benhabib asks:

> Is it possible to reconcile the insight of feminist theory that gender difference is both central and ubiquitous in our lives with the kind of interactive universalism advocated in this book? Is not universalism of any sort, whether Kantian or Habermasian, incompatible with the goals and insights of feminism? (Benhabib, 1992, p. 146)

3.1 □ *The Unhappy Marriage of Marxism and Feminism: towards a more progressive union*

Heidi Hartmann

The 'marriage' of Marxism and feminism has been like the marriage of husband and wife depicted in English common law: Marxism and feminism are one, and that one is Marxism.[1] Recent attempts to integrate Marxism and feminism are unsatisfactory to us as feminists because they subsume the feminist struggle into the 'larger' struggle against capital. To continue our simile further, either we need a healthier marriage or we need a divorce.

The inequalities in this marriage, like most social phenomena, are no accident. Many Marxists typically argue that feminism is at best less important than class conflict and at worst divisive of the working class. This political stance produces an analysis that absorbs feminism into the class struggle. Moreover, the analytic power

Earlier drafts of this essay appeared in 1975 and 1977 co-authored with Amy B. Bridges. Unfortunately, because of the press of current commitments, Amy was unable to continue with this project, joint from its inception and throughout most of its long and controversial history. Over the years many individuals and groups offered us comments, debate, and support. Among them I would like to thank Marxist Feminist Group I, the Women's Studies College at SUNY Buffalo, the Women's Studies Program at the University of Michigan, various groups of the Union for Radical Political Economics, and Temma Kaplan, Anne Markusen, and Jane Flax for particularly careful, recent readings. A version substantially similar to the current one was published in *Capital and Class* in the summer of 1979. I would like to thank the editors of *Capital and Class*, Lydia Sargent, and other members of South End Press for their interest in this essay.

From Sargent, L. (ed.), *Women and Revolution: A discussion of the unhappy marriage of Marxism and feminism*, South End Press, Boston, MA, 1981, pp. 2–4, 9–11, 14–24, 27–41.

of Marxism with respect to capital has obscured its limitations with respect to sexism. We will argue here that while Marxist analysis provides essential insight into the laws of historical development, and those of capital in particular, the categories of Marxism are sex-blind. Only a specifically feminist analysis reveals the systemic character of relations between men and women. Yet feminist analysis by itself is inadequate because it has been blind to history and insufficiently materialist. Both Marxist analysis, particularly its historical and materialist method, and feminist analysis, especially the identification of patriarchy as a social and historical structure, must be drawn upon if we are to understand the development of Western capitalist societies and the predicament of women within them. In this essay we suggest a new direction for Marxist feminist analysis.

[. . .]

I. Marxism and the Woman Question

The woman question has never been the 'feminist question'. The feminist question is directed at the causes of sexual inequality between women and men, of male dominance over women. Most Marxist analyses of women's position take as their question the relationship of women to the economic system, rather than that of women to men, apparently assuming the latter will be explained in their discussion of the former. Marxist analysis of the woman question has taken three main forms. All see women's oppression in our connection (or lack of it) to production. Defining women as part of the working class, these analyses consistently subsume women's relation to men under workers' relation to capital. First, early Marxists, including Marx, Engels, Kautsky, and Lenin, saw capitalism drawing all women into the wage labor force, and saw this process destroying the sexual division of labor. Second, contemporary Marxists have incorporated women into an analysts of everyday life in capitalism. In this view, all aspects of our lives are seen to reproduce the capitalist system and we are all workers in the system. And third, Marxist feminists have focused on housework and its relation to capital, some arguing that housework produces surplus value and that houseworkers work directly for capitalists.

[. . .]

While the approach of the early Marxists ignored housework and stressed women's labor force participation, the two more recent approaches emphasize housework to such an extent they ignore women's current role in the labor market. Nevertheless, all three attempt to include women in the category working class and to understand women's oppression as another aspect of class oppression. In doing so all give short shrift to the object of feminist analysis, the relations between women and men. While our 'problems' have been elegantly analyzed, they have been misunderstood. The focus of Marxist analysis has been class relations; the object of Marxist analysis has been understanding the laws of motion of capitalist society. While we believe Marxist methodology *can* be used to formulate feminist strategy, these Marxist feminist approaches discussed above clearly do not do so, their Marxism clearly dominates their feminism.

As we have already suggested, this is due in part to the analytical power of Marxism itself. Marxism is a theory of the development of class society, of the accumulation process in capitalist societies, of the reproduction of class dominance, and of the development of contradictions and class struggle. Capitalist societies are driven by the demands of the accumulation process, most succinctly summarized by the fact that production is oriented to exchange, not use. In a capitalist system production is important only in so far as it contributes to the making of profits, and the use value of products is only an incidental consideration. Profits derive from the capitalists' ability to exploit labor-power, to pay laborers less than the value of what they produce. The accumulation of profits systematically transforms social structure as it transforms the relations of production. The reserve army of labor, the poverty of great numbers of people and the near-poverty of still more, these human reproaches to capital are by-products of the accumulation process itself. From the capitalist's point of view, the reproduction of the working class may 'safely be left to itself'.[2] At the same time, capital creates an ideology, which grows up along side it, of individualism, competitiveness, domination, and in our time, consumption of a particular kind. Whatever one's theory of the genesis of ideology one must recognize these as the dominant values of capitalist societies.

Marxism enables us to understand many aspects of capitalist societies: the structure of production, the generation of a particular occupational structure, and the nature of the dominant ideology. Marx's theory of the development of capitalism is a theory of the development of 'empty places'. Marx predicted, for example, the growth of the proletariat and the demise of the petty bourgeoisie. More precisely and in more detail, Braverman among others has explained the creation of the 'places' clerical worker and service worker in advanced capitalist societies.[3] Just as capital creates these places indifferent to the individuals who fill them, the categories of Marxist analysis, class, reserve army of labor, wage-laborer, do not explain why particular people fill particular places. They give no clues about why *women* are subordinate to *men* inside and outside the family and why it is not the other way around. *Marxist categories, like capital itself, are sex-blind.* The categories of Marxism cannot tell us who will fill the empty places. Marxist analysis of the woman question has suffered from this basic problem.

[. . .]

II. Radical Feminism and Patriarchy

[. . .]

Towards a Definition of Patriarchy

We can usefully define patriarchy as a set of social relations between n have a material base, and which, though hierarchical, establish interdependence and solidarity among men that enable them to dominate women. Though patriarchy is hierarchical and men of different classes, races, or ethnic groups have different places in the patriarchy, they also are united in their shared relationship of dominance over their women; they are dependent on each other to maintain that domination. Hierarchies 'work' at least in part because they create vested interests in the status quo. Those at the higher levels can 'buy off' those at the lower levels by offering them power over those still lower. In the hierarchy of patriarchy, all men, whatever their rank in the patriarchy, are bought off by being able to control at least some women. There is some evidence to suggest that when patriarchy was first institutionalized in state societies, the ascending rulers literally made men the heads of their families (enforcing their control over their wives and children) in exchange for the men's ceding some of their tribal resources to the new rulers.[4] Men are dependent on one another (despite their hierarchical ordering) to maintain their control over women.

The material base upon which patriarchy rests lies most fundamentally in men's control over women's labor-power. Men maintain this control by excluding women from access to some essential productive resources (in capitalist societies, for example, jobs that pay living wages) and by restricting women's sexuality.[5] Monogamous heterosexual marriage is one relatively recent and efficient form that seems to allow men to control both these areas. Controlling women's access to resources and their sexuality, in turn, allows men to control women's labor-power, both for the purpose of serving men in many personal and sexual ways and for the purpose of rearing children. The services women render men, and which exonerate men from having to perform many unpleasant tasks (like cleaning toilets), occur outside as well as inside the family setting. Examples outside the family include the harassment of women workers and students by male bosses and professors as well as the common use of secretaries to run personal errands, make coffee, and provide 'sexy' surroundings. Rearing children, whether or not the children's labor-power is of immediate benefit to their fathers, is nevertheless a crucial task in perpetuating patriarchy as a system. Just as class society must be reproduced by schools, workplaces, consumption norms, etc., so must patriarchal social relations. In our society children are generally reared by women at home, women socially defined and recognized as inferior to men, while men appear in the domestic picture only rarely. Children raised in this way generally learn their places in the gender hierarchy well. Central to this process, however, are the areas outside the home where patriarchal behaviors are taught and the inferior position of women enforced and reinforced: churches, schools, sports, clubs, unions, armies, factories, offices, health centers, the media, etc.

The material base of patriarchy, then, does not rest solely on childrearing in the family, but on all the social structures that enable men to control women's labor. The aspects of social structures that perpetuate patriarchy are theoretically identifiable, hence separable from their other aspects. Gayle Rubin has increased our ability to identify the patriarchal element of these social structures enormously by identifying 'sex/gender systems':

> a 'sex/gender system' is the set of arrangements by which a society transforms biological sexuality into products of human activity, and in which these transformed sexual needs are satisfied.[6]

We are born female and male, biological sexes, but we are created woman and man, socially recognized genders. *How* we are so created is that second aspect of the *mode* of production of which Engels spoke, 'the production of human beings themselves, the propagation of the species'.

How people propagate the species is socially determined. If, biologically, people are sexually polymorphous, and society were organized in such a way that all forms of sexual expression were equally permissible, reproduction would result only from some sexual encounters, the heterosexual ones. The strict division of labor by sex, a social invention common to all known societies, creates two very separate genders and a need for men and women to get together for economic reasons. It thus helps to direct their sexual needs toward heterosexual fulfillment, and helps to ensure biological reproduction. In more imaginative societies, biological reproduction might be ensured by other techniques, but the division of labor by sex appears to be the universal solution to date. Although it is theoretically possible that a sexual division of labor does not imply inequality between the sexes, in most known societies, the socially acceptable division of labor by sex is one which accords lower status to women's work. The sexual division of labor is also the underpinning of sexual subcultures in which men and women experience life differently; it is the material base of male power which is exercised (in our society) not just in not doing housework and in securing superior employment, but psychologically as well.

How people meet their sexual needs, how they reproduce, how they inculcate social norms in new generations, how they learn gender, how it feels to be a man or a woman – all occur in the realm Rubin labels the sex/gender system. Rubin emphasizes the influence of kinship (which tells you with whom you can satisfy sexual needs) and the development of gender-specific personalities via childrearing and the 'Oedipal machine'. In addition, however, we can use the concept of the sex/gender system to examine all other social institutions for the roles they play in defining and reinforcing gender hierarchies. Rubin notes that theoretically a sex/gender system could be female dominant, male dominant, or egalitarian, but declines to label various known sex/gender systems or to periodize history accordingly. We choose to label our present sex/gender system patriarchy, because it appropriately captures the notion of hierarchy and male dominance which we see as central to the present system.

Economic production (what Marxists are used to referring to as *the* mode of production) and the production of people in the sex/gender sphere both determine 'the social organization under which the people of a particular historical epoch and a particular country live', according to Engels. The whole of society, then, can be understood by looking at both these types of production and reproduction, people and things.[7] There is no such thing as 'pure capitalism', nor does 'pure patriarchy' exist, for they must of necessity coexist. What exists is patriarchal capitalism, or patriarchal feudalism, or egalitarian hunting/gathering societies, or matriarchal horticultural societies, or patriarchal horticultural societies, and so on. There appears to be no necessary connection between *changes* in the one aspect of production and changes in the other. A society could undergo transition from capitalism to socialism, for example, and remain patriarchal.[8] Common sense, history, and our experience tell us, however, that these two aspects of production are so closely intertwined that change in one ordinarily creates movement, tension, or contradiction in the other.

Racial hierarchies can also be understood in this context. Further elaboration may be possible along the lines of defining color/race systems, arenas of social life that take biological color and turn it into a social category, race. Racial hierarchies, like gender hierarchies, are aspects of our social organization, of how people are produced and reproduced. They are not fundamentally ideological; they constitute that second aspect of our mode of production, the production and reproduction of people. It might be most accurate, then, to refer to our societies not as, for example, simply capitalist, but as patriarchal capitalist white supremacist. In Part III below, we illustrate one case of capitalism adapting to and making use of racial orders, and several examples of the interrelations between capitalism and patriarchy.

Capitalist development creates the places for a hierarchy of workers, but traditional Marxist categories cannot tell us who will fill which places. Gender and racial hierarchies determine who fills the empty places. *Patriarchy is not simply hierarchical organization*, but hierarchy in which *particular* people fill *particular* places. It is in studying patriarchy that we learn why it is women who are dominated and how. While we believe that most known societies have been patriarchal, we do not view patriarchy as a universal, unchanging phenomenon. Rather, patriarchy, the set of interrelations among men that allow men to dominate women, has changed in form and intensity over time. It is crucial that the hierarchy among men, and their differential access to patriarchal benefits, be examined. Surely, class, race, nationality, and even marital status and sexual orientation, as well as the obvious age, come into play here. And women of different class, race, national, marital status, or sexual orientation groups are subjected to different degrees of patriarchal power. Women may themselves exercise class, race, or national power, or even patriarchal power (through their family connections) over men lower in the patriarchal hierarchy than their own male kin.

To recapitulate, we define patriarchy as a set of social relations which has a material base and in which there are hierarchical relations between men and solidarity among them which enable them in turn to dominate women. The material base of patriarchy is men's control over women's labor-power. That control is maintained by excluding women from access to necessary economically productive resources, and by restricting women's sexuality. Men exercise their control in receiving personal service work from women, in not having to do housework or rear children, in having access to women's bodies for sex, and in feeling powerful and being powerful. The crucial elements of patriarchy as we *currently* experience them are: heterosexual marriage (and consequent homophobia), female childrearing and housework, women's economic dependence on men (enforced by arrangements in the labor market), the state, and numerous institutions based on social relations among men – clubs, sports, unions, professions, universities, churches, corporations, and armies. All of these elements need to be examined if we are to understand patriarchal capitalism.

Both hierarchy and interdependence among men and the subordination of women are *integral* to the functioning of our society; that is, these relationships are *systemic*. We leave aside the question of the creation of these relations and ask: can we recognize patriarchal relations in capitalist societies? Within capitalist societies we must discover those same bonds between men which both bourgeois and Marxist social scientists claim no longer exist or are, at the most, unimportant leftovers. Can we understand how these relations among men are perpetuated in capitalist societies? Can we identify ways in which patriarchy has shaped the course of capitalist development?

III. The Partnership of Patriarchy and Capital

How are we to recognize patriarchal social relations in capitalist societies? It appears as if each woman is oppressed by her own man alone; her oppression seems a private affair. Relationships among men and among families seem equally fragmented. It is hard to recognize relationships among men, and between men and women, as *systematically* patriarchal. We argue, however, that patriarchy as a system of relations between men and women exists in capitalism, and that in capitalist societies a healthy and strong partnership exists between patriarchy and capital. Yet if one begins with the concept of patriarchy and an understanding of the capitalist mode of production, one recognizes immediately that the partnership of patriarchy and capital was not inevitable; men and capitalists often have conflicting interests, particularly over the use of women's labor-power. Here is one way in which this conflict might manifest itself: the vast majority of men might want their women at home to personally service them. A smaller number of men, who are capitalists, might want most women (not their own) to work in the wage labor market. In examining the tensions of this conflict over women's labor-power historically, we will be able to identify the material base of patriarchal relations in capitalist societies, as well as the basis for the partnership between capital and patriarchy.

Industrialization and the Development of Family Wages

Marxists made quite logical inferences from a selection of the social phenomena they witnessed in the nineteenth century. But Marxists ultimately underestimated the strength of the preexisting patriarchal social forces with which fledgling capital had to contend and the need for capital to adjust to these forces. The Industrial Revolution was drawing all people into the labor force, including women and children; in fact the first factories used child and female labor almost exclusively.[9] That women and children could earn wages separately from men both undermined authority relations [. . .] and kept wages low for everyone.

[. . .]

While the problem of cheap competition could have been solved by organizing the wage-earning women and youths, the problem of disrupted family life could not be. Men reserved union protection for men and argued for protective labor laws for women and children.[10] Protective labor laws, while they may have ameliorated some of the worst abuses of female and child labor, also limited the participation of adult women in many 'male' jobs.[11] Men sought to keep high-wage jobs for themselves and to raise male wages generally. They argued for wages sufficient for their wage labor alone to support their families. This 'family wage' system gradually came to be the norm for stable working-class families at the end of the nineteenth century and the beginning of the twentieth.[12] Several observers have declared the non-wage-working wife to be part of the standard of living of male workers.[13] Instead of fighting for equal wages for men and women, male workers sought the family wage, wanting to retain their wives' services at home. In the absence of patriarchy a unified working class might have confronted capitalism, but patriarchal social relations divided the working class, allowing one part (men) to be bought off at the expense of the other (women). Both the hierarchy between men and the solidarity among them were crucial in this process of resolution. Family wages may be understood as a resolution of the conflict over women's labor-power which was occurring between patriarchal and capitalist interests at that time.

Family wages for most adult men imply men's acceptance, and collusion in, lower wages for others – young people, women and socially defined inferior men as well (Irish, blacks, etc., the lowest groups in the patriarchal hierarchy who are denied many of the patriarchal benefits). Lower wages for women and children and inferior men are enforced by job segregation in the labor market, in turn maintained by unions and management as well as by auxiliary institutions like schools, training programs, and even families. Job segregation by sex, by insuring that women have the lower-paid jobs, both assures women's economic dependence on men and reinforces notions of appropriate spheres for women and men. For most men, then, the development of family wages secured the material base of male domination in two ways. First, men have the better jobs in the labor market and earn higher wages than women. The lower pay women receive in the labor market both perpetuates men's material advantage over women and encourages women to choose wifery as a career. Second, then, women do housework, childcare, and perform other services at home which benefit men directly.[14] Women's home responsibilities in turn reinforce their inferior labor market position.[15]

The resolution that developed in the early twentieth century can be seen to benefit capitalist interests as well as patriarchal interests. Capitalists, it is often argued, recognized that in the extreme conditions which prevailed in the early nineteenth century industrialization, working-class families could not adequately reproduce themselves. They realized that housewives produced and maintained healthier workers than wage-working wives and that educated children became better workers than noneducated ones. The bargain, paying family wages to men and keeping women home, suited the capitalists at the time as well as the male workers. Although the terms of the bargain have altered over time, it is still true that the family and women's work in the family serve capital by providing a labor force and serve men as the space in which they exercise their privilege. Women, working to serve men and their families, also serve capital as consumers.[16] The family is also the place where dominance and submission are learned, as Firestone, the Frankfurt School, and many others have explained.[17] Obedient children become obedient workers; girls and boys each learn their proper roles.

While the family wage shows that capitalism adjusts to patriarchy, the changing status of children shows that patriarchy adjusts to capital. Children, like women, came to be excluded from wage labor. As children's ability to earn money declined, their legal relationship to their parents changed. At the beginning of the industrial era in the United States, fulfilling children's need for their fathers was thought to be crucial, even primary, to their happy development; fathers had legal priority in cases of contested custody. As children's ability to contribute to the economic well-being of the family declined, mothers came increasingly to be viewed as crucial to the happy development of their children, and gained legal priority in cases of contested custody.[18] Here patriarchy adapted to the changing economic role of children: when children were productive, men claimed them; as children became unproductive, they were given to women.

The Partnership in the Twentieth Century

The prediction of nineteenth century Marxists that patriarchy would wither away in the face of capitalism's need to proletarianize everyone has not come true. Not only did Marxists underestimate the strength and flexibility of patriarchy, they also overestimated the strength of capital. They envisioned the new social force of capitalism, which had torn feudal relations apart, as virtually all powerful. Contemporary observers are in a better position to see the difference between the tendencies of 'pure' capitalism and those of 'actual' capitalism as it confronts historical forces in everyday practice. Discussions of the partnership between capital and racial orders and of labor market segmentation provide additional examples of how 'pure' capitalist forces meet up with historical reality. Great flexibility has been displayed by capitalism in this process.

[. . .]

If the first element of our argument about the course of capitalist development is that capital is not all-powerful, the second is that capital is tremendously flexible. Capital accumulation encounters preexisting social forms, and both destroys them and adapts to them. The adaptation of capital can be seen as a reflection of the *strength* of these preexisting forms to persevere in new environments. Yet even as they persevere, they are not unchanged. The ideology with which race and sex are understood today, for example, is strongly shaped by the particular ways racial and sexual divisions are reinforced in the accumulation process.

[. . .]

Ideology in the Twentieth Century

Patriarchy, by establishing and legitimating hierarchy among men (by allowing men of all groups to control at least some women), reinforces capitalist control, and capitalist values shape the definition of patriarchal good.

The psychological phenomena Shulamith Firestone identifies are particular examples of what happens in relationships of dependence and domination. They follow from the realities of men's social power – which women are denied – but they are shaped by the fact that they happen in the context of a capitalist society.[19] If we examine the characteristics of men as radical feminists describe them – competitive, rationalistic, dominating – they are much like our description of the dominant values of capitalist society.

This 'coincidence' may be explained in two ways. In the first instance, men, as wage laborers, are absorbed in capitalist social relations at work, driven into the competition these relations prescribe, and absorb the corresponding values.[20] The radical feminist description of men was not altogether out of line for capitalist societies. Secondly, even when men and women do not actually behave in the way sexual norms prescribe, men *claim for themselves* those characteristics which are valued in the dominant ideology. So, for example, the authors of *Crestwood Heights* found that while the men, who were professionals, spent their days manipulating subordinates (often using techniques that appeal to fundamentally irrational motives to elicit the preferred behavior), men and women characterized men as 'rational and pragmatic'. And while the women devoted great energies to studying scientific methods of childrearing and child development, men and women in Crestwood Heights characterized women as 'irrational and emotional'.[21]

This helps to account not only for 'male' and 'female' characteristics in capitalist societies, but for the particular form sexist ideology takes in capitalist societies. Just as women's work serves the dual purpose of perpetuating male domination and capitalist production, so sexist ideology serves the dual purpose of glorifying male characteristics/capitalist values, and denigrating female characteristics/social need. If women were degraded or powerless in other societies, the reasons (rationalizations) men had for this were different. Only in a capitalist society does it make sense to look down on women as emotional or irrational. As epithets, they would not have made sense in the Renaissance. Only in a capitalist society does it make sense to look down on women as 'dependent'. 'Dependent' as an epithet would not make sense in feudal societies. Since the division of labor ensures that women as wives and mothers in the family are largely concerned with the production of use values, the denigration of these activities obscures capital's inability to meet socially determined need at the same time that it degrades women in the eyes of men, providing a rationale for male dominance. An example of this may be seen in the peculiar ambivalance of television commercials. On one hand, they address themselves to the real obstacles to providing for socially determined needs: detergents that destroy clothes and irritate skin, shoddily made goods of all sorts. On the other hand, concern with these problems must be denigrated; this is accomplished by mocking women, the workers who must deal with these problems.

A parallel argument demonstrating the partnership of patriarchy and capitalism may be made about the sexual division of labor in the workforce. The sexual division of labor places women in low-paying jobs, and in tasks thought to be appropriate to women's role. Women are teachers, welfare workers, and the great majority of workers in the health fields. The nurturant roles that women play in these jobs are of low status because capitalism emphasizes personal independence and the ability of private enterprise to meet social needs, emphases contradicted by the need for collectively provided social services. As long as the social importance of nurturant tasks can be denigrated because women perform them, the confrontation of capital's priority on exchange value by a demand for use values can be avoided. In this way, it is not feminism, but sexism that divides and debilitates the working class.

IV. Towards a More Progressive Union

Many problems remain for us to explore. Patriarchy as we have used it here remains more a descriptive term than an analytic one. If we think Marxism alone inadequate, and radical feminism itself insufficient, then we need to develop new categories. What makes our task a difficult one is that the same features, such as the division of labor, often reinforce both patriarchy and capitalism, and in a thoroughly patriarchal capitalist society, it is hard to isolate the mechanisms of patriarchy. Nevertheless, this is what we must do. We have pointed to some starting places: looking at who benefits from women's labor-power, uncovering the material base of patriarchy, investigating the mechanisms of hierarchy and solidarity among men. The questions we must ask are endless.

Can we speak of the laws of motion of a patriarchal system? How does patriarchy generate feminist struggle? What kinds of sexual politics and struggle between the sexes can we see in societies other than advanced capitalist ones? What are the contradictions of the patriarchal system and what is their relation to the contradictions of capitalism? We know that patriarchal relations gave rise to the feminist movement, and that capital generates class struggle – but how has the relation of feminism to class struggle been played out in historical contexts? In this section we attempt to provide an answer to this last question.

Feminism and the Class Struggle

Historically and in the present, the relation of feminism and class struggle has been either that of fully separate paths ('bourgeois' feminism on one hand, class struggle on the other), or, within the left, the dominance of feminism by Marxism. With respect to the latter, this has been a consequence both of the analytic power of Marxism, and of the power of men within the left. These have produced both open struggles on the left, and a contradictory position for Marxist feminists.

Most feminists who also see themselves as radicals (anti-system, anti-capitalist, anti-imperialist, socialist, communist, Marxist, whatever) agree that the radical wing of the women's movement has lost momentum while the liberal sector seems to have seized the time and forged ahead. Our movement is no longer in that exciting, energetic period when no matter what we did, it worked – to raise consciousness, to bring more women (more even than could be easily incorporated) into the movement, to increase the visibility of women's issues in the society, often in ways fundamentally challenging to both the capitalist and patriarchal relations in society. Now we sense parts of the movement are being coopted and 'feminism' is being used against women – for example, in court cases when judges argue that women coming out of long-term marriages in which they were housewives don't need alimony because we all know women are liberated now. The failure to date to secure the passage of the Equal Rights Amendment in the United States indicates the presence of legitimate fears among many women that feminism will continue to be used against women, and it indicates a real need for us to reassess our movement, to analyze why it has been coopted in this way. It is logical for us to turn to Marxism for help in that reassessment because it is a developed theory of social change. Marxist theory is well developed compared to feminist theory, and in our attempt to use it, we have sometimes been sidetracked from feminist objectives.

The left has always been ambivalent about the women's movement, often viewing it as dangerous to the cause of socialist revolution. When left women espouse feminism, it may be personally threatening to left men. And of course many left organizations benefit from the labor of women. Therefore, many left analyses (both in progressive and traditional forms) are self-serving, both theoretically and politically. They seek to influence women to abandon attempts to develop an independent understanding of women's situation and to adopt the 'left's' analyses of the situation. As for our response to this pressure, it is natural that, as we ourselves have turned to Marxist analysis, we would try to join the 'fraternity' using this paradigm, and we may end up trying to justify our struggle to the fraternity rather than trying to analyze the situation of women to improve our political practice. Finally, many Marxists are satisfied with the traditional Marxist analysis of the women question. They see class as the correct framework with which to understand women's position. Women should be understood as part of the working class; the working class's struggle against capitalism should take precedence over any conflict between men and women. Sex conflict must not be allowed to interfere with class solidarity.

As the economic situation in the United States has worsened in the last few years, traditional Marxist analysis has reasserted itself. In the sixties the civil rights movement, the student free speech movement, the antiwar movement, the women's movement, the environmental movement, and the increased militancy of professional and white-collar groups all raised new questions for Marxists. But now the return of obvious economic problems such as inflation and unemployment had eclipsed the importance of these demands and the left has returned to the 'fundamentals' – working-class (narrowly defined) politics. The growing 'Marxist–Leninist preparty' sects are committed antifeminists, in both doctrine and practice. And there are signs that the presence of feminist issues in the academic left is declining as well. Day care is disappearing from left conferences. As Marxism or political economy become intellectually acceptable, the 'old boys' network of liberal academia is replicated in a sidekick 'young boys' network of Marxists and radicals, none the less male in membership and outlook despite its youth and radicalism.

The pressures on radical women to abandon this silly stuff and become 'serious' revolutionaries have increased. Our work seems a waste of time compared to inflation and unemployment. It is symptomatic of male dominance that *our* unemployment was never considered in a crisis. In the last major economic crisis, the 1930s, the vast unemployment was partially dealt with by excluding women from many kinds of jobs – one wage job per family, and that job was the man's. Capitalism and patriarchy recovered – strengthened from the crisis. Just as economic crises serve a restorative function for capitalism by correcting imbalances, so they might serve patriarchy. The thirties put women back in their place.

The struggle against capital and patriarchy cannot be successful if the study and practice of the issues of feminism is abandoned. A struggle aimed only at capitalist relations of oppression will fail, since their underlying supports in patriarchal relations of oppression will be overlooked. And the analysis of patriarchy is essential to a definition of the kind of socialism useful to women. While men and women share a need to overthrow capitalism they retain interests particular to their gender group. It is not clear – from our sketch, from history, or from male socialists – that the socialism being struggled for is the same for both men and women. For a humane socialism would require not only consensus on what the new society should look like and what a healthy person should look like, but more concretely, it would require that men relinquish their privilege.

As women we must not allow ourselves to be talked out of the urgency and importance of our tasks, as we have so many times in the past. We must fight the attempted coercion, both subtle and not so subtle, to abandon feminist objectives.

This suggests two strategic considerations. First, a struggle to establish socialism must be a struggle in which groups with different interests form an alliance. Women should not trust men to liberate them after the revolution, in part, because there is no reason to think they would know how; in part, because there is no necessity for them to do so. In fact their immediate self-interest lies in our continued oppression. Instead we must have our own organizations and our own power base. Second, we think the sexual division of labor within capitalism has given women a practice in which we have learned to understand what human interdependence and needs are. While men have long struggled *against* capital, women know what to struggle *for*.[22] As a general rule, men's position in patriarchy and capitalism prevents them from recognizing both human needs for nurturance, sharing, and growth, and the potential for meeting those needs in a nonhierarchical, nonpatriarchal society. But even if we raise their consciousness, men might assess the potential gains against the potential losses and choose the status quo. Men have more to lose than their chains.

As feminist socialists, we must organize a practice which addresses both the struggle against patriarchy and the struggle against capitalism. We must insist that the society we want to create is a society in which recognition of interdependence is liberation rather than shame, nurturance is a universal, not an oppressive practice, and in which women do not continue to support the false as well as the concrete freedoms of men.

Notes

1. Often paraphrased as 'the husband and wife are one and that one is the husband', English law held that 'by marriage, the husband and wife are one person in law: that is, the very being or legal existence of the women is suspended during the marriage, or at least is incorporated and consolidated into that of the Husband', I. Blackstone, *Commentaries*, 1965, pp. 442–5, cited in Kenneth M. Davidson, Ruth B. Ginsburg and Herma H. Kay, *Sex Based Discrimination* (St. Paul, MN: West Publishing Co., 1974), p. 117.
2. This is a paraphrase. Karl Marx wrote: 'The maintenance and reproduction of the working class is, and must ever be, a necessary condition to the reproduction of capital. But the capitalist may safely leave its fulfillment to the labourer's instincts of self-preservation and propagation'. [*Capital* (New York: International Publishers, 1967), vol. 1, p. 572.]
3. Harry Braverman, *Labor and Monopoly Capital* (New York: Monthly Review Press, 1975).
4. See Viana Muller, 'The formation of the state and the oppression of women: some theoretical considerations and a case study in England and Wales', *Review of Radical Political Economics*, vol. 9, no. 3 (Fall 1977), pp. 7–21.
5. The particular ways in which men control women's access to important economic resources and restrict their sexuality vary enormously, both from society to society, from subgroup to subgroup, and across time. The examples we use to illustrate patriarchy in this section, however, are drawn primarily from the experience of whites in Western capitalist countries. The diversity is shown in *Toward an Anthropology of Women*, ed. Rayna Rapp Reiter (New York: Monthly Review Press, 1975), *Woman, Culture and Society*, ed. Michelle Rosaldo and Louise Lamphere (Stanford, CA: Stanford University Press, 1974), and *Females, Males, Families: A biosocial approach*, by Liba Leibowitz (North Scituate, MA: Duxbury Press, 1978). The control of women's sexuality is tightly

linked to the place of children. An understanding of the demand (by men and capitalists) for children is crucial to understanding changes in women's subordination.

Where children are needed for their present or future labor-power, women's sexuality will tend to be directed toward reproduction and childrearing. When children are seen as superfluous, women's sexuality for other than reproductive purposes is encouraged, but men will attempt to direct it toward satisfying male needs. The Cosmo girl is a good example of a woman 'liberated' from childrearing only to find herself turning all her energies toward attracting and satisfying men. Capitalists can also use female sexuality to their own ends, as the success of Cosmo in advertising consumer products shows.

6. Gayle Rubin, 'The traffic in women', in *Anthropology of Women*, ed. Reiter, p. 159.
7. Himmelweit and Mohun point out that both aspects of production (people and things) are logically necessary to describe a mode of production because by definition a mode of production must be capable of reproducing itself. Either aspect alone is not self-sufficient. To put it simply, the production of things requires people, and the production of people requires things. Marx, though recognizing capitalism's need for people, did not concern himself with how they were produced or what the connections between the two aspects of production were. See Susan Himmelweit and Simon Mohun, 'Domestic labour and capital', *Cambridge Journal of Economics*, vol. 1, no. 1 (March 1977), pp. 15–31.
8. For an excellent discussion of one such transition to socialism, see Batya Weinbaum, 'Women in transition to socialism: perspectives on the Chinese case', *Review of Radical Political Economics*, vol. 8, no. 1 (Spring 1976), pp. 34–58.
9. It is important to remember that in the preindustrial period, women contributed a large share to their families' subsistence – either by participating in a family craft or by agricultural activities. The initiation of wage work for women both allowed and required this contribution to take place independently from the men in the family. The new departure, then, was not that women earned income, but that they did so beyond their husbands' or fathers' control. Alice Clark, *The Working Life of Women in the Seventeenth Century* (New York: Kelly, 1969) describes women's preindustrial economic roles and the changes that occurred as capitalism progressed. It seems to be the case that Marx, Engels, and Kautsky were not fully aware of women's economic role before capitalism.
10. Just as the factory laws were enacted for the benefit of all capitalists against the protest of some, so too, protective legislation for women and children may have been enacted by the state with a view toward the reproduction of the working class. Only a completely instrumentalist view of the state would deny that the factory laws and protective legislation legitimate the state by providing concessions and are responses to the demands of the working class itself.
11. For a more complete discussion of protective labor legislation and women, see Ann C. Hill, 'Protective labor legislation for women: its origin and effect', mimeographed (New Haven, CT: Yale Law School, 1970) parts of which have been published in Barbara A. Babcock, Ann E. Freedman, Eleanor H. Norton and Susan C. Ross, *Sex Discrimination and the Law: Causes and remedies* (Boston, MA: Little Brown & Co., 1975), an excellent law text. See also Hartmann, 'Capitalism, patriarchy, and job segregation by sex', *Signs: Journal of Women in Culture and Society*, vol. 1, no. 3, pt 2 (Spring 1976), pp. 164–6.
12. A reading of Alice Clark, *The Working Life of Women*, and Ivy Pinchbeck, *Women Workers*, suggests that the expropriation of production from the home was followed by a social adjustment process creating the social norm of the family wage. Heidi Hartmann, in *Capitalism and Women's Work in the Home, 1900–1930* (Unpublished Ph.D. dissertation, Yale University, 1974; forthcoming Temple University Press) argues, based on qualitative data, that this process occurred in the U.S. in the early twentieth

century. One should be able to test this hypothesis quantitatively by examining family budget studies for different years and noting the trend of the proportion of the family income for different income groups, provided by the husband. However, these data were not available in comparable form for our period. The family wage resolution has probably been undermined in the post World War II period. Carolyn Shaw Bell, in 'Working women's contribution to family income', *Eastern Economic Journal*, vol. 1, no. 3 (July 1974), pp. 185–201, presents current data and argues that it is now incorrect to assume that the man is the primary earner of the family. Yet whatever the *actual* situation today or earlier in the century, we would argue that the social norm *was* and *is* that men should earn enough to support their families. To say it has been the norm is not to say it has been universally achieved. In fact, it is precisely the failure to achieve the norm that is noteworthy. Hence the observation that in the absence of sufficiently high wages, 'normative' family patterns disappear, as for example among immigrants in the nineteenth century and Third World Americans today. Oscar Handlin, *Boston's Immigrants* (New York: Atheneum, 1968) discusses mid-nineteenth-century Boston, where Irish women were employed in textiles; women constituted more than half of all wage laborers and often supported unemployed husbands. The debate about family structure among Black Americans today still rages; see Carol B. Stack, *All Our Kin: strategies for survival in a Black community* (New York: Harper & Row, 1974), esp. Chap. 1. We would also argue (see below) that for most families the norm is upheld by the relative places men and women hold in the labor market.

13. Hartmann, *Women's Work*, argues that the non-working wife was generally regarded as part of the male standard of living in the early twentieth century (see p. 136, no. 6) and Ira Gerstein, 'Domestic work and capitalism', *Radical America*, vol. 7, no. 4–5 (July–October 1973) pp. 101–28, suggests that the norm of the working wife enters into the determination of the value of male labor-power (see p. 121).

14. The importance of the fact that women perform labor services for men in the home cannot be overemphasized. As Pat Mainardi said in 'The politics of housework', '[t]he measure of your oppression is his resistance' (in *Sisterhood is Powerful*, ed. Robin Morgan [New York: Vintage Books, 1970], p. 451). Her article, perhaps as important for us as Firestone on love, is an analysis of power relations between women and men as exemplified by housework.

15. Libby Zimmerman has explored the relation of membership in the primary and secondary labor markets to family patterns in New England. See her *Women in the Economy: A case study of Lynn, Massachusetts, 1760–1974* (Unpublished Ph.D dissertation, Heller School, Brandeis, 1977). Batya Weinbaum is currently exploring the relationship between family roles and places in the labor market. See her 'Redefining the question of revolution', *Review of Radical Political Economics*, vol. 9, no. 3 (Fall 1977), pp. 54, 78, and *The Curious Courtship of Women's Liberation and Socialism* (Boston, MA: South End Press, 1978). Additional studies of the interaction of capitalism and patriarchy can be found in Zillah Eisenstein, ed., *Capitalist Patriarchy and the case for Socialist Feminism* (New York: Monthly Review Press, 1978).

16. See Batya Weinbaum and Amy Bridges, 'The other side of the paycheck: monopoly capital and the structure of consumption', *Monthly Review*, vol. 28, no. 3 (July–August 1976), pp. 88–103, for a discussion of women's consumption work.

17. For the view of the Frankfurt School, see Max Horkheimer, 'Authority and the family', in *Critical Theory* (New York: Herder & Herder, 1972) and Frankfurt Institute of Social Research, 'The family', in *Aspects of Sociology* (Boston, MA: Beacon, 1972).

18. Carol Brown, 'Patriarchal capitalism and the female-headed family', *Social Scientist* (India), no. 40–41 (November–December 1975), pp. 28–39.

19. Richard Sennett's and Jonathan Cobb's *The Hidden Injuries of Class* (New York: Random House, 1973) examines similar kinds of psychological phenomena within hierarchical relationships between men at work.

20. This should provide some clues to class differences in sexism, which we cannot explore here.
21. See John R. Seeley *et al.*, *Crestwood Heights* (Toronto: University of Toronto Press, 1956), pp. 382–94. While men's place may be characterized as 'in production' this does not mean that women's place is simply 'not in production' – her tasks, too, are shaped by capital. Her nonwage work is the resolution, on a day-to-day basis, of production for exchange with socially determined need, the provision of use values in a capitalist society (this is the context of consumption). See Weinbaum and Bridges, 'The other side of the paycheck', for a more complete discussion of this argument. The fact that women provide 'merely' use values in a society dominated by exchange values can be used to denigrate women.
22. Lise Vogel, 'The earthly family', *Radical America*, vol. 7, no. 4–5 (July–October 1973), pp. 9–50.

3.2 □ *Sorties: Out and Out: attacks/ways out/forays*

Hélène Cixous

[. . .]

A Woman's Coming to Writing:
Who
Invisible, foreign, secret, hidden, mysterious, black, forbidden
Am I ...
Is this me, this no-body that is dressed up, wrapped in veils, carefully kept distant, pushed to the side of History and change, nullified, kept out of the way, on the edge of the stage, on the kitchen side, the bedside?
For you?
Is that me, a phantom doll, the cause of sufferings and wars, the pretext, 'because of her beautiful eyes', for what men do, says Freud, for their divine illusions, their conquests, their havoc? Not for the sake of 'me', of course. But for my 'eyes', so that I will look at you, so that he will be looked at, so that he will see himself seen as he wants to be. Or as he fears he is not. Me, nobody, therefore, or else the mother that the Eternal Male always returns to when seeking admiration.
Men say that it is for her that the Greeks launched a thousand ships, destroyed, killed, waged a fabulous war for ten-times-ten years – among men! For the sake of her, yonder, the idol, carried off, hidden, lost. Because it is for-her and without-her that they live it up at the celebration of death that they call their life.
Murder of the Other:
I come, biographically, from a rebellion, from a violent and anguished direct refusal to accept what is happening on the stage on whose edge I find I am placed, as a result of the combined accidents of History. I had this strange 'luck': a couple

From Cixous, H. and Clément, C., *The Newly Born Woman*, trans. B. Wing, Manchester University Press, Manchester, 1986, pp. 69–73, 78–86, 131.

200

of rolls of the dice, a meeting between two trajectories of the diaspora,[1] and, at the end of these routes of expulsion and dispersion that mark the functioning of Western History through the displacements of Jews, I fall. – I am born – right in the middle of a scene that is the perfect example, the naked model, the raw idea of this very process: I learned to read, to write, to scream, and to vomit in Algeria. Today I know from experience that one cannot imagine what an Algerian French girl was; you have to have been it, to have gone through it. To have seen 'Frenchmen' at the 'height' of imperialist blindness, behaving in a country that was inhabited by humans as if it were peopled by nonbeings, born-slaves. I learned everything from this first spectacle: I saw how the white (French), superior, plutocratic, civilized world founded its power on the repression of populations who had suddenly become 'invisible', like proletarians, immigrant workers, minorities who are not the right 'color'. Women.[2] Invisible as humans. But, of course, perceived as tools – dirty, stupid, lazy, underhanded, etc. Thanks to some annihilating dialectical magic. I saw that the great, noble, 'advanced' countries established themselves by expelling what was 'strange'; excluding it but not dismissing it; enslaving it. A commonplace gesture of History: there have to be *two* races – the masters and the slaves.

We know the implied irony in the master/slave dialectic: the *body* of what is strange must not disappear, but its force must be conquered and returned to the master. Both the appropriate and the inappropriate must exist: the clean, hence the dirty; the rich, hence the poor; etc.

So I am three or four years old and the first thing I see in the street is that the world is divided in half, organized hierarchically, and that it maintains this distribution through violence. I see that there are those who beg, who die of hunger, misery, and despair, and that there are offenders who die of wealth and pride, who stuff themselves, who crush and humiliate. Who kill. And who walk around in a stolen country as if they had had the eyes of their souls put out. Without seeing that the others are alive.

Already I know all about the 'reality' that supports History's progress: everything throughout the centuries depends on the distinction between the Selfsame, the ownself (– what is mine, hence what is good) and that which limits it: so now what menaces my-own-good (good never being anything other than what is good-for-me) is the 'other'. What is the 'Other'? If it is truly the 'other', there is nothing to say; it cannot be theorized. The 'other' escapes me. It is elsewhere, outside: absolutely other. It doesn't settle down. But in History, of course, what is called 'other' is an alterity that does settle down, that falls into the dialectical circle. It is the other in a hierarchically organized relationship in which the same is what rules, names, defines, and assigns 'its' other. With the dreadful simplicity that orders the movement Hegel erected as a system, society trots along before my eyes reproducing to perfection the mechanism of the death struggle: the reduction of a 'person' to a 'nobody' to the position of 'other' – the inexorable plot of racism. There has to be some 'other' – no master without a slave, no economico-political power without exploitation, no dominant class without cattle under the yoke, no 'Frenchmen' without wogs, no Nazis without Jews, no property without exclusion – an exclusion that has its limits and is part of the dialectic. If there were no other, one would invent it. Besides, that is what masters do: they have their slaves made to order. Line for line. They assemble the machine and keep the alternator supplied so that it reproduces all the oppositions that make economy and thought run.

The paradox of otherness is that, of course, at no moment in History is it tolerated or possible as such. The other is there only to be reappropriated, recaptured, and destroyed as other. Even the exclusion is not an exclusion. Algeria was not France, but it was 'French'.

Me too. The routine 'our ancestors, the Gauls' was pulled on me. But I was born in Algeria, and my ancestors lived in Spain, Morocco, Austria, Hungary, Czechoslovakia, Germany; my brothers by birth are Arab. So where are we in history? I side with those who are injured, trespassed upon, colonized. I am (not) Arab. Who am I? I am 'doing' French history. I am a Jewish woman. In which ghetto was I penned up during your wars and your revolutions? I want to fight. What is my name? I want to change life. Who is this 'I'? Where is my place? I am looking. I search everywhere. I read, I ask. I begin to speak. Which language is mine? French? German? Arabic? Who spoke for me throughout the generations? It's my luck. What an accident! Being born in Algeria, not in France, not in Germany; a little earlier and, like some members of my family, I would not be writing today. I would anonymiserate eternally from Auschwitz. Luck: if I had been born a hundred years earlier, I told myself, I would have been part of the Commune. How? – you? Where are my battles? my fellow soldiers? What am I saying ... the comrades, women, my companions-in-arms?

I am looking everywhere. A daughter of chance. One year earlier. A miracle. I know it; I hate it: I might never have been anything but dead. Yesterday, what could I have been? Can I imagine my elsewhere?

– I live all of my childhood in this knowledge: several times I have miraculously survived. In the previous generation, I would not have existed. And I live in this rebellion: it is impossible for me to live, to breathe, to eat in a world where my people don't breathe, don't eat, are crushed and humiliated. My people: all those that I am, whose same I am. History's condemned, the exiled, colonized, and burned.

Yes, Algeria is unliveable. Not to mention France.
Germany! Europe the accomplice! ...

– There has to be somewhere else, I tell myself. And everyone knows that to go somewhere else there are routes, signs, 'maps' – for an exploration, a trip. – That's what books are. Everyone knows that a place exists which is not economically or politically indebted to all the vileness and compromise. That is not obliged to reproduce the system. That is writing. If there is a somewhere else that can escape the infernal repetition, it lies in that direction, where *it* writes itself, where *it* dreams, where *it* invents new worlds.

And that is where I go. I take books; I leave the real, colonial space; I go away. Often I go read in a tree. Far from the ground and the shit. I don't go and read just to read, to forget – No! Not to shut myself up in some imaginary paradise. I am searching: somewhere there must be people who are like me in their rebellion and in their hope. Because I don't despair: if I myself shout in disgust, if I can't be alive without being angry, there must be others like me. I don't know who, but when I am big, I'll find them and I'll join them, I don't yet know where. While waiting, I want to have only my true ancestors for company (and even at that I forgive the Gauls a great deal, thanks to their defeat, they, too, were alienated, deceived, enslaved, it's true) – my true allies, my true 'race'. Not this comical, repulsive species that exercises power in the place where I was born.

And naturally I focused on all the texts in which there is struggle. Warlike texts; rebellious texts. For a long time I read, I lived, in a territory made of spaces taken from all the countries to which I had access through fiction, an antiland (I can never say the word 'patrie', 'fatherland', even if it is provided with an 'anti-') where distinctions of races, classes, and origins would not be put to use without someone's rebelling. Where there are people who are ready for anything – to live, to die for the sake of ideas that are right and *just*. And where it was not impossible or pathetic to be generous. I knew, I have always known, what I hated. I located the enemy and all his destructive figures: authority, repression, censorship, the unquenchable thirst for wealth and power. The ceaseless work of death – the constant of evil. But that couldn't last. Death had to be destroyed. I saw that reality, history, was a series of struggles, without which we would have long ago been dead. And in my mental voyage, I gave great importance to battlefields, conflicts, the confrontation between the forces of death and the forces of life, between wrong ideas and right ideas. Actually, I have always wanted war; I did not believe that changes would be made except through revolutionary movements. I saw the enormity of power every day. Nazism, colonialism, centuries of violent inequality, the massacre of peoples, religious wars. Only one answer – struggle. And without theorizing any of that, of course – I forged through the texts where there was struggle.

I questioned might – its use, its value; through a world of fiction and myths, I followed closely those who had it and who used it. I asked everywhere: where does your strength come from? What have you done with your power? What cause have you served? I watched the 'masters' especially closely – the kings, chiefs, judges, leaders, all those who I thought could have changed society; and then the 'heroes': that is to say, the persons endowed with an individual strength but without authority, those who were isolated, eccentric, the intruders: great, undaunted, sturdy beings, who were at odds with the Law.

[. . .]

The Empire of the Selfsame (Empirically from Bad to Worse)

For, unfortunately, Hegel isn't inventing things. What I mean is that the dialectic, its syllogistic system, the subject's going out into the other *in order to come back* to itself, this entire process, particularly described in the *Phenomenology of the Mind*, is, in fact, what is commonly at work in our everyday banality. Nothing is more frightening or more ordinary than Society's functioning the way it is laid out with the perfect smoothness of Hegelian machinery, exhibited in the movement through which one passes, in three stages, from the family to the State.

A historical process dynamized by the drama of the Selfsame [*Propre*]. Impossible to conceive of a desire that does not entail conflict and destruction. We are still living under the Empire of the Selfsame. The same masters dominate history from the beginning, inscribing on it the marks of their appropriating economy: history, as a story of phallocentrism, hasn't moved except to repeat itself. 'With a difference', as Joyce says. Always the same, with other clothes.

Nor has Freud (who is, moreover, the heir of Hegel and Nietzsche) made anything up. All the great theorists of destiny or of human history have reproduced the most commonplace logic of desire, the one that keeps the movement toward the other staged in a patriarchal production, under Man's law.

History, history of phallocentrism, history of propriation: a single history. History of an identity: that of man's becoming recognized by the other (son or woman), reminding him that, as Hegel says, death is his master.

It is true that recognition, following the phallocentric lead, passes through a conflict the brunt of which is borne by woman; and that desire, in a world thus determined, is a desire for appropriation. This is how that logic goes:

(1) Where does desire come from? From a mixture of difference and *inequality*. No movement toward, if the two terms of the couple are in a state of equality. It is always a difference of forces which results in movement. (Reasoning that is, therefore, based on 'physical' laws.)

(2) A little surreptitious slippage: the *sexual* difference with an *equality* of force, therefore, does not produce the movement of desire. It is *inequality* that triggers desire, as a desire – for appropriation. Without inequality, without struggle, there is inertia – death.

It is on this level of analysis (more or less conscious, depending on the supposed-masters) that what I consider to be the great masculine imposture operates:

One could, in fact, imagine that difference or inequality – if one understands by that noncoincidence, asymmetry – lead to desire without negativity, without one of the partner's succumbing: we would recognize each other in a type of exchange in which each one would keep the *other* alive and different. But in the (Hegelian) schema of recognition, there is no place for the other, for an equal other, for a whole and living woman. She must recognize and recuntnize the male partner, and in the time it takes to do this, she must disappear, leaving him to gain Imaginary profit, to win Imaginary victory. The good woman, therefore, is the one who 'resists' long enough for him to feel both his power over her and his desire (I mean one who 'exists'), and not too much, to give him the pleasure of enjoying, without too many obstacles, the return to himself which he, grown greater – reassured in his own eyes, is making.

All women have more or less experienced this cuntditionality of masculine desire. And all its secuntdary effects. The fragility of a desire that must (pretend to) kill its object. Fantasizing rape or making the transition to the act of rape. And plenty of women, sensing what is at stake there, cuntsent to play the part of object. ...

Why did this comedy, whose final act is the master's flirtation with death, make Bataille laugh so hard, as he amused himself by pushing Hegel to the edge of the abyss that a civilized man keeps himself from falling into? This abyss that functions as a metaphor both of death and of the feminine sex.

All history is inseparable from economy in the limited sense of the word, that of a certain kind of savings. Man's return – the relationship linking him profitably to man-being, conserving it. This economy, as a law of appropriation, is a phallocentric production. The opposition appropriate/inappropriate, proper/improper, clean/unclean, mine/not mine (the valorization of the selfsame), organizes the opposition identity/difference. Everything takes place as if, in a split second, man and being had propriated each other. And as if his relationship to woman was still at play as the possibility – though threatening, of the not-proper, not-clean, not-mine: desire is inscribed as the desire to reappropriate for himself that which seems able to escape him. The (unconscious?) stratagem and violence of masculine economy consists in making sexual difference hierarchical by valorizing one of the terms of the relationship, by reaffirming what Freud calls *phallic primacy*. And the 'difference' is always perceived and carried out as an opposition. Masculinity/femininity are opposed in such a way that it is male privilege that is affirmed in a movement of conflict played out in advance.

And one becomes aware that the Empire of the Selfsame is erected from a fear that, in fact, is typically masculine: the fear of expropriation, of separation, of losing the attribute. In other words, the threat of castration has an impact. Thus, there is a relationship between the problematic of the not-selfsame, not-mine (hence of desire and the urgency of reappropriation) and the constitution of a subjectivity that experiences itself only when it makes its law, its strength, and its mastery felt, and it can all be understood on the basis of masculinity because this subjectivity is structured around a loss. Which is not the case with femininity.

What does one give?

All the difference determining history's movement as property's movement is articulated between two economies that are defined in relation to the problematic of the gift.

The (political) economy of the masculine and the feminine is organized by different demands and constraints, which, as they become socialized and metaphorized, produce signs, relations of power, relationships of production and reproduction, a whole huge system of cultural inscription that is legible as masculine or feminine.

I make a point of using the *qualifiers* of sexual difference here to avoid the confusion man/masculine, woman/feminine: for there are some men who do not repress their femininity, some women who, more or less strongly, inscribe their masculinity. Difference is not distributed, of course, on the basis of socially determined 'sexes'. On the other hand, when I speak of political economy and libidinal economy, connecting them, I am not bringing into play the false question of origins – a story made to order for male privilege. We have to be careful not to lapse smugly or blindly into an essentialist ideological interpretation, as both Freud and Jones, for example, risked doing in their different ways. In the quarrel that brought them into conflict on the subject of feminine sexuality, both of them, starting from opposite points of view, came to support the formidable thesis of a 'natural', anatomical determination of sexual difference-opposition. On that basis, both of them implicitly back phallocentrism's position of strength.

We can recall the main lines of the opposing positions: Jones (in *Early Feminine Sexuality*) in an ambiguous move attacks the Freudian theses that make woman out to be a flawed man.

For Freud:

(1) The 'fate' of the feminine situation is an effect of an anatomical 'defect'.

(2) There is only one libido and it is male in essence; sexual difference is inscribed at the beginning of the *phallic phase* that both boys and girls go through. Until that point, the girl will have been a sort of little boy: the genital organization of the infantile libido is articulated through the equivalence activity/masculinity. The vagina has not yet been 'discovered'.

(3) Since the first object of love, for both sexes, is the mother, it is only in the boy that the love of the opposite sex is 'natural'.

For Jones: femininity is an autonomous 'essence'.

From the beginning (starting at the age of six months) the girl has a 'feminine' desire for her father; analysis of the little girl's most primitive fantasies would show, in fact, that in place of the breast, which is perceived as disappointing, the penis or (by an analogical shift) an object shaped like it is desired. One is already in the chain of substitutions, which means that the child, in the series of partial objects, would come to take the place of the penis ... for, to counter Freud, Jones obediently reenlists in Freudian territory. And overdoes it! He concludes from the equation breast-penis-child that the little girl feels a primary desire toward her father. (And the desire to have the father's child would be primary also.) He concludes that, of course, the girl has a primary love for the opposite sex as well. Therefore, she too has a right to her own Oedipus complex as a primary formation and to the threat of mutilation by the mother. In the end – a woman, that is what she is and with no anatomical defect: her clitoris is not a minipenis. Clitoral masturbation is not, as Freud claims, a masculine practice. And seeing the early fantasies, it would seem that the vagina is discovered extremely early.

In fact, by affirming that there is a specific femininity (all the while preserving orthodox theses elsewhere), Jones is still reenforcing phallocentrism under the pretext of taking femininity's side (and God's too, who, he reminds us, created them male and female!). And bisexuality disappears in the unbridged abyss separating the opponents here.

As for Freud, if one subscribes to what he says in his article on the *Disappearance of the Oedipus Complex* (1933) in which he identifies himself with Napoleon: 'anatomy is destiny', one participates in condemning woman to death. And in wrapping up all of History.

It is undeniable that there are psychic consequences of the difference between the sexes. But they certainly cannot be reduced to the ones that Freudian analysis designates. Starting from the relationship of the two sexes to the Oedipus complex, the boy and the girl are steered toward a division of social roles such that women 'inevitably' have a lesser productivity because they 'sublimate' less than men and that symbolic activity, hence the production of culture, is the work of men.[3]

Elsewhere, Freud starts from what he calls the *anatomical* difference between the sexes. And we know how that is represented in his eyes: by the difference between having/not having the phallus. By reference to those precious parts. Starting from what will take shape as the transcendental signifier with Lacan.

But *sexual difference* is not determined simply by the fantasized relation to anatomy, which depends to a great extent on catching *sight* of something, thus on the strange importance that is accorded to exteriority and to that which is specular in sexuality's development. A voyeur's theory, of course.

No, the difference, in my opinion, becomes most clearly perceived on the level of *jouissance*, inasmuch as a woman's instinctual economy cannot be identified by a man or referred to the masculine economy.

For me, the question asked of woman – 'What does she want?' – is a question that woman asks herself, in fact, because she is asked it. It is precisely because there is so little room for her desire in society that, because of not knowing what to do with it, she ends up not knowing where to put it or if she even has it. This question conceals the most immediate and most urgent question: 'How do I pleasure?' What is it – feminine *jouissance* – where does it happen, how does it inscribe itself – on the level of her body or of her unconscious? And then, how does it write itself?

One can ramble on for a long time about hypothetical pre-history and a matriarchal epoch. Or, like Bachofen,[4] one can attempt to prefigure a gynarchic society, drawing from it poetic and mythical effects, which have a powerfully subversive impact regarding the history of family and male power.

All the ways of differently thinking the history of power, property, masculine domination, the formation of the State, and the ideological equipment have some effect. But the change that is in process concerns more than just the question of 'origin'. There is phallocentrism. History has never produced or recorded anything else – which does not mean that this form is destinal or natural. Phallocentrism is the enemy. Of everyone. Men's loss in phallocentrism is different from but as serious as women's. And it is time to change. To invent the other history.

There is 'destiny' no more than there is 'nature' or 'essence' as such. Rather, there are living structures that are caught and sometimes rigidly set within historicocultural limits so mixed up with the scene of History that for a long time it has been impossible (and it is still very difficult) to think or even imagine an 'elsewhere'. We are presently living in a transitional period – one in which it seems possible that the classic structure might be split.

It is impossible to predict what will become of sexual difference – in another time (in two or three hundred years?). But we must make no mistake: men and women are caught up in a web of age-old cultural determinations that are almost unanalyzable in their complexity. One can no more speak of 'woman' than of 'man' without being trapped within an ideological theater where the proliferation of representations, images, reflections, myths, identifications, transform, deform, constantly change everyone's Imaginary and invalidate in advance any conceptualization.[5]

Nothing allows us to rule out the possibility of radical transformation of behaviors, mentalities, roles, political economy – whose effects on libidinal economy are unthinkable – today. Let us simultaneously imagine a general change in all the structures of training, education, supervision – hence in the structures of reproduction of ideological results. And let us imagine a real liberation of sexuality, that is to say, a transformation of each one's relationship to his or her body (and to the other body), an approximation to the vast, material, organic, sensuous universe that we are. This cannot be accomplished, of course, without political transformations that are equally radical. (Imagine!) Then 'femininity' and 'masculinity' would inscribe quite differently their effects of difference, their economy, their relationship to expenditure, to lack, to the gift. What today appears to be 'feminine' or 'masculine' would no longer amount to the same thing. No longer would the common logic of difference be organized with the opposition that remains dominant. Difference would be a bunch of new differences.

But we are still floundering – with few exceptions – in Ancient History.

The Masculine Future

There are some exceptions. There have always been those uncertain, poetic persons who have not let themselves be reduced to dummies programmed by pitiless repression of the homosexual element. Men or women: beings who are complex, mobile, open. Accepting the other sex as a component makes them much richer, more various, stronger, and – to the extent that they are mobile – very fragile. It is only in this condition that we invent. Thinkers, artists, those who create new values, 'philosophers' in the mad Nietzschean manner, inventors and wreckers of concepts and forms, those who change life cannot help but be stirred by anomalies – complementary or contradictory. That doesn't mean that you have to be homosexual to create. But it does mean that there is no *invention* possible, whether it be philosophical or poetic, without there being in the inventing subject an abundance of the other, of variety: separate-people, thought-/people, whole populations issuing from the unconscious, and in each suddenly animated desert, the springing up of selves one didn't know – our women, our monsters, our jackals, our Arabs, our aliases, our frights. That there is no invention of any other I, no poetry, no fiction without a certain homosexuality (the I/play of bisexuality) acting as a crystallization of my ultrasubjectivities.[6] I is this exuberant, gay, personal matter, masculine, feminine or other where I enchants, I agonizes me. And in the concert of personalizations called I, at the same time that a certain homosexuality is repressed, symbolically, substitutively, it comes through by various signs, conduct-character, behavior-acts. And it is even more clearly seen in writing.

Thus, what is inscribed under Jean Genêt's name, in the movement of a text that divides itself, pulls itself to pieces, dismembers itself, regroups, remembers itself, is a proliferating, maternal femininity. A phantasmic meld of men, males, gentlemen, monarchs, princes, orphans, flowers, mothers, breasts gravitates about a wonderful 'sun of energy' – love – that bombards and disintegrates these ephemeral amorous anomalies so that they can be recomposed in other bodies for new passions.

She is bisexual:

What I propose here leads directly to a reconsideration of *bixexuality*. To reassert the value of bisexuality;[7] hence to snatch it from the fate classically reserved for it in which it is conceptualized as 'neuter' because, as such, it would aim at warding off castration. Therefore, I shall distinguish between two bisexualities, two opposite ways of imagining the possibility and practice of bisexuality.

(1) Bisexuality as a fantasy of a complete being, which replaces the fear of castration and veils sexual difference in so far as this is perceived as the mark of a mythical separation – the trace, therefore, of a dangerous and painful ability to be cut. Ovid's Hermaphrodite, less bisexual than asexual, not made up of two genders but of two halves. Hence, a fantasy of unity. Two within one, and not even two wholes.

(2) To this bisexuality that melts together and effaces, wishing to avert castration, I oppose the *other bisexuality*, the one with which every subject, who is not shut up inside the spurious Phallocentric Performing Theater, sets up his or her erotic universe. Bisexuality – that is to say the location within oneself of the presence of both sexes, evident and insistent in different ways according to the individual, the nonexclusion of difference or of a sex, and starting with this 'permission' one gives oneself, the multiplication of the effects of desire's inscription on every part of the body and the other body.

For historical reasons, at the present time it is woman who benefits from and opens up within this bisexuality beside itself, which does not annihilate differences but cheers them on, pursues them, adds more: in a certain way *woman is bisexual* – man having been trained to aim for glorious phallic monosexuality. By insisting on the primacy of the phallus and implementing it, phallocratic ideology has produced more than one victim. As a woman, I could be obsessed by the scepter's great shadow, and they told me: adore it, that thing you don't wield.

But at the same time, man has been given the grotesque and unenviable fate of being reduced to a single idol with clay balls. And terrified of homosexuality, as Freud and his followers remark. Why does man fear *being* a woman? Why this refusal [*Ablehnung*] of femininity? The question that stumps Freud. The 'bare rock' of castration. For Freud, the repressed is not the other sex defeated by the dominant sex, as his friend Fliess (to whom Freud owes the theory of bisexuality) believed; what is repressed is leaning toward one's own sex.

Psychoanalysis is formed on the basis of woman and has repressed (not all that successfully) the femininity of masculine sexuality, and now the account it gives is hard to disprove.

We women, the derangers, know it only too well. But nothing compels us to deposit our lives in these lack-banks; to think that the subject is constituted as the last stage in a drama of bruising rehearsals; to endlessly bail out the father's religion. Because we don't desire it. We don't go round and round the supreme hole. We have no *woman's* reason to pay allegiance to the negative. What is feminine (the poets suspected it) affirms: ... and yes I said yes I will Yes, says Molly (in her rapture), carrying *Ulysses* with her in the direction of a new writing; I said yes, I will Yes.

To say that woman is somehow bisexual is an apparently paradoxical way of displacing and reviving the question of difference. And therefore of writing as 'feminine' or 'masculine'.

I will say: today, writing is woman's. That is not a provocation, it means that woman admits there is an other. In her becoming-woman, she has not erased the bisexuality latent in the girl as in the boy. Femininity and bisexuality go together, in a combination that varies according to the individual, spreading the intensity of its force differently and (depending on the moments of their history) privileging one component or another. It is much harder for man to let the other come through him. Writing is the passageway, the entrance, the exit, the dwelling place of the other in me – the other that I am and am not, that I don't know how to be, but that I feel passing, that makes me live – that tears me apart, disturbs me, changes me, who? – a feminine one, a masculine one, some? – several, some unknown, which is indeed what gives me the desire to know and from which all life soars. This peopling gives neither rest nor security, always disturbs the relationship to 'reality', produces an uncertainty that gets in the way of the subject's socialization. It is distressing, it wears you out; and for men this permeability, this nonexclusion, is a threat, something intolerable.

Notes

1. My father, Sephardic – Spain – Morocco – Algeria – my mother, Ashkenazy – Austria – Hungary – Czechoslavakia (her father) and Spain (her mother) passing by chance through a Paris that was short-lived.
2. Women: at that time I wasn't thinking about them. At first, occupying the stage in a way that I could plainly see, the battle to death was the battle pitting colonial power against its victims. Beyond that I perceived that it was the imperialist result of capitalist structure and that it intensified the class struggle by deepening it and making it more monstrous and inhuman: the exploited were not even 'workers' but, with racism's assistance, something worse – subhuman; and the universe could pretend to obey 'natural' laws. War was on the horizon, partially concealed from me. I wasn't in France. I didn't see betrayal and collaboration with my own eyes. We were living under Vichy: I perceived its effects without knowing their causes. I had to guess why my father couldn't do his work, why I couldn't go to school, et cetera. And I had to guess why, as a little white girl informed me, 'all Jews are liars'.
3. Freud's thesis is the following: when the Oedipus complex disappears, the *superego* becomes its heir. The moment a boy starts to feel the threat of castration, he begins to overcome the Oedipus complex, with the help of a very harsh superego. For the boy, the

Oedipus complex is a primary formation – his first love object is the mother, as it is for the girl. But the girl's history is inevitably constituted under the pressure of a superego that is less harsh: because she is castrated, her superego will not be as strong. She never completely overcomes the Oedipus complex. The feminine Oedipus complex is not a primary formation. The pre-Oedipal attachment to the mother entails a difficulty for the girl from which, Freud says, she never recovers. It is having to change objects (to love the father) along the way – a painful conversion, which is accompanied by a supplementary renunciation: the passage from pre-Oedipal sexuality to 'normal' sexuality supposes the abandonment of the clitoris for the vagina. In the terms of this 'destiny', women have a reduced symbolic activity: they have nothing to lose, to win, or to defend.

4. J.-J. Bachofen (1815–76), a Swiss historian of 'gynocracy', 'historian' of a nonhistory. His aim is to show that the various peoples (Greek, Roman, Hebrew) have passed through an age of 'gynocracy', the reign of the Mother, before arriving at patriarchy. This age can only be deduced, for it remains without history. This situation, which was humiliating for men, has been repressed, according to Bachofen's theory, and covered by historical oblivion. And he attempts (particularly in *Das Mutterrecht* [*Mother Right*] 1861) to make an archeology of the matriarchal system, which is very beautiful, beginning with a reading of the first historical texts on the level of the symptom, of what is unsaid in them. Gynocracy, he says, is organized materialism.

5. There are encoded paradigms projecting the robot couple man/woman, as seen by contemporary societies that are symptomatic of a consensus of repetition. See the UNESCO issue of 1975, which is devoted to the International Woman's Year.

6. *Prénoms de Personne* [*Nobody's First Names*], Cixous, Éditions du Seuil: 'Les Comtes de Hoffmann' ['Tales of Hoffmann'], pp. 112 ff.

7. See *Nouvelle Revue de Psychoanalyse*, no. 7, *Bisexualité et différence des sexes* (Spring 1973).

3.3 □ *Feminism and Deconstruction, Again: negotiations*

Gayatri Chakravorty Spivak

[. . .]

It is not just that deconstruction cannot found a politics, while other ways of thinking can. It is that deconstruction can make founded political programs more useful by making their in-built problems more visible. To act is therefore not to ignore deconstruction, but actively to transgress it without giving it up. (A slightly tougher formulation which clarity-fetishists can ignore: deconstruction does not aim at *praxis* or theoretical practice but lives in the persistent crisis or unease of the moment of *techñe* or crafting.) Feminism has a special situation here because, among the many names that Derrida gives to the problem/solution of founded programs, one is 'woman'. I explain in this chapter [of *Outside in the Teaching Machine*] why feminism should keep to the critical intimacy of deconstruction but give up its attachment to that specific name for the problem/solution of founded programs (also named 'writing'). I put it so awkwardly because so-called 'political' academics will still insist that writing is only script and make the blindingly brilliant critique that Derrida ignores mothers speaking to infants, or ignores orature.[1]

This is a more charitable position on the usefulness of deconstruction for feminism than I have supported in the past. It is a negotiation and an acknowledgment of complicity. This is a result of a growing sense that, at home and abroad, postcolonials and migrants are still coming to terms with unacknowledged complicity with the culture of imperialism, in a whole range of experiences including the failure of secularism and the Eurocentrism of economic migration. There may be something like a relationship with how feminists and indeed women in general deal with patriarchy and feminist theory.[2]

The chapter is written in the musing style of speaking to my 'school-mates', the occasion being Teresa Brennan's invitation to speak to feminists generally sympathetic to poststructuralism and psychoanalysis in a seminar series at Cambridge in 1987.

Spivak, G. C., *Outside in the Teaching Machine*, Routledge, New York, 1993, pp. 121–40, 305–9.

I first conceived of the line of thought pursued in the following pages immediately after six months of teaching in Delhi and Calcutta. Teaching for the first time in the country of my citizenship, and occasionally in my own language, was an unsettling and ambivalent experience. The measure of my unease will be sensed when I point out that I found a resonance in Thomas Nagel's reflections on the Vietnam years:

> the United States was engaged in a criminal war, criminally conducted. This produced a heightened sense of the absurdity of my theoretical pursuits. Citizenship is a surprisingly strong bond, even for those of us whose patriotic feelings are weak. We read the newspaper every day with rage and horror, and it was different from reading about the crimes of another country. Those feelings led to the growth in the late 1960s of serious professional work by philosophers on public issues.[3]

Rajiv Gandhi and his centralized power-structure were attempting to redefine India as the habitation of the tiny percentage of the taxpaying upper crust. That is my class alliance, which I felt much more strongly than my class-position as an academic in a trivial discipline in the United States. Those were also the months of the crisis of the Bofors arms scandal, not much publicized in the international press but certainly disturbing to a critic who regularly theorized the 'epistemic violence' of imperialism. It did not help that that particular crisis was later managed by the Indian intervention in the Sri Lankan Civil War. (Again, the intervening years have left their mark on this narrative. Does one ever catch up with the history of the present? I have come to sense that my unease had something to do not only with the culture of 'old' imperialisms, but with the relationship between the new economic migrant to the United States and the country of her origin, thus the 'new' imperialism; citizenship as a pious mark of perceived difference rather than sameness, on both sides. This sense bleeds into forthcoming work. In that balance, two fresh entries, adding to the bond of [a] citizenship there, [b] migrancy here: [a] Religious fundamentalism and the relationship between secularism and the culture of 'old' imperialism [...] [b] the Gulf War and the New World Order, the breakup of the remnants of India's old protected economy and the much greater role played by the IMF and the World Bank in the new 'liberalized' polity, perceived by the *New York Times* as the end of 'the political era in which India emerged from colonialism'.)[4]

The position of academic feminism in the elite universities in the two Indian cities where I worked was not strikingly different from the United States, where I habitually teach. And I am not given to unquestioning benevolence towards that dubious category – 'Third World Woman'. Yet, there was produced in me, not infrequently during my time in India, 'a heightened sense of the absurdity of my theoretical pursuits'. When I spoke in Cambridge in response to Teresa Brennan's invitation, immediately after leaving India, I found myself considering the relationship between feminism and deconstruction in terms of that sense of absurdity.

Before I could embark on such a chastening project, it seemed necessary to situate a sympathetic misrepresentation of the connection between the two movements. In that spirit I offered a reading of a few pages from a book then recently out, Jacqueline Rose's *Sexuality in the Field of Vision*.[5]

At the end of Rose's introduction to her book, there is a dismissal of Derrida as a certain kind of subjectivist essentialist. Unlike Elaine Showalter's or, more recently, Margaret Homan's dismissals of deconstruction, Rose's text is based on a *reading* of Derrida.[6] When I deal with this dismissal, you see me defending a sort-of-Derrida against Rose defending a sort-of-Lacan. This is yet another instance of 'the [necessary] absurdity of [our] theoretical pursuits'. Those few months in India, spent as a diasporic Indian and a working academic, gave me a sense of how peculiarly uneasy people were about the cultural legacy of imperialism. This was certainly true in my own class but was also pervasive, however inarticulately, across the classes. The unease straddled the genders, and in its context, varieties of elite nativism or isolationist nationalism seemed peculiarly out of touch with national and international 'realities'. The practical effects of this legacy will escape theoretical negotiations into the veining of traces even as those negotiations become more possible, more authoritative.[7] As a reminder of this unease, and in response to Brennan's specific invitation, I felt I must reckon with the legacy of patriarchy which, like the culture of imperialism, is a dubious gift that we can only transform if we acknowledge it. In the strictest sense, feminism is 'subsumed' in patriarchy. My entire discussion of Rose must be read as framed by this necessary absurdity.

I agree with Rose that 'to understand subjectivity, sexual difference and fantasy, in a way that neither entrenches the terms nor denies them' remains a crucial task for today.[8] On these terms, in fact, there is not much difference between how she understands Lacan and how I understand deconstruction. For Rose, 'only the concept of a subjectivity at odds with itself gives back to women the right to an impasse at the point of sexual identity, with no nostalgia whatsoever for its possible or future integration into a norm'.[9] This desire for an impasse is not unlike the desire for the abyss or infinite regression for which deconstruction must perpetually account. I do, of course, declare myself bound by that desire. The difference between Rose and myself here is that what she feels is a right to be claimed, I am obliged to recognize as a bind to be watched.[10] I think the difference between us in this context comes from Rose's understanding of deconstruction as *only* a narrative of the fully dispersed and decentered subject. I am not myself suggesting a strict opposition between structure and narrative, or morphology and narrative. But I do want to insist that when it is understood only as a narrative, deconstruction is only the picture of an impossibility that cannot help *any* political position. Or perhaps it can, only too easily. (I am thinking here of other arguments, relying on a trivialized description of deconstruction as a narrative, arguments which suggest, for example, that since women are naturally decentered, deconstruction is good for feminism and vice versa.)

In her introduction to *Sexuality in the Field of Vision*, Rose is by no means a trivializer, but seems still to understand deconstruction only as a narrative. One way of showing this is to bring a different understanding of deconstruction to bear on Jacqueline Rose's general presentation of psychoanalysis as a project.

It seems to me that, for Rose, the psychoanalytic project is a kind of epistemological project, through which women and men understand their ontology in terms of (or at least not excluding) sexual difference:

> Feminism must depend on psychoanalysis because the issue of how individuals recognize themselves as male or female, the demand that they do so, seems to stand in such fundamental relation to the forms of inequality and subordination which it is feminism's objective to change.[11]

This sentence is, I think, about male and female subjects construing themselves as knowable objects, especially if I am right in thinking that the word 'recognize' is doing duty here for the more critical 'cognize'. Now the antisexist project of feminism bases itself upon the conviction that distinctions arising in social practice out of the declaration of a fundamental ontic difference are, more often than not, incorrect, because, like most declarations of difference, these involve a dissimulated ranking. The range of such social practices runs from sociobiology to corporate (civil) and familial (domestic) practice. Rose's new epistemological itinerary will allow us to correct this. It will use the epistemology of sexual difference as an answer to the ontological question: what am I (woman)? and then to an accounting of that epistemology: how do I recognize myself (woman)?

It is, however, the next step, contained in the last part of the sentence from Rose quoted above, which gives me trouble. That step covers the quick shift from epistemology/ontology to the ethicopolitical project. The subject recognizing herself (woman) seems in Rose's reading to do so in order to act in the interests of psychosocial justice: in a 'fundamental relation to the forms of inequality and subordination which it is feminism's objective to change'. Rose's position is of course sufficiently subtle. She is aware that 'femininity [the formula for this ontic secret that we discover through the epistemological itinerary of the divided subject – woman] in psychoanalysis, is neither simply achieved nor is it ever complete'. It none the less involves that unacknowledged shift I have described between epistemology/ontology on the one hand and ethicopolitics on the other. If, as Rose suggests, it is crucial to admit the division in the subject, it seems to me no less crucial to admit the irreducible difference between the subject (woman) of that epistemology, and the subject (feminist) of this ethicopolitics.[12] In the previous chapter, I have touched upon the fact that Marxism foundered on this difference. In my new and forthcoming work, I am concentrating upon this difference straddling the division between the women's movement and feminist theory.

If one looks at the deconstructive *morphology* (rather than simply reading it as the narrative of the decentered subject), then one is obliged to notice that deconstruction has always been about the limits of epistemology. It sees the ontological impetus as a program implicated in the writing of the name of Man.[13]

Let me emphasize this by reopening *Spurs*, where Derrida comments on Heidegger and his reading of Nietzsche.[14] Simplifying Derrida's argument a little, we could read it as follows: there is a question which is precomprehended even by the careful

subtlety of the Heideggerian articulation of the ontico-ontological difference. Simplifying that Heideggerian subtlety, we might summarize it as follows: Heidegger
suggests that *Dasein* is ontically programmed to ask the ontological question, *and*
not to be able to answer it. This is undoubtedly a corrective for any account which
assumes that when we look for an epistemological itinerary to cleanse the
ontological account of ourselves, this might contribute or, indeed, lead to correct
psychosexual ethicopolitical action. (One may argue that 'correct' epistemologies
can be the basis of 'correct' public policy – but that seems not to be Rose's argument.
Indeed, the relationship between research and public policy is another link in the
chain of knowing/doing [*pouvoir/savoir*] that is under discussion.)

Even this Heideggerian corrective is critiqued by Derrida because it does not
attend to the naming of woman.

> For not having posed the sexual question, or at least for having subsumed it in the
> general question of truth, Heidegger's reading of Nietzsche has been idling offshore ever
> since it missed the woman in the *affabulation* of truth.[15]

Spurs gives an account of how one can read Nietzsche's master concept-metaphors.
The most interesting one for Derrida is 'woman'. Like all concept-metaphors,
'woman' is here used in such a way that one cannot locate an adequate literal
referent for the word. There *is* something special about it, however, for the question
of sexual difference in Nietzsche is not 'a regional question in a larger order which
would subordinate it first to the domain of a general ontology, subsequently to that
of a fundamental ontology, and finally to the question of the truth of being itself'.[16]

Derrida rescues this reading of the concept-metaphor 'woman' in Nietzsche, and
also suggests that Nietzsche's own *analysis* of sexual difference is caught within a
historical or narrative understanding/misunderstanding of 'propriation', making a
being proper to itself.

(This notion, of the originary and therefore structurally inaccessible autoposition
of the subject, is a fairly common one in generally non-foundationalist 'Marxist'
philosophers such as Louis Althusser or Theodor Adorno. Althusser's ill-fated
remark about the 'apparently paradoxical proposition which I shall express in the
following terms: *ideology has no history*' belongs to this family of notions; as does
Adorno's carefully articulated statement, 'the subject is appearance in its self-
positing and at the same time something historically altogether real'.[17] Derrida
places the question of sexual difference, at least, as he sees it in Nietzsche, in this
space. (For Althusser, by contrast, sexual difference is one of the ideologies [rather
than Ideology], which are within history: 'it is in this implacable and more or less
pathological … structure of the familial ideological configuration that the former
subject-to-be will have to … [become] the sexual subject [boy or girl] which it
already is in advance'.[18] For Adorno the question of sexual difference cannot be
entertained on this level.)

In Derrida's reading, Nietzsche is able to sketch sexual difference as preontological
propriation perhaps *because* he is bound by and gives his assent to significations and

values that define sexual difference in terms of the eternal war between the sexes, and the mortal hatred of the sexes in love, eroticism, etc. Thus propriation in Nietzsche may at first glance seem to have nothing but a series of restricted meanings: appropriation, expropriation, taking possession, gift and barter, mastering, servitude.[19] You have, then, on the one side, Heidegger with his extraordinarily subtle account of the ontological difference, *not* posing the sexual question, at least in this context. You have, on the other, Nietzsche, using or having to use the concept-metaphor 'woman' to point at preontological difference, using it, none the less, inside male-dominated historical narratives of propriation.

Jacqueline Rose, when she writes about propriation in a couple of sentences in her introduction, is obliged to keep within the Nietzschean historical assumptions about propriation, without the emancipating moment of emergence of woman as 'catachresis', as a metaphor without a literal referent standing in for a concept that is the condition of conceptuality: Nietzsche privileges the metaphor as condition of possibility of 'truth'. 'Woman' is a necessary and irreducible misnomer for this prior or primal figurative. Any program which assumes continuity between the subject of epistemology/ontology and that of ethicopolitics, must actively forget that the call to/of the wholly-other, that which is the undifferentiated (radically precontinuous) ethical, is the condition of possibility of the political, and that the propriation of a subject for ontology/epistemology has already also become possible by way of this condition. [...]

The distinction between the narrow sense and the general sense of catachresis is never clear-cut in deconstruction, although the difference is always acknowledged. According to Derrida, if one looks at propriation in the general sense in Nietzsche, one sees a question that is 'more powerful than the question, 'what is?', more powerful than 'the veil of truth or the meaning of being',[20] because before one can even say that *there is being*, there must be a decision that being can be proper to itself to the extent of being part of that proposition. (In German, before the gift of being in *Es gibt Sein*, one has to think the propriety to itself of the *Es*.) Outside of all philosophical game playing, the irreducible predicament pointed at here is that the ontological question cannot be asked in terms of a cleansed epistemology, for propriation organizes the totality of 'language's process and symbolic exchange in general', caught in the catachresis, snarled in the false analogy, not in 'pure' metaphor.[21]

I believe that in 'Displacement and the Discourse of Woman', I missed the fact that in Derrida's reading of Nietzsche in *Spurs*, there is an insistence that 'woman' in that text was a concept-metaphor that was also a *name* marking the preontological as propriation in sexual difference.[22]

When one of us defends Derrida against the other of us defending Lacan we are moving away from the suggestion in deconstruction (indeed European post-Hegelian theory in general) that a thinker does not make a point on the full steam of his sovereign subjectivity. Nietzsche, even as he depends upon propriation in the patriarchal, restricted, or narrow sense, reaches the general sense of propriation by putting the *name* of woman on it through the conduct of his text. And Derrida, grasping his reach as reader, does it not to trump Nietzsche but to make his text more useful for us. I hope the rest of this chapter will make clear how crucial it is not to ignore the powerful currents of European antihumanist thought that influence us, yet not to excuse them of their masculism while using them. This is what I am calling 'negotiation'.

Thus we can read Nietzsche's text in a way that suggests that the name of woman makes the question of propriation indeterminate. Let us look at the sentence: 'there is no truth of woman, but because of that abyssal self-apartness of truth, this non-truth is "truth"'.[23] If one takes the crucial term 'woman' out of the sentence, it would be possible to suggest that this is what Nietzsche thinks is new about his philosophy of truth, that the nature of truth is such that it is always abyssally (in a structure of repeated indefinite mirroring) apart from what one appropriates as the truth in terms of which one can act. This non-truth is 'truth'. The quotation marks indicate a catachrestical setting apart [...] 'Truth' here is not only not the literal, it is rather that for which there is no *adequate* literal referent.

Because, in Nietzsche's understanding of propriation in the narrow sense, woman is seen as the custodian of irreducibly inadequate literal referents; she is also seen as a model. In other words, when Nietzsche suggests there is no truth of woman in his historical understanding, a certain *kind* of woman is a model for the 'no truth'. Woman is thus 'one name for that non-truth of truth':[24] *one name* for that nontruth of truth.

My previous position on this essay of Derrida's was polemical. I suggested that it was not right to see the figure of woman as a sign for indeterminancy. Reading my analysis of appropriation in this polemic, Jacqueline Rose gives me the benefit of the doubt by claiming solidarity on this particular position.[25] And, within its own context, I accept this gesture. But today, negotiating, I want to give the assent for the moment to Derrida's argument. Affirmative deconstruction says 'yes' to a text twice, sees complicity when it could rather easily be oppositional. As we have seen in the previous chapter, Derrida has described his first phase as 'guarding the question', 'keeping the question alive'. The question is no particular question, of course, but its slippage into the form of *a* particular question is a 'necessary transgression'. In that spirit, and in this case, let us protect the question that we urge Rose to ask: is there not a difference between knowing-being – epistemo/ontological – and right doing – the ethicopolitical?[26] He described the second phase as calling to the wholly other. (If sexual difference is indeed pre-comprehended by the onto-logical question then, miming Derrida's Nietzsche, *we* might think 'philosopher', by way of the same historical narrative that gave Nietzsche 'woman', as one misname for the forgetfulness of the nontruth of 'truth'; The quick defensiveness to save philosophy from this charge, discussed in the previous chapter, will then match our anger at these 'philosophers' use of the name of 'woman', and show that the difference between the philosopher and woman conceals a violence (truth/non-truth::theory/practice) that will not be undone by repeating the theory-practice quarrel in the women's quarter. Luce Irigaray's 'ethics of sexual difference' [...] gives us a way out in the thinking of ethics. I have tried to think a politics that will not repeat that violence, more carefully than I have been able to in this book, in 'Gender in Contemporary Colonization', as yet unpublished.

At this stage, still discussing feminism and deconstruction, let us consider how this shift from the first phase to the second translates into a strategy of reading, a strategy of giving assent. Let us look at Derrida's relatively recent study of Nietzsche, *The Ear of the Other*, a piece on the politics of reading.[27] He suggests there that the reader should not excuse the texts of Nietzsche for their use by the Nazis. There is no reason to say that that was a mere misreading. On the contrary, the reader should note that there is something in Nietzsche's text which leads exactly to that kind of appropriation. This is one paradoxical way of saying 'yes' to the text, but it entails understanding from within, as it were, so that the moments that lend themselves to the so-called misappropriation are understood in the text's own terms. It is then that one can begin to develop a politics of reading, which will open up a text towards an as yet unknown horizon so that it can be of use without excuse. Let us now call this: negotiating with structures of violence. It is in that spirit of negotiation that I propose to give assent to Derrida's text about woman as a name for the nontruth of truth, upon the broader terrain of negotiation with other established structures, daily practiced but often disavowed, like the Law, institutional education, and, ultimately, capitalism. Negotiation, not collaboration; producing a new politics through critical intimacy.

Affirmative deconstruction of this kind was already signaled in *Grammatology*. Let us repeat that passage:

> The movements of deconstruction do not destroy structures from the outside. They are not possible and effective, nor can they take active aim, except by inhabiting those structures. Inhabiting them *in a certain way*, because one always inhabits, *and all the more when one does not suspect it*. Operating necessarily from the inside, borrowing all the strategic and economic resources of subversion from the old structure, borrowing them structurally, that is to say without being able to isolate their elements and atoms, the enterprise of deconstruction always *in a certain way* falls prey to its own work (*OG*, 24; emphasis mine).

It is this particular attitude that presages the crucial difference between the first and the second phases. The second attitude towards that which is critiqued, the giving of assent without excuse, so much that one inhabits its discourse – a short word for this might be 'love'.[28]

Deconstruction is not an exposure of error, nor a tabulation of error; logocentrism is not a pathology, nor is the metaphysical closure a prison to overthrow by violent means. Looking for irreducibles, realizing the theoretical absurdity of my position, it is with that 'love' that I am reading texts already read, and questioning the usefulness of reading deconstruction merely as the narrative of the decentered subject, of the fully dispersed subject. This is where I began, with the suggestion that Rose's case against deconstruction was based on such a reading.

Let us look in more detail at why it is unsatisfactory to reduce deconstruction to a narrative.

One focus of deconstruction as a morphology is the graphematic structure. In this brief compass, I will present the morphology also as a narrative (perhaps this is inescapable) – the narrative of a narrative if you like – and contrast it to the narrative of a decentered subject which deconstruction offers not only to Jacqueline Rose, but to readers such as Jürgen Habermas and Fredric Jameson.

One focus, then, of deconstruction is the graphematic structure. The adjective 'graphematic' comes from Derrida's analysis that writing is historically the structure that is supposed necessarily to operate in the presumed absence of its origin, the sender.

Any act must assume unified terms to get started. The implicit mechanics by which these assumptions are established or taken for granted spell out, if examined, a structure of repetition, which yet overtly posits self-evidence. These mechanics are generally found to be suppressed or finessed, so that beginnings do not seem problematic. Nearly all of Derrida's writing has been a discussion of such gestures – sometimes even self-conscious gestures of dismissal as difficulties or counter-examples – performed in different ways in different discourses. Let us decide to call this gesture the suppression of a graphematic structure. The graphematic structure that seems to orchestrate the inauguration of all acts (including acts of thought) is a structure *like* writing (although it is passed off as the self-identity of definitions present to themselves), something that looks more like the mark of an absent presence, writing commonly conceived. As in the case of writing commonly conceived, we cannot be necessarily sure of the identity of the originator, so in the case of the graphematic structure, we cannot endorse the 'fact' that it *is* an absent presence of which the trace-structure at the origin is the mark. (I remind the reader of the origin of Marx's socialist teleology in a 'convenient error' [....].) This unendorsable naming of the discovery of the repetition at the origin as 'graphematic', by way of 'writing' as a catachresis, is the double bind that founds all deconstruction. In other words, hidden agendas might pass themselves off as the goes-without-saying-ness of truth, to fools and knaves alike; but to show them up as writing *and mean it* is to buy into that very agenda, unless we put scare-quotes around the word, and say: can't do better for the time being, must keep moving. To call by the name of man all human reality is move number one: humanism; to substitute the name of woman in that mode is move number two; to put scare-quotes around 'woman' is move number three, not a synthesis but a provisional half-solution that always creates problems because it is or is not mistaken for the second move; therefore always looking forward, while making do, toward a fourth move, that never happens but always might.

By these alleyways, human beings think themselves unified also by finessing the assumption of a repressed graphematic structure. There is no way to get hold of a subject before this two-step. This is the narrative of the famous decentered subject. In early work such as 'Structure, Sign, and Play' and the first chapter of *Of Grammatology*, Derrida does invoke 'our epoch', meaning, specifically, an 'epoch' that privileges language and thinks (impossibly) to have got rid of centrisms.[29] To turn this critique – of a claim to have decentered method, by pointing out that the subject can only ever be posited by the finessing of a graphematic structure at the origin – into merely the story of the individual becoming decentered with late capitalism (Jameson), the passing of the pre-Socratics (Heidegger), the inception of modernity (Habermas via Weber), or with Derrida's new tricky bolstering of Eurocentric patriarchy (Rose), is a plausible but unexamined move.

The useful part of deconstruction is in the suggestion that the subject is always centered. Deconstruction persistently notices that this centering is an effect-structure with indeterminable boundaries that can only be deciphered as determining. No politics can occupy itself with only this enabling epistemological double bind. But when a political analysis or program forgets this it runs the risk of declaring ruptures where there is also a repetition – a risk that can result in varieties of fundamentalism, of which the onto/epistemo/ethicopolitical confusion is a characteristic symptom. International communism has died of the risk.

Différance is one of the names for the necessity to obliterate the graphematic structure, *and* the necessity to misname it 'graphematic', since there is no other way one can call it. This double bind – the double session of 'defering' – is at the origin of practice.[30]

Rose suggests, and she is not alone, that there is in Derrida a desire to suppress sexual difference in the interest of *différance*, and a privileging of *différance* as *the* name. (It seems to go unnoticed that, in his later work, the word is hardly ever used.)

Différance is, and it cannot be repeated often enough, only *one* name for the irreducible double bind that allows the very possibility of difference(s). Sexual *identity* is sexual *différance*, not sexual difference; it produces sexual difference. We are obliged to assume a pre-originary wholly other space without differences in the interest of suppressing that 'graphematic' structure at the inauguration of our texts; and *différance* is only *one* name for that necessity. There is no harm in admitting that it's not just the production of *sexual* difference that's being framed here but the possibility of thinking difference itself.

I invite you to consider again that, in the discourse of this critic of phallogocentrism, 'woman' is another name for this irreducible double bind. This is a difficult consideration when we want to claim deconstruction for or against feminism, but I now see no way around it. Here *différance* as the ungraspable ground of propriation *is* (but the copula is a supplement) sexual difference.[31] The *name* (of) woman occupies this site in Derrida. *Différance* and 'woman' are two names on a chain of nominal displacements where, unmotivated names, neither can claim priority. 'Man' is the duped name of the undivided origin. We are rather far away from the 'subject' of feminist ethicopolitics. In fact, we are still looking at the (im)possibility of broaching the epistemo/ontological.[32]

If *différance* (or 'woman', as well as the other names) opens up the question of symbolic possibility in general, it is not, as Rose writes, by suppression of thoughts of cultural form. The thought of cultural forms, which implies the differentiation of one culture from another, or of sexual difference, and indeed all other kinds of difference; the difference between being and nonbeing, if you like the ontico-ontological difference in this particular understanding, our desire to have an impasse which can only be between two things, our desire even for the undecidable; all of these are limited by the possibility that at the beginning is a suppression which we cannot get a handle on. *Différance* is in a (con)text, never pure. That's all it is, it's no big deal, but it's *not* a story-line which dismisses these differences as culturally unacceptable. We are still circling around the possibility of story-lines, even the story-lines that put one 'culture' over against another. (I have learned this all the better in terms of the politics of the postcolonial clamor for cultural difference and the current demands of liberal multiculturalism.) If all this seems too ethereal remember we wouldn't have to do this if 'deconstruction' had not been diagnosed in the first place as a story-line suppressing sexual and cultural difference in the interest of *différance*. As you will, I hope, see in the end, I prefer a more pragmatic line of reasoning (by way of a persistent active and only immediately forgetful transgression of theory) myself when I am thinking/doing as a feminist.[33]

'Woman', then, is a name that is the nontruth of 'truth' in Derrida reading Nietzsche. [. . .] This particular species of nominalism, an obsession with names that are necessarily misnames, names that are necessarily catachreses, 'writing', '*différance*', 'power' ('woman' in this case), names that have no adequate literal referent, characterizes poststructuralism in general, in spite of local differences (and via 'Value', and the 'Social', makes one suspect a kinship between the Marxian project and the implicit politics of poststructuralism – thinking of Marx's critical intimacy with Hegel's *Verhältnis*-obsessed dialectical structuralism – so inaccessible to the polemical eye, yet perhaps among the most important reasons for its failure in the hands of positivist sentimentalists). It is important to remember that each of these names is determined by their historical burden in the most empirical way. (Derrida calls this 'paleonymy'.) I hope it is by now clear that Nietzsche uses a name such as 'woman' because he has inherited it, and thus he uses all the contemporary allegorical, sociological, historical, and dismissive stereotypes about woman. On the other hand, since Nietzsche also wants to welcome this name as a name for his own practice – 'my truths' – what one sees in his text is the site of a conflict or a negotiation. Nietzsche, or Derrida, or for that matter Lacan, is here fully complicit with masculism (quite as Nietzsche is with the possibility of the grafting of Nazism onto his left), yet it is also possible to see, and Derrida is asking us to see this in Nietzsche because if we do this we can make the text useful, that within this itinerary there is that peculiar affirmation. This is the model Nietzsche wants – woman in that sense is *twice* model (modeling the nontruth of 'truth', and being as unlike the dogmatic philosopher of truth as possible by way of some of the dubious historical stereotypes). It might be useful for us to *accuse* the text responsibly, and then lift this lever and *ab-use* the text, rather than not use it at all and follow the mistake of the truth of (wo)man. Derrida himself is also bound (as is Lacan, and as are we in our taste for a pragmatic feminism that claims to be theoretical even as it forgets the difference between the subjects of onto/epistemology and ethico-politics) by a certain set of historical presuppositions. After all, one never hears a claim not to use anything from the other side except as it is made possible through institutional affiliation, the International Book Trade, fiscal support of a nation-state, consumerist support of transnational ('postmodern') capitalism, and so on. It is never heard from women involved in primary health care, literacy, or alternative (not 'sustainable' – that new cant word) development. (The crisis of so-called national liberation is a different case and must have its share of gesture politics.) In the persistent struggle against gendering ('internalized constraint seen as choice')[34] it is better to ab-use the enemy's enemies than to be a purist while sitting in the enemy's lap – a lap so colossal and shape-changing that you can forget you are sitting in it.

Derrida gives proof of being bound by the paleonymy of 'woman' when, at the end of *The Ear of the Other*, speaking still about his politics of reading, he sounds a theme that has been sounded by him before: the patronymic (the father's name), because through it the man can continue to survive after death, is a kiss of death. By contrast, the nameless feminine is the name of living. And it is this peculiar *livingness* of the feminine that is in some ways contaminated or betrayed by what Derrida perhaps understands as 'feminism'. 'No woman or trace of woman. And I do not make this remark in order to benefit from that supplement of seduction which today enters into all courtships or courtrooms. This vulgar procedure is what I propose to call "gynegogy"'.[35]

It must be acknowledged that this perspective, constituted by the historico-legal tradition of the patronymic in patriarchy, exists in Derrida's text just as much as a perspective constituted by *his* historical legacy exists in Nietzsche's catachrestical use of 'woman' as name. Thus, because of the necessity of the historical determination of the name 'woman' for the double bind at the origin of the production of 'truth(s)', there is no sense in talking about the relationship between deconstruction and feminism as if women were naturally decentered.[36] It takes its place, in its productivity, with the claim that women are naturally anything.

Yet the name of woman as the nontruth of 'truth' *can* have a significant message for us if we, refusing fully to honor the historically bound catachresis, give the name of woman to that *disenfranchised* woman who is *historically* different from ourselves, the subjects of feminist theory, and yet acknowledge that she has the right to the construction of a subject-effect of sovereignty in the narrow sense. Then we, as those by now relatively enfranchised agents, will share and understand the philosophers' anxiety about the nasty historical determinations which allow this name to exist. Since these philosophers are not essentialists, they have a real anxiety about the loss of the name 'woman' because it survives on these precariously sketched, basically essentialist historical generalizations. This is what is reflected in the kind of masculinist noises we noticed above at the conclusion of *The Ear of the Other*.[37]

There is a passage in Lacan's 'Love Letter', an essay translated by Jacqueline Rose in *Feminine Sexuality*, where he talks about the understanding of the place of woman beyond the question of sex, in soul-making and in naming God, which I think can be put together with Nietzsche's longing for affirming the name of woman as the nontruth of 'truth', and Derrida's anxiety about compromising the living feminine in the interest of a gynegogy which would sell itself to the death-story of the patronymic.[38] This, to my mind, marks a moment of the need for taking the name of woman in the interest of a philosophical practice. It is, in fact, no more and indeed no less than the need for a name. It is easier to grasp this if we look at the way in which Derrida writes about *différance*. In 'Différance', the essay by that name, he repeats tediously that *différance* is neither a concept nor a metaphor, nor indeed a word, and yet, in the end, the entire essay is argued in terms of the conceptuality and metaphoricity of the term. This particular tactic, of marking the anxiety by keeping the name intact against all disavowals unreadable without the name of that graphematic structure which can only be misnamed, makes work open to traditional masculism, in the case of the name of 'woman', as it makes it open to traditional modes of language use in the case of *différance*.

What can we do about this? I have already mentioned that I welcome the idea of the embattled love of the text that is given to us by deconstruction. Yet I cannot err too long on that path. Deconstruction is not androgyny, phallocentrism is not a pathology. After we have repeated these lessons, we must still insist on the project of antisexism, because sexism *is* also a pathology.[39] In that perspective, women can no longer only be names for 'writing' or the nontruth of *différance*. We cannot claim both the desire to identify with the oppression of woman in terms of an ontological deception, and the desire for the right to an impasse, to a deconstructive feminism which would take woman as a name for the graphematic structure and the nontruth of truth. We have to give up the one or the other. I would propose that we should not share this anxiety for the name, we should not identify the guarding of the question with *this* particular name. This would allow us to use the ontological and epistemological critiques found in deconstruction (and indeed psychoanalysis) and appreciate poststructuralist 'nominalism'. We must remember that this *particular name*, the name of 'woman', misfires for feminism. Yet, a feminism that takes the traditionalist line *against* deconstruction falls into a historical determinism where 'history' becomes a gender-fetish.

What I have described in the paragraph above is an ethical aporia, backed up by intellectual preparation and its relationship to a political decision. 'Pessimism of the intellect and optimism of the will', if you like formulas, or, 'ethics as the experience of the impossible'. Derrida has written about this with the philosopher's anxiety in 'The Force of Law'. By contrast, guarding this particular name for the graphematic structure is perhaps the most essentialist move of all – this turning of deconstruction into a narrative whether in praise or dispraise. If *we* lose the 'name' of specifically woman for writing there is no cause for lament.

It is *in the interest of* diagnosing the ontological ruse, on the basis of which there is oppression of woman, that we have to bring our understanding of the relationship between the name 'woman' and deconstruction into crisis. If we do not take the time to understand this in our zeal to be 'political', then I fear we act out the kind of play that Nietzsche figured out in *The Genealogy of Mortals*: in the interest of giving an alibi to his desire to punish, which is written into his way of being, in other words in the interest of a survival game, man produces an alibi which is called justice. And in the interest of that alibi, man has to define and articulate, over and over again, the name of man. It seems to me that if *we* forget that *we* cannot have a deconstructive feminism which decides to transform the usefulness of the name 'woman', itself based on a certain kind of historical anxiety for the graphematic structure, into a narrative, and thus take up arms against what we sometimes call essentialism, *then* we might be acting out this particular scenario, adequately contradicting and thus legitimizing it – by devising newer names of woman – in the interest of giving the desire to punish the alibi of justice. And if you ask me whether the disenfranchised can think this critique, I would say yes. It is the disenfranchised who teaches us most often by saying: I do not recognize myself in the object of your benevolence. I do not recognize my share in your naming. Although the vocabulary is not that of high theory, she tells us if we *care* to hear (without identifying our onto/epistemological subjectivity with *her* anxiety for the subjectship of ethics and the agency of the political) that she is not the literal referent for our frenzied naming of woman in the scramble for legitimacy in the house of theory. She reminds us that the name of 'woman', however political, is, like any other name, a catachresis.

(I am not being ethereal here. I know the kind of woman I am thinking about. And I also know that this person is not imaginable by most friends reading these words. I cannot enter into the immense and complicated logic of why this is so. Let this remain a lost parenthesis, being fleshed out through a laborious program of a learning not yet accessible to the production of knowledge – a promissory note that you are under no obligation to endorse in the competition for 'the most oppressed feminist'.)

The claim to deconstructive feminism (and deconstructive antisexism – the political claim of deconstructive feminists) cannot be sustained in the name of 'woman' within the Derridian problematic. Like class consciousness, which justifies its own production so that this historical class-formation can be undone, 'woman' as the name of writing must be erased in so far as it is a necessarily historical catachresis.

The name of woman cannot be the 'reality' of writing or of the necessary graphematic structure unless you turn the theory into nonsense. Let us say, speaking from within, that we have to deconstruct our desire for the impasse, neutralize the name of 'woman' *for deconstruction* and be deconstructive feminists in that sense. If we want to make political claims that are more useful all around than the general bourgeois academic feminist toothsome euphoria, this seems now to be the only way.

This point is not quite identical with the other note I have been sounding on and off: the object that is known to us through the epistemic project, the cleansed object that knows the itinerary of its recognition of itself as male or female, cannot be identical with the constituency of antisexism, the subject of ethicopolitics. I will bring the two together by way of a consideration of Foucault's double-play with 'power' and power, and compare it to ours with 'woman' and woman: the name and, as it were, the thing, the phenomenal essence. It should be a lesson to us that *if* we do not watch out for the historical determinations for the name of woman as catachresis in deconstruction, and merely seek to delegitimize the name of man, we legitimize what is diagnosed by Nietzsche and acted out by Foucault.

'Objective' precedes the famous chapter on 'Method' in *History of Sexuality I*. By the end of this section, everything happens as if the lessons learned from Nietzsche, precisely the alibi for the ontological compulsion to articulate as epistemology (name of man as subject of justice as alibi for the ontological need to punish), could be undone by an act of will. Thus Foucault is able to say, 'We must at the same time conceive of sex without the law, and power without the king' (*HS*, 91). This sentence leads into the section entitled 'Method'. Arrived here, the *name* 'power' is systematically sold short for the 'thing' power, and we are able to get a method because we know the objective, not reduced to an act of willed thought. (The best way to deconstruct this is through Foucault's own notion of the 'referential' in the *Archaeology of Knowledge* [....]

This bit of short-circuiting is comparable to the way that we would naturalize the *name* 'woman' if we transformed it into the central character in that narrative of woman's recognition within gendering, however deferred. Foucault's naturalizing of the *name* 'power' allows the coding of the phenomenality of power as something like an arithmetical system of equivalences: 'And it is doubltless the strategic codification of these points of resistance that makes a revolution possible somewhat similar to the way in which the state relies on the institutional integration of power relationships.'[40] We see here a case of Foucault's desire to get beyond the ontological/epistemological bind, comparable to our equation of the subject of ontoepistemology and ethicopolitics.

I have warned against an abuse of theory, because we cannot stop when the analytic philosopher can stop, with 'the heritage of Socrates' behind him.[41] I quote the following words, continuing my very first quotation in this essay not in mockery, but recognizing how self-critical they are. 'Moral judgment' Nagel writes, 'and moral theory certainly apply to public questions, but they are notably ineffective.' What I have been arguing so far about the relationship between feminism and deconstructive feminism, feminism and the confusion between the object of the epistemic project and the constituency of antisexism might translate to what is being said here.

Moral judgment and moral theory certainly apply to public questions, but they are notably ineffective. When powerful interests are involved it is very difficult to change anything by arguments, however cogent, which appeal to decency, humanity, compassion, and fairness. These considerations also have to compete with the more primitive moral sentiments of honor and retribution and respect for strength. The conditions under which moral argument can have an influence are rather special, and not very well understood by me. They need to be investigated through the history and psychology of morals, important but underdeveloped subjects much neglected by philosophers since Nietzsche. It certainly is not enough that the injustice of a practice of the wrongness of policy should be made glaringly evident. People have to be ready to listen, and that is not determined by argument.[42]

In the end Nagel says, in a kind of melancholy self-distancing from Marx's Eleventh Thesis on Feuerbach: 'I do not know whether it is important to change the world or to understand it, but philosophy is best judged by its contribution to understanding, not to the course of events.' [...] Marx tried to redo the role of philosophy in the divided but related activities of interpreting and changing the world. Yet Marxism foundered in the relationship between class-*consciousness* and agency of 'revolution', not to mention the running of a bounded 'post-revolutionary state'. If, in fact, we do not acknowledge that the object of the epistemic search and the constituency of antisexist work are not identical, that gendering is within 'the history and psychology of morals', and we simply finesse the fact that the feminist challenge must combine method *and* act, we might be able to echo the nobility of Thomas Nagel's sentiments. I myself think we cannot stop here, because in the cultures now dominating the world, women have not had an acknowledged code of 'honor and retribution and respect for strength' except as victims/supporters. I will, then, repeat my modest solution.

Incanting to ourselves all the perils of transforming a 'name' to a referent – making a catechism, in other words, of catachresis – let us none the less name (as) 'woman' that disenfranchised woman whom we strictly, historically, geopolitically *cannot imagine*, as literal referent. 'Subaltern' is the name of the social space that is different from the classed social circuit, the track of hegemony. By proposing the irreducible other in that space as holding the name 'woman', I am attempting to deflect attention from the 'poor little rich girl speaking *personal* pain as victim of the *greatest* oppression'-act that multiculturalist capitalism – with its emphasis on individuation and competition – would thrust upon us. Let us divide the name of woman so that we see ourselves as naming, not merely named. Let us acknowledge that we must change a morphology to a story-line, acknowledge that we participated in obliterating the traces of her production, stage the scene of the effacing of the graphematic – her biography – in the crudest possible way. The anxiety of this naming will be that, if we must think a relationship between the subject of onto/epistemology (ourselves, roughly, in this room at Cambridge, or Elaine Showalter at Princeton) and the object of onto/axiology (that disenfranchised woman, not even graduated into that subject, whose historicity or subjectship we cannot imagine beyond the regulation 'women's union' or 'personal pain' human interest anecdote), the hope behind the political desire will be that the possibility for the name will be finally erased. Today, here, what I call the 'gendered subaltern', especially in decolonized space, has become the name 'woman' for me. 'Douloti' ... traffic-in-wealth – financialization – may be one such name. In search of irreducibles, after the chastening experience of coming close to the person who provides that imagined name, I want to be able not to lament when the material possibility for the name will have disappeared.

[. . .]

Notes

1. With reference to this complaint, see Derrida's spirited defense of the Nambikwara against the charge that peoples without a recognizably phono- or ideo-graphic writing were 'without writing,' (*Of Grammatology*, trans. Gayatri Chakravorty Spivak (Baltimore: The Johns Hopkins University Press, 1976), pp. 101–40. Hereafter cited as *OG*)

2. For two different approaches to this question, see Ashis Nandy, *The Intimate Enemy: Loss and Recovery of Self Under Colonialism* (Oxford: Oxford University Press, 1983) and Dipesh Chakrabarty, 'Postcoloniality and the Artifice of History: Who Speaks for "Indian" Pasts?,' *Representations*, 37 (Winter 1992): pp. 1–26.

3. Thomas Nagel, *Mortal Questions* (Cambridge: Cambridge University Press, 1979), p. xii.

4. Edward A. Gargan, 'India Flirts with Hope, Despite Disasters,' *New York Times* (March 1, 1992).

5. Jacqueline Rose, *Sexuality in the Field of Vision* (London: Verso, 1986).

6. Margaret Homan, 'Feminist Criticism and Theory: The Ghost of Creusa', *Yale Journal of Criticism* 1: 1 (Fall 1987), pp. 153–182. Showalter quoted by Elizabeth Skolbert, 'Literary Feminism Comes of Age', *New York Times Sunday Magazine* (December 6, 1987): p. 112.

7. See Partha Chatterjee, *Nationalist Thought and the Colonial World: A Derivative Discourse?* (London: Zed, 1986).

8. Rose, *Sexuality*, p. 23.

9. Rose, *Sexuality*, p. 15.

10. The difference between the desire for an impasse and negotiating with an enabling double bind seems important if we wish to acknowledge that we are 'free agents' produced by and written in history. Ignoring of the double bind in nonfoundationalist philosophy is now affecting Euroamerican Marxism as well: 'a justification of Marxian theory on the grounds of its social context and consequences amounts to warranting a theory by the means of the self-same theory … we are not bothered by the nature of [the alternative antiessentialist] infinite regress that is independent of these "independent terms" and can serve as an ultimate ground of truth for these meanings.' (Stephen A. Resnick and Richard D. Wolff, *Knowledge and Class: A Marxian Critique of Political Economy* [Chicago: University of Chicago Press, 1987], p. 28.)

11. Rose, *Sexuality*, p. 5.

12. It would be to belabor the obvious to point out that there is rather a straight and self-conscious line here between Kant and Freud. See, for example, Freud, *Standard Edition*, vol. 22, pp. 61, 163. The relationship between the knowing and acting subject is a rupture rather than a continuous progression. It is surely one of the gifts of structuralist and poststructuralist psychoanalysis to make us productively uneasy about that relationship. (I use 'productive' where I should perhaps say 'potentially productive.' I mean that the unease can be less intransigent than a mere privileging of either theory or practice, or the assumption of achievable continuity between them.)

13. Again, this is rather a prominent cornerstone of the critique of humanism. The lines here fall unevenly between Nietzsche, Heidegger, Foucault, and Derrida. Foucault, having decided to name the problem itself the empirico-transcendental-discursive mark of the modern, went off in other interesting directions. Derrida has kept patiently producing its implications. He stated the problem simply in 1963 (in a sentence that I often quote) with special reference to the anthropologizing of philosophy, a project, in which the later Rose as a feminist (Derrida is speaking of Sartre as a humanist) is perhaps also engaged: 'Everything occurs as if the sign(man) has no origin, no historical, cultural, linguistic limit' (*Margins of Philosophy*, p. 116).

14. Jacques Derrida, *Spurs*, trans. Barbara Harlow (Chicago: University of Chicago Press, 1978).
15. Derrida, *Spurs*, p. 109. The essay 'Geschlecht: différence sexuelle, différence ontologique,' in *Psyche: Inventions de l'autre* (Paris: Galilée, 1987) should be considered if one wants to engage Derrida specifically on the issue of the place of sexual duality in Heidegger's thought. It has little to do with the argument here.
16. Derrida, *Spurs*, p. 109.
17. Louis Althusser, 'Ideology and Ideological State Apparatuses (Notes Towards an investigation),' in *Lenin and Philosophy and Other Essays*, trans. Ben Brewster (New York: Monthly Review Press, 1971), p. 159. Theodor Adorno, 'Subject and Object', in *The Essential Frankfurt School Reader*, trans. Andrew Arato and Eike Gebhardt (New York: Urizen, 1978), p. 508.
18. Althusser, 'Ideology,' p. 176.
19. Derrida, *Spurs*, p. 110.
20. Derrida, *Spurs*, p. 111.
21. Derrida, *Spurs*, p. 110.
22. Gayatri Chakravorty Spivak, 'Displacement and the Discourse of Woman', in Mark Krupnick, ed., *Displacement: Derrida and After* (Bloomington: Indiana University Press, 1983). I do mention the fact of the 'name', but do not seem to grasp its import.
23. Derrida, *Spurs*, p. 51.
24. Derrida, *Spurs*, p. 51.
25. Rose, *Sexuality*, p. 21 n. 38.
26. This phase in Derrida begins as early as his deconstructive reading of the philosophy of Emmanual Levinas in 'Violence and Metaphysics', published in 1964 (and in *Writing and Difference*, trans. Alan Bass [Chicago: University of Chicago Press, 1978]). Levinas argues there that Husserl and Heidegger, both within the Greek tradition, ultimately write philosophies of oppression. Neutralizing the other, fundamental ontology and phenomenology perform the same structural operation as philosophies of knowledge, appropriating the other as object. By contrast, Levinas suggests, the gaze toward the other must always be open, an open question, the possibility of the ethical. 'Before the ontological level, the ethical level' (p. 98). Derrida reads Levinas critically, suggesting that he too is complicit with philosophy in the Greek. But about the openness of the question, the prior claim of responsibility to the trace of the other (which will be for him the possibility of 'the non-ethical opening of ethics': *Of Grammatology*, p. 140), he is in agreement.
27. Jacques Derrida, *The Ear of the Other: Otobiography, Transference, Translation*, trans. Peggy Kamuf (New York: Schocken, 1985).
28. The paleonymic burden of the word 'love' for a feminist is to be distinguished rigorously from the gentlemanly or belle-lettristic attitude of 'love for the text'.
29. 'Structure, Sign, and Play in the Discourse of the Human Sciences', in *Writing and Difference*.
30. Part of the idea behind spelling 'différance' with an 'a' was that it would be a neographism, be visible, not audible. To keep the word in English and to pronounce it in the French way has foiled that project. Since another part of the idea was to include both 'differ' and 'defer' and indicate that this was the spacing/time structure of the inevitable break between, among other things, theory and method (epistemo/ontology and axiology, too, of course), I propose 'difering' in English. l will do nothing to give this translation currency.
31. 'The Supplement of Copula: Philosophy Before Linguistics' in *Margins of Philosophy*. The 'supplement' – both adding to a preexisting whole and filling a preexisting hole – is something like the 'difering' that every 'is' pretends or professes it isn't doing.

32. ... [T]he '(im)' in such a formulation marks the enabling double bind at the inauguration of practice that, literalizing a catachresis, allows the possibility of practice as craft. I believe there is no particular virtue in making it sound less abstract in its formulation, and thus taking away precision. If the reader wants the 'concrete', she will have to check it out in doing, not grasping easily.

33. I add this parenthesis because, when I gave a version of this paper at the University of Virginia, so clear a thinker as Richard Rorty thought that my message was that feminism must 'ignore' deconstruction altogether in order to act. To spell it out this way sounds bizarre. In the doing it is something like a reflex, the 'faith' (habit?) that Gramsci refers to in 'The Formation of Intellectuals' (Antonio Gramsci, *Selections from the Prison Notebooks*, trans. Quintin Hoare and Geoffrey Nowell-Smith [New York: International Publishers, 1971], p. 339). I think, although it does not matter to me very much, that Derrida himself is aware of this at all times, and that it is because of this that in the introduction to his 1987 collection *Psyche*, he calls the unifying themes of his writings of the last decade *a théorie distraite* – the best English translation of which would be, in my judgment, 'an inattentive theory' (*Psyche*, p. 9). ... Such 'inattention' – pointing toward the constancy of a habit – has interesting connections with the Freudian notion of hypercathexis.

34. Sheila Allen and Carol Wolkowitz, *Homeworking: Myths and Realities* (London: Macmillan, 1987), p. 73.

35. Derrida, *The Ear of the Other*, pp. 16–17, 38.

36. It is interesting to see that Derrida falls back on the most 'orthodox' model of deconstructive method-reversal and displacement – when he makes a somewhat similar point and does not, of course, refer to his own position within patriarchal presuppositions: Derrida, 'Women in the Beehive,' in Paul Smith and Alice Jardine, eds., *Men in Feminism* (New York: Methuen, 1987), pp. 194–5. It is these presuppositions of the name 'woman', rather than the morphology of 'différance', that will not allow for the acknowledgment of class and race specifically in women – racial heterogeneity in another guise – that I go on to discuss in my text.

37. Foucault fabulates this anxiety poignantly in the adult male Greek's anxiety about the loss of the boyhood of the boy as erotic object in *The Use of Pleasure: The History of Sexuality*, trans. Robert Hurley (New York: Vintage, 1986), vol. 2.

38. Jacques Lacan, 'God and the Jouissance of Woman, A Love Letter', in *Feminine Sexuality*, trans. Jacqueline Rose (London: Macmillan, 1982), p. 155f.

39. An interested insistence of this sort, not absolutely justified by theory, is, of course, pervasively crucial to deconstructive method. The two articulations that I still find most useful are *OG*, 62, and 'The Double Session,' in *Dissemination*, trans. Barbara Johnson (Chicago: University of Chicago Press, 1981), p. 235.

40. Foucault, *Archaeology*, p. 96.

41. For this particular bonding, see Richard Rorty, 'Solidarity or Objectivity?', in Cornel West and John Rajchman, eds., *Post-Analytical Philosophy* (New York: Columbia University Press, 1985).

42. Nagel, *Mortal Questions*, p. xiii.

3.4 □ *Difference: 'A special Third World women issue'*

Trinh T. Minh-ha

[. . .]

Words empty out with age. Die and rise again, accordingly invested with new meanings, and always equipped with a secondhand memory. In trying to tell something, a woman is told, shredding herself into opaque words while her voice dissolves on the walls of silence. Writing: a commitment of language. The web of her gestures, like all modes of writing, denotes a historical solidarity (on the understanding that her story remains separable from history). She has been warned of the risk she incurs by letting words run off the rails, time and again tempted by the desire to gear herself to the accepted norms. But where has obedience led her? At best, to the satisfaction of a 'made-woman', capable of achieving as high a mastery of discourse as that of the male establishment in power. Immediately gratified, she will, as years go by, sink into oblivion, a fate she inescapably shares with her foresisters. How many, already, have been condemned to premature deaths for having borrowed the master's tools and thereby played into his hands? Solitude is a common prerequisite, even though this may only mean solitude in the immediate surroundings. Elsewhere, in every corner of the world, there exist women who, despite the threat of rejection, resolutely work toward the unlearning of institutionalized language, while staying alert to every deflection of their body compass needles. *Survival*, as Audre Lorde comments, '*is not an academic skill. ... It is learning how to take our differences and make them strengths. For the master's tools will never dismantle the master's house.* They may allow us temporarily to beat him at his own game, but they will never enable us to bring about genuine change.'[1] The more one depends on the master's house for support, the less one hears what

Trinh, T. M.-H., *Woman, Native, Other: Writing, postcoloniality and feminism*, University of Indiana Press, Bloomington, 1989, pp. 79–83, 85–6, 90, 95–101, 102–4, 157–9.

he doesn't want to hear. Difference is not difference to some ears, but awkwardness or incompleteness. Aphasia. Unable or unwilling? Many have come to tolerate this dissimilarity and have decided to suspend their judgments (only) whenever the other is concerned. Such an attitude is a step forward; at least the danger of speaking for the other has emerged into consciousness. But it is a very small step indeed, since it serves as an excuse for their complacent ignorance and their reluctance to involve themselves in the issue. You who understand the dehumanization of forced removal-relocation-reeducation-redefinition, the humiliation of having to falsify your own reality, your voice – you know. And often cannot *say* it. You try and keep on trying to unsay it, for if you don't, they will not fail to fill in the blanks on your behalf, and you will be said.

The Policy of 'Separate Development'

With a kind of perverted logic, they work toward your erasure while urging you to keep your way of life and ethnic values *within the borders of your homelands*. This is called the policy of 'separate development' in apartheid language. Tactics have changed since the colonial times and indigenous cultures are no longer (overtly) destroyed (preserve the form but remove the content, or vice versa). You may keep your traditional law and tribal customs among yourselves, as long as you and your own kind are careful not to step beyond the assigned limits. Nothing has been left to chance when one considers the efforts made by the White South African authorities to distort and use the tools of Western liberalism for the defense of their racialistic-ally indefensible cause. Since no integration is possible when terror has become the order of the day, I (not you) will give you freedom. I will grant you autonomy – not complete autonomy, however, for 'it is a liberal fallacy to suppose that those to whom freedom is given will use it only as foreseen by those who gave it'.[2] (Confidentially, I live in a state of intense fear, knowing that Western education has taught you aggression in equality. Now I sleep with a gun under my pillow and lock the gate at the top of my stairway; a single second of carelessness may cost me my life – for life and domination are synonyms to me – and I tremble at the slightest movement of my servants. Better intern you 'for your own good' than be interned or 'driven to the sea' by you.) Self-determination begins with the division of the land (on condition that I cut the cake), and I will make sure each of you gets the part s/he *deserves*. The delimitation of territories is my answer to what I perceive as some liberals' dream for 'the inauguration, namely, of a system in which South Africa's many peoples would resolve themselves unreluctantly into one'.[3] The governed do not (should not) compose a single people; this is why I am eager to show that South Africa is not one but ten separate nations (of which the White nation is the only one to be skin-defined; the other nine being determined largely on the basis of language – the Zulu nation, the Swazi nation, and so on). This philosophy – I will not call it 'policy' – of 'differentiation' will allow me to have better control over my nation while looking after yours, helping you thereby to gradually stand on your own. It will enable you to return to 'where you belong' whenever you are not satisfied with my law and customs or whenever you are no longer useful to me. Too bad if you consider what has been given to you as the leftovers of my meals. Call it 'reserves of cheap labor' or 'bantustans' if you wish; 'separate development' means that each one of us minds her/his own business (I will interfere when my rights are concerned since I represent the State) and that your economical poverty is of your own making. As for 'the Asiatic cancer, which has already eaten so deeply into the vitals of South Africa, [it] ought to be resolutely eradicated'.[4] Non-white foreigners have no part whatsoever in my plans and I 'will undertake to drive the coolies [Indians] out of the country within four years'.[5] My 'passionate concern for the future of a European-type white society, and ... that society's right to self-preservation' is not a question of color feeling, but of nationalism, the 'Afrikaner nationalism [which] is a form of collective selfishness; but to say this is simply to say that it is an authentic case of nationalism'.[6]

Words manipulated at will. As you can see, 'difference' is essentially 'division' in the understanding of many. It is no more than a tool of self-defense and conquest. You and I might as well not walk into this semantic trap which sets us up against each other as expected by a certain ideology of separatism. Have you read the grievances some of our sisters express on being among the few women chosen for a 'Special Third World Women's Issue' or on being the only Third World woman at readings, workshops, and meetings? It is as if everywhere we go, we become Someone's private zoo. Gayatri Chakravorty Spivak spoke of their remarking 'the maids upstairs in the guest quarters were women of color' in a symposium;[7] Gloria Anzaldúa, of their using her as a token woman and her friend Nellie Wong as a 'purveyor of resource lists';[8] Mitsuye Yamada, of having to start from scratch each time, as if she were 'speaking to a brand new audience of people who had never known an Asian Pacific woman who is other than the passive, sweet, etc., stereotype of the "Oriental" woman';[9] Audre Lorde, of the lack of interracial cooperation between academic feminists whose sole explanation for the issue remains: 'We did not know who to ask';[10] and Alice Walker, of the necessity of learning to discern the true feminist – for whom racism is inherently an impossibility' – from the white female opportunist – for whom racism, inasmuch as it assures white privilege, is an accepted way of life'.[11] The decision you and I are called upon to make is fraught with far-reaching consequences. On the one hand, it is difficult for us to sit at table with them (the master and/or his substitutes) without feeling that our presence, like that of the 'native' (who happens to be invited) among the anthropologists, serves to mask the refined sexist and/or racist tone of their discourse, reinforcing thereby its pretensions to universality. Given the permanent status of 'foreign workers', we – like the South African blacks who are allowed to toil on white territories as 'migrants', but are gotten rid of and resettled to the homeland area as soon as they become unprofitable labor units – continue in most cases to be treated as 'temporary sojourners', even though we may spend our whole lifetime by their side pleading a common cause.

[. . .]

'Why do we have to be concerned with the question of Third World women? After all, it is only one issue among many others.' Delete 'Third World' and the sentence immediately unveils its value-loaded clichés. Generally speaking, a similar result is obtained through the substitution of words like *racist* for *sexist*, or vice versa, and the established image of the *Third World Woman* in the context of (pseudo-) feminism readily merges with that of the *Native* in the context of (neo-colonialist) anthropology. The problems are interconnected. Here, a plural, angry reply may be expected: what else do you wish? It seems as if no matter what We do We are being resented. Now, 'in response to complaints of exclusionary practices, special care is always taken to notify minority organizations and women of color of conferences, planning meetings, job openings, and workshops'.[12] Once again, re-read the statement with the master's voice and with 'woman' in place of 'minority'. Much remains to be said about the attitude adopted in this 'special care' program and its (unavowed or unavowable) intent. Viewing the question through the eyes of a white sister, Ellen Pence thus writes:

> Gradually, I began to realize the tremendous gap between my rhetoric about solidarity with Third World women and my gut feelings. ... Our idea of including women of color was to send out notices. We never came to the business table as equals. Women of color joined us on our terms. ... I started seeing the similarities with how men have excluded the participation of women in their work through Roberts Rules of Order, encouraging us to set up subcommittees to discuss *our* problems but never seeing sexism as their problem. It became clear that in many ways I act the same way toward women of color, supporting them in dealing with *their* issues. ... I'm now beginning to realize that in many cases men do not understand because they have never committed themselves to understanding and by understanding, choosing to share their power. The lessons we've learned so well as women must be the basis for our understanding of ourselves as oppressive to the Third World women we work with.[13]

No matter which side i belong to, once i step down into the mud pit to fight my adversary, i can only climb out from it stained. This is the story of the duper who turns her/himself into a dupe while thinking s/he has made a dupe of the other. The close dependency that characterizes the master–servant relationship and binds the two to each other for life is an old, patent fact one can no longer deny. Thus, in so far as I/i understand how 'sexism dehumanizes men', I/i shall also see how 'my racism must dehumanize me' (Pence). The inability to relate the two issues, and to feel them in my bones, has allowed me to indulge in the illusion that I will remain safe from all my *neighbors' problems* and can go on leading an undisturbed, secure life of my own. Hegemony and racism are, therefore, a pressing feminist issue; 'as usual, the impetus comes from the grass-roots, activist women's movement'. Feminism, as Barbara Smith defines it, 'is the political theory and practice that struggles to free *all* women. ... Anything less than this vision of total freedom is not feminism, but merely female self-aggrandizement'.[14]

[. . .]

Infinite Layers: I Am Not i Can Be You and Me

A critical difference from myself means that I am not i, am within and without i. I/i can be I or i, you and me both involved. We (with capital W) sometimes include(s), other times exclude(s) me. You and I are close, we intertwine; you may stand on the other side of the hill once in a while, but you may also be me, while remaining what you are and what i am not. The differences made *between* entities comprehended as absolute presences – hence the notions of *pure origin* and *true* self – are an outgrowth of a dualistic system of thought peculiar to the Occident (the 'onto-theology' which characterizes Western metaphysics). They should be distinguished from the differences grasped *both between* and *within* entities, each of these being understood as multiple presence.[15] Not One, not two either. 'I' is, therefore, not a unified subject, a fixed identity, or that solid mass covered with layers of superficialities one has gradually to peel off before one can see its true face. 'I' is, itself, *infinite layers*. Its complexity can hardly be conveyed through such typographic conventions as I, i, or I/i. Thus, I/i am compelled by the will to say/unsay, to resort to the entire gamut of personal pronouns to stay near this fleeing *and* static essence of Not-I. Whether I accept it or not, the natures of *I, i, you, s/he, We, we, they*, and *wo/man* constantly overlap. They all display a necessary ambivalence, for the line dividing *I* and *Not-I*, *us* and *them*, or *him* and *her* is not (cannot) always (be) as clear as we would like it to be. Despite our desperate, eternal attempt to separate, contain, and mend, categories always leak. Of all the layers that form the open (never finite) totality of 'I', which is to be filtered out as superfluous, fake, corrupt, and which is to be called pure, true, real, genuine, original, authentic? Which, indeed, since all interchange, revolving in an endless process? (According to the context in which they operate, the superfluous can become the real; the authentic can prove fake; and so on.) *Authenticity*, as a need to rely on an 'undisputed origin', is prey to an obsessive *fear*: that of *losing a connection*. Everything must hold together. In my craving for a logic of being, I cannot help but loathe the threats of interruptions, disseminations, and suspensions. To begin, to develop to a climax, then, to end. To fill, to join, to unify. The order and the links create an illusion of continuity, which I highly prize for fear of nonsense and emptiness. Thus, a clear origin will give me a connection back through time, and I shall, by all means, search for that genuine layer of myself to which I can always cling. To abolish it in such a perspective is to remove the basis, the prop, the overture, or the finale – giving thereby free rein to indeterminancy: the result, forefeared, is either an anarchic succession of climaxes or a de(inex)pressive, uninterrupted monotony – and to enter into the limitless process of interactions and changes that nothing will stop, not even death. In other words, things may be said to be what they are, not exclusively in relation to what was and what will be (they should not solely be seen as clusters chained together by the temporal sequence of cause and effect), but also in relation to each other's immediate presences and to themselves as non/presences. The *real*, nothing else than a *code of representation*, does not (cannot) coincide with the lived or the performed. This is what Vine Deloria, Jr accounts for when he exclaims: 'Not even Indians can relate themselves to this type of creature who, to anthropologists, is the "real" Indian.'[16] A realistic identification with such a code has, therefore, no reality whatsoever: it is like 'stopping the ear while trying to steal the bell' (Chinese saying).

[. . .]

The Female Identity Enclosure

Difference as uniqueness or special identity is both limiting and deceiving. If identity refers to the whole pattern of sameness within a human life, the style of a continuing me that permeates all the changes undergone, then difference remains within the boundary of that which distinguishes one identity from another. This means that *at heart*, X must be X, Y must be Y, and X *cannot* be Y. Those who run around yelling that X is not X and X *can* be Y usually land in a hospital, a 'rehabilitation' center, a concentration camp, or a res-er-va-tion. All deviations from the dominant stream of thought, that is to say, the belief in a permanent essence of wo/man and in an invariant but fragile identity, whose 'loss' is considered to be a 'specifically human danger', can easily fit into the categories of the 'mentally ill' or the 'mentally underdeveloped'. It is probably difficult for a 'normal', probing mind to recognize that to seek is to lose, for seeking presupposes a separation between the seeker and the sought, the continuing me and the changes it undergoes. What if the popularized story of the identity crisis proves to be only a story and nothing else? Can identity, indeed, be viewed other than as a by-product of a 'manhandling' of life, one that, in fact, refers no more to a consistent 'pattern of sameness' than to an inconsequential process of otherness? How am I to lose, maintain, or gain an (fe/male) identity when it is impossible to me to take up a position outside this identity from which I presumably reach in and feel for it? Perhaps a way to portray it is to borrow these verses from the *Cheng-tao-ke*:

> You cannot take hold of it,
> But you cannot lose it.
> In not being able to get it, you get it.
> When you are silent, it speaks;
> When you speak, it is silent.[17]

Difference in such an insituable context is *that which undermines the very idea of identity*, deferring to infinity the layers whose totality forms 'I'. It subverts the foundations of any affirmation or vindication of value and cannot, thereby, ever bear in itself an absolute value. The difference (within) between *difference* itself and *identity* has so often been ignored, and the use of the two terms so readily confused, that claiming a female/ethnic identity/difference is commonly tantamount to reviving a kind of naive 'male-tinted' romanticism. If feminism is set forth as a demystifying force, then it will have to question thoroughly the belief in its own identity. To suppose, like Judith Kegan Gardiner, that 'the concept of female identity provides a key to understanding the *special qualities* of contemporary writing by women ... , the diverse ways in which writing by women *differs* from writing by men', and to 'propose the preliminary metaphor "female identity is a process" for the most fundamental of these differences' does not, obviously, allow us to radically depart from the master's logic. Such a formulation endeavors to 'reach a theory of female-identity ... that *varies from the male model*', and to demonstrate that:

> primary identity for women is more flexible and relational *than for men*. Female gender identity is *more* stable *than male gender identity*. Female infantile identifications are *less* predictable *than male ones* ... the *female counterpart* of the male identity crisis may occur more diffusely, at a different stage, or not at all. (emphasis added)

It seems quite content with reforms that, at best, contribute to the improvement and/or enlargement of the identity enclosure, but do not, in any way, attempt to remove its fence. The constant need to refer to the 'male model' for comparisons unavoidably maintains the subject under tutelage. For the point is not to carve one's space in 'identity theories that ignore women' and describe some of the faces of female identity, saying, like Gardiner: 'I picture female identity as typically less fixed, less unitary, and more flexible than male individuality, both in its primary core and in the entire maturational complex developed from this core',[18] but patiently to dismantle the very notion of core (be it static or not) and identity.

Woman can never be defined. Bat, dog, chick, mutton, tart. Queen, madam, lady of pleasure. MISTRESS. *Belle-de-nuit*, woman of the streets, fruitwoman, fallen woman. Cow, vixen, bitch. Call girl, joy girl, working girl. Lady and whore are both bred to please. The old Woman image-repertoire says She is a Womb, a mere baby's pouch, or 'nothing but sexuality'. She is a passive substance, a parasite, an enigma whose mystery proves to be a snare and a delusion. She wallows in night, disorder, and immanence and is at the same time the 'disturbing factor (between men)' and the key to the beyond. The further the repertoire unfolds its images, the more entangled it gets in its attempts at capturing Her. 'Truth, Beauty, Poetry – she is All: once more all under the form of the Other. All except herself',[19] Simone de Beauvoir wrote. Yet, even with or because of Her capacity to embody All, Woman is the lesser man, and among male athletes, to be called a woman is still resented as the worst of insults. 'Wo-' appended to 'man' in sexist contexts is not unlike 'Third World', 'Third', 'minority', or *color* affixed to *woman* in pseudo-feminist contexts. Yearning for universality, the generic 'woman', like its counterpart, the generic 'man', tends to efface difference within itself. Not every female is 'a real woman', one knows this through hearsay. ... Just as 'man' provides an example of how the part played by women has been ignored, undervalued, distorted, or omitted through the use of terminology presumed to be generic, 'woman' more often than not reflects the subtle power of linguistic exclusion, for its set of referents rarely includes those relevant to Third World 'female persons'. 'All the Women Are White, All the Blacks are Men, But Some of Us Are Brave' is the title given to an anthology edited by Gloria T. Hull, Patricia Bell Scott and Barbara Smith. It is, indeed, somehow devious to think that WOMAN also encompasses the Chinese with bound feet, the genitally mutilated Africans, and the one thousand Indians who committed *suttee* for one royal male. Sister Cinderella's foot is also enviably tiny but never crooked! And European witches were also burnt to purify the body of Christ, but they do not pretend to 'self-immolation'. 'Third World', therefore, belongs to a category apart, a 'special' one that is meant to be both complimentary and complementary, for First and Second went out of fashion, leaving a serious Lack behind to be filled.

Third World?

To survive, 'Third World' must necessarily have negative *and* positive connotations: negative when viewed in a vertical ranking system – 'underdeveloped' compared to over-industrialized, 'underprivileged' within the already Second sex – and positive when understood sociopolitically as a subversive, 'non-aligned' force. Whether 'Third World' sounds negative or positive also depends on *who* uses it. Coming from you Westerners, the word can hardly mean the same as when it comes from Us members of the Third World. Quite predictably, you/we who condemn it most are both we who buy in and they who deny any participation in the bourgeois mentality of the West. For it was in the context of such mentality that 'Third World' stood out as a new semantic finding to designate what was known as 'the savages' before the Independences. Today, hegemony is much more subtle, much more pernicious than the form of blatant racism once exercised by the colonial West. I/i always find myself asking, in this one-dimensional society, where I/i should draw the line between tracking down the oppressive mechanisms of the system and aiding their spread. 'Third World' commonly refers to those states in Africa, Asia and Latin America which called themselves 'non-aligned', that is to say, affiliated with neither the Western (capitalist) nor the Eastern (communist) power bloc. Thus, if 'Third World' is often rejected for its judged-to-be-derogative connotations, it is not so much because of the hierarchical, first-second-third order implied, as some invariably repeat, but because of the growing threat 'Third World' consistently presents to the Western bloc the last few decades. The emergence of repressed voices into the worldwide political arena has already prompted her (Julia Kristeva) to ask: 'How will the West greet the awakening of the "third world" as the Chinese call it? Can we [Westerners] participate, actively and lucidly, in this awakening when the center of the planet is in the process of moving toward the East?'.[20] Exploited, looked down upon, and lumped together in a convenient term that denies their individualities, a group of 'poor' (nations), having once sided with neither of the dominating forces, has slowly learned to turn this denial to the best account. 'The Third World to Third World peoples' thus becomes an empowering tool, and one which politically includes all non-whites in their solidarist struggle against all forms of Western dominance. And since 'Third World' now refers to more than the geographically and economically determined nations of the 'South' (versus 'North'), since the term comprises such 'developed' countries as Japan and those which have opted for socialist reconstruction of their system (China, Cuba, Ethiopia, Angola, Mozambique) as well as those which have favored a capitalist mode of development (Nigeria, India, Brazil), there no longer exists such a thing as a unified unaligned Third World bloc. Moreover, Third World has moved West (or North, depending on where the dividing line falls) and has expanded so as to include even the remote parts of the First World. What is at stake is not only the hegemony of Western cultures, but also their identities as unified cultures. Third World dwells on diversity; so does First World. This is our strength and our misery. The West is painfully made to realize the existence of a Third World in the First World, and vice versa. The Master is bound to recognize that His Culture is not as homogeneous, as monolithic as He believed it to be. He discovers, with much reluctance, He is just an other among others.

Thus, whenever it is a question of 'Third World women' or, more disquietingly, of 'Third World Women in the US', the reaction provoked among many whites almost never fails to be that of annoyance, irritation, or vexation. 'Why Third World in the US?' they say angrily; 'You mean those who still have relatives in South East Asia?' 'Third World! I don't understand how one can use such a term, it doesn't mean anything.' Or even better, 'Why use such a term to defeat yourself?' Alternatives like 'Western' and 'non-western' or 'Euro-American' and 'non-Euro-American' may sound a bit less charged, but they are certainly neither neutral nor satisfactory, for they still take the dominant group as point of reference, and they reflect well the West's ideology of dominance (it is as if we were to use the term 'non-Afro-Asian', for example, to designate all white peoples). More recently, we have been hearing of the Fourth World which, we are told, 'is a world populated by indigenous people who still continue to bear a spiritual relationship to their traditional lands'. The colonialist creed 'Divide and Conquer' is here again, alive and well. Often ill at ease with the outspoken educated natives who represent the Third World in debates and paternalistically scornful of those who remain reserved, the dominant thus decides to weaken this term of solidarity, both by invalidating it as empowering tool and by inciting divisiveness within the Third World – a Third World within the Third World. Aggressive Third World (educated 'savages') with its awareness and resistance to domination must therefore be classified apart from gentle Fourth World (uneducated 'savages'). Every unaligned voice should necessarily/consequently be either a personal or a minority voice. The (impersonal) majority, as logic dictates, has to be the (aligned) dominant.

> It is, apparently, inconvenient, if not downright mind stretching [notes Alice Walker], for white women scholars to think of black women as women, perhaps because 'woman' (like 'man' among white males) is a name they are claiming for themselves, and themselves alone. Racism decrees that if they are now women (years ago they were ladies, but fashions change) then black women must, perforce, be something else. (While they were 'ladies' black women could be 'women' and so on.)[21]

Another revealing example of this separatist majority mentality is the story Walker relates of an exhibit of women painters at the Brooklyn Museum: when asked 'Are there no black women painters represented here?' (none of them is, apparently), a white woman feminist simply replies 'It's a *women's* exhibit!'[22] Different historical contexts, different semantic contents. ...

'Woman' and the Subtle Power of Linguistic Exclusion

What is *woman*? Long ago, during one of the forceful speeches she delivered in defense of her people, Sojourner Truth was asked by a threatened white doctor in the audience to prove to all those present that she was truly a woman:

> 'There are those among us', he began in a tone characteristic of institutional training, 'who question whether or not you are a woman. Some feel that maybe you are a man in a woman's disguise. To satisfy our curiosity, why don't you show your breasts to the women [sic] in this audience?'[23]

It seemed, indeed, profoundly puzzling for this man-child doctor's mind to see the Woman (or Breasts) in someone who had 'never been helped into carriages, lifted over ditches, nor given the best places everywhere', who had 'plowed, and planted, and gathered into barns', and who, beyond measure, triumphantly affirmed elsewhere: 'Look at me! Look at my arm! ... and no man could head me – and *ar'nt I a woman*!'[24] Definitions of '*woman*', 'womanhood', 'femininity', 'femaleness', and, more recently, of 'female identity', have brought about the arrogance of such a sham anatomical curiosity – whose needs must be 'satisfied' – and the legitimation of a shamelessly dehumanizing form of Indiscretion. Difference reduced to sexual identity is thus posited to justify and conceal exploitation. The Body, the most visible difference between men and women, the only one to offer a secure ground for those who seek the permanent, the feminine 'nature' and 'essence', remains thereby the safest basis for racist and sexist ideologies. The two merging themes of Otherness and the Identity-Body are precisely what Simone de Beauvoir discussed at length in *The Second Sex*, and continued until the time of her death to argue in the French journal she edited, *Questions Féministes*. The lead article written by the Editorial Collective under the title of 'Variations on Common Themes' explains the purpose of the journal – to destroy the notion of differences between the sexes, 'which gives a shape and a base to the concept of "woman"':

> Now, after centuries of men constantly repeating that *we* were different, here are women screaming, as if they were afraid of not being heard and as if it were an exciting discovery: 'We are different!' Are you going fishing? No, I am going fishing.

> The very theme of difference, whatever the differences are represented to be, is useful to the oppressing group ... any allegedly natural feature attributed to an oppressed group is used to imprison this group within the boundaries of a Nature which, since the group is oppressed, ideological confusion labels 'nature of oppressed person' ... to demand the right to Difference without analyzing its social character is to give back the enemy an effective weapon.[25]

Difference as the Editorial Collective of *Questions Féministes* understands and condemns it is bound to remain an integral part of naturalist ideology. It is the very kind of colonized-anthropo-logized difference the master has always happily granted his subordinates. The search and the claim for an essential female/ethnic identity-difference today can never be anything more than a move within the male-is-norm-divide-and-conquer trap. The malady lingers on. As long as words of difference serve to legitimate a discourse instead of delaying its authority to infinity, they are, to borrow an image from Audre Lorde, 'noteworthy only as *decorations*'. In 'An open letter to Mary Daly', Lorde reproaches Daly (whose vision of non-European women in *Gyn/Ecology* mainly results from her insistence on universalizing women's oppression) with utilizing Lorde's words 'only to testify against myself as a woman of color'. She further expands this comment by specifying:

> I feel you do celebrate differences between white women as a creative force towards change, rather than a reason for misunderstanding and separation. But you fail to recognize that, as women, those differences expose all women to various forms and degrees of partriarchal oppression, some of which we share, some of which we do not. ... The oppression of women knows no ethnic nor racial boundaries, true, but that does not mean it is identical within those boundaries.

In other words,

> to imply ... that all women suffer the same oppression simply because we are women, is to lose sight of the many varied tools of patriarchy.[26]

Here you probably smile, for none of us is safe from such a critique, including I who quote Lorde in my attempts at disentangling Difference. The process of differentiation, however, continues, and speaking nearby or together with certainly differs from speaking for and about. The latter aims at the finite and dwells in the realm of fixed oppositions (subject/object difference; man/woman sexual difference), tending thereby to valorize the privileged father-daughter relationship.

[. . .]

Subject-in-the-Making

'In "woman"', says Julia Kristeva, 'I see something that cannot be represented, something that is not said, something above and beyond nomenclatures and ideologies'.[27] Since there can be no social-political r-evolution without a r-evolution of subjects, in order to shatter the social codes, women must assume, in every (non-dualist) sense of the word, 'a *negative* function: reject everything ... definite, structured, loaded with meaning, in the existing state of society'. Such a responsibility does not exclusively devolve upon women, but it is women who are in a better position to accept it, 'because in social, sexual and symbolic experiences being a woman has always provided a means to another end, to becoming something else: a subject-in-the-making, a subject on trial'.[28] In a book written after her visit to China, Kristeva remarks how little Chinese women differ from Chinese men – these women 'whose ancestors knew better than anyone the secrets of erotic art, now so sober and so absorbed in their gray-blue suits, relaxed and austere ... stand[ing] before their lathes or in the arms of their children ... the "pill" in their pockets ...':

> One can say that they 'censure the sexual difference' ... what if this reproach, insofar as it is one, were to have no meaning except in our framework of paternal dominance, where any trace of a 'central mother figure' is completely lost? What if their tradition, on condition one could strip it of its hierarchical-bureaucratic-patriarchal weight, allowed no more separation between two metaphysical entities (Men and Women); no more symbolic difference, that is, outside the biological difference, except *a subtle differentiation on both sides of the biological barrier, structured by the recognition of a social law to be assumed in order ceaselessly to be contested?* ...
>
> If ... one considered the family, women, and the sexual difference in the way they determine a social ethic, one could say ... that the basic question there is the building of a society whose active power is represented by no one ... not even women.[29] (emphasis added)

The point raised by this apparent indifference to a physical distinction between men and women is not simple repression of a sexual difference, but a *different* distribution *of* sexual *difference*, therefore a challenge to the notion of (sexual) identity as commonly defined in the West and the entire gamut of concepts that ensues: femininity-femaleness-feminitude-woman-womanhood/masculinity-maleness-virility-man-manhood, and so on. In other words, sexual difference has no absolute value and is interior to the praxis of every subject. What is known as the 'Phallic principle' in one part of the world (despite the dominance this part exerts over the rest) does not necessarily apply to the other parts. A thorough undermining of all power-based values would require the dismantling of the sovereign, authority-claiming subject, without which it is bound to be co-opted by power. 'On a deeper level', observes Kristeva, 'a woman cannot "be"; it is something which does not even belong in the order of *being*. It follows that a feminist practice can only be negative ['our negativity is not Nietzschean anger'], at odds with what already exists so that we may say "that's not it" and "that's still not it"'.[30]

Ethnicity or Womanhood: Whose Duality?

Voices of theories. Unlike Kristeva, while understanding the necessity of a 'negative' feminist practice which continuously reminds us that 'woman cannot be' or that we can no more speak about 'woman' than about 'man', I would not 'try to go against metaphysical theories that censure what [she] just labeled "a woman"' and to 'dissolve identity'.[31] Although these statements belong to a context of active questioning of the search for a woman's identity (and, by extension, of a straight celebration of ethnic identity), they tend to invite accusations of privileging 'woman' as attitude over 'woman' as sex. One does not go without the other, and 'woman', with its undefinable specificity (the difference, as mentioned above, both between and within entities), cannot exclusively be apprehended in relation to an apparently unsexed or supposedly beyond-the-sex 'negative function'. The perception of sex as a secondary attribute – a property or an adjective that one can add or subtract – to woman is a perception that still dwells in the prevailing logic of acquisition and separation. Difference understood not as an irreducible quality but as a drifting apart within 'woman' articulates upon the infinity of 'woman' as entities of inseparable 'I's' and 'Not-I's'. In any case, 'woman' here is not interchangeable with 'man'; and to declare provocatively, as Kristeva does, that one should dissolve 'even sexual identities' is, in a way, to disregard the importance of the shift that the notion of identity has undergone in woman's discourses. That shift does not lead to 'a theory of female identity ... that varies from the male model' (Gardiner), as mentioned earlier, but rather to identity as points of re-departure of the critical processes by which I have come to understand how the personal – the ethnic me, the female me – is political. Difference does not annul identity. It is beyond and alongside identity. Thus, there is simply no point outside Kristeva's 'sexual identities' from which to take up a position ('When you are silent, it speaks;/When you speak, it is silent'). The same holds true for the choice many women of color feel obliged to make between ethnicity and womanhood: how can they? You never have/are one without the other. The idea of two illusorily separated identities, one ethnic, the other woman (or, more precisely, female), again, partakes in the Euro-American system of dualistic reasoning and its age-old divide-and-conquer tactics. Triple jeopardy means here that whenever a woman of color takes up the feminist fight, she immediately qualifies for three possible 'betrayals': she can be accused of betraying either man (the 'man-hater'), or her community ('people of color should stay together to fight racism'), or woman herself ('you should fight first on the women's side'). The pitting of anti-racist and anti-sexist struggles against one another allows some vocal fighters to dismiss blatantly the existence of either racism or sexism within their lines of action, as if oppression only comes in separate, monolithic forms. Thus, to understand how pervasively dominance operates via the concept of hegemony or of absent totality in plurality is to understand that the work of decolonization will have to continue within the women's movements.

[. . .]

Notes

1. Audre Lorde, 'The master's tools will never dismantle the master's house', in *This Bridge Called My Back: Writings by radical women of color*, ed. C. Morraga and G. Anzaldúa (Watertown, MA.: Persephone Press, 1981), p. 99.
2. Charles A. W. Manning. 'In defense of apartheid', in *Africa Yesterday and Today*, ed. C. D. Moore and A. Dunbar (New York: Bantam, 1968), p. 287.
3. *Ibid.*, p. 289.
4. Jan Christiaan Smuts, quoted in Louis Fischer, *Gandhi: His life and message for the world* (New York: New American Library, 1954), p. 25.
5. General Louis Botha, quoted in *ibid.*
6. Manning, 'In defense of apartheid', p. 287.
7. Gayatri Chakravorty Spivak, 'The politics of interpretations', *Critical Inquiry* 9, no. 1 (1982), p. 278.
8. Gloria Anzaldúa, 'Speaking in tongues: a letter to 3rd World women writers', *This Bridge*, pp. 167–8.
9. Mitsuye Yamada, 'Asian Pacific American women and feminism', *This Bridge*, p. 71.
10. Lorde, 'The master's tools', p. 100.
11. Alice Walker, 'One child of one's own: a meaningful digression within the work(s)', in *The Writer on Her Work*, ed. J. Sternburg (New York: W. W. Norton, 1980), p. 137.
12. Ellen Pence, 'Racism – a white issue', in *But Some of Us Are Brave*, ed. G. T. Hull, P. B. Scott and B. Smith (Old Westbury, NY.: Feminist Press, 1982), p. 46.
13. *Ibid.*, pp. 46–7.
14. Barbara Smith, 'Racism and women's studies', *But Some of Us Are Brave*, p. 49.
15. I have discussed at length the notions of non-dualistic thinking and of multiple presence in Trinh T. Minh-ha, *Un Art sans oeuvre. L'Anonymat dans les arts contemporains* (Troy, MI.: International Books Pubs, 1981).
16. Vine Deloria, Jr, *Custer Died for Your Sins* (New York: Avon Books, 1969), p. 86.
17. Quoted in Alan W. Watts, *Nature, Man, and Woman* (1958, rpt. New York: Vintage Books, 1970), p. 121.
18. 'On female identity and writings by women', *Critical Inquiry* 8 (Special Issue on *Writing and Sexual Difference*, ed. E. Abel), no. 2 (1981), pp. 348–9, 354, 353.
19. Simone de Beauvoir, *The Second Sex* (1952, rpt. New York: Bantam, 1970), p. 223.
20. Julia Kristeva, 'Woman can never be defined', trans. Marily A. August, in *New French Feminisims*, ed. E. Marks and I. De Courtivon (Amherst: University of Massachusetts Press, 1980), p. 139.
21. 'One child of one's own', pp. 133–4.
22. *Ibid.*, p. 136.

23. Quoted in *Sturdy Black Bridges. Visions of Black women in literature*, ed. R. P. Bell, B. J. Parker and B. Guy-Sheftall (Garden City, NY.: Anchor/Doubleday, 1979), p. xxv.
24. Sojourner Truth, 'Speech of woman's suffrage', *The Ethnic American Woman*, p. 335.
25. In *New French Feminisms*, pp. 214, 219.
26. In *This Bridge*, pp. 95, 97.
27. 'Woman can never be defined', p. 137.
28. Kristeva in an interview with Xavière Gauthier, 'Oscillation between power and denial', *New French Feminisms*, pp. 166–7.
29. Julia Kristeva, 'On the women of China', trans. E. Conroy Kennedy, *Signs* 1, no. 1 (1975), pp. 79, 81.
30. 'Woman can never be defined', p. 137.
31. *Ibid.*, p. 138.

3.5 □ *The Straight Mind*[1]

Monique Wittig

In recent years in Paris, language as a phenomenon has dominated modern theoretical systems and the social sciences and has entered the political discussions of the lesbian and women's liberation movements. This is because it relates to an important political field where what is at play is power, or more than that, a network of powers, since there is a multiplicity of languages that constantly act upon the social reality. The importance of language as such as a political stake has only recently been perceived.[2] But the gigantic development of linguistics, the multiplication of schools of linguistics, the advent of the sciences of communication, and the technicality of the metalanguages that these sciences utilize, represent the symptoms of the importance of what is politically at stake. The science of language has invaded other sciences, such as anthropology through Lévi-Strauss, psychoanalysis through Lacan, and all the disciplines which have developed from the basis of structuralism.

The early semiology of Roland Barthes nearly escaped from linguistic domination to become a political analysis of the different systems of signs, to establish a relationship between this or that system of signs – for example, the myths of the petty-bourgeois class – and the class struggle within capitalism that this system tends to conceal. We were almost saved, for political semiology is a weapon (a method) that we need to analyze what is called ideology. But the miracle did not last. Rather than introducing into semiology concepts which are foreign to it – in this case Marxist concepts – Barthes quickly stated that semiology was only a branch of linguistics and that language was its only object.

Thus, the entire world is only a great register where the most diverse languages come to have themselves recorded, such as the language of the Unconscious,[3] the language of fashion, the language of the exchange of women where human beings are literally the signs which are used to communicate. These languages, or rather these discourses, fit into one another, interpenetrate one another, support one another, reinforce one another, auto-engender, and engender one another. Linguistics engenders

From Wittig, M., *The Straight Mind and Other Essays*, Harvester Wheatsheaf, Hemel Hempstead, 1992, pp. 21–32, 102–3.

semiology and structural linguistics, structural linguistics engenders structuralism, which engenders the Structural Unconscious. The ensemble of these discourses produces a confusing static for the oppressed, which makes them lose sight of the material cause of their oppression and plunges them into a kind of ahistoric vacuum.

For they produce a scientific reading of the social reality in which human beings are given as invariants, untouched by history and unworked by class conflicts, with identical psyches because genetically programmed. This psyche, equally untouched by history and unworked by class conflicts, provides the specialists, from the beginning of the twentieth century, with a whole arsenal of invariants: the symbolic language which very advantageously functions with very few elements, since, like digits (0–9), the symbols 'unconsciously' produced by the psyche are not very numerous. Therefore, these symbols are very easy to impose, through therapy and theorization, upon the collective and individual unconscious. We are taught that the Unconscious, with perfectly good taste, structures itself upon metaphors, for example, the Name-of-the-father, the Oedipus complex, castration, the murder-or-death-of-the-father, the exchange of women, etc. If the Unconscious, however, is easy to control, it is not just by anybody. Similar to mystical revelations, the apparition of symbols in the psyche demands multiple interpretations. Only specialists can accomplish the deciphering of the Unconscious. Only they, the psychoanalysts, are allowed (authorized?) to organize and interpret psychic manifestations which will show the symbol in its full meaning. And while the symbolic language is extremely poor and essentially lacunary, the languages or metalanguages which interpret it are developing, each one of them, with a richness, a display, that only theological exegeses of the Bible have equalled.

Who gave the psychoanalysts their knowledge? For example, for Lacan, what he calls the 'psychoanalytic discourse', or the 'analytical experience', both 'teach' him what he already knows. And each one teaches him what the other one taught him. But can we deny that Lacan scientifically discovered, through the 'analytical experience' (somehow an experiment), the structures of the Unconscious? Will we be irresponsible enough to disregard the discourses of the psychoanalyzed people lying on their couches? In my opinion, there is no doubt that Lacan found in the Unconscious the structures he said he found there, since he had previously put them there. People who did not fall into the power of the psychoanalytic institution may experience an immeasurable feeling of sadness at the degree of oppression (of manipulation) that the psychoanalyzed discourses show. In the analytic experience there is an oppressed person, the psychoanalyzed, whose need for communication is exploited and who (in the same way as the witches could, under torture, only repeat the language that the inquisitors wanted to hear) has no other choice, (if s/he does not want to destroy the implicit contract which allows her/him to communicate and which s/he needs), than to attempt to say what s/he is supposed to say. They say that this can last for a lifetime – cruel contract which constrains a human being to display her/his misery to an oppressor who is directly responsible for it, who exploits her/him economically, politically, ideologically and whose interpretation reduces this misery to a few figures of speech.

But can the need to communicate that this contract implies only be satisfied in the psychoanalytic situation, in being cured or 'experimented' with? If we believe recent testimonies[4] by lesbians, feminists, and gay men, this is not the case. All their testimonies emphasize the political significance of the impossibility that lesbians, feminists, and gay men face in the attempt to communicate in heterosexual society, other than with a psychoanalyst. When the general state of things is understood (one is not sick or to be cured, one has an enemy) the result is that the oppressed person breaks the psychoanalytic contract. This is what appears in the testimonies, along with the teaching that the psychoanalytic contract was not a contract of consent but a forced one.

The discourses which particularly oppress all of us, lesbians, women, and homosexual men, are those which take for granted that what founds society, any society, is heterosexuality.[5] These discourses speak about us and claim to say the truth in an apolitical field, as if anything of that which signifies could escape the political in this moment of history, and as if, in what concerns us, politically insignificant signs could exist. These discourses of heterosexuality oppress us in the sense that they prevent us from speaking unless we speak in their terms. Everything which puts them into question is at once disregarded as elementary. Our refusal of the totalizing interpretation of psychoanalysis makes the theoreticians say that we neglect the symbolic dimension. These discourses deny us every possibility of creating our own categories. But their most ferocious action is the unrelenting tyranny that they exert upon our physical and mental selves.

When we use the overgeneralizing term 'ideology' to designate all the discourses of the dominating group, we relegate these discourses to the domain of Irreal Ideas; we forget the material (physical) violence that they directly do to the oppressed people, a violence produced by the abstract and 'scientific' discourses as well as by the discourses of the mass media. I would like to insist on the material oppression of individuals by discourses, and I would like to underline its immediate effects through the example of pornography.

Pornographic images, films, magazine photos, publicity posters on the walls of the cities, constitute a discourse, and this discourse covers our world with its signs, and this discourse has a meaning: it signifies that women are dominated. Semioticians can interpret the system of this discourse, describe its disposition. What they read in that discourse are signs whose function is not to signify and which have no *raison d'être* except to be elements of a certain system or disposition. But for us this discourse is not divorced from the real as it is for semioticians. Not only does it maintain very close relations with the social reality which is our oppression (economically and politically), but also it is in itself real since it is one of the aspects of oppression, since it exerts a precise power over us. The pornographic discourse is one of the strategies of violence which are exercised upon us: it humiliates, it degrades, it is a crime against our 'humanity'. As a harassing tactic it has another function, that of a warning. It orders us to stay in line, and it keeps those who would tend to forget who they are in step; it calls upon fear. These same experts in semiotics, referred to earlier, reproach us for confusing, when we demonstrate against pornography, the discourses with the reality. They do not see that this discourse *is* reality for us, one of the facets of the reality of our oppression. They believe that we are mistaken in our level of analysis.

I have chosen pornography as an example because its discourse is the most symptomatic and the most demonstrative of the violence which is done to us through discourses, as well as in the society at large. There is nothing abstract about the power that sciences and theories have to act materially and actually upon our bodies and our minds, even if the discourse that produces it is abstract. It is one of the forms of domination, its very expression. I would say, rather, one of its exercises. All of the oppressed know this power and have had to deal with it. It is the one which says: you do not have the right to speech because your discourse is not scientific and not theoretical, you are on the wrong level of analysis, you are confusing discourse and reality, your discourse is naive, you misunderstand this or that science.

If the discourse of modern theoretical systems and social science exert a power upon us, it is because it works with concepts which closely touch us. In spite of the historic advent of the lesbian, feminist, and gay liberation movements, whose proceedings have already upset the philosophical and political categories of the discourses of the social sciences, their categories (thus brutally put into question) are nevertheless utilized without examination by contemporary science. They function like primitive concepts in a conglomerate of all kinds of disciplines, theories, and current ideas that I will call the straight mind. (See The *Savage Mind* by Claude Lévi-Strauss.) They concern 'woman', 'man', 'sex', 'difference', and all of the series of concepts which bear this mark, including such concepts as 'history', 'culture', and the 'real'. And although it has been accepted in recent years that there is no such thing as nature, that everything is culture, there remains within that culture a core of nature which resists examination, a relationship excluded from the social in the analysis – a relationship whose characteristic is ineluctability in culture, as well as in nature, and which is the heterosexual relationship. I will call it the obligatory social relationship between 'man' and 'woman'. (Here I refer to Ti-Grace Atkinson and her analysis of sexual intercourse as an institution.[6]) With its ineluctability as knowledge, as an obvious principle, as a given prior to any science, the straight mind develops a totalizing interpretation of history, social reality, culture, language, and all the subjective phenomena at the same time. I can only underline the oppressive character that the straight mind is clothed in in its tendency to immediately universalize its production of concepts into general laws which claim to hold true for all societies, all epochs, all individuals. Thus one speaks of *the* exchange of women, *the* difference between the sexes, *the* symbolic order, *the* Unconscious, Desire, *Jouissance*, Culture, History, giving an absolute meaning to these concepts when they are only categories founded upon heterosexuality, or thought which produces the difference between the sexes as a political and philosophical dogma.

The consequence of this tendency toward universality is that the straight mind cannot conceive of a culture, a society where heterosexuality would not order not only all human relationships but also its very production of concepts and all the processes which escape consciousness, as well. Additionally, these unconscious processes are historically more and more imperative in what they teach us about ourselves through the instrumentality of specialists. The rhetoric which expresses them (and whose seduction I do not underestimate) envelops itself in myths, resorts to enigma, proceeds by accumulating metaphors, and its function is to poeticize the obligatory character of the 'you-will-be-straight-or-you-will-not-be'.

In this thought, to reject the obligation of coitus and the institutions that this obligation has produced as necessary for the constitution of a society, is simply an impossibility, since to do this would mean to reject the possibility of the constitution of the other and to reject the 'symbolic order', to make the constitution of meaning impossible, without which no one can maintain an internal coherence. Thus lesbianism, homosexuality, and the societies that we form cannot be thought of or spoken of, even though they have always existed. Thus, the straight mind continues to affirm that incest, and not homosexuality, represents its major interdiction. Thus, when thought by the straight mind, homosexuality is nothing but heterosexuality.

Yes, straight society is based on the necessity of the different/other at every level. It cannot work economically, symbolically, linguistically, or politically without this concept. This necessity of the different/other is an ontological one for the whole conglomerate of sciences and disciplines that I call the straight mind. But what is the different/other if not the dominated? For heterosexual society is the society which not only oppresses lesbians and gay men, it oppresses many different/others, it oppresses all women and many categories of men, all those who are in the position of the dominated. To constitute a difference and to control it is an 'act of power, since it is essentially a normative act. Everybody tries to show the other as different. But not everybody succeeds in doing so. One has to be socially dominant to succeed in it.'[7]

For example, the concept of difference between the sexes ontologically constitutes women into different/others. Men are not different, whites are not different, nor are the masters. But the blacks, as well as the slaves, are. This ontological characteristic of the difference between the sexes affects all the concepts which are part of the same conglomerate. But for us there is no such thing as being-woman or being-man. 'Man' and 'woman' are political concepts of opposition, and the copula which dialectically unites them is, at the same time, the one which abolishes them.[8] It is the class struggle between women and men which will abolish men and women.[9] The concept of difference has nothing ontological about it. It is only the way that the masters interpret a historical situation of domination. The function of difference is to mask at every level the conflicts of interest, including ideological ones.

In other words, for us, this means there cannot any longer be women and men, and that as classes and categories of thought or language they have to disappear, politically, economically, ideologically. If we, as lesbians and gay men, continue to speak of ourselves and to conceive of ourselves as women and as men, we are instrumental in maintaining heterosexuality. I am sure that an economic and political transformation will not dedramatize these categories of language. Can we redeem *slave*? Can we redeem *nigger, negress*? How is *woman* different? Will we continue to write *white, master, man*? The transformation of economic relationships will not suffice. We must produce a political transformation of the key concepts, that is, of the concepts which are strategic for us. For there is another order of materiality, that of language, and language is worked upon from within by these strategic concepts. It is at the same time tightly connected to the political field, where everything that concerns language, science and thought refers to the person as subjectivity and to her/his relationship to society. And we cannot leave this within the power of the straight mind or the thought of domination.

If among all the productions of the straight mind I especially challenge the models of the Structural Unconscious, it is because: at the moment in history when the domination of social groups can no longer appear as a logical necessity to the dominated, because they revolt, because they question the differences, Lévi-Strauss, Lacan, and their epigones call upon necessities which escape the control of consciousness and therefore the responsibility of individuals.

They call upon unconscious processes, for example, which require the exchange of women as a necessary condition for every society. According to them, that is what the unconscious tells us with authority, and the symbolic order, without which there is no meaning, no language, no society, depends on it. But what does women being exchanged mean if not that they are dominated? No wonder then that there is only one Unconscious, and that it is heterosexual. It is an Unconscious which looks too consciously after the interests of the masters[10] in whom it lives for them to be dispossessed of their concepts so easily. Besides, domination is denied; there is no slavery of women, there is difference. To which I will answer with this statement made by a Romanian peasant at a public meeting in 1848: 'Why do the gentlemen say it was not slavery, for we know it to have been slavery, this sorrow that we have sorrowed.' Yes, we know it, and this science of oppression cannot be taken away from us.

It is from this science that we must track down the 'what-goes-without-saying' heterosexual, and (I paraphrase the early Roland Barthes) we must not bear 'seeing Nature and History confused at every turn'.[11] We must make it brutally apparent that psychoanalysis after Freud and particularly Lacan have rigidly turned their concepts into myths – Difference, Desire, the Name-of-the-father, etc. They have even 'over-mythified' the myths, an operation that was necessary for them in order to systematically heterosexualize that personal dimension which suddenly emerged through the dominated individuals into the historical field, particularly through women, who started their struggle almost two centuries ago. And it has been done systematically, in a concert of interdisciplinarity, never more harmonious than since the heterosexual myths started to circulate with ease from one formal system to another, like sure values that can be invested in anthropology as well as in psychoanalysis and in all the social sciences.

This ensemble of heterosexual myths is a system of signs which uses figures of speech, and thus it can be politically studied from within the science of our oppression; 'for-we-know-it-to-have-been-slavery' is the dynamic which introduces the diachronism of history into the fixed discourse of eternal essences. This undertaking should somehow be a political semiology, although with 'this sorrow that we have sorrowed' we work also at the level of language/manifesto, of language/action, that which transforms, that which makes history.

In the meantime, in the systems that seemed so eternal and universal that laws could be extracted from them, laws that could be stuffed into computers, and in any case for the moment stuffed into the unconscious machinery, in these systems, thanks to our action and our language, shifts are happening. Such a model, as for example, the exchange of women, reengulfs history in so violent and brutal a way that the whole system, which was believed to be formal, topples over into another dimension of knowledge. This dimension of history belongs to us, since somehow we have been designated, and since, as Lévi-Strauss said, we talk, let us say that we break off the heterosexual contract.

So, this is what lesbians say everywhere in this country and in some others, if not with theories at least through their social practice, whose repercussions upon straight culture and society are still unenvisionable. An anthropologist might say that we have to wait for fifty years. Yes, if one wants to universalize the functioning of these societies and make their invariants appear. Meanwhile the straight concepts are undermined. What is woman? Panic, general alarm for an active defense. Frankly, it is a problem that the lesbians do not have because of a change of perspective, and it would be incorrect to say that lesbians associate, make love, live with women, for 'woman' has meaning only in heterosexual systems of thought and heterosexual economic systems. Lesbians are not women.

Notes

1. This text was first read in New York at the Modern Language Association Convention in 1978 and dedicated to American lesbians.
2. However, the classical Greeks knew that there was no political power without mastery of the art of rhetoric, especially in a democracy.
3. Throughout this paper, when Lacan's use of the term 'the Unconscious' is referred to it is capitalized, following his style.
4. For example, see Karla Jay and Allen Young, (eds), *Out of the Closets* (New York: Links Books, 1972).
5. Heterosexuality: a word which first appears in the French language in 1911.
6. Ti-Grace Atkinson, *Amazon Odyssey* (New York: Links Books, 1974), pp. 13–23.
7. Claude Faugeron and Philippe Robert, *La Justice et son public et les représentations sociales du système pénal* (Paris: Masson, 1978).
8. See, for her definition of 'social sex', Nicole-Claude Mathieu, 'Notes pour une définition sociologique des catégories de sexe', *Épistémologie Sociologique* 11 (1971). Translated as *Ignored by Some, Denied by Others: The social sex category in sociology* (pamphlet), Explorations in Feminism 2 (London: Women's Research and Resources Centre Publications, 1977), pp. 16–37.
9. In the same way that in every other class struggle the categories of opposition are 'reconciled' by the struggle whose goal is to make them disappear.
10. Are the millions of dollars a year made by the psychoanalysts symbolic?
11. Roland Barthes, *Mythologies* (New York: Hill & Wang, 1972), p. 11.

3.6 □ *From* In a Different Voice: Psychological theory and women's development

Carol Gilligan

Concepts of Self and Morality

[. . .]

Norma Haan's (1975) research on college students and Constance Holstein's (1976) three-year study of adolescents and their parents indicate that the moral judgments of women differ from those of men in the greater extent to which women's judgments are tied to feelings of empathy and compassion and are concerned with the resolution of real as opposed to hypothetical dilemmas. However, as long as the categories by which development is assessed are derived from research on men, divergence from the masculine standard can be seen only as a failure of development. As a result, the thinking of women is often classified with that of children. The absence of alternative criteria that might better encompass the development of women, however, points not only to the limitations of theories framed by men and validated by research samples disproportionately male and adolescent, but also to the diffidence prevalent among women, their reluctance to speak publicly in their own voice, given the constraints imposed on them by their lack of power and the politics of relations between the sexes.

From Gilligan, C., *In a Different Voice: Psychological theory and women's development*, Harvard University Press, Cambridge, MA, 1982, pp. 69–74, 79, 82–3, 98, 100–01, 102–3, 105, 172–4, 177–80.

In order to go beyond the question 'How much like men do women think, how capable are they of engaging in the abstract and hypothetical construction of reality?' it is necessary to identify and define developmental criteria that encompass the categories of women's thought. Haan points out the necessity to derive such criteria from the resolution of the 'more frequently occurring, real-life moral dilemmas of interpersonal, empathic, fellow-feeling concerns' (p. 34) which have long been the center of women's moral concern. But to derive developmental criteria from the language of women's moral discourse, it is necessary first to see whether women's construction of the moral domain relies on a language different from that of men and one that deserves equal credence in the definition of development. This in turn requires finding places where women have the power to choose and thus are willing to speak in their own voice.

When birth control and abortion provide women with effective means for controlling their fertility, the dilemma of choice enters a central arena of women's lives. Then the relationships that have traditionally defined women's identities and framed their moral judgments no longer flow inevitably from their reproductive capacity but become matters of decision over which they have control. Released from the passivity and reticence of a sexuality that binds them in dependence, women can question with Freud what it is that they want and can assert their own answers to that question. However, while society may affirm publicly the woman's right to choose for herself, the exercise of such choice brings her privately into conflict with the conventions of femininity, particularly the moral equation of goodness with self-sacrifice. Although independent assertion in judgment and action is considered to be the hallmark of adulthood, it is rather in their care and concern for others that women have both judged themselves and been judged.

The conflict between self and other thus constitutes the central moral problem for women, posing a dilemma whose resolution requires a reconciliation between femininity and adulthood. In the absence of such a reconciliation, the moral problem cannot be resolved. The 'good woman' masks assertion in evasion, denying responsibility by claiming only to meet the needs of others, while the 'bad woman' forgoes or renounces the commitments that bind her in self-deception and betrayal. It is precisely this dilemma – the conflict between compassion and autonomy, between virtue and power – which the feminine voice struggles to resolve in its effort to reclaim the self and to solve the moral problem in such a way that no one is hurt.

When a woman considers whether to continue or abort a pregnancy, she contemplates a decision that affects both self and others and engages directly the critical moral issue of hurting. Since the choice is ultimately hers, and therefore one for which she is responsible, it raises precisely those questions of judgment that have been most problematic for women. Now she is asked whether she wishes to interrupt that stream of life which for centuries has immersed her in the passivity of dependence while at the same time imposing on her the responsibility for care. Thus the abortion decision brings to the core of feminine apprehension, to what Joan Didion (1972) calls 'the irreconcilable difference of it – that sense of living one's deepest life underwater, that dark involvement with blood and birth and death' (p. 14), the adult questions of responsibility and choice.

How women deal with such choices was the subject of the abortion study, designed to clarify the ways in which women construct and resolve abortion decisions. Twenty-nine women, ranging in age from fifteen to thirty-three and diverse in ethnic background and social class, were referred for the study by abortion and pregnancy counseling services. The women participated in the study for a variety of reasons – some to gain further clarification with respect to a decision about which they were in conflict, some in response to a counselor's concern about repeated abortions, and others to contribute to ongoing research. Although the pregnancies occurred under a variety of circumstances in the lives of these women, certain commonalities were discerned. The adolescents often failed to use birth control because they denied or discredited their capacity to bear children. Some women became pregnant due to the omission of contraceptive measures in circumstances where intercourse had not been anticipated. Some pregnancies coincided with efforts on the part of the women to end a relationship and may be seen as a manifestation of ambivalence or as a way of putting the relationship to the ultimate test of commitment. For these women, the pregnancy appeared to be a way of testing truth, making the baby an ally in the search for male support and protection or, that failing, a companion victim of male rejection. Finally, some women became pregnant as a result either of a failure of birth control or of a joint decision that was later reconsidered. Of the twenty-nine women, four decided to have the baby, two miscarried, twenty-one chose abortion, and two who were in doubt about the decision at the time of the interview could not be contacted for the follow-up research.

The women were interviewed twice, first at the time they were making the decision, in the first trimester of a confirmed pregnancy, and then at the end of the following year. The referral procedure required that there be an interval between the woman's contacting a counselor or clinic and the time the abortion was performed. Given this factor and the fact that some counselors saw participation in the study as an effective means of crisis-intervention, there is reason to believe that the women interviewed were in greater than usual conflict over the decision. Since the study focused on the relation between judgment and action rather than on the issue of abortion *per se*, no effort was made to select a sample that would be representative of women considering, seeking, or having abortions. Thus the findings pertain to the different ways in which women think about dilemmas in their lives rather than to the ways in which women in general think about the abortion choice.

In the initial part of the interview, the women were asked to discuss the decision they faced, how they were dealing with it, the alternatives they were considering, their reasons both for and against each option, the people involved, the conflicts entailed, and the ways in which making this decision affected their views of themselves and their relationships with others. In the second part of the interview, the women were asked to resolve three hypothetical moral dilemmas, including the Heinz dilemma from Kohlberg's research.

In extending Piaget's description of children's moral judgment to the moral judgment of adolescents and adults, Kohlberg (1976) distinguishes three perspectives on moral conflict and choice. Tying moral development in adolescence to the growth of reflective thought at that time, Kohlberg terms these three views of morality preconventional, conventional, and postconventional, to reflect the expansion in moral understanding from an individual to a societal to a universal point of view. In this scheme, conventional morality, or the equation of the right or good with the maintenance of existing social norms and values, is always the point of departure. Whereas preconventional moral judgment denotes an inability to construct a shared or societal viewpoint, postconventional judgment transcends that vision. Preconventional judgment is egocentric and derives moral constructs from individual needs; conventional judgment is based on the shared norms and values that sustain relationships, groups, communities, and societies; and postconventional judgment adopts a reflective perspective on societal values and constructs moral principles that are universal in application.

This shift in perspective toward increasingly differentiated, comprehensive, and reflective forms of thought appears in women's responses to both actual and hypothetical dilemmas. But just as the conventions that shape women's moral judgment differ from those that apply to men, so also women's definition of the moral domain diverges from that derived from studies of men. Women's construction of the moral problem as a problem of care and responsibility in relationships rather than as one of rights and rules ties the development of their moral thinking to changes in their understanding of responsibility and relationships, just as the conception of morality as justice ties development to the logic of equality and reciprocity. Thus the logic underlying an ethic of care is a psychological logic of relationships, which contrasts with the formal logic of fairness that informs the justice approach.

Women's constructions of the abortion dilemma in particular reveal the existence of a distinct moral language whose evolution traces a sequence of development. This is the language of selfishness and responsibility, which defines the moral problem as one of obligation to exercise care and avoid hurt. The inflicting of hurt is considered selfish and immoral in its reflection of unconcern, while the expression of care is seen as the fulfillment of moral responsibility. The reiterative use by the women of the words *selfish* and *responsible* in talking about moral conflict and choice, given the underlying moral orientation that this language reflects, sets the women apart from the men whom Kohlberg studied and points toward a different understanding of moral development.

The three moral perspectives revealed by the abortion decision study denote a sequence in the development of the ethic of care. These different views of care and the transitions between them emerged from an analysis of the ways in which the women used moral language – words such as *should, ought, better, right, good,* and *bad*, by the changes and shifts that appeared in their thinking, and by the way in which they reflected on and judged their thought. In this sequence, an initial focus on caring for the self in order to ensure survival is followed by a transitional phase in which this judgment is criticized as selfish. The criticism signals a new understanding of the connection between self and others which is articulated by the concept of responsibility. The elaboration of this concept of responsibility and its fusion with a maternal morality that seeks to ensure care for the dependent and unequal characterizes the second perspective. At this point, the good is equated with caring for others. However, when only others are legitimized as the recipients of the woman's care, the exclusion of herself gives rise to problems in relationships, creating a disequilibrium that initiates the second transition. The equation of conformity with care, in its conventional definition, and the illogic of the inequality between other and self, lead to a reconsideration of relationships in an effort to sort out the confusion between self-sacrifice and care inherent in the conventions of feminine goodness. The third perspective focuses on the dynamics of relationships and dissipates the tension between selfishness and responsibility through a new understanding of the interconnection between other and self. Care becomes the self-chosen principle of a judgment that remains psychological in its concern with relationships and response but becomes universal in its condemnation of exploitation and hurt. Thus a progressively more adequate understanding of the psychology of human relationships – an increasing differentiation of self and other and a growing comprehension of the dynamics of social interaction – informs the development of an ethic of care. This ethic, which reflects a cumulative knowledge of human relationships, evolves around a central insight, that self and other are interdependent. The different ways of thinking about this connection or the different modes of its apprehension mark the three perspectives and their transitional phases. In this sequence, the fact of interconnection informs the central, recurring recognition that just as the incidence of violence is in the end destructive to all, so the activity of care enhances both others and self.

[. . .]

The transition from the first to the second perspective, the shift from selfishness to responsibility, is a move toward social participation. Whereas from the first perspective, morality is a matter of sanctions imposed by a society of which one is more subject than citizen, from the second perspective, moral judgment relies on shared norms and expectations. The woman at this point validates her claim to social membership through the adoption of societal values. Consensual judgment about goodness becomes the overriding concern as survival is now seen to depend on acceptance by others.

Here the conventional feminine voice emerges with great clarity, defining the self and proclaiming its worth on the basis of the ability to care for and protect others. The woman now constructs a world perfused with the assumptions about feminine goodness that are reflected in the stereotypes of the Broverman *et al.* studies (1972), where all the attributes considered desirable for women presume an other – the recipient of the 'tact, gentleness and easy expression of feeling' which allow the woman to respond sensitively while evoking in return the care that meets her 'very strong need for security' (p. 63). The strength of this position lies in its capacity for caring; the limitation of this position lies in the restriction it imposes on direct expression.

[. . .]

This notion of responsibility, backwards in its assumptions about control, disguises assertion as response. By reversing responsibility, it generates a series of indirect actions, which in the end leave everyone feeling manipulated and betrayed. The logic of this position is confused in that the morality of mutual care is embedded in the psychology of dependence. Assertion becomes potentially immoral in its power to hurt. This confusion is captured in Kohlberg's definition of the third stage of moral development which joins the need for approval with the wish to care for and help others. When thus caught between the passivity of dependence and the activity of care, the woman becomes suspended in a paralysis of initiative with respect to both action and thought. Thus Denise [one of the women interviewed] speaks of herself as 'just going along with the tide'.

The transitional phase that follows this judgment is marked by a shift in concern from goodness to truth. The transition begins with reconsideration of the relationship between self and other, as the woman starts to scrutinize the logic of self-sacrifice in the service of a morality of care. In the abortion interviews this transition is announced by the reappearance of the word *selfish*. Retrieving the judgmental initiative, the woman begins to ask whether it is selfish or responsible, moral or immoral, to include her own needs within the compass of her care and concern. This question leads her to reexamine the concept of responsibility, juxtaposing the concern with what other people think with a new inner judgment.

In separating the voice of the self from the voices of others, the woman asks if it is possible to be responsible to herself as well as to others and thus to reconcile the disparity between hurt and care. The exercise of such responsibility requires a new kind of judgment, whose first demand is for honesty. To be responsible for oneself, it is first necessary to acknowledge what one is doing. The criterion for judgment thus shifts from goodness to truth when the morality of action is assessed not on the basis of its appearance in the eyes of others, but in terms of the realities of its intention and consequence.

[. . .]

To admit the truth of the women's perspective to the conception of moral development is to recognize for both sexes the importance throughout life of the connection between self and other, the universality of the need for compassion and care. The concept of the separate self and of moral principles uncompromised by the constraints of reality is an adolescent ideal, the elaborately wrought philosophy of a Stephen Daedalus whose flight we know to be in jeopardy. Erikson (1964), in contrasting the ideological morality of the adolescent with the adult ethic of taking care, attempts to grapple with this problem of integration. But when he charts a developmental path where the sole precursor to the intimacy of adult love and the generativity of adult work and relationships is the trust established in infancy, and where all intervening experience is marked as steps toward autonomy and independence, then separation itself becomes the model and the measure of growth. Though Erikson observes that, for women, identity has as much to do with intimacy as with separation, this observation is not integrated into his developmental chart.

The morality of responsibility that women describe stands, like their concept of self, apart from the path marked to maturity. The progress to moral maturity is depicted as leading through the adolescent questioning of conventional morality to the discovery of individual rights.

[. . .]

The moral imperative that emerges repeatedly in interviews with women is an injunction to care, a responsibility to discern and alleviate the 'real and recognizable trouble' of this world. For men, the moral imperative appears rather as an injunction to respect the rights of others and thus to protect from interference the rights to life and self-fulfillment. Women's insistence on care is at first self-critical rather than self-protective, while men initially conceive obligation to others negatively in terms of noninterference. Development for both sexes would therefore seem to entail an integration of rights and responsibilities through the discovery of the complementarity of these disparate views. For women, the integration of rights and responsibilities takes place through an understanding of the psychological logic of relationships. This understanding tempers the self-destructive potential of a self-critical morality by asserting the need of all persons for care. For men, recognition through experience of the need for more active responsibility in taking care corrects the potential indifference of a morality of noninterference and turns attention from the logic to the consequences of choice (Gilligan and Murphy, 1979; Gilligan, 1981). In the development of a postconventional ethical understanding, women come to see the violence inherent in inequality, while men come to see the limitations of a conception of justice blinded to the differences in human life.

Hypothetical dilemmas, in the abstraction of their presentation, divest moral actors from the history and psychology of their individual lives and separate the moral problem from the social contingencies of its possible occurrence. In doing so, these dilemmas are useful for the distillation and refinement of objective principles of justice and for measuring the formal logic of equality and reciprocity. However, the reconstruction of the dilemma in its contextual particularity allows the understanding of cause and consequence which engages the compassion and tolerance repeatedly noted to distinguish the moral judgments of women. Only when substance is given to the skeletal lives of hypothetical people is it possible to consider the social injustice that their moral problems may reflect and to imagine the individual suffering their occurrence may signify or their resolution engender.

The proclivity of women to reconstruct hypothetical dilemmas in terms of the real, to request or to supply missing information about the nature of the people and the places where they live, shifts their judgment away from the hierarchical ordering of principles and the formal procedures of decision-making. This insistence on the particular signifies an orientation to the dilemma and to moral problems in general that differs from any current developmental stage descriptions. Consequently, though several of the women in the abortion study clearly articulate a postconventional metaethical position, none of them is considered principled in their normative moral judgments of Kohlberg's hypothetical dilemmas. Instead, the women's judgments point toward an identification of the violence inherent in the dilemma itself, which is seen to compromise the justice of any of its possible resolutions. This construction of the dilemma leads the women to recast the moral judgment from a consideration of the good to a choice between evils.

[. . .]

The reluctance to judge remains a reluctance to hurt, but one that stems not from a sense of personal vulnerability but rather from a recognition of the limitation of judgment itself. The deference of the conventional feminine perspective thus continues at the postconventional level, not as moral relativism but rather as part of a reconstructed moral understanding. Moral judgment is renounced in an awareness of the psychological and social determination of human behavior, at the same time that moral concern is reaffirmed in recognition of the reality of human pain and suffering.

[. . .]

The abortion study suggests that women impose a distinctive construction on moral problems, seeing moral dilemmas in terms of conflicting responsibilities. This construction was traced through a sequence of three perspectives, each perspective representing a more complex understanding of the relationship between self and other and each transition involving a critical reinterpretation of the conflict between selfishness and responsibility. The sequence of women's moral judgment proceeds from an initial concern with survival to a focus on goodness and finally to a reflective understanding of care as the most adequate guide to the resolution of conflicts in human relationships. The abortion study demonstrates the centrality of the concepts of responsibility and care in women's constructions of the moral domain, the close tie in women's thinking between conceptions of the self and of morality, and ultimately the need for an expanded developmental theory that includes, rather than rules out from consideration, the differences in the feminine voice. Such an inclusion seems essential, not only for explaining the development of women but also for understanding in both sexes the characteristics and precursors of an adult moral conception.

[. . .]

Visions of Maturity

[. . .]

There seems at present to be only partial agreement between men and women about the adulthood they commonly share. In the absence of mutual understanding, relationships between the sexes continue in varying degrees of constraint, manifesting the 'paradox of egocentrism' which Piaget describes, a mystical respect for rules combined with everyone playing more or less as he pleases and paying no attention to his neighbor (p. 61). For a life-cycle understanding to address the development in adulthood of relationships characterized by cooperation, generosity, and care, that understanding must include the lives of women as well as of men.

Among the most pressing items on the agenda for research on adult development is the need to delineate *in women's own terms* the experience of their adult life. My own work in that direction indicates that the inclusion of women's experience brings to developmental understanding a new perspective on relationships that changes the basic constructs of interpretation. The concept of identity expands to include the experience of interconnection. The moral domain is similarly enlarged by the inclusion of responsibility and care in relationships. And the underlying epistemology correspondingly shifts from the Greek ideal of knowledge as a correspondence between mind and form to the biblical conception of knowing as a process of human relationship.

Given the evidence of different perspectives in the representation of adulthood by women and men, there is a need for research that elucidates the effects of these differences in marriage, family, and work relationships. My research suggests that men and women may speak different languages that they assume are the same, using similar words to encode disparate experiences of self and social relationships. Because these languages share an overlapping moral vocabulary, they contain a propensity for systematic mistranslation, creating misunderstandings which impede communication and limit the potential for cooperation and care in relationships. At the same time, however, these languages articulate with one another in critical ways. Just as the language of responsibilities provides a weblike imagery of relationships to replace a hierarchical ordering that dissolves with the coming of equality, so the language of rights underlines the importance of including in the network of care not only the other but also the self.

As we have listened for centuries to the voices of men and the theories of development that their experience informs, so we have come more recently to notice not only the silence of women but the difficulty in hearing what they say when they speak. Yet in the different voice of women lies the truth of an ethic of care, the tie between relationship and responsibility, and the origins of aggression in the failure of connection. The failure to see the different reality of women's lives and to hear the differences in their voices stems in part from the assumption that there is a single mode of social experience and interpretation. By positing instead two different modes, we arrive at a more complex rendition of human experience which sees the truth of separation and attachment in the lives of women and men and recognizes how these truths are carried by different modes of language and thought.

To understand how the tension between responsibilities and rights sustains the dialectic of human development is to see the integrity of two disparate modes of experience that are in the end connected. While an ethic of justice proceeds from the premise of equality – that everyone should be treated the same – an ethic of care rests on the premise of nonviolence – that no one should be hurt. In the representation of maturity, both perspectives converge in the realization that just as inequality adversely affects both parties in an unequal relationship, so too violence is destructive for everyone involved. This dialogue between fairness and care not only provides a better understanding of relations between the sexes but also gives rise to a more comprehensive portrayal of adult work and family relationships.

As Freud and Piaget call our attention to the differences in children's feelings and thought, enabling us to respond to children with greater care and respect, so a recognition of the differences in women's experience and understanding expands our vision of maturity and points to the contextual nature of developmental truths. Through this expansion in perspective, we can begin to envision how a marriage between adult development as it is currently portrayed and women's development as it begins to be seen could lead to a changed understanding of human development and a more generative view of human life.

References

Broverman, I., Vogel, S., Broverman, D., Clarkson, F. and Rosenkrantz, P. 'Sex-role stereotypes: a current appraisal', *Journal of Social Issues* 28 (1972): 59–78.

Didion, Joan, 'The women's movement', *New York Times Book Review*, 30 July 1972, pp. 1–2, 14.

Erikson, Erik H. *Childhood and Society*, New York: W. W. Norton, 1950.

Erikson, Erik H. *Young Man Luther*, New York: W. W. Norton, 1958.

Erikson, Erik H. *Insight and Responsibility*, New York: W. W. Norton, 1964.

Erikson, Erik H. *Identity: Youth and crisis*, New York: W. W. Norton, 1968.

Erikson, Erik H. *Gandhi's Truth.*, New York: W. W. Norton, 1969.

Erikson, Erik H. 'Reflections on Dr. Borg's life cycle', *Daedalus 105* (1976): 1–29. (Also in Erikson (ed.), *Adulthood*, New York: W. W. Norton, 1978.)

Freud, Sigmund, *The Standard Edition of the Complete Psychological Works of Sigmund Freud*, trans. and ed. James Strachey, London: Hogarth, 1961.

Freud, Sigmund, *Three Essays on the Theory of Sexuality* (1905) vol. VII.

Freud, Sigmund, 'Civilized sexual morality and modern nervous illness' (1908) vol. IX.

Freud, Sigmund, 'On narcissism: an introduction' (1914) vol. XIV.

Freud, Sigmund, 'Some psychical consequences of the anatomical distinction between the sexes' (1925), vol. XIX.

Freud, Sigmund, *The Question of Lay Analysis* (1926), vol. XX.

Freud, Sigmund, *Civilization and its discontents* (1930/1929), vol. XXI.

Freud, Sigmund, 'Female sexuality' (1931), vol. XXI.

Freud, Sigmund, *New Introductory Lectures on Psycho-Analysis* (1933/1932), vol. XXII.

Gilligan, Carol, 'Moral development in the college years', in A. Chickering (ed.), *The Modern American College*. San Francisco: Jossey-Bass, 1981.

Gilligan, Carol and Belenky, Mary F. 'A naturalislic study of abortion decisions', in R. Selman and R. Yando (eds), *Clinical-Developmental Psychology*, New Directions for Child Development, no. 7. San Francisco: Jossey-Bass, 1980.

Gilligan, Carol and Murphy, John Michael, 'Development from adolescence to adulthood: the philosopher and the 'dilemma of the fact'. In D. Kuhn (ed.), *Intellectual Development Beyond Childhood*. New Directions for Child Development, no. 5. San Francisco: Jossey-Bass, 1979.

Haan, Norma, 'Hypothetical and actual moral reasoning in a situation of civil disobedience', *Journal of Personality and Social Psychology* 32 (1975): 255–70.

Holstein, Constance, 'Development of moral judgment: a longitudinal study of males and females', *Child Development* 47 (1976): 51–61.

Joyce, James, *A Portrait of the Artist as a Young Man* (1916), New York: The Viking Press, 1956.

Kohlberg, Lawrence, 'The development of modes of thinking and choices in years 10 to 16', Ph.D. Diss., University of Chicago, 1958.

Kohlberg, Lawrence, 'Stage and sequence: the cognitive-development approach to socialization', in D. A. Goslin (ed.), *Handbook of Socialization Theory and Research*, Chicago: Rand McNally, 1969.

Kohlberg, Lawrence, 'Continuities and discontinuities in childhood and adult moral development revisited', in *Collected Papers on Moral Development and Moral Education*, Moral Education Research Foundation, Harvard University, 1973.

Kohlberg, Lawrence, 'Moral stages and moralization: the cognitive-development approach', in T. Lickona (ed.), *Moral Development and Behavior: Theory, research and social issues.*, New York: Holt, Rinehart & Winston, 1976.

Kohlberg, Lawrence, *The Philosophy of Moral Development.*, San Francisco: Harper & Row, 1981.

Kohlberg, L. and Gilligan, C. 'The adolescent as a philosopher: the discovery of the self in a post-conventional world', *Daedalus* 100 (1971): 1051–86.

Kohlberg, L. and Kramer, R. 'Continuities and discontinuities in child and adult moral development', *Human Development* 12 (1969): 93–120.

Piaget, Jean, *The Moral Judgment of the Child* (1932), New York: The Free Press, 1965.

Piaget, Jean, *Six Psychological Studies*, New York: Viking Books, 1968.

Piaget, Jean, *Structuralism*, New York: Basic Books, 1970.

4 □ Marxism

Introduction

Louis Althusser acknowledges the determining power of economic conditions 'in the last instance', adding – it is not clear how seriously – that this instance 'never comes'. If there is a way to approach the selection of Readings in this Section, it may be the extent to which each theorist endorses such qualifications of a Marxist tradition which flourished in Eastern and Western Europe before World War I but has been severely discredited whenever the opportunity has arisen to make it the ruling tradition. In the loosest sense, all the Readings below – bar Ernesto Laclau and Chantal Mouffe's (Reading 4.7) – fall within the category of 'Western Marxism', and they at least measure their point of departure from Marx. Attempts to define Western Marxism have a history, beginning in the disputes with Georg Lukács and Karl Korsch by the Comintern in 1923 but becoming more judicious in Maurice Merleau-Ponty's *Adventures of the Dialectic* (1955) and Perry Anderson's *Considerations on Western Marxism* (1979). Anderson's is the broadest sweep – since he comes at the concept generationally, geographically and intellectually – and includes Louis Althusser and anti-Hegelian Marxists.

Western Marxism, in Anderson's definition, can be construed theoretically as setting itself against the scientific model of orthodox Eastern Marxism and the theoretical work of Engels at the end of his life and Kautsky and Plekhanov from the late 1880s, all of whom expounded a more confident historical materialism than can be found in a consistent way in Marx himself. Their 'text' is Marx's *Capital*, as it is, less immediately, in Luxemburg's, Bukharin's and Lenin's accounts of the advances of monopoly and finance capitalism through to the early years of the First World War. Western Marxism lacks this insistent economism, and is also missing the promulgation of Marxist political theory to be found in Lenin especially, but also in Trotsky. The work of the Frankfurt School in particular – but other strands in Western Marxism, too – came out of the disappointments and defeats which began in the 1920s in Western Europe with the revival of capitalism and reformism, and accompanied the increasing isolation of the Soviet Revolution and its aftermath; and they were fuelled by the trajectory of the Soviet state from the 1930s and its cultural manifestation in the Popular Front against fascism. After 1945, capitalism went into overdrive in the USA and, eventually, in Europe and, in its various manifestations, made more and more confident claims that it was best fitted also to deliver democratic ends. Anderson sums up the consequences for Western Marxism: 'Henceforward, it was to speak its own enciphered language, at an increasingly remote distance from the class whose fortunes it formally sought to serve or articulate' (Anderson, 1979, p. 32). Intellectually, stimulation came from the rediscovery in the 1920s of Marx's early writings which emphasized alienation, reification and cultural critique, sometimes at the expense of economic developments. It was the founding in 1923 of the Institute for Social Research – invariably known since the 1960s as the Frankfurt School – which gave Western Marxism the academic space to become remote – or, to put it more positively, to develop theoretically, initially in Germany and between 1934 and 1949 in the USA.

'Cultural Criticism and Society' (Reading 4.2) is the lead essay in Adorno's 1955 book *Prisms*, written after his return to Frankfurt in 1949 after exile in England (1934–8) and the USA (1938–49). These essays come out of a period in which reflection upon the Holocaust came together with a continuing analysis of mass culture, most forcefully in 'The culture industry' (1944) and other essays written with his Frankfurt School colleague Max Horkheimer, and published as *The Dialectic of Enlightenment*. Their attack on domination through reification is relentless, and the fierceness of the attack on Hollywood intimates that this critique is still dealing with the manipulation of consciousness by the fascist regimes of the 1930s. The Frankfurt School idea that an 'administered world' and 'repressive tolerance' were the chief outcomes of the promise of the Enlightenment is evident in *Prisms*, which takes up Max Weber's theme in the closing pages of *The Protestant Ethic and the Spirit of Capitalism* (1930): that rationality, with its Reformation origins, had constructed a rationalised world, an 'iron cage'. In Adorno's words near the end of 'Cultural Criticism and Society':

> the sinister, integrated society of today no longer tolerates even those relatively independent, distinct moments to which the theory of the causal dependence of superstructure on base once referred. In the open-air prison which the world is becoming, it is no longer so important to know what depends on what, such is the extent to which everything is one. ... Absolute reification, which presupposed intellectual progress as one of its elements, is now preparing to absorb the mind entirely. (Adorno, 1967, p. 34)

Adorno's pessimism about the relationship between theory and practice predates his experience of fascism, and may be discerned in his inaugural lecture of 1931, 'The actuality of philosophy'; but by the 1950s it is openly expressed and may even be generalized as an element in Western Marxism. From the late 1920s political connections were sparse among Western Marxists. Indeed, Gramsci's *'revolution against Capital'* together with a loss of the confidence that runs through Marx's text that thought and practice can be united in scientific socialism and historical inevitability, became motifs in a wholesale turn towards philosophical critique and the project of the unmasking of ideological structures. In Adorno, Horkheimer and Marcuse the power of the administered world left the working class without its classical revolutionary role, so that Critical Theory remained their only way to be radical. Invariably, the sphere left open to what Adorno calls an immanent critique is culture. Incidentally, the borrowing of 'Critical Theory' to describe the loose agglomeration of self-reflective, interdisciplinary theorizing presented in a *Reader* such as this implies a common problem in relating theory to action which runs through the whole field from the Frankfurt School in the 1930s to a post-structuralist hegemony in the 1970s and 1980s.

Even 'in theory' a 'way out' is difficult to envisage, and certainly in Adorno there is nothing of Marcuse's radicalization of Freud in the service of utopian speculation, though a Frankfurt School conference on Freud the year after *Eros and Civilization* (1955) was published provided an opportunity. It was left to avant-garde modernism to put up some resistance to mass culture and its hegemonic power, as Martin Jay explains: 'The wholeness of art, including music, was ... a prefiguration of the normative totality of the future society' (Jay, 1984b, pp. 54–5). Adorno insists (in a discussion of Baudelaire's modernism) that this is no mere aestheticism:

> 'Essence' itself in this poetry is no abstract thing in itself; it is a social phenomenon. The objectively dominant idea in Baudelaire's work is that the new, the products of historical progress, are what has to be conjured up in his verse. To use Benjamin's expression, we find not an archaic, but a 'dialectical' image in his work. (Adorno, 1980, p. 158)

Like Walter Benjamin (see Reading 4.1), Adorno rejects symbolism as the basis of art and a Hegelian expressive totality as the basis for philosophy: 'philosophy ... must learn to do without the symbolic function, in which for a long time, at least in idealism, the particular appeared to represent the general' (Adorno, 1977, p. 127). At the other end of the aesthetic spectrum, realism was rejected (the crux of Adorno's case against Lukács) because it was too easily co-opted and the solidarity with readers which it encouraged was a false, 'populist' unity which threatened critical, revolutionary independence. Adorno and Benjamin – along with Lukács, Bertolt Brecht and, in a different way, Louis Althusser (see Reading 4.3) – have made a remarkable contribution to Marxist aesthetic and cultural theory. The extent and quality of these contributions, however, are a measure of their distance from the economic and political concerns of nineteenth- and early-twentieth-century Marxism.

Prisms also contains Adorno's first essay on Walter Benjamin. Apart from a passing regret in this essay at 'Benjamin's tendency to cede his intellectual power to objects diametrically opposed to it, the most extreme example of which was his study on 'The Work of Art in the Era of its Mechanical Reproduction' (Adorno, 1967, p. 233), Adorno does not confront his worry that Benjamin's interest in new media (photography and film, especially) brings him too close to one of the mechanisms of domination in the modern world. Benjamin's view in 'The work of art', 'The author as producer' and 'Paris – capital of the nineteenth century' is that although technology destroys the aura of an original work of art and a remembered moment of unity, it reveals the logic of capitalist repetition and, as a technology of reproduction, holds out the possibility of a genuinely popular culture. In connection with Benjamin's enigmatic 'Theses on the philosophy of history' (completed in 1940, just before he died), his openness to technology points towards an allegorical theory of history; in Fredric Jameson's words: 'an exercise ... in the locating of some fitting emblem in which to anchor the peculiar and nervous modern state of mind which was Benjamin's subject matter' (Jameson, 1974, p. 76). 'The allegorically significant', Benjamin remarks in *The Origin of German Tragic Drama*, 'is prevented by guilt from finding fulfillment in its meaning in itself' (Benjamin, 1977, p. 224). This rejection of the expressive totality of the symbol, which collapses subject into object, object into subject, is the crucial, if highly mediated, step towards historical explanation. Allegory becomes Benjamin's dialectics; it is, in Adorno's phrase, 'the thinking of materialism' (Adorno, 1977).

In an anti-Marxist reading of Benjamin's 'Theses on the philosophy of history', Gershom Scholem points out that historical materialism, in the immediate aftermath of the shock of the Nazi–Soviet Pact and the massing storm clouds of fascism, needed theology to win through. However, it does not take a lot of rereading, especially in the context of Adorno's, Marcuse's and Benjamin's comments on allegory, to take this as the utopian, rather than theological, dimension in Marxism reasserting itself in dark times. It is not theological because the universal, like the symbolic, is decisively rejected (there is no 'eternal image'); but there is the hope, located in the most enigmatic of Benjamin's theses (number IX), that 'the storm blowing from Paradise' will hurl 'the angel of history' into the future (Benjamin, 1973, p. 259).

If Perry Anderson's contextual account gives a degree of coherence to most of the figures in this Section, then Louis Althusser's work, beginning in 1953 with expository accounts of Marx, is the clearest indication that Western Marxism is nothing like a homogeneous body of theory. Where for Herbert Marcuse, among others, the rediscovery of Marx's early works gave philosophical, even humanistic, critique an authorised role and potential, for Althusser these texts had to be read but then put in their place – a place of significantly less importance than that occupied by Marx's mature work. In terms which bear comparison with Michel Foucault, and Thomas Kuhn's *The Structure of Scientific Revolutions* (1962), but seem to have been derived from his former teacher Gaston Bachelard, Althusser argues for an epistemological break in Marx's thought. *For Marx* (1965) and *Reading Capital* (1968) are the relevant texts. In returning to Marx, Althusser does not, as the foregoing discussion of Western Marxism might suggest, return to a reflection model, the superstructure corresponding to the base in a directly determinate relationship. Rather, in *For Marx*, he fashions an argument within theory:

> a science always works on existing concepts. ... It does not work on a purely objective 'given', that of pure and absolute 'facts'. On the contrary, its particular labour consists of *elaborating its own scientific facts* through a critique of the *ideological 'facts'* elaborated by an earlier ideological theoretical practice. To elaborate its own specific 'facts' is simultaneously to elaborate its own 'theory', since a scientific fact – and not the self-styled pure phenomenon – can only be identified in the field of a theoretical practice. (Althusser, 1970, p. 184)

The seemingly enclosed feel to this remarkable formulation recalls the debate covered in Section 1, on Structuralism and Post-Structuralism, especially the former. Just as Barthes, in *Mythologies* (see Reading 1.1), draws on a Marxist critique of ideology, so Althusser's work can be usefully read in conjunction with structuralism. The structuralist tenets of the priority of the system to its constituent parts, the questioning of reference (used, in part, to insist that totality could not be read off from the economic base in pre-1917 fashion), and the attack on the subject all inform Althusser's rejection of Lukács's *expressive* totality and, more broadly, the Hegelian tradition in Marxism. Where that tradition understands the parts of the historical process as revealed in the totality, Althusser talks of the 'relative autonomy' of different spheres. For Althusser, a scientific theory alone, and not the humanistic, consciousness-centred Marxism of E.P. Thompson (who gives a firm reply to Althusser in *The Poverty of Theory* [1978]), could supply a total view free from subjectivism. Structuralism's anti-subjectivism is utilised by Althusser to argue that ideology is not the product of individual false consciousness or a conspiracy, but has a materiality to it. Ideology is inseparable from representations, and 'in the majority of cases these representations have nothing to do with "consciousness": they are usually images and occasionally concepts, but it is above all as *structures* that they impose on the vast majority of men, not via their "consciousness"' (Althusser, 1970, p. 233). The links with Saussurean linguistics may be discerned in this not altogether persuasive assertion (materiality seems to mean systematicity); but so, too, can links with Lacanian psychoanalytic theory, and these assist Althusser in arguing that it is the centred self which is the pre-eminent subject of ideology:

> there is no ideology except by the subject and for subjects. ... The category of the subject ... is the constitutive category of all ideology, whatever its determination (regional or class) and whatever its historical date – since ideology has no history. (Althusser, 1971, pp. 170–71)

It is the repetitive character of the construction of a subject, the subject as 'interpellated', which Althusser takes from Lacan. Ideology in what Althusser calls a 'general' sense (as opposed to 'particular ideologies' in specific institutions and practices) seems permanent, even under communism, in the way that the unconscious is permanent. Science alone can see through ideology, as Althusser explains in the passage from *For Marx* quoted above, which suggests a comparison with Lenin's understanding of the way in which science could transform the working class into a knowledgeable class.

It is hard to tell whether it is Althusser's theoretical position, as partially laid out in Reading 4.3, or the continuing story of defeats which so moulded the Frankfurt School, which accounts for his highly abstract and seemingly transhistorical (virtually Idealist) concept of ideology; and, therefore, for a concept of science which would match this view of ideology and replace Marx's epistemology, in which knowledge comes through action in the midst of changing conditions and manifested contradictions. Althusser's position can be a recipe for detachment, even quiescence, and he was noticeably silent over the Soviet invasion of Czechoslovakia in 1968.

In *The Political Unconscious* (1983), a book which far outweighs his somewhat overexposed studies of postmodernism, Fredric Jameson (see Reading 4.5) engages with Althusser, a figure from whom he had largely kept his distance in earlier works. Jameson's attempt to incorporate elements of Althusser's work as a vital element in any 'negative Marxist hermeneutic' is pursued while, on another front, he advances a continued critique of post-structuralism – its 'ideology of the text' – and a re-evaluation of the work of Lukács. On post-structuralism – which Jameson takes seriously and has, therefore, to argue with and around – there is a sharp reminder not to take various textual manifestations of heterogeneity as all that politically radical. 'Paradoxically', Jameson points out in an important note to Reading 4.5, 'the extrinsic, "contextual" or situational references repudiated by [post-structuralism] turn out to be precisely what is *heterogeneous* to it' (Jameson, 1983, p. 283). This is a theme Jameson has expanded upon ever since his 1972 book *The Prison-House of Language*.

In *Marxism and Form* (1974), Jameson assembles Lukács, Adorno, Benjamin, Marcuse, and Sartre into a tradition of thinkers (a subset of Western Marxism itself) who have engaged with formal and, especially, narrative issues. More than any other theorist, it is Lukács who prompts Jameson towards narrative as *the* epistemological form capable of *forming* a historical consciousness. Lukács – who in many ways announces the onset of Western Marxism with *History and Class Consciousness* (1923) – holds out against various forms of reification, including symbolism as an aspect of modernism. Instead, he promotes the nineteenth-century realistic novel. Thus, the lesson Jameson learns from Lukács is, crudely, to keep things moving:

> realism itself comes to be distinguished by its movement, its storytelling and dramatization of its content; comes, following the title of one of Lukács' finest essays, to be characterized by narration rather than description. ... for him, symbolism ... is always a second best, always a kind of admission of defeat on the part of the novelist; for by having recourse to it the writer implies that some original, objective meaning in objects is henceforth inaccessible to him. (Jameson, 1974, pp. 196, 197)

Jameson also finds in Lukács the expression of a utopian potential, frowned upon within scientific Marxism and present only intermittently in Western Marxism in times of despair, 'when it becomes clear to us that there is a sense in which the development from [the utopian socialist] Fourier to Marx remains, both theoretically and practically, a task for the future' (quoted in Jameson, 1988c, p. 76). In an explicit reversal of Adorno and Horkheimer's domination thesis in 'The culture industry', Jameson recognises the necessity for a positive hermeneutics. This must accompany a Marxist critique of ideology and must confront, rather than back away from, the 'degraded' products of mass culture in an effort to release their utopian dimension, that which still points to an unrealised and better future associated with the needs and interests of the class most subdued by the product's ideological functioning. Jameson's optimism in seeking ways to release a subdued utopian impulse is an important theoretical move, even if it cannot fully answer Frankfurt School pessimism about the power of culture industries such as Hollywood. What is apparent from reading Jameson alongside Adorno's 'Cultural Criticism and Society', however, is how at home Jameson is with the sphere of cultural criticism. The turn to culture (and the superstructure) which marks Western Marxism seems less of a denial of a Marxist project than it can in older Marxists. Jameson is quite open about the new circumstances in the Preface to *The Political Unconscious*:

> as the traditional dialectic teaches us, the historicizing operation can follow two distinct paths, which only ultimately meet in the same place: the path of the object and the path of the subject, the historical origins of the things themselves and that more intangible historicity of the concepts and categories by which we attempt to understand those things. ... For better or for worse, it is this second path we have chosen to follow here. (Jameson, 1983, p. 9)

Jameson posits Marxism as the horizon against which the shortcomings of other theoretical models must be measured and accorded 'local' or 'sectoral validity' within 'the intellectual marketplace today' (Jameson, 1983, p. 10). In this acknowledgement, as in Jameson's willingness to read the past through his own moment of late monopoly capitalism, it is easy to appreciate why he feels it important to come to terms with postmodernism. His analysis of postmodern culture is familiar, but – for the purposes of this *Reader* – it is still worth quoting the claim that postmodernism, as a period concept, gives explanatory leverage upon the post-structuralist theory which has been a persistent antagonist for Jameson and post-1960s Marxism:

> This is perhaps the moment to say something about contemporary theory, which has, among other things, been committed to the mission of criticizing and discrediting this very hermeneutic model of the inside and the outside and of stigmatizing such models as ideological and metaphysical. But what is today called contemporary theory – or better still, theoretical discourse – is also, I would want to argue, itself very precisely a postmodernist phenomenon. It would therefore be inconsistent to defend the truth of its theoretical insights in a situation in which the very concept of 'truth' itself is part of the metaphysical baggage which poststructuralism seeks to abandon. What we can at least suggest is that the poststructuralist critique of the hermeneutic, of ... the depth model, is useful for us as a very significant symptom of the very postmodernist culture which is our subject here. (Jameson, 1991, p. 12)

From time to time, Jameson has relied upon Raymond Williams (see Reading 4.4), though without much awareness of the social and historical context which formed Williams and gives substance to his stress upon lived experience and the 'structure of feeling' in any culture. The importance of culture as a concept in Williams – beginning with *Culture and Society, 1780–1950* (1958) and leading to his influence upon British Cultural Studies – is enough to justify his inclusion under the category

Western Marxism. But Terry Eagleton catches another aspect of Williams's highly individualistic membership of this potpourri of a tradition when he remarks that 'if a Marxist criticism comes about in English society, one might risk the paradox that one of its sources will be the fact that Williams had in his own time to reject it' (Eagleton, 1978, p. 23). Eagleton goes on, however, to criticise Williams's 'Romantic populism', which idealises the ordinary, day-to-day dimension of culture, without a full understanding of the structural character of late capitalism and of culture as itself an ideological term. Williams's assumption, which he shares with E.P. Thompson, is that the culture of a rooted community is indeed *its* culture (Eagleton, 1978, pp. 27–35). In his *Marxism and Literature* (1977; Reading 4.4), Williams responds to but does not necessarily answer Eagleton's criticism that his concept of culture is too unified, and lacks awareness of the invasive power of cultural and social institutions beyond the local and immediate. Williams distinguishes hegemony from the more formal concept of ideology, remarking on the 'saturation of the whole process of living' by which 'domination' and 'subordination' (Williams's words) are enacted. But Williams interprets the move from more direct forms of control to 'saturation' in a positive way:

> If the pressures and limits of a given form of domination are to this extent experienced *and in practice internalized*, the whole question of class rule, and of opposition to it, is transformed. Gramsci's emphasis on the creation of an alternative hegemony, by the practical connection of many different forms of struggle, including those not easily recognizable as and indeed not primarily 'political' and 'economic', thus leads to a much more profound and more active sense of revolutionary activity in a highly developed society than the persistently abstract models derived from very different historical situations. (Williams, 1977, pp. 110–11)

While he accepts that a certain idealism is built into his notion of culture, Williams warns against seeing hegemony as seamless and as total. If hegemony is a process rather than an imposed structure and if, in order to work, it must be translated into local discourses, then it cannot be total:

> The reality of any hegemony, in the extended political and cultural sense, is that, while by definition it is always dominant, it is never either total or exclusive. At any time, forms of alternative or directly oppositional politics and culture exist as significant elements in the society. (Williams, 1977, p. 113)

Jameson finds in Williams's notions of 'dominant, residual and emergent' culture the sense of movement necessary to resist the temptation to assume that post-modernism and, with it, theories of textuality mark the limits of any critique, and that analysis can take place only inside the text or in a thoroughly textual culture. If postmodernism is recategorised in Williams's term as only a 'dominant', then alternative cultural resources exist: those which have not been wiped out by an 'affectless' culture of simulacra, and those which are generated by contradictions within the dominant culture. Jameson has proposed 'cognitive mapping' in an attempt to reconnect, from within, the local with the general or totality, but the vagueness of this notion and the apparent dilution of Marxist praxis into the critical reading of a culture calls for further elaboration (Jameson, 1988a).

Counter-hegemonic thinking has considerable potential, but if it is adopted it throws up one particular problem for Marxism: if a local focus is adopted to demonstrate that hegemony is not total, it is not at all clear that the micro-politics that can be recovered can ever come together in a coherent manner capable of opposing, in more general ways, the ruling class. It is odd that Quentin Skinner entitles his perceptive overview of contemporary theory *The Return of Grand Theory* (1985), because the drift of developments within and across each of the Sections in this *Reader* – with the implications becoming most patent in this Section – is towards micro-analysis and difference. Of late, it has been Michel Foucault who has often seemed the most likely alternative for Marxists troubled by the subsuming of race, gender and region within an overarching narrative of class conflict. But when Foucault himself arrives, theoretically, at the diversity and multi-sitedness of micro-political activity, this only serves to highlight the macro-dimension once more, because even a cursory survey of post-1945 history reveals that when the big decisions are made, they are still made by a class-based alliance of 'the power elite' at the highest levels of the military–industrial–governmental complex. At which recognition Foucault has to resort, somewhat hopefully, to 'specific intellectuals' (Foucault, 1980, pp. 126–33) to provide the junctures which link the particular to the general.

The text around which much Marxist unease has concentrated is Ernesto Laclau and Chantal Mouffe's *Hegemony and Socialist Strategy: Towards a radical democratic politics* (1985; see Reading 4.7). Together with the British journal *Marxism Today* and its 'New Times' project of 1988–9, Laclau and Mouffe have brought Gramsci and the concept of hegemony to the centre of revisionist left-of-centre thinking in an attempt to explain the strength of capitalism's hold over minds and hearts as well as bodies, but also to carve out an area for resistance. Tony Bennett is just one of those who refer to 'the Gramscian moment in cultural studies', critically from his perspective (Bennett, 1992, p. 29). In a later text from the one included here, *New Reflections on the Revolutions of Our Time* (1990), Laclau states his position: 'I haven't rejected Marxism. Something different has occurred. It is Marxism that has broken up and I believe I am holding on to its best fragments' (Laclau, 1990). Although a top–down, structural (rather than structuralist) explanation of class power has plenty of mileage in it, emancipation through working-class solidarity is difficult to defend through examples and, theoretically, is liable to relegate in importance or get theoretically mixed up with other forms of resistance and liberation (through the identity politics of race, gender, ecology, etc.). In the absence of the priority of class, according to Laclau and Mouffe, what is needed is an explanation of how a dominant culture is contested through often contingent relations between groups. Protest and the articulation of grievances are not funnelled through class but become part of 'chains of equivalence'.

Although Laclau and Mouffe's analysis is entirely relevant to the cultural dimension which figures so strongly in Western Marxism – particularly in its later and, some would argue, virtually non-Marxist phase – its importance lies in the explicit focus upon the political sphere, rather than that of culture. Thus, in Thomas Docherty's *Postmodernism: A reader* (1993), Laclau's 'Politics and the limits of modernity' (1988) is included as an instance of 'post-Marxism or postmodern Marxism' (Docherty, 1993, p. 319); and, as far as the latter category goes, there are a number of familiar aspects: first, heterogeneity, difference and – in its least stringent formulation – pluralism as descriptions of a politics that takes full account of the variety of new social movements; second, a scepticism about the emancipatory, dialectical metanarrative; third (a closely related point), a scepticism about the Enlightenment search for a totality and for Truth which finds expression in difference politics but also in a revival of American Pragmatism which has a particular relevance in the sphere of local or regional political action; and, fourth, an acceptance that 'democracy' is the contested concept (after 1989 this is so in the ex-communist states as well) and is, simultaneously, a call to liberatory action and the means of containing and diffusing democratic claims. These arguments seek to recover a radical politics after the defeats of socialism and communism across the world, even drawing strength from the subsequent detailed discrediting of less-than-glorious models of what socialism and communism can be. However, this unhappy history may require a still more dramatic rethink; at least, this is Richard Rorty's view in his attempt to put 'Western leftist intellectuals' on the spot in these deliberately irritating observations (from 'The intellectuals at the end of socialism' [1992]):

> Visitors from postrevolutionary Eastern and Central Europe are going to stare at us incredulously if we continue to use the word *socialism* when we describe our political goals. For these people take it as self-evident that nobody could, any longer, wish to nationalize the means of production or abolish private property. To them, *socialism* means the absence of a market economy. They are not prepared to fudge, as we have for so long, the difference between socialism and social democracy. … We ['Western leftist intellectuals'] are not only going to have to stop using the term *capitalist economy* as though we knew what a functioning non-capitalist economy looked like, we are going to have to stop using the term *bourgeois culture* as though we knew what a viable *non*-bourgeois culture in an industrialized society would look like. (Rorty, 1992, pp. 1, 2)

By way of contrast to much of the above – but from a position within Western Marxism, and specifically within the Italian Marxism which includes Gramsci – Sebastiano Timpanaro (see Reading 4.6) steadfastly adopts a long and, in some respects, fundamental point of view. In *On Materialism* (1970), Timpanaro returns to what initially brought Marx and Engels into an agreement with Darwin: the materialism of nature within a historical perspective. While there is a superficial similarity with Althusser, in so far as both argue for the scientific status of Marxism, Timpanaro goes back to Engels's materialist science of socialism and the study of the capitalism of his own time. This is a project continued, in *Late Capitalism* (1975), by Ernst Mandel who, in his long-wave theory of economic change, shares something of Timpanaro's appreciation of the time-scale of historical change. Thus, Timpanaro warns against the historicism which takes from Gramsci only what Gramsci's constrained circumstances in prison permitted him: a limited, localised understanding of praxis: 'the appeal to praxis often represents, within the Marxist camp, a way of not talking about or of talking very little about materialism' (Timpanaro, 1980, p. 56). And, in a polemic against 'structuralism and its successors', Timpanaro inveighs against Althusser's conception of Marx: 'But can one possibly see [Marx] as the precursor of a theory like structuralism, which emerged from the anti-materialist (and, more or less indirectly, anti-Marxist) reaction of the late nineteenth century and represents a renewal of the schism between history and science?' (Timpanaro, 1980, p. 196). Raymond Williams invokes Timpanaro when he defends his own stress on 'experience' and comments upon the linguistic turn in which 'the epistemological wholly absorbs the ontological':

> To formalist friends, of whom I have many, who affect to doubt the very possibility of an 'external' referent, it is necessary to recall an absolutely founding presumption of materialism: namely that the natural world exists whether anyone signifies it or not. The fact is that we have been passing through a phase of rabid idealism on the left in the sixties and seventies. It is a positive relief to read Timpanaro's reminder that physical organisms exist in an undeniably material world whether or not they have even been signified. (Williams, 1981, p. 167)

Perry Anderson, who provides the parameters for any account of Western Marxism, is another contemporary Marxist who seems to find in Timpanaro an overlooked dimension of the material. He sees in this 'privative' understanding of human nature the basis for the ethics which is largely missing in Marxism and which creates a commonality of analysis between the two poles of nature and history, between Marxism and (Anderson's two examples) feminism and ecological movements, the latter spurred on by the prospects of global – or at least, very far-reaching – catastrophes.

4.1 □ *Theses on the Philosophy of History*

Walter Benjamin

I

The story is told of an automaton constructed in such a way that it could play a winning game of chess, answering each move of an opponent with a countermove. A puppet in Turkish attire and with a hookah in its mouth sat before a chessboard placed on a large table. A system of mirrors created the illusion that this table was transparent from all sides. Actually, a little hunchback who was an expert chess player sat inside and guided the puppet's hand by means of strings. One can imagine a philosophical counterpart to this device. The puppet called 'historical materialism' is to win all the time. It can easily be a match for anyone if it enlists the services of theology, which today, as we know, is wizened and has to keep out of sight.

II

'One of the most remarkable characteristics of human nature', writes Lotze, 'is, alongside so much selfishness in specific instances, the freedom from envy which the present displays toward the future.' Reflection shows us that our image of happiness is thoroughly colored by the time to which the course of our own existence has assigned us. The kind of happiness that could arouse envy in us exists only in the air we have breathed, among people we could have talked to, women who could have given themselves to us. In other words, our image of happiness is indissolubly bound up with the image of redemption. The same applies to our view of the past, which is the concern of history. The past carries with it a temporal index by which it is referred to redemption. There is a secret agreement between past generations and the present one. Our coming was expected on earth. Like every generation that

From Benjamin, W., *Illuminations*, trans. H. Zohn, ed. H. Arendt, Fontana, London, 1973, pp. 255–66.

preceded us, we have been endowed with a *weak* Messianic power, a power to which the past has a claim. That claim cannot be settled cheaply. Historical materialists are aware of that.

III

A chronicler who recites events without distinguishing between major and minor ones acts in accordance with the following truth: nothing that has ever happened should be regarded as lost for history. To be sure, only a redeemed mankind receives the fullness of its past — which is to say, only for a redeemed mankind has its past become citable in all its moments. Each moment it has lived becomes a *citation à l'ordre du jour* — and that day is Judgment Day.

IV

> Seek for food and clothing first, then
> the Kingdom of God shall be added unto you.
> (HEGEL, 1807)

The class struggle, which is always present to a historian influenced by Marx, is a fight for the crude and material things without which no refined and spiritual things could exist. Nevertheless, it is not in the form of the spoils which fall to the victor that the latter make their presence felt in the class struggle. They manifest themselves in this struggle as courage, humor, cunning, and fortitude. They have retroactive force and will constantly call in question every victory, past and present, of the rulers. As flowers turn toward the sun, by dint of a secret heliotropism the past strives to turn toward that sun which is rising in the sky of history. A historical materialist must be aware of this most inconspicuous of all transformations.

V

The true picture of the past flits by. The past can be seized only as an image which flashes up at the instant when it can be recognized and is never seen again. 'The truth will not run away from us': in the historical outlook of historicism these words of Gottfried Keller mark the exact point where historical materialism cuts through historicism. For every image of the past that is not recognized by the present as one of its own concerns threatens to disappear irretrievably. (The good tidings which the historian of the past brings with throbbing heart may be lost in a void the very moment he opens his mouth.)

VI

To articulate the past historically does not mean to recognize it 'the way it really was' (Ranke). It means to seize hold of a memory as it flashes up at a moment of danger. Historical materialism wishes to retain that image of the past which unexpectedly appears to man singled out by history at a moment of danger. The danger affects both the content of the tradition and its receivers. The same threat hangs over both: that of becoming a tool of the ruling classes. In every era the attempt must be made anew to wrest tradition away from a conformism that is about to overpower it. The Messiah comes not only as the redeemer, he comes as the subduer of Antichrist. Only that historian will have the gift of fanning the spark of hope in the past who is firmly convinced that *even the dead* will not be safe from the enemy if he wins. And this enemy has not ceased to be victorious.

VII

> Consider the darkness and the great cold
> In this vale which resounds with misery.
>   (BRECHT, *The Threepenny Opera*)

To historians who wish to relive an era, Fustel de Coulanges recommends that they blot out everything they know about the later course of history. There is no better way of characterizing the method with which historical materialism has broken. It is a process of empathy whose origin is the indolence of the heart, *acedia*, which despairs of grasping and holding the genuine historical image as it flares up briefly. Among medieval theologians it was regarded as the root cause of sadness. Flaubert, who was familiar with it, wrote: '*Peu de gens devineront combien il a fallu être triste pour ressusciter Carthage.*' ('Few will be able to guess how sad one had to be in order to resuscitate Carthage.') The nature of this sadness stands out more clearly if one asks with whom the adherents of historicism actually empathize. The answer is inevitable: with the victor. And all rulers are the heirs of those who conquered before them. Hence, empathy with the victor invariably benefits the rulers. Historical materialists know what that means. Whoever has emerged victorious participates to this day in the triumphal procession in which the present rulers step over those who are lying prostrate. According to traditional practice, the spoils are carried along in the procession. They are called cultural treasures, and a historical materialist views them with cautious detachment. For without exception the cultural treasures he surveys have an origin which he cannot contemplate without horror. They owe their existence not only to the efforts of the great minds and talents who have created them, but also to the anonymous toil of their contemporaries. There is no document of civilization which is not at the same time a document of barbarism. And just as such a document is not free of barbarism, barbarism taints also the manner in which it was transmitted from one owner to another A historical materialist therefore dissociates himself from it as far as possible. He regards it as his task to brush history against the grain.

VIII

The tradition of the oppressed teaches us that the 'state of emergency' in which we live is not the exception but the rule. We must attain to a conception of history that is in keeping with this insight. Then we shall clearly realize that it is our task to bring about a real state of emergency, and this will improve our position in the struggle against Fascism. One reason why Fascism has a chance is that in the name of progress its opponents treat it as a historical norm. The current amazement that the things we are experiencing are 'still' possible in the twentieth century is *not* philosophical. This amazement is not the beginning of knowledge – unless it is the knowledge that the view of history which gives rise to it is untenable.

IX

> Mein Flügel ist zum Schwung bereit,
> ich kehrte gern zurück,
> denn blieb ich auch lebendige Zeit,
> ich hätte wenig Glück.

> (My wing is ready for flight,
> I would like to turn back.
> If I stayed timeless time,
> I would have little luck.)
> (GERHARD SCHOLEM, '*Gruss vom Angelus*')

A Klee painting named 'Angelus Novus' shows an angel looking as though he is about to move away from something he is fixedly contemplating. His eyes are staring, his mouth is open, his wings are spread. This is how one pictures the angel of history. His face is turned toward the past. Where we perceive a chain of events, he sees one single catastrophe which keeps piling wreckage upon wreckage and hurls it in front of his feet. The angel would like to stay, awaken the dead, and make whole what has been smashed. But a storm is blowing from Paradise; it has got caught in his wings with such violence that the angel can no longer close them. This storm irresistibly propels him into the future to which his back is turned, while the pile of debris before him grows skyward. This storm is what we call progress.

X

The themes which monastic discipline assigned to friars for meditation were designed to turn them away from the world and its affairs. The thoughts which we are developing here originate from similar considerations. At a moment when the politicians in whom the opponents of Fascism had placed their hopes are prostrate and confirm their defeat by betraying their own cause, these observations are intended to disentangle the political worldlings from the snares in which the traitors have entrapped them. Our consideration proceeds from the insight that the politicians' stubborn faith in progress, their confidence in their 'mass basis', and, finally, their servile integration in an uncontrollable apparatus have been three aspects of the same thing. It seeks to convey an idea of the high price our accustomed thinking will have to pay for a conception of history that avoids any complicity with the thinking to which these politicians continue to adhere.

XI

The conformism which has been part and parcel of Social Democracy from the beginning attaches not only to its political tactics but to its economic views as well. It is one reason for its later breakdown. Nothing has corrupted the German working class so much as the notion that it was moving with the current. It regarded technological developments as the fall of the stream with which it thought it was moving. From there it was but a step to the illusion that the factory work which was supposed to tend toward technological progress constituted a political achievement. The old Protestant ethics of work was resurrected among German workers in secularized form. The Gotha Program[1] already bears traces of this confusion, defining labor as 'the source of all wealth and all culture'. Smelling a rat, Marx countered that 'the man who possesses no other property than his labor-power' must of necessity become 'the slave of other men who have made themselves the owners. ...' However, the confusion spread, and soon thereafter Josef Dietzgen proclaimed: 'The savior of modern times is called work. The ... improvement ... of labor constitutes the wealth which is now able to accomplish what no redeemer has ever been able to do.' This vulgar-Marxist conception of the nature of labor bypasses the question of how its products might benefit the workers while still not being at their disposal. It recognizes only the progress in the mastery of nature, not the retrogression of society; it already displays the technocratic features later encountered in Fascism. Among these is a conception of nature which differs ominously from the one in the Socialist utopias before the 1848 revolution. The new conception of labor amounts to the exploitation of nature, which with naive complacency is contrasted with the exploitation of the proletariat. Compared with this positivistic conception, Fourier's fantasies, which have so often been ridiculed, prove to be surprisingly sound. According to Fourier, as a result of efficient cooperative labor, four moons would illuminate the earthly night, the ice would recede from the poles, sea water would no longer taste salty, and beasts of prey would do man's bidding. All this illustrates a kind of labor which, far from exploiting nature, is capable of delivering her of the creations which lie dormant in her womb as potentials. Nature, which, as Dietzgen puts it, 'exists gratis', is a complement to the corrupted conception of labor.

XII

> We need history, but not the way a spoiled loafer
> in the garden of knowledge needs it.
> (NIETZSCHE, *Of the Use and Abuse of History*)

Not man or men but the struggling, oppressed class itself is the depository of historical knowledge. In Marx it appears as the last enslaved class, as the avenger that completes the task of liberation in the name of generations of the downtrodden. This conviction, which had a brief resurgence in the Spartacist group,[2] has always been objectionable to Social Democrats. Within three decades they managed virtually to erase the name of Blanqui, though it had been the rallying sound that had reverberated through the preceding century. Social Democracy thought fit to assign to the working class the role of the redeemer of future generations, in this way cutting the sinews of its greatest strength. This training made the working class forget both its hatred and its spirit of sacrifice, for both are nourished by the image of enslaved ancestors rather than that of liberated grandchildren.

XIII

> Every day our cause becomes clearer and people get smarter.
> (WILHELM DIETZGEN, *Die Religion der Sozialdemokratie*)

Social Democratic theory, and even more its practice, have been formed by a conception of progress which did not adhere to reality but made dogmatic claims. Progress as pictured in the minds of Social Democrats was, first of all, the progress of mankind itself (and not just advances in men's ability and knowledge). Secondly, it was something boundless, in keeping with the infinite perfectibility of mankind. Thirdly, progress was regarded as irresistible, something that automatically pursued a straight or spiral course. Each of these predicates is controversial and open to criticism. However, when the chips are down, criticism must penetrate beyond these predicates and focus on something that they have in common. The concept of the historical progress of mankind cannot be sundered from the concept of its progression through a homogeneous, empty time. A critique of the concept of such a progression must be the basis of any criticism of the concept of progress itself.

XIV

Origin is the goal.
(KARL KRAUS, *Worte in Versen*, vol. I)

History is the subject of a structure whose site is not homogeneous, empty time, but time filled by the presence of the now [*Jetztzeit*].[3] Thus, to Robespierre ancient Rome was a past charged with the time of the now which he blasted out of the continuum of history. The French Revolution viewed itself as Rome reincarnate. It evoked ancient Rome the way fashion evokes costumes of the past. Fashion has a flair for the topical, no matter where it stirs in the thickets of long ago; it is a tiger's leap into the past. This jump, however, takes place in an arena where the ruling class gives the commands. The same leap in the open air of history is the dialectical one, which is how Marx understood the revolution.

XV

The awareness that they are about to make the continuum of history explode is characteristic of the revolutionary classes at the moment of their action. The great revolution introduced a new calendar. The initial day of a calendar serves as a historical time-lapse camera. And, basically, it is the same day that keeps recurring in the guise of holidays, which are days of remembrance. Thus the calendars do not measure time as clocks do; they are monuments of a historical consciousness of which not the slightest trace has been apparent in Europe in the past hundred years. In the July revolution an incident occurred which showed this consciousness still alive. On the first evening of fighting it turned out that the clocks in towers were being fired on simultaneously and independently from several places in Paris. An eye-witness, who may have owed his insight to the rhyme, wrote as follows:

> Qui le croirait! on dit, qu'irrités contre l'heure
> De nouveaux Josués au pied de chaque tour,
> Tiraient sur les cadrans pour arrêter le jour.

> (Who would have believed it! we are told that new Joshuas
> at the foot of every tower, as though irritated with
> time itself, fired at the dials in order to stop the day.)

XVI

A historical materialist cannot do without the notion of a present which is not a transition, but in which time stands still and has come to a stop. For this notion defines the present in which he himself is writing history. Historicism gives the 'eternal' image of the past; historical materialism supplies a unique experience with the past. The historical materialist leaves it to others to be drained by the whore called 'Once upon a time' in historicism's bordello. He remains in control of his powers, man enough to blast open the continuum of history.

XVII

Historicism rightly culminates in universal history. Materialistic historiography differs from it as to method more clearly than from any other kind. Universal history has no theoretical armature. Its method is additive; it musters a mass of data to fill the homogeneous, empty time. Materialistic historiography, on the other hand, is based on a constructive principle. Thinking involves not only the flow of thoughts, but their arrest as well. Where thinking suddenly stops in a configuration pregnant with tensions, it gives that configuration a shock, by which it crystallizes into a monad. A historical materialist approaches a historical subject only where he encounters it as a monad. In this structure he recognizes the sign of a Messianic cessation of happening, or, put differently, a revolutionary chance in the fight for the oppressed past. He takes cognizance of it in order to blast a specific era out of the homogeneous course of history – blasting a specific life out of the era or a specific work out of the lifework. As a result of this method the lifework is preserved in this work and at the same time canceled;[4] in the lifework, the era; and in the era, the entire course of history. The nourishing fruit of the historically understood contains time as a precious but tasteless seed.

XVIII

'In relation to the history of organic life on earth,' writes a modern biologist, 'the paltry fifty millennia of *homo sapiens* constitute something like two seconds at the close of a twenty-four-hour day. On this scale, the history of civilized mankind would fill one-fifth of the last second of the last hour.' The present, which, as a model of Messianic time, comprises the entire history of mankind in an enormous abridgment, coincides exactly with the stature which the history of mankind has in the universe.

A

Historicism contents itself with establishing a causal connection between various moments in history. But no fact that is a cause is for that very reason historical. It became historical posthumously, as it were, through events that may be separated from it by thousands of years. A historian who takes this as his point of departure stops telling the sequence of events like the beads of a rosary. Instead, he grasps the constellation which his own era has formed with a definite earlier one. Thus he establishes a conception of the present as the 'time of the now' which is shot through with chips of Messianic time.

B

The soothsayers who found out from time what it had in store certainly did not experience time as either homogeneous or empty. Anyone who keeps this in mind will perhaps get an idea of how past times were experienced in remembrance – namely, in just the same way. We know that the Jews were prohibited from investigating the future. The Torah and the prayers instruct them in remembrance, however. This stripped the future of its magic, to which all those succumb who turn to the soothsayers for enlightenment. This does not imply, however, that for the Jews the future turned into homogeneous, empty time. For every second of time was the strait gate through which the Messiah might enter.

Editor's notes

1. The Gotha Congress of 1875 united the two German Socialist parties, one led by Ferdinand Lassalle, the other by Karl Marx and Wilhelm Liebknecht. The program, drafted by Liebknecht and Lassalle, was severely attacked by Marx in London. See his 'Critique of the Gotha Program'.
2. Leftist group, founded by Karl Liebknecht and Rosa Luxemburg at the beginning of World War I in opposition to the pro-war policies of the German Socialist Party, later absorbed by the Communist Party.
3. Benjamin says '*Jetztzeit*' and indicates by the quotation marks that he does not simply mean an equivalent to *Gegenwart*, that is, present. He is clearly thinking of the mystical *nunc stans*.
4. The Hegelian term *aufheben* in its threefold meaning: to preserve, to elevate, to cancel.

4.2 □ *Cultural Criticism and Society*

Theodor W. Adorno

[. . .]

The complicity of cultural criticism with culture lies not in the mere mentality of the critic. Far more, it is dictated by his relation to that with which he deals. By making culture his object, he objectifies it once more. Its very meaning, however, is the suspension of objectification. Once culture itself has been debased to 'cultural goods', with its hideous philosophical rationalization, 'cultural values', it has already defamed its *raison d'être*. The distillation of such 'values' – the echo of commercial language is by no means accidental – places culture at the will of the market. Even the enthusiasm for foreign cultures includes the excitement over the rarity in which money may be invested. If cultural criticism, even at its best with Valéry, sides with conservativism, it is because of its unconscious adherence to a notion of culture which, during the era of late capitalism, aims at a form of property which is stable and independent of stock-market fluctuations. This idea of culture asserts its distance from the system in order, as it were, to offer universal security in the middle of a universal dynamic. The model of the cultural critic is no less the appraising collector than the art critic. In general, cultural criticism recalls the gesture of bargaining, of the expert questioning the authenticity of a painting or classifying it among the Master's lesser works. One devaluates in order to get more. The cultural critic evaluates and hence is inevitably involved in a sphere stained with 'cultural values', even when he rants against the mortgaging of culture. His contemplative stance towards culture necessarily entails scrutinizing, surveying, balancing, selecting: this piece suits him, that he rejects. Yet his very sovereignty, the claim to a more profound knowledge of the object, the separation of the idea from its object through the independence of the critical judgment, threatens to succumb to the thinglike form of the object when cultural criticism appeals to a

From Adorno, T. W. *Prisms*, trans. S. and S. Weber, Neville Spearman, London, 1967, pp. 22–34.

collection of ideas on display, as it were, and fetishizes isolated categories such as mind, life and the individual.

But the greatest fetish of cultural criticism is the notion of culture as such. For no authentic work of art and no true philosophy, according to their very meaning, has ever exhausted itself in itself alone, in its being-in-itself. They have always stood in relation to the actual life-process of society from which they distinguished themselves. Their very rejection of the guilt of a life which blindly and callously reproduces itself, their insistence on independence and autonomy, on separation from the prevailing realm of purposes, implies, at least as an unconscious element, the promise of a condition in which freedom were realized. This remains an equivocal promise of culture as long as its existence depends on a bewitched reality and, ultimately, on control over the work of others. That European culture in all its breadth – that which reached the consumer and which today is prescribed for whole populations by managers and psychotechnicians – degenerated to mere ideology resulted from a change in its function with regard to material praxis: its renunciation of interference. Far from being culture's 'sin', the change was forced upon culture by history. For it is only in the process of withdrawing into itself, only indirectly that is, that bourgeois culture conceives of a purity from the corrupting traces of a totalitarian disorder which embraces all areas of existence. Only in so far as it withdraws from a praxis which has degenerated into its opposite, from the ever-changing production of what is always the same, from the service of the customer who himself serves the manipulator – only in so far as it withdraws from Man, can culture be faithful to man. But such concentration on substance which is absolutely one's own, the greatest example of which is to be found in the poetry and theoretical writings of Paul Valéry, contributes at the same time to the impoverishment of that substance. Once the mind is no longer directed at reality, its meaning is changed despite the strictest preservation of meaning. Through its resignation before the facts of life and, even more, through its isolation as one 'field' among others, the mind aids the existing order and takes its place within it. The emasculation of culture has angered philosophers since the time of Rousseau and the 'ink-splattering age' of Schiller's *Robbers*, to Nietzsche and, finally, to the preachers of commitment for its own sake. This is the result of culture's becoming self-consciously cultural, which in turn places culture in vigorous and consistent opposition to the growing barbarism of economic hegemony. What appears to be the decline of culture is its coming to pure self-consciousness. Only when neutralized and reified does Culture allow itself to be idolized. Fetishism gravitates towards mythology. In general, cultural critics become intoxicated with idols drawn from antiquity to the dubious, long-evaporated warmth of the liberalist era, which recalled the origins of culture in its decline. Cultural criticism rejects the progressive integration of all aspects of consciousness within the apparatus of material production. But because it fails to see through the apparatus, it turns towards the past, lured by the promise of immediacy. This is necessitated by its own momentum and not merely by the influence of an order which sees itself obliged to drown out its progress in dehumanization with cries against dehumanization and progress. The isolation of the mind from material production heightens its esteem but also makes it a scapegoat in the general consciousness for that which is perpetrated in practice. Enlightenment as such – not as an instrument of actual domination – is held responsible. Hence, the irrationalism of cultural criticism. Once it has wrenched the mind out of its dialectic with the material conditions of life, it seizes it unequivocally and straightforwardly as the principle of fatality, thus undercutting the mind's own resistance. The cultural critic is barred from the insight that the reification of life results not from too much enlightenment but from too little, and that the mutilation of man which is the result of the present particularistic rationality is the stigma of the total irrationality. The abolition of this irrationality, which would coincide with the abolition of the divorce between mental and physical work, appears as chaos to the blindness of cultural criticism: whoever glorifies order and form as such must see in the petrified divorce an archetype of the Eternal. That the fatal fragmentation of society might some day end is, for the cultural critic, a fatal destiny. He would rather that everything end than for mankind to put an end to reification. This fear harmonizes with the interests of those interested in the perpetuation of material denial. Whenever cultural criticism complains of 'materialism', it furthers the belief that the sin lies in man's desire for consumer goods, and not in the organization of the whole which withholds these goods from man: for the cultural critic, the sin is satiety, not hunger. Were mankind to possess the wealth of goods, it would shake off the chains of that civilized barbarism which cultural critics ascribe to the advanced state of the human spirit rather than to the retarded state of society. The 'eternal values' of which cultural criticism is so fond reflect the perennial catastrophe. The cultural critic thrives on the mythical obduracy of culture.

Because the existence of cultural criticism, no matter what its content, depends on the economic system, it is involved in the fate of the system. The more completely the life-process, including leisure, is dominated by modern social orders – those in the East, above all – the more all spiritual phenomena bear the mark of the order. Either they may contribute directly to the perpetuation of the system as entertainment or edification, and are enjoyed as exponents of the system precisely because of their socially preformed character. Familiar, stamped and Approved by Good Housekeeping[5] as it were, they insinuate themselves into a regressive consciousness, present themselves as 'natural', and permit identification with powers whose preponderance leaves no alternative but that of false love. Or, by being different, they become rarities and once again marketable. Throughout the liberalist era, culture fell within the sphere of circulation. Hence, the gradual withering away of this sphere strikes culture to the quick. With the elimination of trade and its irrational loopholes by the calculated distributive apparatus of industry, the commercialization of culture culminates in absurdity. Completely subdued, administered, thoroughly 'cultivated' in a sense, it dies out. Spengler's denunciation – that mind and money go together – proves correct. But because of his sympathy with direct rule, he advocated a structure of existence divested of all economic as well as spiritual mediations. He maliciously threw the mind together with an economic type which was in fact obsolete. What Spengler failed to understand was that no matter to what extent the mind is a product of that type, it implies at the same time the objective possibility of overcoming it. Just as culture sprang up in the marketplace, in the traffic of trade, in communication and negotiation, as something distinct from the immediate struggle for individual self-preservation, just as it was closely tied to trade in the era of mature capitalism, just as its representatives were counted among the class of 'third persons' who supported themselves in life as middlemen, so culture, considered 'socially necessary' according to classical rules, in the sense of reproducing itself economically, is in the end reduced to that as which it began, to mere communication. Its alienation from human affairs terminates in its absolute docility before a humanity which has been enchanted and transformed into clientele by the suppliers. In the name of the consumer, the manipulators suppress everything in culture which enables it to go beyond the total immanence in the existing society and allow only that to remain which serves society's unequivocal purpose. Hence, 'consumer culture' can boast of being not a luxury but rather the simple extension of production. Political slogans, designed for mass manipulation, unanimously stigmatize, as 'luxury', 'snobbism'. and 'highbrow', everything cultural which displeases the commissars. Only when the established order has become the measure of all things does its mere reproduction in the realm of consciousness become truth. Cultural criticism points to this and rails against 'superficiality' and 'loss of substance'. But by limiting its attention the entanglement of culture in commerce, such criticism itself becomes superficial. It follows the pattern of reactionary social critics who pit 'productive' against 'predatory' capital. In fact, all culture shares the guilt of society. It ekes out its existence only by virtue of injustice already perpetrated in the sphere of production much as does commerce (cf. *Dialektik der Aufklärung*). Consequently, cultural criticism shifts the guilt: such criticism is ideology as long as it remains mere criticism of ideology. Totalitarian regimes of both kinds, seeking to protect the status quo from even the last traces of insubordination which they ascribe to culture even at its most servile, can conclusively convict culture and its introspection of servility. They suppress the mind, in itself already grown intolerable, and so feel themselves to be purifiers and revolutionaries. The ideological function of cultural criticism bridles its very truth which lies in its opposition to ideology. The struggle against deceit works to the advantage of naked terror. 'When I hear the word "culture", I reach for my gun,' said the spokesman of Hitler's Imperial Chamber of Culture.

Cultural criticism is, however, only able to reproach culture so penetratingly for prostituting itself, for violating in its decline the pure autonomy of the mind, because culture originates in the radical separation of mental and physical work. It is from this separation – the original sin[5] as it were – that culture draws its strength. When culture simply denies the separation and feigns harmonious union, it falls back behind its own notion. Only the mind which, in the delusion of being absolute, removes itself entirely from the merely existent, truly defines the existent in its negativity. As long as even the least part of the mind remains engaged in the reproduction of life, it is its sworn bondsman. The anti-philistinism of Athens was both the most arrogant contempt of the man who need not soil his hands for the man from whose work he lives, and the preservation of an image of existence beyond the constraint which underlies all work. In projecting its own uneasy conscience on to its victims as their 'baseness', such an attitude also accuses that which they endure: the subjugation of men to the prevailing form in which their lives are reproduced. All 'pure culture' has always been a source of discomfort to the spokesmen of power. Plato and Aristotle knew why they would not permit the notion to arise. Instead, in questions concerning the evaluation of art, they advocated a pragmatism which contrasts curiously with the *pathos* of the two great metaphysicians. Modern bourgeois cultural criticism has, of course, been too prudent to follow them openly in this respect. But such criticism secretly finds a source of comfort in the divorce between 'high' and 'popular' culture, art and entertainment, knowledge and noncommittal *Weltanschauung*. Its anti-philistinism exceeds that of the Athenian upper class to the extent that the proletariat is more dangerous than the slaves. The modern notion of a pure, autonomous culture indicates that the antagonism has become irreconcilable. This is the result both of an uncompromising opposition to being-for-something else, and of an ideology which in its hybris enthrones itself as being-in-itself.

Cultural criticism shares the blindness of its object. It is incapable of allowing the recognition of its frailty to arise, a frailty set in the division of mental and physical work. No society which contradicts its very notion – that of mankind – can have full consciousness of itself. A display of subjective ideology is not required to obstruct this consciousness, although in times of historical upheaval it tends to contribute to the objective blindness. Rather, the fact that every form of repression, depending on the level of technology, has been necessary for the survival of society, and that society as it is, despite all absurdity, does indeed reproduce its life under the existing conditions, objectively produces the semblance of society's legitimation. As the epitome of the self-consciousness of an antagonistic society, culture can no more divest itself of this semblance than can cultural criticism, which measures culture against culture's own ideal. The semblance has become total in a phase in which irrationality and objective falsity hide behind rationality and objective necessity. Nevertheless, by virtue of their real force, the antagonisms reassert themselves in the realm of consciousness. Just because culture affirms the validity of the principle of harmony within an antagonistic society, albeit in order to glorify that society, it cannot avoid confronting society with its own notion of harmony and thereby stumbling on discord. The ideology which affirms life is forced into opposition to life by the immanent drive of the ideal. The mind which sees that reality does not resemble it in every respect but is instead subject to an unconscious and fatal dynamic, is impelled even against its will beyond apologetics. The fact that theory becomes real force when it moves men is founded in the objectivity of the mind itself which, through the fulfilment of its ideological function, must lose faith in ideology. Prompted by the incompatibility of ideology and existence, the mind, in displaying its blindness, also displays its effort to free itself of ideology. Disenchanted, the mind perceives naked existence in its nakedness and delivers it up to criticism. The mind either damns the material base, in accordance with the ever-questionable criterion of its 'pure principle', or it becomes aware of its own questionable position, by virtue of its incompatibility with the base. As a result of the social dynamic, culture becomes cultural criticism, which preserves the notion of culture while demolishing its present manifestations as mere commodities and means of brutalization. Such critical consciousness remains subservient to culture in so far as its concern with culture distracts from the true horrors. From this arises the ambivalent attitude of social theory towards cultural criticism. The procedure of cultural criticism is itself the object of permanent criticism, both in its general presuppositions – its immanence in the existing society – and in its concrete judgments. For the subservience of cultural criticism is revealed in its specific content, and only in this may it be grasped conclusively. At the same time, a dialectical theory which does not wish to succumb to 'Economism', the sentiment which holds that the transformation of the work is exhausted in the increase of production, must absorb cultural criticism, the truth of which consists in bringing untruth to consciousness of itself. A dialectical theory which is uninterested in culture as a mere epiphenomenon aids pseudo-culture to run rampant and collaborates in the reproduction of the evil. Cultural traditionalism and the terror of the new Russian despots are in basic agreement. Both affirm culture as a whole, sight-unseen, while at the same time prescribing all forms of consciousness which are not made-to-order. They are thus no less ideological than is criticism when it calls a disembodied culture before its tribunal, or holds the alleged negativity of culture responsible for real catastrophes. To accept culture as a whole is to deprive it of the ferment which is its very truth – negation. The joyous appropriation of culture harmonizes with a climate of military music and paintings of battle-scenes. What distinguishes dialectical from cultural criticism is that it heightens cultural criticism until the notion of culture is itself negated, fulfilled and surmounted in one.

Immanent criticism of culture, it may be argued, overlooks what is decisive: the role of ideology in social conflicts. To suppose, if only methodologically, anything like an independent logic of culture is to collaborate in the hypostasis of culture, the ideological *proton pseudos*. The substance of culture, according to this argument, resides not in culture alone but in its relation to something external, to the material life-process. Culture, as Marx observed of juridical and political systems, cannot be fully 'understood either in terms of itself ... or in terms of the so-called universal development of the mind'. To ignore this, the argument concludes, is to make ideology the basic matter and thus to establish it firmly. And in fact, having taken a dialectical turn, cultural criticism must not hypothesize the criteria of culture. Criticism retains its mobility in regard to culture by recognizing the latter's position within the whole. Without such freedom, without consciousness transcending the immanence of culture, immanent criticism itself would be inconceivable: the spontaneous movement of the object can be followed only by someone who is not entirely engulfed by it. But the traditional demand of the ideology-critique is itself subject to a historical dynamic. The critique was conceived against idealism, the philosophical form which reflects the fetishization of culture. Today, however, the definition of consciousness in terms of being has become a means of dispensing with all consciousness which does not conform to existence. The objectivity of truth, without which the dialectic is inconceivable, is tacitly replaced by vulgar positivism and pragmatism – ultimately, that is, by bourgeois subjectivism. During the bourgeois era, the prevailing theory was the ideology and the opposing praxis was in direct contradiction. Today, theory hardly exists any longer and the ideology drones, as it were, from the gears of an irresistible praxis. No notion dares to be conceived any more which does not cheerfully include, in all camps, explicit instructions as to who its beneficiaries are – exactly what the polemics once sought to expose. But the unideological thought is that which does not permit itself to be reduced to 'operational terms' and instead strives solely to help the things themselves to that articulation from which they are otherwise cut off by the prevailing language. Since the moment arrived when every advanced economic and political council agreed that what was important was to change the world and that to interpret it was *allotria*, it has become difficult simply to invoke the *Theses* against Feuerbach. Dialectics also includes the relation between action and contemplation. In an epoch in which bourgeois social science has, in Scheler's words, 'plundered' the Marxian notion of ideology and diluted it to universal relativism, the danger involved in overlooking the function of ideologies has become less than that of judging intellectual phenomena in a subsumptive, uninformed and administrative manner and assimilating them into the prevailing constellations of power which the intellect ought to expose. As with many other elements of dialectical materialism, the notion of ideology has changed from an instrument of knowledge into its straitjacket. In the name of the dependence of superstructure on base, all use of ideology is controlled instead of criticized. No one is concerned with the objective substance of an ideology as long as it is expedient.

Yet the very function of ideologies becomes increasingly abstract. The suspicion held by earlier cultural critics is confirmed: in a world which denies the mass of human beings the authentic experience of intellectual phenomena by making genuine education a privilege and by shackling consciousness, the specific ideological content of these phenomena is less important than the fact that there should be anything at all to fill the vacuum of the expropriated consciousness and to distract from the open secret. Within the context of its social effect, the particular ideological doctrine which a film imparts to its audience is presumably far less important than the interest of the homeward-bound movie-goer in the names and marital affairs of the stars. Vulgar notions such as 'amusement' and 'diversion' are more appropriate than pretentious explanations which designate one writer as a representative of the lower-middle class, another of the upper-middle. Culture has become ideological not only as the quintessence of subjectively devised manifestations of the objective mind, but even more as the sphere of private life. The illusory importance and autonomy of private life conceals the fact that private life drags on only as an appendage of the social process. Life transforms itself into the ideology of reification – a death mask. Hence, the task of criticism must be not so much to search for the particular interest-groups to which cultural phenomena are to be assigned, but rather to decipher the general social tendencies which are expressed in these phenomena and through which the most powerful interests realize themselves. Cultural criticism must become social physiognomy. The more the whole divests itself of all spontaneous elements, is socially mediated and filtered, is 'consciousness', the more it becomes 'culture'. In addition to being the means of subsistence, the material process of production finally unveils itself as that which it always was, from its origins in the exchange-relationship as the false consciousness which the two contracting parties have of each other: ideology. Inversely, however, consciousness becomes at the same time increasingly a mere transitional moment in the functioning of the whole. Today, ideology means society as appearance. Although mediated by the totality behind which stands the rule of partiality, ideology is not simply reducible to a partial interest. It is, as it were, equally near the centre in all its pieces.

The alternatives – either calling culture as a whole into question from outside under the general notion of ideology, or confronting it with the norms which it itself has crystallized – cannot be accepted by critical theory. To insist on the choice between immanence and transcendence is to revert to the traditional logic criticized in Hegel's polemic against Kant. As Hegel argued, every method which sets limits and restricts itself to the limits of its object thereby goes beyond them. The position transcending culture is in a certain sense presupposed by dialectics as the consciousness which does succumb in advance to the fetishization of the intellectual sphere. Dialectics means intransigence towards all reification. The transcendent method, which aims at totality, seems more radical than the immanent method, which presupposes the questionable whole. The transcendent critic assumes an as it were Archimedean position above culture and the blindness of society, from which consciousness can bring the totality, no matter how massive, into flux. The attack on the whole draws strength from the fact that the semblance of unity and wholeness in the world grows with the advance of reification; that is, with division. But the summary dismissal of ideology which in the Soviet sphere has already become a pretext for cynical terror, taking the form of a ban on 'objectivism', pays that wholeness too high an honour. Such an attitude buys up culture *en bloc* from society, regardless of the use to which it is put. If ideology is defined as socially necessary appearance, then the ideology today is society itself in so far as its integral power and inevitability, its overwhelming existence-in-itself, surrogates the meaning which that existence has exterminated. The choice of a standpoint outside the sway of existing society is as fictitious as only the construction of abstract utopias can be. Hence, the transcendent criticism of culture, much like bourgeois cultural criticism, sees itself obliged to fall back upon the idea of 'naturalness', which itself forms a central element of bourgeois ideology. The transcendent attack on culture regularly speaks the language of false escape, that of the 'nature boy'. It despises the mind and its works, contending that they are, after all, only man-made and serve only to cover up 'natural' life. Because of this alleged worthlessness, the phenomena allow themselves to be manipulated and degraded for purposes of domination.

This explains the inadequacy of most socialist contributions to cultural criticism: they lack the experience of that with which they deal. In wishing to wipe away the whole as if with a sponge, they develop an affinity to barbarism. Their sympathies are inevitably with the more primitive, more undifferentiated, no matter how much it may contradict the level of intellectual productive forces. The blanket rejection of culture becomes a pretext for promoting what is crudest, 'healthiest', even repressive; above all, the perennial conflict between individual and society, both drawn in like manner, which is obstinately resolved in favour of society according to the criteria of the administrators who have appropriated it. From there it is only a step to the official reinstatement of culture. Against this struggles the immanent procedure as the more essentially dialectical. It takes seriously the principle that it is not ideology in itself which is untrue but, rather, its pretension to correspond to reality. Immanent criticism of intellectual and artistic phenomena seeks to grasp, through the analysis of their form and meaning, the contradiction between their objective idea and that pretension. It names what the consistency or inconsistency of the work itself expresses of the structure of the existent. Such criticism does not stop at a general recognition of the servitude of the objective mind, but seeks rather to transform this knowledge into a heightened perception of the thing itself. Insight into the negativity of culture is binding only when it reveals the truth or untruth of a perception, the consequence or lameness of a thought, the coherence or incoherence of a structure, the substantiality or emptiness of a figure of speech. Where it finds inadequacies it does not ascribe them hastily to the individual and his psychology, which are merely the façade of the failure, but instead seeks to derive them from the irreconcilability of the object's moments. It pursues the logic of its aporias, the insolubility of the task itself. In such antinomies criticism perceives those of society. A successful work, according to immanent criticism, is not one which resolves objective contradictions in a spurious harmony, but one which expresses the idea of harmony negatively by embodying the contradictions, pure and uncompromised, in its innermost structure. Confronted with this kind of work, the verdict 'mere ideology' loses its meaning. At the same time, however, immanent criticism holds in evidence the fact that the mind has always been under a spell. On its own it is unable to resolve the contradictions under which it labours. Even the most radical reflection of the mind on its own failure is limited by the fact that it remains only reflection, without altering the existence to which its failure bears witness. Hence immanent criticism cannot take comfort in its own idea. It can neither be vain enough to believe that it can liberate the mind directly by immersing itself in it, nor naive enough to believe that unflinching immersion in the object will inevitably lead to truth by virtue of the logic of things if only the subjective knowledge of the false whole is kept from intruding from the outside, as it were, in the determination of the object. The less the dialectical method can today presuppose the Hegelian identity of subject and object, the more it is obliged to be mindful of the duality of the moments. It must relate the knowledge of society as a totality and of the mind's involvement in it to the claim inherent in the specific content of the object that it be apprehended as such. Dialectics cannot, therefore, permit any insistence on logical neatness to encroach on its right to go from one *genus* to another, to shed light on an object in itself hermetic by casting a glance at society, to present society with the bill which the object does not redeem. Finally, the very opposition between knowledge which penetrates from without and that which bores from within becomes suspect to the dialectical method, which sees in it a symptom of precisely that reification which the dialectic is obliged to accuse. The abstract categorizing and, as it were, administrative thinking of the former corresponds in the latter to the fetishism of an object blind to its genesis, which has become the prerogative of the expert. But if stubbornly immanent contemplation threatens to revert to idealism, to the illusion of the self-sufficient mind in command of both itself and of reality, transcendent contemplation threatens to forget the effort of conceptualization required and content itself instead with the prescribed label, the petrified invective, most often 'petty-bourgeois', the ukase dispatched from above. Topological thinking, which knows the place of every phenomenon and the essence of none, is secretly related to the paranoic system of delusions which is cut off from experience of the object. With the aid of mechanically functioning categories, the world is divided into black and white and thus made ready for the very domination against which concepts were once conceived. No theory, not even that which is true, is safe from perversion into delusion once it has renounced a spontaneous relation to the object. Dialectics must guard against this no less than against enthralment in the cultural object. It can subscribe neither to the cult of the mind nor to hatred of it. The dialectical critic of culture must both participate in culture and not participate. Only then does he do justice to his object and to himself.

The traditional transcendent critique of ideology is obsolete. In principle, the method succumbs to the very reification which is its critical theme. By transferring the notion of causality directly from the realm of physical nature to society, it falls back behind its own object. Nevertheless, the transcendent method can still appeal to the fact that it employs reified notions only in so far as society itself is reified. Through the crudity and severity of the notion of causality, it claims to hold up a mirror to society's own crudity and severity, to its debasement of the mind. But the sinister, integrated society of today no longer tolerates even those relatively independent, distinct moments to which the theory of the causal dependence of superstructure on base once referred. In the open-air prison which the world is becoming, it is no longer so important to know what depends on what, such is the extent to which everything is one. All phenomena rigidify, become insignias of the absolute rule of that which is. There are no more ideologies in the authentic sense of false consciousness, only advertisements for the world through its duplication and the provocative lie which does not seek belief but commands silence. Hence, the question of the causal dependence of culture, a question which seems to embody the voice of that on which culture is thought only to depend, takes on a backwoods ring. Of course, even the immanent method is eventually overtaken by this. It is dragged into the abyss by its object. The materialistic transparency of culture has not made it more honest, only more vulgar. By relinquishing its own particularity, culture has also relinquished the salt of truth, which once consisted in its opposition to other particularities. To call it to account before a responsibility which it denies is only to confirm cultural pomposity. Neutralized and ready-made, traditional culture has become worthless today. Through an irrevocable process its heritage, hypocritically reclaimed by the Russians, has become expendable to the highest degree, super-fluous, trash. And the hucksters of mass culture can point to it with a grin, for they treat it as such. The more total society becomes, the greater the reification of the mind and the more paradoxical its effort to escape reification on its own. Even the most extreme consciousness of doom threatens to degenerate into idle chatter. Cultural criticism finds itself faced with the final stage of the dialectic of culture and barbarism. To write poetry after Auschwitz is barbaric. And this corrodes even the knowledge of why it has become impossible to write poetry today. Absolute reification, which presupposed intellectual progress as one of its elements, is now preparing to absorb the mind entirely. Critical intelligence cannot be equal to this challenge as long as it confines itself to self-satisfied contemplation.

4.3 □ *Ideology and Ideological State Apparatuses (Notes towards an Investigation)*[1]

Louis Althusser

[. . .]

Infrastructure and Superstructure

On a number of occasions[2] I have insisted on the revolutionary character of the Marxist conception of the 'social whole' in so far as it is distinct from the Hegelian 'totality'. I said (and this thesis only repeats famous propositions of historical materialism) that Marx conceived the structure of every society as constituted by 'levels' or 'instances' articulated by a specific determination: the *infrastructure*, or economic base (the 'unity' of the productive forces and the relations of production) and the *superstructure*, which itself contains two 'levels' or 'instances': the politico-legal (law and the State) and ideology (the different ideologies, religious, ethical, legal, political, etc.).

Besides its theoretico-didactic interest (it reveals the difference between Marx and Hegel), this representation has the following crucial theoretical advantage: it makes it possible to inscribe in the theoretical apparatus of its essential concepts what I have called their *respective indices of effectivity*. What does this mean?

It is easy to see that this representation of the structure of every society as an edifice containing a base (infrastructure) on which are erected the two 'floors' of the superstructure, is a metaphor, to be quite precise, a spatial metaphor: the metaphor

From Althusser, L., *Lenin and Philosophy and Other Essays*, trans. B. Brewster, Monthly Review Press, New York, 1971, pp. 134–6, 141–50, 159–62, 164–7, 170–75, 183–6.

of a topography [*topique*].[3] Like every metaphor, this metaphor suggests something, makes something visible. What? Precisely this: that the upper floors could not 'stay up' (in the air) alone, if they did not rest precisely on their base.

Thus the object of the metaphor of the edifice is to represent above all the 'determination in the last instance' by the economic base. The effect of this spatial metaphor is to endow the base with an index of effectivity known by the famous terms: the determination in the last instance of what happens in the upper 'floors' (of the superstructure) by what happens in the economic base.

Given this index of effectivity 'in the last instance', the 'floors' of the superstructure are clearly endowed with different indices of effectivity. What kind of indices?

It is possible to say that the floors of the superstructure are not determinant in the last instance, but that they are determined by the effectivity of the base; that if they are determinant in their own (as yet undefined) ways, this is true only in so far as they are determined by the base.

Their index of effectivity (or determination), as determined by the determination in the last instance of the base, is thought by the Marxist tradition in two ways: (1) there is a 'relative autonomy' of the superstructure with respect to the base; (2) there is a 'reciprocal action' of the superstructure on the base.

We can therefore say that the great theoretical advantage of the Marxist topography, i.e. of the spatial metaphor of the edifice (base and superstructure), is simultaneously that it reveals that questions of determination (or of index of effectivity) are crucial; that it reveals that it is the base which in the last instance determines the whole edifice; and that, as a consequence, it obliges us to pose the theoretical problem of the types of 'derivatory' effectivity peculiar to the superstructure, i.e. it obliges us to think what the Marxist tradition calls conjointly the relative autonomy of the superstructure and the reciprocal action of the superstructure on the base.

The greatest disadvantage of this representation of the structure of every society by the spatial metaphor of an edifice, is obviously the fact that it is metaphorical: i.e. it remains *descriptive*.

It now seems to me that it is possible and desirable to represent things differently. NB, I do not mean by this that I want to reject the classical metaphor, for that metaphor itself requires that we go beyond it. And I am not going beyond it in order to reject it as outworn. I simply want to attempt to think what it gives us in the form of a description.

I believe that it is possible and necessary to think what characterizes the essential of the existence and nature of the superstructure *on the basis of reproduction*. Once one takes the point of view of reproduction, many of the questions whose existence was indicated by the spatial metaphor of the edifice, but to which it could not give a conceptual answer, are immediately illuminated.

My basic thesis is that it is not possible to pose these questions (and therefore to answer them) *except from the point of view of reproduction*.

[. . .]

The State

[. . .]

To summarize the 'Marxist theory of the State' [. . .], it can be said that the Marxist classics have always claimed that (1) the State is the repressive State apparatus, (2) State power and State apparatus must be distinguished, (3) the objective of the class struggle concerns State power, and in consequence the use of the State apparatus by the classes (or alliance of classes or of fractions of classes) holding State power as a function of their class objectives, and (4) the proletariat must seize State power in order to destroy the existing bourgeois State apparatus and, in a first phase, replace it with a quite different, proletarian, State apparatus, then in later phases set in motion a radical process, that of the destruction of the State (the end of State power, the end of every State apparatus).

In this perspective, therefore, what I would propose to add to the 'Marxist theory' of the State is already there in so many words. But it seems to me that even with this supplement, this theory is still in part descriptive, although it does now contain complex and differential elements whose functioning and action cannot be understood without recourse to further supplementary theoretical development.

The State Ideological Apparatuses

Thus, what has to be added to the 'Marxist theory' of the State is something else.

Here we must advance cautiously in a terrain which, in fact, the Marxist classics entered long before us, but without having systematized in theoretical form the decisive advances implied by their experiences and procedures. Their experiences and procedures were indeed restricted in the main to the terrain of political practice.

In fact, i.e. in their political practice, the Marxist classics treated the State as a more complex reality than the definition of it given in the 'Marxist theory of the State', even when it has been supplemented as I have just suggested. They recognized this complexity in their practice, but they did not express it in a corresponding theory.[4]

I should like to attempt a very schematic outline of this corresponding theory. To that end, I propose the following thesis.

In order to advance the theory of the State it is indispensable to take into account not only the distinction between *State power* and *State apparatus*, but also another reality which is clearly on the side of the (repressive) State apparatus, but must not be confused with it. I shall call this reality by its concept: *the Ideological State Apparatuses*.

What are the Ideological State Apparatuses (ISAs)?

They must not be confused with the (Repressive) State Apparatus. Remember that in Marxist theory, the State Apparatus (SA) contains: the Government, the Administration, the Army, the Police, the Courts, the Prisons, etc., which constitute what I shall in future call the Repressive State Apparatus. Repressive suggests that the State Apparatus in question 'functions by violence' – at least ultimately (since repression, e.g. administrative repression, may take non-physical forms).

I shall call Ideological State Apparatuses a certain number of realities which present themselves to the immediate observer in the form of distinct and specialized institutions. I propose an empirical list of these which will obviously have to be examined in detail, tested, corrected and reorganized. With all the reservations implied by this requirement, we can for the moment regard the following institutions as Ideological State Apparatuses (the order in which I have listed them has no particular significance):

- the religious ISA (the system of the different Churches);
- the educational ISA (the system of the different public and private 'Schools');
- the family ISA;[5]
- the legal ISA;[6]
- the political ISA (the political system, including the different Parties);
- the trade-union ISA;
- the communications ISA (press, radio and television, etc.);
- the cultural ISA (Literature, the Arts, sports, etc.).

I have said that the ISAs must not be confused with the (Repressive) State Apparatus. What constitutes the difference?

As a first moment, it is clear that while there is *one* (Repressive) State Apparatus, there is a *plurality* of Ideological State Apparatuses. Even presupposing that it exists, the unity that constitutes this plurality of ISAs as a body is not immediately visible.

As a second moment, it is clear that whereas the – unified – (Repressive) State Apparatus belongs entirely to the *public* domain, much the larger part of the Ideological State Apparatuses (in their apparent dispersion) are part, on the contrary, of the *private* domain. Churches, Parties, Trade Unions, families, some schools, most newspapers, cultural ventures, etc., etc., are private.

We can ignore the first observation for the moment. But someone is bound to question the second, asking me by what right I regard as Ideological *State* Apparatuses, institutions which for the most part do not possess public status, but are quite simply *private* institutions. As a conscious Marxist, Gramsci already forestalled this objection in one sentence. The distinction between the public and the private is a distinction internal to bourgeois law, and valid in the (subordinate) domains in which bourgeois law exercises its 'authority'. The domain of the State escapes it because the latter is 'above the law': the State, which is the State *of* the ruling class, is neither public nor private; on the contrary, it is the precondition for any distinction between public and private. The same thing can be said from the starting point of our State Ideological Apparatuses. It is unimportant whether the institutions in which they are realized are 'public' or 'private'. What matters is how they function. Private institutions can perfectly well 'function' as Ideological State Apparatuses. A reasonably thorough analysis of any one of the ISAs proves it.

But now for what is essential. What distinguishes the ISAs from the (Repressive) State Apparatus is the following basic difference: the Repressive State Apparatus functions 'by violence', whereas the Ideological State Apparatuses *function 'by ideology'*.

I can clarify matters by correcting this distinction. I shall say rather that every State Apparatus, whether Repressive or Ideological, 'functions' both by violence and by ideology, but with one very important distinction which makes it imperative not to confuse the Ideological State Apparatuses with the (Repressive) State Apparatus.

This is the fact that the (Repressive) State Apparatus functions massively and predominantly *by repression* (including physical repression), while functioning secondarily by ideology. (There is no such thing as a purely repressive apparatus.) For example, the Army and the Police also function by ideology both to ensure their own cohesion and reproduction, and in the 'values' they propound externally.

In the same way, but inversely, it is essential to say that for their part the Ideological State Apparatuses function massively and predominantly *by ideology*, but they also function secondarily by repression, even if ultimately, but only ultimately, this is very attenuated and concealed, even symbolic. (There is no such thing as a purely ideological apparatus.) Thus Schools and Churches use suitable methods of punishment, expulsion, selection, etc., to 'discipline' not only their shepherds, but also their flocks. The same is true of the Family. ... The same is true of the cultural IS Apparatus (censorship, among other things), etc.

Is it necessary to add that this determination of the double 'functioning' (predominantly, secondarily) by repression and by ideology, according to whether it is a matter of the (Repressive) State Apparatus or the Ideological State Apparatuses, makes it clear that very subtle explicit or tacit combinations may be woven from the interplay of the (Repressive) State Apparatus and the Ideological State Apparatuses? Everyday life provides us with innumerable examples of this, but they must be studied in detail if we are to go further than this mere observation.

Nevertheless, this remark leads us towards an understanding of what constitutes the unity of the apparently disparate body of the ISAs. If the ISAs 'function' massively and predominantly by ideology, what unifies their diversity is precisely this functioning, in so far as the ideology by which they function is always in fact unified, despite its diversity and its contradictions, *beneath the ruling ideology*, which is the ideology of 'the ruling class'. Given the fact that the 'ruling class' in principle holds State power (openly or more often by means of alliances between classes or class fractions), and therefore has at its disposal the (Repressive) State Apparatus, we can accept the fact that this same ruling class is active in the Ideological State Apparatuses in so far as it is ultimately the ruling ideology which is realized in the Ideological State Apparatuses, precisely in its contradictions. Of course, it is a quite different thing to act by laws and decrees in the (Repressive) State Apparatus and to 'act' through the intermediary of the ruling ideology in the Ideological State Apparatuses. We must go into the details of this difference – but it cannot mask the reality of a profound identity. To my knowledge, *no class can hold State power over a long period without at the same time exercising its hegemony over and in the State Ideological Apparatuses*. I only need one example and proof of this: Lenin's anguished concern to revolutionize the educational Ideological State Apparatus (among others), simply to make it possible for the Soviet proletariat, who had seized State power, to secure the future of the dictatorship of the proletariat and the transition to socialism.[7]

This last comment puts us in a position to understand that the Ideological State Apparatuses may be not only the *stake*, but also the *site* of class struggle, and often of bitter forms of class struggle. The class (or class alliance) in power cannot lay down the law in the ISAs as easily as it can in the (Repressive) State Apparatus, not only because the former ruling classes are able to retain strong positions there for a long time, but also because the resistance of the exploited classes is able to find means and occasions to express itself there, either by the utilization of their contradictions, or by conquering combat positions in them in struggle.[8]

Let me run through my comments.

If the thesis I have proposed is well-founded, it leads me back to the classical Marxist theory of the State, while making it more precise in one point. I argue that it is necessary to distinguish between State power (and its possession by ...) on the one hand, and the State Apparatus on the other. But I add that the State Apparatus contains two bodies: the body of institutions which represent the Repressive State Apparatus on the one hand, and the body of institutions which represent the body of Ideological State Apparatuses on the other.

But if this is the case, the following question is bound to be asked, even in the very summary state of my suggestions: what exactly is the extent of the role of the Ideological State Apparatuses ? What is their importance based on ? In other words: to what does the 'function' of these Ideological State Apparatuses, which do not function by repression but by ideology, correspond?

On the Reproduction of the Relations of Production

I can now answer the central question which I have left in suspense for many long pages: *how is the reproduction of the relations of production secured?*

In the topographical language (Infrastructure, Superstructure), I can say: for the most part,[9] it is secured by the legal-political and ideological superstructure.

But as I have argued that it is essential to go beyond this still descriptive language, I shall say: for the most part, it is secured by the exercise of State power in the State Apparatuses, on the one hand the (Repressive) State Apparatus, on the other the Ideological State Apparatuses.

What I have just said must also be taken into account, and it can be assembled in the form of the following three features:

1. All the State Apparatuses function both by repression and by ideology, with the difference that the (Repressive) State Apparatus functions massively and

predominantly by repression, whereas the Ideological State Apparatuses function massively and predominantly by ideology.

2. Whereas the (Repressive) State Apparatus constitutes an organized whole whose different parts are centralized beneath a commanding unity, that of the politics of class struggle applied by the political representatives of the ruling classes in possession of State power, the Ideological State Apparatuses are multiple, distinct, 'relatively autonomous' and capable of providing an objective field to contradictions which express, in forms which may be limited or extreme, the effects of the clashes between the capitalist class struggle and the proletarian class struggle, as well as their subordinate forms.

3. Whereas the unity of the (Repressive) State Apparatus is secured by its unified and centralized organization under the leadership of the representatives of the classes in power executing the politics of the class struggle of the classes in power, the unity of the different Ideological State Apparatuses is secured, usually in contradictory forms, by the ruling ideology, the ideology of the ruling class.

Taking these features into account, it is possible to represent the reproduction of the relations of production[10] in the following way, according to a kind of 'division of labour'.

The role of the Repressive State Apparatus, in so far as it is a repressive apparatus, consists essentially in securing by force (physical or otherwise) the political conditions of the reproduction of relations of production which are in the last resort *relations of exploitation*. Not only does the State apparatus contribute generously to its own reproduction (the capitalist State contains political dynasties, military dynasties, etc.), but also, and above all, the State apparatus secures by repression (from the most brutal physical force, via mere administrative commands and interdictions, to open and tacit censorship) the political conditions for the action of the Ideological State Apparatuses.

In fact, it is the latter which largely secure the reproduction specifically of the relations of production, behind a 'shield' provided by the Repressive State Apparatus. It is here that the role of the ruling ideology is heavily concentrated, the ideology of the ruling class, which holds State power. It is the intermediation of the ruling ideology that ensures a (sometimes teeth-gritting) 'harmony' between the Repressive State Apparatus and the Ideological State Apparatuses, and between the different Ideological State Apparatuses.

[. . .]

On Ideology

[. . .]

Ideology has no History

One word first of all to expound the reason in principle which seems to me to found, or at least to justify, the project of a theory of ideology *in general*, and not a theory of particular ideolog*ies*, which, whatever their form (religious, ethical, legal, political), always express *class positions*.

It is quite obvious that it is necessary to proceed towards a theory of ideolog*ies* in the two respects I have just suggested. It will then be clear that a theory of ideolog*ies* depends in the last resort on the history of social formations, and thus of the modes of production combined in social formations, and of the class struggles which develop in them. In this sense it is clear that there can be no question of a theory of ideolog*ies in general*, since ideolog*ies* (defined in the double respect suggested above: regional and class) have a history, whose determination in the last instance is clearly situated outside ideologies alone, although it involves them.

On the contrary, if I am able to put forward the project of a theory of ideology *in general*, and if this theory really is one of the elements on which theories of ideolog*ies* depend, that entails an apparently paradoxical proposition which I shall express in the following terms: *ideology has no history*.

As we know, this formulation appears in so many words, in a passage from *The German Ideology*. Marx utters it with respect to metaphysics, which, he says, has no more history than ethics (meaning also the other forms of ideology)

In *The German Ideology*, this formulation appears in a plainly positivist context. Ideology is conceived as a pure illusion, a pure dream, i.e. as nothingness. All its reality is external to it. Ideology is thus thought as an imaginary construction whose status is exactly like the theoretical status of the dream among writers before Freud. For these writers, the dream was the purely imaginary, i.e. null, result of 'day's residues', presented in an arbitrary arrangement and order, sometimes even 'inverted', in other words, in 'disorder'. For them, the dream was the imaginary, it was empty, null and arbitrarily 'stuck together' [*bricolé*], once the eyes had closed, from the residues of the only full and positive reality, the reality of the day. This is exactly the status of philosophy and ideology (since in this book philosophy is ideology *par excellence*) in *The German Ideology*.

Ideology, then, is for Marx an imaginary assemblage [*bricolage*], a pure dream, empty and vain, constituted by the 'day's residues' from the only full and positive reality, that of the concrete history of concrete material individuals materially producing their existence. It is on this basis that ideology has no history in *The German Ideology*, since its history is outside it, where the only existing history is, the history of concrete individuals, etc. In *The German Ideology*, the thesis that ideology has no history is therefore a purely negative thesis, since it means both:

1. ideology is nothing in so far as it is a pure dream (manufactured by who knows what power: if not by the alienation of the division of labour, but that, too, is a *negative* determination);
2. ideology has no history, which emphatically does not mean that there is no history in it (on the contrary, for it is merely the pale, empty and inverted reflection of real history) but that it has no history *of its own*.

Now, while the thesis I wish to defend formally speaking adopts the terms of

The German Ideology ('ideology has no history'), it is radically different from the positivist and historicist thesis of *The German Ideology*.

For on the one hand, I think it is possible to hold that ideologies *have a history of their own* (although it is determined in the last instance by the class struggle); and on the other, I think it is possible to hold that ideology *in general has no history*, not in a negative sense (its history is external to it), but in an absolutely positive sense.

This sense is a positive one if it is true that the peculiarity of ideology is that it is endowed with a structure and a functioning such as to make it a non-historical reality, i.e. an *omni-historical* reality, in the sense in which that structure and functioning are immutable, present in the same form throughout what we can call history, in the sense in which the *Communist Manifesto* defines history as the history of class struggles, i.e. the history of class societies.

To give a theoretical reference-point here, I might say that, to return to our example of the dream, in its Freudian conception this time, our proposition: ideology has no history, can and must (and in a way which has absolutely nothing arbitrary about it, but, quite the reverse, is theoretically necessary, for there is an organic link between the two propositions) be related directly to Freud's proposition that the *unconscious is eternal*, i.e. that it has no history.

If eternal means, not transcendent to all (temporal) history, but omnipresent, transhistorical and therefore immutable in form throughout the extent of history, I shall adopt Freud's expression word for word, and write *ideology is eternal*, exactly like the unconscious. And I add that I find this comparison theoretically justified by the fact that the eternity of the unconscious is not unrelated to the eternity of ideology in general.

That is why I believe I am justified, hypothetically at least, in proposing a theory of ideology *in general*, in the sense that Freud presented a theory of the unconscious *in general*.

To simplify the phrase, it is convenient, taking into account what has been said about ideologies, to use the plain term ideology to designate ideology in general, which I have just said has no history, or, what comes to the same thing, is eternal, i.e. omnipresent in its immutable form throughout history (= the history of social formations containing social classes). For the moment I shall restrict myself to 'class societies' and their history.

Ideology is a 'Representation' of the Imaginary Relationship of Individuals to their Real Conditions of Existence

In order to approach my central thesis on the structure and functioning of ideology, I shall first present two theses, one negative, the other positive. The first concerns the object which is 'represented' in the imaginary form of ideology, the second concerns the materiality of ideology.

THESIS I: Ideology represents the imaginary relationship of individuals to their real conditions of existence.

[. . .]

To speak in a Marxist language, if it is true that the representation of the real conditions of existence of the individuals occupying the posts of agents of production, exploitation, repression, ideologization and scientific practice, does in the last analysis arise from the relations of production, and from relations deriving from the relations of production, we can say the following: all ideology represents in its necessarily imaginary distortion not the existing relations of production (and the other relations that derive from them), but above all the (imaginary) relationship of individuals to the relations of production and the relations that derive from them. What is represented in ideology is therefore not the system of the real relations which govern the existence of individuals, but the imaginary relation of those individuals to the real relations in which they live.

If this is the case, the question of the 'cause' of the imaginary distortion of the real relations in ideology disappears and must be replaced by a different question: why is the representation given to individuals of their (individual) relation to the social relations which govern their conditions of existence and their collective and individual life necessarily an imaginary relation? And what is the nature of this imaginariness? Posed in this way, the question explodes the solution by a 'clique',[11] by a group of individuals (Priests or Despots) who are the authors of the great ideological mystification, just as it explodes the solution by the alienated character of the real world. We shall see why later in my exposition. For the moment I shall go no further.

THESIS II: Ideology has a material existence.

I have already touched on this thesis by saying that the 'ideas' or 'representations', etc., which seem to make up ideology do not have an ideal [*idéale* or *idéelle*] or spiritual existence, but a material existence. I even suggested that the ideal [*idéale, idéelle*] and spiritual existence of 'ideas' arises exclusively in an ideology of the 'idea' and of ideology, and, let me add, in an ideology of what seems to have 'founded' this conception since the emergence of the sciences, i.e. what the practicians of the sciences represent to themselves in their spontaneous ideology as 'ideas', true or false. Of course, presented in affirmative form, this thesis is unproven. I simply ask that the reader be favourably disposed towards it, say, in the name of materialism. A long series of arguments would be necessary to prove it.

This hypothetical thesis of the not spiritual but material existence of 'ideas' or other 'representations' is indeed necessary if we are to advance in our analysis of the nature of ideology. Or rather, it is merely useful to us in order the better to reveal what every at all serious analysis of any ideology will immediately and empirically show to every observer, however critical.

While discussing the Ideological State Apparatuses and their practices, I said that each of them was the realization of an ideology (the unity of these different regional ideologies – religious, ethical, legal, political, aesthetic, etc. – being assured by their subjection to the ruling ideology). I now return to this thesis: an ideology always exists in an apparatus, and its practice, or practices. This existence is material.

Of course, the material existence of the ideology in an apparatus and its practices does not have the same modality as the material existence of a paving-stone or a rifle. But, at the risk of being taken for a Neo-Aristotelian (NB, Marx had a very high regard for Aristotle), I shall say that 'matter is discussed in many senses', or rather that it exists in different modalities, all rooted in the last instance in 'physical' matter.

Having said this, let me move straight on and see what happens to the 'individuals' who live in ideology, i.e. in a determinate (religious, ethical, etc.) representation of the world whose imaginary distortion depends on their imaginary relation to their conditions of existence, in other words, in the last instance, to the relations of production and to class relations (ideology = an imaginary relation to real relations). I shall say that this imaginary relation is itself endowed with a material existence.

[. . .]

I shall immediately set down two conjoint theses:

1. there is no practice except by and in an ideology;
2. there is no ideology except by the subject and for subjects.

I can now come to my central thesis.

Ideology Interpellates Individuals as Subjects

This thesis is simply a matter of making my last proposition explicit: there is no ideology except by the subject and for subjects. Meaning, there is no ideology except for concrete subjects, and this destination for ideology is only made possible by the subject: meaning, *by the category of the subject* and its functioning.

By this I mean that, even if it only appears under this name (the subject) with the rise of bourgeois ideology, above all with the rise of legal ideology,[12] the category of the subject (which may function under other names: e.g. as the soul in Plato, as God, etc.) is the constitutive category of all ideology, whatever its determination (regional or class) and whatever its historical date – since ideology has no history.

I say: the category of the subject is constitutive of all ideology, but at the same time and immediately I add that *the category of the subject is only constitutive of all ideology in so far as all ideology has the function (which defines it) of 'constituting' concrete individuals as subjects*. In the interaction of this double constitution exists the functioning of all ideology, ideology being nothing but its functioning in the material forms of existence of that functioning.

In order to grasp what follows, it is essential to realize that both he who is writing these lines and the reader who reads them are themselves subjects, and therefore ideological subjects (a tautological proposition), i.e. that the author and the reader of these lines both live 'spontaneously' or 'naturally' in ideology in the sense in which I have said that 'man is an ideological animal by nature'.

[. . .]

I only wish to point out that you and I are *always-already* subjects, and as such constantly practice the rituals of ideological recognition, which guarantee for us that we are indeed concrete, individual, distinguishable and (naturally) irreplaceable subjects. The writing I am currently executing and the reading you are currently[13] performing are also in this respect rituals of ideological recognition, including the 'obviousness' with which the 'truth' or 'error' of my reflections may impose itself on you.

But to recognize that we are subjects and that we function in the practical rituals of the most elementary everyday life (the handshake, the fact of calling you by your name, the fact of knowing, even if I do not know what it is, that you 'have' a name of your own, which means that you are recognized as a unique subject, etc.) – this recognition only gives us the 'consciousness' of our incessant (eternal) practice of ideological recognition – its consciousness, i.e. its *recognition* – but in no sense does it give us the (scientific) *knowledge* of the mechanism of this recognition. Now it is this knowledge that we have to reach, if you will, while speaking in ideology, and from within ideology we have to outline a discourse which tries to break with ideology, in order to dare to be the beginning of a scientific (i.e. subjectless) discourse on ideology.

Thus in order to represent why the category of the 'subject' is constitutive of ideology, which only exists by constituting concrete subjects as subjects, I shall employ a special mode of exposition: 'concrete' enough to be recognized, but abstract enough to be thinkable and thought, giving rise to a knowledge.

As a first formulation I shall say: *all ideology hails or interpellates concrete individuals as concrete subjects*, by the functioning of the category of the subject.

This is a proposition which entails that we distinguish for the moment between concrete individuals on the one hand and concrete subjects on the other, although at this level concrete subjects only exist in so far as they are supported by a concrete individual.

I shall then suggest that ideology 'acts' or 'functions' in such a way that it 'recruits' subjects among the individuals (it recruits them all), or 'transforms' the individuals into subjects (it transforms them all) by that very precise operation which I have called *interpellation* or hailing, and which can be imagined along the lines of the most commonplace everyday police (or other) hailing: 'Hey, you there!'[14]

Assuming that the theoretical scene I have imagined takes place in the street, the hailed individual will turn round. By this mere one-hundred-and-eighty-degree physical conversion, he becomes a *subject*. Why? Because he has recognized that the hail was 'really' addressed to him, and that 'it was *really him* who was hailed' (and not someone else). Experience shows that the practical telecommunication of hailings is such that they hardly ever miss their man: verbal call or whistle, the one hailed always recognizes that it is really him who is being hailed. And yet it is a strange phenomenon, and one which cannot be explained solely by 'guilt feelings', despite the large numbers who 'have something on their consciences'.

Naturally for the convenience and clarity of my little theoretical theatre I have had to present things in the form of a sequence, with a before and an after, and thus in the form of a temporal succession. There are individuals walking along. Somewhere (usually behind them) the hail rings out: 'Hey, you there!' One individual (nine times out of ten it is the right one) turns round, believing/suspecting/knowing that it is for him, i.e. recognizing that 'it really is he' who is meant by the hailing. But in reality these things happen without any succession. The existence of ideology and the hailing or interpellation of individuals as subjects are one and the same thing.

I might add: what thus seems to take place outside ideology (to be precise, in the street), in reality takes place in ideology. What really takes place in ideology seems therefore to take place outside it. That is why those who are in ideology believe themselves by definition outside ideology: one of the effects of ideology is the practical *denegation* of the ideological character of ideology by ideology: ideology never says, 'I am ideological'. It is necessary to be outside ideology, i.e. in scientific knowledge, to be able to say: I am in ideology (a quite exceptional case) or (the general case): I was in ideology. As is well known, the accusation of being in ideology only applies to others, never to oneself (unless one is really a Spinozist or a Marxist, which, in this matter, is to be exactly the same thing). Which amounts to saying that ideology *has no outside* (for itself), but at the same time *that it is nothing but outside* (for science and reality).

[. . .]

P.S. If these few schematic theses allow me to illuminate certain aspects of the functioning of the Superstructure and its mode of intervention in the Infrastructure, they are obviously *abstract* and necessarily leave several important problems unanswered, which should be mentioned:

1. The problem of the *total process* of the realization of the reproduction of the relations of production.

As an element of this process, the ISAs *contribute* to this reproduction. But the point of view of their contribution alone is still an abstract one.

It is only within the processes of production and circulation that this reproduction is realized. It is realized by the mechanisms of those processes, in which the training of the workers is 'completed', their posts are assigned them, etc. It is in the internal mechanisms of these processes that the effect of the different ideologies is felt (above all the effect of legal-ethical ideology).

But this point of view is still an abstract one. For in a class society the relations of production are relations of exploitation, and therefore relations between antagonistic classes. The reproduction of the relations of production, the ultimate aim of the ruling class, cannot therefore be a merely technical operation training and distributing individuals for the different posts in the 'technical division' of labour. In fact there is no 'technical division' of labour except in the ideology of the ruling class: every 'technical' division, every 'technical' organization of labour is the form and mask of a *social* (= class) division and organization of labour. The reproduction of the relations of production can therefore only be a class undertaking. It is realized through a class struggle which counterposes the ruling class and the exploited class.

The *total process* of the realization of the reproduction of the relations of production is therefore still abstract, in so far as it has not adopted the point of view of this class struggle. To adopt the point of view of reproduction is therefore, in the last instance, to adopt the point of view of the class struggle.

2. The problem of the class nature of the ideolog*ies* existing in a social formation.

The 'mechanism' of ideology *in general* is one thing. We have seen that it can be reduced to a few principles expressed in a few words (as 'poor' as those which, according to Marx, define production *in general* or in Freud, define *the* unconscious *in general*). If there is any truth in it, this mechanism must be *abstract* with respect to every real ideological formation.

I have suggested that the ideologies were *realized* in institutions, in their rituals and their practices, in the ISAs. We have seen that on this basis they contribute to that form of class struggle, vital for the ruling class, the reproduction of the relations of production. But the point of view itself, however real, is still an abstract one.

In fact, the State and its Apparatuses only have meaning from the point of view of the class struggle, as an apparatus of class struggle ensuring class oppression and guaranteeing the conditions of exploitation and its reproduction. But there is no class struggle without antagonistic classes. Whoever says class struggle of the ruling class says resistance, revolt and class struggle of the ruled class.

That is why the ISAs are not the realization of ideology *in general*, nor even the conflict-free realization of the ideology of the ruling class. The ideology of the ruling class does not become the ruling ideology by the grace of God, nor even by virtue of the seizure of State power alone. It is by the installation of the ISAs in which this ideology is realized and realizes itself that it becomes the ruling ideology. But this installation is not achieved all by itself; on the contrary, it is the stake in a very bitter and continuous class struggle: first against the former ruling classes and their positions in the old and new ISAs, then against the exploited class.

But this point of view of the class struggle in the ISAs is still an abstract one. In fact, the class struggle in the ISAs is indeed an aspect of the class struggle, sometimes an important and symptomatic one: e.g. the anti-religious struggle in the eighteenth century, or the 'crisis' of the educational ISA in every capitalist country today. But the class struggles in the ISAs is only one aspect of a class struggle which goes beyond the ISAs. The ideology that a class in power makes the ruling ideology in its ISAs is indeed 'realized' in those ISAs, but it goes beyond them, for it comes from elsewhere. Similarly, the ideology that a ruled class manages to defend in and against such ISAs goes beyond them, for it comes from elsewhere.

It is only from the point of view of the classes, i.e. of the class struggle, that it is possible to explain the ideolog*ies* existing in a social formation. Not only is it from this starting point that it is possible to explain the realization of the ruling ideology in the ISAs and of the forms of class struggle for which the ISAs are the seat and the stake. But it is also and above all from this starting point that it is possible to understand the provenance of the ideologies which are realized in the ISAs and confront one another there. For if it is true that the ISAs represent the *form* in which the ideology of the ruling class must *necessarily* be realized, and the form in which the ideology of the ruled class must *necessarily* be measured and confronted, ideologies are not 'born' in the ISAs but from the social classes at grips in the class struggle: from their conditions of existence, their practices, their experience of the struggle, etc.

April 1970

Notes

1. This text is made up of two extracts from an ongoing study. The subtitle 'Notes towards an Investigation' is the author's own. The ideas expounded should not be regarded as more than the introduction to a discussion.
2. In *For Marx* and *Reading Capital*, 1965 (English editions 1969 and 1970 respectively).
3. *Topography* from the Greek *topos*: place. A topography represents in a definite space the respective *sites* occupied by several realities: thus the economic is *at the bottom* (the base), the superstructure *above it*.
4. To my knowledge, Gramsci is the only one who went any distance in the road I am taking. He had the 'remarkable' idea that the State could not be reduced to the (Repressive) State Apparatus, but included, as he put it, a certain number of institutions from '*civil society*': the Church, the Schools, the trade unions, etc. Unfortunately, Gramsci did not systematize his institutions, which remained in the state of acute but fragmentary notes (cf. Gramsci, *Selections from the Prison Notebooks*, International Publishers, 1971, pp. 12, 259, 260–63; see also the letters to Tatiana Schucht, 7 September 1931, in *Lettre del Carcere*, Einaudi, 1968, p. 479. English-language translation in preparation.
5. The family obviously has other 'functions' than that of an ISA. It intervenes in the reproduction of labour-power. In different modes of production it is the unit of production and/or the unit of consumption.
6. The 'Law' belongs both to the (Repressive) State Apparatus and to the system of the ISAs.
7. In a pathetic text written in 1937, Krupskaya relates the history of Lenin's desperate efforts and what she regards as his failure.
8. What I have said in these few brief words about the class struggle in the ISAs is obviously far from exhausting the question of the class struggle.
   To approach this question, two principles must be borne in mind:
   The first principle was formulated by Marx in the Preface to *A Contribution to the Critique of Political Economy*:

   > In considering such transformations [a social revolution] a distinction should always be made between the material transformation of the economic conditions of production, which can be determined with the precision of natural science, and the legal, political, religious, aesthetic or philosophic – in short, ideological forms in which men become conscious of this conflict and fight it out.

   The class struggle is thus expressed and exercised in ideological forms, thus also in the ideological forms of the ISAs. But the class struggle *extends far beyond* these forms, and it is because it extends beyond them that the struggle of the exploited classes may also be exercised in the forms of the ISAs, and thus turn the weapon of ideology against the classes in power.

This by virtue of the *second principle*: the class struggle extends beyond the ISAs because it is rooted elsewhere than in ideology, in the Infrastructure, in the relations of production, which are relations of exploitation and constitute the base for class relations.

9. For the most part. For the relations of production are first reproduced by the materiality of the processes of production and circulation. But it should not be forgotten that ideological relations are immediately present in these same processes.

10. *For that part* of reproduction to which the Repressive State Apparatus and the Ideological State Apparatus *contribute*.

11. I use this very modern term deliberately. For even in Communist circles, unfortunately, it is a commonplace to 'explain' some political deviation (left or right opportunism) by the action of a 'clique'.

12. Which borrowed the legal category of 'subject in law' to make an ideological notion: man is by nature a subject.

13. NB: this double 'currently' is one more proof of the fact that ideology is 'eternal', since these two 'currentlys' are separated by an indefinite interval; I am writing these lines on 6 April 1969, you may read them at any subsequent time.

14. Hailing as an everyday practice subject to a precise ritual takes a quite 'special' form in the policeman's practice of 'hailing' which concerns the hailing of 'suspects'.

4.4 □ *Dominant,*
Residual, and Emergent

Raymond Williams

The complexity of a culture is to be found not only in its variable processes and their social definitions – traditions, institutions, and formations – but also in the dynamic interrelations, at every point in the process, of historically varied and variable elements. In what I have called 'epochal' analysis, a cultural process is seized as a cultural system, with determinate dominant features: feudal culture or bourgeois culture or a transition from one to the other. This emphasis on dominant and definitive lineaments and features is important and often, in practice, effective. But it then often happens that its methodology is preserved for the very different function of historical analysis, in which a sense of movement within what is ordinarily abstracted as a system is crucially necessary, especially if it is to connect with the future as well as with the past. In authentic historical analysis it is necessary at every point to recognize the complex interrelations between movements and tendencies both within and beyond a specific and effective dominance. It is necessary to examine how these relate to the whole cultural process rather than only to the selected and abstracted dominant system. Thus 'bourgeois culture' is a significant generalizing description and hypothesis, expressed within epochal analysis by fundamental comparisons with 'feudal culture' or 'socialist culture'. However, as a description of cultural process, over four or five centuries and in scores of different societies, it requires immediate historical and internally comparative differentiation. Moreover, even if this is acknowledged or practically carried out, the 'epochal' definition can exert its pressure as a static type against which all real cultural process is measured, either to show 'stages' or 'variations' of the type (which is still historical analysis), or, at its worst, to select supporting and exclude 'marginal' or 'incidental' or 'secondary' evidence.

Such errors are avoidable, if, while retaining the epochal hypothesis, we can find terms which recognize not only 'stages' and 'variations' but the internal dynamic

From Williams, R., *Marxism and Literature*, Oxford University Press, Oxford, 1977, pp. 121–7.

relations of any actual process. We have certainly still to speak of the 'dominant' and the 'effective', and in these senses of the hegemonic. But we find that we have also to speak, and indeed with further differentiation of each, of the 'residual' and the 'emergent', which in any real process. and at any moment in the process, are significant both in themselves and in what they reveal of the characteristics of the 'dominant'.

By 'residual' I mean something different from the 'archaic', though in practice these are often very difficult to distinguish. Any culture includes available elements of its past, but their place in the contemporary cultural process is profoundly variable. I would call the 'archaic' that which is wholly recognized as an element of the past, to be observed, to be examined, or even on occasion to be consciously 'revived', in a deliberately specializing way. What I mean by the 'residual' is very different. The residual, by definition, has been effectively formed in the past, but it is still active in the cultural process, not only and often not at all as an element of the past, but as an effective element of the present. Thus certain experiences, meanings, and values which cannot be expressed or substantially verified in terms of the dominant culture, are nevertheless lived and practised on the basis of the residue – cultural as well as social – of some previous social and cultural institution or formation. It is crucial to distinguish this aspect of the residual, which may have an alternative or even oppositional relation to the dominant culture, from that active manifestation of the residual (this being its distinction from the archaic) which has been wholly or largely incorporated into the dominant culture. In three characteristic cases in contemporary English culture this distinction can become a precise term of analysis. Thus organized religion is predominantly residual, but within this there is a significant difference between some practically alternative and oppositional meanings and values (absolute brotherhood, service to others without reward) and a larger body of incorporated meanings and values (official morality, or the social order of which the other-worldly is a separated neutralizing or ratifying component). Again, the idea of rural community is predominantly residual, but is in some limited respects alternative or oppositional to urban industrial capitalism, though for the most part it is incorporated, as idealization or fantasy, or as an exotic – residential or escape – leisure function of the dominant order itself. Again, in monarchy, there is virtually nothing that is actively residual (alternative or oppositional), but, with a heavy and deliberate additional use of the archaic, a residual function has been wholly incorporated as a specific political and cultural function – marking the limits as well as the methods – of a form of capitalist democracy.

A residual cultural element is usually at some distance from the effective dominant culture, but some part of it, some version of it – and especially if the residue is from some major area of the past – will in most cases have had to be incorporated if the effective dominant culture is to make sense in these areas. Moreover, at certain points the dominant culture cannot allow too much residual experience and practice outside itself, at least without risk. It is in the incorporation of the actively residual – by reinterpretation, dilution, projection, discriminating inclusion and exclusion

– that the work of the selective tradition is especially evident. This is very notable in the case of versions of 'the literary tradition', passing through selective versions of the character of literature to connecting and incorporated definitions of what literature now is and should be. This is one among several crucial areas, since it is in some alternative or even oppositional versions of what literature is (has been) and what literary experience (and in one common derivation, other significant experience) is and must be, that, against the pressures of incorporation, actively residual meanings and values are sustained.

By 'emergent' I mean, first, that new meanings and values, new practices, new relationships and kinds of relationship are continually being created. But it is exceptionally difficult to distinguish between those which are really elements of some new phase of the dominant culture (and in this sense 'species-specific') and those which are substantially alternative or oppositional to it: emergent in the strict sense, rather than merely novel. Since we are always considering relations within a cultural process, definitions of the emergent, as of the residual, can be made only in relation to a full sense of the dominant. Yet the social location of the residual is always easier to understand, since a large part of it (though not all) relates to earlier social formations and phases of the cultural process, in which certain real meanings and values were generated. In the subsequent default of a particular phase of a dominant culture there is then a reaching back to those meanings and values which were created in actual societies and actual situations in the past, and which still seem to have significance because they represent areas of human experience, aspiration, and achievement which the dominant culture neglects, undervalues, opposes, represses, or even cannot recognize.

The case of the emergent is radically different. It is true that in the structure of any actual society, and especially in its class structure, there is always a social basis for elements of the cultural process that are alternative or oppositional to the dominant elements. One kind of basis has been valuably described in the central body of Marxist theory: the formation of a new class, the coming to consciousness of a new class, and within this, in actual process, the (often uneven) emergence of elements of a new cultural formation. Thus the emergence of the working class as a class was immediately evident (for example, in nineteenth-century England) in the cultural process. But there was extreme unevenness of contribution in different parts of the process. The making of new social values and institutions far outpaced the making of strictly cultural institutions, while specific cultural contributions, though significant, were less vigorous and autonomous than either general or institutional innovation. A new class is always a source of emergent cultural practice, but while it is still, as a class, relatively subordinate, this is always likely to be uneven and is certain to be incomplete. For new practice is not, of course, an isolated process. To the degree that it emerges, and especially to the degree that it is oppositional rather than alternative, the process of attempted incorporation significantly begins. This can be seen, in the same period in England, in the emergence and then the effective incorporation of a radical popular press. It can be seen in the emergence and incorporation of working-class writing, where the fundamental problem of emergence is clearly revealed, since the basis of incorporation, in such cases, is the effective predominance of received literary forms – an incorporation, so to say, which already conditions and limits the emergence. But the development is always uneven. Straight incorporation is most directly attempted against the visibly alternative and oppositional class elements: trade unions, working-class political parties, working-class life styles (as incorporated into 'popular' journalism, advertising, and commercial entertainment). The process of emergence, in such conditions, is then a constantly repeated, an always renewable, move beyond a phase of practical incorporation: usually made much more difficult by the fact that much incorporation looks like recognition, acknowledgement, and thus a form of *acceptance*. In this complex process there is indeed regular confusion between the locally residual (as a form of resistance to incorporation) and the generally emergent.

Cultural emergence in relation to the emergence and growing strength of a class is then always of major importance, and always complex. But we have also to see that it is not the only kind of emergence. This recognition is very difficult, theoretically, though the practical evidence is abundant. What has really to be said, as a way of defining important elements of both the residual and the emergent, and as a way of understanding the character of the dominant, is that *no mode of production and therefore no dominant social order and therefore no dominant culture ever in reality includes or exhausts all human practice, human energy, and human intention.* This is not merely a negative proposition, allowing us to account for significant things which happen outside or against the dominant mode. On the contrary it is a fact about the modes of domination, that they select from and consequently exclude the full range of human practice. What they exclude may often be seen as the personal or the private, or as the natural or even the metaphysical. Indeed it is usually in one or other of these terms that the excluded area is expressed, since what the dominant has effectively seized is indeed the ruling definition of the social.

It is this seizure that has especially to be resisted. For there is always, though in varying degrees, practical consciousness, in specific relationships, specific skills, specific perceptions, that is unquestionably social and that a specifically dominant social order neglects, excludes, represses, or simply fails to recognize. A distinctive and comparative feature of any dominant social order is how far it reaches into the whole range of practices and experiences in an attempt at incorporation. There can be areas of experience it is willing to ignore or dispense with: to assign as private or to specialize as aesthetic or to generalize as natural. Moreover, as a social order changes, in terms of its own developing needs, these relations are variable. Thus in advanced capitalism, because of changes in the social character of labour, in the social character of communications, and in the social character of decision-making, the dominant culture reaches much further than ever before in capitalist society into hitherto 'reserved' or 'resigned' areas of experience and practice and meaning. The area of effective penetration of the dominant order into the whole social and cultural process is thus now significantly greater. This in turn makes the problem of emergence especially acute, and narrows the gap between alternative and oppositional elements.

The alternative, especially in areas that impinge on significant areas of the dominant, is often seen as oppositional and, by pressure, often converted into it. Yet even here there can be spheres of practice and meaning which, almost by definition from its own limited character, or in its profound deformation, the dominant culture is unable in any real terms to recognize. Elements of emergence may indeed be incorporated, but just as often the incorporated forms are merely facsimiles of the genuinely emergent cultural practice. Any significant emergence, beyond or against a dominant mode, is very difficult under these conditions; in itself and in its repeated confusion with the facsimiles and novelties of the incorporated phase. Yet, in our own period as in others, the fact of emergent cultural practice is still undeniable, and together with the fact of actively residual practice is a necessary complication of the would-be dominant culture.

This complex process can still in part be described in class terms. But there is always other social being and consciousness which is neglected and excluded: alternative perceptions of others, in immediate relationships; new perceptions and practices of the material world. In practice these are different in quality from the developing and articulated interests of a rising class. The relations between these two sources of the emergent – the class and the excluded social (human) area – are by no means necessarily contradictory. At times they can be very close and on the relations between them much in political practice depends. But culturally and as a matter of theory the areas can be seen as distinct.

What matters, finally, in understanding emergent culture, as distinct from both the dominant and the residual, is that it is never only a matter of immediate practice; indeed it depends crucially on finding new forms or adaptations of form. Again and again what we have to observe is in effect a *pre-emergence*, active and pressing but not yet fully articulated, rather than the evident emergence which could be more confidently named. It is to understand more closely this condition of pre-emergence, as well as the more evident forms of the emergent, the residual, and the dominant, that we need to explore the concept of structures of feeling.

4.5 □ The Dialectic of Utopia and Ideology

Fredric Jameson

As in all previous history, whoever emerges as victor still participates in that triumph in which today's rulers march over the prostrate bodies of their victims. As is customary, the spoils are borne aloft in that triumphal parade. These are generally called the cultural heritage. The latter finds a rather distanced observer in the historical materialist. For such cultural riches, as he surveys them, everywhere betray an origin which he cannot but contemplate with horror. They owe their existence, not merely to the toil of the great creators who have produced them, but equally to the anonymous forced labor of the latters' contemporaries. There has never been a document of culture which was not at one and the same time a document of barbarism.

(WALTER BENJAMIN, 'Theses on the Philosophy of History', VII)

The conception of the political unconscious ... has tended to distance itself, at certain strategic moments, from those implacably polemic and demystifying procedures traditionally associated with the Marxist practice of ideological analysis. It is now time to confront the latter directly and to spell out such modifications in more detail. The most influential lesson of Marx – the one which ranges him alongside Freud and Nietzsche as one of the great negative diagnosticians of contemporary culture and social life – has, of course, rightly been taken to be the lesson of false consciousness, of class bias and ideological programming, the lesson of the structural limits of the values and attitudes of particular social classes, or in other words of the constitutive relationship between the praxis of such groups and what they conceptualize as value or desire and project in the form of culture.

From Jameson, F., *The Political Unconscious: Narrative as a socially symbolic act*, Methuen, London, 1983, pp. 281–92, 296–7, 298–9.

In a splendidly argued confrontation with Marxism, the anthropologist Marshall Sahlins has attempted to demonstrate that it is by its very philosophical structure locked into an approach to culture which must thus remain functional or instrumental in the broadest sense.[1] Given the Marxian orientation toward the reading or demystification of superstructures in terms of their base, or relations of production, even the most sophisticated Marxian analyses of cultural texts must, according to Sahlins, necessarily always presuppose a certain structural functionality about culture: the latter will always 'ultimately' (if not far more immediately) be grasped as the instrument, witting or unwitting, of class domination, legitimation, and social mystification. Sahlins is untroubled by the paradox that Marx himself reserved his most brilliant polemic onslaughts for the classical form taken by an instrumental theory of culture in his own time, namely utilitarianism; nor does Sahlins seem aware that his own targets – economism, technological determinism, the primacy of the forces of production – are also those that have been subjected to powerful critiques by a range of contemporary Marxisms which regard them as deviations from the authentic Marxist spirit. It may, however, readily be admitted that what he calls the instrumentalization of culture is a temptation or tendency within all Marxisms, without, for all that, being a necessary and fatal consequence.

Before offering a perspective in which this particular problem becomes a false one, we must clarify the troubled position of the individual subject within it. We suggested ... that most forms of contemporary criticism tend, as toward their ideal, toward a model of immanence: on the theoretical level that concerns us here, this is to say that the phenomenological ideal – that of some ideal unity of consciousness or thinking and experience or the 'objective' fact – continues to dominate modern thought even where phenomenology as such is explicitly repudiated.[2] Even the Freudian model of the unconscious, which has been exemplary in our own proposal of a properly political unconscious here, is everywhere subverted by the neo-Freudian nostalgia for some ultimate moment of *cure*, in which the dynamics of the unconscious proper rise to the light of day and of consciousness and are somehow 'integrated' in an active lucidity about ourselves and the determinations of our desires and our behavior. But the cure in that sense is a myth, as is the equivalent mirage within a Marxian ideological analysis: namely, the vision of a moment in which the individual subject would be somehow fully conscious of his or her determination by class and would be able to square the circle of ideological conditioning by sheer lucidity and the taking of thought. But in the Marxian system, only a collective unity – whether that of a particular class, the proletariat, or of its 'organ of consciousness', the revolutionary party – can achieve this transparency; the individual subject is always positioned within the social totality (and this is the sense of Althusser's insistence on the *permanence* of ideology).

What this impossibility of immanence means in practice is that the dialectical reversal must always involve a painful 'decentering' of the consciousness of the individual subject, whom it confronts with a determination (whether of the Freudian or the political unconscious) that must necessarily be felt as extrinsic or external to conscious experience. It would be a mistake to think that anyone ever really learns to live with this ideological 'Copernican revolution', any more than the most lucid subjects of psychoanalysis ever really achieve the habit of lucidity and self-knowledge; the approach to the Real is at best fitful, the retreat from it into this or that form of intellectual comfort perpetual. But if this is so, it follows that we must bracket that whole dimension of the critique of the Marxist doctrine of determination by social being which springs from exasperation with this unpleasant reflexivity. In particular, it should be stressed that the process of totalization ... offers no way out of this the 'labor and suffering of the negative', but must necessarily be accompanied by it, if the process is to be authentically realized.

Once this unavoidable experiential accompaniment of the dialectic is granted, however, the theoretical problem of interpretive alternatives to an instrumental or functional theory of culture may more adequately be raised. That such alternatives are at least abstractly conceivable may be demonstrated by Paul Ricoeur's seminal reflections on the dual nature of the hermeneutic process:

> At one pole, hermeneutics is understood as the manifestation and restoration of a meaning addressed to me in the manner of a message, a proclamation, or as is sometimes said, a kerygma; according to the other pole, it is understood as a demystification, as a reduction of illusion. ... The situation in which language finds itself today comprises this double possibility, this double solicitation and urgency: on the one hand, to purify discourse of its excrescences, liquidate the idols, go from drunkenness to sobriety, realize our state of poverty once and for all; on the other hand, to use the most 'nihilistic', destructive, iconoclastic movement so as to *let speak* what once, what each time, was *said*, when meaning appeared anew, when meaning was at its fullest. Hermeneutics seems to me to be animated by this double motivation: willingness to suspect, willingness to listen: vow of rigor, vow of obedience. In our time we have not finished doing away with *idols* and we have barely begun to listen to *symbols*.[3]

It is unnecessary to underscore the obvious, namely the origins of Ricoeur's thought and figures in the tradition of religious exegesis and Christian historicism. The limits of Ricoeur's formulation are, however, not specifically theological ones, but are attributable to the persistence of categories of the individual subject: specifically, his conception of 'positive' meaning as a kerygma or interpellation (retained in Althusser's theory of ideology[4]) is modeled on the act of communication between individual subjects, and cannot therefore be appropriated as such for any view of meaning as a collective process.

As far as the religious framework of Ricoeur's account is concerned, I have throughout the present work implied what I have suggested explicitly elsewhere, that any comparison of Marxism with religion is a two-way street, in which the former is not necessarily discredited by its association with the latter. On the contrary, such a comparison may also function to rewrite certain religious concepts – most notably Christian historicism and the 'concept' of providence, but also the pretheological systems of primitive magic – as anticipatory foreshadowings of historical materialism within precapitalist social formations in which scientific thinking is unavailable as such. Marx's own notion of the so-called Asiatic mode of production (or 'Oriental despotism') is the very locus for such reinterpretation of religious categories, as we will see below.

Meanwhile, the historically original form of the negative dialectic in Marxism – whether ideology is in it grasped as mere 'false consciousness', or, more comprehensively, as structural limitation – should not be allowed to overshadow the presence in the Marxian tradition of a whole series of equivalents to Ricoeur's doctrine of meaning or positive hermeneutic. Ernst Bloch's ideal of hope or of the Utopian impulse; Mikhail Bakhtin's notion of the dialogical as a rupture of the one-dimensional text of bourgeois narrative, as a carnivalesque dispersal of the hegemonic order of a dominant culture; the Frankfurt School's conception of strong memory as the trace of gratification, of the revolutionary power of that *promesse de bonheur* most immediately inscribed in the aesthetic text: all these formulations hint at a variety of options for articulating a properly Marxian version of meaning beyond the purely ideological.

Yet we have also suggested ... that even within an ostensibly religious framework such varied options can be measured against the standard of the medieval system of four levels, which helped us to distinguish the resonance of the 'moral' level – that of the individual soul, or of the libidinal Utopia of the individual body – from that ultimate, and logically prior level traditionally termed the 'anagogical', in which even such individual visions of Utopian transfiguration are rewritten in terms of the collective, of the destiny of the human race. Such a distinction allows us to spell out the priority, within the Marxist tradition, of a 'positive hermeneutic' based on social class from those still limited by anarchist categories of the individual subject and individual experience. The concept of class is thus the space in which, if anywhere, a Marxian version of the hermeneutics of meaning, of some noninstrumental conception of culture, may be tested, particularly in so far as it is from this same concept of social class that the strongest form of a Marxian 'negative hermeneutic' – of the class character and functionality of ideology as such – also derives.

Such a demonstration might be staged under a reversal of Walter Benjamin's great dictum that 'there is no document of civilization which is not at one and the same time a document of barbarism', and would seek to argue the proposition that the effectively ideological is also, at the same time, necessarily Utopian. What is logically paradoxical about such a proposition can be understood, if not 'resolved', by considering the conceptual limits imposed on our thinking and our language by categories that we have had frequent enough occasion to unmask in the preceding pages, namely those of the ethical code of good and evil, in which even our own terminology of 'positive' and 'negative' remains unavoidably imprisoned. We have suggested that the vocation of the dialectic lies in the transcendence of this opposition toward some collective logic 'beyond good and evil', while noting that the language of the classics of dialectical thought has historically failed to overcome this opposition, which it can only neutralize by reflexive play across these categories. Nor is this particularly surprising, if we take dialectical thought to be the anticipation of the logic of a collectivity which has not yet come into being. In this sense, to project an imperative to thought in which the ideological would be grasped as somehow at one with the Utopian, and the Utopian at one with the ideological, is to formulate a question to which a collective dialectic is the only conceivable answer.

Yet at a lower and more practical level of cultural analysis this proposition is perhaps somewhat less paradoxical in its consequences, and may initially be argued in terms of a manipulatory theory of culture. Such theories, which are strongest in areas like the study of the media and mass culture in contemporary society, must otherwise rest on a peculiarly unconvincing notion of the psychology of the viewer, as some inert and passive material on which the manipulatory operation works. Yet it does not take much reflection to see that a process of compensatory exchange must be involved here, in which the henceforth manipulated viewer is offered specific gratifications in return for his or her consent to passivity. In other words, if the ideological function of mass culture is understood as a process whereby otherwise dangerous and protopolitical impulses are 'managed' and defused, rechanneled and offered spurious objects, then some preliminary step must also be theorized in which these same impulses – the raw material upon which the process works – are initially awakened within the very text that seeks to still them. If the function of the mass cultural text is meanwhile seen rather as the production of false consciousness and the symbolic reaffirmation of this or that legitimizing strategy, even this process cannot be grasped as one of sheer violence (the theory of hegemony is explicitly distinguished from control by brute force) nor as one inscribing the appropriate attitudes upon a blank slate, but must necessarily involve a complex strategy of rhetorical persuasion in which substantial incentives are offered for ideological adherence. We will say that such incentives, as well as the impulses to be managed by the mass cultural text, are necessarily Utopian in nature. Ernst Bloch's luminous recovery of the Utopian impulses at work in that most degraded of all mass cultural texts, advertising slogans – visions of external life, of the transfigured body, of preternatural sexual gratification – may serve as the model for an analysis of the dependence of the crudest forms of manipulation on the oldest Utopian longings of humankind.[5] As for the influential Adorno-Horkheimer denunciation of the 'culture industry', this same Utopian hermeneutic – implicit in their system as well – is in their *Dialectic of Enlightenment* obscured by an embattled commitment to high culture; yet it has not sufficiently been noticed that it has been displaced to the succeeding chapter of that work,[6] where a similar, yet even more difficult analysis is undertaken, in which one of the ugliest of all human passions, anti-Semitism, is shown to be profoundly Utopian in character, as a form of cultural envy which is at the same time a repressed recognition of the Utopian impulse.

Still, such analyses, methodologically suggestive though they are, do not go far enough along the lines proposed above. In particular, they depend on an initial separation between means and ends – between Utopian gratification and ideological manipulation – which might well serve as evidence for the opposite of what was to have been demonstrated, and might be invoked to deny the profound identity between these two dimensions of the cultural text. It is possible, indeed, that such a separation springs objectively from the peculiar structure of the mass cultural texts themselves; and that culture proper, by which we may understand the 'organic' culture of older societies fully as much as the 'high' culture of the present day,[7] may be expected to embody such identity in a rather different form.

We must therefore return to the 'strong' form of the problem, and to the class terms in which we began by posing it. Its traditional Marxist formulation would then run as follows: how is it possible for a cultural text which fulfills a demonstrably ideological function, as a hegemonic work whose formal categories as well as its content secure the legitimation of this or that form of class domination – how is it possible for such a text to embody a properly Utopian impulse, or to resonate a universal value inconsistent with the narrower limits of class privilege which inform its more immediate ideological vocation? The dilemma is intensified when we deny ourselves, as we just have, the solution of a coexistence of different functions, as when, for instance, it is suggested that the greatness of a given writer may be separated from his deplorable opinions, and is achieved in spite of them or even against them. Such a separation is possible only for a world-view – liberalism – in which the political and the ideological are mere secondary or 'public' adjuncts to the content of a real 'private' life, which alone is authentic and genuine. It is not possible for any world-view – whether conservative or radical and revolutionary – that takes politics seriously.

There can, I think, be only one consequent 'solution' to the problem thus posed: it is the proposition that *all* class consciousness – or in other words, all ideology in the strongest sense, including the most exclusive forms of ruling-class consciousness just as much as that of oppositional or oppressed classes – is in its very nature Utopian. This proposition rests on a specific analysis of the dynamics of class consciousness which can only briefly be summarized here,[8] and whose informing idea grasps the emergence of class consciousness as such (what in Hegelian language is sometimes called the emergence of a class-for-itself, as opposed to the merely potential class-in-itself of the positioning of a social group within the economic structure) as a result of the struggle between groups or classes. According to this analysis, the prior moment of class consciousness is that of the oppressed classes (whose structural identity – whether a peasantry, slaves, serfs, or a genuine proletariat – evidently derives from the mode of production). On such a view, those who must work and produce surplus-value for others will necessarily grasp their own solidarity – initially, in the unarticulated form of rage, helplessness, victimization, oppression by a common enemy – *before* the dominant or ruling class has any particular incentive for doing so. Indeed, it is the glimpse of such sullen resistance, and the sense of the nascent political dangers of such potential unification of the laboring population, which generates the mirror-image of class solidarity among the ruling groups (or the possessors of the means of production). This suggests, to use another Hegelian formula, that the *truth* of ruling-class consciousness (that is, of hegemonic ideology and cultural production) is to be found in working-class consciousness. It suggests, even more strongly, that the index of all class consciousness is to be found not in the latter's 'contents' or ideological motifs, but first and foremost in the dawning sense of solidarity with other members of a particular group or class, whether the latter happen to be your fellow landowners, those who enjoy structural privileges linked to your own, or, on the contrary, fellow workers and producers, slaves, serfs, or peasants. Only an ethical politics, linked to those ethical categories we have often had occasion to criticize and to deconstruct in the preceding pages [of *The Political Unconscious*], will feel the need to 'prove' that one of these forms of class consciousness is good or positive and the other reprehensible or wicked: on the grounds, for example, that working-class consciousness is potentially more universal than ruling-class consciousness, or that the latter is essentially linked to violence and repression. It is unnecessary to argue these quite correct propositions; ideological commitment is not first and foremost a matter of moral choice but of the taking of sides in a struggle between embattled groups. In a fragmented social life – that is, essentially in all class societies – the political thrust of the struggle of all groups against each other can never be immediately universal but must always necessarily be focused on the class enemy. Even in preclass society (what is called tribal or segmentary society, or in the Marxian tradition, primitive communism), collective consciousness is similarly organized around the perception of what threatens the survival of the group: indeed, the most powerful contemporary vision of 'primitive communism', Colin Turnbull's description of pygmy society,[9] suggests that the culture of prepolitical society organizes itself around the external threat of the nonhuman or of nature, in the form of the rainforest, conceived as the overarching spirit of the world.

The preceding analysis entitles us to conclude that all class consciousness of whatever type is Utopian in so far as it expresses the unity of a collectivity; yet it must be added that this proposition is an allogorical one. The achieved collectivity or organic group of whatever kind – oppressors fully as much as oppressed – is Utopian not in itself, but only in so far as all such collectivities are themselves *figures* for the ultimate concrete collective life of an achieved Utopian or classless society. Now we are in a better position to understand how even hegemonic or ruling-class culture and ideology are Utopian, not in spite of their instrumental function to secure and perpetuate class privilege and power, but rather precisely because that function is also in and of itself the affirmation of collective solidarity.

Such a view dictates an enlarged perspective for any Marxist analysis of culture, which can no longer be content with its demystifying vocation to unmask and to demonstrate the ways in which a cultural artifact fulfills a specific ideological mission, in legitimating a given power structure, in perpetuating and reproducing the latter, and in generating specific forms of false consciousness (or ideology in the narrower sense). It must not cease to practice this essentially negative hermeneutic function (which Marxism is virtually the only current critical method to assume today) but must also seek, through and beyond this demonstration of the instrumental function of a given cultural object, to project its simultaneously Utopian power as the symbolic affirmation of a specific historical and class form of collective unity.[10] This is a unified perspective and not the juxtaposition of two options or analytic alternatives: neither is satisfactory in itself. The Marxian 'negative hermeneutic', indeed, practiced in isolation, fully justifies Sahlins's complaints about the 'mechanical' or purely instrumental nature of certain Marxian cultural analyses; while the Utopian or 'positive hermeneutic', practiced in similar isolation as it is in Frye's doctrine of the collective origins of art, relaxes into the religious or the theological, the edifying and the moralistic, if it is not informed by a sense of the class dynamics of social life and cultural production.

[. . .]

Such is then the general theoretical framework in which I would wish to argue the methodological proposition outlined here: that a Marxist negative hermeneutic, a Marxist practice of ideological analysis proper, must in the practical work of reading and interpretation be exercised *simultaneously* with a Marxist positive hermeneutic, or a decipherment of the Utopian impulses of these same still ideological cultural texts. If the Mannheimian overtones of this dual perspective – ideology and Utopia – remain active enough to offer communicational noise and conceptual interference, then alternative formulations may be proposed, in which an *instrumental* analysis is coordinated with a *collective-associational* or *communal* reading of culture, or in which a *functional* method for describing cultural texts is articulated with an *anticipatory* one.

I would not want to conclude, however, without observing that the issues and dilemmas such a proposal seeks to address greatly transcend the limited field of literary or even cultural criticism. One hesitates to defend the privileged position of cultural criticism in a self-serving way. Still, it is a historical fact that the 'structuralist' or textual revolution – as, mainly through Althusserianism, it has transformed a whole range of other disciplines, from political science to anthropology, and from economics to legal and juridical studies – takes as its model a kind of decipherment of which literary and textual criticism is in many ways the strong form. This 'revolution', essentially antiempiricist, drives the wedge of the concept of a 'text' into the traditional disciplines by extrapolating the notion of 'discourse' or 'writing' onto objects previously thought to be 'realities' or objects in the real world, such as the various levels or instances of a social formation: political power, social class, institutions, and events themselves. When properly used, the concept of the 'text' does not, as in garden-variety semiotic practice today, 'reduce' these realities to small and manageable written documents of one kind or another, but rather liberates us from the empirical object – whether institution, event, or individual work – by displacing our attention to its *constitution* as an object and its *relationship* to the other objects thus constituted.

[. . .]

Finally, I will take Tom Nairn's pathbreaking book on the national question, *The Break-up of Britain*, as an example of an analogous theoretical solution to that proposed here in an area which remains one of the fundamental ones of contemporary world politics but about which Nairn rightly observes that it stands as 'Marxism's great historical failure', blocked precisely by a practice of the traditional Marxian negative hermeneutic for which the national question is a mere ideological epiphenomenon of the economic.

> The task of a theory of nationalism ... must be to embrace both horns of the dilemma. It must be to see the phenomenon as a whole, in a way that rises above these 'positive' and 'negative' sides. ... [Such] distinctions do not imply the existence of two brands of nationalism, one healthy and one morbid. The point is that, as the most elementary comparative analysis will show, all nationalism is both healthy and morbid. Both progress and regress are inscribed in its genetic code from the start.[11]

Nor is this insistence on the simultaneously ideological and Utopian character of the national phenomenon a merely theoretical issue. On the contrary, it is increasingly clear in today's world (if it had ever been in doubt) that a Left which cannot grasp the immense Utopian appeal of nationalism (any more than it can grasp that of religion or of fascism) can scarcely hope to 'reappropriate' such collective energies and must effectively doom itself to political impotence.

But at this point, we must restore Benjamin's identification of culture and barbarism to its proper sequence, as the affirmation not merely of the Utopian dimension of ideological texts, but also and above all of the ideological dimension of all high culture. So it is that a Marxist hermeneutic – the decipherment by historical materialism of the cultural monuments and traces of the past – must come to terms with the certainty that all the works of class history, as they have survived and been transmitted to people the various museums, canons and 'traditions' of our own time, are all in one way or another profoundly ideological, have all had a vested interest in and a functional relationship to social formations based on violence and exploitation; and that, finally, the restoration of the meaning of the greatest cultural monuments cannot be separated from a passionate and partisan assessment of everything that is oppressive in them and that knows complicity with privilege and class domination, stained with the guilt not merely of culture in particular but of History itself as one long nightmare.

Yet Benjamin's slogan is a hard saying, and not only for liberal and apoliticizing critics of art and literature, for whom it spells the return of class realities and the painful recollection of the dark underside of even the most seemingly innocent and 'life-enhancing' masterpieces of the canon. For a certain radicalism also, Benjamin's formulation comes as a rebuke and a warning against the facile reappropriation of the classics as humanistic expressions of this or that historically 'progressive' force. It comes, finally, as an appropriate corrective to the doctrine of the political unconscious which has been developed in these pages, reasserting the undiminished power of ideological distortion that persists even within the restored Utopian meaning of cultural artifacts, and reminding us that within the symbolic power of art and culture the will to domination perseveres intact. It is only at this price – that of the simultaneous recognition of the ideological and Utopian functions of the artistic text – that a Marxist cultural study can hope to play its part in political praxis, which remains, of course, what Marxism is all about.

Notes

1. Marshall Sahlins, *Culture and Practical Reason* (Chicago: University of Chicago Press, 1976).
2. As far as literary criticism is concerned, it is often easier to denounce this mirage of immanence on the level of theory than to resist its hold on the level of practical exegesis. An instructive and influential example of this contradiction may be found in the contemporary reaction against an 'old-fashioned' Lukácsean 'content analysis' (as documented in the important Cluny colloquium held by *La Nouvelle Critique* in April 1970, and published as *Littérature et idéologies*): the codification of a whole new alternate method – which explores the inscription of ideology in an ensemble of purely formal categories, such as representation, narrative closure, the organization around the centered subject, or the illusion of presence – is generally associated with the *Tel quel* and *Screen* groups, and also, in a different way, with the work of Jacques Derrida (see in particular 'Hors Livre', in *La Dissémination* [Paris: Seuil, 1972], pp. 9–67. The unmasking of such categories and their ideological consequences is then achieved in the name of newer aesthetic, psychoanalytic, and moral values variously termed heterogeneity, dissemination, discontinuity, schizophrenia, and *écriture*, that is, in the name of explicitly anti-immanent (but also antitranscendent) concepts. Yet the impulse behind the critical practice thereby theorized is often precisely an immanent one, which brackets the historical situations in which texts are effective and insists that ideological positions can be identified by the identification of inner-textual or purely formal features. Such an approach is thereby able to confine its work to individual printed texts, and projects the ahistorical view that the formal features in question always and everywhere bear the same ideological charge. Paradoxically, then, the extrinsic, 'contextual' or situational references repudiated by this system turn out to be precisely what is *heterogeneous* to it.
3. Paul Ricoeur, *Freud and Philosophy*, trans. D. Savage (New Haven, CT: Yale, 1970), p. 27.
4. See Louis Althusser, 'Ideological State Apparatuses', in *Lenin and Philosophy*, trans. Ben Brewster (New York: Monthly Review, 1971), pp. 170–77. (See Reading 4.3 above.)
5. Ernst Bloch, *Das Prinzip Hoffnung* (Frankfurt: Suhrkamp, 1959), pp. 395–409.
6. Max Horkheimer and Theodor W. Adorno, *Dialectic of Enlightenment*, trans. J. Cumming, (New York: Herder & Herder, 1972), pp. 168–208.
7. In 'Reification and Utopia in mass culture' (*Social Text*, no. 1 [1979], pp. 130–48), I suggest, however, that it may well be more adequate to study contemporary 'high culture' (that is to say, modernism) as part of a larger cultural unity in which mass culture stands as its inseparable dialectical counterpole.
8. See *Marxism and Form*, pp. 376–90; and the related reflections in 'Class and allegory in contemporary mass culture: *Dog Day Afternoon* as a political film', *College English*, vol. 38, No. 7 (March 1977), reprinted in *Screen Education*, no. 30 (Spring, 1979). These formulations draw on Ralf Dahrendorf, *Class and Class Conflict in Industrial Society* (Palo Alto, CA: Stanford University Press, 1959), pp. 280–89; on E. P. Thompson, *The Making of the English Working Class* (New York: Vintage, 1966), Preface (but see also his 'Eighteenth century English society: class struggle without class?', *Social History*, 3 [May, 1978]; and *The Poverty of Theory* [London: Merlin, 1979], pp. 298 ff.); and finally on Jean-Paul Sartre, *Critique of Dialectical Reason*, trans.

A. Sheridan-Smith (London: New Left Books, 1976), esp. pp. 363–404, on the 'fused group'.

9. Colin Turnbull, *The Forest People* (New York: Simon & Schuster, 1962).
10. That this is no mere theoretical or literary-critical issue may be demonstrated by the renewal of interest in the nature and dynamics of fascism, and the urgency of grasping this phenomenon in some more adequate way than as the mere epiphenomenal 'false consciousness' of a certain moment of monopoly capitalism. Such attempts, many of them grounded on Reich and seeking to measure the mass 'libidinal investment' in fascism, constitute the attempt, in our current terminology, to complete an 'ideological' analysis of fascism by one which identifies its 'Utopian' power and sources. See, for example, Jean-Pierre Faye, *Langages totalitaires* (Paris: Hermann, 1972); Maria Antonietta Macciochi (ed.), *Eléments pur une analyse du fascisme*, 2 vols (Paris: 10/18, 1976); as well as Ernst Bloch's *Erbschaft dieser Zeit* (1935; Frankfurt: Suhrkamp, 1973).
11. Tom Nairn, *The Break-up of Britain* (London: New Left Books, 1977), pp. 332, 347–8.

4.6 □ *Considerations on Materialism*

Sebastiano Timpanaro

Perhaps the sole characteristic common to virtually all contemporary varieties of Western Marxism is their concern to defend themselves against the accusation of materialism. Gramscian or Togliattian Marxists, Hegelian-Existentialist Marxists, Neo-Positivizing Marxists, Freudian or Structuralist Marxists, despite the profound dissensions which otherwise divide them, are at one in rejecting all suspicion of collusion with 'vulgar' or 'mechanical' materialism; and they do so with such zeal as to cast out, together with mechanism or vulgarity, materialism *tout court*. Much of the polemical debate between various Marxist groups turns precisely on the selection of the most effective safeguard against the danger of falling into vulgar materialism: whether this safeguard is to be the dialectic or historicism, an appeal to Marxist humanism or an association of Marxism with an empirio-critical or pragmatist or Platonist epistemology.

[. . .]

This ostensible self-purification of Marxism is typically concretized and symbolized by a devaluation of Engels, who for many holds prime responsibility for the decline of Marxism from its true philosophical heights to the depths of a 'popular philosophy'. Because of its dramatically contradictory character (which deserves a more profound study), Engels's work is particularly liable to attack from both main contemporary Marxist currents, Hegelian and empirio-pragmatist. On the one hand, Engels was much more sensible than Marx of the necessity to come to terms with the natural sciences, to link 'historical' materialism (in the human sciences) to physical and biological materialism – all the more so, at a time when Darwin had finally opened the way to an historical understanding of nature itself. On the other hand, in his effort to reject any reduction of Marxism to a banal evolutionism or eclectic positivism, Engels undertook to apply the Hegelian dialectic to the sciences

From Timpanaro, S., *On Materialism*, trans. L. Garner, Verso, London, 1975, pp. 29, 32–6, 40–45, 47–8, 51–4.

with a certain punctilio, and to translate phenomena of physics or biology into the language of the 'negation of the negation' and the 'conversion of quantity into quality'. It is for this reason that he can be accused in turn of archaic Hegelianism and contamination by positivism, abandonment of the great German philosophical tradition and neglect of the pragmatist hints in the *Theses on Feuerbach*, scientism and a retrogressive and superficial scientific culture.

It might be argued that polemics against the deformations of vulgar materialism are justified by the need to struggle against Stalinist dogmatism and to restore its free creative force to Marxism. It is true that in Stalin's opuscule *On Dialectical and Historical Materialism*, which became the most widely diffused elementary text on Marxism, not merely in the USSR but throughout the world communist movement, it is easy to find extremely schematic and crude assertions, especially as regards relations between structure and superstructure. But a crude conception and exposition of Marxism does not necessarily mean an accentuation of its materialist aspect. In fact, Stalin's brochure, as well as his other writings, lack any specific interest in the natural sciences or the relationship between man and nature; there is a complete absence of any emphasis on the 'passive side' of consciousness, on the way in which man is conditioned by his own physical structure and the natural environment. Indeed, certain of Stalin's positions, such as his patronage of Lysenko, or his very theory of socialism and even communism in one country, can well be defined as idealist and voluntarist. It is no mistake that critics have spoken of 'Stalinist subjectivism'. The so-called dogmatism of Stalin and his followers did not in reality consist of a coherent materialist position, but rather of a 'politicization' (in the pejorative sense) of Marxist theory – in other words an immediate reduction not only of science to ideology, but of ideology itself to an instrument of propaganda and petty justification of adventitious political positions, whereby the most abrupt changes of policy were in each case legitimated with pseudo-theoretical arguments and presented as congruent with the most orthodox Marxism.[1]

[. . .]

But what are we to understand by materialism? Moreover, how is materialism to escape from the accusation of itself being a metaphysic too, and one of the most naive ones at that?

By materialism we understand above all acknowledgement of the priority of nature over 'mind', or if you like, of the physical level over the biological level, and of the biological level over the socioeconomic and cultural level; both in the sense of chronological priority (the very long time which supervened before life appeared on earth, and between the origin of life and the origin of man), and in the sense of the conditioning which nature *still* exercises on man and will continue to exercise at least for the foreseeable future. Cognitively, therefore, the materialist maintains that experience cannot be reduced either to a production of reality by a subject (however such production is conceived) or to a reciprocal implication of subject and object. We cannot, in other words, deny or evade the element of passivity in experience: the external situation which we do not create but which imposes itself on us. Nor can we in any way reabsorb this external datum by making it a mere negative moment in the activity of the subject, or by making both the subject and the object mere moments, distinguishable only in abstraction, of a single effective reality constituted by experience.

This emphasis on the passive element in experience certainly does not claim to be a theory of knowledge – something which in any case can be constructed only by experimental research on the physiology of the brain and the sense organs, and not by merely conceptual or philosophical exercises. But it is the preliminary condition for any theory of knowledge which is not content with verbalistic and illusory solutions.

This implies a polemical position towards a major part of modern philosophy, which has entangled and exhausted itself in the setting up of 'epistemological traps' to catch and tame the external datum, in order to make it something which exists solely as a function of the activity of the subject. It is important to realize that epistemology has undergone such an enormous (and sophistical) development in modern thought because it has not only corresponded to the need to understand how knowledge arises, but has been charged with the task of founding the absolute liberty of man, by eliminating everything which commonly seems to restrict that freedom. Whether this task has been executed in the direction of a romantic idealism of the absolute ego, or in that of a critical empiricism, whether the subject–object relation is conceived as relation of creation, or scission within an original unity, or reciprocal action or 'transaction', or any other variant, certainly implies a whole series of important differences in cultural formation and social ambience, and explains the fierce polemics of both past and present among the proponents of these various idealisms. It does not, however, alter their common character as illusions. It should be added that the attacks on epistemologism by pragmatists and actualists of the left also serve, indeed in exasperated form, the same purpose of 'annihilating external reality' and founding human freedom which generated epistemologism itself. They thus form a type of polemic which from our point of view can be situated within the general orientation that we hold must be rejected.

It will be said that if the idealism of the absolute ego is the expression of a culture strongly imbued with romantic and anti-scientific irrationalism, empirio-criticist and pragmatist positions arose precisely from reflections on science, and that it is therefore illegitimate to counterpose a materialism based on the sciences of a century ago, or even on naive common sense, to these conceptions as 'more scientific'.

But it is on this very point that mistakes are particularly easy to make. It is true that scientific knowledge is the only exact and rigorous form of knowledge. But if philosophy displaces all its attention from the results and objects of scientific research to the research as such, and if, omitting to consider man's condition in the world as it is established by the *results* of scientific research, it confines itself to a methodology of the activity of the scientist, then it relapses into idealism, because it then suggests that there is only one reality – not nature, but man the investigator of nature and constructor of his *own* science. The results of scientific research teach us that man occupies a marginal position in the universe; that for a very long time life did not exist on earth, and that its origin depended on very special conditions; that human thought is conditioned by determinate anatomical and physiological structures, and is clouded or impeded by determinate pathological alterations of these; and so on. But let us consider these results as mere contents of our thoughts as it cogitates or of our activity as it experiments and modifies nature, let us emphasize that they do not exist outside our thought and our activity, and the trick is done: external reality has been conjured away, and not by an antiquated humanism hostile to science, but instead with all the blessings of science and of modernity!

[. . .]

The very uncertainty which has always existed within the camp of Marxism as to the way in which materialism should be understood, and the ease with which versions of Marxism have prevailed that have attenuated or directly denied its materialist character, are undoubtedly due to the influences of bourgeois culture. [...] But I also believe that they have found a propitious terrain because of a lack of clarity that goes right back to the origin of Marxist theory and was perhaps never completely overcome even in Marx's mature thought.

Marxism was born as an affirmation of the *decisive primacy* of the socioeconomic level over juridical, political and cultural phenomena, and as an affirmation of the historicity of the economy. It might be said that in the expression 'historical materialism', the noun was a polemic against Hegel and a whole philosophical tradition which affirmed the primacy of the spirit over any economic structure, whereas the adjective was a polemic against Feuerbach and English classical economics, in short against any statically naturalist conception of human society.

If a critique of anthropocentrism and an emphasis on the conditioning of man by nature are considered essential to materialism, it must be said that Marxism, especially in its first phase (up to and including *The German Ideology*), is not materialism proper. Physical and biological nature is certainly not denied by Marx, but it constitutes more a prehistoric antecedent to human history than a reality which still limits and conditions man. From the time when man started to labour and to produce, it appears that he enters into relationship with nature (according to a famous passage in *The German Ideology*) only through work. This was to relapse into a pragmatic conception of the relationship between man and nature which illegitimately annuls the 'passive side' of this relationship itself; to pass over in silence the fact that man enters into relation with nature also through heredity and, even more, through the innumerable other influences of the natural environment on his body and hence on his intellectual, moral and psychological personality. To deny all this by affixing the label of positivism or of vulgar materialism to it is not possible, whether for the fundamental reason that facts do not allow themselves to be vanquished by labels or because, even historically, materialism has not been a privilege or a blemish only of the positivist age (among positivists, indeed, it has been a minority position), but characterized a whole strand of the eighteenth-century Enlightenment (not to speak of earlier philosophical positions, or later ones such as those of Leopardi or Feuerbach) which cannot be liquidated with a couple of polemic strokes.

Marx in his maturity – who admired Darwin and wanted to dedicate the second volume of *Capital* to him, who declared in the preface to *Capital* itself that he 'viewed the evolution of the economic formation of society as a process of natural history', – was certainly much more materialist than the Marx of the *Theses on Feuerbach*. But the gigantic labour to which he had dedicated himself in the field of political economy did not permit him to develop a new conception of the relation between man and nature which would fully replace that outlined in his youthful writings.

Even more than by Marx – though evidently not in dissent from him – the need for the construction of a materialism which was not purely socioeconomic but also 'natural' was felt by Engels, and this was a great merit of his. The impulse to deepen their materialism in this way came not only from the general philosophical and scientific climate of the second half of the nineteenth century, but more specifically from the radical change which Darwinism introduced in the natural sciences, by its definitive demonstration (against the concept of nature accepted by Hegel and materialists of Hegelian derivation such as Moleschott) of the historicity of nature. The task was now no longer to counterpose the historicity of human society to the ahistoricity of nature, but to establish both the linkage and the distinction between the two historicities. Engels contributed to this task most especially in his splendid book on *The Origin of the Family*, as well as in his general expositions of Marxism. However, as we have already mentioned, he remained torn between a tendency to develop physical-biological materialism and a tendency to counterpose the last great 'classical' philosophy of Hegelianism to the 'eclectic soup' of positivist professors.

[. . .]

When Marxists affirm the 'decisive primacy' of economic and social structures, and therefore designate this level and not the biological level underlying it as the 'base' of human society and culture, they are right in relation to the great transformations and differentiations of society, which arise fundamentally as consequences of changes in economic structures and not of the geographical environment or physical constitution of man. The division of humanity into social classes explains its history infinitely better than its division into races or peoples; and although, as a given fact, racial hatreds and national conflicts have existed and continue to exist, and although the ambiguous and composite concepts of nation and of homeland always have a racist component, there is nevertheless no doubt that these conflicts, at least from the end of prehistory onwards, are fundamentally disguised or diverted economic and social conflicts (increasingly so), not 'genuinely' biological or ethnic contrasts. Hence the immense methodological superiority of Marx's historiography by comparison, not merely with a vulgar racist historiography, but even with an ethnic historiography such as that of Thierry.[2]

By comparison with the evolutionary pace of economic and social structures (and of the superstructures determined by them), nature, including man as a biological entity, also changes, as evolutionism has taught us, but at an immensely slower tempo. 'Nature is ever green, or rather goes/by such long paths/that she seems still', says Leopardi.[3] If therefore we are studying even a very long period of human history to examine the transformations of society, we may legitimately pass over the physical and biological level, inasmuch as relative to that period it is a constant. Similarly, we may agree it is permissible for a Marxist, when writing the history of political or cultural events within the restricted context of a fundamentally unitary and stable socioeconomic situation, to take the latter as a constant and study the history of the superstructure alone. Engels, and later Gramsci, warned that it would be naive to think that each single superstructural fact was the repercussion of a change in the infrastructure. Luporini has recalled that Marx himself, in the 1859 preface to *A Critique of Political Economy*, explicitly affirms the dependence of the superstructure on the structure only 'in its macroscopic and catastrophic aspects, so to speak, that is, in relation to social revolutions'.[4]

But if, basing ourselves on this relatively immobile character (over a certain period) of the economic and social structure, we were to conclude that it has no conditioning power over the superstructure, or even no real existence, we should be committing a typical 'historicist' fallacy. Now, it is a precisely similar sophism to deny the conditioning which nature exercises on humanity in general, just because this conditioning does not conspicuously differentiate individual epochs of human history. Marxists put themselves in a scientifically and polemically weak position if, after rejecting the idealist arguments which claim to show that the only reality is that of the Spirit and that cultural facts are in no way dependent on economic structures, they then borrow the same arguments to deny the dependence of man on nature.

[. . .]

The historicist polemic against 'man in general', which is completely correct as long as it denies that certain historical and social forms such as private property or class divisions are inherent in humanity in general, errs when it overlooks the fact that man as a biological being, endowed with a certain (not unlimited) adaptability to his external environment, and with certain impulses towards activity and the pursuit of happiness, subject to old age and death, is not an abstract construction, nor one of our prehistoric ancestors, a species of pithecanthropus now superseded by historical and social man, but still exists in each of us and in all probability will still exist in the future. It is certainly true that the development of society changes men's ways of feeling pain, pleasure and other elementary psycho-physical reactions, and that there is hardly anything that is 'purely natural' left in contemporary man, that has not been enriched and remoulded by the social and cultural environment. But the general aspects of the 'human condition' still remain, and the specific characteristics introduced into it by the various forms of associated life have not been such as to overthrow them completely. To maintain that, since the 'biological' is always presented to us as mediated by the 'social', the 'biological' is nothing and the 'social' is everything, would once again be idealist sophistry. If we make it ours, how are we to defend ourselves from those who will in turn maintain that, since all reality (including economic and social reality) is knowable only through language (or through the thinking mind), language (or the thinking mind) is the sole reality, and all the rest is abstraction?

[. . .]

It is certainly necessary to warn that the dependence of the superstructure on the structure must not be conceived in a simplistic way. It is still more necessary, as Luporini has recently observed[5] not to content oneself with generic refutations of simplism and mechanism ('reciprocal action between structure and superstructure', 'dependence of the superstructure on the structure, but only in the *last instance*'), but finally to proceed to deepen actual study of the processes by which the superstructure acquires autonomy (always within certain limits) of the structure, and exercises a reaction on it, which will yet remain secondary by comparison with the action exercised on it by the structure. However, it seems to me that the concept of superstructure, *even understood non-mechanically*, cannot include the totality of cultural activities.

Interest in mathematics or physics or philology only arises, it is true, in a definite social environment; the adoption of particular techniques of research is only conceivable in a particular society; furthermore ideology itself (this is aimed specifically at the many modern historians who consider themselves immune from all 'practical political' interests) is a perilous but irreplaceable instrument of research, at least as long as a perfectly classless society has not been achieved. But the *objective* truths which the sciences have already attained in pre-socialist societies (sometimes the work of politically and socially conservative scientists) are not reducible to slave-owning or feudal or bourgeois ideology. Otherwise we should really fall into a debased historicism, into a relativist conception of knowledge and, at the end of the day, into a denial of external reality or of its knowability.[6] Thus, just as scientific knowledge is not *sic et simpliciter* superstructure (although, we repeat, it is necessarily connected with elements of the superstructure), so the *instrumental*, ideologically neutral and therefore extra-class dimensions that exist in all human institutions – in language more than in legal, political and cultural institutions in the strict sense[7] – are not reducible without residue to superstructures.

[. . .]

The constant dimensions (hardly modified hitherto, and perhaps scarcely modifiable in the future) of the human condition are not, be it clearly understood, metaphysical or metahistorical. 'Man in general' as we understand it – who is none other than natural man – is not 'eternal man'; so much so that he has an origin and will have an end (or a transformation by Darwinian evolution). But though they are not actually eternal, these aspects are nevertheless *long-lasting*: that is to say, they have, relative to the existence of the human species, much greater stability than historical or social institutions.[8] To attempt to reduce them to the latter is merely to provide an easy polemical target for those who will exploit the inevitable failure of such a reduction to reaffirm once again the existence of 'eternal man' – just as any attempt to derive religion exclusively from economic and social conditions, overlooking the fact that religion is also an illusory compensation for the fear of death and in general for the oppression which nature exercises on man, plays into the hands of those who exalt the independent and privileged value of the 'religious experience'.[9] The problem of 'historical and cultural inheritance' and of the 'permanence and transmission of values' through successive and variant forms of society (the importance of which is rightly emphasized by Luporini in the article we have already had occasion to cite) will doubtless find a large measure of its solution in a more articulated conception of the relations between structure and super-structure and in a closer study of the function of intellectuals as bearers of the continuity of culture. But we should not forget either that this cultural continuity – through which, as Marx observed, we feel so near to the poetry of Homer – has also been rendered possible by the fact that man as a biological being has remained essentially unchanged from the beginnings of civilization to the present; and those sentiments and representations which are closest to the biological facts of human existence have changed little.

At this point it will, I think, be sufficiently clear in what respect one can, from a materialist point of view, agree or disagree with recent orientations which may be summarized by such formulas as 'Marxism plus psychoanalysis' or 'Marxism plus structuralism plus psychoanalysis'. These trends must be conceded the merit of rejecting the reduction of Marxism to 'historicism' (with all the idealist and intuitionist errors connoted by this term),[10] of emphasizing the need for scientific study of historical and literary disciplines, and finally of seeking to connect the study of historical man with the study of natural man (hence their interest in psychology, in anthropology, and in language as a more or less intermediate formation between natural organisms and social institutions).

However, psychoanalysis and structuralism, if they contain an appeal to science against the claims of a purely humanistic culture, are at the same time deeply permeated with anti-materialist ideology. The attacks to which psychoanalysis has been and is subjected 'from the Right' should not lead us to forget the fact that this scientific current arose in polemical opposition to materialist psychology, and sought to render psychic phenomena independent of anatomical and physiological data. That linguists with a Crocean or Vosslerian background[11] attack structuralism in the name of an identification of language with art, does not alter the fact that structuralism makes the 'system' it studies into something closed and intrinsically coherent, and reveals no interest in its genesis 'from below', or in the relations between human activities and their material determinations – whether socio-economic or biophysical. Its truly Cuvierian concept of 'system' is inherently ahistorical, not merely anti-historicist. Polarization of the distinction between synchrony and diachrony, and contempt or indifference towards diachronic studies, are essential characteristics of structuralism, which cannot be overcome by any eclectic blending of it.

Surveying these two tendencies, it is more necessary than ever to separate their scientific achievements from all that is ideological and unverifiable in them (I refer in particular to psychoanalysis), or even tantamount to charlatanry (I refer, as a limiting case, to the colossal presumptions and ridiculous coquetries of a Lévi-Strauss). What is needed is an ideological confrontation between Marxism and these tendencies, an antagonistic and not merely receptive stance: antagonistic not only in the sense of a critique of their lack of interest in economic and social facts and in the link between theory and practice, but also in the sense of a critique of their anti-materialism. Failing this, any *rapprochement* with structuralism or psycho-analysis will merely end in yet another 'modernization' of Marxism, through which it will be culturally enriched but will always remain subaltern.

It is also wrong, in my view, to assume that a Marxist interest in linguistics or psychology today must obligatorily be directed towards the *latest* schools within these disciplines. If we are convinced (and as a matter of principle we should all be) that the development of bourgeois culture does not follow a trajectory of absolute progress, but of progress-and-involution (progress in methodological refinement and in certain areas of knowledge, involution in ideology and therewith partial falsification or misinterpretation of properly scientific results), then it may be that Pavlov will have more to tell us than Freud, at least in certain respects, and Ascoli[12] more than Roman Jakobson. It may also be that the vanguard role within the sciences at present assigned by bourgeois culture to linguistics and psychology will prove debatable, and a more important position be attributed to the historical sciences of nature. But of course all these options depend on a choice for or against materialism.

Notes

1. This aspect of Stalinism was first analyzed by Trotsky: see especially *The Revolution Betrayed* (New York 1965), pp. 32–5. Note also Lukác's comments in *Nuovi Argomenti*, no. 57–8, July–October 1962, pp. 120–24.
2. Augustin Thierry (1795–1856): French historian who concentrated on national conflicts in European history. (NLB)
3. *La Ginestra*, lines 292–4. (NLB)
4. Engels, letters to Bloch and Schmidt, in Marx–Engels, *Selected Correspondence*, (Moscow 1965), pp. 417–25; Gramsci, *Prison Notebooks*, (London 1971), pp. 407 ff. See also C. Luporini, 'Realtà e Storicità: Economia e Dialettica nel Marxismo', *Critica Marxista*, IV, 1966, p. 105, and now in *Dialettica e materialismo*, p. 207.
5. Realtà e Storicità', pp. 104–6.
6. It must be remembered that the concept of superstructure historically arose from a critique of religion and law, that is to say, of constructions which were both eminently devoid of objective validity, and especially profuse in universalistic pretensions, vaunting a divine or 'natural' origin. The concept of superstructure played an extremely important role in demystifying these claims. But transferred without modification to the domain of scientific knowledge, it risks making the latter as relative and subjective a phenomenon as religion or law; that is, it can have an anti-materialist and anthropocentric effect. The very theory of knowledge as a mirror-reflection, which appears to be a *ne plus ultra* of objectivism, can acquire a relativist character if it is only historical and social reality, and not also natural reality, that is taken as the object of the reflection: Kepler's laws or

Pascal's principle then become mere expressions of the sociocultural ambience in which their authors were reared, and not also formulations of *objective* relations between phenomena — relations which antedate their discoverers. There is a way of writing the history of science as the history of culture, and of equating science with the history of science, which may represent a major advance over historical or literary idealism, but itself remains too humanistic.

7. See Stalin's only writing of any theoretical interest, *Marxism and Linguistics*, and my comment on it in *Belfagor*, XVIII, 1963, pp. 9–14.

8. Of course, there are also very considerable differences in the duration of historical and social superstructures. Marx and Engels noted in *The Communist Manifesto* that certain forms of consciousness were common to all successive civil societies hitherto, since they were all societies divided into classes. Probably basing himself on this passage from the *Manifesto*, the Triestine writer and scholar Guido Voghera sought to develop from a Marxist point of view the idea that certain moral principles correspond to the inherent needs of any society (including communist society), and are therefore certainly superstructures, but superstructures 'of sociality in general'. Although the dangers of a regression to an ahistorical conception of ethics are evident, I think that this notion nevertheless deserves close consideration.

9. It may be noted that the role of the relationship between man and nature in the genesis and perdurance of religion was precisely perceived by Lenin in a letter to Gorky of December 1913: 'God is (in history and in real life) first of all the complex of ideas generated by the brutish subjection of man both by external nature and by the class yoke.' Lenin, *Collected Works* (Moscow 1966), vol. 35, p. 128.

10. See Louis Althusser, *Reading Capital* (London 1979), and Luporini. 'Realtà e Storicità'. However, it should be said that the profession of historicism by Italian Marxists did not merely have the inferior humanist or intuitionist connotation that is rightly repudiated today; it also had the sense of a polemic against the metaphysical or 'actualistic' aspects of Italian neo-idealism. Especially in the field of literary history, historicism meant a rejection of the aesthetics of pure intention, and of monographic essays; in other words, what was summarily defined as a 'return to De Sanctis'. It should also be noted that well before Althusser or Luporini, there were Italian Marxists who denounced the ambiguities inherent in the notion of 'historicism': see especially A. La Penna in *La Riforma della Scuola*, VI, no. 2, February 1959.

11. Karl Vossler (1872–1949): German linguist and follower of Croce, who equated language and poetry. (NLB)

12. Graziadio Ascoli (1829–1907): the greatest Italian linguistic scholar of the last century, a specialist in neo-Latin and Celtic languages. (NLB)

4.7 □ *From* Hegemony and Socialist Strategy

Ernesto Laclau and Chantal Mouffe

Introduction

Left-wing thought today stands at a crossroads. The 'evident truths' of the past – the classical forms of analysis and political calculation, the nature of the forces in conflict, the very meaning of the Left's struggles and objectives – have been seriously challenged by an avalanche of historical mutations which have riven the ground on which those truths were constituted. Some of these mutations doubtless correspond to failures and disappointments: from Budapest to Prague and the Polish *coup d'état*, from Kabul to the sequels of Communist victory in Vietnam and Cambodia, a question mark has fallen more and more heavily over a whole way of conceiving both socialism and the roads that should lead to it. This has recharged critical thinking, at once corrosive and necessary, on the theoretical and political bases on which the intellectual horizon of the Left was traditionally constituted. But there is more to it than this. A whole series of positive new phenomena underlie those mutations which have made so urgent the task of theoretical reconsideration: the rise of the new feminism, the protest movements of ethnic, national and sexual minorities, the anti-institutional ecology struggles waged by marginalized layers of the population, the anti-nuclear movement, the atypical forms of social struggle in countries on the capitalist periphery – all these imply an extension of social conflictuality to a wide range of areas, which creates the potential, but no more than the potential, for an advance towards more free, democratic and egalitarian societies.

This proliferation of struggles presents itself, first of all, as a 'surplus' of the social *vis-à-vis* the rational and organized structures of society – that is, of the social 'order'. Numerous voices, deriving especially from the liberal-conservative camp, have insistently argued that Western societies face a crisis of governability and a

From Laclau, E. and Mouffe, C., *Hegemony and Socialist Strategy: Towards a radical democratic politics*, Verso, London, 1985, pp. 1–4, 149, 152–4, 159–61, 163–9, 176–8, 193–4.

threat of dissolution at the hands of the egalitarian danger. However, the new forms of social conflict have also thrown into crisis theoretical and political frameworks closer to the ones that we shall seek to engage in dialogue in the major part of this book. These correspond to the classical discourses of the Left, and the characteristic modes in which it has conceived the agents of social change, the structuring of political spaces, and the privileged points for the unleashing of historical transformations. What is now in crisis is a whole conception of socialism which rests upon the ontological centrality of the working class, upon the role of Revolution, with a capital 'r', as the founding moment in the transition from one type of society to another, and upon the illusory prospect of a perfectly unitary and homogeneous collective will that will render pointless the moment of politics. The plural and multifarious character of contemporary social struggles has finally dissolved the last foundation for that political imaginary. Peopled with 'universal' subjects and conceptually built around History in the singular, it has postulated 'society' as an intelligible structure that could be intellectually mastered on the basis of certain class positions and reconstituted, as a rational, transparent order, through a founding act of a political character. Today, the Left is witnessing the final act of the dissolution of that Jacobin imaginary.

[. . .]

The guiding thread of our analysis has been the transformations in the concept of hegemony, considered as a discursive surface and fundamental nodal point of Marxist political theorization. Our principal conclusion is that behind the concept of 'hegemony' lies hidden something more than a type of political relation *complementary* to the basic categories of Marxist theory. In fact, it introduces a *logic of the social* which is incompatible with those categories. Faced with the rationalism of classical Marxism, which presented history and society as intelligible totalities constituted around conceptually explicable laws, the logic of hegemony presented itself from the outset as a *complementary* and *contingent* operation, required for conjunctural imbalances within an evolutionary paradigm whose essential or 'morphological' validity was not for a moment placed in question. (One of the central tasks of this book will be to determine this specific logic of contingency.) As the areas of the concept's application grew broader, from Lenin to Gramsci, the field of contingent articulations also expanded, and the category of 'historical necessity' – which had been the cornerstone of classical Marxism – withdrew to the horizon of theory. ... The expansion and determination of the social logic implicit in the concept of 'hegemony' – in a direction that goes far beyond Gramsci – will provide us with an *anchorage* from which contemporary social struggles are *thinkable* in their specificity, as well as permitting us to outline a new politics for the Left based upon the project of a radical democracy.

One question remains to be answered: why should we broach this task through a critique and a deconstruction of the various discursive surfaces of classical Marxism? Let us first say that there is not *one* discourse and *one* system of categories through which the 'real' might speak without mediations. In operating deconstructively within Marxist categories, we do not claim to be writing 'universal history', to be inscribing our discourse as a moment of a single, linear process of knowledge. Just as the era of normative epistemologies has come to an end, so too has the era of universal discourses. Political conclusions similar to those set forth in this book could have been approximated from very different discursive formations – for example, from certain forms of Christianity, or from libertarian discourses alien to the socialist tradition – none of which could aspire to be *the* truth of society (or 'the insurpassable philosophy of our time', as Sartre put it). For this very reason, however, Marxism is *one* of the traditions through which it becomes possible to formulate this new conception of politics. For us, the validity of this point of departure is simply based on the fact that it constitutes our own past.

Is it not the case that, in scaling down the pretensions and the area of validity of Marxist theory, we are breaking with something deeply inherent in that theory: namely, its monist aspiration to capture with its categories the essence or underlying meaning of History? The answer can only be in the affirmative. Only if we renounce any epistemological prerogative based upon the ontologically privileged position of a 'universal class' will it be possible seriously to discuss the present degree of validity of the Marxist categories. At this point we should state quite plainly that we are now situated in a post-Marxist terrain. It is no longer possible to maintain the conception of subjectivity and classes elaborated by Marxism, nor its vision of the historical course of capitalist development, nor, of course, the conception of communism as a transparent society from which antagonisms have disappeared. But if our intellectual project in this book is *post*-Marxist, it is evidently also post-*Marxist*. It has been through the development of certain intuitions and discursive forms constituted within Marxism, and the inhibition or elimination of certain others, that we have constructed a concept of hegemony which, in our view, may be a useful instrument in the struggle for a radical, libertarian and plural democracy.

[. . .]

Hegemony and Radical Democracy

[. . .]

In this chapter we shall defend the thesis that it is [the] moment of continuity between the Jacobin and the Marxist political imaginary which has to be put in question by the project for a radical democracy. The rejection of privileged points of rupture and the confluence of struggles into a unified political space, and the acceptance, on the contrary, of the plurality and indeterminacy of the social, seem to us the two fundamental bases from which a new political imaginary can be constructed, radically libertarian and infinitely more ambitious in its objectives than that of the classic Left. This demands, in the first place, a description of the historical terrain in which it emerged, which is the field of what we shall call the 'democratic revolution'.

The Democratic Revolution

The theoretical problematic which we have presented excludes not only the concentration of social conflict on *a priori* privileged agents, but also reference to any *general* principle or substratum of an anthropological nature which, at the same time that it unified the different subject positions, would assign a character of inevitability to resistance against the diverse forms of subordination. There is therefore nothing inevitable or natural in the different struggles against power, and it is necessary to explain in each case the reasons for their emergence and the different modulations they may adopt. The struggle against subordination cannot be the result of the situation of subordination itself. Although we can affirm, with Foucault, that wherever there is power there is resistance, it must also be recognized that the forms of resistance may be extremely varied. Only in certain cases do these forms of resistance take on a political character and become struggles directed towards putting an end to relations of subordination as such. If throughout the centuries there have been multiple forms of resistance by women against male domination, it is only under certain conditions and specific forms that a feminist movement which demands equality (equality before the law in the first place, and subsequently in other areas) has been able to emerge. Clearly, when we speak here of the 'political' character of these struggles, we do not do so in the restricted sense of demands which are situated at the level of parties and of the State. What we are referring to is a type of action whose objective is the transformation of a social relation which constructs a subject in a relationship of subordination. Certain contemporary feminist practices, for example, tend to transform the relationship between masculinity and femininity without passing in any way through parties or the State. Of course, we are not seeking to deny that certain practices require the intervention of the political in its restricted sense. What we wish to point out is that politics as a practice of creation, reproduction and transformation of social relations cannot be located at a determinate level of the social, as the problem of the political is the problem of the institution of the social, that is, of the definition and articulation of social relations in a field crisscrossed with antagonisms.

Our central problem is to identify the discursive conditions for the emergence of a collective action, directed towards struggling against inequalities and challenging relations of subordination. We might also say that our task is to identify the conditions in which a relation of subordination becomes a relation of oppression, and thereby constitutes itself into the site of an antagonism. We enter here onto a terrain constituted by numerous terminological shifts which have ended by establishing a synonymity between 'subordination', 'oppression', and 'domination'. The base which makes this synonymity possible is, as is evident, the anthropological assumption of a 'human nature' and of a unified subject: if we can determine *a priori* the essence of a subject, every relation of subordination which denies it automatically becomes a relation of oppression. But if we reject this essentialist perspective, we need to differentiate 'subordination' from 'oppression' and explain the precise conditions in which subordination becomes oppressive. We shall understand by a *relation of subordination* that in which an agent is subjected to the decisions of another – an employee with respect to an employer, for example, or in certain forms of family organization the woman with respect to the man, and so on. We shall call *relations of oppression*, in contrast, those relations of subordination which have transformed themselves into sites of antagonisms. Finally, we shall call *relations of domination* the set of those relations of subordination which are considered as illegitimate from the perspective, or in the judgement, of a social agent external to them, and which, as a consequence, may or may not coincide with the relations of oppression actually existing in a determinate social formation. The problem is, therefore, to explain how relations of oppression are constituted out of relations of subordination. It is clear why relations of subordination, considered in themselves, cannot be antagonistic relations: a relation of subordination establishes, simply, a set of differential positions between social agents, and we already know that a system of differences which constructs each social identity as *positivity* not only cannot be antagonistic, but would bring about the ideal conditions for the elimination of all antagonisms – we would be faced with a sutured social space, from which every equivalence would be excluded. It is only to the extent that the positive differential character of the subordinated subject position is subverted that the antagonism can emerge. 'Serf', 'slave', and so on, do not designate in themselves antagonistic positions; it is only in the terms of a different discursive formation, such as 'the rights inherent to every human being', that the differential positivity of these categories can be subverted and the subordination constructed as oppression. This means that there is no relation of oppression without the presence of a discursive 'exterior' from which the discourse of subordination can be interrupted.[1] The logic of equivalence in this sense displaces the effects of some discourses towards others. If, as was the case with women until the seventeenth century, the ensemble of discourses which constructed them as subjects fixed them purely and simply in a subordinated position, feminism as a movement of struggle against women's subordination could not emerge. Our thesis is that it is only from the moment when the democratic discourse becomes available to articulate the different forms of resistance to subordination that the conditions will exist to make possible the struggle against different types of inequality. In the case of women we may cite as an example the role played in England by Mary Wollstonecraft, whose book *Vindication of the Rights of Woman*, published in 1792, determined the birth of feminism through the use made in it of the democratic discourse, which was thus displaced from the field of political equality between citizens to the field of equality between the sexes.

[. . .]

Democratic Revolution and New Antagonisms

The equivalential displacement between distinct subject positions – which is a condition for the emergence of an antagonism – may thus present itself in two fundamental variants. Firstly, it may be a question of relations of subordination already in existence which, thanks to a displacement of the democratic imaginary, are rearticulated as relations of oppression. To take the case of feminism once again: it is because women as women are denied a right which the democratic ideology recognizes in principle for all citizens that there appears a fissure in the construction of the subordinated feminine subject from which an antagonism *may* arise. It is also the case with the ethnic minorities who demand their civil rights. But the antagonism can also arise in other circumstances – for example, when acquired rights are being called into question, or when social relations which had not been constructed under the form of subordination begin to be so under the impact of certain social transformations. In this case it is because it is negated by practices and discourses bearing new forms of inequality that a subject position can become the site of an antagonism. But in every case what allows the forms of resistance to assume the character of collective struggles is the existence of an external discourse which impedes the stabilization of subordination as difference.

The unsatisfactory term 'new social movements' groups together a series of highly diverse struggles: urban, ecological, anti-authoritarian, anti-institutional, feminist, anti-racist, ethnic, regional or that of sexual minorities. The common denominator of all of them would be their differentiation from workers' struggles, considered as 'class' struggles. It is pointless to insist upon the problematic nature of this latter notion: it amalgamates a series of very different struggles at the level of the relations of production, which are set apart from the 'new antagonisms' for reasons that display all too clearly the persistence of a discourse founded upon the privileged status of 'classes'. What interests us about these new social movements, then, is not the idea of arbitrarily grouping them into a category opposed to that of class, but the *novel* role they play in articulating that rapid diffusion of social conflictuality to more and more numerous relations which is characteristic today of advanced industrial societies. This is what we shall seek to analyse through the theoretical problematic presented above, which leads us to conceive these movements as an extension of the democratic revolution to a whole new series of social relations. As for their novelty, that is conferred upon them by the fact that they call into question new forms of subordination. We should distinguish two aspects of this relation of continuity/discontinuity. The aspect of continuity basically involves the fact that the conversion of liberal-democratic ideology into the 'common sense' of Western societies laid the foundation for that progressive challenge to the hierarchical principle which Tocqueville called the 'equalization of conditions'. It is the permanence of this egalitarian imaginary which permits us to establish a continuity between the struggles of the nineteenth century against the inequalities bequeathed by the *ancien régime* and the social movements of the present. But from a second point of view we can speak of discontinuity, as a good proportion of the new political subjects have been constituted through their antagonistic relationship to recent forms of subordination, derived from the implanting and expansion of capitalist relations of production and the growing intervention of the state. It is to these new relations of subordination and to the antagonisms constituted within them that we shall now address ourselves.

It was in the context of the reorganization which took place after the Second World War that a series of changes occurred at the level of social relations and a new hegemonic formation was consolidated. The latter articulated modifications at the level of the labour process, the form of state and the dominant modes of cultural diffusion which were to bring about a profound transformation in the existing forms of social intercourse. If we examine the problem from an economic point of view, the decisive change is what Michel Aglietta has termed the transition from an extensive to an intensive regime of accumulation. The latter is characterized by the spread of capitalist relations of production to the whole set of social relations, and the subordination of the latter to the logic of production for profit. According to Aglietta the fundamental moment of this transition is the introduction of Fordism, which he describes as 'the principle of an articulation between process of production and mode of consumption'.[2] More specifically, it is the articulation between a labour process organized around the semi-automatic production line, and a mode of consumption characterized by the individual acquisition of commodities produced on a large scale for private consumption. This penetration of capitalist relations of production, initiated at the beginning of the century and stepped up from the 1940s on, was to transform society into a vast market in which new 'needs' were ceaselessly created, and in which more and more of the products of human labour were turned into commodities. This 'commodification' of social life destroyed previous social relations, replacing them with commodity relations through which the logic of capitalist accumulation penetrated into increasingly numerous spheres. Today it is not only as a seller of labour-power that the individual is subordinated to capital, but also through his or her incorporation into a multitude of other social relations: culture, free time, illness, education, sex, and even death. There is practically no domain of individual or collective life which escapes capitalist relations.

But this 'consumer society' has not led to the end of ideology, as Daniel Bell announced, nor to the creation of a one-dimensional man, as Marcuse feared. On the contrary, numerous new struggles have expressed resistance against the new forms of subordination, and this from within the very heart of the new society. Thus it is that the waste of natural resources, the pollution and destruction of the environment, the consequences of productivism have given birth to the ecology movement. Other struggles, which Manuel Castells terms 'urban',[3] express diverse forms of resistance to the capitalist occupation of social space. The general urbanization which has accompanied economic growth, the transfer of the popular classes to the urban periphery or their relegation to the decaying inner cities, and the general lack of collective goods and services have caused a series of new problems which affect the organization of the whole of social life outside work. Hence the multiplicity of social relations from which antagonisms and struggles may originate: habitat, consumption, various services can all constitute terrains for the struggle against inequalities and the claiming of new rights.

[. . .]

One cannot understand the present expansion of the field of social conflictuality and the consequent emergence of new political subjects without situating both in the context of the commodification and bureaucratization of social relations on the one hand and the reformulation of the liberal-democratic ideology – resuiting from the expansion of struggles for equality – on the other. For this reason we have proposed that this proliferation of antagonisms and calling into question of relations of subordination should be considered as a moment of deepening of the democratic revolution. This has also been stimulated by the third important aspect in the mutation of social relations which has characterized the hegemonic formation of the post-war period: namely, the new cultural forms linked to the expansion of the means of mass communication. These were to make possible a new mass culture which would profoundly shake traditional identities. Once again, the effects here are ambiguous, as along with the undeniable effects of massification and uniformization, this media-based culture also contains powerful elements for the subversion of inequalities: the dominant discourses in consumer society present it as social progress and the advance of democracy, to the extent that it allows the vast majority of the population access to an ever-increasing range of goods. Now, while Baudrillard is right to say that we are 'ever further away from an equality *vis-à-vis* the object',[4] the reigning appearance of equality and the cultural democratization which is the inevitable consequence of the action of the media permit the questioning of privileges based upon older forms of status. Interpellated as equals in their capacity as consumers, ever more numerous groups are impelled to reject the real inequalities which continue to exist. This 'democratic consumer culture' has undoubtedly stimulated the emergence of new struggles which have played an important part in the rejection of old forms of subordination, as was the case in the United States with the struggle of the black movement for civil rights. The phenomenon of the young is particularly interesting, and it is no cause for wonder that they should constitute a new axis for the emergence of antagonisms. In order to create new necessities, they are increasingly constructed as a specific category of consumer, which stimulates them to seek a financial autonomy that society is in no condition to give them. On the contrary, the economic crisis and unemployment make their situation difficult indeed. If we add to this the disintegration of the family cell and its growing reduction to pure functions of consumption, along with the absence of social forms of integration of these 'new subjects' who have received the impact of the general questioning of existing hierarchies, we easily understand the different forms which the rebellion of the young has adopted in industrial societies.

The fact that these 'new antagonisms' are the expression of forms of resistance to the commodification, bureaucratization and increasing homogenization of social life itself explains why they should frequently manifest themselves through a proliferation of particularisms, and crystallize into a demand for autonomy itself. It is also for this reason that there is an identifiable tendency towards the valorization of 'differences' and the creation of new identities which tend to privilege 'cultural' criteria (clothes, music, language, regional traditions, and so on). In so far as of the two great themes of the democratic imaginary – equality and liberty – it was that of equality which was traditionally predominant, the demands for autonomy bestow an increasingly central role upon liberty. For this reason many of these forms of resistance are made manifest not in the form of collective struggles, but through an increasingly affirmed individualism. (The Left, of course, is ill prepared to take into account these struggles, which even today it tends to dismiss as 'liberal'. Hence the danger that they may be articulated by a discourse of the Right, of the defence of privileges.) But in any case, and whatever the political orientation through which the antagonism crystallizes (this will depend upon the chains of equivalence which construct it), *the form of the antagonism as such* is identical in all cases. That is to say, it always consists in the construction of a social identity – of an overdetermined subject position – on the basis of the equivalence between a set of elements or values which expel or externalize those others to which they are opposed. Once again, we find ourselves confronting the *division* of social space.

[. . .]

The central idea which we have defended thus far is that the new struggles – and the radicalization of older struggles such as those of women or ethnic minorities – should be understood from the double perspective of the transformation of social relations characteristic of the new hegemonic formation of the post-war period, and of the effects of the displacement into new areas of social life of the egalitarian imaginary constituted around the liberal-democratic discourse. It is this which has provided the framework necessary for the questioning of the different relations of subordination and the demanding of new rights. That the democratic imaginary has played a fundamental role in the eruption of new demands since the 1960s is perfectly well understood by the American neo-conservatives, who denounce the 'excess of democracy' and the wave of 'egalitarianism' which in their view caused an overload in the political systems of the West. Samuel Huntington, in his report to the Trilateral Commission in 1975, argued that the struggles in the United States in the 1960s for greater equality and participation had provoked a 'democratic surge' which had made society 'ungovernable'. He concluded that 'the strength of the democratic ideal poses a problem for the governability of democracy'.[5] The increasingly numerous demands for real equality have led society, according to the neo-conservatives, to the edge of the 'egalitarian precipice'. This is where they see the origins of the double transformation which, in their opinion, the idea of equality has undergone: it has passed from equality of opportunity to equality of results, and from equality between individuals to equality between groups. Daniel Bell considers that this 'new egalitarianism' puts in jeopardy the true ideal of equality, whose objective cannot be equality of results, but a 'just meritocracy'.[6] The present crisis is, then, seen as the result of a 'crisis of values', the consequence of the development of an 'adversary culture' and of the 'cultural contradictions of capitalism'.

Thus far we have presented the emergence of new antagonisms and political subjects as linked to the expansion and generalization of the democratic revolution. In reality, it can also be seen as a prolongation of various other areas of political effects which we have come across frequently throughout our analysis. In particular, the proliferation of these antagonisms makes us see in a new light the problem of the fragmentation of the 'unitary' subjects of the social struggles with which Marxism found itself confronted in the wake of its first crisis, at the end of the last century. All the discussion on strategies for recomposition of working-class unity, seen in perspective, is nothing other than the first act of a recognition – reluctant, it is true – of the plurality of the social, and the unsutured character of all political identity. If we read *sous rature* the texts of Rosa Luxemburg, Labriola, and of Kautsky himself, we shall see that this unassimilable moment of plurality is in one way or another present in their discourse, undermining the coherence of their categories. It is clear that this multiformity was not necessarily a negative moment of fragmentation or the reflection of an artificial division resulting from the logic of capitalism, as the theorists of the Second International thought, but the very terrain which made *possible* a deepening of the democratic revolution. As we shall see, this deepening is revealed even in the ambiguities and difficulties which every practice of articulation and recomposition has to face. Renunciation of the category of subject as a unitary, transparent and sutured entity opens the way to the recognition of the specificity of the antagonisms constituted on the basis of different subject positions, and, hence, the possibility of the deepening of a pluralist and democratic conception. The critique of the category of unified subject, and the recognition of the discursive dispersion within which every subject position is constituted, therefore involve something more than the enunciation of a general theoretical position: they are the *sine qua non* for thinking the multiplicity out of which antagonisms emerge in societies in which the democratic revolution has crossed a certain threshold. This gives us a theoretical terrain on the basis of which the notion of *radical and plural democracy* – which will be central to our argument from this point on – finds the first conditions under which it can be apprehended. Only if it is accepted that the subject positions cannot be led back to a positive and unitary founding principle – only then can pluralism be considered radical. Pluralism is *radical* only to the extent that each term of this plurality of identities finds within itself the principle of its own validity, without this having to be sought in a transcendent or underlying positive ground for the hierarchy of meaning of them all and the source and guarantee of their legitimacy. And this radical pluralism is *democratic* to the extent that the autoconstitutivity of each one of its terms is the result of displacements of the egalitarian imaginary. Hence, the project for a radical and plural democracy, *in a primary sense*, is nothing other than the struggle for a maximum autonomization of spheres on the basis of the generalization of the equivalential-egalitarian logic.

This approach permits us to redimension and do justice to workers' struggles themselves, whose character is distorted when they are contrasted *en bloc* to the struggles of the 'new political subjects'. Once the conception of the working class as a 'universal class' is rejected, it becomes possible to recognize the plurality of the antagonisms which take place in the field of what is arbitrarily grouped under the label of 'workers' struggles', and the inestimable importance of the great majority of them for the deepening of the democratic process. Workers' struggles have been numerous, and have assumed an extraordinary variety of forms as a function of transformations in the role of the state, the trade-union practices of different categories of workers, the antagonisms within and outside the factories, and the existing hegemonic equilibria. An excellent example is afforded us by the so-called 'new workers' struggles', which took place in France and in Italy at the end of the 1960s. They show well how the forms of struggles within the factory depend upon a discursive context much vaster than that of simple relations of production. The evident influence of the struggles and slogans of the student movement; the central role played by young workers, whose culture was radically different from that of their older colleagues; the importance of immigrants in France and southerners in Italy – all this reveals to us that the other social relations in which workers are enrolled will determine the manner in which they react inside the factory, and that as a result the plurality of these relations cannot be magically erased to constitute a *single* working class. Nor, then, can workers' demands be reduced to a unique antagonism whose nature is ontologically different from that of other social and political subjects.

Thus far we have spoken of a multiplicity of antagonisms whose effects, converging and overdetermined, are registered within the framework of what we have called the 'democratic revolution'. At this point it is necessary, nevertheless, to make it clear that the democratic revolution is simply the terrain upon which there operates a logic of displacement supported by an egalitarian imaginary, but that it does not predetermine the *direction* in which this imaginary will operate. If this direction were predetermined we should simply have constructed a new teleology – we would be on a terrain similar to that of Bernstein's *Entwicklung*. But in that case there would be no room at all for a hegemonic practice. The reason why it is not thus, and why no teleology can account for social articulations, is that the discursive compass of the democratic revolution opens the way for political logics as diverse as right-wing populism and totalitarianism on the one hand, and a radical democracy on the other. Therefore, if we wish to construct the hegemonic articulations which allow us to set ourselves in the direction of the latter, we must understand in all their radical heterogeneity the range of possibilities which are opened in the terrain of democracy itself.

It cannot be doubted that the proliferation of new antagonisms and of 'new rights' is leading to a crisis of the hegemonic formation of the post-war period. But the form in which this crisis will be overcome is far from being predetermined, as the manner in which rights will be defined and the forms which struggle against subordination will adopt are not unequivocally established. We are faced here with a true polysemia. Feminism or ecology, for example, exist in multiple forms, which depend upon the manner in which the antagonism is discursively constituted. Thus we have a radical feminism which attacks men as such; a feminism of difference which seeks to revalorize 'femininity'; and a Marxist feminism for which the fundamental enemy is capitalism, considered as linked indissolubly to patriarchy. There are therefore a plurality of discursive forms of constructing an antagonism on the basis of the different modes of women's subordination. Ecology, in the same way, may be anti-capitalist, anti-industrialist, authoritarian, libertarian, socialist, reactionary, and so on. The forms of articulation of an antagonism, therefore, far from being predetermined, are the result of a hegemonic struggle. This affirmation has important consequences, as it implies that these new struggles do not necessarily have a progressive character, and that it is therefore an error to think, as many do, that they spontaneously take their place in the context of left-wing politics. Many have devoted themselves since the 1960s to the search for a new privileged revolutionary subject which might come to replace the working class, with the latter seen as having failed in its historical mission of emancipation. The ecological movements, the student movements, feminism and the marginal masses have been the most popular candidates for the carrying out of this new role. But it is clear that such an approach does not escape the traditional problematic, but simply displaces it. There is no *unique* privileged position from which a uniform continuity of effects will follow, concluding with the transformation of society as a whole. All struggles, whether those of workers or other political subjects left to themselves, have a partial character, and can be articulated to very different discourses. It is this articulation which gives them their character, not the place from which they come. There is therefore no subject – nor, further, any 'necessity' – which is absolutely radical and irrecuperable by the dominant order, and which constitutes an absolutely guaranteed point of departure for a total transformation. (Equally, there is nothing which permanently assures the stability of an established order.)

[. . .]

Radical Democracy: Alternative for a New Left

[. . .]

It is clear, therefore, that a left alternative can *only* consist of the construction of a different system of equivalents, which establishes social division on a new basis. In the face of the project for the reconstruction of a hierarchic society, the alternative of the Left should consist of locating itself fully in the field of the democratic revolution and expanding the chains of equivalents between the different struggles against oppression. *The task of the Left therefore cannot be to renounce liberal-democratic ideology, but on the contrary, to deepen and expand it in the direction of a radical and plural democracy.* We shall explain the dimensions of this task in the following pages, but the very fact that it is possible arises out of the fact that the *meaning* of liberal discourse on individual rights is not definitively fixed; and just as this unfixity permits their articulation with elements of conservative discourse, it also permits different forms of articulation and redefinition which accentuate the democratic moment. That is to say, as with any other social element, the elements making up the liberal discourse never appear as crystallized, and may be the field of hegemonic struggle. It is not in the abandonment of the democratic terrain but, on the contrary, in the extension of the field of democratic struggles to the whole of civil society and the state, that the possibility resides for a hegemonic strategy of the Left. It is nevertheless important to understand the radical extent of the changes which are necessary in the political imaginary of the Left, if it wishes to succeed in founding a political practice fully located in the field of the democratic revolution and conscious of the depth and variety of the hegemonic articulations which the present conjuncture requires. The fundamental obstacle in this task is the one to which we have been drawing attention from the beginning of this book: essentialist apriorism, the conviction that the social is sutured at some point, from which it is possible to fix the meaning of any event independently of any articulatory practice. This has led to a failure to understand the constant displacement of the nodal points structuring a social formation, and to an organization of discourse in terms of a logic of '*a priori* privileged points' which seriously limits the Left's capacity for action and political analysis. This logic of privileged points has operated in a variety of directions. From the point of view of the determining of the fundamental antagonisms, the basic obstacle, as we have seen, has been *classism*: that is to say, the idea that the working class represents the privileged agent in which the fundamental impulse of social change resides – without perceiving that the very orientation of the working class depends upon a political balance of forces and the radicalization of a plurality of democratic struggles which are decided in good part *outside* the class itself. From the point of view of the *social levels* at which the possibility of implementing changes is concentrated, the fundamental obstacles have been *statism* – the idea that the expansion of the role of the state is the panacea for all problems; and *economism* (particularly in its technocratic version) – the idea that from a successful economic strategy there necessarily follows a continuity of political effects which can be clearly specified.

But if we look for the ultimate core of this essentialist fixity, we shall find it in the fundamental nodal point which has galvanized the political imagination of the Left: the classic concept of 'revolution', cast in the Jacobin mould. Of course, there would be nothing in the concept of 'revolution' to which objection could be made if we understood by it the overdetermination of a set of struggles in a point of political rupture, from which there follow a variety of effects spread across the whole of the fabric of society. If this were all that was involved, there is no doubt that in many cases the violent overthrow of a repressive regime is the condition of every democratic advance. But the classic concept of revolution implied much more than this: it implied the *foundational* character of the revolutionary act, the institution of a point of concentration of power from which society could be 'rationally' reorganized. This is the perspective which is incompatible with the plurality and the opening which a radical democracy requires. Once again radicalizing certain of Gramsci's concepts, we find the theoretical instruments which allow us to redimension the revolutionary act itself. The concept of a 'war of position' implies precisely the *process* character of every radical transformation – the revolutionary act is, simply, an internal moment of this process. The multiplication of political spaces and the preventing of the concentration of power in one point are, then, preconditions of every truly democratic transformation of society. The classic conception of socialism supposed that the disappearance of private ownership of the means of production would set up a chain of effects which, over a whole historical epoch, would lead to the extinction of all forms of subordination. Today we know that this is not so. *There are not*, for example, necessary links between anti-sexism and anti-capitalism, and a unity between the two can only be the result of a hegemonic articulation. It follows that it is only possible to construct this articulation on the basis of separate struggles, which only exercise their equivalential and overdetermining effects in *certain* spheres of the social. This requires the autonomization of the spheres of struggle and the multiplication of political spaces, which is incompatible with the concentration of power and knowledge that classic Jacobinism and its different socialist variants imply. Of course, every project for radical democracy implies a socialist dimension, as it is necessary to put an end to capitalist relations of production, which are at the root of numerous relations of subordination; but socialism is *one* of the components of a project for radical democracy, not vice versa. For this very reason, when one speaks of the socialization of the means of production as one element in the strategy for a radical and plural democracy, one must insist that this cannot mean only workers' self-management, as what is at stake is true participation by all subjects in decisions about what is to be produced, how it is to be produced, and the forms in which the product is to be distributed.

[. . .]

Notes

1. On the concept of 'interruption', see D. Siverman and B. Torode, *The Material Word* (London 1980), ch. 1.
2. M. Aglietta, *A Theory of Capitalist Regulation* (London 1979), p. 117.
3. Cf. M. Castells, *La question urbaine* (Paris 1972).
4. Baudrillard, *Le système des objets* (Paris 1968), p. 183.
5. S. Huntington, 'The democratic distemper', in N. Glazer and I. Kristol (eds), *The American Commonwealth* (New York 1976), p. 37.
6. D. Bell, 'On meritocracy and equality', *The Public Interest*, Fall 1972.

5 □ *Post-Foundational Ethics and Politics*

Introduction*

The previous Section titles refer to canonic categories in Critical Theory, even if some of their contents have been chosen to convey the permeability and imprecision of those categories. To collect seven pieces under the heading Post-Foundational Ethics and Politics requires a different kind of Section introduction: less an introduction to the individual theorists within the framework of an established field and more an extended rationale which maps a series of enquiries and alerts readers to the significance of some figures (notably Hannah Arendt) whose relevance and importance to Critical Theory registered too late in the compiling of this book to have been included.

The first thing to say is that this section is not a comprehensive summary of where Theory is currently 'at' – certainly not in a chronological sense because although ethical preoccupations seem to have come late to some theorists, Emmanuel Lévinas's first book (on Husserl) was published in 1930 (see Reading 5.5). Perhaps, though, it is the rediscovery of Lévinas, dating from Jacques Derrida's 1964 essay 'Violence and metaphysics', which prompts his inclusion. Even so, it has to be admitted that post-foundational ethics and politics would not be many readers' version of where most interest and energy in pursuing objectives are currently concentrated. Colonial discourse and post-colonial theory (see Williams and Chrisman, 1993) exert a stronger claim, probably even a stronger claim than postmodernism (see Docherty, 1993). Of course, postmodernism might be one way of talking about a post-foundational crisis in Theory, except that the Readings which follow are a step back from – or on from – postmodernism, because there is little interest in defining it or investigating its cultural manifestations in architecture, art and literature. Moreover, there is no intent, here, to explain the theoretical positions as mere signs of the postmodern era.

The second thing to say – or, rather, to repeat from the main Introduction – is that there is no suggestion that theorists included in earlier Sections could not be included here: 'Choreographies', Christie McDonald's 1982 interview with Jacques Derrida; or his and J. Hillis Miller's responses to the accusations of anti-Semitism and collaboration with the Nazis levelled at Paul de Man would be many readers' choices. Miller's recent work has been explicitly about what he calls 'the ethics of

---

* This Introduction and Section owe a lot to my colleague Richard King, though I feel sure that his selection of Readings would have been a more determined and principled questioning of a post-structuralist and Marxist canon.

reading', and Derrida has, arguably, always been vitally interested in ethical and political questions, rather than in the nihilistic or playful. Richard Bernstein's view, though, is that these concerns have become more marked as the implications of key theoretical breakthroughs have been acknowledged:

> Initially it appears that ethical-political questions about *praxis* are excluded and marginalized. In the early writings of Heidegger, Derrida, Foucault and Rorty these questions do not even seem to be considered. Yet as we follow the pathways of their thinking and writings something curious begins to happen – for each of these thinkers begins to gravitate more and more to confronting the ethical-political consequences of their own thinking. (Bernstein, 1991, p. 11)

That is to say, the ethical-political dimension is not a formal alternative to the texts and categories above but a development in the work of Derrida, Foucault, and others. Gayatri Spivak is just one of many other theorists included in this *Reader* (see Reading 3.3) to be explicit about the increasingly urgent intersection between ethics and politics in their work – for instance, in a 1993 interview with Sara Danius and Stefan Jonsson:

> more than critiquing Western ethics [in *The Postcolonial Critic*] I am more interested now in imagining the other ethical subject ... moving from the critical phase into a more affirmative phase, into areas from where agencies of critique can come. (Spivak, 1993, p. 27)

There is another defining feature of post-foundational ethical and political thought, and this is the overdue involvement in its problematics by thinkers who are working in different fields – primarily political and moral thought – or do not easily fit the categories employed in the Sections above: Richard Rorty (Reading 5.1), Seyla Benhabib (Reading 5.3), Martha Nussbaum (Reading 5.7), and Jürgen Habermas (Reading 5.2; Habermas's connections with the original Frankfurt School are often quite tenuous). But fully to register the importance of this changing personnel, other theorists, besides those represented in their own words, need to be mentioned: Charles Taylor, John Rawls (who at least features prominently in Rorty's essay), Hannah Arendt, Alasdair MacIntyre, Michael Walzer, Jean Bethke Elshtain, Cornel West, Stanley Cavell, and Bernstein. The traffic has not been one-way, and moral and political theory have been revitalised by a growing awareness of developments in Critical Theory. Judging by recent surveys of this renaissance, thinkers are grappling with a problem familiar to those on the Critical Theory side: namely, how to respond to the widely recognised limitations of any foundational theory of truth, whether founded in transcendental conceptions of truth or in an acceptance of the self's unchallenged place at the centre of any analysis. From the Critical Theory side, the concentration upon cultural, aesthetic and philosophical questions – even in Marxism, where Western Marxism is defined by just these preoccupations at the expense of economics and politics – indicates the value in more of an exchange with neo-Kantian liberals such as Rawls; neo-Hegelian communitarians such as Taylor; and neo-Aristotelians, such as Nussbaum and Arendt, who compete as much with more orthodox liberals as with Marxists and post-structuralists in their assertion of the importance of the political and public sphere. Bernstein's explanation of the subtitle to *The New Constellation: The ethical-political horizons of modernity/postmodernity* – a book which seeks to repair the intellectual apartheid between the Anglo-American and European traditions – underlines the expanded focus of this exchange between traditions:

> the hyphenated expression 'ethical-political' ... invoke[s] and recall[s] the classical (Greek) understanding of the symbiotic relation between ethics and politics. Ethics is concerned with *ethos*, with those habits, customs and modes of response that shape and define our *praxis*. Politics is concerned with our public lives in the *polis* – with the communal bonds that at once unite and separate us as citizens. (Bernstein, 1991, p. 9)

Politics and ethics are posited, therefore, as antidotes to the narrowing of this enquiry in modern thought, equally in positivistic moral and political philosophy and, less obviously, in Critical Theory.

Bernstein poses, as an organising theme for *The New Constellation*, questions provoked by Rorty as well as Derrida: critique or deconstruction or the exercise of pragmatic, non-essentialising reason, but in the service of what? What is being stood for, and what is being critiqued? Critique and deconstruction are critical of the Enlightenment, but does not this undermine the basis for critique and deconstruction? How should one live? By quoting Derrida, Bernstein accepts that these questions are not foreign to the continental tradition, even if the vocabulary is different from that used by Anglo-American thinkers: 'I cannot conceive of a radical critique which would not be ultimately motivated by some sort of affirmation, acknowledged or not' (quoted in Bernstein, 1991, p. 7). Nevertheless, what is at issue in reassessments of critique and deconstruction are the implications of a logic of deferral, the necessity for an immanent reading (a reading rather than an interpretation), and the general caution at using concepts such as freedom in a world defined in terms of an imagery of imprisonment from Weber through the Frankfurt School to Foucault. Charles Taylor, who is a contributor to this debate in his own right in *Sources of the Self* (1989), puts the case against Foucault in a 1984 article originally published in *Political Theory*, a journal with more and more to say to Critical Theorists. Taylor respects Foucault's 'unmasking' of different regimes of power, but questions Foucault's apparent unwillingness to theorise his own position:

> The idea of liberating truth [in Foucault] is a profound illusion. There is no truth which can be espoused, defended, rescued against systems of power. On the contrary, each such system defines its own variant of truth. And there is no escape from power into freedom for such systems of power are co-extensive with human society. (Taylor, 1986, p. 70)

For Taylor:

> The Foucaultian notion of power not only requires for its sense the correlative notions of truth and liberation, but even the standard link between them, which makes truth the condition of liberation. To speak of power, and to want to deny a place to liberation and truth as well as the link between them, is to speak incoherently. (Taylor, 1986, p. 93)

Even in the specific, local site where, Foucault insists, resistance must be concentrated (because a general source of power either cannot be located or cannot practically be attacked head-on), it is still not clear in Foucault *why* one should act this way rather than that way. The desirable end is, for Foucault, constructed by the imposing authority.

As so often, a diagnosis of a general malaise seems less convincing when a number of examples are investigated. It would be interesting to hear whether Charles Taylor could maintain his thesis with reference to Foucault's last writings. Similarly, while Jean-François Lyotard's *The Postmodern Condition* (1979) is short on persuasive responses to the crisis of legitimation which is his main theme, *The Differend* (1983) undoubtedly addresses the related issues of post-foundational ethics and politics. In a variety of ways, all the Readings below signal a reconsideration of how to respond to a world in which there is no broadly assumed external, context-free standard of truth, and conflict seems endemic. In some cases, the reconsideration directly faces up to the perceived dangers of relativism, which structuralism inaugurated in its postmodern phase but which is an aspect of all anti-foundational thinking. In other cases, relativism is seen more positively, and is therefore to be explored. Rorty has been prominent in proposing that we learn the lessons of (mostly French) post-structuralism: that philosophy in its traditional metaphysical role is not going to decide anything once and for all; and the more important and pressing the issue, the less likely that there will be agreement on foundational principles. Rorty differs from Derrida, for example, in concluding that this failure of philosophy in its epistemological and ontological modes is actually a good thing: look at what happens when fundamentals are adhered to, is the lesson he would derive from the crises of twentieth-century history, notably those of the 1930s and 1940s. It may be, though, that Rorty's low-key, non-polemical defence of Western liberalism derives more from the failures of left and right ideologies than from the strengths of what is left after the Cold War. But to return to Rorty's post-foundationalism: in his view Derrida unnecessarily worries away at the metaphysical tradition rather than considering other forms of legitimation and engaging in the process of redescription of cultural and political vocabularies. Incidentally, Christopher Norris's vigorous rejection of Rorty's postmodern Derrida stands as an indication that 'Anglo-American' is hardly a reliable category in surveying current debates (see Norris, 1985, ch. 6).

In accordance with his espousal of a post-Philosophical (with a capital letter) culture in favour of cultural criticism and 'conversation', Rorty is intellectually in touch with most of the figures centrally involved in responding to doubts about (if not the end of) foundational thinking. His preference for essayistic interventions in the broader sphere of 'the humanities' that will grease the wheels of debate across intellectual traditions and disciplines which have not had much to say to each other is consistent with what he thinks intellectuals should be doing. His tone has upset the cultural Left and Right, as it once upset Philosophers, and for a while the debates that are now going on across disciplines and fields of enquiry will almost certainly continue to generate some kneejerk reactions – for example, that Rortyean liberalism is inescapably the prop for American cultural imperialism; or, on the other hand, that French esoterics are a radical alternative to practical political action. But one can hope that the example of some of the participants in the debates will be salutary, and there will be more genuine interchange of ideas.

On the first count – that liberalism is merely symptomatic of Western, and particularly American, power – Reading 5.2 is some indication of the complexity of liberalism. But more important is the fact that only a minority of those now entering the debates out of an Anglo-American intellectual background would count themselves as liberals, and all have different versions of the separation between private and public spheres which Rorty makes central to his version of liberalism: 'the idea that politics can be separated from beliefs about matters of ultimate importance – that shared beliefs among citizens on such matters are not essential to a democratic society' (Rorty, 1991, vol. 2, p. 175). Rorty's account of Rawls suggests that the latter's notion of procedural liberalism ought to be taken far more seriously outside of Anglo-American political theory because it faces up to the necessity, in a multicultural society, that different discourses engage with each other in the absence of any way in which objective (meta-physical) judgements can be reached about their truth or falsity. There is also more common ground – or, at a minimum, the basis for productive dialogue – than one would think between Rawls and his communitarian opponents (Taylor and MacIntyre, for instance) and Lyotard – in *The Differend*, at least.

To the second kneejerk reaction – that French (and especially French post-structuralist) theory lends itself to a disappointing political and ethical acquiescence masquerading as radicalism – the most significant recent rejoinder is to be found in *The Differend*. While it is close to Derrida, Lyotard's work has given greater prominence to narrative and to a 'philosophy of sentences' rather than simply to the deconstruction of the structure of the sign with which Derrida announced himself in two of his 1967 books, *Speech and Phenomena* and *Of Grammatology*. The activity and sense of agency, which is sometimes difficult to make out after the linguistic turn in philosophy, is realised in narrative which, Lyotard argues, is never totalised but has to be begun over and over, thereby manifesting a storytelling impulse in humans. Lyotard recognises that political action is provoked, rather than curtailed, by the breakdown of the binary opposition between the metanarratives of Marxism and capitalism; and that the loss of transcendental foundations is an argument for, rather than against, a democratic, consensual form of legitimacy. In *The Differend*, he brings politics and ethics down to sentences: each sentence proposes another sentence, but this linkage, this What next?, is both contingent and necessary, in so far as sentences get corralled into genres. Ethical and political questions arise in the attempt to transform contingency into necessity, sentences into genres or 'regimes of sentences' which are in an agonistic relationship to each other. Importantly, Lyotard does not substitute 'dissensus' for 'consensus' because 'it would only be the case if the concatenation of phrases had nothing to do with any finality tied to a genre, and took place without genres if their heterogeneity completely disjoined them and left their linkage unforeseeable and inexplicable. ... Now, this is not possible' (Lyotard, 1988 p. 129). To locate a 'differend' is an injunction to enter the public realm. Thus, it is Lyotard's post-foundationalism which is the motor for politics: 'One side's legitimacy does not imply the other's lack of legitimacy' (Lyotard, 1988, p. xi). If this sounds like an acceptance of relativism, Lyotard makes it clear that the public sphere, that of litigation, does not consist of a mere balancing or reconciling of *existing* argumentations:

> The differend is the unstable state and instant of language wherein something which must be able to be put into phrases cannot yet be. ... A lot of searching must be done to find new rules for forming and linking phrases that are able to express the differend. ... What is at stake in a literature, a philosophy, in a politics perhaps, is to bear witness to differends by finding idioms for them. (Lyotard, 1988, p. 13)

Lyotard hesitates over politics because it requires a degree of normalisation, and his own experience of politics-turned-into-a-genre, complete with a grand narrative of communism ('teleology begins with genres of discourse, not with sentences'), perhaps makes him suspicious of any hint of totalisation. Here, Jürgen Habermas and Hannah Arendt offer concepts of the political which can usefully be compared and contrasted with Lyotard's.

In Arendt's case, compared, in so far as both she and Lyotard react against forms of totalitarianism; but contrasted, up to a point, in so far as Arendt finds what she is willing to call 'freedom' precisely in the public (and presumably normalised) sphere of politics. Arendt's analysis in *The Origins of Totalitarianism* (1951) persuaded a generation of mostly American intellectuals who had come up from the chastening experiences of the 1930s and 1940s to doubt politics as a 'vocation' (Max Weber's description), or at least politics understood as Messianic politics of Left or Right. She anticipates concern about metanarratives in her indictment of the totalitarianism of fascism and communism for its adherence to 'laws of movement', whether of Nature or History. Yet, in striking contrast to those American intellectuals whom she influenced, Arendt's theoretical explanation of totalitarianism is not completely dominated by the experiences of the 1930s and the war years, even though these brought her ideas together. In tracing the genealogy of totalitarianism and its relationship with modernity, she goes back to the nineteenth century in Europe and the vacating of the public arena as a place of common interests by the middle classes. There was still talk of the public, of course, but, in Arendt's words, 'the whole thing is a delusion. Public life takes on the deceptive aspect of a total of private interests as though these interests could create a new quality through sheer addition' (Arendt, 1986, p. 145). This is what she largely means when she talks of the 'rise of the social' at the expense of a political public realm defined by the common good and inhabited by citizens. And this phenomenon occurred well in advance of totalitarianism. It then became possible to exclude and victimise those who had been propelled into the discredited public sphere by other historical changes, notably the break-up of nation-states. These peoples became 'homeless', 'stateless' and 'rightless'. The redefinition – in effect, loss – of public space did not produce totalitarianism but created the conditions in which it could flourish. Terror and ideological manipulation colonised the public spaces, the spaces between people which ought to precipitate communication.

Arendt ought to have been entirely disenchanted with the public political sphere after her analysis of what totalitarianism does to it; instead, she foregrounds it, concentrating in particular upon the importance of the spaces between people, the places where communication can go on. Rather in the manner of the American Pragmatist William James, who, faced by philosophical arguments which denied freedom, decided one day simply to believe in freedom, Arendt, in a 1960 essay, 'What is freedom?', sets herself the task of thinking about freedom and its connection with politics in spite of the insights into totalitarianism which she herself had provided ten years earlier. She acknowledges the difficulty, and her account is an indirect gloss on the intellectual problem of thinking affirmatively in the wake of some of the intellectual trends represented in previous Sections:

> Yet it is precisely this coincidence of politics and freedom which we cannot take for granted in the light of our present political experience. The rise of totalitarianism, its claim to having subordinated all spheres of life to the demands of politics and its consistent nonrecognition of civil rights, above all the rights of privacy and the right to freedom from politics, makes us doubt not only the coincidence of politics and freedom but their very compatibility. We are inclined to believe that freedom begins where politics ends because we have seen that freedom has disappeared when so-called political considerations overruled everything else. Was not the liberal credo, 'The less politics the more freedom' right after all? (Arendt, 1961, p. 149)

Arendt goes after this liberal definition of freedom as 'freedom *from* politics', and does so just in advance of the 1960s revival of a view of politics as public participation, and with a theoretical acumen which has allowed her defence to survive a rerun of the end of ideology crisis post-1968, to which Lyotard and Foucault allude.

Arendt seeks to rescue politics as inseparable from freedom, and she resorts, in the absence of better models, to the classical tradition of republican or civic virtue in which citizens must appear, debate and act in public. For Arendt, with the loss of the public political space which the Greek *polis* symbolised, people behave solely as economic producers and consumers. This, incidentally, is the gist of her difference with Marx. The *polis*, it is necessary to stress, *symbolises* public participation, because Arendt does not seriously envisage the return of elite rule, dependent upon the labour of the excluded. The public sphere is not an exclusive space, since entry does not depend upon status, as it did in the Greek *polis*; nevertheless, it is still not an easy space in which to appear because it is, by definition, agonistic. But what must be emphasised is that in an increasingly privatised society, Arendt's work argues that the modern philosophical tradition (Rousseau and Kant are her antagonists) has unwittingly conspired with socioeconomic developments to transpose the idea of freedom 'from its original field, the field of politics and human affairs in general, to an inward domain, the will, where it would be open to self-inspection' (Arendt, 1961, p. 145). She goes on to defend freedom as acting in concert with others in public:

> the very opposite of 'inner freedom', the inward space into which men may escape from external coercion and *feel* free. This inner feeling remains without outer manifestations and hence is by definition politically irrelevant. ... it was originally the result of an estrangement from the world in which worldly experiences were transformed into experiences within one's own self. (Arendt, 1961, p. 146)

For Arendt, the political is the recognition that we live in a society with others who are both similar to and different from us. This is where her pluralism differs from the assumed pluralism of some of her consensus-theory contemporaries, who refused to acknowledge its ideological character. But it also suggests that Arendt has something to offer to the understanding of contemporary identity and difference politics, because politics, for her, requires the common condition of citizenship, especially when cross-cultural decisions are involved.

Richard Bernstein was introduced above as an American philosopher interested in linking the American and European traditions (where Britain figures in all of this intellectual excitement is a depressing thought), and he gives a good summary of why the work of Arendt, who was exiled in the United States, is so worthwhile:

> It is action which is exhibited in the public space of political debate, action that presupposes the human condition of plurality and natality that is the highest form of the *vita activa*. ... We have become blind and forgetful of what is distinctive about action, and are on the verge of becoming a 'laboring society'. But Arendt's analysis of action is intended as an act of retrieval, to reveal a possibility that can never be obliterated. (Bernstein, 1991, p. 127; see also Bernstein, 1985; King, 1984)

The reference to natality is motivated by Arendt's claim, in *Origins of Totalitarianism*, that 'with each new birth' in the camps 'a new beginning is born into the world, a new world has potentially come into being' (Arendt, 1986, p. 465). Arguably, there is something in common between the critique of metaphysics in, say, Derrida, and Arendt's insistence that freedom is an intersubjective concept which needs a space, needs civil society, and should not be confined to 'an inward domain ... where it would be open to self-inspection'. However, it is only in a very cautious – even precious – sense, subject to constant deferral, that Derrida has helped us to function in 'the realm of politics ... whose *raison d'être* ... is freedom, and [whose] ... field of experience is action' (Arendt, 1961, p. 146). And as Taylor observes in his admiring but critical account of Michel Foucault: 'it is certainly not the case that all [political] patterns *issue* from conscious action, but all patterns have to be made *intelligible* in relation to conscious action' (Taylor, 1986, p. 88). Taylor is particularly critical of the Nietzschean deconstruction of the self, in case it undermines the self-determination and self-realisation through experience which the philosophy of the subject initially voiced, and which is most needed by the exploited and marginalised (see King, 1992). There is a related worry that theoretical discourses may become so disengaged from each other that common purposes cannot be articulated, nor projects carried through; and that interventions in the public, political sphere will always be skirmishes around the edges because of the assumption (and it can be an intellectually comforting assumption) that this sphere is under hegemonic control. The very assumption that there is hegemonic control can de-legitimate critical discourses.

Reading 5.2, by Jürgen Habermas, is a direct response to comments on his work by a number of critics, Rorty and Bernstein among them, all of which are collected in Bernstein's *Habermas and Modernity* (Bernstein, 1986a). Lyotard, Adorno and Horkheimer are also strong presences in the book, because Habermas's defence of what he elsewhere calls 'modernity: an incomplete project' (Habermas, 1985) is a partial response to the postmodern end of metanarratives, including that of the Enlightenment project which had suffered at the hands of his former Frankfurt School colleagues. Habermas's essay is also part of a defence of the public sphere which he has been conducting since *The Structural Transformation of the Public Sphere*, first published in German in 1962 (Habermas, 1989a). Rather like Arendt, Habermas effects a recovery from the nadir of modernity that was (knowledge of) the Holocaust to argue determinedly for a revision of the tradition of emancipatory reason, located in the public world. Where Adorno and Horkheimer's reading of Weber led them to a concept of totality in some ways more entrenched than Weber's 'iron cage' of instrumental rationality (from which the only conceivable exit for Adorno was through negative dialectics), Habermas arrives at a theory of communicative reason which, he maintains, produces understanding of the other, and of society and its potential for emancipation, even though philosophy cannot give access to objective meaning. Habermas defends his claim to have steered between relativism and absolutism in Reading 5.2, so comments can be reserved for the related question of what Habermas means by the public sphere, since this concept is one way of formulating the different responses to post-foundationalism from an ethical and political point of view.

In one of the essays in *Situating the Self* (1992) Seyla Benhabib (Reading 5.3) compares Habermas's discursive model of the public sphere with Arendt's republican model and the liberal one in John Rawls, among others. Benhabib commends Habermas for challenging the assumption that the public dimension and, with it, participation is an inevitable casualty of modernity and, further, for broadening Arendt's (understandable but limiting) view that politics is the only and pre-eminent sphere of participation. There is also a dynamic quality to Habermas's public sphere which contrasts with the taint of supposed neutrality attached to the liberal definition. In Benhabib's account, 'the public sphere comes into existence whenever and wherever all affected by general social and political norms of action engage in a practical discourse, evaluating their validity' (Benhabib, 1992, p. 105). In contrast to the liberal limitation of the public sphere of discussion and legislation to those subjects necessary for what Rorty calls 'political cohesion', Benhabib (*ibid.*, p. 106) develops the view that 'in communicative ethics and in democratic politics we assume critical and reflective distance precisely toward those rules and practices which we also cannot avoid but uphold'. Earlier, she defines those rules and practices as the 'constitutive and regulative institutional norms of debate in democratic societies which cannot be transformed and abrogated by simple majority decisions' (*ibid.*, p. 107). Where Lyotard might come back is in the matter of whether such a model can account for the recognition 'that what remains to be phrased exceeds what [humans] can presently phrase, and that they must be allowed to institute idioms which do not yet exist' (Lyotard, 1988, p. 13). This is not central to Benhabib's analysis, however, and elsewhere in her book she invokes a feminist critique of Lyotard's version of postmodernism as damaging to the 'regulative ideal of enhancing the agency, autonomy and selfhood of women' (p. 214); however, using Carol Gilligan's work (see Reading 3.6), she also advances a feminist modification to the gender-blindness of discursive, liberal and republican models of the public sphere and their relation to the supposedly private sphere.

It is not surprising to find that the discussion of ethics and politics, within the context of arguments about post-foundationalism, has spread into the field of colonial discourse, subaltern studies and feminism via the concepts of difference and otherness. There is no easy way to generalise this new concern, since alongside the revised and more circumspect ethics of sameness (Nussbaum; Habermas and, in Rorty's reporting of him, John Rawls to an extent), the Readings below include an ethics and a politics of radical alterity (Emmanuel Lévinas, Lyotard, to the degree indicated in the comments above, and Luce Irigaray [Reading 5.6]). Lévinas, for instance, offers an ethics which starts from an acceptance not of commonality but of irreducible otherness. In rejecting the Hegelian subsumption of otherness in an 'absolute freedom', Lévinas proposes an absolute otherness 'with an alterity that is not formal, is not the simple reverse of identity, and is not formed out of resistance to the same, but is prior to every initiative, to all imperialism of the same. It is other with an alterity constitutive of the very content of the other' (Lévinas, 1969, p. 38). Since this radical otherness disturbs one's own self, a response is required which is also a responsibility for the other. It is this sense of obligation – sometimes regarded as a form of violence – which Lyotard translates into the form of senders and addressees of sentences. For Lévinas, however, this is the ethical encounter, indicating that he regards the ethical as absolutely prior to all other relations: it is 'the face to face'. Lévinas does not look for the collapsing of the other into the same but asks what we do about the other. There is reciprocity in this relationship. The self's autonomy is questioned but not dispersed. The self, meeting the other, becomes itself, and philosophy begins from this encounter: 'The fact that the other, my neighbor, is also a third party with respect to another, who is also a neighbor, is the birth of thought, consciousness, justice and philosophy' (Lévinas, 1981, p. 128).

Luce Irigaray's significance for psychoanalytic and feminist thought has already been introduced in earlier Sections, but since the late 1980s she has drawn out the ethical challenge latent in her own intentions in both of those intellectual spheres. Thus, her 'Questions to Emmanuel Lévinas' expands upon the suggestion that when Lévinas cares for the other precisely as other, he risks denying the feminine other. The feminine other is in danger of being reduced to the stimulus for Lévinas's own 'birth' in the general senses identified in the statement above. For Irigaray, Lévinas's laudable effort to respect 'the mystery of the other' makes it likely that when he theorises woman he will have no way back from the patriarchal equation between mystery and nature, 'the darkness of a pseudo-animality'. 'The feminine other', she remarks, 'is left without her own specific face. On this point his philosophy falls radically short of ethics' (Irigaray, 1991). However, as the earlier discussion of the essays in *This Sex Which Is Not One* indicates, to deconstruct sexual difference, even – or perhaps especially – when woman becomes the crucial excess which dismantles any system (the idea of 'reading as a woman'), is to fail to confront the power of essentialism both to confine women and as the focus for self-definition. Essentialism or nature, here, functions as a strategic risk. Men, too, fail to achieve self-definition by exporting 'nature' to the feminine domain through symbolisation. But Irigaray's chief concern in Reading 5.6 and in a related essay, 'The necessity for sexuate rights', is with the urgent need to recognise sexual difference in law through rights, a concept which has been reinvigorated by the attention it is now receiving from contrasting spheres of political thought (John Rawls comes to mind again, as does the rediscovery of Hannah Arendt through the work of Benhabib and Habermas) and from feminist theory.

It is Derrida, however, who prompts the most surprising criticism of Lévinas, and it has a particular use in post-colonial theory. 'If the other was not recognized as ego,' Derrida observes, 'its entire alterity would collapse.' He adds that 'the other is absolutely other only if he is an ego, that is, in a certain way, if he is the same as I' (Derrida, 1978, pp. 125, 127). Martha Nussbaum's incautious characterisation of Derrida at the end of Reading 5.7 is less to be recommended than her determined (and controversial) attempt to reconstruct a non-essentialist sameness which we can discern from time to time in Derrida. She has important things to say, notably that to recognise the other as human is to recognise a degree of commonality. She rejects the prevailing orthodoxy that to respond with sympathy, recognition and under-standing is necessarily to enter an imperialist engagement. It is worth stressing that she situates her cautioning against the possible blindnesses of difference as a concept in the international context of development economics. How to connect is not a question that can be evaded in such a context; which is not to say that Nussbaum comes up with a wholly satisfying explanation of what 'an essentialism of a kind' might be (for a different approach, see Fuss, 1989); but she wants to urge critical consideration of what levels of justice a society without any essentialism might achieve by way of recognising and reforming wrongs. Richard Bernstein is more circumspect than Nussbaum, but he also is worried at the easy recourse to difference and incommensurability in contemporary theory. He accepts that

> we can never escape the real practical possibility that we will fail to do justice to the alterity of 'the Other'. ... But the response to this practical failure should be an ethical one – to assume the responsibility to acknowledge, appreciate and not to violate the alterity of 'the Other'. Without such acknowledgement and recognition no ethics is possible. (Bernstein, 1991, p. 74)

The implied contrast is between an ethical response and a theoretical one which would turn any failure to communicate and any limit case into an absolute theory – this time, of difference.

5.1 □ *The Priority of Democracy to Philosophy*

Richard Rorty

Thomas Jefferson set the tone for American liberal politics when he said 'it does me no injury for my neighbor to say that there are twenty Gods or no God'.[1] His example helped make respectable the idea that politics can be separated from beliefs about matters of ultimate importance – that shared beliefs among citizens on such matters are not essential to a democratic society. Like many other figures of the Enlightenment, Jefferson assumed that a moral faculty common to the typical theist and the typical atheist suffices for civic virtue.

Many Enlightenment intellectuals were willing to go further and say that since religious beliefs turn out to be inessential for political cohesion, they should simply be discarded as mumbo jumbo – perhaps to be replaced (as in twentieth-century totalitarian Marxist states) with some sort of explicitly secular political faith that will form the moral consciousness of the citizen. Jefferson again set the tone when he refused to go that far. He thought it enough to privatize religion, to view it as irrelevant to social order but relevant to, and possibly essential for, individual perfection. Citizens of a Jeffersonian democracy can be as religious or irreligious as they please as long as they are not 'fanatical'. That is, they must abandon or modify opinions on matters of ultimate importance, the opinions that may hitherto have given sense and point to their lives, if these opinions entail public actions that cannot be justified to most of their fellow citizens.

This Jeffersonian compromise concerning the relation of spiritual perfection to public policy has two sides. Its absolutist side says that every human being, without the benefit of special revelation, has all the beliefs necessary for civic virtue. These beliefs spring from a universal human faculty, conscience – possession of which constitutes the specifically human essence of each human being. This is the faculty

From Rorty, R., *Objectivity, Relativism, and Truth: Philosophical papers*, vol. 1, Cambridge University Press, Cambridge, 1991, pp. 175–81, 183–96.

that gives the individual human dignity and rights. But there is also a pragmatic side. This side says that when the individual finds in her conscience beliefs that are relevant to public policy but incapable of defense on the basis of beliefs common to her fellow citizens, she must sacrifice her conscience on the altar of public expediency.

The tension between these two sides can be eliminated by a philosophical theory that identifies justifiability to humanity at large with truth. The Enlightenment idea of 'reason' embodies such a theory: the theory that there is a relation between the ahistorical essence of the human soul and moral truth, a relation which ensures that free and open discussion will produce 'one right answer' to moral as well as to scientific questions.[2] Such a theory guarantees that a moral belief that cannot be justified to the mass of mankind is 'irrational', and thus is not really a product of our moral faculty at all. Rather, it is a 'prejudice', a belief that comes from some other part of the soul than 'reason'. It does not share in the sanctity of conscience, for it is the product of a sort of pseudoconscience – something whose loss is no sacrifice, but a purgation.

In our century, this rationalist justification of the Enlightenment compromise has been discredited. Contemporary intellectuals have given up the Enlightenment assumption that religion, myth, and tradition can be opposed to something ahistorical, something common to all human beings *qua* human. Anthropologists and historians of science have blurred the distinction between innate rationality and the products of acculturation. Philosophers such as Heidegger and Gadamer have given us ways of seeing human beings as historical all the way through. Other philosophers, such as Quine and Davidson, have blurred the distinction between permanent truths of reason and temporary truths of fact. Psychoanalysis has blurred the distinction between conscience and the emotions of love, hate, and fear, and thus the distinction between morality and prudence. The result is to erase the picture of the self common to Greek metaphysics, Christian theology and Enlightenment rationalism: the picture of an ahistorical natural center, the locus of human dignity, surrounded by an adventitious and inessential periphery.

The effect of erasing this picture is to break the link between truth and justifiability. This, in turn, breaks down the bridge between the two sides of the Enlightenment compromise. The effect is to polarize liberal social theory. If we stay on the absolutist side, we shall talk about inalienable 'human rights' and about 'one right answer' to moral and political dilemmas without trying to back up such talk with a theory of human nature. We shall abandon metaphysical accounts of what a right is while nevertheless insisting that everywhere, in all times and cultures, members of our species have had the same rights. But if we swing to the pragmatist side, and consider talk of 'rights' an attempt to enjoy the benefits of metaphysics without assuming the appropriate responsibilities, we shall still need something to distinguish the sort of individual conscience we respect from the sort we condemn as 'fanatical'. This can only be something relatively local and ethnocentric – the tradition of a particular community, the consensus of a particular culture. According to this view, what counts as rational or as fanatical is relative to the group to which we think it necessary to justify ourselves – to the body of shared belief that determines the reference of the word 'we'. The Kantian identification with a central transcultural and ahistorical self is thus replaced by a quasi-Hegelian identification with our own community, thought of as a historical product. For pragmatist social theory, the question of whether justifiability to the community with which we identify entails truth is simply irrelevant.

Ronald Dworkin and others who take the notion of ahistorical human 'rights' seriously serve as examples of the first, absolutist, pole. John Dewey and, as I shall shortly be arguing, John Rawls serve as examples of the second pole. But there is a third type of social theory – often dubbed 'communitarianism' – which is less easy to place. Roughly speaking, the writers tagged with this label are those who reject both the individualistic rationalism of the Enlightenment and the idea of 'rights', but unlike the pragmatists, see this rejection as throwing doubt on the institutions and culture of the surviving democratic states. Such theorists include Robert Bellah, Alasdair MacIntyre, Michael Sandel, Charles Taylor, early Roberto Unger, and many others. These writers share some measure of agreement with a view found in an extreme form both in Heidegger and in Horkheimer and Adorno's *Dialectic of Enlightenment*. This is the view that liberal institutions and culture either should not or cannot survive the collapse of the philosophical justification that the Enlightenment provided for them.

There are three strands in communitarianism that need to be disentangled. First, there is the empirical prediction that no society that sets aside the idea of ahistorical moral truth in the insouciant way that Dewey recommended can survive. Horkheimer and Adorno, for example, suspect that you cannot have a moral community in a disenchanted world because toleration leads to pragmatism, and it is not clear how we can prevent 'blindly pragmatized thought' from losing 'its transcending quality and its relation to truth'.[3] They think that pragmatism was the inevitable outcome of Enlightenment rationalism and that pragmatism is not a strong enough philosophy to make moral community possible.[4] Second, there is the moral judgment that the sort of human being who is produced by liberal institutions and culture is undesirable. MacIntyre for example, thinks that our culture – a culture he says is dominated by 'the Rich Aesthete, the Manager, and the Therapist' – is a *reductio ad absurdum* both of the philosophical views that helped create it and of those now invoked in its defense. Third, there is the claim that political institutions 'presuppose' a doctrine about the nature of human beings and that such a doctrine must, unlike Enlightenment rationalism, make clear the essentially historical character of the self. So we find writers like Taylor and Sandel saying that we need a theory of the self that incorporates Hegel's and Heidegger's sense of the self's historicity.

The first claim is a straightforward empirical, sociological-historical one about the sort of glue that is required to hold a community together. The second is a straightforward moral judgment that the advantages of contemporary liberal democracy are outweighed by the disadvantages, by the ignoble and sordid character of the culture and the individual human beings that it produces. The third claim, however, is the most puzzling and complex. I shall concentrate on this third, most puzzling, claim, although toward the end I shall return briefly to the first two.

To evaluate this third claim, we need to ask two questions. The first is whether there is any sense in which liberal democracy 'needs' philosophical justification at all. Those who share Dewey's pragmatism will say that although it may need philosophical articulation, it does not need philosophical backup. On this view, the philosopher of liberal democracy may wish to develop a theory of the human self that comports with the institutions he or she admires. But such a philosopher is not thereby justifying these institutions by reference to more fundamental premises, but the reverse: He or she is putting politics first and tailoring a philosophy to suit. Communitarians, by contrast, often speak as though political institutions were no better than their philosophical foundations.

The second question is one that we can ask even if we put the opposition between justification and articulation to one side. It is the question of whether a conception of the self that, as Taylor says, makes 'the community constitutive of the individual'[5] does in fact comport better with liberal democracy than does the Enlightenment conception of the self. Taylor summarizes the latter as 'an ideal of disengagement' that defines a 'typically modern notion' of human dignity: 'the ability to act on one's own, without outside interference or subordination to outside authority'. On Taylor's view, as on Heidegger's, these Enlightenment notions are closely linked with characteristically modern ideas of 'efficacy, power, unperturbability'.[6] They are also closely linked with the contemporary form of the doctrine of the sacredness of the individual conscience – Dworkin's claim that appeals to rights 'trump' all other appeals. Taylor, like Heidegger, would like to substitute a less individualistic conception of what it is to be properly human – one that makes less of autonomy and more of interdependence.

I can preview what is to come by saying that I shall answer 'no' to the first question about the communitarians' third claim and 'yes' to the second. I shall be arguing that Rawls, following up on Dewey, shows us how liberal democracy can get along without philosophical presuppositions. He has thus shown us how we can disregard the third communitarian claim. But I shall also argue that communitarians like Taylor are right in saying that a conception of the self that makes the community constitutive of the self does comport well with liberal democracy. That is, if we *want* to flesh out our self-image as citizens of such a democracy with a philosophical view of the self, Taylor gives us pretty much the right view. But this sort of philosophical fleshing-out does not have the importance that writers like Horkheimer and Adorno, or Heidegger, have attributed to it.

Without further preface, I turn now to Rawls. I shall begin by pointing out that both in *A Theory of Justice* and subsequently, he has linked his own position to the Jeffersonian ideal of religious toleration. In an article called 'Justice as fairness:

political not metaphysical', he says that he is 'going to apply the principle of toleration to philosophy itself', and goes on to say:

> The essential point is this: as a practical political matter no general moral conception can provide the basis for a public conception of justice in a modern democratic society. The social and historical conditions of such a society have their origins in the Wars of Religion following the Reformation and the development of the principle of toleration, and in the growth of constitutional government and the institutions of large market economies. These conditions profoundly affect the requirements of a workable conception of political justice: such a conception must allow for a diversity of doctrines and the plurality of conflicting, and indeed incommensurable conceptions of the good affirmed by the members of existing democratic societies.[7]

We can think of Rawls as saying that just as the principle of religious toleration and the social thought of the Enlightenment proposed to bracket many standard theological topics when deliberating about public policy and constructing political institutions, so we need to bracket many standard topics of philosophical inquiry. For purposes of social theory, we can put aside such topics as an ahistorical human nature, the nature of selfhood, the motive of moral behavior, and the meaning of human life. We treat these as irrelevant to politics as Jefferson thought questions about the Trinity and about transubstantiation.

In so far as he adopts this stance, Rawls disarms many of the criticisms that, in the wake of Horkheimer and Adorno, have been directed at American liberalism. Rawls can agree that Jefferson and his circle shared a lot of dubious philosophical views, views that we might now wish to reject. He can even agree with Horkheimer and Adorno, as Dewey would have, that these views contained the seeds of their own destruction. But he thinks that the remedy may be not to formulate better philosophical views on the same topics, but (for purposes of political theory) benignly to neglect these topics. As he says:

> since justice as fairness is intended as a political conception of justice for a democratic society, it tries to draw solely upon basic intuitive ideas that are embedded in the political institutions of a democratic society and the public traditions of their interpretation. Justice as fairness is a political conception in part because it starts from within a certain political tradition. We hope that this political conception of justice may be at least supported by what we may call 'overlapping consensus', that is, by a consensus that includes all the opposing philosophical and religious doctrines likely to persist and gain adherents in a more or less just constitutional democratic society.[8]

Rawls thinks that 'philosophy as the search for truth about an independent metaphysical and moral order cannot ... provide a workable and shared basis for a political conception of justice in a democratic society'.[9] So he suggests that we confine ourselves to collecting 'such settled convictions as the belief in religious toleration and the rejection of slavery', and then 'try to organize the basic intuitive ideas and principles implicit in these convictions into a coherent conception of justice'.[10]

This attitude is thoroughly historicist and antiuniversalist.[11] Rawls can wholeheartedly agree with Hegel and Dewey against Kant and can say that the Enlightenment attempt to free oneself from tradition and history, to appeal to 'Nature' or 'Reason' was self-deceptive.[12] He can see such an appeal as a misguided attempt to make philosophy do what theology failed to do. Rawls's effort to, in his words, 'stay on the surface, philosophically speaking' can be seen as taking Jefferson's avoidance of theology one step further.

[. . .]

Rawls wants views about man's nature and purpose to be detached from politics. As he says, he wants his conception of justice to 'avoid ... claims about the essential nature and identity of persons'.[13] So presumably, he wants questions about the point of human existence, or the meaning of human life, to be reserved for private life. A liberal democracy will not only exempt opinions on such matters from legal coercion, but also aim at disengaging discussions of such questions from discussions of social policy. Yet it will use force against the individual conscience, just in so far as conscience leads individuals to act so as to threaten democratic institutions. Unlike Jefferson's, Rawls's argument against fanaticism is not that it threatens truth about the characteristics of an antecedent metaphysical and moral order by threatening free discussion, but *simply* that it threatens freedom, and thus threatens justice. Truth about the existence or nature of that order drops out.

The definition of 'philosophy' I have just suggested is not as artificial and *ad hoc* as it may appear. Intellectual historians commonly treat 'the nature of the human subject' as the topic that gradually replaced 'God' as European culture secularized itself. This has been the central topic of metaphysics and epistemology from the seventeenth century to the present, and, for better or worse, metaphysics and epistemology have been taken to be the 'core' of philosophy.[14] In so far as one thinks that political conclusions require extrapolitical grounding – that is, in so far as one thinks Rawls's method of reflective equilibrium[15] is not good enough – one will want an account of the 'authority' of those general principles.

If one feels a need for such legitimation, one will want either a religious or a philosophical preface to politics.[16] One will be likely to share Horkheimer and Adorno's fear that pragmatism is not strong enough to hold a free society together. But Rawls echoes Dewey in suggesting that in so far as justice becomes the first virtue of a society, the need for such legitimation may gradually cease to be felt. Such a society will become accustomed to the thought that social policy needs no more authority than successful accommodation among individuals, individuals who find themselves heir to the same historical traditions and faced with the same problems. It will be a society that encourages the 'end of ideology', that takes reflective equilibrium as the only method needed in discussing social policy. When such a society deliberates, when it collects the principles and intuitions to be brought into equilibrium, it will tend to discard those drawn from philosophical accounts of the self or of rationality. For such a society will view such accounts not as the foundations of political institutions, but as, at worst, philosophical mumbo jumbo, or, at best, relevant to private searches for perfection, but not to social policy.[17]

In order to spell out the contrast between Rawls's attempt to 'stay on the surface, philosophically speaking' and the traditional attempt to dig down to 'philosophical foundations of democracy', I shall turn briefly to Sandel's *Liberalism and the Limits of Justice*. This clear and forceful book provides very elegant and cogent arguments against the attempt to use a certain conception of the self, a certain metaphysical view of what human beings are like, to legitimize liberal politics. Sandel attributes this attempt to Rawls. Many people, including myself, initially took Rawls's *A Theory of Justice* to be such an attempt. We read it as a continuation of the Enlightenment attempt to ground our moral intuitions on a conception of human nature (and, more specifically, as a neo-Kantian attempt to ground them on the notion of 'rationality').

[. . .]

But reading *A Theory of Justice* as political rather than metaphysical, one can see that when Rawls says that 'the self is prior to the ends which are affirmed by it',[18] he need not mean that there is an entity called 'the self' that is something distinct from the web of beliefs and desires that that self 'has'. When he says that 'we should not attempt to give form to our life by first looking to the good independently defined',[19] he is not basing this 'should' on a claim about the nature of the self. 'Should' is not to be glossed by 'because of the intrinsic nature of morality'[20] or 'because a capacity for choice is the essence of personhood', but by something like 'because *we* – we modern inheritors of the traditions of religious tolerance and constitutional government – put liberty ahead of perfection'.

This willingness to invoke what *we* do raises, as I have said, the specters of ethnocentrism and of relativism. Because Sandel is convinced that Rawls shares Kant's fear of these specters, he is convinced that Rawls is looking for an '"Archimedean point" from which to assess the basic structure of society' – a 'standpoint neither compromised by its implication in the world nor dissociated and so disqualified by detachment'.[21] It is just this idea that a standpoint can be 'compromised by its implication in the world' that Rawls rejects in his recent writings. Philosophically inclined communitarians like Sandel are unable to envisage a middle ground between relativism and a 'theory of the moral subject' – a theory that is not about, for example, religious tolerance and large market economies, but about human beings as such, viewed ahistorically. Rawls is trying to stake out just such a middle ground.[22] When he speaks of an 'Archimedian point', he does not mean a point outside history, but simply the kind of settled social habits that allow much latitude for further choices.

[. . .]

[We] heirs of the Enlightenment think of enemies of liberal democracy like Nietzsche or Loyola as, to use Rawls's word, 'mad'. We do so because there is no way to see them as fellow citizens of our constitutional democracy, people whose life plans might, given ingenuity and goodwill, be fitted in with those of other citizens. They are not crazy because they have mistaken the ahistorical nature of human beings. They are crazy because the limits of sanity are set by what we can take seriously. This, in turn, is determined by our upbringing, our historical situation.[23]

If this short way of dealing with Nietzsche and Loyola seems shockingly ethnocentric, it is because the philosophical tradition has accustomed us to the idea that anybody who is willing to listen to reason – to hear out all the arguments – can be brought around to the truth. This view, which Kierkegaard called 'Socratism' and contrasted with the claim that our point of departure may be simply a historical event, is intertwined with the idea that the human self has a center (a divine spark, or a truth-tracking faculty called 'reason') and that argumentation will, given time and patience, penetrate to this center. For Rawls's purposes, we do not need this picture. We are free to see the self as centerless, as a historical contingency all the way through. Rawls neither needs nor wants to defend the priority of the right to the good as Kant defended it, by invoking a theory of the self that makes it more than an 'empirical self', more than a 'radically situated subject'. He presumably thinks of Kant as, although largely right about the nature of justice, largely wrong about the nature and function of philosophy.

More specifically, he can reject Sandel's Kantian claim that there is a 'distance between subject and situation which is necessary to any measure of detachment, is essential to the ineliminably *possessive* aspect of any coherent conception of the self'.[24] Sandel defines this aspect by saying, 'I can never fully be constituted by my attributes ... there must always be some attributes I *have* rather than am'. On the interpretation of Rawls I am offering, we do not need a categorical distinction between the self and its situation. We can dismiss the distinction between an attribute of the self and a constituent of the self, between the self's accidents and its essence, as 'merely' metaphysical.[25] If we are inclined to philosophize, we shall want the vocabulary offered by Dewey, Heidegger, Davidson, and Derrida, with its built-in cautions against metaphysics, rather than that offered by Descartes, Hume, and Kant.[26] For if we use the former vocabulary, we shall be able to see moral progress as a history of making rather than finding, of poetic achievement by 'radically situated' individuals and communities, rather than as the gradual unveiling, through the use of 'reason', of 'principles' or 'rights' or 'values'.

Sandel's claim that 'the concept of a subject given prior to and independent of its objects offers a foundation for the moral law that ... powerfully completes the deontological vision' is true enough. But to suggest such a powerful completion to Rawls is to offer him a poisoned gift. It is like offering Jefferson an argument for religious tolerance based on exegesis of the Christian Scriptures'.[27] Rejecting the assumption that the moral law needs a 'foundation' is just what distinguishes Rawls from Jefferson. It is just this that permits him to be a Deweyan naturalist who needs neither the distinction between will and intellect nor the distinction between the self's constituents and its attributes. He does not *want* a 'complete deontological vision', one that would explain *why* we should give justice priority over our conception of the good. He is filling out the consequences of the claim that it is prior, not its presuppositions.[28] Rawls is not interested in conditions for the identity of the self, but only in conditions for citizenship in a liberal society.

Suppose one grants that Rawls is not attempting a transcendental deduction of American liberalism or supplying philosophical foundations for democratic institutions, but simply trying to systematize the principles and intuitions typical of American liberals. Still, it may seem that the important questions raised by the critics of liberalism have been begged. Consider the claim that we liberals can simply dismiss Nietzsche and Loyola as crazy. One imagines these two rejoining that they are quite aware that their views unfit them for citizenship in a constitutional democracy and that the typical inhabitant of such a democracy would regard them as crazy. But they take these facts as further counts against constitutional democracy. They think that the kind of person created by such a democracy is not what a human being should be.

In finding a dialectical stance to adopt toward Nietzsche or Loyola, we liberal democrats are faced with a dilemma. To refuse to argue about what human beings should be like seems to show a contempt for the spirit of accommodation and tolerance, which is essential to democracy. But it is not clear how to argue for the claim that human beings ought to be liberals rather than fanatics without being driven back on a theory of human nature, on philosophy. I think that we must grasp the first horn. We have to insist that not every argument needs to be met in the terms in which it is presented. Accommodation and tolerance must stop short of a willingness to work within any vocabulary that one's interlocutor wishes to use, to take seriously any topic that he puts forward for discussion. To take this view is of a piece with dropping the idea that a single moral vocabulary and a single set of moral beliefs are appropriate for every human community everywhere, and to grant that historical developments may lead us to simply *drop* questions and the vocabulary in which those questions are posed.

Just as Jefferson refused to let the Christian Scriptures set the terms in which to discuss alternative political institutions, so we either must refuse to answer the question 'What sort of human being are you hoping to produce?' or, at least, must not let our answer to this question dictate our answer to the question 'Is justice primary?'[29] It is no more evident that democratic institutions are to be measured by the sort of person they create than that they are to be measured against divine commands. It is not evident that they are to be measured by anything more specific than the moral intuitions of the particular historical community that has created those institutions. The idea that moral and political controversies should always be 'brought back to first principles' is reasonable if it means merely that we should seek common ground in the hope of attaining agreement. But it is misleading if it is taken as the claim that there is a natural order of premises from which moral and political conclusions are to be inferred – not to mention the claim that some particular interlocutor (for example, Nietzsche or Loyola) has already discerned that order. The liberal response to the communitarians' second claim must be, therefore, that even if the typical character types of liberal democracies *are* bland, calculating, petty, and unheroic, the prevalence of such people may be a reasonable price to pay for political freedom.

The spirit of accommodation and tolerance certainly suggests that we should seek common ground with Nietzsche and Loyola, but there is no predicting where, or whether, such common ground will be found. The philosophical tradition has assumed that there are certain topics (for example, 'What is God's will?', 'What is man?', 'What rights are intrinsic to the species?') on which everyone has, or should have, views, and that these topics are prior in the order of justification to those at issue in political deliberation. This assumption goes along with the assumption that human beings have a natural center that philosophical inquiry can locate and illuminate. By contrast, the view that human beings are centerless networks of beliefs and desires and that their vocabularies and opinions are determined by historical circumstance allows for the possibility that there may not be enough overlap between two such networks to make possible agreement about political topics, or even profitable discussion of such topics.[30] We do not conclude that Nietzsche and Loyola are crazy because they hold unusual views on certain 'fundamental' topics; rather, we conclude this only after extensive attempts at an exchange of political views have made us realize that we are not going to get anywhere.[31]

One can sum up this way of grasping the first horn of the dilemma I sketched earlier by saying that Rawls puts democratic politics first, and philosophy second. He retains the Socratic commitment to free exchange of views without the Platonic commitment to the possibility of universal agreement – a possibility underwritten by epistemological doctrines like Plato's Theory of Recollection[32] or Kant's theory of the relation between pure and empirical concepts. He disengages the question of whether we ought to be tolerant and Socratic from the question of whether this strategy will lead to truth. He is content that it should lead to whatever intersubjective reflective equilibrium may be obtainable, given the contingent make-up of the subjects in question. Truth, viewed in the Platonic way, as the grasp of what Rawls calls 'an order antecedent to and given to us', is simply not relevant to democratic politics. So philosophy, as the explanation of the relation between such an order and human nature, is not relevant either. When the two come into conflict, democracy takes precedence over philosophy.

This conclusion may seem liable to an obvious objection. It may seem that I have been rejecting a concern with philosophical theories about the nature of men and women on the basis of just such a theory. But notice that although I have frequently said that Rawls *can be content* with a notion of the human self as a centerless web of historically conditioned beliefs and desires, I have not suggested that he *needs* such a theory. Such a theory does not offer liberal social theory a *basis*. If one *wants* a model of the human self, then this picture of a centerless web will fill the need. But for purposes of liberal social theory, one can do without such a model. One can get along with common sense and social science, areas of discourse in which the term 'the self' rarely occurs.

If, however, one has a taste for philosophy – if one's vocation, one's private pursuit of perfection, entails constructing models of such entities as 'the self', 'knowledge', 'language', 'nature', 'God', or 'history', and then tinkering with them until they mesh with one another – one *will* want a picture of the self. Since my own vocation is of this sort, and the moral identity around which I wish to build such models is that of a citizen of a liberal democratic state, I commend the picture of the self as a centerless and contingent web to those with similar tastes and similar identities. But I would not commend it to those with a similar vocation but dissimilar moral identities – identities built, for example, around the love of God, Nietzschean self-overcoming, the accurate representation of reality as it is in itself, the quest for 'one right answer' to moral questions, or the natural superiority of a given character type. Such persons need a more complex and interesting, less simple-minded model of the self – one that meshes in complex ways with complex models of such things as 'nature' or 'history'. Nevertheless, such persons may, for pragmatic rather than moral reasons, be loyal citizens of a liberal democratic society. They may despise most of their fellow citizens, but be prepared to grant that the prevalence of such despicable character types is a lesser evil than the loss of political freedom. They may be ruefully grateful that their private senses of moral identity and the models of the human self that they develop to articulate this sense – the ways in which they deal with their aloneness – are not the concern of such a state. Rawls and Dewey have shown how the liberal state can ignore the difference between the moral identities of Glaucon and of Thrasymachus, just as it ignores the difference between the religious identities of a Catholic archbishop and a Mormon prophet.

There is, however, a flavor of paradox in this attitude toward theories of the self. One might be inclined to say that I have evaded one sort of self-referential paradox only by falling into another sort. For I am presupposing that one is at liberty to rig up a model of the self to suit oneself, to tailor it to one's politics, one's religion, or one's private sense of the meaning of one's life. This, in turn, presupposes that there is no 'objective truth' about what the human self is *really* like. That, in turn, seems a claim that could be justified only on the basis of a metaphysico-epistemological view of the traditional sort. For surely, if anything is the province of such a view, it is the question of what there is and is not a 'fact of the matter' about. So my argument must ultimately come back to philosophical first principles.

Here I can only say that if there were a discoverable fact of the matter about what there is a fact of the matter about, then it would doubtless be metaphysics and epistemology that would discover that meta-fact. But I think that the very idea of a 'fact of the matter' is one we would be better off without. Philosophers like Davidson and Derrida have, I think, given us good reason to think that the *physis–nomos*, *in se–ad nos*, and objective–subjective distinctions were steps on a ladder that we can now safely throw away. The question of whether the reasons such philosophers have given for this claim are themselves metaphysico-epistemological reasons, and if not, what sort of reasons they are, strikes me as pointless and sterile. Once again, I fall back on the holist's strategy of insisting that reflective equilibrium is all we need try for – that there is no natural order of justification of beliefs, no predestined outline for argument to trace. Getting rid of the idea of such an outline seems to me one of the many benefits of a conception of the self as a centerless web. Another benefit is that questions about whom we need justify ourselves to – questions about who counts as a fanatic and who deserves an answer – can be treated as just further matters to be sorted out in the course of attaining reflective equilibrium.

I can, however, make one point to offset the air of light-minded aestheticism I am adopting toward traditional philosophical questions. This is that there is a moral purpose behind this light-mindedness. The encouragement of light-mindedness about traditional philosophical topics serves the same purposes as does the encouragement of light-mindedness about traditional theological topics. Like the rise of large market economies, the increase in literacy, the proliferation of artistic genres, and the insouciant pluralism of contemporary culture, such philosophical superficiality and light-mindedness helps along the disenchantment of the world. It helps make the world's inhabitants more pragmatic, more tolerant, more liberal, more receptive to the appeal of instrumental rationality.

If one's moral identity consists in being a citizen of a liberal polity, then to encourage light-mindedness may serve one's moral purposes. Moral commitment, after all, does not require taking seriously all the matters that are, for moral reasons, taken seriously by one's fellow citizens. It may require just the opposite. It may require trying to josh them out of the habit of taking those topics so seriously. There may be serious reasons for so joshing them. More generally, we should not assume that the aesthetic is always the enemy of the moral. I should argue that in the recent history of liberal societies, the willingness to view matters aesthetically – to be content to indulge in what Schiller called 'play' and to discard what Nietzsche called 'the spirit of seriousness' – has been an important vehicle of moral progress.

I have now said everything I have to say about the third of the communitarian claims that I distinguished at the outset: the claim that the social theory of the liberal state rests on false philosophical presuppositions. I hope I have given reasons for thinking that in so far as the communitarian is a critic of liberalism, he should drop this claim and should instead develop either of the first two claims: the empirical claim that democratic institutions cannot be combined with the sense of common purpose predemocratic societies enjoyed, or the moral judgment that the products of the liberal state are too high a price to pay for the elimination of the evils that preceded it. If communitarian critics of liberalism stuck to these two claims, they would avoid the sort of terminal wistfulness with which their books typically end. Heidegger, for example, tells us that 'we are too late for the gods, and too early for Being'. Unger ends *Knowledge and Politics* with an appeal to a *Deus absconditus*. MacIntyre ends *After Virtue* by saying that we 'are waiting not for a Godot, but for another – doubtless very different – St. Benedict'.[33] Sandel ends his book by saying that liberalism 'forgets the possibility that when politics goes well, we can know a good in common that we cannot know alone', but he does not suggest a candidate for this common good.

Instead of thus suggesting that philosophical reflection, or a return to religion, might enable us to re-enchant the world, I think that communitarians should stick to the question of whether disenchantment has, on balance, done us more harm than good, or created more dangers than it has evaded. For Dewey, communal and public disenchantment is the price we pay for individual and private spiritual liberation, the kind of liberation that Emerson thought characteristically American. Dewey was as well aware as Weber that there is a price to be paid, but he thought it well worth paying. He assumed that no good achieved by earlier societies would be worth recapturing if the price were a diminution in our ability to leave people alone, to let them try out their private visions of perfection in peace. He admired the American habit of giving democracy priority over philosophy by asking, about any vision of the meaning of life, 'Would not acting out this vision interfere with the ability of others to work out their own salvation?' Giving priority to that question is no more 'natural' than giving priority to, say, MacIntyre's question 'What sorts of human beings emerge in the culture of liberalism?' or Sandel's question 'Can a community of those who put justice first ever be more than a community of strangers?' The question of which of these questions is prior to which others is, necessarily, begged by *everybody*. Nobody is being any more arbitrary than anybody else. But that is to say that nobody is being arbitrary at all. Everybody is just insisting that the beliefs and desires they hold most dear should come first in the order of discussion. That is not arbitrariness, but sincerity.

The danger of re-enchanting the world, from a Deweyan point of view, is that it might interfere with the development of what Rawls calls 'a social union of social unions',[34] some of which may be (and in Emerson's view, should be) very small indeed. For it is hard to be both enchanted with one version of the world and tolerant of all the others. I have not tried to argue the question of whether Dewey was right in this judgment of relative danger and promise. I have merely argued that such a judgment neither presupposes nor supports a theory of the self. Nor have I tried to deal with Horkheimer and Adorno's prediction that the 'dissolvent rationality' of the Enlightenment will eventually cause the liberal democracies to come unstuck.

The only thing I have to say about this prediction is that the collapse of the liberal democracies would not, in itself, provide much evidence for the claim that human societies cannot survive without widely shared opinions on matters of ultimate importance – shared conceptions of our place in the universe and our mission on earth. Perhaps they cannot survive under such conditions, but the eventual collapse of the democracies would not, in itself, show that this was the case – any more than it would show that human societies require kings or an established religion, or that political community cannot exist outside of small city-states.

Both Jefferson and Dewey described America as an 'experiment'. If the experiment fails, our descendants may learn something important. But they will not learn a philosophical truth, any more than they will learn a religious one. They will simply get some hints about what to watch out for when setting up their next experiment. Even if nothing else survives from the age of the democratic revolutions, perhaps our descendants will remember that social institutions *can* be viewed as experiments in cooperation rather than as attempts to embody a universal and ahistorical order. It is hard to believe that this memory would not be worth having.

Notes

1. Thomas Jefferson, *Notes on the State of Virginia*, Query XVII, in *The Writings of Thomas Jefferson*, ed. A. A. Lipscomb and A. E. Bergh (Washington, DC, 1905), 2: 217.
2. Jefferson included a statement of this familiar Scriptural claim (roughly in the form in which it had been restated by Milton in *Areopagitica*) in the preamble to the Virginia Statute for Religious Freedom: 'truth is great and will prevail if left to herself, ... she is the proper and sufficient antagonist to error, and has nothing to fear from the conflict, unless by human interposition disarmed of her natural weapons, free argument and debate, errors ceasing to be dangerous when it is permitted freely to contradict them' (*ibid.*, 2: 302).
3. Max Horkheimer and Theodor W. Adorno, *Dialectic of Enlightenment* (New York: Seabury Press, 1972), p. xiii.
4. 'For the Enlightenment, whatever does not conform to the rule of computation and utility is suspect. So long as it can develop undisturbed by any outward repression, there is no holding it. In the process, it treats its own ideas of human rights exactly as it does the older universals ... Enlightenment is totalitarian' (*ibid.*, p. 6). This line of thought recurs repeatedly in communitarian accounts of the present state of the liberal democracies; see, for example, Robert Bellah, Richard Madsen, William Sullivan, Ann Swidler and Steven Tipton, *Habits of the Heart: Individualism and commitment in American life* (Berkeley: University of California Press, 1985): 'There is a widespread feeling that the promise of the modern era is slipping away from us. A movement of enlightenment and liberation that was to have freed us from superstition and tyranny has led in the twentieth century to a world in which ideological fanaticism and political oppression have reached extremes unknown in previous history' (p. 277).
5. Charles Taylor, *Philosophy and the Human Sciences*, vol. 2 of *Philosophical Papers* (Cambridge: Cambridge University Press, 1985), p. 8.
6. *Ibid.*, p. 5.
7. John Rawls, 'Justice as fairness: political not metaphysical', *Philosophy and Public Affairs*, 14 (1985): 225. Religious toleration is a constantly recurring theme in Rawls's writing. Early in *A Theory of Justice* (Cambridge, MA.: Harvard University Press, 1971), when giving examples of the sort of common opinions that a theory of justice must take into account and systematize, he cites our conviction that religious intolerance is unjust (p. 19). His example of the fact that 'a well-ordered society tends to eliminate or at least to control men's inclinations to injustice' is that 'warring and intolerant sects are much less likely to exist' (p. 247). Another relevant passage (which I shall discuss below) is his diagnosis of Ignatius Loyola's attempt to make the love of God the 'dominant good'. 'Although to subordinate all our aims to one end does not strictly

speaking violate the principles of rational choice ... it still strikes us as irrational, or more likely as mad' (pp. 553–4).

8. Rawls, 'Justice as fairness', pp. 225–6. The suggestion that there are many philosophical views that will *not* survive in such conditions is analogous to the Enlightenment suggestion that the adoption of democratic institutions will cause 'superstitious' forms of religious belief gradually to die off.

9. *Ibid.*, p. 230.

10. *Ibid.*

11. For Rawls's historicism see, for example, *Theory of Justice*, p. 547. There, Rawls says that the people in the original position are assumed to know 'the general facts about society', including the fact that 'institutions are not fixed but change over time, altered by natural circumstances and the activities and conflicts of social groups'. He uses this point to rule out, as original choosers of principles of justice, those 'in a feudal or a caste system', and those who are unaware of events such as the French Revolution. This is one of many passages that make clear (at least read in the light of Rawls's later work) that a great deal of knowledge that came late to the mind of Europe is present to the minds of those behind the veil of ignorance. Or, to put it another way, such passages make clear that those original choosers behind the view exemplify a certain modern type of human being, not an ahistorical human nature. See also p. 548, where Rawls says 'Of course in working out what the requisite principles [of justice] are, we must rely upon current knowledge as recognized by common sense and the existing scientific consensus. We have to concede that as established beliefs change, it is possible that the principles of justice which it seems rational to choose may likewise change.'

12. See Bellah *et al.*, *Habits of the Heart*, p. 141, for a recent restatement of this 'counter-Enlightenment' line of thought. For the authors' view of the problems created by persistence in Enlightenment rhetoric and by the prevalence of the conception of human dignity that Taylor identifies as 'distinctively modern', see p. 21: 'For most of us, it is easier to think about to get what we want than to know exactly what we should want. Thus Brian, Joe, Margaret and Wayne [some of the Americans interviewed by the authors] are each in his or her own way confused about how to define for themselves such things as the nature of success, the meaning of freedom, and the requirements of justice. Those difficulties are in an important way created by the limitations in the common tradition of moral discourse they – and we – share.' Compare p. 290: 'the language of individualism, the primary American language of self-understanding, limits the way in which people think.'

   To my mind, the authors of *Habits of the Heart* undermine their own conclusions in the passages where they point to actual moral progress being made in recent American history, notably in their discussion of the civil rights movement. There, they say that Martin Luther King, Jr, made the struggle for freedom 'a practice of commitment within a vision of America as a community of memory', and that the response King elicited 'came from the reawakened recognition by many Americans that their own sense of self was rooted in companionship with others who, though not necessarily like themselves, nevertheless shared with them a common history and whose appeals to justice and solidarity made powerful claims on our loyalty' (p. 252). These descriptions of King's achievement seem exactly right, but they can be read as evidence that the rhetoric of the Enlightenment offers at least as many opportunities as it does obstacles for the renewal of a sense of community. The civil rights movement combined, without much strain, the language of Christian fellowship and the 'language of individualism', about which Bellah and his colleagues are dubious.

13. Rawls, 'Justice as fairness', p. 223.

14. In fact, it has been for the worse. A view that made politics more central to philosophy and subjectivity less would both permit more effective defenses of democracy than those

that purport to supply it with 'foundations' and permit liberals to meet Marxists on their own, political, ground. Dewey's explicit attempt to make the central philosophical question 'What serves democracy?' rather than 'What permits us to argue for democracy?' has been, unfortunately, neglected. I try to make this point in 'Philosophy as science, as metaphor, and as politics' (in *Essays on Heidegger and Others*).

15. That is, give-and-take between intuitions about the desirability of particular consequences of particular actions and intuitions about general principles, with neither having the determining voice.

16. One will also, as I did on first reading Rawls, take him to be attempting to supply such legitimation by an appeal to the rationality of the choosers in the original position. Rawls warned his readers that the original position (the position of those who, behind a veil of ignorance that hides them from their life chances and their conceptions of the good, select from among alternative principles of justice) served simply 'to make vivid ... the restrictions that it seems reasonable to impose on arguments for principles of justice and therefore on those principles themselves' (*Theory of Justice*, p. 18).

   But this warning went unheeded by myself and others, in part because of an ambiguity between 'reasonable' as defined by ahistorical criteria and as meaning something like 'in accord with the moral sentiments characteristic of the heirs of the Enlightenment'. Rawls's later work has, as I have said, helped us come down on the historicist side of this ambiguity; see, for example, 'Kantian constructivism': 'the original position is not an axiomatic (or deductive) basis from which principles are derived but a procedure for singling out principles most fitting to the conception of the person most likely to be held, at least implicitly, in a democratic society' (p. 572). It is tempting to suggest that one could eliminate all reference to the original position from *A Theory of Justice* without loss, but this is as daring a suggestion as that one might rewrite (as many have wished to do) Kant's *Critique of Pure Reason* without reference to the thing-in-itself. T. M. Scanlon has suggested that we can, at least, safely eliminate reference, in the description of the choosers in the original position, to an appeal to self-interest. 'Contractualism and utilitarianism', in *Utilitarianism and Beyond*, ed. Bernard Williams and Amartya Sen [Cambridge: Cambridge University Press, 1982]). Since justifiability is, more evidently than self-interest, relative to historical circumstance, Scanlon's proposal seems to be more faithful to Rawls's overall philosophical program than Rawls's own formulation.

17. In particular, there will be no principles or intuitions concerning the universal features of human psychology relevant to motivation. Sandel thinks that since assumptions about motivation are part of the description of the original position, 'what issues at one end in a theory of justice must issue at the other in a theory of the person, or more precisely, a theory of the moral subject' (*Liberalism and the Limits of Justice*, p. 47). I would argue that if we follow Scanlon's lead (Note 16) in dropping reference to self-interest in our description of the original choosers and replacing this with reference to their desire to justify their choices to their fellows, then the only 'theory of the person' we get is a sociological description of the inhabitants of contemporary liberal democracies.

18. Rawls, *Theory of Justice*, p. 560.

19. *Ibid.*

20. It is important to note that Rawls explicitly distances himself from the idea that he is analyzing the very idea of morality, and from conceptual analysis as the method of social theory (*ibid.*, p. 130). Some of his critics have suggested that Rawls is practicing 'reductive logical analysis' of the sort characteristic of 'analytic philosophy'; see, for example, William M. Sullivan, *Reconstructing Public Philosophy* (Berkeley: University of California Press, 1982), pp. 94 ff. Sullivan says that 'this ideal of reductive logical analysis lends legitimacy to the notion that moral philosophy is summed up in the task of discovering, through the analysis of moral rules, both primitive elements and governing principles that must apply to any rational moral system, *rational* here meaning

"logically coherent"' (p. 96). He goes on to grant that 'Nozick and Rawls are more sensitive to the importance of history and social experience in human life than were the classic liberal thinkers' (p. 97). But this concession is too slight and is misleading. Rawls's willingness to adopt 'reflective equilibrium' rather than 'conceptual analysis' as a methodological watchword sets him apart from the epistemologically oriented moral philosophy that was dominant prior to the appearance of *A Theory of Justice*. Rawls represents a reaction against the Kantian idea of 'morality' as having an ahistorical essence, the same sort of reaction found in Hegel and in Dewey.

21. Sandel, *Liberalism and the Limits of Justice*, p. 17.
22. '... liberty of conscience and freedom of thought should not be founded on philosophical or ethical skepticism, nor on indifference to religious and moral interests. The principles of justice define an appropriate path between dogmatism and intolerance on the one side, and a reductionism which regards religion and morality as mere preferences on the other' (Rawls, *Theory of Justice*, p. 243). I take it that Rawls is identifying 'philosophical or ethical skepticism' with the idea that everything is just a matter of 'preference', even religion, philosophy, and morals. So we should distinguish his suggestion that we 'extend the principle of toleration to philosophy itself' from the suggestion that we dismiss philosophy as epiphenomenal. That is the sort of suggestion that is backed up by reductionist accounts of philosophical doctrines as 'preferences' or 'wish fulfillments' or 'expressions of emotion' (see Rawls's criticism of Freudian reductionism in *ibid.*, pp. 539 ff.). Neither psychology nor logic nor any other theoretical discipline can supply non-question-begging reasons why philosophy should be set aside, any more than philosophy can supply such reasons why theology should be set aside. But this is compatible with saying that the general course of historical experience may lead us to neglect theological topics and bring us to the point at which, like Jefferson, we find a theological vocabulary 'meaninglesss' (or, more precisely, useless). I am suggesting that the course of historical experience since Jefferson's time has led us to a point at which we find much of the vocabulary of modern philosophy no longer useful.
23. 'Aristotle remarks that it is a peculiarity of men that they possess a sense of the just and the unjust and that their sharing a common understanding of justice makes a polis. Analogously one might say, in view of our discussion, that a common understanding of justice as fairness makes a constitutional democracy' (Rawls, *Theory of Justice*, p. 243). In the interpretation of Rawls I am offering, it is unrealistic to expect Aristotle to have developed a conception of justice as fairness, since he simply lacked the kind of historical experience that we have accumulated since his day. More generally, it is pointless to assume (with, for example, Leo Strauss) that the Greeks had already canvassed the alternatives available for social life and institutions. When we discuss justice, we cannot agree to bracket our knowledge of recent history.
24. Sandel, *Liberalism and the Limits of Justice*, p. 20.
25. We can dismiss other distinctions that Sandel draws in the same way. Examples are the distinction between a voluntarist and a cognitive account of the original position (*ibid.*, p. 121), that between 'the identity of the subject', as the 'product' rather than the 'premise' of its agency (*ibid.*, p. 152), and that between the question 'Who am I?'and its rival as 'the paradigmatic moral question', 'What shall I choose?' (*ibid.*, p. 153). These distinctions are all to be analyzed away as products of the 'Kantian dualism' that Rawls praises Hegel and Dewey for having overcome.
26. For some similarities between Dewey and Heidegger with respect to anti-Cartesianism, see my 'Overcoming the tradition', in Richard Rorty, *Consequences of Pragmatism* (Minneapolis: University of Minnesota Press, 1982).
27. David Levin has pointed out to me that Jefferson was not above borrowing such arguments. I take this to show that Jefferson, like Kant, found himself in an untenable halfway position between theology and Deweyan social experimentalism.

28. Sandel takes 'the primacy of the subject' to be not only a way of filling out the deontological picture, but also a necessary condition of its correctness: 'If the claim for the primacy of justice is to succeed, if the right is to be prior to the good in the interlocking moral and foundational sense we have distinguished, then some version of the claim for the primacy of the subject must succeed as well' (*Liberalism and the Limits of Justice*, p. 7). Sandel quotes Rawls as saying that 'the essential unity of the self is already provided by the conception of the right', and takes this passage as evidence that Rawls holds a doctrine of the 'priority of the self' (*ibid.*, p. 21). But consider the context of this sentence. Rawls says: 'The principles of justice and their realization in social forms define the bounds within which our deliberations take place. The essential unity of the self is already provided by the conception of right. Moreover, in a well-ordered society this unity is the same for all; everyone's conception of the good as given by his rational plan is a sub-plan of the larger comprehensive plan that regulates the community as a social union of social unions' (*Theory of Justice*, p. 563). The 'essential unity of the self', which is in question here, is simply the system of moral sentiments, habits, and internalized traditions that is typical of the politically aware citizen of a constitutional democracy. This self is, once again, a historical product. It has nothing to do with the nonempirical self, which Kant had to postulate in the interests of Enlightenment universalism.

29. This is the kernel of truth in Dworkin's claim that Rawls rejects 'goal-based' social theory, but this point should not lead us to think that he is thereby driven back on a 'rights-based' theory.

30. But one should not press this point so far as to raise the specter of 'untranslatable languages'. As Donald Davidson has remarked, we would not recognize other organisms as actual or potential language users – or, therefore, as persons – unless there were enough overlap in belief and desire to make translation possible. The point is merely that efficient and frequent communication is only a necessary, not a sufficient, condition of agreement.

31. Further, such a conclusion is *restricted* to politics. It does not cast doubt on the ability of these men to follow the rules of logic, or their ability to do many other things skillfully and well. It is thus not equivalent to the traditional philosophical charge of 'irrationality'. That charge presupposes that inability to 'see' certain truths is evidence of the lack of an organ that is essential for human functioning generally.

32. In Kierkegaard's *Philosophical Fragments*, we find the Platonic Theory of Recollection treated as the archetypal justification of 'Socratism' and thus as the symbol of all forms (especially Hegel's) of what Bernard Williams has recently called 'the rationalist theory of rationality' – the idea that one is rational only if one can appeal to universally accepted criteria, criteria whose truth and applicability all human beings can find 'in their heart'. This is the philosophical core of the Scriptural idea that 'truth is great, and will prevail', when the idea is dissociated from the idea of 'a New Being' (in the way that Kierkegaard refused to dissociate it).

33. See Jeffrey Stout's discussion of the manifold ambiguities of this conclusion in 'Virtue among the ruins: an essay on MacIntyre', *Newe Zeitschrift für Systematische Theologie und Religionsphilosophie*, 26 (1984): 256–73, especially 269.

34. This is Rawls's description of 'a well-ordered society (corresponding to justice as fairness)' (*Theory of Justice*, p. 527). Sandel finds these passages metaphorical, and complains that 'intersubjective and individualistic images appear in uneasy, sometimes unfelicitous combination, as if to betray the incompatible commitments contending within' (*Liberalism and the Limits of Justice*, pp. 150 ff.). He concludes that 'the moral vocabulary of community in the strong sense cannot in all cases be captured by a conception that [as Rawls has said his is] 'in its theoretical bases is individualistic'. I am claiming that these commitments will look incompatible only if one attempts to define

their philosophical presuppositions (which Rawls himself may occasionally have done too much of), and that this is a good reason for not making such attempts. Compare the Enlightenment view that attempts to sharpen up the theological presuppositions of social commitments had done more harm than good, and that if theology cannot simply be discarded, it should at least be left as fuzzy (or, one might say, 'liberal') as possible. Oakeshott has a point when he insists on the value of theoretical muddle for the health of the state.

Elsewhere Rawls has claimed that 'there is no reason why a well-ordered society should encourage primarily individualistic values if this means ways of life that lead individuals to pursue their own way and to have no concern for the interest of others' ('Fairness to goodness', *Philosophical Review*, 84 [1975]: 550). Sandel's discussion of this passage says that it 'suggests a deeper sense in which Rawls' conception is individualistic', but his argument that this suggestion is correct is, once again, the claim that 'the Rawlsian self is not only a subject of possession, but an antecedently individuated subject' (*Liberalism and the Limits of Justice*, pp. 61 ff.). This is just the claim I have been arguing against by arguing that there is no such thing as 'the Rawlsian self', and that Rawls does not want or need a 'theory of the person'. Sandel says (p. 62) that Rawls 'takes for granted that every individual consists of one and only one system of desires', but it is hard to find evidence for this claim in the texts. At worst, Rawls simplifies his presentation by imagining each of his citizens as having only one such set, but this simplifying assumption does not seem central to his view.

5.2 □ Questions and Counterquestions*

Jürgen Habermas

[. . .]

Scarcely anyone would disagree that [. . .] distances and oppositions have increased and intensified in the modern age, which has itself become a philosophical theme of the first rank since the eighteenth century. Individuals, groups, and nations have drifted far apart in their backgrounds of biographical and social-cultural experience. This pluralization of diverging universes of discourse belongs to specifically modern experience; the shattering of naive consensus is the impetus for what Hegel calls 'the experience of reflection'. We cannot now simply wish this experience away; we can only negate it. In the framework of our culture, invested as it is with reflection, the thrust of this experience had to be worked through not only politically but also philosophically. Today we can survey the spectrum of answers given by philosophers: roughly speaking, it extends all the way from historicism to transcendentalism.

On the one side, Dilthey, Weber, Jaspers, and Kolakowski take an affirmative position on the growing pluralism of 'gods and demons' [*Glaubensmächte*], existential modes of being, myths, value attitudes, and metaphysical or religious world-views. A philosophy that treats forms of truth in the plural is supposed to leave to the sciences the job of providing an adequate reserve of consensual knowledge. On the other side, philosophers such as Husserl, the early Wittgenstein, Popper, and Apel, all attempt to maintain, at a higher level of abstraction, the unity of reason, even if only in a procedural sense. They distill the common characteristics of rational activity that *must* be implicitly presupposed in the pluralism of 'gods and demons' and in the argumentative collisions between universes of discourse. In this way, there arise what Rorty calls 'metanarratives', that is, the theories of rationality

* Habermas is responding to articles collected in *Habermas and Modernity*.

From Bernstein, R. J. (ed.), *Habermas and Modernity*, Polity Press, Cambridge, 1985, pp. 192–8, 203–11, 228–30.

that are supposed to account for why and in what sense we can still connect our convictions and our descriptive, normative, and evaluative statements, with a transcending validity claim that goes beyond merely local contexts.

These are philosophical answers to the *unavoidable* experience of modernity; when they are sharpened into the opposition between relativism and absolutism, an *unmediated* confrontation emerges between pure historicism and pure transcendentalism. At that point the failures of both positions become clear: the one side carries the burden of self-referential, pragmatic contradictions and paradoxes that violate our need for consistency; the other side is burdened with a foundationalism that conflicts with our consciousness of the fallibility of human knowledge. No one who gives this situation much thought would want to be left in this bind.

In the context of our discussion here, this reading of the present situation is not really in dispute, although Rorty, Bernstein, and I react to it in different ways. Forcefully freeing himself from the straitjacket of analytic philosophy, Richard Rorty has undertaken the most ambitious project: he wants to destroy the tradition of the philosophy of consciousness, from its Cartesian beginnings, with the aim of showing the pointlessness of the entire discussion of the foundations and limits of knowledge. He concludes that philosophers need only recognize the hybrid character of their controversies and give the field over to the practitioners of science, politics, and daily life to be rid of the problem. Like the later Wittgenstein, Rorty sees philosophy itself as the sickness whose symptoms it previously and unsuccessfully tried to cure. But Rorty is still enough of a philosopher to give a reason for his recommendation that we avoid the *Holzweg* of philosophical justification: one shouldn't scratch where it doesn't itch. It is just this assumption that 'it doesn't itch' that I find problematic.

Forms of life are totalities which always emerge in the plural. Their coexistence may cause friction, but this *difference* does not automatically result in their *incompatibility*. Something similar is the case for the pluralism of values and belief systems. The closer the proximity in which competing 'gods and demons' have to live with each other in political communities, the more tolerance they demand; but they are not incompatible. Convictions can contradict one another only when those who are concerned with problems define them in a similar way, believe them to need resolution, and want to decide issues on the basis of good reasons.

To be sure, it is also a characteristic of modernity that we have grown accustomed to living with dissent in the realm of questions that admit of 'truth'; we simply put controversial validity claims to one side 'for the time being'. None the less, we perceive *this* pluralism of contradictory convictions as an incentive for learning processes; we live in the expectation of *future* resolutions. As long as we take part and do not merely look over our own shoulders as historians and ethnographers, we maintain precisely the distinctions that Rorty wants to retract: between valid and socially accepted views, between good arguments and those which are merely successful for a certain audience at a certain time.

In believing that he can consistently replace the implicitly normative conception of 'valid arguments' with the descriptive concept of 'arguments held to be true for us at this time', Rorty commits an objectivistic fallacy. We could not even understand the meaning of what we describe from a third-person perspective as argumentative conduct if we had not already learned the performative attitude of a participant in argumentation; that is, what it means from the perspective of the first person to raise a validity claim that points beyond the provincial agreements of the specific local context. Only this capacity gives our *opinions* the character of *convictions*. (This is no less true for the practice of everyday communication than for argumentative disputes about the hypothetical validity of statements.) Any mutual understanding produced in communication and reproduced in the life-world is based on a potential reserve of reasons that may be challenged, reasons that force us to take a rationally motivated position of yes or no. This calls for a *different* type of attitude from that which we bring to the claims of merely influential ideas. From the perspective of the participant, a moment of *unconditionedness* is built into the *conditions* of action oriented toward reaching understanding. From the perspective of the first person, the question of which beliefs are justified is a question of which beliefs are based on good reasons; it is not a function of life-habits that enjoy social currency in some places and not in others.

And because in the modern age the gaps between competing convictions reach deep into the domain of questions that 'admit of truth', there exists, contrary to Rorty, a philosophical interest 'to see social practices of justification as more than just such practices'.[1] The stubbornness with which philosophy clings to the role of the 'guardian of reason' can hardly be dismissed as an idiosyncrasy of self-absorbed intellectuals, especially in a period in which basic irrationalist undercurrents are transmuted once again into a dubious form of politics. In my opinion, it is precisely the neoconservatives who articulate, intensify, and spread this mood of the times via the mass media – with such an effect that 'it itches'.

II

In his latest book Richard Bernstein gives us another answer: instead of bidding farewell to philosophy from an artificially alienated viewpoint of an ethnologist, he turns it toward the practical. While Rorty absolutizes the perspective of the observer, Bernstein remains within the perspective of the participant and enters into a debate which today leads beyond the mistaken alternatives of historicism and trancendentalism, a debate going on between Gadamer, Arendt, Rorty, and myself, among others.[2] Bernstein does not end his splendid reconstruction of the diverse paths of this discussion – a discussion that has not yet come to a close – with a proposal for a theoretical solution, but with a practical recommendation: we ought to *act* under the presupposition of the unifying power of communicative reason. In order to make this argumentative move intelligible, let me cite a thesis of Herbert Schnädelbach with which Bernstein would probably agree: 'that the difference between what we always claim for our rationality and what we are actually able to explicate as rational can in principle never be eliminated'.[3] If I understand the conclusion of his book correctly, it is for this reason that Bernstein from the start locates the moment of unconditionedness built into the universalistic validity *claims* of our communicative practices in the horizon of *practical* reason; he finds in the communicative infrastructure of the life-world a practical postulate, one that is dictated by reason itself. He refuses to regard the procedural unity of rationality within the historical and cultural multiplicity of standards of rationality as a question that is accessible to *theoretical* treatment.

I suspect that behind Bernstein's argumentative strategy there lies an absolutizing of the perspective of the participant which is complementary to Rorty's absolutizing of that of the observer. I don't see why one could not, at least in a preliminary way, explore a *third path*, which I have embarked upon with my 'theory of communicative action'. In this approach, philosophy surrenders its claim to be the sole representative in matters of rationality and enters into a nonexclusive division of labor with the reconstructive sciences. It has the aim of clarifying the presuppositions of the rationality of processes of reaching understanding, which may be presumed to be universal because they are unavoidable. Then philosophy shares with the sciences a falliblistic consciousness, in that its strong universalistic suppositions require confirmation in an interplay with empirical theories of competence.[4] This revisionary self-understanding of the role of philosophy marks a break with the aspirations of first philosophy [*Ursprungsphilosophie*] in any form, even that of the theory of knowledge; but it does not mean that philosophy abandons its role as the guardian of rationality. With its self-imposed modesty of method, a philosophy starting from formal pragmatics preserves the possibility of speaking of rationality in the singular. Unlike the sciences, it has to account reflectively for its own context of emergence and thus its own place in history.[5] Thus, 'metanarratives', in the sense of foundational 'ultimate groundings' or totalizing philosophies of history, could never even arise.

The most important achievement of such an approach is the possibility of clarifying a concept of communicative rationality that escapes the snares of Western logocentrism. Instead of following Nietzsche's path of a totalizing and self-referential critique of reason, whether it be via Heidegger to Derrida, or via Bataille to Foucault,[6] and throwing the baby out with the bathwater, it is more promising to seek this end through the analysis of the *already* operative potential for rationality contained in the everyday practices of communication. Here the validity dimensions of propositional truth, normative rightness, and subjective truthfulness or authenticity are intermeshed with each other. From this network of a bodily and interactively shaped, historically situated reason, our philosophical tradition selected out only the single thread of propositional truth and theoretical reason and stylized it into the monopoly of humanity. The common ground that unites both von Humboldt and pragmatism with the later Wittgenstein and Austin is the opposition to the *ontological* privileging of the world of beings, the *epistemological* privileging of contact with objects or existing states of affairs, and the *semantic* privileging of assertoric sentences and propositional truth. Logocentrism means neglecting the complexity of reason effectively operating in the life-world, and restricting reason to its cognitive-instrumental dimension (a dimension, we might add, that has been noticeably privileged and selectively utilized in processes of capitalist modernization).

Rorty takes Western logocentrism as an indication of the exhaustion of our philosophical discourse and a reason to bid adieu to philosophy as such. This way of reading the tradition cannot be maintained if philosophy can be transformed so as to enable it to cope with the entire spectrum of aspects of rationality – and with the historical fate of a reason that has been arrested again and again, ideologically misused and distorted, but that also stubbornly raises its voice in every inconspicuous act of successful communication. Such a transformation is possible only if philosophy does not remain fixated on the natural sciences. Had Rorty not shared this fixation, he might have entertained a more flexible and accepting relationship to the philosophical tradition. Fortunately, not all philosophizing can be subsumed under the paradigm of the philosophy of consciousness.

Rorty believes that the need in the modern age for self-reassurance is a capricious problem created by intellectuals – indeed, even a typically German problem. In his view, it arises from the esoteric *Weltschmerz* of small intellectual circles, from their preoccupation with a world that was lost along with the religious beliefs of their fathers. But does it not remain an open question whether or not the social integrative powers of the religious tradition shaken by enlightenment can find an equivalent in the unifying, consensus-creating power of reason? This was indeed the motivation behind German Idealism; this type of idealism has found equally influential proponents in the tradition of Peirce, Royce, Mead, and Dewey, in which Rorty prefers to place himself. What is perhaps specifically German is the philosophical concept of alienation, both in the Hegelian–Marxist version and the early Romantic version taken up by Nietzsche. This same theme resonates not only in post-structuralist France; since the sixties, and I need not remind Rorty of this, the discussion of modernity in conflict with itself had been nowhere so lively as in the USA – admittedly, more so among social scientists and psychologists than among analytic philosophers. Carl Schorske even thought he could see intellectual affinities between the contemporary American scene and Weimar Germany. While the expression 'postmodern' was not invented by American neoconservatives, they at least popularized it.

Do not these and similar signs indicate that intellectuals articulate shifts in mood, which they in no way invent, but which have instead palpable social and often economic causes? As a good pragmatist, I hold the view that a philosopher's capacity to create problems through intentionally inciting doubt is quite limited. I share Peirce's doubt about any type of Cartesian doubt. Problems emerge in situations over which we are not in control; they are something which objectively happens to us. The slogan that leftist intellectuals are the cause of the misery they analyze has already been bandied about for too long among rightist intellectuals in Germany to be credible. It is no more credible in the attractive packaging of a theory of the new class.

To me, the notion of intellectual 'value elites' is absolutely worthless. Like Rorty, I have for a long time identified myself with that radical democratic mentality which is present in the best American traditions and articulated in American pragmatism. This mentality takes seriously what appears to so-called radical thinkers as so much reformist naivety. Dewey's 'attempt to make concrete concerns with the daily problems of one's community' expresses both a practice and an attitude. It is a maxim of action about which it is in fact superfluous to philosophize.

[. . .]

IV

Thomas McCarthy raises two sorts of objections: first, against my systematic interpretation of Weber's diagnosis of the times; and second, against my analysis of interpretative understanding. Since I believe that the relationship between the two problems established by McCarthy is artificial, I will first deal separately with the problem of the objectivity of understanding.

In the field of meaning theory I hold the view that we understand a literally meant speech act when we know the conditions under which it could be accepted as valid by a hearer. This pragmatically extended version of truth conditional semantics is supported by the fact that we connect the execution of speech acts to various validity claims: claims to the truth of propositions (or of the existential presuppositions of the propositional contents), claims to the rightness of an utterance (with respect to existing normative contexts), and claims to the truthfulness of an expressed intention. With these claims we take on, as it were, a warrant for their redemption, should it be necessary – above all, in that we offer, at least implicitly, reasons for the validity of our speech acts. A hearer knows the content of what is said when he knows what reasons (or what sort of reasons) the speaker would give for the validity of his speech act (under appropriate circumstances). The interpreter (even the social scientific interpreter who deals with linguistically formed data) does not understand symbolically prestructured objects (in the normal case, communicative utterances), if he or she does not also understand the reasons potentially related to their validity claims.

Now the interesting point is that reasons are of a special nature. They can always be expanded into arguments which we then understand only when we *recapitulate* [*nachvollziehen*] them in the light of some standards of rationality. This 'recapitulation' requires a reconstructive activity in which we bring into play our own standards of rationality, at least intuitively. From the perspective of a participant, however, one's own rationality standards must always claim general validity; this claim to general validity can be restricted only subsequently, from the perspective of a third person. In short, the interpretative reconstruction of reasons makes it necessary that for us to place 'their' standards in relation to 'ours', so that in the case of a contradiction we either revise our preconceptions or relativize 'their' standards of rationality against 'ours'.

These reflections do indeed lead to the rather 'strong' thesis that we *cannot* understand reasons without at least implicitly evaluating them. McCarthy argues that this conclusion is false, since, even if it is the case that it is necessary to take up a rationally motivated yes or no position on reasons in order to understand them, the interpreter can not only agree or disagree with them but, can also practice a kind of abstention; he or she has the option of 'leaving to one side' the question of the validity of 'their' rationality standards (and hence of the reasons themselves). However, I think that such an abstention is also a rationally motivated position, as much as a 'yes' or a 'no', and in no way relieves us of the necessity of taking a position. Abstention in this context does not really signify a true declaration of neutrality, but only signals that we are putting off problems for the time being and wish to suspend our interpretative efforts. For example, so long as we are unable to see a perspicuous internal relation between the categorial frameworks of Aristotelian and Newtonian physics, we do not know precisely in what sense Aristotle, in contrast to Newton, wanted to 'explain' natural processes. Simply noting the competition between various paradigms comes close to confessing that we do not yet understand the physics and metaphysics of Aristotle as well as we do the basic assumptions about nature in classical mechanics.

The rational character of understanding, which Gadamer always emphasized, becomes especially clear in limit cases, as, for example, in the interpretation of mythical narratives. Undercutting or leaving to one side (or merely shaking one's head while accepting) the totalistic categories of a world-view within which the narrative interweaving and (as it appears to *us*) the categorial confusion of surface phenomena lay claim to explanatory power, merely indicate that we are putting off, prematurely breaking off, the interpretative process. This is tantamount to confessing that we do not yet understand the point of mythical modes of thought. We understand them only when we can say why the participants had good reasons for their confidence in this *type* of explanation. But in order to achieve this degree of understanding, we have to establish an internal relation between 'their' sort of explanation and the kind we accept as correct. We must be able to reconstruct the successful and unsuccessful learning processes which separate 'us' from 'them'; both modes of explanation have to be located within the same universe of discourse. As long as this is not achieved, the feeling remains that one does not understand something. It is this perplexity which finds its appropriate expression in suspension.

But it does not follow from this that the sciences which have to establish hermeneutic access to their object domain have to renounce the objectivity of knowledge. I have criticized this hermeneutistic position in various ways.[7] In principle, I do not see any difficulty in achieving some theoretical knowledge even in those domains of reality with which we have contact primarily through norm-conforming or expressive attitudes. My reservations concern only those theoretical positions which ignore the hermeneutic dimension of access to the object domain entirely.[8] If the sentence McCarthy criticizes is to be read as reporting my own view, 'that nothing can be learned in the objectivating attitude about inner nature qua subjectivity',[9] then it may be understood only in the sense of a rejection of *purely* objectivistic approaches to psychology.

McCarthy is further interested in the question whether or not the rationality complexes which have been differentiated in modern Europe and achieved a certain autonomy do not, as it were, also communicate with one another and have their roots in one and the same reason. In my view, this theme can be treated independently of the problem of interpretative understanding. For this purpose, the schema reproduced by McCarthy is not really a fruitful point of departure. Its purpose was only to represent the content of Max Weber's famous '*Zwischenbetrachtung*'.[10] Unfortunately, in response to earlier objections I made the mistake of referring to this schema in a systematic way.[11] And McCarthy does the same here. My previous carelessness thus makes it necessary in what follows to distinguish more carefully between my interpretation of Weber and my own views.

V

I want first to isolate those elements of Weber's theory of culture that I appropriated into my own view (1). In so doing, we then encounter McCarthy's concern for the costs of a process of disenchantment that now leaves open the possibility of only a procedural unity of reason cutting across different forms of argumentation (2). McCarthy finally treats the question of the synthesis of the differentiated moments of reason under three quite distinct aspects. He lists three problems that cannot be subsumed under the *same* analytical perspective (that is, the perspective of varying basic attitudes toward the objective, the social, and the subjective worlds) (3).

1. To begin with, let me turn to what I have appropriated from Weber's theory of culture. In Weber's view, the assertion of a differentiation of 'value spheres', each with its own inner logic – which was inspired by the Neo-Kantians Emil Lask and Heinrich Rickert – can be plausibly defended in regard to modern Europe on two levels: first, on the level of ideas that can be transmitted in traditions (scientific theories, moral and legal beliefs, as well as artistic productions); but also, second, on the level of cultural action systems, in which corresponding 'discourses' and activities are given professionally and institutionally organized form. The differentiation of value spheres corresponds to a decentered understanding of the world which is an important internal condition for the professionalized treatment of cultural traditions separated into questions of truth, justice, and taste. This modern understanding of the world makes possible a hypothetical approach to phenomena and experiences, which are isolated from the complexity of life-world contexts and analyzed under experimentally varied conditions. This is equally true for the states of an objectified nature, for norms and modes of acting, and for the reflective experiences of an 'unbound' subjectivity (set free from the practical constraints of everyday life). The well-known distinction of cognitive developmental psychology between structurally defined levels of learning, on the one hand, and the learning of contents, on the other, certainly may not be applied in the same way to science, morality, and art. In this respect my formulations were not careful enough.

Compared to the growth of theoretical knowledge, described by McCarthy as accumulation of contents across paradigm shifts, the trends in the development of art [. . .] do not so much signify an accumulation of contents as the progressive constitution of a particular domain of autonomous art and aesthetic experience purified of cognitive and moral admixtures; they also signify expanding explorations that illuminate more and more of this realm of experience. Yet this concentric expansion is not accompanied by the familiar effects of a devaluation of formerly held insights typical for cumulative learning processes. Moral and legal theories occupy a middle position. Here, too, we can observe the constitution of a domain of autonomous morality and moral universalism that distills a class of rationally solvable problems from the complexity of the contexts of ethical life under the single aspect of justice. Learning processes in this sphere are similar to a theoretical progress achieved within the limits of a single paradigm. Thus, in the modern age the explication and justification of moral intuitions make a certain 'progress': this progress is not exhausted in ever new reinterpretations of the same moral principle.

However, the thesis that capitalist modernization can be grasped as a selective actualization of the rationality potential contained in modern structures of consciousness requires the counterfactual supposition of a non-selective model of societal rationalization.[12] In this connection I have suggested that for the value spheres of science, morality, and art in modern Europe 'we should be able to demonstrate plausible correspondences with typical forms of argumentation, each of which is specialized in accord with a universal validity claim'.[13] Thus, the burden of proof is put on the theory of argumentation; leaving aside explicative discourse and therapeutic critique, it has to distinguish and clarify the systematic content of three different forms of argumentation: namely, empirical-theoretical discourse, moral discourse, and aesthetic critique.[14] It was due to the context of Weber's diagnosis of the times that I did not introduce the three rationality complexes via argumentation theory but by way of a schema that was supposed to represent the characteristics of a decentered understanding of the world. Indeed, the modern understanding of the world structurally opens up the possibility of taking objectivating, norm-conforming or expressive attitudes towards three different worlds (objective, social or subjective – in short, to states of affairs, norms, or subjective experiences); it also allows us to vary these attitudes in relation to elements of one and the same world.

[. . .]

2. Based on reflections in the theory of meaning, I take as my starting point that facts, norms, and subjective experiences have their *originary* locus in 'their' corresponding worlds (objective, social, or subjective), and, *in the first instance*, are accessible, or identifiable, only from the perspective of an actor who takes a corresponding attitude (be it objectivating, norm-conforming, or expressive). It is with this linear ordering that the first of the three questions McCarthy treats at the end of his article arises.

How is it that we can talk in an objectivating attitude about something in the subjective or social world, that is, about those elements that we *first* experience as something subjective or which we *first* encounter as something normative? In theoretical discourse (scientific discourse, for example) we can only incorporate these elements if we thematize subjective experiences and norms as states of affairs after having transformed them into components of the objective world. In everyday communication we certainly succeed, without much trouble, in transforming expressive utterances (or first-person sentences) into equivalent statements in the third person, or in accurately reporting the content of normative utterances or imperatives from the third-person point of view. On the level of scientific discourse, however, there is a tendency to delimit the object domains of, for example, psychology or sociology, by neglecting their hermeneutic dimensions, in such a way that the components of the subjective or social world are naturalistically assimilated to physical entities or to observable behavior. In each case they are made into components of the objective world, inherently accessible only in the objectivating attitude; that is, they are forced into the basic conceptual framework of physicalism or behaviorism. As opposed to this naturalistic reduction, the point here is only to defend non-objectivistic approaches in psychology and the social sciences.

Mutatis mutandis, the same questions arise for moral-practical discourse, and, indirectly, for aesthetic criticism. These forms of argumentation are also inherently related to components of one specific world, the social or the subjective. Here too, elements of the other two worlds must be brought into play in such a way as to avoid the dangers of, respectively, *moralism* and *aestheticism*, just as previously the danger of *objectivism* had to be avoided. We can thus observe that science, morality, and art have not only been differentiated *from each other*; they also communicate *with each other*. But within the boundaries of each expert culture, the different moments of reason come into contact with one another in such a way as to avoid violating the inner logic of the dominant form of argumentation specialized either in truth, normative correctness, or aesthetic harmony. This is one concern of the last chapter of *The Theory of Communicative Action*.[15]

At this point the motivation behind McCarthy's criticism becomes clear: an interest in the question of how the moments of reason retain their unity within differentiation, and of how this unity can be adequately expressed in philosophical analysis. Unfortunately, my schematic presentation of Weber's diagnosis of the times leads McCarthy to conflate three quite distinct questions under a single aspect. As just shown, the formal–pragmatic relations play a role in the analysis of those interactions between the cognitive, moral, and expressive moments of reason. But the other two questions really have nothing to do with this problem: first, the question of how the knowledge produced in expert cultures can be mediated with everyday practices (which I touched upon above in relation to the constellation 'art' and 'life'); and second, the question of whether we can provide an equivalent for the meaning of traditional world-views – for their function of 'Sinngebung'.

3. With the emergence of autonomous art and science, problems of mediation arise – such as the relation of art and life, or of theory and practice. Since Hegel a corresponding problem has emerged in terms of the relation of morality and ethical life (*Sittlichkeit*). This problem has less to do with an expressive attitude toward the social world than with the fact that the insights of a postconventional morality would remain without any impact on real life unless morality is anchored in concrete forms of ethical life. The deontological ethics developed in the Kantian tradition do indeed offer a solution to the problem of justification; they show how to choose between controversial norms of action with good reasons (in light of what might be willed by all). But they do not offer any solution for two resultant problems: first, that of the *application* of justified norms which are general and abstracted from any content; and second, that of the *efficacy* of pure moral insights that have been gained under the condition of abstracting from available motivations. Autonomous morality owes its gain in rationality to the transformation of questions of the good life into problems of justice. As a consequence of this deontological abstraction, it can only provide answers to questions lacking specific contexts. This necessary disregard for the complexity of concrete forms of life, in which moral moments are always interlaced with evaluative, cognitive, and expressive moments, calls for specific compensations that make good the deficits with regard to the application and realization of moral insights. I am not able to go further into this question here.[16]

The discussions of morality and ethical life, theory and practice, art and life, all center around the idea of a non-reified everyday communicative practice, a form of life with structures of an undistorted intersubjectivity. Such a possibility must today be wrung from the professional, specialized, self-sufficient culture of experts and from the systems-imperatives of state and economy which destructively invade the ecological basis of life and the communicative infrastructure of our life-world. This same intuition is expressed in Marx's utopian perspective on the realization of philosophy: to the extent that the reason expressed in Hegel's philosophy can be embodied in the forms of life of an emancipated society, philosophy somehow becomes pointless. For Marx, philosophy realized is philosophy *aufgehoben*. The theory of communicative action gives this idea another reading: the unity of reason cannot be reestablished on the level of cultural traditions in terms of a substantive world-view, but only on this side of the expert cultures, in a non-reified, communicative practice of everyday life. Indeed, in a certain way the unity of reason is *a tergo* always-already realized in communicative action – namely, in such a way that we have an intuitive knowledge of it. A philosophy that wants to bring this intuition to a conceptual level must retrieve the scattered traces of reason in communicative practices themselves, no matter how muted they may be. However, it cannot simply repeat the attempt, long since discredited, to project some theoretical picture of the world as a whole.

I think I have learned from the tradition of Hegelian–Marxism, from the history of critical social theory from Marx to Benjamin, Bloch, Marcuse, and Adorno that any attempt to embed the perspective of reconciliation in a philosophy of history of nature, however indirectly it is done, must pay the price of dedifferentiating forms of knowledge behind whose categorial distinctions we can no longer retreat in good conscience. All this is not really an argument, but more an expression of skepticism in the face of so many failed attempts to have one's cake and eat it too: to retain both Kant's insights and, at the same time, to return to the 'home' [*Behausung*] from which these same insights have driven us. But, perhaps, McCarthy or others will some day succeed in formulating the continuities between human history and natural history so carefully that they are weak enough to be plausible and yet strong enough to permit us to recognize man's place in the cosmos (Scheler), at least in broad outlines.

Notes

1. Richard Rorty, *Philosophy and the Mirror of Nature* (Princeton, NJ, 1979), p. 390.
2. R. J. Bernstein, *Beyond Objectivism and Relativism* (Philadelphia, 1983).
3. H. Schnädelbach, in *Kommunikation und Reflexion*, ed. W. Kuhlmann and D. Böhler (Frankfurt, 1983), p. 361.
4. J. Habermas, 'Die Philosophie als Platzhalter und Interpret', in *Moralbewusstsein und kommunikatives Handeln* (Frankfurt, 1983), pp. 9 ff.
5. Habermas, *Theorie des kommunikativen Handelns*, vol. 2 (Frankfurt, 1981), pp. 586 ff.
6. I have never used the term 'neoconservative', in this connection. I did once, in passing, compare the critique of reason in Foucault and Derrida to the '*Young Conservatives*' of the Weimar Republic. Usually Hans Freyer, Arnold Gehlen, Martin Heidegger, Ernst Jünger, and Carl Schmidt are numbered among this group. They all take from Nietzsche the radical gesture of a break with modernity and a revolutionary renewal of pre-modern energies, most often reaching back to archaic times. Like any comparison, it has its weaknesses, but in the German context it does illuminate intellectual affinities that, notwithstanding the politically contrary positions, stem from the authority of Nietzsche. (See my 'Modernity versus post-modernity', *New German Critique*, 22 (1981), 3–22.)
7. Habermas, *The Theory of Communicative Action*, vol. 1, pp. 120 ff., 130 ff. Also, 'Interpretative social science and Hermeneuticism', in *Social Science as Moral Inquiry*, ed. N. Hann, R. Bellah, P. Rabinow and W. Sullivan (Berkeley, CA, 1983), pp. 251–70.
8. Habermas, *Zur Logik der Sozialwissenschaften* (Frankfurt, 1982).
9. Habermas, *The Theory of Communicative Action*, vol. I, p. 237.
10. *Ibid.*, p. 238.
11. Habermas, *Vorstudien und Ergänzungen zur Theorie des kommunikativen Handelns* (Frankfurt, 1982).
12. On this 'rather risky model', see *The Theory of Communicative Action*, vol. I, pp. 239 ff.
13. *Ibid.*
14. See my 'Excursus' on argumentation theory, *ibid.*, pp. 18–42.
15. 'In each of these spheres, the process of differentiation is accompanied by a countermovement which always re-incorporates the other two, at first excluded validity aspects under the primacy of the dominant one. In this way, non-objectivist approaches to the human sciences also bring into play the perspectives of moral and aesthetic critique, while not endangering the primacy of the question of truth; only in this way is an encompassing theory of society possible. The discussion of an ethics of responsibility and the more pronounced consideration of utilitarian motives bring the

perspectives of the calculation of consequences and the interpretation of needs into play in universalistic ethics, perspectives which lie within the cognitive and expressive validity domains; in this way, materialistic ideas can also be given their due, without endangering the autonomy of the moral perspective. Finally, post-avant-garde art is characterized by the simultaneous presence of realistic and engaged intentions, along with the authentic continuation of classical modernity, which distilled out the internal meaning of the aesthetic sphere. With realistic and engaged art, once again the cognitive and moral-practical moments enter into art, at the level of the wealth of form set free by the avant-garde.' Habermas, *Theorie des kommunikativen Handelns*, vol. II, pp. 585–6.

16. See Habermas, 'Über Moralität und Sittlichkeit: was macht eine Lebensform rational?', in *Rationalität*, ed. H. Schnädelbach (Frankfurt, 1984), pp. 218 ff.

5.3 □ Communicative Ethics and the Claims of Gender, Community and Postmodernism

Seyla Benhabib

As the twentieth century draws to a close, there is a little question that we are living through more than the chronological end of an epoch. To invoke a distinction familiar to the Greeks, it is not only *kronos* which is holding sway over our lives; but our *kairos* as well, our lived time, time as imbued with symbolic meaning, is caught in the throes of forces of which we only have a dim understanding at the present. The many 'postisms', like posthumanism, post-structuralism, postmodernism, post-Fordism, post-Keynesianism, and post-histoire, circulating in our intellectual and cultural lives, are at one level only expressions of a deeply shared sense that certain aspects of our social, symbolic and political universe have been profoundly and most likely irretrievably transformed.

During periods of profound transformations such as these, as contemporaries of an epoch, we are more often than not in the position of staring through the glass darkly. We do not have the privilege of hindsight; we are not like the 'owl of Minerva' which spreads its wings only at dusk. As engaged intellectuals we cannot write from the vantage point of 'the grey which paints itself on green', and we do not even want to. Contrary to this Hegelian prognosis of 'standing at the end of history', which has been recently revived by Francis Fukuyama – this late student of Hegel as read through the eyes of Alexandre Kojève[1] – the present harbors many ironies, contradictions and perplexities. Ernst Bloch's phrase of 'non-contemporaneous contemporaneities', or *ungleichzeitige Gleichzeitigkeiten*, is more appropriate to capture the fractured spirit of our times.[2]

From Benhabib, S., *Situating the Self: Gender, community and postmodernism in contemporary ethics*, Polity Press, Cambridge, 1992, pp. 1–19.

Among the many ironies nourished by this fractured spirit is certainly the fact that while the cultural and political ideals of modernity, and among them what Richard Rorty has called 'the metanarratives of liberal democracies',[3] have become suspect to the humanistic and artistic avant-garde of Western late-capitalist societies, political developments in Eastern Europe and the Soviet Union have given these ideals a new purchase on life. While the peoples of Eastern Europe and the Soviet Union have taken to the streets and defied state police as well as the potential threat of foreign troops in the name of parliamentary democracy, the rule of law and a market economy, the academic discourse of the last decades, particularly under the label of 'postmodernism', has produced an intellectual climate profoundly skeptical toward the moral and political ideals of modernity, the Enlightenment and liberal democracy.

This current mood of skepticism among intellectual, academic and artistic circles toward continuing the 'project of modernity' is based upon an understandable disillusionment with a form of life that still perpetrates war, armament, environmental destruction and economic exploitation at the cost of satisfying basic human needs with human dignity, a form of life that still relegates many women, non-Christian and non-white peoples to second-class moral and political status, a form of life that saps the bases of solidaristic coexistence in the name of profit and competition. Whether the form of life of advanced capitalist mass democracies can reform itself from within is a pressing one. It is my conviction, however, that the project of modernity can only be reformed from within the intellectual, moral and political resources made possible and available to us by the development of modernity on a global scale since the sixteenth century. Among the legacies of modernity which today need reconstructing but not wholesale dismantling are moral and political universalism, committed to the now seemingly 'old-fashioned' and suspect ideals of universal respect for each person in virtue of their humanity; the moral autonomy of the individual; economic and social justice and equality; democratic participation; the most extensive civil and political liberties compatible with principles of justice; and the formation of solidaristic human associations.

This book [*Situating the Self*] attempts a reconstruction of this legacy by addressing the following question: what is living and what is dead in universalist moral and political theories of the present, after their criticism in the hands of communitarians, feminists and postmodernists? More specifically, this book is an attempt to defend the tradition of universalism in the face of this triple-pronged critique by engaging with the claims of feminism, communitarianism and postmodernism, and by learning from them.

Communitarian critics of liberalism like Alasdair MacIntyre, Michael Sandel, Charles Taylor and Michael Walzer have questioned the epistemological assumptions as well as the normative vision of liberal political theories. Feminist thinkers like Carol Gilligan, Carole Pateman, Susan Moller Okin, Virginia Held, Iris Young, Nancy Fraser, and Drucilla Cornell have continued the communitarian critique of liberal visions of the 'unencumbered self'. They have also pointed out that neither liberals nor communitarians have overcome their gender blindness such as to include women and their activities in their theories of justice and community.

Postmodernists, a somewhat vague label by which we have come to designate the works of Michel Foucault, Jacques Derrida and Jean-François Lyotard among others, while sharing the communitarian and feminist skepticism toward the metanarratives of liberal Enlightenment and modernity, have radicalized this critique to the point of questioning the idea of an autonomous subject of ethics and politics and the normative foundations of democratic politics altogether. Each of these lines of thought has contributed to a forceful rethinking of the Enlightenment tradition in ethics and politics extending from Immanuel Kant to John Rawls and Jürgen Habermas.

I wish to isolate three general themes around which the rethinking of Enlightenment universalism initiated by feminism, communitarianism and postmodernism ought to be continued. Communitarians, feminists and postmodernists have (1) voiced skepticism toward the claims of a 'legislating' reason to be able to articulate the necessary conditions of a 'moral point of view', an 'original position', or an 'ideal speech situation'; (2) they have questioned the abstract and disembedded, distorting and nostalgic ideal of the autonomous male ego which the universalist tradition privileges; (3) they have unmasked the inability of such universalist, legislative reason to deal with the indeterminacy and multiplicity of contexts and life-situations with which practical reason is always confronted. I shall argue in this book that there is a powerful kernel of truth in these criticisms, and that contemporary universalist theories must take seriously the claims of community, gender and postmodernism. Nevertheless, neither the pretenses of a legislative reason, nor the fiction of a disembedded autonomous male ego, nor for that matter indifference and insensitivity to contextual reasoning, are the *sine qua non* of the universalist tradition in practical philosophy. A post-Enlightenment defense of universalism, without metaphysical props and historical conceits, is still viable. Such universalism would be interactive not legislative, cognizant of gender difference not gender blind, contextually sensitive and not situation indifferent. The goal of the essays collected in this volume is to argue for such a post-Enlightenment project of interactive universalism.

By bringing competing intellectual discourses of the present into dialogue, and by measuring their claims against each other, I intend to soften the boundaries which have often been drawn around universalist theories and feminist positions, communitarian aspirations and postmodernist skepticism. These oppositions and juxtapositions are too simple to grasp the complex crisscrossing of theoretical and political commitments in the present. Not only is a feminist universalism, for example, a discursive possibility rather than a sheer contradiction in terms; no matter how contradictory their political messages may be, in their critique of progress and modernity communitarianism and postmodernism are allies rather than opponents. By focusing on the fragile and shifting nature of such conceptual alliances and confrontations, I hope to illuminate the contradictory potentials of the present moment in our intellectual lives. It is my hope to create cracks and fissures in the edifice of discursive traditions large enough so that a new ray of reason which still reflects the dignity of justice along with the promise of happiness may shine through them.

A central premise of this book is that the crucial insights of the universalist tradition in practical philosophy can be reformulated today without committing oneself to the metaphysical illusions of the Enlightenment. These are the illusions of a self-transparent and self-grounding reason, the illusion of a disembedded and disembodied subject, and the illusion of having found an Archimedean standpoint, situated beyond historical and cultural contingency. They have long ceased to convince. But since how long one lingers on in their company and basks in their comforting warmth more often than not depends upon the intensity of the original farewell, let me state here my own adieu to these ideals. Enlightenment thinkers from Hobbes and Descartes to Rousseau, Locke and Kant believed that reason is a natural disposition of the human mind, which when governed by proper education can discover certain truths. It was furthermore assumed that the clarity and distinctness of these truths or the vivacity of their impact upon our senses would be sufficient to ensure intersubjective agreement among like-thinking rational minds. Even Kant, whose Copernican revolution uncovered the active contribution of the knower to the process of knowing, nevertheless conflated the discovery of those conditions under which the objectivity of experience was possible with those conditions under which the truth or falsehood of propositions concerning experience could be ascertained. By contrast, I proceed from the premise that we must distinguish between the conditions for ascertaining the validity of statements and those characteristics pertaining to the cognitive apparatus of the human subject and which lead it to organize perceptual and experiential reality in a certain fashion.[4] Such a universal-pragmatic reformulation of transcendental philosophy, as undertaken by Karl-Otto Apel and Jürgen Habermas,[5] is postmetaphysical in the sense that truth is no longer regarded as the psychological attribute of human consciousness, or to be the property of a reality distinct from the mind, or even to consist in the process by which 'givens' in consciousness are correlated with 'givens' in experience. In the discursive justification and validation of truth claims no moment is privileged as a given, evidential structure which cannot be further questioned. It is the discourse of the community of inquirers (Charles Sanders Peirce) which first assigns an evidential or other type of value to aspects of our consciousness or experience, and brings them into play as factors which support our claims to the veracity of our beliefs. In the continuing and potentially unending discourse of the community of inquiry there are no 'givens', there are only those aspects of consciousness and reality which at any point in time may enter into our deliberations as evidence and which we find cogent in backing our statements. The first step, then, in the formulation of a post-metaphysical universalist position is to shift from a substantialistic to a discursive, communicative concept of rationality.

The second step comes with the recognition that the subjects of reason are finite, embodied and fragile creatures, and not disembodied cogitos or abstract unities of transcendental apperception to which may belong one or more bodies. The empiricist tradition, which in contradistinction from Descartes and Kant, let us say, would describe the self as an 'I know not what', or as a 'bundle of impressions', does not so much ignore the body as it tries to formulate the unity of the self along the model of the continuity of a substance in time. As opposed to the dismissal of the body in the one case, and the reduction of self-identity to the continuity of a substance in the other, I assume that the subject of reason is a human infant whose body can only be kept alive, whose needs can only be satisfied, and whose self can only develop within the human community into which it is born. The human infant becomes a 'self', a being capable of speech and action, only by learning to interact in a human community. The self becomes an individual in that it becomes a 'social' being capable of language, interaction and cognition. The identity of the self is constituted by a narrative unity which integrates what 'I' can do, have done and will accomplish with what you expect of 'me', interpret my acts and intentions to mean, wish for me in the future, etc. The Enlightenment conception of the disembedded cogito no less than the empiricist illusion of a substance-like self cannot do justice to those contingent processes of socialization through which an infant becomes a person, acquires language and reason, develops a sense of justice and autonomy, and becomes capable of projecting a narrative into the world of which she is not only the author but the actor as well. The 'narrative structure of actions and personal identity' is the second premise which allows one to move beyond the metaphysical assumptions of Enlightenment universalism.

If reason is the contingent achievement of linguistically socialized, finite and embodied creatures, then the legislative claims of practical reason must also be understood in interactionist terms. We may mark a shift here from *legislative to interactive rationality*.[6] This shift radically alters the conceptualization of 'the moral point of view'. The moral point of view is not an Archimedean center from which the moral philosopher pretends to be able to move the world. The moral point of view articulates rather a certain stage in the development of linguistically socialized human beings when they start to reason about general rules governing their mutual existence from the standpoint of a hypothetical questioning: under what conditions can we say that these general rules of action are valid not simply because it is what you and I have been brought up to believe or because my parents, the synagogue, my neighbors, my tribe say so, but because they are fair, just, impartial, in the mutual interest of all? The moral point of view corresponds to the stage of reasoning reached by individuals for whom a disjunction emerges between the social validity of norms and of normative institutional arrangements on the one hand, and their hypothetical validity from the standpoint of some standard of justice, fairness, impartiality. 'Tell me Euthyphro', is the Socratic question, 'is something pious because the gods love it, or do the gods love it because it is pious?' In the first case, the morally valid is dictated by the gods of my city, in the second, even the gods of my city recognize the presence of standards of piety and justice which would be valid for all. The moral point of view corresponds to the developmental stage of individuals and collectivities who have moved beyond identifying the 'ought' with the 'socially valid', and thus beyond a 'conventional' understanding of ethical life, to a stance of questioning and hypothetical reasoning. Most high cultures in human history which differentiate between the natural and the social worlds are capable of producing such questioning, and such a disjunction between 'the moral ought' (*das moralische Sollen*) and 'social validity or acceptability' (*soziale Geltung*).[7]

The elements of a postmetaphysical, interactive universalism are: the universal pragmatic reformulation of the basis of the validity of truth claims in terms of a discourse theory of justification; the vision of an embodied and embedded human self whose identity is constituted narratively, and the reformulation of the moral point of view as the contingent achievement of an interactive form of rationality rather than as the timeless standpoint of a legislative reason. Taken together, these premises form a broad conception of reason, self and society. What is their status in the project of a postmetaphysical and interactive universalism?

Perhaps this question can be best approached by contrasting John Rawls's claims for a 'political conception of justice' with the broad vision of reason, self and society outlined above. In the wake of objections raised by communitarians like Michael Sandel in particular to the concept of the self and the vision of the good presupposed or at least implied by his theory of justice, John Rawls distinguished between 'metaphysical' and 'political' conceptions of justice. While the former view would entail fundamental philosophical premises about the nature of the self, one's vision of society and even one's concept of human rationality, the political conception of justice proceeded from assumptions about self, society and reason which were 'formulated not in terms of any comprehensive doctrine but in terms of certain fundamental intuitive ideas viewed as latent in the public political culture of a democratic society'.[8] Rawls believes in the legislative task of reason and he limits the scope of philosophical inquiry in accordance with conceptions of what is appropriate for the public culture of liberal democracies. He formulates his philosophical presuppositions in such a fashion as would elicit an 'overlapping consensus' and thus be acceptable to the implicit self-understanding of the public actors of a democratic polity. The essays collected in this volume do not restrict the scope of normative inquiry to the actually existing limitations on the public discourses of actually existing democracies. In the final analysis, conceptions of self, reason and society and visions of ethics and politics are inseparable. One should regard such conceptions of self, reason and society not as elements of a 'comprehensive' *Weltanschauung* which cannot be further challenged, but as presuppositions which are themselves always also subject to challenge and inquiry. As I will argue below, such assumptions about self, reason and society are the 'substantive' presuppositions without which no 'proceduralism', including Rawls's own program of an 'overlapping consensus', can be cogently formulated. There is a kind of normative philosophical analysis of fundamental presuppositions which serves to place ethical inquiry in the larger context of epistemic and cultural debates in a society. Such analysis of presuppositions should be viewed not as the attempt to put forth a comprehensive moral doctrine acceptable to all, but as the dialectical uncovering of premises and arguments which are implicit not only in contemporary cultural and intellectual debates but in the institutions and social practices of our lives as well. In Hegelian language this would be the study of ethics as a doctrine of 'objective spirit'. In my language this is a study of ethics in the context of a critical theory of society and culture.[9]

While continuing the broad philosophical shift from legislative to interactive reason initiated by the work of Jürgen Habermas in particular, in this book I depart from his version of a discourse or communicative ethic in crucial ways. I attempt to highlight, emphasize and even radicalize those aspects of a discourse ethic which are universalist without being rationalistic, which seek understanding among humans while considering the consensus of all to be a counterfactual illusion, and which are sensitive to differences of identity, needs and modes of reasoning without obliterating these behind some conception of uniform rational moral autonomy. There are three decisive foci around which I propose to save discourse ethics from the excesses of its own rationalistic Enlightenment legacy. These are the conceptualization of the moral point of view in light of the reversibility of perspectives and the cultivation in Hannah Arendt's terms of 'representative thinking', to 'engender' the subject of moral reasoning, not in order to relativize moral claims to fit gender differences but to make them gender sensitive and cognizant of gender difference; to develop a rudimentary phenomenology of moral judgment in order to show how a principled, universalist morality and context-sensitive moral judgment can fit together. My goal is to situate reason and the moral self more decisively in contexts of gender and community, while insisting upon the discursive power of individuals to challenge such situatedness in the name of universalistic principles, future identities and as yet undiscovered communities.

Chapter 1, entitled 'In the Shadow of Aristotle and Hegel: Communicative Ethics and Current Controversies in Practical Philosophy', presents the general outlines of my attempt to defend communicative ethics while heeding the criticism of neo-Aristotelians like Hans-Georg Gadamer and Alasdair MacIntyre on the one hand and of neo-Hegelians like Charles Taylor on the other. I begin by seeking an answer to the standard Hegelian objection to formalist ethical universalism that procedures of universalizability are at best inconsistent and at worst empty. Applying this objection to the case of discourse ethics, I maintain that neither inconsistency nor emptiness are unavoidable defects of a conversationally conceived model of moral reasoning. What I propose is a procedural reformulation of the universalizability principle along the model of a moral conversation in which the capacity to reverse perspectives, that is, the willingness to reason from the others' point of view, and the sensitivity to hear their voice is paramount. Following Kant, Hannah Arendt has given this core intuition of universalistic ethical and political theories a brilliant formulation:

> The power of judgment rests on a potential agreement with others, and the thinking process which is active in judging something is not, like the thought process of pure reasoning, a dialogue between me and myself, but finds itself always and primarily, even if I am quite alone in making up my mind, in an anticipated communication with others with whom I know I must finally come to some agreement. And this enlarged way of thinking, which as judgment knows how to transcend its individual limitations, cannot function in strict isolation or solitude; it needs the presence of others 'in whose place' it must think, whose perspective it must take into consideration, and without whom it never has the opportunity to operate at all. [10]

The nerve of my reformulation of the universalist tradition in ethics is this construction of the 'moral point of view' along the model of a moral conversation, exercising the art of 'enlarged thinking'. The goal of such conversation is not consensus or unanimity (*Einstimmigkeit* or *Konsens*) but the 'anticipated communication with others with whom I know I must finally come to some agreement' (*Verständigung*). This distinction between 'consensus' and 'reaching an agreement' has not always been heeded in objections to communicative ethics. At times Habermas himself has overstated the case by insisting that the purpose of universalizability procedures in ethics must be the uncovering or discovering of some 'general interest' to which all could consent.[11] I propose to view the concept of 'general interest' in ethics and politics more as a regulative ideal and less as the subject matter of a substantive consensus. In ethics, the universalizability procedure, if it is understood as a reversing of perspectives and the willingness to reason from the other's (others') point of view, does not guarantee consent; it demonstrates the will and the readiness to seek understanding with the other and to reach some reasonable agreement in an open-ended moral conversation. Likewise, in politics, it is less significant that 'we' discover 'the' general interest, but more significant that collective decisions be reached through procedures which are radically open and fair to all. Above all these decisions should not exclude the voice of those whose 'interests' may not be formulable in the accepted language of public discourse, but whose very presence in public life may force the boundaries between private needs and public claims, individual misfortunes and collectively representable grievances.

One consequence of reformulating universalizability in terms of the model of reversibility of perspectives and the cultivation of 'enlarged thinking' is that the *identity of the moral self* must be reconceptualized as well. More precisely, this reformulation allows us to challenge those presuppositions of 'legalistic universalism' from Kant to Rawls which have privileged a certain vision of the moral self. In order to think of universalizability as reversing of perspectives and a seeking to understand the standpoint of the other(s), they must be viewed not only as generalized but also as concrete others. According to the standpoint of the 'generalized other', each individual is a moral person endowed with the same moral rights as ourselves; this moral person is also a reasoning and acting being, capable of a sense of justice, of formulating a vision of the good, and of engaging in activity to pursue the latter. The standpoint of the concrete other, by contrast, enjoins us to view every moral person as a unique individual, with a certain life history, disposition and endowment, as well as needs and limitations. One consequence of limiting procedures of universalizability to the standpoint of the generalized other has been that the other as distinct from the self has disappeared in universalizing moral discourse. [. . .] [T]here can be no coherent reversibility of perspectives and positions unless the identity of the other as distinct from the self, not merely in the sense of bodily otherness but as a concrete other, is retained.

I envision the relationship of the generalized to the concrete other as along the model of a continuum. In the first place there is the universalistic commitment to the consideration of every human individual as a being worthy of universal moral respect. This norm which I share with the liberal tradition is institutionalized in a democratic polity through the recognition of civil, legal and political rights – all of which reflect the morality of the law or, if you wish, the principles of justice in a well-ordered polity. The standpoint of the concrete other, by contrast, is implicit in those ethical relationships in which we are always already immersed in the lifeworld. To be a family member, a parent, a spouse, a sister or a brother means to know how to reason from the standpoint of the concrete other. One cannot act within these ethical relationships in the way in which standing in this kind of a relationship to someone else demands of us without being able to think from the standpoint of our child, our spouse, our sister or brother, mother or father. To stand in such an ethical relationship means that we as concrete individuals know what is expected of us in virtue of the kind of social bonds which tie us to the other.

If the standpoint of the generalized and the concrete other(s) are thought of as existing along a continuum, extending from universal respect for all as moral persons at one end to the care, solidarity and solicitation demanded of us and shown to us by those to whom we stand in the closest relationship at the other,[12] then the privileging in traditional universalistic theories of the legal domain and the exclusive focus upon relationships of justice must be altered. I argue against Kohlberg and Habermas that relations of justice do not exhaust the moral domain, even if they occupy a privileged position within it [. . .]. Again to introduce a Hegelian locution, ethical life encompasses much more than the relationship of right-bearing generalized others to each other. Even if the Kantian tradition distinguishes between legality and morality, a tendency in Kantian ethics which has persisted till our own days is to model ethical bonds along juridical (*rechtsfroemmig*) ones. Viewed from the standpoint of the interactive universalism which I seek to develop in this book, the problem appears differently: my question is how ethical life must be thought of – life in the family no less than life in the modern constitutional state – from the standpoint of a postconventional and universalist morality. Sometimes Hegel argued as if 'the moral point of view' and Sittlichkeit were incompatible, but the really challenging task suggested by his *Philosophy of Right* is to envisage a universalistic moral point of view as situated within an ethical community. Call this the vision of a *postconventional Sittlichkeit*.

It is this search for a 'postconventional Sittlichkeit' which distinguishes my vision from that of communitarian thinkers like Michael Sandel and Alasdair MacIntyre in particular. In the chapter on 'Autonomy, Modernity and Community: Communitarianism and Critical Society Theory in Dialogue', I argue that there are two strands of communitarian thinking on the question of reconstituting a community under conditions of modernity. The first I describe as the 'integrationist' and the second as the 'participationist'. While the first group of thinkers seek to reconstitute community via recouping and reclaiming an integrative vision of fundamental values and principles, the participationists envisage such a community as emerging from common action, engagement and debate in the civic and public realms of democratic societies. I reject the integrationist vision of community as being incompatible with the values of autonomy, pluralism, reflexivity and tolerance in modern societies.

In the constitution of such a postconventional Sittlichkeit via participatory politics in a democratic polity, the faculty of 'enlarged thinking' plays a crucial role. This was one of Hannah Arendt's cardinal insights, and ultimately why she considered judgment a political rather than a moral faculty. In 'thinking with Arendt against Arendt' in several of the chapters below, I will attempt to make her conception of enlarged thinking useful both for morality and for politics. In the democratic polity, the gap between the demands of justice, as these articulate principles of moral right, and the demands of virtue, as this defines the quality of our relations to others in the lifeworld, can be bridged by cultivating qualities of civic friendship and solidarity. These qualities of civic friendship and solidarity mediate between the standpoints of the 'generalized' and the 'concrete others', by teaching us to reason, to understand and to appreciate the standpoint of 'collective concrete others'. Such understanding, however, is a product of political activity. It cannot be performed either by the political theorist or by the moral agent *in vacuo*. For, as Arendt well knew, the multiplicity of perspectives which constitute the political can only be revealed to those who are willing to engage in the foray of public contestation. The perspectival quality of the public world can only manifest itself to those who 'join together in action in concert'. Public space is formed through such action in concert. In a postconventional Sittlichkeit, the public sphere is the crucial domain of interaction which mediates between the macropolitical institutions of a democratic polity and the private sphere.

The public sphere is a common theme in several chapters of this book. I set up a contrast between the liberal, the Arendtian and the Habermasian models of the public sphere. As representative of the liberal position, Bruce Ackerman's model of a public conversation under the constraints of neutrality is chosen. My argument is that the constraint of neutrality illicitly limits the agenda of public conversation and excludes particularly those groups like women and blacks who have not been traditional partners in the liberal dialogue. I maintain that democratic politics redefines and reconstitutes the line between the right and the good, justice and the good life. Although this agonal and contestatory dimension of politics is at the heart of Hannah Arendt's work, what makes her concept of public space so deficient from the standpoint of complex, modern societies is a constraint similar to that introduced by Ackerman with his concept of 'liberal neutrality'. Arendt also seeks to limit the scope and the agenda of the public sphere via essentialist assumptions about the 'natural place' of human activities and the 'political' or 'non-political' nature of certain topoi of debate. By contrast, I plead for a radically proceduralist model of the public sphere, neither the scope nor the agenda of which can be limited *a priori*, and whose lines can be redrawn by the participants in the conversation. Habermas's concept of a public sphere embodying the principles of a discourse ethics is my model here.

One of the chief contributions of feminist thought to political theory in the Western tradition is to have questioned the line dividing the public and the private. Feminists have argued that the 'privacy' of the private sphere, which has always included the relations of the male head of household to his spouse and children, has been an opaque glass rendering women and their traditional spheres of activity invisible and inaudible. Women, and the activities to which they have been historically confined, like childrearing, housekeeping, satisfying the emotional and sexual needs of the male, tending to the sick and the elderly, have been placed until very recently beyond the pale of justice. The norms of freedom, equality and reciprocity have stopped at the household door. Two centuries after the American and the French revolutions, the entry of women into the public sphere is far from complete, the gender division of labor in the family is still not the object of moral and political reflection, and women and their concerns are still invisible in contemporary theories of justice and community. It is not my purpose to lament the invisibility of gender in contemporary thought, but rather to ask the question: what consequences does this invisibility have for the theories under consideration? A theory of universalist morality or of the public sphere cannot simply 'ignore' women and be subsequently 'corrected' by their reinsertion into the picture from which they were missing. Women's absence points to some categorical distortions within these theories; that is to say, because they exclude women these theories are systematically skewed. The exclusion of women and their point of view is not just a political omission and a moral blind spot but constitutes an epistemological deficit as well.

I call attention to the epistemological deficits of contemporary universalism in the following areas. First, I argue that the neglect by universalist theories of the moral emotions and of everyday moral interactions with concrete others has everything to do with the gender division of labor in Western societies subsequent to modernity. Justice becomes the core of collective moral life when the extended households of antiquity and the Middle Ages lose their productive functions with the rise of the capitalist exchange economy, and become mere reproductive units whose function is to satisfy the daily bodily and psychosexual needs of their members. Second, every concept of public space presupposes a corresponding delimitation of the private. In the chapter entitled 'Models of Public Space: Hannah Arendt, the Liberal Tradition and Jürgen Habermas', I show that these theories of the public sphere are gender blind to the extent that they either draw a rigid and dogmatic boundary between the public and the private (Arendt), or, as is the case with Habermas, because they develop binary oppositions which exclude the thematization of issues most important for women from public discussion. The oppositions between, 'justice' and 'the good life', 'generalizable interests' versus 'private need interpretations', between 'public norms' and 'private values', have the consequence of leaving the line between the public and the private pretty much where it has always been, namely between the public spheres of the polity and the economy on the one hand and the familial-domestic realm on the other. Engaging in a dialectical battle with Habermas, I try to reconstruct his model of the public sphere in a way which would both accommodate feminist criticisms and also help feminists in our own thinking about alternative public spheres.

Finally, there is a relationship between the neglect of the problem of moral judgment in universalist moral theories and the neglect of women and their activities. Because women's sphere of activity has traditionally been and still today is so concentrated in the private sphere in which children are raised, human relationships maintained and traditions handed down and continued, the female experience has been more attuned to the 'narrative structure of action' and the 'standpoint of the concrete other'. Since they have had to deal with concrete individuals, with their needs, endowments, wants and abilities, dreams as well as failures, women in their capacities as primary caregivers have had to exercise insight into the claims of the particular. In a sense the art of the particular has been their domain, as has the 'web of stories', which in Hannah Arendt's words constitutes the who and the what of our shared world. It is in the context of discussing Hannah Arendt's theory of judgment that I provide the outlines of a phenomenology of moral judgment, which would none the less be compatible with a universalist and principled morality.

The claim that the gender blindness of universalist theories is not merely a matter of moral indifference or political inclination but that it points to a deeper epistemic failure has been one of the cornerstones of the postmodernist critique of the grand narratives of the logocentric Western tradition. If there is one commitment which unites postmodernists from Foucault to Derrida to Lyotard it is this critique of Western rationality as seen from the perspective of the margins, from the standpoint of what and whom it excludes, suppresses, delegitimizes, renders mad, imbecilic or childish. In his impressive genealogies of reason Foucault uncovers the discursive practices which have drawn the line between madness and civilization, mental health and sickness, criminality and normality, sexual deviance and sexual conformism. [13] Foucault shows that the other of reason comes to haunt this very reason. The persistence of the other within the text of Western metaphysics, the continuing attempts of this metaphysics to erase the presence of the other in the endless game of binary oppositions, has been a guiding vision of Jacques Derrida's thought from his early essay on 'the ends of man' to his most recent comments on the 'force of law'. [14] Of course, it would be a mistake to think that the other in Jacques Derrida's thought is merely a nomer for an excluded gender, race, people or geopolitical region of the world. For Derrida, as for Hegel, no identity can be constituted without difference; the other is never merely an other but always also an in- and for-itself. But for Hegel there is a moment of identity which overcomes difference by 'appropriating' it, by pretending that the 'other' is something merely posited (*etwas gesetzt*) which the one self-identical subject presupposes (*vorausgesetzt*), for Derrida difference is irreducible and never evaporates into the imperialist game of positing one's presuppositions which Hegel's subjects always play. Difference which is ineliminable is *différance*, the continuing act and process of differing. Although there is no identity, none the less there is more than merely a contingent relationship between the logocentrism of the West and the imperialist gesture with which the West 'appropriates' its other(s), pretending, much like the Hegelian concept, that they were its own presuppositions on the way to self-fulfillment. The Orient is there to enable the Occident, Africa is there to enable Western civilization to fulfill its mission, the woman is there to help man actualize himself in her womb, etc. ... The logic of binary oppositions is also a logic of subordination and domination.

In Jean-François Lyotard's work the epistemic exclusion of the other also has moral and political implications, although it can by no means be reduced to these. In *The Postmodern Condition* Lyotard contrasted the 'grand narratives' of the Enlightenment to the '*petits récits*' of women, children, fools and primitives. The exclusion of small narrativity, argued Lyotard, was an aspect of the grandiose vision of the modernizing Western tradition. *The Postmodern Condition* left ambiguous, however, whether by 'narrativity' Lyotard meant a kind of ordinary language philosophy *à la* Wittgenstein, a hermeneutic tradition of judgment *à la* Gadamer, or a kind of poetic imagination like the one Richard Rorty defends. Perhaps all three were envisioned. In subsequent works like *Le Différend*, *Just Gaming* and *Heidegger and the Jews*[15] there is a linking of the limits of rationalism to the ethics and politics of the other.

As the chapter on 'Feminism and the Question of Postmodernism' clarifies, in their critique of the illusions of logocentrism and in their championing of the standpoint of the 'other(s)', postmodernist thinkers have been crucial allies for contemporary feminism. By focusing on the problem of the subject, the question of grand narratives, and the standards of rationality and critique, I construct a dialogue here between weak and strong postmodernist claims and feminist positions/oppositions. Postmodernism is an ally with whom feminism cannot claim identity but only partial and strategic solidarity. Postmodernism, in its infinitely skeptical and subversive attitude toward normative claims, institutional justice and political struggles, is certainly refreshing. Yet, it is also debilitating. The so-called critique of 'identity politics', which is now dominating feminist thought, is not only an acknowledgment of the necessity of 'rainbow politics', as Iris Young has claimed.[16] The critique of 'identity politics' attempts to replace the vision of an autonomous and engendered subject with that of a fractured, opaque self; the 'deed without the doer' becomes the paradigm of subversive activity for selves who joyfully deny their own coherence and relish their opacity and multiplicity. This problematic vision of the self is a radicalization of the Nietzschean critique of modernity in the name of an aesthetics of the everyday. It is Zarathustra who can be lamb and lion, sage and rebel at once. For women the aesthetic transcendence of the everyday is of course a temptation. But precisely because women's stories have so often been written for them by others, precisely because their own sense of self has been so fragile, and their ability to assert control over the conditions of their existence so rare, this vision of the self appears to me to be making a virtue out of necessity. No less important is that social criticism of the kind required for women's struggles is not even possible without positing the legal, moral and political norms of autonomy, choice and self-determination. Aesthetic modernism has always parasitically depended upon the achievements of modernity in the spheres of law and morality – in so far as the right of the moral person to pursue her sense of the good, be it ever so fractured, incoherent and opaque, has first to be anchored in law and morality before it can become an everyday option for playful selves. In this respect, as in many others, postmodernism presupposes a superliberalism, more pluralistic, more tolerant, more open to the right of difference and otherness than the rather staid and sober versions presented by John Rawls, Ronald Dworkin and Thomas Nagel. As far as I am concerned this is not troublesome. What is baffling, though, is the lightheartedness with which postmodernists simply assume or even posit those hyper-universalist and super-liberal values of diversity, heterogeneity, eccentricity and otherness. In doing so they rely on the very norms of the autonomy of subjects and the rationality of democratic procedures which otherwise they seem to so blithely dismiss. What concept of reason, which vision of autonomy allows us to retain these values and the institutions within which these values flourish and become ways of life? To this question postmodernists have no answer; perhaps because, more often than not, as sons of the French Revolution, they have enjoyed the privileges of the modern to the point of growing blasé *vis-à-vis* them.

This book ends as it began in a tug with Hegel. 'On Hegel, Women and Irony' brings together many strands of argumentation. By examining Hegel's relationship to the movement of the early romantics in the Jena circle, and in particular by looking at the life of one of these early 'modernist' women, Caroline Michaelis von Schlegel Schelling, I show that the women's question in Hegel's philosophy is not only a conceptual result necessitated by a series of binary oppositions which define the logic of gender relations in his philosophy. Nor is the confinement of women to a traditionalist vision of Sittlichkeit in the *Philosophy of Right* merely a consequence of the historical limitations of Hegel's times. Hegel could have argued otherwise, just as some of his contemporaries and most notably the early Friedrich von Schlegel did. Yet he chose not to; he was not necessitated to do so. He chose not to follow the consequences of modernity in ethical life all the way into the sphere of personal, intimate, sexual relations between men and women. He refused to accept the ideals of heterosexual equality and egalitarian reciprocity which his romantic friends, for a short while at least, advocated. Yet as the person of Caroline von Schlegel Schelling shows, women cannot but have an ambivalent relationship to modernity, which on the one hand promises them so much and which yet on the other constantly subverts its own *promesse du bonheur*. In joining the French revolutionary armies and the shortlived republic of Mainz, Caroline appears to me to have appreciated the dialectic of bourgeois republicanism which initially allowed women as participants into the public sphere, only at a second stage to send them scurrying home. The recovery of a sense of irony in the face of the modernist project and bemusement at its dialectical twists and turns is truer not only to the dilemmas of contemporary feminism but in the face of an epoch approaching its end as well.

Notes

1. F. Fukuyama has argued that transformations in the Soviet Union and Eastern Europe show that we have in effect reached 'the end of history'. F. Fukuyama, 'The end of history?', *The National Interest* (Summer 1989), pp. 3–18. Of course, this is not meant in the trivial chronological sense that time will now stand still, but rather in the sense that the economic and political *kairos* of the future (how long is the future?) will not add

anything new to the principles of Western capitalism and liberal democracy. Just as Hegel saw the post-French revolutionary modern state, based on the principles of the right of persons and property, to represent the conceptual end of the history of freedom, Fukuyama also believes that the second half of the twentieth century has vindicated capitalism and liberal democracy over their enemies, namely fascism and communism. See *ibid.*, pp. 9 ff.

2. See Ernst Bloch, *Erbschaft dieser Zeit*, first published 1935 (Suhrkamp, Frankfurt, 1973), pp. 110 ff.

3. See Richard Rorty, 'Habermas and Lyotard on postmodernity', *Praxis International*, 4.1 (April 1984), pp. 34 ff. Also see 'The contingency of a liberal community', in *Contingency, Irony and Solidarity* (Cambridge University Press, Cambridge, 1989), pp. 44 ff.

4. Wilfried Sellars's discussion of this point, which is, after all, a restatement of Hegel's critique of 'Sense Certainty' in the first chapter of *The Phenomenology of Spirit*, has been very influential on my thinking. See Wilfried Sellars, 'Empiricism and the philosophy of mind', in *Science, Perception and Reality* (Humanities, New York, 1963), pp. 127 ff.; and Michael Williams, *Groundless Belief: An essay on the possibility of epistemology* (Yale University Press, New Haven, CT, 1977), esp. pp. 25 ff. for a more recent statement.

5. See Karl-Otto Apel, 'From Kant to Peirce: the semiotic transformation of transcendental logic', in *Towards a Transformation of Philosophy*, trans. Glyn Adey and David Frisby (Routledge & Kegan Paul, London, 1980), pp. 77–93; see also J. Habermas, 'What is universal pragmatics?', in *Communication and the Evolution of Society*, trans. Thomas McCarthy (Beacon, Boston, MA, 1979), pp. 1–69, and 'Wahrheitstheorien', in *Wirklichkeit und Reflexion*, ed. H. Fahrenbach (Neske, Pfüllingen, 1973), and most recently Jürgen Habermas, *Postmetaphysisches Denken* (Suhrkamp, Frankfurt, 1989).

6. In chapter 5 [of *Situating the Self*], 'The Generalized and the Concrete Other: The Kohlberg–Gilligan Controversy and Moral Theory', I use the terms 'substitutionalist' and 'interactive' universalisms to mark this contrast.

7. The kind of developmental universalism defended by Kohlberg and Habermas has at times been subject to the misleading reading that Socrates and Jesus, Buddha or Francis of Assisi, as members of cultures and societies which were prior in world history to Western Enlightenment and modernity, should be considered for that reason to be on a 'lower level of moral development' than Voltaire or Nietzsche, Kant or Karl Marx! Obviously, an absurd view which reeks of the self-satisfied evolutionism of the eighteenth and nineteenth centuries. I have argued elsewhere that this is a gross misunderstanding of Habermas's work; in particular, see S. Benhabib, *Critique, Norm and Utopia: A study of the foundations of critical theory* (Columbia University Press, New York, 1986) pp. 253 ff. Although the relationship of cognitive universalist moral positions to modernity is a complex one, which I shall address in various chapters below, the developmental interpretation of the moral point of view in no way sanctions the construal of world history and human cultures as if they were stages in the growth of a superego writ large. I reject attempts to apply a cognitive developmental scheme with a teleological endpoint to world history and cultures. One can utilize a much weaker scheme of distinctions between preconventional, conventional, and postconventional modalities of cultural traditions, without also having to maintain that these are 'natural' sequences of evolution which will invariably take place in a normal course of 'development'. For in the case of individual development it is the interaction of a finite bodily individual with the social and the physical world which initiates learning in this individual, activates memory and reflection and brings about progressions to 'higher', more integrated stages of situation comprehension and problem solving. The 'subject' of world history, by contrast, is an abstraction at best and a fiction at worst. One cannot

attribute to this fiction a dynamic source of interaction and learning such as propels individuals. Although I find the categories of 'pre, post and conventional moralities' descriptively useful in thinking about patterns of normative reasoning in cultures, I attribute no teleological necessity to the progression from one stage to another.

8. John Rawls, 'The priority of right and ideas of the good', *Philosophy and Public Affairs*, 17.4 (Fall 1988), pp. 251–76, here p. 252.

9. I have dealt with the logic and presuppositions of critical social theory in my book *Critique, Norm and Utopia*. The current volume continues the exploration of the project of communicative ethics, outlined in Chapter 8 of that book.

10. Hannah Arendt, 'The crisis in culture', in *Between Past and Future: Six exercises in political thought* (Meridian, New York, 1961), pp. 220–21.

11. See in particular Habermas's continuing reliance on the concept of 'general interest', formulated first in the context of his theory of legitimation crisis, and subsequently in the context of his moral theory. J. Habermas, *Legitimation Crisis*, trans. Thomas McCarthy (Beacon, Boston, MA, 1975), pp. 111 ff, and 'Discourse ethics: notes on a program of philosophical justification', in *Moral Consciousness and Communicative Action*, trans. Christian Lehnhardt and Shierry Weber Nicholsen (MIT Press, Boston, MA, 1990), pp. 43 ff; and my critique in chapter 1 [of *Situating the Self*].

12. This, of course, does not mean that only family or kinship groups can define such a space for us. In modern societies most individuals re-create family and kinlike structures for themselves on the basis of ties other than blood lineage; the relationship of friendship, which is a special bonding of two individuals, beyond and sometimes against the demands of kinship, nationality, ethnicity and politics, is one of the most cherished dimensions of ordinary lives under conditions of modernity.

13. For an early but extremely illuminating statement of the purpose of 'genealogical inquiry', see Michel Foucault, 'Nietzsche, genealogy, history', in *Language, Counter-Memory, Practice: Selected essays and interviews*, ed. and introd. Donald F. Bouchard (Cornell University Press, New York, 1977), pp. 139–65.

14. Jacques Derrida, 'The ends of man', reprinted in *After Philosophy*, ed. Kenneth Baynes, James Bohman and Thomas McCarthy (MIT Press, Boston, MA, 1987), pp. 125–61, and 'The force of law: The "mythical foundation of authority"', in special issue on Deconstruction and the Possibility of Justice, *Benjamin N. Cardozo Law Review*, 11.5–6 (July–August 1990), pp. 919–1047.

15. See Jean-François Lyotard, *The Differend: Phrases in dispute*, trans. G. van den Abbeele (University of Minnesota Press, Minneapolis, 1988); Jean-François Lyotard and Jean-Loup Thebaud, *Just Gaming*, trans. Wald Godzich (University of Minnesota Press, Minneapolis, 1979); and Lyotard, *Heidegger and the Jews*, trans. Andreas Michel and Mark Roberts (University of Minnesota Press, Minneapolis, 1990).

16. See Iris Young, 'The ideal of community and the politics of difference', reprinted in *Feminism and Postmodernism*, ed. Linda Nicholson (Routledge, New York, 1990), pp. 300–01.

5.4 □ *From* The Differend: Phrases in dispute

Jean-François Lyotard

Preface: Reading Dossier

Title

As distinguished from a litigation, a differend [*différend*] would be a case of conflict, between (at least) two parties, that cannot be equitably resolved for lack of a rule of judgment applicable to both arguments. One side's legitimacy does not imply the other's lack of legitimacy. However, applying a single rule of judgment to both in order to settle their differend as though it were merely a litigation would wrong (at least) one of them (and both of them if neither side admits this rule). Damages result from an injury which is inflicted upon the rules of a genre of discourse but which is reparable according to those rules. A wrong results from the fact that the rules of the genre of discourse by which one judges are not those of the judged genre or genres of discourse. The ownership of a literary or artistic work can incur damages (as when the moral rights of the author are assailed); but the very principle that one ought to treat a work as an object of ownership may constitute a wrong (as when it is not recognized that the 'author' is its hostage). The title of this book suggests (through the generic value of the definite article) that a universal rule of judgment between heterogeneous genres is lacking in general.

Object

The only one that is indubitable, the phrase, because it is immediately presupposed. (To doubt that one phrases is still to phrase, one's silence makes a phrase.) Or better

From Lyotard, J.-F., *The Differend: Phrases in dispute*, trans. G. Van Den Abbeele, Manchester University Press, Manchester, 1983, pp. xi–xvi, 3–14.

yet, phrases: because the singular calls forth the plural (as the plural does the singular) and because the singular and the plural are together already the plural.

Thesis

A phrase, even the most ordinary one, is constituted according to a set of rules (its regimen). There are a number of phrase regimens: reasoning, knowing, describing, recounting, questioning, showing, ordering, etc. Phrases from heterogeneous regimens cannot be translated from one into the other. They can be linked one onto the other in accordance with an end fixed by a genre of discourse. For example, dialogue links an ostension (showing) or a definition (describing) onto a question; at stake in it is the two parties coming to an agreement about the sense of a referent. Genres of discourse supply rules for linking together heterogeneous phrases, rules that are proper for attaining certain goals: to know, to teach, to be just, to seduce, to justify, to evaluate, to rouse emotion, to over-see. ... There is no 'language' in general, except as the object of an Idea.

Question

A phrase 'happens'. How can it be linked onto? By its rule, a genre of discourse supplies a set of possible phrases, each arising from some phrase regimen. Another genre of discourse supplies another set of other possible phrases. There is a differend between these two sets (or between the genres that call them forth) because they are heterogeneous. And linkage must happen 'now'; another phrase cannot not happen. It's a necessity; time, that is. There is no non-phrase. Silence is a phrase. There is no last phrase. In the absence of a phrase regimen or of a genre of discourse that enjoys a universal authority to decide, does not the linkage (whichever one it is) necessarily wrong the regimens or genres whose possible phrases remain unactualized?

Problem

Given (1) the impossibility of avoiding conflicts (the impossibility of indifference) and (2) the absence of a universal genre of discourse to regulate them (or, if you prefer, the inevitable partiality of the judge): to find, if not what can legitimate judgment (the 'good' linkage), then at least how to save the honor of thinking.

Stakes

To convince the reader (including the first one, the A.) that thought, cognition, ethics, politics, history or being, depending on the case, are in play when one phrase is linked onto another. To refute the prejudice anchored in the reader by centuries of humanism and of 'human sciences' that there is 'man,' that there is 'language', that the former makes use of the latter for his own ends, and that if he does not succeed in attaining these ends, it is for want of good control over language 'by means' of a 'better' language. To defend and illustrate philosophy in its differend with its two adversaries: on its outside, the genre of economic discourse (exchange, capital); on its inside, the genre of academic discourse (mastery). By showing that the linking of one phrase onto another is problematic and that this problem is the problem of politics, to set up a philosophical politics apart from the politics of 'intellectuals' and of politicians. To bear witness to the differend.

Context

The 'linguistic turn' of Western philosophy (Heidegger's later works, the penetration of Anglo-American philosophies into European thought, the development of language technologies); and correlatively, the decline of universalist discourses (the metaphysical doctrines of modern times: narratives of progress, of socialism, of abundance, of knowledge). The weariness with regard to 'theory', and the miserable slackening that goes along with it (new this, new that, post-this, post-that, etc.). The time has come to philosophize.

Pretext

The two thoughts which beckon to the A.: the Kant of the third *Critique* and the historical-political texts (the 'fourth Critique'); the Wittgenstein of the *Philosophical Investigations* and the posthumous writings. In the context imagined by the A., they are epilogues to modernity and prologues to an honorable postmodernity. They draw up the affidavit ascertaining the decline of universalist doctrines (Leibnizian or Russellian metaphysics). They question the terms in which these doctrines thought they could settle differends (reality, subject, community, finality). They question them more rigorously than does Husserl's 'rigorous science', which proceeds by eidetic variation and transcendental evidence, the ultimate expedient of Cartesian modernity. At the opposite pole, Kant says that there is no such thing as intellectual intuition, and Wittgenstein that the signification of a term is its use. The free examination of phrases leads to the (critical) dissociation of their regimens (the separation of the faculties and their conflict in Kant; the disentanglement of language games in Wittgenstein). They lay the ground for the thought of dispersion (diaspora, writes Kant) which, according to the A., shapes our context. Their legacy ought to be relieved today of its cumbersome debt to anthropomorphism (the notion of 'use' in both, an anthropomorphism that is transcendental in Kant, empirical in Wittgenstein).

Mode

The book's mode is philosophic, reflective. Thc A.'s only rule here is to examine cases of differend and to find the rules for the heterogeneous genres of discourse that bring about these cases. Unlike a theoretician, he does not presuppose the rules of his own discourse, but only that this discourse too must obey rules. The mode of the book is philosophical, and not theoretical (or anything else) to the extent that its stakes are in discovering its rules rather than in supposing their knowledge as a principle. In this very way, it denies itself the possibility of settling, on the basis of its own rules, the differends it examines (contrary to the speculative genre, for instance, or the analytic). The mode is that of a metalanguage in the linguist's sense (phrases are its object) but not in the logician's sense (it does not constitute the grammar of an object-language).

Genre

In the sense of poetics, the genre is that of Observations, Remarks, Thoughts, and Notes which are relative to an object; in other words, a discontinuous form of the Essay. A notebook of sketches? The reflections are arranged in a series of numbers and grouped into sections. The series is interrupted on occasion by Notices, which are reading notes for philosophical texts, but the whole is to be read in sequence.

Style

The A.'s naive ideal is to attain a zero degree style and for the reader to have the thought in hand, as it were. There sometimes ensues a tone of wisdom, a sententious one, which should be disregarded. The book's tempo is not that of 'our time'. A little out of date? The A. explains himself at the end about the time of 'our time'.

Reader

A philosophical one, that is, anybody on the condition that he or she agrees not to be done with 'language' and not to 'gain time'. Nevertheless, the present reading dossier will allow the reader, if the fancy grabs him or her, to 'talk about the book', without having read it. (For the Notices, a little more professional a reader.)

Author

Announced the present reflections in the 'Prière de désinsérer' of *Rudiments païens* (1977) [*Pagan Rudiments*] and in the Introduction to *The Postmodern Condition*

(1979). Were he not afraid of being tedious, he would confess that he had begun this work right after the publication of *Economie libidinale* (1974). Or for that matter. ... These reflections could not in the end have seen the light of day without an agreement reached between the University of Paris VIII (Vincennes in Saint-Denis) and the CNRS, and without the obliging help of Maurice Caveing and Simone Debout-Oleszkiewicz, researchers at the CNRS. The A., if not the reader, thanks them for this.

Address

So, in the next century there will be no more books. It takes too long to read, when success comes from gaining time. What will be called a book will be a printed object whose 'message' (its information content) and name and title will first have been broadcast by the media, a film, a newspaper interview, a television program, and a cassette recording. It will be an object from whose sales the publisher (who will also have produced the film, the interview, the program, etc.) will obtain a certain profit margin, because people will think that they must 'have' it (and therefore buy it) so as not to be taken for idiots or to break (my goodness) the social bond! The book will be distributed at a premium, yielding a financial profit for the publisher and a symbolic one for the reader. This particular book, along with others, belongs to the last of last year's line [*fin de série*]. Despite every effort to make his thought communicable, the A. knows that he has failed, that this is too voluminous, too long, and too difficult. The promoters have hidden away. Or more exactly, his timidity kept him from 'contacting' them. Contented enough that one publisher (condemned also by this very act) has agreed to publish this pile of phrases.

Philosophers have never had instituted addressees, which is nothing new. The reflection's destination is also an object of reflection. The last of last year's line has been around a long time. So has solitude. Still there is something new: the relation to time (I am tempted to write the 'use of time') that reigns today in the 'public space'. Reflection is not thrust aside today because it is dangerous or upsetting, but simply because it is a waste of time. It is 'good for nothing', it is not good for gaining time. For success is gaining time. A book, for example, is a success if its first printing is rapidly sold out. This finality is the finality of the economic genre. Philosophy has been able to publish its reflections under the guise of many genres (artistic, political, theological, scientific, anthropological), at the price, of course, of misunderstandings and grave wrongs, but still ... – whereas economic calculation seems fatal to it. The differend does not bear upon the content of the reflection. It concerns (and tampers with) its ultimate presuppositions. Reflection requires that you watch out for occurrences, that you don't already know what's happening. It leaves open the question: *Is it happening?* [*Arrive-t-il?*] It tries to keep up with the now [*maintenir le maintenant*] (to use a belabored word). In the economic genre, the rule is that what happens can happen only if it has already been paid back, and therefore has already happened. Exchange presupposes that the cession is canceled in advance by a countercession, the circulation of the book being canceled by its sales. And the sooner this is done, the better the book is.

In writing this book, the A. had the feeling that his sole addressee was the *Is it happening?* It is to it that the phrases which happen call forth. And, of course, he will never know whether or not the phrases happen to arrive at their destination, and by hypothesis, he must not know it. He knows only that this ignorance is the ultimate resistance that the event can oppose to the accountable or countable [*comptable*] use of time.

[. . .]

The Differend

1. You are informed that human beings endowed with language were placed in a situation such that none of them is now able to tell about it. Most of them disappeared then, and the survivors rarely speak about it. When they do speak about it, their testimony bears only upon a minute part of this situation. How can you know that the situation itself existed? That it is not the fruit of your informant's imagination? Either the situation did not exist as such. Or else it did exist, in which case your informant's testimony is false, either because he or she should have disappeared, or else because he or she should remain silent, or else because, if he or she does speak, he or she can bear witness only to the particular experience he had, it remaining to be established whether this experience was a component of the situation in question.

2. 'I have analyzed thousands of documents. I have tirelessly pursued specialists and historians with my questions. I have tried in vain to find a single former deportee capable of proving to me that he had really seen, with his own eyes, a gas chamber'. (Faurisson [. . .]). To have 'really seen with his own eyes' a gas chamber would be the condition which gives one the authority to say that it exists and to persuade the unbeliever. Yet it is still necessary to prove that the gas chamber was used to kill at the time it was seen. The only acceptable proof that it was used to kill is that one died from it. But if one is dead, one cannot testify that it is on account of the gas chamber. – The plaintiff complains that he has been fooled about the existence of gas chambers, fooled that is, about the so-called Final Solution. His argument is: in order for a place to be identified as a gas chamber, the only eyewitness I will accept would be a victim of this gas chamber: now, according to my opponent, there is no victim that is not dead; otherwise, this gas chamber would not be what he or she claims it to be. There is, therefore, no gas chamber.

3. Can you give me, says an editor defending his or her profession, the title of a work of major importance which would have been rejected by every editor and which would therefore remain unknown? Most likely, you do not know any

masterpiece of this kind because. if it does exist, it remains unknown. And if you think you know one, since it has not been made public, you cannot say that it is of major importance, except in your eyes. You do not know of any, therefore, and the editor is right. – This argument takes the same form as those in the preceding numbers. Reality is not what is 'given' to this or that 'subject', it is a state of the referent (that about which one speaks) which results from the effectuation of establishment procedures defined by a unanimously agreed-upon protocol, and from the possibility offered to anyone to recommence this effectuation as often as he or she wants. The publishing industry would be one of these protocols, historical inquiry another.

4. Either the Ibanskian* witness is not a communist, or else he is. If he is, he has no need to to testify that Ibanskian society is communist, since he admits that the communist authorities are the only ones competent to effectuate the establishment procedures for the reality of the communist character of that society. He defers to them then just as the layperson defers to the biologist or to the astronomer for the affirmation of the existence of a virus or a nebula. If he ceases to give his agreement to these authorities, he ceases to be a communist. We come back then to the first case: he is not a communist. This means that he ignores or wishes to ignore the establishment procedures for the reality of the communist character of Ibanskian society. There is, in this case, no more credit to be accorded his testimony than to that of a human being who says he has communicated with Martians. 'There is therefore nothing surprising in the fact that the [Ibanskian] State regards opposition activity in general as a criminal activity on the same level as robbery, gangsterism, speculation and so on ... It is a non-political society (Zinoviev [. . .]). More exactly, it is a learned State [. . .] it knows no reality other than the established one, and it holds the monopoly on procedures for the establishment of reality.

5. The difference, though, between communism, on the one hand, and a virus or a nebula, on the other hand, is that there are means to observe the latter – they are objects of cognition – while the former is the object of an idea of historical-political reason, and this object is not observable (Kant Notice 4, §1). There are no procedures, defined by a protocol unanimously approved and renewable on demand, for establishing in general the reality of the object of an idea. For example, even in physics, there exists no such protocol for establishing the reality of the universe, because the universe is the object of an idea. As a general rule, an object which is thought under the category of the whole (or of the absolute) is not an object of cognition (whose reality could be subjected to a protocol, etc.). The principle affirming the contrary could be called totalitarianism. If the requirement of establishing the reality of a phrase's referent according to the protocol of cognition is extended to any given phrase, especially to those phrases that refer to a whole, then this requirement is totalitarian in its principle. That's why it is important to

---

* The term is from Alexander Zinoviev's satirical novel *The Yawning Heights*, set in a fictitious locale – Ibansk – whose name is a derivative of Ivan, the stereotypical Russian name. [*Trans.*]

distinguish between phrase regimens, and this comes down to limiting the competence of a given tribunal to a given kind of phrase.

6. The plaintiff's conclusion (No. 2) should have been that since the only witnesses are the victims, and since there are no victims but dead ones, no place can be identified as a gas chamber. He should not have said that there are none, but rather that his opponent cannot prove that there are any, and that should have been sufficient to confound the tribunal. It is up to the opponent (the victim) to adduce the proof of the wrong done to him or her!

7. This is what a wrong [*tort*] would be: a damage [*dommage*] accompanied by the loss of the means to prove the damage. This is the case if the victim is deprived of life, or of all his or her liberties, or of the freedom to make his or her ideas or opinions public, or simply of the right to testify to the damage, or even more simply if the testifying phrase is itself deprived of authority (Nos 24–27). In all of these cases, to the privation constituted by the damage there is added the impossibility of bringing it to the knowledge of others, and in particular to the knowledge of a tribunal. Should the victim seek to bypass this impossibility and testify anyway to the wrong done to him or to her, he or she comes up against the following argumentation: either the damages you complain about never took place, and your testimony is false; or else they took place, and since you are able to testify to them, it is not a wrong that has been done to you, but merely a damage, and your testimony is still false.

8. Either you are the victim of a wrong, or you are not. If you are not, you are deceived (or lying) in testifying that you are. If you are, since you can bear witness to this wrong, it is not a wrong, and you are deceived (or lying) in testifying that you are the victim of a wrong. Let p be: you are the victim of a wrong; *not-p*: you are not; Tp: phrase p is true; Fp: it is false. The argument is: either p or *not-p*; if *not-p*, then Fp; if p, then *not-p*, then Fp. The ancients called this argument a dilemma. It contains the mechanism of the *double bind* as studied by the Palo Alto School,[*] it is a linchpin of Hegelian dialectical logic (Hegel Notice, §2). This mechanism consists in applying to two contradictory propositions, p and *not-p*, two logical operators: exclusion (*either ...*, *or*) and implication (*if ...*, *then*). So, at once [(*either p or not-p*) and (*if p, then not-p*)]. It's as if you said both, *either it is white*, or *it is not white*; and *if it is white, it is not white*.

Protagoras

1. 'A story is told of the time Protagoras demanded his fee [*misthos*] from Euathlus, a pupil of his. Euathlus refused to pay, saying, "But I haven't won a victory yet" [*oudèpô nikèn nenikèkà*]. Protagoras replied, "But if I win this dispute [*ègô mèn an*

---

[*] The foremost member of which was, of course, Gregory Bateson. [*Trans*]

nikèsô], I must be paid because I've won [*oti égô énikèsa*], and if you win it I must be paid because you've won"' [. . .]. As is proved by the frequency of its occurrences in various guises [. . .], the fable has a didactic value. It contains several paradoxes [. . .]. The master and the pupil have concluded a contract: the former will be paid only if the latter has been able to win, thanks to the teaching he receives, at least one of the cases he will plead before the tribunals during the period of said teaching. The alternative is simple and the judgment easy: if Euathlus has won at least once, he pays; if not, he is absolved. And since he has not won, there is nothing to pay. In its brachylogical conciseness, Protagoras' reply transforms the alternative into a dilemma. If Euathlus has won at least once, he must pay. If he never won, he still won at least once, and must pay.

How can it be affirmed that Euathlus won when he always lost? It suffices to include the present litigation between him and Protagoras among the series of litigations to be considered in order to decide whether he always lost. In every previous litigation, he lost. Therefore, in the case against Protagoras who maintains that he won one time, he triumphs by ascertaining that he never won. But, if he thereby prevails in a litigation against Protagoras, he has indeed won at least once.

2. The paradox rests on the faculty a phrase has to take itself as its referent. I did not win, I say it, and in saying it I win. Protagoras confuses the modus (the declarative prefix: Euathlus says that) with the dictum, the negative universal that denotes a reality (Euathlus did not win once). It is in order to prohibit this kind of confusion that Russell introduced the theory of types: a proposition (here, the verdict in the litigation between master and pupil) that refers to a totality of propositions (here, the set of prior verdicts) cannot be a part of that totality. Or else, it ceases to be pertinent with regard to negation (that is, to the principle of non-contradiction). It is not decidable in terms of its truth value.

The phrase whose referent is *all phrases* must not be part of its referent. Otherwise, it is 'poorly formed', and it is rejected by the logician. (This is the case for the Paradox of the Liar in the form *I lie.*) The logician has nothing but scorn for the sophist who ignores this principle; but the sophist doesn't ignore it, he unveils it (and in laughter, while Ibanskian power makes one weep) (No. 4).

The Russellian axiom of types is a rule for forming logical phrases (propositions). It delimits a genre of discourse, logic, in terms of its finality: deciding the truth of a phrase. Protagoras' argument is not acceptable within logic because it bars coming to a decision. Is it acceptable within another genre?

3. The totality upon which the argument bears is serial: there are n litigations, the 'current' litigation between master and pupil is added to the preceding ones, $n + 1$. When Protagoras takes it into account, he makes $n = n + 1$. It is true that this synthesis requires an additional 'act': $(n + 1) + 1$. This act corresponds to Protagoras' judgment. That is why he phrases his decision using the aorist [*enikèsa*], the tense for the indeterminate: *If you win, then I'm the winner.* The seriality of totality introduces the consideration of time, which is excluded from the genre of logic. There are, though, logics of time that at least allow for this aspect of the litigation to be made evident.

From this aspect, Euathlus' affirmation wouldn't be: *None of my pleas is a winning one* (a negative universal, which we can designate by *not-p*); but: *None of my pleas was a winning one.* Expressed in a logic of time [. . .], this last phrase could be written: *For all times prior to now, it is true during that time that not-p.* The pinpointing of the true is axed on the 'now.' It is thus not ruled out for Protagoras to say: *There exists at least one time and that time is now or later, and it is true during that time that p.*

Now is indeed the same temporal-logical operator, even though in Protagoras' phrase it is not in the same place in the series as is Euathlus' now. If we situate them in relation to an arbitrary origin t_0, the latter is called t_1 and Protagoras' now t_2. But the arbitrary origin t_0 is precisely what one calls now.

In this respect, Protagoras has done nothing more than use the faculty given him by the temporal deictic 'now' for it to be both the origin of temporal series (before and after) and an element in these series [. . .]. Aristotle encounters and elaborates the same problem when he analyzes the dyad before/after in its relation to the now (Aristotle Notice). The paradoxical phrase cannot be eliminated here simply for its poor formulation. The genre of discourse which ought to accept it is not logic, but 'physics' whose referent is not the phrase, but all moving objects (including phrases). Generalized relativity will confer upon that phrase citizenship rights in the physics of the universe.

4. Phrases form a physical universe if they are grasped as moving objects which form an infinite series. The phrase referring to this universe is therefore by hypothesis part of that universe: it will become part of it in the following instant. If we call history the series of phrases considered in this way (physically), then the historian's phrase 'will become part' of the universe to which it refers. The difficulties raised by historicism and dogmatism stem from this situation. The former declares that his phrase is part of its referent, history; the latter that his phrase is not part of it.

In the solution to the antinomies of pure reason, Kant writes that the question of the series resumes in itself all the conflicts that are raised by cosmological Ideas. The 'last' phrase synthesizes the preceding ones. Is it or is it not part of their set? Dogmatism answers no, empiricism yes. Criticism remarks that the series is never given [*gegeben*], but only proposed [*aufgegeben*], because its synthesis is always deferred. The phrase that synthesizes the series (the judgment actually born upon the set of Euathlus' pleas) is not part of the series when it 'takes place' (as an occurrence), but it is inevitably destined to become part of the series synthesized by the following phrase. The series formed by the world, in particular the world of human history, is neither finite or infinite (we can argue either one indifferently), but the synthesis of the series, for its sake, is 'indefinite'.

5. Protagoras' argument is an *antistrephon*. It is reversible. In the version given by Aulus-Gellius, the dispute between master and pupil takes place before a tribunal. It could be retranscribed as follows: Protagoras: If you win (against me), you will have won; if you lose (against me), even if you say you always lose (against others), then you will still have won. The judges are perplexed. Euathlus: If I lose (against you), I will have lost; if I win (against you), even if I say I always lose, then I will still have lost. The judges decide to put off their pronouncement until later. The history of the world cannot pass a last judgment. It is made out of judged judgments.

9. It is in the nature of a victim not to be able to prove that one has been done a wrong. A plaintiff is someone who has incurred damages and who disposes of the means to prove it. One becomes a victim if one loses these means. One loses them, for example, if the author of the damages turns out directly or indirectly to be one's judge. The latter has the authority to reject one's testimony as false or the ability to impede its publication. But this is only a particular case. In general, the plaintiff becomes a victim when no presentation is possible of the wrong he or she says he or she has suffered. Reciprocally, the 'perfect crime' does not consist in killing the victim or the witnesses (that adds new crimes to the first one and aggravates the difficulty of effacing everything), but rather in obtaining the silence of the witnesses, the deafness of the judges, and the inconsistency (insanity) of the testimony. You neutralize the addressor, the addressee, and the sense of the testimony: then everything is as if there were no referent (no damages). If there is nobody to adduce the proof, nobody to admit it, and/or if the argument which upholds it is judged to be absurd, then the plaintiff is dismissed, the wrong he or she complains of cannot be attested. He or she becomes a victim. If he or she persists in invoking this wrong as if it existed, the others (addressor, addressee, expert commentator on the testimony) will easily be able to make him or her pass for mad. Doesn't paranoia confuse the *As if it were the case* with the *it is the case*?

10. But aren't the others acting for their part as if this were not the case, when it is perhaps the case? Why should there be less paranoia in denying the existence of gas chambers than in affirming it? Because, writes Leibniz, 'nothing is simpler and easier than something'. The one who says there is something is the plaintiff, it is up to him or her to bring forth a demonstration, by means of well-formed phrases and of procedures for establishing the existence of their referent. Reality is always the plaintiff's responsibility. For the defense, it is sufficient to refute the argumentation and to impugn the proof by a counter example. This is the defense's advantage, as recognized by Aristotle (*Rhetoric* 1402 b 24–25) and by strategists. Likewise, it cannot be said that a hypothesis is verified, but only that until further notice it has not yet been falsified. The defense is nihilistic, the prosecution pleads for existents [*l'étant*]. That is why it is up to the victims of extermination camps to prove that extermination. This is our way of thinking that reality is not a given, but an occasion to require that establishment procedures be effectuated in regard to it.

11. The death penalty is suppressed out of nihilism, out of a cognitive consideration for the referent, out of a prejudice in favor of the defense. The odds that it is not the case are greater than the odds that it is. This statistical estimation belongs to the family of cognitive phrases. The presumed innocence of the accused, which obligates the prosecution with adducing the proof of the offense, is the 'humanist' version of the same playing rule of cognition. – If the rules of the game are inverted, if everyone accused is presumed guilty, then the defense has the task of establishing innocence while the prosecution has only to refute the argumentation

and to impugn the proofs advanced by the defense. Now, it may be impossible to establish that the referent of a phrase does not have a given property, unless we have the right to resort to a refutation of the phrase in which the referent does have that property. How can I prove that I am not a drug dealer without asking my accuser to bring forth some proof of it and without refuting that proof? How can it be established that labor-power is not a commodity without refuting the hypothesis that it is? How can you establish what is not without criticizing what is? The undetermined cannot be established. It is necessary that negation be the negation of a determination. – This inversion of the tasks expected on one side and on the other may suffice to transform the accused into a victim, if he or she does not have the right to criticize the prosecution, as we see in political trials. Kafka warned us about this. It is impossible to establish one's innocence, in and of itself. It is a nothingness.

12. The plaintiff lodges his or her complaint before the tribunal, the accused argues in such a way as to show the inanity of the accusation. Litigation takes place. I would like to call a *differend* [*différend*] the case where the plaintiff is divested of the means to argue and becomes for that reason a victim. If the addressor, the addressee, and the sense of the testimony are neutralized, everything takes place as if there were no damages (No. 9). A case of differend between two parties takes place when the 'regulation' of the conflict that opposes them is done in the idiom of one of the parties while the wrong suffered by the other is not signified in that idiom. For example, contracts and agreements between economic partners do not prevent – on the contrary, they presuppose – that the laborer or his or her representative has had to and will have to speak of his or her work as though it were the temporary cession of a commodity, the 'service', which he or she putatively owns. This 'abstraction' as Marx calls it (but the term is bad, what concreteness does it allege?), is required by the idiom in which the litigation is regulated ('bourgeois' social and economic law). In failing to have recourse to this idiom, the laborer would not exist within its field of reference, he or she would be a slave. In using it, he or she becomes a plaintiff. Does he or she also cease for that matter to be a victim?

13. One remains a victim at the same time that one becomes a plaintiff. Does one have the means to establish that one is a victim? No. How can you know then that one is a victim? What tribunal can pass judgment in this matter? In effect, the differend is not a matter for litigation; economic and social law can regulate the litigation between economic and social partners but not the differend between labor-power and capital. By what well-formed phrase and by means of what establishment procedure can the worker affirm before the labor arbitrator that what one yields to one's boss for so many hours per week in exchange for a salary is *not* a commodity? One is presumed to be the owner of something. One is in the case of the accused who has to establish a non-existent or at least a non-attribute. It is easy to refute him or her. It all happens as if what one is could only be expressed in an idiom other than that of social and economic law. In the latter, one can only express what one

has, and if one has nothing, what one does not have either will not be expressed or will be expressed in a certifiable manner as if one had it. If the laborer evokes his or her essence (labor-power), he or she cannot be heard by this tribunal, which is not competent. The differend is signaled by this inability to prove. The one who lodges a complaint is heard, but the one who is a victim, and who is perhaps the same one, is reduced to silence.

14. 'The survivors rarely speak' (no. 1). But isn't there an entire literature of testimonies ... ? – That's not it, though. Not to speak is part of the ability to speak, since ability is a possibility and a possibility implies something and its opposite. *Possible that p* and *Possible that not-p* are equally true. It is in the very definition of the possible to imply opposites at the same time. That the opposite of speaking is possible does not entail the necessity of keeping quiet. To be able not to speak is not the same as not to be able to speak. The latter is a deprivation, the former a negation. (Aristotle, *De Interpretatione* 21 b 12–17; *Metaphysics* IV 1022 b 22 ff). If the survivors do not speak, is it because they cannot speak, or because they avail themselves of the possibility of not speaking that is given them by the ability to speak? Do they keep quiet out of necessity, or freely, as it is said? Or is the question poorly stated?

15. It would be absurd to suppose that human beings 'endowed with language' cannot speak in the strict sense, as is the case for stones. Necessity would signify here: they do not speak because they are threatened with the worst in the case that they would speak, or when in general a direct or indirect attempt is made against their ability to speak. Let's suppose that they keep quiet under threat. A contrary ability needs to be presupposed if the threat is to have an effect, since this threat bears upon the hypothesis of the opposite case, the one in which the survivors would speak. But how could a threat work when it is exerted upon something (here, the eventuality that the survivors will speak) which does not currently exist? What is threatened? This is said to be the life, or happiness, etc., of the one who would speak. But the one who *would* speak (an unreal, conditional state) has no life, no happiness, etc., which can be threatened, since one is oneself unreal or conditional as long as one has not spoken, – if indeed it is that I am never but the addressor of a current phrase.

16. What is subject to threats is not an identifiable individual, but the ability to speak or to keep quiet. This ability is threatened with destruction. There are two means to achieve this: making it impossible to speak, making it impossible to keep quiet. These two means are compatible: it is made impossible for *x* to speak about this (through incarceration, for example); it is made impossible for him or her to keep quiet about that (through torture, for example). The ability is destroyed as an ability: *x* may speak about this *and* keep quiet about that, but he or she ceases to be able *either* to speak *or* not to speak about this or about that. The threat ('If you

were to tell (signify) this, it would be your last phrase' or, 'If you were to keep quiet about that, it would be your last silence') is only a threat because the ability to speak or not to speak is identified with x's existence.

17. The paradox of the last phrase (or of the last silence), which is also the paradox of the series, should give x not the vertigo of what cannot be phrased (which is also called the fear of death), but rather the irrefutable conviction that phrasing is endless. For a phrase to be the last one, another one is needed to declare it, and it is then not the last one. At the least, the paradox should give x both this vertigo and this conviction. – Never mind that the last phrase is the last one that x says! – No, it is the last one that has x as its direct or 'current' addressor.

18. It should be said that addressor and addressee are instances, either marked or unmarked, presented by a phrase. The latter is not a message passing from an addressor to an addressee both of whom are independent of it [. . .]. They are situated in the universe the phrase presents, as are its referent and its sense. 'X's phrase, *my* phrase, *your* silence': do *we*, identifiable individuals, x, y, speak phrases or make silences, in the sense that we would be their authors? Or is it that phrases or silences take place (happen, come to pass), presenting universes in which individuals x, y, you, me are situated as the addressors of these phrases or silences? And if this is so, at the price of what misunderstanding can a threat exerted against x threaten 'his' or 'her' phrase?

19. To say that x can be threatened for what he or she might say or keep quiet is to presuppose that one is free to use language or not and therefore that this freedom to use can be revoked by a threat. This is not false, it is a way of talking about language, humanity, and their interrelations which obeys the rules of the family of certain cognitive phrases (the human sciences). The phrase 'Under threat, under torture, in conditions of incarceration, in conditions of "sensory deprivation" etc., the linguistic behavior of a human being can be dictated to him or to her', is a well-formed phrase, and examples can, alas, be presented for which the scientist can say: here are some cases of it. But the human and linguistic sciences are like the juries of labor arbitration boards.

20. Just as these juries presuppose that the opponents they are supposed to judge are in possession of something they exchange, so do the human and linguistic sciences presuppose that the human beings they are supposed to know are in possession of something they communicate. And the powers that be (ideological, political, religious, police, etc.) presuppose that the human beings they are supposed to guide, or at least control, are in possession of something they communicate. Communication is the exchange of messages, exchange the communication of goods. The instances of communication like those of exchange are definable only in terms of property or propriety [*propriété*]: the propriety of information,

analogous to the propriety of uses. And just as the flow of uses can be controlled, so can the flow of information. As a perverse use is repressed, a dangerous bit of information is banned. As a need is diverted and a motivation created, an addressor is led to say something other than what he or she was going to say. The problem of language, thus posited in terms of communication, leads to that of the needs and beliefs of interlocutors. The linguist becomes an expert before the communication arbitration board. The essential problem he or she has to regulate is that of sense as a unit of exchange independent of the needs and beliefs of interlocutors. Similarly, for the economist, the problem is that of the value of goods and services as units independent of the demands and offers of economic partners.

21. Would you say that interlocutors are victims of the science and politics of language understood as communication to the same extent that the worker is transformed into a victim through the assimilation of his or her labor-power to a commodity? Must it be imagined that there exists a 'phrase-power', analogous to labor-power, and which cannot find a way to express itself in the idiom of this science and this politics? – Whatever this power might be, the parallel must be broken right away. It can be conceived that work is something other than the exchange of a commodity, and an idiom other than that of the labor arbitrator must be found in order to express it. It can be conceived that language is something other than the communication of a bit of information, and an idiom other than that of the human and linguistic sciences is needed in order to express it. This is where the parallel ends: in the case of language, recourse is made to another family of phrases; but in the case of work, recourse is not made to another family of work, recourse is still made to another family of phrases. The same goes for every differend buried in litigation, no matter what the subject matter. To give the differend its due is to institute new addressees, new addressors, new significations, and new referents in order for the wrong to find an expression and for the plaintiff to cease being a victim. This requires new rules for the formation and linking of phrases. No one doubts that language is capable of admitting these new phrase families or new genres of discourse. Every wrong ought to be able to be put into phrases. A new competence (or 'prudence') must be found.

22. The differend is the unstable state and instant of language wherein something which must be able to be put into phrases cannot yet be. This state includes silence, which is a negative phrase, but it also calls upon phrases which are in principle possible. This state is signaled by what one ordinarily calls a feeling: 'One cannot find the words', etc. A lot of searching must be done to find new rules for forming and linking phrases that are able to express the differend disclosed by the feeling, unless one wants this differend to be smothered right away in a litigation and for the alarm sounded by the feeling to have been useless. What is at stake in a literature, in a philosophy, in a politics perhaps, is to bear witness to differends by finding idioms for them.

23. In the differend, something 'asks' to be put into phrases, and suffers from the wrong of not being able to be put into phrases right away. This is when the human beings who thought they could use language as an instrument of communication learn through the feeling of pain which accompanies silence (and of pleasure which accompanies the invention of a new idiom) that they are summoned by language, not to augment to their profit the quantity of information communicable through existing idioms, but to recognize that what remains to be phrased exceeds what they can presently phrase, and that they must be allowed to institute idioms which do not yet exist.

24. It is possible then that the survivors do not speak even though they are not threatened in their ability to speak should they speak later. The socio-linguist, the psycho-linguist, the bio-linguist seek the reasons, the passions, the interests, the context for these silences. Let us first seek their logic. We find that they are substitutes for phrases. They come in the place of phrases during a conversation, during an interrogation, during a debate, during the *talking* of a psychoanalytic session, during a confession, during a critical review, during a metaphysical exposition. The phrase replaced by silence would be a negative one. Negated by it is at least one of the four instances that constitute a phrase universe: the addressee, the referent, the sense, the addressor. The negative phrase that the silence implies could be formulated respectively: *This case does not fall within your competence, This case does not exist, It cannot be signified, It does not fall within my competence.* A single silence could be formulated by several of these phrases. – Moreover, these negative formulations, which deny the ability of the referent, the addressor, the addressee and the sense to be presented in the current idiom, do not point to the other idiom in which these instances could be presented.

25. It should be said by way of simplification that a phrase presents what it is about, the case, *ta pragmata*, which is its referent; what is signified about the case. the sense, *der Sinn*; that to which or addressed to which this is signified about the case, the addressee; that 'through' which or in the name of which this is signified about the case, the addressor. The disposition of a phrase universe consists in the situating of these instances in relation to each other. A phrase may entail several referents, several senses, several addressees, several addressors. Each of these four instances may be marked in the phrase or not [. . .].

26. Silence does not indicate which instance is denied, it signals the denial of one or more of the instances. The survivors remain silent, and it can be understood (1) that the situation in question (the case) is not the addressee's business (he or she lacks the competence, or he or she is not worthy of being spoken to about it, etc.); or (2) that it never took place (this is what Faurisson understands); or (3) that there is nothing to say about it (the situation is senseless, inexpressible); or (4) that it is not the survivors' business to be talking about it (they are not worthy, etc.). Or, several of these negations together.

27. The silence of the survivors does not necessarily testify in favor of the non-existence of gas chambers, as Faurisson believes or pretends to believe. It can just as well testify against the addressee's authority (we are not answerable to Faurisson), against the authority of the witness him- or herself (we, the rescued, do not have the authority to speak about it), finally against language's ability to signify gas chambers (an inexpressible absurdity). If one wishes to establish the existence of gas chambers, the four silent negations must be withdrawn: There were no gas chambers, were there? Yes, there were. – But even if there were, that cannot be formulated, can it? Yes, it can. – But even if it can be formulated, there is no one, at least, who has the authority to formulate it, and no one with the authority to hear it (it is not communicable), is there? Yes, there is.

5.5 □ Ethics of the Infinite

Emmanuel Lévinas

Interview with
Richard Kearney

[. . .]

Richard Kearney: How does the ethical relation to the other, so central a theme in your philosophy, serve to subvert the ontology of a presence in its Greek and Heideggerian forms?

Emmanuel Lévinas: The interhuman relationship emerges with our history, with out being-in-the-world as intelligibility and presence. The interhuman realm can thus be construed as a part of the disclosure of the world as presence. But it can also be considered from another perspective – the ethical or biblical perspective which transcends the Greek language of intelligibility – as a theme of justice and concern for the other as other, as a theme of love and desire which carries us beyond the finite Being of the world as presence. The interhuman is thus an interface: a double axis where what is 'of the world' *qua phenomenological intelligibility* is juxtaposed with what is 'not of the world' *qua ethical responsibility*. It is in this ethical perspective that God must be thought and not in the ontological perspective of our being-there or of some Supreme Being and Creator correlative to the world, as traditional metaphysics often held. God, as the God of alterity and transcendence, can only be understood in terms of the interhuman dimension which, to be sure, emerges in the phenomenological–ontological perspective of the intelligible world, but which cuts through and perforates the totality of presence and points towards the absolutely Other. In this sense one could say that biblical thought has, to some extent, influenced my ethical reading of the interhuman, whereas Greek thought has largely determined its philosophical expression in language. So that I would maintain, against Heidegger, that philosophy can be ethical as well as ontological, can be at once Greek and non-Greek in its inspiration. These two sources of inspiration coexist as two different tendencies in modern philosophy and it is my

From Kearney, R., *Dialogues with Contemporary Continental Thinkers: The phenomenological heritage*, Manchester University Press, Manchester, 1984, pp. 56–61, 63–6, 68–9.

own personal task to try to identify this dual origin of meaning – *der Ursprung der Sinnhaften* – in the interhuman relationship.

RK: One of the most complex and indeed central themes in your philosophy is the rapport between the interhuman and time. Could you elucidate this rapport by situating it in terms of the ethics/ontology distinction?

EL: I am trying to show that man's ethical relation to the other is ultimately prior to his ontological relation to himself (egology) or to the totality of things which we call the world (cosmology). The relationship with the other is *time*: it is an untotalizable diachrony in which one moment pursues another without ever being able to retrieve it, to catch up with or coincide with it. The non-simultaneous and non-present is my primary rapport with the other in time. Time means that the other is forever beyond me, irreducible to the synchrony of the same. The temporality of the interhuman opens up the meaning of otherness and the otherness of meaning. But because there are more than two people in the world, we invariably pass from the ethical perspective of alterity to the ontological perspective of totality. There are always at least three persons. This means that we are obliged to ask who is the other, to try to objectively define the undefinable, to compare the incomparable in an effort to juridically hold different positions together. So that the first type of simultaneity is the simultaneity of equality, the attempt to reconcile and balance the conflicting claims of each person. If there were only two people in the world, there would be no need for law courts because I would always be responsible for, and before, the other. As soon as there are three, the ethical relationship with the other becomes political and enters into the totalizing discourse of ontology. We can never completely escape from the language of ontology and politics. Even when we deconstruct ontology we are obliged to use its language. Derrida's work of deconstruction, for example, possesses the speculative and methodological rigour of the philosophy which he is seeking to deconstruct. It's like the argument of the sceptics: how can we know that we can't know anything? The greatest virtue of philosophy is that it can put itself in question, try to deconstruct what it has constructed and unsay what it has said. Science, on the contrary, does not try to unsay itself, does not interrogate or challenge its own concepts, terms or foundations; it forges ahead, progresses. In this respect, science attempts to ignore language by constructing its own abstract non-language of calculable symbols and formulae. But science is merely a secondary bracketing of philosophical language from which it is ultimately derived; it can never have the last word. Heidegger summed this up admirably when he declared that science *calculates* but does not *think*. Now what I am interested in is precisely this ability of philosophy to think, to question itself and ultimately to unsay itself. And I wonder if this capacity for interrogation and for unsaying (*dédire*) is not itself derived from the pre-ontological interhuman relationship with the other. The fact that philosophy cannot fully totalize the alterity of meaning in some final presence or simultaneity is not for me a deficiency or fault. Or to put it in another way, the best thing about philosophy is that it fails. It is better that philosophy fail to totalize meaning – even though, as ontology, it has attempted just this – for it thereby remains open to the irreducible otherness of transcendence. Greek ontology, to be sure, expressed the strong sentiment that the last word is unity, the many becoming one, the truth as synthesis. Hence Plato defined love – *eros* – as only *half*-divine in so far as it lacks the full coincidence or unification of differences which he defined as divinity. The whole Romantic tradition in European poetry tends to conform to this Platonic ontology by inferring that love is perfect when two people become *one*. I am trying to work against this identification of the Divine with unification or totality. Man's relationship with the other is *better* as difference than as unity: sociality is better than fusion. The very value of love is the impossibility of reducing the other to myself, of coinciding into sameness. From an ethical perspective, two have a better time than one (*on s'amuse mieux à deux*)!

RK: Is it possible to conceive of an eschatology of non-coincidence wherein man and God could coexist eternally without fusing into oneness?

EL: But why eschatology? Why should we wish to reduce time to eternity? Time is the most profound relationship that man can have with God precisely as a going towards God. There is an excellence in time which would be lost in eternity. To desire eternity is to desire to perpetuate oneself, to go on living as oneself, to *be* always. Can one conceive of an eternal life that would not suspend time or reduce it to a contemporaneous presence? To accept time is to accept death as the impossibility of presence. To be in eternity is to be *one*, to be *oneself* eternally. To be in time is to be for God (*être à Dieu*), a perpetual leavetaking (*adieu*).

RK: But how can one be for God or go towards God as the absolutely Other? Is it by going towards the human other?

EL: Yes, and it is essential to point out that the relation implied in the preposition *towards* [à] is ultimately a relation derived from time. Time fashions man's relation to the other, and to the absolutely Other or God, as a diachronic relation irreducible to correlation. 'Going towards God' is not to be understood here in the classical ontological sense of a return to, or reunification with, God as the Beginning or End of temporal existence. 'Going towards God' is meaningless unless seen in terms of my primary going towards the other person. I can only go towards God by being ethically concerned by and for the other person. I am not saying that ethics presupposes belief. On the contrary, belief presupposes ethics as that disruption of our being-in-the-world which opens us to the other. The ethical exigency to be responsible for the other undermines the ontological primacy of the meaning of Being; it unsettles the natural and political positions we have taken up in the world and predisposes us to a meaning that is other than Being, that is otherwise than Being (*autrement qu'être*).

RK: What role does your analysis of the 'face' (*visage*) of the other play in this disruption of ontology?

EL: The approach to the face is the most basic mode of responsibility. As such, the face of the other is verticality and uprightness; it spells a relation of rectitude. The face is not in front of me (*en face de moi*) but above me; it is the other before death, looking through and exposing death. Secondly, the face is the other who asks me not to let him die alone, as if to do so were to become an accomplice in his death.

Thus the face says to me: you shall not kill. In the relation to the face I am exposed as a usurper of the place of the other. The celebrated 'right to existence' which Spinoza called the *conatus essendi* and defined as the basic principle of all intelligibility, is challenged by the relation to the face. Accordingly, my duty to respond to the other suspends my natural right to self-survival, *le droit vitale*. My ethical relation of love for the other stems from the fact that the self cannot survive by itself alone, cannot find meaning within its own being-in-the-world, within the ontology of sameness. That is why I prefaced *Totality and Infinity* with Pascal's phrase, '*Ma place au soleil, le commencement de toute usurpation*'. Pascal makes the same point when he declares that '*le moi est haïssable*'. Pascal's ethical sentiments here go against the ontological privileging of 'the right to exist'. To expose myself to the vulnerability of the face is to put my ontological right to existence into question. In ethics, the other's right to exist has primacy over my own, a primacy epitomized in the ethical edict: you shall not kill, you shall not jeopardize the life of the other. The ethical rapport with the face is asymmetrical in that it subordinates my existence to the other. This principle recurs in Darwinian biology as the 'survival of the fittest', and in psychoanalysis as the natural instinct of the 'id' for gratification, possession and power – the *libido dominandi*.

RK: So I owe more to the other than to myself …

EL: Absolutely, and this ethical exigency undermines the Hellenic endorsement, still prevalent today, of the *conatus essendi*. There is a Jewish proverb which says that 'the other's material needs are my spiritual needs'; it is this disproportion or asymmetry which characterizes the ethical refusal of the first truth of ontology – the struggle to *be*. Ethics is, therefore, *against nature* because it forbids the murderousness of my natural will to put my own existence first.

RK: Does going towards God always require that we go against nature?

EL: God cannot appear as the cause or creator of nature. The word of God speaks through the glory of the face and calls for an ethical conversion or reversal of our nature. What we call lay morality, that is, humanistic concern for our fellow human beings, already speaks the voice of God. But the moral priority of the other over myself could not come to be if it were not motivated by something beyond nature. The ethical situation is a human situation, beyond human nature, in which the idea of God comes to mind (*Gott fällt mir ein*). In this respect, we could say that God is the other who turns our nature inside out, who calls our ontological will-to-be into question. This ethical call of conscience occurs, no doubt, in other religious systems besides the Judeo-Christian, but it remains an essentially religious vocation. God does indeed go against nature for He is not of this world. God is other than Being.

RK: How does one distil the ethico-religious meaning of existence from its natural or ontological sedimentation?

EL: But your question already assumes that ethics is derived from ontology. I believe, on the contrary, that the ethical relationship with the other is just as primary and original (*ursprünglich*) as ontology – if not more so. Ethics is not derived from an ontology of nature; it is its opposite, a meontology which affirms a meaning beyond Being, a primary mode of non-Being (*me-on*).

RK: And yet you claim that the ethical and the ontological coexist as two inspirations without Western philosophy?

EL: Already in Greek philosophy one can discern traces of the ethical breaking through the ontological, for example in Plato's idea of the 'Good existing beyond Being' (*agathon epekeina tes ousias*). (Heidegger, of course, contests this ethical reading of the Good in Plato, maintaining that it is merely one among other descriptions of Being itself.) One can also cite in this connection Descartes's discovery of the 'Idea of the Infinite', which surpasses the finite limits of human nature and the human mind. And similarly supra-ontological notions are to be found in the pseudo-Dionysian doctrine of the *via eminentiae* with its surplus of the Divine over Being, or in the Augustinian distinction in the *Confessions* between the truth which challenges (*veritas redarguens*) and the ontological truth which shines (*veritas lucens*), etc.

[. . .]

RK: In the structuralist and post-structuralist debates which have tended to dominate continental philosophy in recent years, there has been much talk of the disappearance or the demise of the subject. Is your ethical thought an attempt to preserve subjectivity in some form?

EL: My thinking on this matter goes in the opposite direction to structuralism. It is not that I wish to preserve, over and against the structuralist critique, the idea of a subject who would be a substantial or mastering centre of meaning, an idealist self-sufficient *cogito*. These traditional ontological versions of subjectivity have nothing to do with the meontological version of subjectivity that I put forward in *Autrement qu'être*. Ethical subjectivity dispenses with the idealizing subjectivity of ontology which reduces everything to itself. The ethical 'I' is subjectivity precisely in so far as it kneels before the other, sacrificing its own liberty to the more primordial call of the other. For me, the freedom of the subject is not the highest or primary value. The heteronomy of our response to the human other, or to God as the absolutely Other, precedes the autonomy of our subjective freedom. As soon as I acknowledge that it is 'I' who am responsible, I accept that my freedom is anteceded by an obligation to the other. Ethics redefines subjectivity as this heteronymous responsibility in contrast to autonomous freedom. Even if I deny my primordial responsibility to the other by affirming my own freedom as primary, I can never escape the fact that the other has demanded a response from me *before* I affirm my freedom not to respond to his demand. Ethical freedom is *une difficile liberté*, a heteronymous freedom obliged to the other. Consequently, the other is the richest and the poorest of beings: the richest, at an ethical level, in that it always comes before me, its right-to-be preceding mine; the poorest, at an ontological or political level, in that without me it can do nothing, it is utterly vulnerable and exposed. The other haunts our ontological existence and keeps the psyche awake, in a state of vigilant insomnia. Even though we are ontologically free to refuse the other, we remain forever accused, with a bad conscience.

RK: Is not the ethical obligation to the other a purely negative ideal, impossible to realize in our everyday being-in-the-world? After all, we live in a concrete historical world governed by ontological drives and practices, be they political and institutional totalities or technological systems of mastery, organization and control. Is ethics practicable in human society as we know it? Or is it merely an invitation to apolitical acquiescence?

EL: This is a fundamental point. Of course we inhabit an ontological world of technological mastery and political self-preservation. Indeed without these political and technological structures of organization we would not be able to feed mankind. This is the great paradox of human existence: we must use the ontological *for the sake of the other*; to ensure the survival of the other we must resort to the technico-political systems of means and ends. This same paradox is also present in our use of language, to return to an earlier point. We have no option but to employ the language and concepts of Greek philosophy even in our attempts to go beyond them. We cannot obviate the language of metaphysics and yet we cannot, ethically speaking, be satisfied with it: it is necessary but not enough. I disagree, however, with Derrida's interpretation of this paradox. Whereas he tends to see the deconstruction of the Western metaphysics of presence as an irredeemable crisis, I see it as a golden opportunity for Western philosophy to open itself to the dimension of otherness and transcendence beyond Being.

RK: Is there any sense in which language can be ethical?

EL: In *Autrement qu'être* I pose this question when I ask: 'What is saying without a said?'. Saying is ethical sincerity in so far as it is exposition. As such this *saying* is irreducible to the ontological definability of the *said*. Saying is what makes the self-exposure of sincerity possible; it is a way of giving everything, of not keeping anything for oneself. In so far as ontology equates truth with the intelligibility of total presence, it reduces the pure exposure of saying to the totalizing closure of the said. The child is a pure exposure of expression in so far as it is pure vulnerability; it has not yet learned to dissemble, to deceive, to be insincere. What distinguishes human language from animal or child expression, for example, is that the human speaker can remain silent, can refuse to be exposed in sincerity. The human being is characterized as human not only because he is a being who can speak but also because he is a being who can lie, who can live in the duplicity of language as the dual possibility of exposure and deception. The animal is incapable of this duplicity; the dog, for instance, cannot suppress its bark, the bird its song. But man can repress his saying, and this ability to keep silent, to withhold oneself, is the ability to be political. Man can give himself in saying to the point of poetry – or he can withdraw into the non-saying of lies. Language as *saying* is an ethical openness to the other; as that which is *said* – reduced to a fixed identity or synchronized presence – it is an ontological closure to the other.

RK: But is there not some sort of 'morality' of the *said* which might reflect the ethics of *saying* in our everyday transactions in society? In other words, if politics cannot be ethical in so far as it is an expression of our ontological nature, can it at least be 'moral' (in your sense of that term)?

EL: This distinction between the ethical and the moral is very important here. By morality I mean a series of rules relating to social behaviour and civic duty. But while morality thus operates in the socio-political order of organizing and improving our human survival, it is ultimately founded on an ethical responsibility towards the other. As *prima philosophia*, ethics cannot itself legislate for society or produce rules of conduct whereby society might be revolutionized or transformed. It does not operate at the level of the manifesto or *rappel à l'ordre*; it is not a *savoir vivre*. When I talk of ethics as a 'disinterestedness' (*dès-intér-essement*), I do not mean that it is indifference; I simply mean that it is a form of vigilant passivity to the call of the other which precedes our interest in Being, our *inter-esse* as a being-in-the-world attached to property and appropriating what is other than itself to itself. Morality is what governs the world of political 'interestedness', the social interchanges between citizens in a society. Ethics, as the extreme exposure and sensitivity of one subjectivity to another, becomes morality and hardens its skin as soon as we move into the political world of the impersonal 'third' – the world of government, institutions, tribunals, prisons, schools, committees, etc. But the norm which must continue to inspire and direct the moral order is the ethical norm of the interhuman. If the moral-political order totally relinquishes its ethical foundation, it must accept all forms of society including the fascist or totalitarian, for it can no longer evaluate or discriminate between them. The state is usually better than anarchy – but not always. In some instances, fascism or totalitarianism, for example, the political order of the state may have to be challenged in the name of our ethical responsibility to the other. This is why ethical philosophy must remain the first philosophy.

[...]

RK: Your analysis of God as an impossibility of Being or being-present would seem to suggest that the ethical relation is entirely utopian and unrealistic.

EL: This is the great objection to my thought. 'Where did you ever see the ethical relation practised?', people say to me. I reply that its being utopian does not prevent it from investing our everyday actions of generosity or goodwill towards the other: even the smallest and most commonplace gestures, such as saying 'after you' as we sit at the dinner table or walk through a door, bear witness to the ethical. This concern for the other remains utopian in the sense that it is always 'out of place', [*u-topos*] in this world, always other than the 'ways of the world'; but there are many examples of it in the world. I remember meeting once with a group of Latin American students, well versed in the terminology of Marxist liberation and terribly concerned by the suffering and unhappiness of their people in Argentina. They asked me rather impatiently if I had ever actually witnessed the utopian rapport with the other which my ethical philosophy speaks of. I replied: 'Yes, indeed, here in this room.'

RK: So you would maintain that Marxism bears witness to a utopian inspiration?

EL: When I spoke of the overcoming of Western ontology as an 'ethical and prophetic cry' in 'Dieu et la philosophie' (*De Dieu qui vient à l'idée*), I was in fact thinking of Marx's critique of Western idealism as a project to understand the world rather than to transform it. In Marx's critique we find an ethical conscience cutting through the ontological identification of truth with an ideal intelligibility and demanding that theory be converted into a concrete praxis of concern for the other. It is this revelatory and prophetic cry which explains the extraordinary attraction which the Marxist utopia exerted over numerous generations. Marxism was, of course, utterly compromised by Stalinism. The 1968 Revolt in Paris was a revolt of sadness, because it came after the Khrushchev Report and the exposure of the corruption of the Communist Church. The year of 1968 epitomized the joy of despair; a last grasping at human justice, happiness and perfection after the truth had dawned that the communist ideal had degenerated into totalitarian bureaucracy. By 1968 only dispersed groups and rebellious pockets of individuals remained to seek their surrealist forms of salvation, no longer confident in a collective movement of humanity, no longer assured that Marxism could survive the Stalinist catastrophe as the prophetic messenger of history.

RK: What role can philosophy serve today? Has it in fact reached that end which so many contemporary continental philosophers have spoken of?

EL: It is true that philosophy, in its traditional forms of ontotheology and logocentrism – to use Heidegger's and Derrida's terms – has come to an end. But it is not true of philosophy in the other sense of critical speculation and interrogation. The speculative practice of philosophy is by no means near its end. Indeed the whole contemporary discourse of overcoming and deconstructing metaphysics is far more speculative in many respects than metaphysics itself. Reason is never so versatile as when it puts itself in question. In the contemporary end of philosophy, philosophy has found a new lease of life.

5.6 □ Why Define Sexed Rights?

Luce Irigaray

Christina Lasagni: Why are you now taking an interest in law, especially as you have approached problems in such a different way before?[1]

Luce Irigaray: As a philosopher, I am interested in theorizing all domains of reality and knowledge. Only very recently in the history of culture have philosophy and the sciences been separated – the result of methodological specialization, making them beyond the reach of anyone and everyone. The hypertechnical tendencies of current science lead to the creation of increasingly complex formulae that correspond, so it's believed, to an increasingly truthful truth. Consequently, it's a truth that escapes consideration in the light of wisdom, the scientist's own included. This doesn't bode well for our culture and its future development (cf. on this subject, 'Sujet de la Science, Sujet Sexué?' in *Sens et place des connaissances dans la societé*).[2]

So I have always been concerned with the issue of law from the perspective of the difference between the sexes. In *Speculum*, for instance, I discuss it quite explicitly on pages 148–54 and 266–81 [of the French edition], but it pervades the whole chapter on Plato. In *This Sex Which Is Not One*,[3] two chapters – 'Women on the Market' and 'Commodities Among Themselves' – consider the problems of economic and social rights. I'm dealing with the question in a more concrete way now. But as far as I'm concerned, there is no break between my earlier and latest texts, especially in this matter.

Why deal with legal questions more concretely? Because since 1970 I have regularly worked with women or groups of women who belong to liberation movements, and in these I've observed problems or impasses that can't be resolved except through the establishment of an equitable legal system for both sexes. In the absence of such social structures, women and men are losing themselves in spiraling demands, legal or otherwise, while in the meantime there's no protection for the

From Irigaray, L., *Je, tu, nous: Toward a Culture of Difference*, trans. A. Martin, Routledge, New York, 1993, pp. 81–92.

basic rights of every individual and global disorder increases. So the reestablishment of a pseudo-order is sought through the restoration of order to another country by nations incapable of managing their own problems. It's better to give aid than to leave people to die. But is it really a question of aid? Or is it more a question of apparently generous alibis in order to remain masters of the situation? It's not clear. And the laws of most use to us here and now, those to do with us, are always put off as if the world had grown accustomed to disorder, and in this quasi-deluge of our civilizations, all we have to do is find a way of rescuing man's identity – without taking any notice of the civilization women transmit. Any old excuse will do for not taking account of their truth. Men are even going back to archaic stages of culture by forcing their largely domesticated animals on the public as their latest totem. Instead of pursuing cultural development, the world is retreating to the minimum grounds for human definition. The consequences are that we no longer have any religion appropriate for our times, nor complete control of language as a tool of social exchange, as a means to acquire or create knowledge. Our legislation is not adequate to regulate private, religious, national, and international conflicts, particularly when it comes to the protection of life. Therefore, we no longer have any God(s), any language, any familiar cultural landscape. ... What do we have, then, to base social groups upon? I know some people think that the great eve of universal well-being has arrived. But which universal? What new imperialism is there lurking in all this? And who will pay the price for it? There is no universal valid for all men and women aside from the natural economy. All other universals are partial constructions and, as a result, authoritarian and unjust. The first universal to establish would be legislation valid for both sexes as a basic element of human culture. That doesn't mean enforcing sexual choices. But we are 'living' women and men, that is to say sexuate, and our identity can't be constructed without the benefit of a framework of relations, horizontal and vertical, that respects this difference.

In the absence of such an order, many people are nowadays looking for an identity-space other than the human one. A man defines himself in relation to his house or his neighbor's, his car or any other means of transport, the number of miles he's covered, the number of matches he's played, his favorite animals, his unique Gods in whose name he kills others and looks down on women, and so on. Man doesn't concern himself with improving the quality of man: 'Oh, I've got no time for that. ... That's old-fashioned. ... It's a thing of the past, that is. ...' All these indifferent responses, expressed passively by irresponsible citizens, are in my view the result of a lack of rights and obligations appropriate to real civil persons. Which leads to a great deal of authoritarianism, violence, and poverty.

CL: You talk about law that is sexed, law that encompasses female gender. It's a very different idea from the traditional notion of 'parity'. So it's not a matter of 'equal laws for all' but rather a notion of law that takes into account the fact that women are not equal to men. Can you explain the concept of sexed law?

LI: I think that, in particular cases, the struggle has to be for equal rights in order to make the differences between women and men apparent. Or at least I used to think that. I now think that what appears to be the reasonable way is utopian or misguided. Why? Women and men are not equal. And the strategy of equality, when there is one,[4] should always aim to get differences recognized. For example, having equal numbers of men and women in all sectors of social activity in order to get them to progress. Of course, on one level this is a totally desirable solution. But it's not enough. And it's this insufficiency that brings about repression and uncertainty concerning the differences between men and women, which women themselves maintain. Why is the equality strategy not enough? First, because the current social order, and that includes the order defining occupations, is not neutral when viewed in terms of the difference of the sexes. Working conditions and production techniques are not equally designed nor equally applied with respect to sexual difference. Working targets and systems are not equally defined by, nor for, women and men. At best, therefore, equality is achieved on pay. Of course, the right to equal pay is legitimate, as is the right of women to work outside the home and gain economic independence. Some people (men and women) think that this is sufficient in order to respect their human identity. Personally, I don't think it is. These new economic conditions can encourage us to rethink the whole of our social organization, unless they give support to the fact that, in order to achieve a minimum of freedom, women have to subject themselves to the imperatives of a culture that is not their own. Hence, should they have to help manufacture armaments or pollutants, or adjust themselves to men's working patterns, or again should they have to submit and contribute to the development of artificial languages unrelated to their natural language, which increasingly depersonalizes them, and so on? That doesn't equate with having equal rights. Because to have a chance of living freely, women are forced to subject themselves to men's means of production and to enhance their capital or sociocultural inheritance. In spite of all this they do enter the workplace, but in so doing they alienate their female identity. And the incentives that exist for women to go back into the home have a good chance of success, not necessarily among the most reactionary women, as is too readily believed, but also among women who wish to try to become women. What I mean by that is that there is still hardly any sort of work that enables a woman to earn her living as a male citizen does without alienating her identity in working conditions and contexts developed to suit men alone. Not considering this problem causes a great deal of misunderstanding and disagreement among people working for women's liberation. A good deal of time is lost in the mistakes that are made, and many misunderstandings are fostered, cynically or unknowingly, by those in power on a micro or macro level. As for women themselves, they are caught in a dilemma: stuck between the minimum social rights they can obtain by going out to work, gaining economic independence, being seen somewhat in society, etc., and the psychological or physical price they pay, and make other women pay, for this minimum, whether they are totally aware of it or not. All these misunderstandings could be resolved by the recognition that different laws exist for each sex and that equivalent social status can only be established after these laws have been encoded by civil society's elected representatives. So this must be aimed at as a priority.

CL: Can you give some examples, in order to explain how current law was created and has developed to suit men? What laws would be created in accordance with sexual difference?

LI: I think it's possible for me to answer both questions at once, in the sense that what has to be defined as women's rights is what the male people, the between-men culture, has appropriated as possessions, including in this respect not only women's and children's bodies, but also natural space, living space, the economy of signs and images, social and religious representation.

I'll deal with the question, then, by way of what has to be asserted now as women's rights:

1. The right to *human dignity*, which means:

   (a) Stopping the commercial use of their bodies and images;
   (b) Valid representations of themselves in actions, words, and images in all public places;
   (c) Stopping the exploitation of motherhood, a functional part of women, by civil and religious powers.

2. The right to *human identity*, that is:

   (a) The legal encodification of *virginity* (or physical and moral integrity) as a component of female identity that is not reducible to money, and not cash-convertible by the family, the State, or religious bodies in any way. This component of female identity enables the girl to be accorded civil status and gives her a right to keep her virginity (including for her own relationship with the divine) as long as she likes, as well as to lodge a complaint, with the support of the law, against anyone who violates this right from within or outside the family. If it is true that girls are less the objects of exchange between men in our cultures, there are still plenty of places where their virginity is traded, and girls' identity status as a cash-convertible body between men has been neither reformulated nor rethought. Girls need a positive identity to refer to as individual and social civil persons. Such an autonomous identity for girls is also essential for the free consent of women to sexual relationships and for the institution of marriage if women are not to be alienated by male power.

   What's more, this institution should be legally modified, especially in relation to the marriage of minors. At the moment, the law allows the family, the State, or religious bodies to be the legal guardians of the young married couple, and especially the woman, who can be married well before she reaches the age of majority. In my opinion we should increase the age of legal marriage or reduce that of civil majority and not allow marriage to operate as, in effect, an uncivil institution – that is, without the couple being in any way legally responsible.

These rights would enable us to get away from simple penal sanctions and to enjoy civil legality as far as women's rights are concerned. I'm thinking of rape and incest cases, for example, or cases against forced prostitution, pornography, etc., which are always enacted with a view to punishing the guilty rather than in accordance with civil society's guarantee of positive rights appropriate to women. But it's not a good thing, either for women or for relations between the sexes, that women as the injured party be put in the position of simply being accusers. If there were civil rights for women, the whole of society would be the injured party in the case of rape or all the other forms of violence inflicted on women; society, then, would be the plaintiff or co-plaintiff against the harm caused to one of its members.

(b) The right to *motherhood* as a component (not a priority) of female identity. If the body is a legal concern, and it is, then the female body must be civilly identified as a virgin and potential mother. Which means the mother will have the right to choose whether to be pregnant and the number of pregnancies. The mother herself, or her legal representative, will be the one to register the child's birth with the civil authorities.

3. The mutual obligations of mothers-children shall be defined by civil law. This is so that the mother can protect her children and be supported in this by law. That will enable her to be the plaintiff in the name of civil society in incest, rape, abuse, and kidnapping cases concerning children, particularly girls. The respective obligations of the mother and the father will be defined separately.

4. Women shall have a right to defend their own and their children's lives, their living space, their traditions, and their religion against all unilateral decisions emanating from male law (including in this respect armaments and pollution).

5. On a strictly financial level:

(a) Celibacy shall not be penalized by the tax system nor any other charges;
(b) If the State grants family benefits, they shall be of equal value for each child;
(c) Media broadcasts, such as television, for which women pay the same taxes as men, shall be half of the time targeted towards women.

6. Systems of exchange, such as linguistic exchange, for example, shall be revised in order to guarantee a right to equivalent exchange for men and women.

7. Women shall be represented in equal numbers in all civil and religious decision-making bodies, given that religion also represents civil authority.

CL: Some women have theorized their exteriority and aversion to law, their lack of interest in these issues. What do you think of this?

LI: I think this position is a poor analysis of what are the current conditions for the recognition of female identity. But I can appreciate that these women – kept by men-citizens (who generally use law in a way that is foreign to female interests) and not being citizens in their own right – forget this essential dimension of the social structure. I can particularly understand it given that, at the time when female law existed, it wasn't generally written and was exercised without the weight of the institutions that have proliferated under patriarchal regimes. But this female law did exist. The era when women governed the social order did not end in chaos, as some claim. Among other things, female law was characterized by:

1. The transmission of possessions and names between mothers and daughters
2. The privilege of sisters and of the last-born in a later transmission
3. The significance of divinity and the religious in filiation
4. The designation of the country of birth as the *motherland*
5. Respect for local places and divinities
6. Respect for naturally produced food: fruits most of all, then cereals
7. A temporality that respects the rhythms of life, the light cycle, the seasons, and the years
8. A higher morality based upon love and peace
9. A community of all the members of humankind
10. Arbitration entrusted to women on matters of alliances and the resolution of conflicts
11. Symbolic systems linked to art

One can find traces of these elements of female law in the works of Johann Jacob Bachofen, as well as in Mircea Eliade's descriptions of aboriginal cultures that still exist in India, for example. These references are far from being exclusive. They, and their bibliographies, may be able to provide a lead for research. I have chosen to cite men partly to illustrate male theorists' recognition of this reality.

In order for these rights to be respected today, rights that seem to me to correspond to female subjectivity, we will have to resort to written law. Otherwise, written law will continue to be enforced to the detriment of girls, who are alienated from it from birth and by their genealogies. Moreover, I think it would be a good thing for women to create a social order in which they can make use of their subjectivity with its symbols, its images, its dreams and realities – thus, the objective means of subjective exchange.

CL: I'd like to finish off this interview by asking you for some advice for women (and men too) who are interested in the law.

LI: As a priority, they should guarantee the conservation of nature in so far as it's what enables everyone to live and feed themselves through work without speculative and alienating mediations.

1. Specify the basic rights for everyone's life: women and men, girls and boys, mothers and fathers, female and male citizens, women and men workers, etc., starting with women and men, or at least retaining this difference as a framework if other priorities come to the fore.
2. Reduce the rights of groups or companies governed by one or only a few people. Democracy itself still does not exist in the sense in which it is invoked, and its principles need to be looked at, particularly in the light of the time and manner in which it was defined and established by men alone.

3. Redefine and value adequate laws on housing, and indeed private property in general. Women, men, and children need a place to live without being cheated of this need, this desire, this rightful investment, by environmental pollution (cars, airplanes, noisy machines, etc.), by lack of safety or faulty construction, liberties taken in building places initially denied permission to be built, and therefore depriving existing residents of light, air, and peace, and forcing them into a semi-nomadism through a lack of legal protection regarding real estate.

4. Reduce the power money has, particularly the surplus-value associated with the capricious desires of the rich or those not so rich (take, for example, real estate agents who speculate on human greed by pretending that a smaller apartment can be more expensive since it's sought after by purchasers having trouble moving, but the sellers know that's not the case), and get back to valid exchanges based on the cost of products and the choice of means of production (which means going back to more natural methods without increasing production or overproducing with respect to the earth, the air, the oceans, and human bodies, too).

5. Question the origins of the law currently in force, particularly in relation to the time when women really were civil persons, a time misleadingly termed Prehistory. This will lead you to consider what has to be changed in current law and to question the notions of the civil and the religious as assimilable or differentiated and guaranteeing free choices.

May 1988

Notes

1. Christina Lasagni asked me these questions for the first issue of *Il diritto delle donne*, journal of Emilia Romagna, published in Bologna, Italy.
2. 'Is the subject of science sexed?' trans. Carol Mastrangelo Bové, *Hypatia* 2 (Fall 1987): 65–87.
3. Trans. Catherine Porter with Carolyn Burke (Ithaca, NY: Cornell University Press, 1985), originally published (Paris: Minuit, 1977).
4. And it's present in the very concept of law, though not simply as a strategy.

5.7 □ Human Functioning and Social Justice: in defense of Aristotelian essentialism [1]

Martha C. Nussbaum

[. . .]

Antiessentialist conversations

[. . .]

At a conference on value and technology, an American economist who has long been considered a radical delivers a paper urging the preservation of traditional ways of life in a rural area of India, now under threat of contamination from Western values. As evidence of the excellence of this rural way of life, he points to the fact that, whereas we Westerners experience a sharp split between the values that prevail in the workplace and the values that prevail in the home, here, by contrast, there exists what the economist calls 'the embedded way of life'. His example: just as in the home a menstruating woman is thought to pollute the kitchen and so may not enter it, so too in the workplace a menstruating woman is taken to pollute the loom and may not enter the room where looms are kept. An economist from India objects that this example is repellent rather than admirable, for surely such practices both degrade the women in question and inhibit their freedom. The first economist's collaborator, an elegant French anthropologist (who would, I suspect, object

From *Political Theory*, vol. 20, no. 2, May 1992, pp. 202–10, 212–34, 237, 239–46.

violently to a purity check at the seminar room door), addresses the objector in contemptuous tones. Doesn't he realize that there is, in these matters, no privileged place to stand? Doesn't he know that he is neglecting the radical otherness of these village people by bringing his Western essentialist values into the picture?

The same French anthropologist now delivers her paper. She expresses regret that the introduction of smallpox vaccination to India by the British eradicated the cult of Sittala Devi, the goddess to whom one used to pray in order to avert smallpox. Here, she says, is another example of Western neglect of difference. Someone (it might have been me) objects that it is surely better to be healthy rather than ill, to live rather than to die. The frosty answer comes back: Western essentialist medicine conceives of things in terms of binary oppositions: life is opposed to death, health to disease. But if we cast away this blinkered way of seeing things, we will comprehend the radical otherness of Indian traditions. At this point, Eric Hobsbawm, who has been listening to the proceedings in increasingly uneasy silence, rises to deliver a blistering indictment of the traditionalism and relativism that prevail in this group. He lists examples of how the appeal to tradition has been used in history to defend various types of oppression and violence.

[. . .]

These examples are not unusual; I could cite many more. What we see in such cases is an odd phenomenon indeed. Highly intelligent people, people deeply committed to the good of women and men in developing countries, people who think of themselves as progressive and feminist and antiracist, are taking up positions that converge, as Hobsbawm correctly saw, with the positions of reaction, oppression, and sexism. Under the banner of their radical and politically correct 'antiessentialism' march ancient religious taboos, the luxury of the pampered husband, ill health, ignorance, and death. (And in my own essentialist way, I say it at the outset. I do hold that death is opposed to life in the most binary way imaginable, and slavery to freedom, and hunger to adequate nutrition, and ignorance to knowledge.)

Essentialism is becoming a dirty word in the academy and in those parts of human life that are influenced by it. Essentialism – which for these purposes I shall understand as the view that human life has certain central defining features – is linked by its opponents with an ignorance of history, with lack of sensitivity to the voices of women and minorities.[2] It is taken, usually without extended argument, to be in league with racism and sexism, with 'patriarchal' thinking generally, whereas extreme relativism is taken to be a recipe for social progress. In this essay, I question these connections. I grant that some criticisms of some forms of essentialism have been fruitful and important: they have established the ethical debate on a more defensible metaphysical foundation and have redirected our gaze from unexamined abstract assumptions to the world and its actual history. But I argue that those who would throw out all appeals to a determinate account of the human being, human functioning, and human flourishing are throwing away far too much – in terms even, and especially, of their own compassionate ends.

I argue, first, that the legitimate criticisms of essentialism still leave room for essentialism of a kind: for a historically sensitive account of the most basic human needs and human functions. I then sketch such an account, which I have developed at length elsewhere, showing how it can meet the legitimate objections. I then argue that without such an account, we do not have an adequate basis for an account of social justice and the ends of social distribution. With it, on the other hand, we have – what we urgently need at this time – the basis for a global ethic and a fully international account of distributive justice. Finally, I argue that without essentialism of a kind, we are deprived of two moral sentiments that are absolutely necessary if we are to live together decently in the world: compassion and respect.[3]

The assault on essentialism

[. . .]

Attacks on Metaphysical-Realist Essentialism

Metaphysical realism claims that there is some determinate way that the world is apart from the interpretive workings of the cognitive faculties of living beings. A description of the world is true just in case it corresponds to that independently existing structure, false in so far as it does not so correspond. Unless the metaphysical realist is also a skeptic – a combination rarely found, since it is hard to sustain confidence in realism without the belief that someone can adequately grasp reality – realism is accompanied by some related account of knowledge. Some mind or other – whether God's alone or certain human minds also – is said to be able to grasp this real structure as it is in itself; knowledge is defined in terms of this grasp.

[. . .]

The common objection to this sort of realism is that this sort of metaphysical truth is not in fact available. Sometimes this is put skeptically: the independent structure may still exist, but we can know nothing of it. More often, today, doubt is cast on the coherence of the whole realist idea that there is some one determinate structure to the way things are, independent of all human interpretation. This is the objection that nonphilosophers tend to associate with Jacques Derrida's assault on the 'metaphysics of presence', which he takes to have dominated the entirety of the Western philosophical tradition.[4] But it actually has a much longer and more complicated history. It begins in the Western tradition at least as early as Kant's assault on transcendent metaphysics – and perhaps far earlier, since some scholars have found a version of it in Aristotle's anti-Platonist arguments.[5] Its contemporary versions are themselves many and complex – involving, frequently, technical issues in the philosophy of science and the philosophy of language. In this sophisticated literature – whose major contributors include such outstanding philosophers as Ludwig Wittgenstein, W.V.O. Quine, Donald Davidson, Hilary Putnam, and Nelson Goodman – the arguments of Derrida are relatively minor contributions, which do not even confront a great many of the pressing questions that are at issue.[6]

The attack on metaphysical realism is far too complex to be summarized here, but its implications for essentialism are clear. If the only available (or perhaps even coherent) picture of reality is one in the derivation of which human interpretations play a part, if the only defensible conceptions of truth and knowledge hold truth and knowledge to be in certain ways dependent on human cognitive activity within history, then the hope for a pure unmediated account of our human essence as it is in itself, apart from history and interpretation, is no hope at all but a deep confusion. To cling to it as a goal is to pretend that it is possible for us to be told from outside what to be and what to do, when in reality the only answers we can ever hope to have must come, in some manner, from ourselves.

Attacks on Internalist Essentialism

But one might accept these conclusions and still be an essentialist. One might, that is, believe that the deepest examination of human history and human cognition *from within* still reveals a more or less determinate account of the human being, one that divides its essential from its accidental properties. Such an account would say: take away properties X, Y, and Z (a suntan, let us say, or a knowledge of Chinese, or an income of $40,000 a year) and we will still have what we count as a human being on our hands. On the other hand, take away properties A, B, and C (the ability to think about the future, say, or the ability to respond to the claims of others, or the ability to choose and act) and we no longer have a human life at all. Separating these two groups of properties requires an evaluative inquiry: for we must ask, which things are so important that we will not count a life as a human life without them? Such an evaluative inquiry into what is deepest and most indispensable in our lives need not presuppose an external metaphysical foundation, clearly: it can be a way of looking at ourselves, asking what we really think about ourselves and what holds our history together. Later on, I shall propose one version of such a historically grounded empirical essentialism – which, since it takes its stand within human experience, I shall now call 'internalist' essentialism.[7] Such internalist conceptions of the human being are still vulnerable to some, if not all, of the charges brought against essentialism generally. So even though the opposition rarely makes the externalist/internalist distinction, I shall myself introduce it, mentioning three charges that I think any good internalist account will need to answer.

1. Neglect of Historical and Cultural Differences

The opposition charges that any attempt to pick out some elements of human life as more fundamental than others, even without appeal to a transhistorical reality, is bound to be insufficiently respectful of actual historical and cultural differences. People, it is claimed, understand human life and humanness in widely different ways, and any attempt to produce a list of 'essential properties' is bound to enshrine certain understandings of the human and to demote others. Usually, the objector continues, this takes the form of enshrining the understanding of a dominant group at the expense of minority understandings. Such objectors usually also suggest that only an actual unanimous agreement would be sufficient to justify an essentialist conclusion. But in practice, such agreements are not forthcoming, so essentialism is bound to consist of the imposition of someone's authority on someone else.

2. *Neglect of Autonomy*

A different objection is pressed by liberal opponents of essentialism; usually these opponents are themselves willing to be essentialist about the central importance of human freedom and autonomy[8] The objection is that by determining in advance what elements of human life have most importance, the essentialist is failing to respect the right of people to choose a plan of life according to their own lights, determining what is most central and what is not. Such evaluative choices must be left to each citizen. For this reason, politics must refuse itself a determinate theory of the human being and the human good.

3. *Prejudicial Application*

If we operate with a determinate conception of the human being that is meant to have some normative moral and political weight, we must also, in applying it, ask which beings we take to fall under the concept. Here, the objector notes that all too easily the powerless can be excluded. Aristotle himself, it is pointed out, held that women and slaves were not full-fledged human beings; and since his politics was based on his essentialism, the failure of these beings (in his view) to exhibit the desired essence led to their political exclusion and oppression. The suggestion is that renouncing the use of such a determinate conception of the human will make it easier for such people to be heard and included.

The Collapse into Subjectivism

Each of these objections has some force. Later on in the essay, I ask how much force each of them has and whether there is a version of essentialism that can survive them. But what is alarming about the current debate in a variety of fields – literary theory, some parts of legal theory, and much of economic theory and development studies – is that this further inquiry has not taken place. Very often, as in my Helsinki examples, the collapse of metaphysical realism is taken to entail not only the collapse of essentialism about the human being but a retreat into an extreme relativism, or even subjectivism, about all questions of evaluation.[9]

The retreat usually takes the following form. First, an impossible demand is made, say, for unmediated presentness to reality as it is in itself or for an actual universal agreement about matters of value. Next, it is claimed that this demand cannot be met. Then, without any further ado – without looking at internal realist positions, such as those of Charles Taylor and Hilary Putnam, and without asking what more moderate cognitive demands *can* be met – the theorist concludes that everything is up for grabs and there are no norms to give us guidance in matters of evaluation. For some theorists, evaluation then becomes a matter of power: the criterion of truth will derive from one's contingent position of social authority. [10] For others, it becomes, instead, a matter of play and self-assertion: what is good is what I (whether for reasons or arbitrarily or whimsically) choose to assert. [11] For still others, as we shall see, value collapses into utility: to judge something good is part of a transaction in which one seeks to maximize one's utility (understood as desire-satisfaction or wealth or whatever).

[. . .]

Furthermore, in a more general attack on distinction-making, all 'binary oppositions' are frequently called into question – as if it is always both illegitimate and somehow *bad* to oppose one thing clearly to another, as if such distinction-making were always a preparation for some cruelty or oppression. [12] By these steps we arrive, in some cases, at the complete banishment of logic – that allegedly male patriarchal imperialist phenomenon.

[. . .]

Confronting the Objections

Let me say very directly where I stand on the objections to essentialism. I believe that Kantian and related contemporary arguments (by Quine, Davidson, Putnam, and Goodman in particular) have indeed successfully established the untenability of extreme metaphysical realism. I cannot argue this here, but I hope it can at least be agreed that it would be extremely unwise for a political proposal to rely on the truth of metaphysical realism, given our current argumentative situation. On the other hand, it does not seem to me that such a result shows anything like what the relativist objectors think it shows. When we get rid of the hope of a transcendent metaphysical grounding for your evaluative judgments – about the human being as about anything else – we are not left with the abyss. We have everything that we always had all along: the exchange of reasons and arguments by human beings within history, in which, for reasons that are historical and human but not the worse for that, we hold some things to be good and others bad, some arguments to be sound and others not sound. Why, indeed, should the relativist conclude that the absence of a transcendent basis for judgment – a basis that, according to them, was never there anyway – should make us despair of doing as we have done all along, distinguishing persuasion from manipulation?

In fact, the collapse into extreme relativism or subjectivism seems to me to betray a deep attachment to metaphysical realism itself. For it is only to one who has pinned everything to that hope that its collapse will seem to entail the collapse of all evaluation – just as it is only to a deeply believing religious person, as Nietzsche saw, that the news of the death of God brings the threat of nihilism. What we see here, I think, is a reaction of *shame* – a turning away of the eyes from our poor humanity, which looks so mean and bare – by contrast to a dream of another sort. What do we have here, these critics seem to say? Only our poor old human conversations, our human bodies that interpret things so imperfectly? Well, if that is all there is, we do not really want to study it too closely, to look into the distinctions it exhibits. We will just say that they are all alike, for, really, they do look pretty similar when compared to the heavenly standard we were seeking. It is like the moment reported by Aristotle when some students arrived at the home of Heraclitus, eager to see the great sage and cosmologist. They found him – not on a hilltop gazing at the heavens but sitting in his kitchen or, perhaps, on the toilet (for there is a philological dispute at this point!). He looked at their disappointed faces, saw that they were about to turn away their eyes, and said, 'Come in, don't be afraid. There are gods here too.' Aristotle uses this story to nudge his reluctant students out of the shame that is preventing them from looking closely at the parts of animals. When you get rid of your shame, he says, you will notice that there is order and structure *in* the animal world.[13]

So too, I think, with realism: the failure to take an interest in studying our practices of analyzing and reasoning, human and historical as they are, the insistence that we would have good arguments only if they came from heaven – all this betrays a shame before the human. On the other hand, if we really think of the hope of a transcendent ground for value as uninteresting and irrelevant, as we should, then the news of its collapse will not change the way we do things: it will just let us get on with the business of reasoning in which we were already engaged.

And as Hilary Putnam argues,[14] the demise of realism may even boost the status of ethical evaluation. For the metaphysical realist frequently made a sharp distinction between fact and value, believing that truth of the sort the realist is after was available in the scientific realm but not in the realm of value. Bringing science inside human history makes what was already believed to be in there look better, not worse – because its claims are no longer contrasted sharply with claims that look 'harder' and more 'factual'. Thus the polarity between scientific fact and subjective ethical value on which much of neoclassical economics rests is called into question by the collapse of realism – from the side of science, to be sure, but this reopens the whole question of the relationship between ethics and science and makes it possible to argue, as does Putnam, that ethics is no worse off than any science.

As for the objections to internalist essentialism, each of them has some force. Many essentialist conceptions have been insular in an arrogant way and neglectful of differences among cultures and ways of life. Some have been neglectful of choice and autonomy. And some have been prejudicially applied – sometimes even by their inventors (as in the cases of Aristotle and Rousseau). But none of this, it seems to me, shows that all essentialism *must* fail in one or more of these ways. And if one feels that there are urgent reasons why we need such an account of human functioning, one will be motivated to try to construct one that will in fact meet the objections. I now propose such an account and then return to the area of development policy, offering my reasons for thinking that we do in fact urgently need such an account.

An Essentialist Proposal: the Basic Human Functions

Here, then, is a sketch of an internal-essentialist proposal, an account of the most important functions of the human being, in terms of which human life is defined.[15] The idea is that once we identify a group of especially important functions in human life, we are then in a position to ask what social and political institutions are doing about them. Are they giving people what they need in order to be capable of functioning in all these human ways? And are they doing this in a minimal way, or are they making it possible for citizens to function *well*? I will consider the political implications of the account in the next section; now I must describe the account itself.

I call this account of the human functions the 'thick vague theory of the good'.[16] The point of this name is to insist, first of all, on the normative character of the list. We are not pretending to discover some value-neutral facts about ourselves, independently of all evaluation; instead, we are conducting an especially probing and basic sort of evaluative inquiry. The name is also chosen to contrast the account with John Rawls's 'thin theory of the good', which insists on confining the list of the 'primary goods' that will be used by the members of the Original Position to a group of allegedly all-purpose means that have a role in any conception of the human good whatever. By contrast, my Aristotelian conception is concerned with *ends* and with the overall shape and content of the human form of life.[17] Finally, the list is 'vague' and this deliberately so and in a good sense, for, as we shall see, it admits of much multiple specification in accordance with varied local and personal conceptions. The idea is that it is better to be vaguely right than precisely wrong; I claim that without the guidance offered by such a list, what we often get in public policy is precise wrongness.

This conception is emphatically *not* metaphysical; that is, it does not claim to derive from any source external to the actual self-interpretations and self-evaluations of human beings in history.[18] Nor is it peculiar to a single metaphysical or religious tradition. It aims to be as universal as possible, and its guiding intuition, in fact, directs it to cross religious, cultural, and metaphysical gulfs. For it begins from two facts: first, that we do recognize others as human across many divisions of time and place. Whatever the differences we encounter, we are rarely in doubt as to when we are dealing with a human being and when we are not. The essentialist account attempts to describe the bases for these recognitions, by mapping out the general shape of the human form of life, those features that constitute a life as human wherever it is. Second, we do have a broadly shared general consensus about the features whose absence means the end of a human form of life. We have in medicine and mythology alike an idea that some transitions or changes just are not compatible with the continued existence of that being as a member of the human kind (and thus as the same individual, since species identity seems to be necessary for personal identity). This is really just another way of coming at the first question, of asking what the most central features of our common humanity *are*, without which no individual can be counted (or counted any longer) as human.[19]

[. . .]

Here, then, as a first approximation, is a story about what seems to be part of any life that we will count as a human life:

Level I of the Thick Vague Conception: The Shape of the Human Form of Life

Mortality. All human beings face death and, after a certain age, know that they face it. This fact shapes more or less every other element of human life. Moreover, all human beings have an aversion to death. Although in many circumstances death will be preferred to the available alternatives, the death of a loved one or the prospect of one's own death is an occasion for grief and/or fear. If we encountered an immortal anthropomorphic being *or* a mortal being that showed no aversion to death and no tendency to avoid death, we would judge, in both these cases, that the form of life was so different from our own that the being could not be acknowledged as human.

The human body. [. . .] The experience of the body is, to be sure, culturally shaped, but the body itself, not culturally variant in its nutritional and other related requirements, sets limits on what can be experienced, ensuring a great deal of overlap.

There is much disagreement, of course, about *how much* of human experience is rooted in the body. Here, religion and metaphysics enter the picture in a nontrivial way. Therefore, in keeping with the nonmetaphysical character of the list, I shall include at this point only those features that would be agreed to be bodily even by determined dualists. The more controversial features, such as thinking, perceiving, and emotion, I shall discuss separately, taking no stand on the question of dualism.[20]

[. . .]

1. *Hunger and thirst; the need for food and drink.*

[. . .]

2. *Need for shelter.*

[. . .]

3. *Sexual desire.*

[. . .]

4. *Mobility.*

[. . .]

Capacity for pleasure and pain. Experiences of pain and pleasure are common to all human life (though once again both their expression and, to some extent, the experience itself may be culturally shaped).

[. . .]

Cognitive capability: perceiving, imagining, thinking. All human beings have sense perception, the ability to imagine, and the ability to think, making distinctions and 'reaching out for understanding'.[21]

[. . .]

Early infant development.

[. . .]

If we encountered a tribe of apparent humans and then discovered that they never had been babies and had never, in consequence, had those experiences of extreme dependency, need, and affection, we would, I think, have to conclude that their form of life was sufficiently different from our own that they could not be considered part of the same kind.

Practical reason. All human beings participate (or try to) in the planning and managing of their own lives, asking and answering questions about what is good and how one should live.

[. . .]

Affiliation with other human beings.

[. . .]

We define ourselves in terms of at least two sorts of affiliation: intimate family and/or personal relations and social or civic relations.

Relatedness to other species and to nature.

[. . .]

[A] creature who treated animals exactly like stones and could not be brought to see any difference would probably be regarded as too strange to be human. So, too, would a creature who did not in any way respond to the beauty and wonder of the natural world.

Humor and play. [. . .] Laughter and play are frequently among the deepest and also the first modes of our mutual recognition.

[. . .]

An entire society that lacked this ability would seem to us both terribly strange and terribly frightening.

Separateness. However much we live with and for others, we are, each of us, 'one in number', proceeding on a separate path through the world from birth to death. Each person feels only his or her own pain and not anyone else's. Each person dies without entailing logically the death of anyone else. When one person walks across the room, no other person follows automatically. When we count the number of human beings in a room, we have no difficulty figuring out where one begins and the other ends. These obvious facts need stating because they might have been otherwise. We should bear them in mind when we hear talk of the absence of individualism in certain societies. Even the most intense forms of human interaction, for example, sexual experience, are experiences of responsiveness, not of fusion. If fusion is made the goal, the result is bound to be bitter disappointment.

[. . .]

[A]s the next level of the conception of the human being, I now specify certain basic functional capabilities at which societies should aim for their citizens (in accordance with the political idea more fully investigated in the next section). In other words, this will be an account of the second threshold – although in some areas, it seems to me to coincide with the first. I shall actually introduce the list as one of related capabilities rather than of actual functionings, since I shall argue that capability to function, not actual functioning, should be the goal of legislation and public planning.

Level 2 of the Thick Vague Conception: Basic Human Functional Capabilities

1. Being able to live to the end of a complete human life, as far as is possible; not dying prematurely, or before one's life is so reduced as to be not worth living.
2. Being able to have good health; to be adequately nourished; to have adequate shelter; having opportunities for sexual satisfaction; being able to move from place to place.
3. Being able to avoid unnecessary and nonbeneficial pain and to have pleasurable experiences.

4. Being able to use the five senses; being able to imagine, to think, and to reason.
5. Being able to have attachments to things and persons outside ourselves; to love those who love and care for us, to grieve at their absence, in general, to love, grieve, to feel longing and gratitude.
6. Being able to form a conception of the good and to engage in critical reflection about the planning of one's own life.
7. Being able to live for and with others, to recognize and show concern for other human beings, to engage in various forms of familial and social interaction.
8. Being able to live with concern for and in relation to animals, plants, and the world of nature.
9. Being able to laugh, to play, to enjoy recreational activities.
10. Being able to live one's own life and nobody else's; being able to live one's own life in one's very own surroundings and context.

The Aristotelian essentialist claims that a life that lacks any one of these, no matter what else it has, will be lacking in humanness. So it would be reasonable to take these things as a focus for concern, in asking how public policy can promote the good of human beings. The list is, emphatically, a list of separate components. We cannot satisfy the need for one of them by giving a larger amount of another one. All are of central importance, and all are distinct in quality. This limits the trade-offs that it will be reasonable to make, and thus limits the applicability of quantitative cost-benefit analysis.

[. . .]

Answering the Objections

I must now try to show how the thick vague theory of the good can answer the objections most commonly made against essentialism. First of all, it should be clear by now that the list does not derive from any extrahistorical metaphysical conception, or rely on the truth of any form of metaphysical realism. As I have said, its guiding intuition is that we do recognize as human, people who do not share our own metaphysical and religious ideas; it aims to get at the root of those recognitions. It does so by conducting an inquiry that is, frankly, both evaluative and internal to human history. Furthermore, the conception does not even demand universal actual agreement among human beings in order to play the moral and political role that we want it to play. I have tried to arrive at a list that will command a very wide consensus, and a consensus that is fully international. Its very close resemblance to other similar lists worked out independently in parts of the world as divergent as Finland and Sri Lanka[22] gives some reason for optimism about consensus. On the other hand, unanimity is not required; for people who have not been willing to engage in the cross-cultural study and the probing evaluation that is behind the list may well refuse assent for varied reasons. Even among those who do engage in the inquiry, there may be differences of opinion. With regard to some components of the list, the very act of entering a disagreement seems to be an acknowledgment of the importance of the component: this seems true, for example, of both practical reasoning and affiliation. But with regard to others, there will be room for ongoing debate and reformulation. The aim is, simply, to achieve enough of a working consensus that we can use the list as a basis for the kind of political reflection that I describe in the next section. (We may usefully compare, at this point, John Rawls's idea of an 'overlapping consensus' that is political and not metaphysical.[23]) So, the objections to essentialism that assume its dependence on realism seem to fail, in this particular case.

As for the three objections to 'internalist' essentialism, each one of them is, and should remain, a central concern of the Aristotelian essentialist. For the list will command the sort of broad consensus she wishes only if these objections can be successfully met.

Concerning *neglect of historical and cultural difference*, the Aristotelian begins by insisting that the thick vague conception is vague for precisely this reason. The list claims to have identified in a very general way components that are fundamental to any human life. But it allows in its very design for the possibility of multiple specifications of each of the components. This is so in several different ways. First, the constitutive circumstances of human life, while broadly shared, are themselves realized in different forms in different societies. The fear of death, the love of play, relationships of friendship and affiliation with others, even the experience of the bodily appetites – these never turn up in simply the vague and general form in which they have been introduced here but always in some specific and historically rich cultural realization, which can profoundly shape not only the conceptions used by the citizens in these areas but their experiences themselves. None the less, we do have in these areas of our common humanity sufficient overlap to sustain a general conversation, focusing on our common problems and prospects. Sometimes, the common conversation will permit us to criticize some conceptions of the grounding experiences themselves, as at odds with other things that human beings want to do and to be.[24]

[. . .]

The liberal charges the Aristotelian with *neglect of autonomy*, arguing that any such determinate conception removes from the citizens the chance to make their own choices about the good life. This is a complicated issue; four points can be stressed.[25] First, the list is a list of capabilities, and not actual functions, precisely because the conception is designed to leave room for choice. Government is not directed to push citizens into acting in certain valued ways; instead, it is directed to make sure that all human beings have the necessary resources and conditions for acting in those ways. It leaves the choice up to them. A person with plenty of food can always choose to fast; a person who has access to subsidized university education can always decide to do something else instead. By making opportunities available, government enhances, and does not remove, choice.[26] Second, this respect for choice is built deeply into the list itself in the architectonic role it gives to practical reasoning. One of the most central capabilities promoted by the conception will be the capability of choosing itself, which is made among the most fundamental elements of the human essence.[27] Third, we should note that the major liberal view in this area, the view of John Rawls, does not shrink from essentialism of our internal sort in just this area. Rawls insists that satisfactions that are not the outgrowth of one's very own choices have no moral worth, and he conceives of the 'two moral powers' (analogous to our practical reasoning) and of sociability (corresponding to our affiliation) as built into the definition of the parties in the original position and thus as necessary constraints on any outcome they will select.[28] In this way, the liberal view and the Aristotelian view converge more than one might initially suppose. Finally, the Aristotelian insists that choice is not pure spontaneity, flourishing independently of material and social conditions. If one cares about autonomy, then one must care about the rest of the form of life that supports it and the material conditions that enable one to live that form of life. Thus the Aristotelian claims that her own comprehensive concern with flourishing across all areas of life is a better way of promoting choice than is the liberal's narrower concern with spontaneity alone, which sometimes tolerates situations in which individuals are in other ways cut off from the fully human use of their faculties.

The Aristotelian conception can indeed be *prejudicially applied*. It is possible to say all the right things about humanness and then to deny that women or blacks or other minorities fall under the concept. How should the essentialist deal with this problem? First of all, it should be stressed that the fact that a conception can be withheld for reasons of prejudice or lack of love undermines not the conception itself but the person who withholds it. One may, looking at a minority whom one hates, speak of them as beetles or ants, and one may carry this refusal of humanity into the sphere of law and public action. Does this undermine our idea that a conception of the human being is a good basis for moral obligation? It seems to me that it does not. For what such cases reveal is the great power of the conception of the human. Acknowledging this other person as a member of the very same kind would have generated a sense of affiliation and responsibility; this was why the self-deceptive stratagem of splitting the other off from one's own species seemed so urgent and so seductive. And the stratagem of denying humanness to beings with whom one lives in conversation and some form of human interaction is a fragile sort of self-deceptive tactic, vulnerable to sustained and consistent reflection and also to experiences that cut through self-deceptive rationalization.[29]

[. . .]

So far, I have focused on the higher-level (developed) human capabilities that make a life a good human life but have not spoken at length about the empirical basis for the application of the concept 'human being' to a creature before us. The basis cannot, of course, be the presence of the higher-level capabilities on my list, for one of the main points of the list is to enable us to say, of some being before us, that this being might possibly come to have these higher-level capabilities but does not now have them. It is that gap between basic (potential) humanness and its full realization that exerts a claim on society and government. What, then, is to be the basis for a determination that this being is one of the human beings, one of the ones whose functioning concerns us? I claim that it is the presence of a lower-level (undeveloped) capability to perform the functions in question, such that with the provision of suitable support and education, the being would be capable of choosing these functions.[30]

[. . .]

Our Need for Essentialism in Public Policy

I have said that we urgently need a version of essentialism in public life. If we reject it, we reject guidance that is crucial if we are to construct an adequate account of distributive justice to guide public policy in many areas. It is time for me to substantiate these claims. I shall focus on the area with which I began: the assessment of the 'quality of life' in developing countries, with a view to formulating policy, both within each separate country and between one country and another. The general direction of my argument should by now be clear: we cannot tell how a country is doing unless we know how the people in it are able to function in the central human ways. And without an account of the good, however vague, that we take to be *shared*, we have no adequate basis for saying what is *missing* from the lives of the poor or marginalized or excluded, no adequate way of justifying the claim that any deeply embedded tradition that we encounter is unjust.

Public policy analyses of the quality of life in developing countries often use measures that are extremely crude.[31] It is still common to find countries ranked in accordance with their gross national product *per capita*, even though this measure does not even concern itself with the distribution of resources and thus can give good marks to a country with enormous inequalities.

[. . .]

One step up in level of sophistication is an approach that measures the quality of life in terms of utility. This would be done, for example, by polling people about whether they are satisfied with their current health status or their current level of education. This approach at least has the merit of focusing on people and viewing resources as valuable because of what they do in human lives. But its narrow focus on subjective expressions of satisfaction brings with it a number of serious problems. First of all, desires and subjective preference are not always reliable indices of what a person really needs, of what would really be required to make that life a flourishing one. Desires and satisfactions are highly malleable. The rich and pampered easily become accustomed to their luxury and view with pain and frustration a life in which they are treated just like everyone else. The poor and deprived frequently adjust their expectations and aspirations to the low level of life they have known; thus their failure to express dissatisfaction can often be a sign that they really do have enough. This is all the more true when the deprivations in question include deprivation of education and other information about alternative ways of life. Circumstances confine the imagination.[32]

Thus, if we rely on utility as our measure of life quality, we most often will get results that support the status quo and oppose radical change.

[. . .]

To treat deep parts of our identity as alienable commodities is to do violence to the conception of the self that we actually have and to the texture of the world of human practice and interaction revealed through this conception. As Marx put it, 'Assume the human being to be the human being and its relation to the world to be a human one, then you can exchange love only for love, trust for trust, etc.'[33]

Finally, utilitarianism, neglecting as it does the inalienability of certain elements of the self, neglects also the ethical salience of the boundaries between persons. As a theory of public measurement, utilitarianism is committed to the aggregation of satisfactions. Individuals are treated as centers of pleasure or pain, satisfaction or dissatisfaction, and the fact of their separateness one from another is not given special weight in the theory, which proceeds by summing. But in the world we actually inhabit, it is a highly relevant fact that my pain is not yours, nor yours mine. If trade-offs between functions are problematic where a single life is concerned, they are all the more problematic when they cross the boundaries of lives, purchasing one person's satisfaction at the price of another's misery. It is easy to see what consequences this can have for policy. For the utilitarian is frequently willing to tolerate huge inequalities for the sake of a larger total or average sum. The Aristotelian's fundamental commitment, by contrast, is to bring each and every person across the threshold into capability for good functioning. This means devoting resources to getting everyone across before any more is given to those who are already capable of functioning at some basic level. If all cannot be brought across the threshold, to this extent the ends of public policy have not been met.

The local tradition relativism endorsed in my Helsinki examples claims to be different from prevailing economic-utilitarian views, on account of its close attention to the fabric of daily life in traditional societies. But it actually shares many of the defects of the utilitarian view, for it refuses to subject preferences, as formed in traditional societies, to any sort of critical scrutiny. It seems to assume that all criticism must be a form of imperialism, the imposition of an outsider's power on local ways. Nor does it simply claim (as do utilitarian economists) to avoid normative judgments altogether, for it actually endorses the locally formed norms as good and even romanticizes them in no small degree. It confers a bogus air of legitimacy on these deeply embedded preferences by refusing to subject them to ethical scrutiny.

[. . .]

One more antiessentialist approach to questions of distributive justice must now be considered. It is by far the most powerful alternative to the Aristotelian approach, and its differences from it are subtle and complex. This is the liberal idea, defended in different forms by John Rawls and Ronald Dworkin, that distribution should aim at an equal allotment of certain basic resources (or, in the case of Rawls, should tolerate inequalities only where this would improve the situation of the worst off).[34]

The Rawlsian liberal insists on distributing basic resources without taking a stand on the human good, even in the vague way in which the 'thick vague theory' has done so. The aim is to leave to each citizen a choice of the conception of the good by which he or she will live. As we have said, Rawls does take a stand on some of the components of our conception. For sociability and practical reason are treated as essential to any conception of human flourishing that can be entertained; liberty is on the list of 'primary goods', as are the 'social conditions of self-respect'; and in argument against utilitarianism, Rawls commits himself very strongly to the centrality of the separateness of persons.[35] On the other hand, as we have seen, the Aristotelian conception does itself insist on the fundamental role of choice and autonomy. But there are still significant differences between the two conceptions, for the Rawlsian view treats income and wealth as 'primary goods' of which more is always better, independently of the concrete conception of the good. And he does define the 'better off' and 'worse off' in terms of quantities of these basic resources rather than in terms of functioning or capability.

To this, the Aristotelian has three replies. First, [. . .] wealth and income are not good in their own right; they are good only in so far as they promote human functioning. Rawls's view, which appears to treat them as having independent significance, obscures the role that they actually play in human life.

Second, human beings have variable needs for resources, and any adequate definition of the better off and worse off must reflect that fact. A pregnant woman has nutritional needs that are different from those of a nonpregnant woman and a child from those of an adult. The child who has exactly the same amount of protein in her diet as an adult is less well off, given her greater needs. A person whose mobility is impaired will need a significantly greater amount of resources than will a person of average mobility in order to achieve the same level of capability to move about. These are not just rare exceptions; they are pervasive facts of life. Thus the failure of the liberal theory to deal with them is a serious defect. And yet, to deal with them, we need a general conception of what functions we are trying to support.[36]

Third, the liberal, by defining being well off in terms of possessions alone, fails to go deep enough in imagining the impediments to functioning that are actually present in many human lives. Marx argued, for example, that workers who lack control over their own activity and its products lead lives less than fully human, even if they do get adequate wages. In general, the structure of labor relations, of class relations, and of race and gender relations in a society can alienate its members from the fully human use of their faculties even when their material needs are met. It is possible to hold that a pampered middle-class housewife is well off, despite the barriers that prevent her from expressing herself fully in employment and education. What is very unclear is whether Rawls – who does indeed decide to postpone

consideration of structures of power within the household – should allow himself
to be in this position, given his commitment to the realization of the two moral
powers for each and every citizen. At the very least, there is a tension internal to
the view, which can be dispelled only by a more explicit consideration of the
relationship between the two moral powers and various other human functions and
their material and institutional necessary conditions.[37] With political liberty, Rawls
fully seizes this problem; therefore he places liberty among the primary goods. My
claim is that he needs to go further in this direction, making the list of primary goods
not a list of resources and commodities at all but a list of basic capabilities of the
person.

[. . .]

Compassion and Respect

A new dimension of our question emerges if we now ask ourselves what moral
sentiments we are encouraged and permitted to have by antiessentialist subjectivism,
on one hand, or by Aristotelian essentialism, on the other. I now argue that two
moral sentiments that we take to be particularly important for the human
community can have their home only within a view that recognizes a determinate
conception of the human being. In so far as relativist and subjectivist views appear
to incorporate them, they do so only by being partially or tacitly essentialist. These
two sentiments are compassion and respect.[38]

 Eleos, pity or compassion, is, according to ancient Greek analyses that are still
unsurpassed, a painful emotion felt toward the pain or suffering of another person.
It has three cognitive requirements: first, the belief that the suffering is not trivial
but serious; second, the belief that the person who is suffering did not cause the
suffering by deliberate fault; third, the belief that one's own possibilities are similar
to those of the person suffering. It involves, then, in its very structure, the injunction
to recognize common human limits and vulnerabilities; and the plausible claim is
that the person who does not recognize him- or herself as sharing a common
humanity with the sufferer will react to the suffering with an arrogant hardness,
rather than with compassion. This structure is built into many literary and historical
situations in which people appeal to others for compassion: and in such situations
we see that the response that acknowledges shared possibilities is a humane
response, closely connected with beneficent action.

[. . .]

 I claim [with the ancient Greek tradition and Rousseau that] compassion does
require the belief in a common humanity. We do not grasp the significance of
suffering or lack or impediment unless and until we set it in the context of a view
of what it is for a human being to flourish. And we do not respond compassionately
to that gap between norm and fulfillment unless we think that this is a possibility

in which we too partake. Compassion requires us to say: however far these people are from us in fortune or class or race or gender, those differences are morally arbitrary and might have befallen me as well. And if we are not in a position to say that, it is not at all clear on what grounds we can be persuaded to give to these people.

[. . .]

There is a deep moral tradition that says that compassion is not required, for we can be sufficiently motivated to other-regarding action by respect for the dignity of humanity. This tradition, exemplified in the thought of the ancient Stoics, Spinoza, Kant, and in a different way, Nietzsche, still makes central use of a notion of common humanity, for respect is not groundless or arbitrary. It has a foundation: the recognition in the object of certain powers or capabilities. Usually, these are taken to be specifically human powers – although one might motivate respect from a broader notion of the animal or, on the other hand, from notions of the rational being or the person that might be narrower in their application. For Kant, respect is due to humanity; a basic moral principle is to treat humanity, wherever it is found, as an end in itself. For the ancient Stoics similarly, respect is owed to that which is recognized as a human being, having certain powers and capabilities. One needs to have an account of what those powers and capabilities are, and it had better be an account that links many times and places together. Otherwise, we will have no moral motive for other-regarding action toward people at a distance or toward people of other races and genders.

I have suggested that without a notion of common human functioning, we will have to do without compassion and without a full-blooded notion of respect. What, by contrast, are the moral sentiments of extreme relativism? Here, we must say, I believe, that most relativists are not fully consistent. In so far as they do show for human life everywhere a concern that they do not show for rocks or stones, or even, in the same way, for all animals, they trade tacitly on beliefs and related sentiments that their official view does not allow them. Some utilitarians, especially those intensely concerned with animal rights, really are willing to jettison the species boundary in favor of a broader generic notion of concern for all creatures capable of the experience of pleasure and pain; some pursue this goal with reasonable consistency. But we must say, I think, that even that view attains what coherence and power it has by being essentialist at the generic level. It is certainly very far from being a subjectivist view. And, unlike these thinkers, most alleged subjectivists cheat. They commend their view to us on the grounds of compassion, saying that it will help the situation of the excluded, of minorities, and of women. Yet the theoretical apparatus they then introduce is insufficient to make sense of that very compassion. It permits only narrow, self-regarding sentiments and a relatively detached and curious attitude to the situation of others.

Even when subjectivism has moderated itself into local tradition relativism, as in the examples given in my Helsinki conversations, its range of moral sentiments seems narrow indeed. How quaint, these theorists seem to be saying, how curious.

They do not appear to be able to delve very deeply into the lives in question, imagining for themselves what it really is like to be told that you cannot work when you have your period or that you must pray to a terrifying goddess to avert a life-threatening disease. There is both distance and a certain condescension in this refusal of imagination and acknowledgment. But anything more would require the admission that it is relevant to ask themselves how *they* would feel in that situation. And this their theory forbids them to do. *That* menstrual period and *that* work they must treat as something different in kind (or at least not the same in kind) as the comparable elements in their own lives. It is not surprising, then, that they do not think of the pain of exclusion as something that might be their own or see its significance in and for a life that could have been their own. The moral sentiments of this sort of relativism, I claim, are the sentiments of the tourist: wonder, curiosity, and amused interest. But the pain of the stranger is seen as pain only if its significance is understood as that of pain: as similar, then, to the pain that we know. And it is only in the light of such an acknowledgment that wonder turns to grief, curiosity to practical determination, and amused interest to compassion.

[. . .]

[C]ompassionate identification need not ignore concrete local differences; in fact, at its best, it demands a searching analysis of differences in order that the general good be appropriately realized in the new concrete case. But the learning about and from the other is motivated as it is in Aristotle's own studies of other cultures: by the conviction that the other is one of us.

Somewhere in the vast reaches of literary-theoretical space, there is a planet known as Textualité. Its inhabitants look very much like human beings – except that they are very large and each one has only a single eye. Their mythology reports that they are the descendants of some emigrants from Earth, who fled that planet in search of a home where they could escape patriarchal authority and binary thinking to take delight in the free play of difference, utility, and power.

There are on Textualité many nations. Some are rich and some are very poor. Within most of the nations, there are also large inequalities that have perceptible effects on the health and mobility and educational level of the inhabitants. The people of Textualité, however, do not see such things as we see them. For they really have discarded – not just in theory but in the fabric of their daily lives – the Earthly tendencies of thought that link the perception of one's neighbor's pain to the memory of one's own and the perception of a stranger's pain to the experience of a neighbor's, all this through the general idea of the human being and human flourishing. To these people, strangers simply look very strange. They are seen as other forms of life, who have nothing in common with their own lives. Occasionally they share perceptions and ideas with a few other beings in locally bounded communities that establish group norms. At other times, each one goes out after his or her own utility or power, treating every other being as foreign.

Do the people of Textualité feel pain when they see a stranger who is hungry or ill or abused? They do dislike the *sight* of such ugly things. But they do not feel the pain of fellow-feeling, for that has been declared a remnant of outmoded Earthly thinking. How should we know, they say, that this being is suffering from lack of food? For that is a different form of life from ours, and we have been brought up to appreciate the play of difference. Saying this, they go on with their play and turn away their eyes. Do the people of Textualité construct government programs to improve literacy or health care or agriculture in the distant poorer regions of their planet? Why, indeed, should they? Doing so is unlikely to maximize their own expected utility, and they cannot bring themselves to make any judgment about the form of life in a strange part of the globe, about people with whom they could never be in conversation. Perhaps those inhabitants are enjoying their embedded way of life, they remark at conferences. Do the people of Textualité feel love for one another? Or isn't love of one's fellow humans one of those shopworn essentialist ideals that they left behind on Earth?

We do not live right now on the planet of Textualité. Right now, the new subjectivism – whether in economics or in literary theory – is false of our experiences and responses. But we can choose to follow theory into our lives, focusing on our differences from one another and refusing to acknowledge what is common to all. And then perhaps one day, the texture of the human world will be differently perceived, perceived through the play of difference and strangeness. Then we will, I think, not *be* human beings any longer.

Notes

1. The argument of this essay is closely related to that of several others, to which I shall refer frequently in what follows: 'Nature, function, and capability', *Oxford Studies in Ancient Philosophy*, suppl. vol. 1 (1988): 145–84 (hereafter NFC); 'Non-relative virtues: an Aristotelian approach', *Midwest Studies in Philosophy* 13 (1988): 32–53, and, in an expanded version, in *The Quality of Life*, edited by M. Nussbaum and A. Sen (Oxford: Clarendon, 1992) (hereafter NRV); 'Aristotelian social democracy', in *Liberalism and the Good*, edited by R. B. Douglass *et al.* (New York: Routledge, 1990) 203–52 (hereafter ASD); 'Aristotle on human nature and the foundations of ethics', forthcoming in a volume on the philosophy of Bernard Williams, edited by R. Harrison and J. Altham (Cambridge: Cambridge University Press, 1992) (hereafter HN); 'Human capabilities, female human beings', in *Human Capabilities: Women, men, and equality*, edited by M. Nussbaum and J. Glover (Oxford: Clarendon, forthcoming) (hereafter HC).
2. Because of such pervasive assumptions, in general I have not used the vocabulary of 'essentialism' in describing my own (historically embedded and historically sensitive) account of the central human functions. I do so here, somewhat polemically, in order to reclaim the word for reasoned debate, and I assume that the reader will look closely at my account of what the 'essentialism' I recommend, in fact, entails. For further comments on this, see HN, ASC, and HC.
3. It is important to note at the outset that my account of an Aristotelian position is very different from other accounts of Aristotle that are well known in current political thought

– in particular, both from the Aristotle that is criticized in Bernard Williams's *Ethics and the Limits of Philosophy* (Cambridge, MA: Harvard University Press, 1985), and from the Aristotle of Alasdair Macintyre's *Whose Justice? Which Rationality?* (Notre Dame, IN: University of Notre Dame Press, 1988). I discuss Williams's Aristotle in HN, MacIntyre's in a review in *The New York Review of Books*, 7 December, 1989.

4. Jacques Derrida, *Of Grammatology*, trans. G. C. Spivak (Baltimore, MD: Johns Hopkins University Press, 1977).

5. For my account of Aristotle's position, see *The Fragility of Goodness: Luck and ethics in Greek tragedy and philosophy* (Cambridge: Cambridge University Press, 1986), ch. 8. Related debates in Indian philosophy are given a most illuminating discussion in B. K. Matilal, *Perception* (Oxford: Clarendon, 1985).

6. In two areas above all, the argument familiar in the literature of deconstruction have gaps: they do not confront debates within the philosophy of science – for example, concerning the interpretation of quantum mechanics – that have great importance for the realism question, and they rarely confront in a detailed way the issues concerning reference and translation that have been debated with considerable subtlety within the philosophy of language.

7. In this category, as close relatives of my view, I would place the 'internal-realist' conception of Hilary Putnam, *Reason, Truth and History* (Cambridge: Cambridge University Press, 1981), *The Many Faces of Realism* (La Salle: Open Court, 1987), and *Realism With a Human Face* (Cambridge, MA: Harvard University Press, 1990); and also Charles Taylor, *Sources of the Self: The making of modern identity* (Cambridge, MA: Harvard University Press, 1989). For my discussion of Taylor's arguments, see *New Republic*, April 1990.

8. See esp. John Rawls, *A Theory of Justice* (Cambridge, MA: Harvard University Press, 1971). Rawls's position and its relationship to the Aristotelian view is discussed in NFC, in HC, and especially in ASD, with references to other later articles in which Rawls has further developed his position concerning the role of a conception of the good in his theory.

9. By relativism I mean the view that the only available standard to value is some local group or individual; by subjectivism I mean the view that the standard is given by each individual's subjective preferences; thus relativism, as I understand it here, is a genus of which subjectivism is one extreme species.

10. A clear example of this view is Stanley Fish: see *Doing What Come Naturally: Change, rhetoric, and the practice of theory and legal studies* (Durham, NC and London: Duke University Press, 1989). I criticized Fish's position in 'Sophistry about conventions', in *Love's Knowledge: Essays on philosophy and literature* (New York: Oxford University Press, 1990), 220–29, and in 'Skepticism about practical reason', a Dewey Lecture delivered at the Harvard University Law School, October 1991, and forthcoming.

11. This is the position that Derrida appeared to take up in a number of works – for example, in *Éperons: Les styles de Nietzsche* (Paris, 1979); he has more recently insisted that his position does leave room for one view to be better than another, see his Afterword to *Limited Inc.*, trans. Samuel Weber and Jeffrey Mehlmann (Evanston, IL: Northwestern University Press, 1988). Certainly, the former position is the one frequently found in the writings of followers of Derrida in literary theory and criticism.

12. S. A. Marglin (pp. 22–3) suggests that this sort of thinking is peculiarly Western. My (entirely typical) epigraphs from non-Western traditions already cast doubt on this. Opponents of such oppositions have not explained how one can speak coherently without bounding off one thing against another, opposing one thing to another.

13. Aristotle, *Parts of Animals* 1.5, 645a5–37. Aristotle notes that anyone who has this shame about looking at the animal world is bound to take up the same attitude to himself, since an animal is what he is.

14. See esp. *Reason, Truth, and History* and also Putnam's chapter in Nussbaum and Sen, eds, *The Quality of Life*.
15. For further elaboration, see HN, ASD, and HC.
16. See ASD; for detailed argument concerning the normative character of such an inquiry into 'essence', see HN.
17. For a detailed account of this contrast, see ASD and NFC.
18. For a closely related idea, see Charles Taylor, *Sources of the Self*.
19. HN discusses the relation of this idea to some debates about the end of life in contemporary medical ethics.
20. On the question of cultural variation in the construction of these basic experiences, see NRV and ASD.
21. See Aristotle, *Metaphysics* 1.1.
22. For Scandinavian conceptions, see the chapters by E. Allardt and R. Erikson in Nussbaum and Sen, eds, *The Quality of Life*. On capabilities in Sri Lanka, see Carlos Fonseka, *Towards a Peaceful Sri Lanka*, WIDER Research for Action series, World Institute for Development Economics Research, Helsinki, 1990.
23. John Rawls, 'The idea of an overlapping consensus', *Oxford Journal of Legal Studies* 7 (1987).
24. For some examples, see NRV.
25. See the longer treatment of this issue in ASD.
26. This distinction is central in the political theory of Amartya Sen. See, among others, 'Equality of what?', in Sen, *Choice, Welfare, and Measurement* (Oxford: Blackwell, 1982) 353–69, and *Commodities and Capabilities* (Amsterdam: North-Holland, 1985).
27. See also Sen, *Commodities and Capabilities*.
28. See esp. Rawls, 'The priority of the right and ideas of the good', *Philosophy and Public Affairs* 17 (1988); for further references and discussions, see ASD.
29. Compare the remarks on slaves in Stanley Cavell, *The Claim of Reason* (New York: Oxford University Press, 1979).
30. This idea is developed more fully in NFC and HC.
31. See Nussbaum and Sen, 'Introduction', *The Quality of Life*.
32. For these objections, see also Sen 'Equality of what?' and *Commodities and Capabilities*. Recent utilitarian work in philosophy has to some extent addressed these objections, introducing many corrections to actual preferences, but the practice of development economists has not been much altered.
33. Marx, *Economics and Philosophical Manuscripts of 1844*, trans. M. Milligan, in *The Marx/Engels Reader*, edited by R. C. Tucker (New York 1978). On the texture of the human work, in connection with a related criticism of utilitarianism, see Putnam, *Reason, Truth and History*. From the debate about the adequacy of economic utilitarianism as a basis for legal judgment, see Margaret Jane Radin's outstanding article 'Market-inalienability', *Harvard Law Review* 100 (1987) 1848 ff., which criticizes Richard Posner for speaking of a woman's body as a commodity of which she may dispose in the market.
34. For a long account of these criticisms, see ASD.
35. Rawls, *A Theory of Justice* (Cambridge, MA: Harvard University Press, 1922) 189–92.
36. See Sen, 'Equality of what?'.
37. On this point, see Okin, *Justice, Gender and the Family*, and my review of her in *New York Review of Books*, forthcoming.
38. I discuss compassion further in 'Tragedy and self-sufficiency: Plato and Aristotle on fear and pity', in *Essays on Aristotle's Poetics*, edited by A. Rorty (Princeton, NJ: Princeton University Press, 1992), and in a longer version in *Oxford Studies in Ancient Philosophy* 10 (1992). Here I use 'compassion' rather than the more usual 'pity' for both Greek *eleos*

and French *pitié* because 'pity' in contemporary use often connotes a condescension toward the sufferer and a lofty distance. These attitudes are not only not implied but are actually repudiated in the accounts standardly given of the original Greek and French words.

Bibliography

A bibliography which tried to reflect both the coherence of such categories as structuralism, post-structuralism, psychoanalytic theory, and so on, and also the permeability of these category divisions, would be confusing and repetitive. Besides, readers use bibliographies for their own purposes, or they browse and follow leads. To meet these more important requirements, this bibliography has a minimalist alphabetical organization.

Abel, E. (ed.) (1982) *Writing and Sexual Difference*, Harvester Wheatsheaf, Hemel Hempstead.

Adorno, T.W. (1967) *Prisms*, trans. S. and S. Weber, Neville Spearman, London.

Adorno, T.W. (1973) *Negative Dialectics*, trans. E.B. Ashton, Routledge, London.

Adorno, T.W. (1977) 'The actuality of philosophy', *Telos*, vol. 31, pp. 120–33.

Adorno, T.W. (1980) 'Reconciliation under duress', trans. R. Livingstone, in E. Bloch *et al.* (1980), pp. 151–76.

Adorno, T.W. (1984) *Aesthetic Theory*, trans. C. Lenhardt, ed. G. Adorno and R. Tiedemann, Routledge, London.

Adorno, T.W. (1991) *The Culture Industry: Selected essays on mass culture*, ed. J.M. Bernstein, Routledge, London.

Adorno, T.W. and Horkheimer, M. (1979) *Dialectic of Enlightenment*, trans. J. Cumming, Verso, London.

Agglietta, M. (1987) *A Theory of Capitalist Regulation: The U.S. experience*, Verso, London.

Althusser, L. (1970) *For Marx*, trans. B. Brewster, Vintage, New York.

Althusser, L. (1971) *Lenin and Philosophy and Other Essays*, trans. B. Brewster, Monthly Review Press, New York.

Althusser, L. (1982) *Montesquieu, Rousseau, Marx: Politics and history*, trans. B. Brewster, Verso, London.

Althusser, L. and Balibar, E. (1983) *Reading Capital*, trans. B. Brewster, Verso, London.

Anderson, P. (1979) *Considerations on Western Marxism*, Verso, London.

Anderson, P. (1983) *In the Tracks of Historical Materialism*, Verso, London.

Arac, J. (1988) *After Foucault: Humanistic knowledge, postmodern challenges*, Rutgers University Press, New Brunswick.

Arac, J., Godzich, W. and Martin, W. (eds) (1983) *The Yale Critics: Deconstruction in America*, University of Minnesota Press, Minneapolis.

Arato, A. and Breines, P. (1979) *The Young Lukács and the Origins of Western Marxism*, Seabury Press, New York.

Arato, A. and Gebhardt, E. (eds) (1978) *The Essential Frankfurt School Reader*, Blackwell, Oxford.

Arendt, H. (1959) *The Human Condition*, University of Chicago Press, Chicago.

Arendt, H. (1961) *Between Past and Future: Six exercises in political thought*, Meridian, Cleveland, OH.

Arendt, H. (1973) *On Revolution*, Penguin, Harmondsworth.

Arendt, H. (1986) *The Origins of Totalitarianism*, André Deutsch, London.

Aronowitz, S. (1981) *The Crisis in Historical Materialism: Class, politics and culture in Marxist theory*, Praeger, New York.

Ashcroft, B., Griffiths, G. and Tiffin, H. (eds) (1989) *The Empire Writes Back: Theory and practice in post-colonial literatures*, Routledge, London.

Attridge, D., Bennington, G. and Young, R. (eds) (1987) *Post-structuralism and the Question of History*, Cambridge University Press, Cambridge.

Bakhtin, M.M. (1981) *The Dialogic Imagination: Four essays*, trans. C. Emerson and M. Holquist, University of Texas Press, Austin.

Barker, F. *et al.* (eds) *The Politics of Theory*, University of Essex Press, Colchester.

Barker, M. and Beezer, A. (eds) *Reading into Cultural Studies*, Routledge, London.

Barker, P. (1993) *Michel Foucault: Subversion of the subject*, Harvester Wheatsheaf, Hemel Hempstead.

Barrett, M. (1980) *Women's Oppression Today: Problems in Marxist feminist analysis*, Verso, London.

Barrett, M. (1991) *The Politics of Theory: From Marx to Foucault*, Polity, Cambridge.

Barthes, R. (1967) *Elements of Semiology*, trans. A. Lavers and C. Smith, Jonathan Cape, London.

Barthes, R. (1972a) *Critical Essays*, trans. R. Howard, Northwestern University Press, Evanston.

Barthes, R. (1972b) *Mythologies*, trans. A. Lavers, Jonathan Cape, London.

Barthes, R. (1975) *S/Z*, trans. R. Miller, Jonathan Cape, London.

Barthes, R. (1977) *Image-Music-Text*, trans. S. Heath, Fontana, London.

Barthes, R. (1980) *The Pleasure of the Text*, trans. R. Miller, Blackwell, Oxford.

Barthes, R. (1981) 'The discourse of history', trans. S. Bann, in E.S. Shaffer (ed.), *Comparative Criticism: A Yearbook 3*, Cambridge University Press, Cambridge, pp. 7–20.

Barthes, R. (1982a), *A Barthes Reader*, ed. S. Sontag, Jonathan Cape, London.

Barthes, R. (1982b) *Empire of Signs*, trans. R. Howard, Hill & Wang, New York.

Baudrillard, J. (1975) *The Mirror of Production*, trans. M. Poster, Telos Press, St Louis.

Baudrillard, J. (1981) *For a Critique of the Political Economy of the Sign*, trans. C. Levin, Telos Press, St Louis.

Baudrillard, J. (1988) *Jean Baudrillard: Selected writings*, ed. M. Poster, Polity, Cambridge.

Baynes, K., Bohman, J. and McCarthy, T. (eds) (1987) *After Philosophy: End or transformation?* MIT, Cambridge, MA.

Beauvoir, S. de (1972) *The Second Sex*, trans. H.M. Pashley, Penguin, Harmondsworth.

Bell, D. (1979) *The Cultural Contradictions of Capitalism*, second edition, Heinemann, London.

Belsey, C. (1980) *Critical Practice*, Methuen, London.

Benhabib, S. (1986) *Critique, Norm and Utopia: A study of the foundations of Critical Theory*, Columbia University Press, New York.

Benhabib, S. (1992) *Situating the Self: Gender, community and postmodernism in contemporary ethics*, Polity, Cambridge.

Benhabib, S. and Cornell, D. (eds) (1987) *Feminism as Critique: Essays on the politics of gender in late capitalist societies*, University of Minnesota Press, Minneapolis.

Benhabib, S. and Dallmayr, F. (eds) (1990) *The Communicative Ethics Controversy*, MIT, Cambridge, MA.

Benjamin, A. (ed.) (1989) *The Problems of Modernity: Adorno and Benjamin*, Routledge, London.

Benjamin, A. (ed.) (1992) *Judging Lyotard*, Routledge, London.

Benjamin, W. (1973) *Illuminations*, trans. H. Zohn, ed. H. Arendt, Fontana, London.

Benjamin, W. (1977) *The Origin of German Tragic Drama*, trans. J. Osborne, Verso, London.

Benjamin, W. (1978) *Reflections: Essays, aphorisms, autobiographical writings*, trans. E. Jephcott, Harcourt Brace Jovanovich, New York.

Benjamin, W. (1979) *One-Way Street and Other Writings*, trans. E. Jephcott and K. Shorter, Verso, London.

Benjamin, W. (1983) *Charles Baudelaire: A lyric poet in the era of high capitalism*, trans. H. Zohn, Verso, London.

Bennett, T. (1979) *Formalism and Marxism*, Methuen, London.

Bennett, T. (1992) 'Putting policy into cultural studies', in L. Grossberg, C. Nelson and P.A. Treichler (eds) (1992), pp. 23–37.

Bennington, G. (1988) *Lyotard: Writing the event*, Manchester University Press, Manchester.

Bennington, G. and Derrida, J. (1993) *Jacques Derrida*, University of Chicago Press, Chicago.

Benton, T. (1984) *The Rise and Fall of Structural Marxism: Althusser and his influence*, St Martin's Press, New York.

Benveniste, E. (1971) *Problems in General Linguistics*, trans. M.E. Meek, University of Miami Press, Coral Gables, FL.

Bernasconi, R. (1986) 'Lévinas and Derrida: The question of the closure of metaphysics' in R.A. Cohen (ed.), *Face to Face with Lévinas*, State University of New York Press, Albany, pp. 181–202.

Bernasconi, R. (1987) 'Deconstruction and the possibility of ethics' in J. Sallis (ed.) (1987), pp. 122–39.

Bernasconi, R. and Critchley, S. (eds) (1991) *Re-Reading Lévinas*, Athlone, London.

Bernasconi, R. and Wood, D. (eds) (1988) *The Provocation of Lévinas: Re-thinking the other*, Routledge, London.

Bernstein, R.J. (1971) *Praxis and Action: Contemporary philosophies of human activity*, University of Pennsylvania Press, Philadelphia.

Bernstein, R.J. (1983) *Beyond Objectivism and Relativism: Science, hermeneutics, and praxis*, University of Pennsylvania Press, Philadelphia.

Bernstein, R.J. (ed.) (1985) *Habermas and Modernity*, Polity, Cambridge.

Bernstein, R.J. (1986) *Philosophical Profiles: Essays in a pragmatic mode*, University of Pennsylvania Press, Philadelphia.

Bernstein, R.J. (1991) *The New Constellation: The ethical-political horizons of modernity/postmodernity*, Polity, Cambridge.

Best, S. and Kellner, D. (1991) *Postmodern Theory: Critical interrogations*, Macmillan, London.

Bhabha, H.K. (ed.) (1990) *Nation and Narration*, Routledge, London.

Bhabha, H.K. (1992) 'Postcolonial authority and postmodern guilt', in L. Grossberg, C. Nelson and P.A. Treichler (eds) (1992), pp. 56–68.

Bhabha, H.K. (1993) *The Location of Culture*, Routledge, London.

Bhaskar, R. (1978) *A Realist Theory of Science*, Harvester, Brighton.

Bhaskar, R. (1979) *The Possibility of Naturalism: A philosophical critique of the contemporary human sciences*, Harvester, Brighton.

Bhaskar, R. (1986) *Scientific Realism and Human Emancipation*, Verso, London.

Bhaskar, R. (1991) *Philosophy and the Idea of Freedom*, Blackwell, Oxford.

Bhaskar, R. (1993) *Dialectic: The pulse of freedom*, Verso, London.

Bloch, E., Lukács, G., Brecht, B., and Adorno, T. (1980) *Aesthetics and Politics*, Verso, London.

Bloom, H. (1973) *The Anxiety of Influence: A theory of poetry*, Oxford University Press, New York.

Bloom, H. (1975) *A Map of Misreading*, Oxford University Press, New York.

Bloom, H., de Man, P., Derrida, J., Hartman, G.H. and Miller, J.H. (1979) *Deconstruction and Criticism*, Seabury Press, New York.

Bogue, R. (1989) *Deleuze and Guattari*, Routledge, London.
Bottomore, T. (1984) *The Frankfurt School*, Ellis Horwood, Chichester and Tavistock, London.
Bové, P. (1986) *Intellectuals in Power: A genealogy of critical humanism*, Columbia University Press, New York.
Bowen-Moore, P. (1989) *Hannah Arendt's Philosophy of Natality*, Macmillan, London.
Bowie, A. (1990) *Aesthetics and Subjectivity from Kant to Nietzsche*, Manchester University Press, Manchester.
Bowie, M. (1987) *Freud, Proust and Lacan: Theory as fiction*, Cambridge University Press, Cambridge.
Bowie, M. (1991) *Lacan*, Harvard University Press, Cambridge, MA.
Boyne, R. (1990) *Foucault and Derrida: The other side of reason*, Unwin Hyman, London.
Braverman, H. (1974) *Labor and Monopoly Capital: The degradation of work in the twentieth century*, Monthly Review Press, New York.
Breines, P. (ed.) (1970) *Critical Interruptions: New Left perspectives on Herbert Marcuse*, Herder, New York.
Brémond, C. (1973) *Logique du récit*, Seuil, Paris.
Brennan, T. (ed.) (1989) *Between Feminism and Psychoanalysis*, Routledge, London.
Brennan, T. (1993) *History after Lacan*, Routledge, London.
Brown, A. (1992) *Roland Barthes: The figures of writing*, Clarendon, Oxford.
Buck-Morss, S. (1977) *The Origin of Negative Dialectics: Theodor W. Adorno, Walter Benjamin, and the Frankfurt School*, Harvester, Brighton.
Bukharin, N. (1969) *Historical Materialism: A system of sociology*, University of Michigan Press, Ann Arbor.
Bunch, C. (1987) *Passionate Politics, 1968–1986: Feminist theory in action*, St Martin's Press, New York.
Bürger, P. (1984) *Theory of the Avant-Garde*, trans. M. Shaw, Manchester University Press, Manchester.
Burke, S. (1992) *The Death and Return of the Author: Criticism and subjectivity in Barthes, Foucault and Derrida*, Edinburgh University Press, Edinburgh.
Butler, J. (1990) *Gender Trouble: Feminism and the subversion of identity*, Routledge, New York.
Calhoun, C. (ed.) (1992) *Habermas and the Public Sphere*, MIT, Cambridge, MA.
Callinicos, A. (1976) *Althusser's Marxism*, Pluto, London.
Carby, H.V. (1987) *Reconstructing Womanhood: The emergence of the Afro-American woman novelist*, Oxford University Press, New York.
Carroll, D. (1987) *Paraesthetics: Foucault, Lyotard, Derrida*, Methuen, New York.
Castoriades, C. (1991) *Philosophy, Politics, Autonomy: Essays in political philosophy*, Oxford University Press, Oxford.
Cavell, S. (1979) *The Claim of Reason: Wittgenstein, skepticism, morality and tragedy*, Clarendon, Oxford.
Cavell, S. (1992) *The Senses of Walden*, expanded edition, University of Chicago Press, Chicago.
Chalier, C. (1991) 'Ethics and the feminine', in R. Bernasconi and S. Critchley (eds) (1991), pp. 119–29.
Chase, C. (1979) 'Oedipal textuality: Reading Freud's reading of *Oedipus*', *Diacritics*, vol. 9, pp. 54–68.
Chodorow, N. (1978) *The Reproduction of Mothering: Psychoanalysis and the sociology of gender*, University of California Press, Berkeley.
Cixous, H. (1981) 'The laugh of the Medusa' in E. Marks and I. de Courtivron (eds) (1981), pp. 245–64.

Cixous, H. and Clément, C. (1986) *The Newly Born Woman*, trans. B. Wing, Manchester University Press, Manchester.

Cohen, G.A. (1978) *Karl Marx's Theory of History: A defence*, Clarendon, Oxford.

Cohen, R.A. (ed.) (1986) *Face to Face with Lévinas*, State University of New York Press, Albany.

Collins, P.H. (1990) *Black Feminist Thought: Knowledge, consciousness and the politics of empowerment*, HarperCollins, London.

Conley, V. A. (1984) *Hélène Cixous: Writing the feminine*, University of Nebraska Press, Lincoln.

Connerton, P. (1980) *The Tragedy of Enlightenment: An essay on the Frankfurt School*, Cambridge University Press, Cambridge.

Coole, D.H. (1988) *Women in Political Theory: From ancient misogyny to contemporary feminism*, Harvester Wheatsheaf, Hemel Hempstead.

Cornell, D., Rosenfeld, M. and Carlson, D.G. (eds) *Deconstruction and the Possibility of Justice*, Routledge, London.

Cousins, M. and Hussain, A. (1984) *Michel Foucault*, Macmillan, London.

Coward, R. (1983) *Patriarchal Precedents: Sexuality and social relations*, Routledge, London.

Coward, R. and Ellis, J. (1977) *Language and Materialism: Developments in semiology and the theory of the subject*, Routledge, London.

Critchley, S. (1992) *The Ethics of Deconstruction: Derrida and Lévinas*, Blackwell, Oxford.

Culler, J. (1976) *Saussure*, Fontana, London.

Culler, J. (1983a) *Barthes*, Fontana, London.

Culler, J. (1983b) *On Deconstruction: Theory and criticism after structuralism*, Routledge, London.

Dallmayr, F. (1981) *Twilight of Subjectivity: Contributions to a post-individualist theory of politics*, University of Massachusetts Press, Amherst.

Daly, M. (1978) *Gyn/Ecology: The meta-ethics of radical feminism*, Beacon Press, Boston, MA.

Daly, M. (1984) *Pure Lust: Elemental female philosophy*, Women's Press, London.

Daniels, N. (ed.) (1975) *Reading Rawls: Critical studies on Rawls' 'A Theory of Justice'*, Blackwell, Oxford.

Davis, A. (1983) *Women, Race and Class*, Vintage, New York.

Davis, R.C. (ed.) (1983) *Lacan and Narration: The psychoanalytic difference in narrative theory*, Johns Hopkins University Press, Baltimore.

Deleuze, G. (1983) *Nietzsche and Philosophy*, trans. H. Tomlinson, Columbia University Press, New York.

Deleuze, G. (1988) *Foucault*, trans. S. Hand, Athlone, London.

Deleuze, G. (1994) *Difference and Repetition*, trans. P. Patton, Athlone, London.

Deleuze, G. (1991) *Bergsonism*, trans. H. Tomlinson and B. Habberjam, Zone Books, New York.

Deleuze, G. and Guattari, F. (1984) *Anti-Oedipus: Capitalism and schizophrenia*, trans. R. Hurley, M. Seem and H.R. Lane, Athlone, London.

Deleuze, G. and Guattari, F. (1987) *A Thousand Plateaus*, trans. B. Massumi, University of Minnesota Press, Minneapolis.

Delphy, C. (1984) *Close to Home: A materialist analysis of women's oppression*, trans. and ed. D. Leonard, Hutchinson, London.

de Man, P. (1970) 'The intentional structure of the romantic image', in H. Bloom (ed.), *Romanticism and Consciousness*, Norton, New York, pp. 65–77.

de Man, P. (1979) *Allegories of Reading: Figural language in Rousseau, Nietzsche, Rilke, and Proust*, Yale University Press, New Haven, CT.

de Man, P. (1982) 'The resistance to theory', *Yale French Studies*, no. 63, pp. 3–20.

de Man, P. (1983) *Blindness and Insight: Essays in the rhetoric of contemporary criticism*, revised edition, Methuen, London.

de Man, P. (1984) *The Rhetoric of Romanticism*, Columbia University Press, New York.

de Man, P. (1986) *The Resistance to Theory*, Manchester University Press, Manchester.

de Man, P. (1988) *Wartime Journalism, 1939–1943*, ed. W. Hamacher, N. Hertz and T. Keenan, University of Nebraska Press, Lincoln.

de Man, P. (1989) *Critical Writings, 1953–1978*, ed. L. Waters, University of Minnesota Press, Minneapolis.

Derrida, J. (1973) *Speech and Phenomena, and Other Essays on Husserl's Theory of Signs*, trans. D.B. Allison, Northwestern University Press, Evanston.

Derrida, J. (1976) *Of Grammatology*, trans. G.C. Spivak, Johns Hopkins University Press, Baltimore, MD.

Derrida, J. (1978) *Writing and Difference*, trans. A. Bass, Routledge, London.

Derrida, J. (1979) *Spurs: Nietzsche's styles*, trans. B. Harlow, University of Chicago Press, Chicago.

Derrida, J. (1981a) *Dissemination*, trans. B. Johnson, Athlone, London.

Derrida, J. (1981b) *Positions*, trans. A. Bass, University of Chicago Press, Chicago.

Derrida, J. (1982) *Margins of Philosophy*, trans. A. Bass, University of Chicago Press, Chicago.

Derrida, J. (1983) 'The principle of reason: The university in the eyes of its pupils', trans. C. Porter and E.P. Morris, *Diacritics*, vol. 13, no. 3, pp. 3–20.

Derrida, J. (1984) 'Of an apocalyptic tone recently adopted in philosophy', trans. J.P. Leavey, *Oxford Literary Review*, vol. 6, no. 2, pp. 3–37.

Derrida, J. (1985) 'Racism's last word', trans. P. Kamuf, *Critical Inquiry*, vol. 12, no. 1, pp. 290–99.

Derrida, J. (1986a) 'But beyond ... (open letter to Anne McClintock and Rob Nixon)', *Critical Inquiry*, vol. 13, no. 1, pp. 155–70.

Derrida, J. (1986b) *Glas*, trans. J.P. Leavey and R. Rand, University of Nebraska Press, Lincoln.

Derrida, J. (1986c) *Mémoires: for Paul de Man*, trans. C. Lindsay, J. Culler and E. Cadava, Columbia University Press, New York.

Derrida, J. (1987a) *The Post Card: From Socrates to Freud and beyond*, trans. A. Bass, University of Chicago Press, Chicago.

Derrida, J. (1987b) 'Some questions and responses', in N. Fabb, D. Attridge, A. Durant and C. McCabe (eds) (1987), pp. 252–64.

Derrida, J. (1988) 'Like the sound of the sea deep within a shell: Paul de Man's war', *Critical Inquiry*, vol. 14, no. 3, pp. 590–652.

Derrida, J. (1989a) *Limited Inc.*, second edition with an Afterword, 'Toward an ethics of discussion', ed. G. Graff, Northwestern University Press, Evanston, IL.

Derrida, J. (1989b) *Of Spirit: Heidegger and the question*, trans. G. Bennington and R. Bowlby, University of Chicago Press, Chicago.

Derrida, J. (1991) *A Derrida Reader: Between the blinds*, ed. P. Kamuf, Harvester Wheatsheaf, Hemel Hempstead.

Derrida, J. (1992) *Given Time: 1. Counterfeit money*, trans. P. Kamuf, University of Chicago Press, Chicago.

Derrida, J. with McDonald, C.V. (1982) 'Choreographies', trans. C.V. McDonald, *Diacritics*, vol. 12, no. 2, pp. 66–76.

Descombes, V. (1980) *Modern French Philosophy*, Cambridge University Press, Cambridge.

Dews, P. (1987) *Logics of Disintegration: Post-structuralist thought and the claims of Critical Theory*, Verso, London.

Diamond, I. and Quinby, L. (1988) *Feminism and Foucault: Reflections on resistance*, Northeastern University Press, Boston, MA.

Dinnerstein, D. (1976) *The Mermaid and the Minotaur: Sexual arrangements and the human malaise*, Harper & Row, New York.

Docherty, T. (1990) *After Theory: Postmodernism/postmarxism*, Routledge, London.

Docherty, T. (ed.) (1993) *Postmodernism: A reader*, Harvester Wheatsheaf, Hemel Hempstead.

Dollimore, J. (1984) *Radical Tragedy: Religion, ideology and power in the drama of Shakespeare and his contemporaries*, Harvester, Brighton.

Dollimore, J. (1991) *Sexual Dissidence: Augustine to Wilde, Freud to Foucault*, Clarendon, Oxford.

Dollimore, J. and Sinfield, A. (1985) *Political Shakespeare: New Essays in Cultural Materialism*, Manchester University Press, Manchester.

Dollimore, J. and Sinfield, A. (1990) 'Culture and textuality: Debating cultural materialism', *Textual Practice*, vol. 4, no. 1, pp. 91–100.

Dreyfuss, H.L. and Rabinow, P. (1983) *Michel Foucault: Beyond structuralism and hermeneutics*, second edition with an Afterword by and an interview with Michel Foucault, University of Chicago Press, Chicago.

Duchen, C. (1986) *Feminism in France: From May '68 to Mitterrand*, Routledge, London.

Dworkin, R. (1977) *Taking Rights Seriously*, Harvard University Press, Cambridge, MA.

Eagleton, T. (1978) *Criticism and Ideology: A study in Marxist literary theory*, Verso, London.

Eagleton, T. (1981) *Walter Benjamin or Towards a Revolutionary Criticism*, Verso, London.

Eagleton, T. (1983) *Literary Theory: An introduction*, Blackwell, Oxford.

Eagleton, T. (1986) *Against the Grain: Essays 1975–1985*, Verso, London.

Eagleton, T. (1990) *The Ideology of the Aesthetic*, Blackwell, Oxford.

Eagleton, T. (1991) *Ideology: An introduction*, Verso, London.

Easthope, A. (1988) *British Post-structuralism since 1968*, Routledge, London.

Easthope, A. (1991) *Literary into Cultural Studies*, Routledge, London.

Ehrmann, J. (ed.) (1970) *Structuralism*, Doubleday, New York.

Eisenstein, H. (1984) *Contemporary Feminist Thought*, Allen & Unwin, London.

Eisenstein, H. and Jardine, A. (eds) (1980) *The Future of Difference*, G.K. Hall, Boston, MA.

Eisenstein, Z.R. (ed.) (1979) *Capitalist Patriarchy and the Case for Socialist Feminism*, Monthly Review Press, New York.

Eisenstein, Z.R. (1986) *The Radical Future of Liberal Feminism*, Northeastern University Press, Boston, MA.

Elliot, G. (1987) *Althusser: The detour of theory*, Verso, London.

Ellmann, M. (1968) *Thinking about Women*, Harcourt, New York.

Elshtain, J.B. (1981) *Public Man, Private Woman: Women in social and political thought*, Princeton University Press, Princeton, NJ.

Evans, J., Hills, J., Hunt, K., Meeham, E., Tusscher, T. ten, Vogel, U. and Waylen, G. (1986) *Feminism and Political Theory*, Sage, London.

Fabb, N., Attridge, D., Durant, A. and McCabe, C. (eds) (1987) *The Linguistics of Writing: Arguments between language and literature*, Manchester University Press, Manchester

Fekete, J. (ed.) (1984) *The Structural Allegory: Reconstructive encounters with the new French thought*, University of Minnesota Press, Minneapolis.

Felman, S. (ed.) (1982) *Literature and Psychoanalysis: The question of reading – otherwise*, Johns Hopkins University Press, Baltimore (originally a special issue of *Yale French Studies*, 1977, nos 55/56).

Felman, S. (1987) *Jacques Lacan and the Adventure of Insight: Psychoanalysis in contemporary culture*, Harvard University Press, Cambridge, MA.

Firestone, S. (1970) *The Dialectic of Sex: The case for feminist revolution*, Bantam Books, New York.

Fletcher, J. and Benjamin, A. (eds) (1990) *Abjection, Melancholia and Love: The work of Julia Kristeva*, Routledge, London.

Forrester, J. (1990) *The Seductions of Psychoanalysis: Freud, Lacan and Derrida*, Cambridge University Press, Cambridge.

Foucault, M. (1970) *The Order of Things: An archaeology of the human sciences*, Tavistock, London.

Foucault, M. (1973a) *The Birth of the Clinic: An archaeology of medical perception*, trans. A.M. Sheridan-Smith, Harper & Row, New York.

Foucault, M. (1973b) *Madness and Civilization: A history of insanity in the age of reason*, trans. R. Howard, Vintage, New York.

Foucault, M. (1974) *The Archaeology of Knowledge*, trans. A.M. Sheridan-Smith, Tavistock, London.

Foucault, M. (1977a) *Discipline and Punish: The birth of the prison*, trans. A. Sheridan, Pantheon, New York.

Foucault, M. (1977b) *Language, Counter-Memory, Practice: Selected essays and interviews*, ed. D.F. Bouchard, Blackwell, Oxford.

Foucault, M. (1978) *The History of Sexuality, vol. 1: An introduction*, trans. R. Hurley, Pantheon, New York.

Foucault, M. (1980) *Power/Knowledge: Selected interviews and other writings, 1972–1977*, trans. C. Gordon, L. Marshall, J. Mepham and K. Soper, ed. C. Gordon, Pantheon, New York.

Foucault, M. (1982) 'Afterword: The subject and power', in H.L. Dreyfus and P. Rabinow (1983), pp. 210–26.

Foucault, M. (1986a) *The Foucault Reader*, ed. P. Rabinow, Penguin, Harmondsworth.

Foucault, M (1986b) *The History of Sexuality, vol. 2: The use of pleasure*, trans. R. Hurley, Viking, London.

Foucault, M (1988a) *The History of Sexuality, vol. 3: The care of the self*, trans. R. Hurley, Harmondsworth, Penguin.

Foucault, M. (1988b) *Politics, Philosophy, Culture: Interviews and other writings, 1977–1984*, trans. A. Sheridan *et al.*, ed. L.D. Kritzman, Routledge, New York.

Foucault, M. (1988c) *Technologies of the Self: A seminar with Michel Foucault*, ed. L.H. Martin, H. Gutman and P.H. Hutton, Tavistock, London.

Foucault, M. (1991) *The Foucault Effect: Studies in governmentality*, ed. G. Burchall, C. Gordon and P. Miller, Harvester Wheatsheaf, Hemel Hempstead.

Fraser, N. (1981) 'Foucault on modern power: empirical insights and normative confusions', *Praxis International*, vol. 3, pp. 272–87.

Fraser, N. (1984) 'The French Derrideans: politicizing deconstruction or deconstructing politics', *New German Critique*, vol. 33, pp. 37–131.

Fraser, N. (1985) 'Michel Foucault: a Young Conservative?', *Ethics*, vol. 96, pp. 165–84.

Fraser, N. (1987) 'What's critical about Critical Theory? The case of Habermas and gender', in S. Benhabib and D. Cornell (eds) (1987), pp. 31–56.

Fraser, N. (1989) *Unruly Practices: Power, discourse and gender in contemporary social theory*, University of Minnesota Press, Minneapolis.

Frazer, E., Hornsby, J. and Lovibond, S. (eds.) (1992) *Ethics: A feminist reader*, Blackwell, Oxford.

Friedan, B. (1963) *The Feminine Mystique*, Dell, New York.

Freud, S. (1964) 'Femininity' in *The Standard Edition of the Complete Psychological Works of Sigmund Freud*, vol. 22. trans. J. Strachey, Hogarth, London.

Fuss, D. (1989) *Essentially Speaking: Feminism, nature and difference*, Routledge, New York.

Gallop, J. (1982) *Feminism and psychoanalysis: The daughter's seduction*, Macmillan, London.

Gallop, J. (1983) '*Quand nos lèvres s'écrivent*: Irigaray's body politic', *Romanic Review*, vol. 74, pp. 77–83.

Gallop, J. (1985) *Reading Lacan*, Cornell University Press, Ithaca, NY.

Gallop, J. (1988) *Thinking through the Body*, Columbia University Press, New York.

Gallop, J. (1990) 'Moving backwards or forwards', in T. Brennan (ed.) (1990), pp. 27–39.

Gasché, R. (1986) *The Tain of the Mirror: Derrida and the philosophy of reflection*, Harvard University Press, Cambridge, MA.

Gates, H.L. Jr (ed.) (1986) '*Race*', *Writing and Difference*, University of Chicago Press, Chicago.

Gates, H.L. Jr (1988) *The Signifying Monkey: A theory of Afro-American literary criticism*, Oxford University Press, New York.

Genette, G. (1980) *Narrative Discourse: An essay in method*, trans. J.E. Lewin, Blackwell, Oxford.

Genette, G. (1982) *Figures of Literary Discourse*, trans. A. Sheridan, Blackwell, Oxford.

Geuss, R. (1981) *The Idea of a Critical Theory: Habermas and the Frankfurt School*, Cambridge University Press, Cambridge.

Gilligan, C. (1982) *In a Different Voice: Psychological theory and women's development*, Harvard University Press, Cambridge, MA.

Giles, S. (ed.) (1993) *Theorizing Modernism: Essays in critical theory*, Routledge, London.

Gilman, C.P. (1966) *Women and Economics: A study of the economic relations between men and women as a factor in social evolution*, Harper & Row, New York.

Gramsci, A. (1971) *Selections from the Prison Notebooks*, trans Q. Hoare and G.N. Smith, Lawrence & Wishart, London.

Greene, G. and Kahn, C. (eds) (1985) *Making a Difference: Feminist literary criticism*, Methuen, London.

Greimas, A.-J. (1966) *Sémantique structurale: Recherche et méthode*, Larousse, Paris.

Griffiths, M. and Whitford, M. (eds) (1988) *Feminist Perspectives in Philosophy*, Macmillan, London.

Griffin, S. (1984) *Woman and Nature*, Women's Press, London.

Grossberg, L., Nelson, C. and Treichler, P.A. (eds) (1992) *Cultural Studies*, Routledge, New York.

Grosz, E. (1990) *Jacques Lacan: A feminist introduction*, Routledge, London.

Grosz, E. (1991) *Sexual Subversions: Three French feminists*, Allen & Unwin, Sydney.

Habermas, J. (1975) *Legitimation Crisis*, trans. T. McCarthy, Beacon Press, Boston, MA.

Habermas, J. (1977) 'Hannah Arendt's communications concept of power', *Social Research, Hannah Arendt Memorial Issue*, no. 44, pp. 3–24.

Habermas, J. (1984) *The Theory of Communicative Action: 1. Reason and the rationalization of society*, trans. T. MacCarthy, Beacon, Boston, MA.

Habermas, J. (1985) 'Modernity: an incomplete project?', in H. Foster (ed.), *Postmodern Culture*, Pluto, London, pp. 3–15.

Habermas, J. (1986a) 'Questions and counterquestions', in R.J. Bernstein (ed.) (1986a), pp. 192–216.

Habermas, J. (1987) *The Philosophical Discourse of Modernity: Twelve lectures*, trans. F. Lawrence, Polity, Cambridge.

Habermas, J. (1988) 'Walter Benjamin: Consciousness-raising or rescuing critique' in G. Smith (ed.) (1988), pp. 90–128.

Habermas, J. (1989a) *The Structural Transformation of the Public Sphere: An inquiry into a category of bourgeois society*, trans. T. Burger and F. Lawrence, MIT, Cambridge, MA.

Habermas, J. (1989b) *The Theory of Communicative Action: 2. Lifeworld and system: A critique of functionalist reason*, trans. T. MacCarthy, Polity, Cambridge.

Habermas, J. (1992) *Autonomy and solidarity: Interviews with Jürgen Habermas*, ed. P. Dews, revised edition, Verso, London.

Hall, S. (1980) 'Cultural studies: two paradigms', *Media, Culture and Society*, vol. 2, no. 2, pp. 57–72.

Hall, S. and Jacques, M. (eds) (1990) *New Times: The changing face of politics in the 1990s*, Lawrence & Wishart, London.

Hamacher, W., Hertz, N. and Keenan, T. (eds) (1989) *Responses: On Paul de Man's wartime journalism*, University of Nebraska Press, Lincoln.

Hamilton, R. and Barrett, M. (eds) (1986) *The Politics of Diversity: Feminism, Marxism and nationalism*, Verso, London.

Hansen, P. (1993) *Hannah Arendt: Politics, history and citizenship*, Polity, Cambridge.

Haraway, D.J. (1989) *Primate Visions: Gender, race, and nature in the world of modern science*, Routledge, New York.

Haraway, D.J. (1991) *Simians, Cyborgs, and Women: The reinvention of nature*, Routledge, New York.

Harding, S. (1986) *The Science Question in Feminism*, Cornell University Press, Ithaca, NY.

Harland, R. (1987) *Superstructuralism: The philosophy of structuralism and post-structuralism*, Methuen, London.

Hartman, G. (1981) *Saving the Text: Literature/Derrida/philosophy*, Johns Hopkins University Press, Baltimore, MD.

Hartmann, H. (1981) 'The unhappy marriage of Marxism and feminism: towards a more progressive union', in L. Sargent (ed.) (1981), pp. 1–41.

Harvey, I.E. (1986) *Derrida and the Economy of Différance*, University of Indiana Press, Bloomington.

Hasan, R. (1987) 'Directions from structuralism' in N. Fabb, D. Attridge, A. Durant and C. McCabe (eds) (1987), pp. 103–22.

Hawkes, T. (1977) *Structuralism and Semiotics*, Methuen, London.

Heidegger, M. (1967) *Being and Time*, trans. J. Macquarrie and E. Robinson, Blackwell, Oxford.

Heidegger, M. (1971) *Poetry, Language, Thought*, Harper Colophon, New York.

Heidegger, M. (1977) *Basic Writings*, ed. D.F. Krell, Harper & Row, New York.

Held, D. (1980) *Introduction to Critical Theory: Horkheimer to Habermas*, University of California Press, Berkeley.

Held, D. (ed.) (1991) *Political Theory Today*, Polity Press, Cambridge.

Hindess, B. and Hirst, P.Q. (1977) *Pre-Capitalist Modes of Production*, Routledge, London.

Hirschkop, K. and Shepherd, D. (eds) (1989) *Bakhtin and Cultural Theory*, Manchester University Press, Manchester.

Hirst, P.Q. (1976) 'Althusser and the theory of ideology', *Economy and Society*, vol. 5, pp. 385–412.

Hirst, P.Q. (1985) *Marxism and Historical Writing*, Routledge, London.

Holquist, M. (1990) *Dialogism: Bakhtin and his world*, Routledge, London.

Holub, R.C. (1991) *Jürgen Habermas: Critic in the public sphere*, Routledge, London.

Honneth, A. (1985) 'An aversion against the universal: A commentary on Lyotard's *Postmodern Condition*', *Theory, Culture and Society*, vol. 2, no. 3, pp. 147–57.

Honneth, A. (1991) *The Critique of Power: Reflective stages in critical social theory*, MIT, Cambridge, MA.

hooks, b. (1981) *Ain't I a Woman: Black women and feminism*, South End Press, Boston, MA.

hooks, b. (1984) *Feminist Theory: From margin to center*, South End Press, Boston, MA.

hooks, b. (1989) *Talking Back: Thinking feminist, thinking black*, Sheba Feminist, London.

hooks, b. (1991) *Yearning: Race, gender and cultural politics*, Turnaround Press, London.

Hoy, D.C. (ed.) (1986) *Foucault: A critical reader*, Blackwell, Oxford.

Hull, G.T., Scott, P.D. and Smith, B. (eds) (1982) *All the Women are White, All the Men are Black, But Some of Us Are Brave*, Feminist Press, Old Westbury, New York.

Humm, M. (ed.) (1992) *Feminisms: A reader*, Harvester Wheatsheaf, Hemel Hempstead.

Irigaray, L. (1985a) *This Sex Which Is Not One*, trans. C. Porter with C. Burke, Cornell University Press, Ithaca, NY.

Irigaray, L (1985b) *Speculum of the other woman*, trans. G.C. Gill, Cornell University Press, Ithaca, NY.

Irigaray, L. (1986) 'The fecundity of the caress: A reading of Lévinas, *Totality and Infinity*, section iv, B, 'The Phenomenology of Eros''', in R.A. Cohen (ed.) (1986), pp. 231–56.

Irigaray, L. (1991) *The Irigaray Reader*, ed. M. Whitford, Blackwell, Oxford.

Irigaray, L. (1992) *Elemental Passions*, trans. J. Collie and J. Still, Athlone, London.

Irigaray, L. (1993a) *An Ethics of Sexual Difference*, trans. C. Burke and G.C. Gill, Athlone, London.

Irigaray, L. (1993b) *Je, tu, nous: Toward a culture of difference*, trans. A. Martin, Routledge, New York.

Jacoby, R. (1981) *Dialectic of Defeat: Contours of Western Marxism*, Cambridge University Press, New York.

Jaggar, A. (1983) *Feminist Politics and Human Nature*, Harvester, Brighton.

Jaggar, A. and Rothenberg, P.S. (eds) (1993), *Feminist Frameworks: Alternative theoretical accounts of the relations between women and men*, third edition, McGraw-Hill, New York.

Jameson, F. (1972) *The Prison-House of Language: A critical account of structuralism and Russian formalism*, Princeton University Press, Princeton, NJ.

Jameson, F. (1974) *Marxism and Form: Twentieth-century dialectical theories of literature*, Princeton University Press, Princeton, NJ.

Jameson, F. (1983) *The Political Unconscious: Narrative as a socially symbolic act*, Methuen, London.

Jameson, F. (1988a) 'Cognitive mapping', in C. Nelson and L. Grossberg (eds) (1988), pp. 347–57.

Jameson, F. (1988b) *The Ideologies of Theory, Essays 1971–1986: 1. Situations of theory*, Routledge, London.

Jameson, F. (1988c) *The Ideologies of Theory, Essays 1971–1986: 2. Syntax of history*, Routledge, London.

Jameson, F. (1990) *Late Marxism: Adorno or the persistence of the dialectic*, Verso, London.

Jameson, F. (1991) *Postmodernism or the Cultural Logic of Late Capitalism*, Verso, London.

Jardine, A. (1985) *Gynesis: Configurations of woman and modernity*, Cornell University Press, Ithaca, NY.

Jardine, A. and Smith, P. (eds) (1987) *Men in Feminism*, Methuen, New York.

Jay, Martin (1973) *The Dialectical Imagination: A history of the Frankfurt School and the Institute of Social Research, 1923–50*, Heinemann, London.

Jay, M. (1984a) *Adorno*, Fontana, London.

Jay, M. (1984b) *Marxism and Totality: The adventures of a concept from Lukács to Habermas*, Polity, Cambridge.

Jefferson, A. and Robey, D. (eds) (1986) *Modern Literary Theory: A comparative introduction*, second, expanded edition, Batsford, London.

Johnson, B. (1980) *The Critical Difference: Essays in the contemporary rhetoric of reading*, Johns Hopkins University Press, Baltimore, MD.

Johnson, C. (1993) *System and Writing in the Philosophy of Jacques Derrida*, Cambridge University Press, New York.

Jones, A.R. (1984) 'Julia Kristeva on femininity: The limits of a semiotic politics', *Feminist Review*, vol. 18, pp. 56–73.

Kaplan, C. (1986) *Sea Changes: Essays on culture and feminism*, Verso, London.

Kaplan, E.A. and Sprinker, M. (eds) (1993) *The Althusserian Legacy*, Verso, London.

Kaplan, G.T. and Kessler, C.S. (eds) (1989) *Hannah Arendt: Thinking, judging, freedom*, Allen & Unwin, Sydney.

Katz, B. (1982) *Herbert Marcuse and the Art of Liberation: An intellectual biography*, Verso, London.

Kautsky, K. (1988) *The Materialist Conception of History*, ed. J.H. Kautsky, Yale University Press, New Haven, CT.

Kearney, R. (ed.) (1984) *Dialogues with Contemporary Continental Thinkers: The phenomenological heritage*, Manchester University Press, Manchester.

Kearney, R. (1987) 'Ethics and the postmodern imagination', *Thought*, vol. 62, pp. 39–58.

Kellner, D. (1984) *Herbert Marcuse and the Crisis of Marxism*, Macmillan, London.

Kelly, M. (1982) *Modern French Marxism*, Blackwell, Oxford.

Keohane, N.O., Rosaldo, M.Z. and Gelpi, B.C. (eds) (1982) *Feminist Theory: A critique of ideology*, Harvester, Brighton.

King, R.H. (1984) 'Endings and beginnings: Politics in Arendt's early thought', *Political Theory*, vol. 12, pp. 235–51.

King, R.H. (1992) *Civil Rights and the Idea of Freedom*, Oxford University Press, New York.

Koedt, A., Levine, E. and Rapone, A. (eds) (1973) *Radical Feminism*, Quadrangle Books, New York.

Kristeva, J. (1977) *About Chinese Women*, trans. A. Barrows, Marion Boyars, London.

Kristeva, J. (1981) *Desire in Language: A semiotic approach to literature and art*, trans. T. Gora, A. Jardine and L.S. Roudiez, Blackwell, Oxford.

Kristeva, J. (1984) *Revolution in Poetic Language*, trans. M. Waller, Columbia University Press, New York.

Kristeva, J. (1986) *The Kristeva Reader*, ed. T. Moi, Blackwell, Oxford.

Krupnik, M. (ed.) (1983) *Displacement: Derrida and after*, University of Indiana Press, Bloomington.

Kuhn, T. (1962) *The Structure of Scientific Revolutions*, University of Chicago Press, Chicago.

Kymlicka, W. (1991) *Contemporary Political Philosophy: An introduction*, Oxford University Press, Oxford.

Lacan, J. (1968) *The Language of the Self: The function of language in psychoanalysis*, trans., with commentary, by A. Wilden, Johns Hopkins University Press, Baltimore, MD.

Lacan, J. (1977) *Écrits: A selection*, trans. A. Sheridan, Tavistock, London.

Lacan, J. (1982) *Feminine Sexuality: Jacques Lacan and the 'école freudienne'*, trans. J. Rose, ed. J. Mitchell and J. Rose, Macmillan, London.

Lacan, J. (1986) *The Four Fundamental Concepts of Psycho-Analysis*, trans. A. Sheridan, ed. J.-A. Miller, Penguin, Harmondsworth.

Laclau, E. (1977) *Politics and Ideology in Marxist Theory: Capitalism-fascism-populism*, New Left Books, London.

Laclau, E. (1988) 'Politics and the limits of modernity', in A. Ross (ed.), *Universal Abandon?*, University of Minnesota Press, Minneapolis, pp. 63–82.

Laclau, E. (1990) *New Reflections on the Revolution of Our Time*, Verso, London.

Laclau, E. and Mouffe, C. (1985) *Hegemony and Socialist Strategy: Towards a radical democratic politics*, Verso, London.

Laplanche, J. (1976) *Life and Death in Psychoanalysis*, Johns Hopkins University Press, Baltimore, MD.

Larrain, J. (1979) *The Concept of Ideology*, Hutchinson, London.

Larrain, J. (1983) *Marxism and Ideology*, Macmillan, London.

Lauretis, T. de. (1984) *Alice Doesn't: Feminism, semiotics, cinema*, Macmillan, London.

Lauretis, T. de (1989) *Technologies of Gender: Essays on theory, film and fiction*, Macmillan, London.

Lavers, A. (1982) *Roland Barthes: Structuralism and after*, Methuen, London.

Lechte, J. (1990) *Julia Kristeva*, Routledge, London.

Lehman, D. (1991) *Signs of the Times: Deconstruction and the fall of Paul de Man*, Deutsch, London.

Leitch, V. (1983) *Deconstructive Criticism: An advanced introduction*, Hutchinson, London.

Lemaire, A. (1977) *Jacques Lacan*, trans. D. Macey, Routledge, London.

Lentricchia, F. (1983) *After the New Criticism*, Methuen, London.

Lévinas, E. (1981) *Otherwise than Being or Beyond Essence*, trans. A. Lingis, Nijhoff, The Hague.

Lévinas, E. (1985) *Ethics and Infinity*, trans. R.A. Cohen, Duquesne University Press, Pittsburg, PA.

Lévinas, E. (1989) *The Lévinas Reader*, ed. S. Hand, Blackwell, Oxford.

Lévinas, E. (1991) *Totality and Infinity: An essay on exteriority*, trans. A. Lingis, Dordrecht, Kluwer.

Lévinas, E. with Kearney, R. (1986) 'Dialogue with Emmanuel Lévinas', in R.A. Cohen (ed.) (1986), pp.13–33.

Lévi-Strauss, C. (1968a) *Structural Anthropology*, vol. 1, trans. C. Jacobson and B.G. Schoepf, Allen Lane, London.

Lévi-Strauss, C. (1968b) *Structural Anthropology*, vol. 2, trans. M. Layton, Allen Lane, London.

Lorde, A. (1984) *Sister Outsider: Essays and speeches*, Crossing Press, Trumansburg, NY.

Lukács, G. (1963) *The Meaning of Contemporary Realism*, Merlin, London.

Lukács, G. (1971) *History and Class Consciousness*, trans. R. Livingstone, Merlin, London.

Lukács, G. (1978) *Writer and Critic and Other Essays*, trans. and ed. A. Kahn, Merlin, London.

Lunn, E. (1985) *Marxism and Modernism: An historical study of Lukács, Brecht, Benjamin, and Adorno*, Verso, London.

Lyotard, J.-F. (1978) 'One of the things at stake in women's struggles', *Sub-stance*, vol. 20, pp. 9–17.

Lyotard, J.-F. (1984) *The Postmodern Condition: A report on knowledge*, trans. G. Bennington and B. Massumi, Manchester University Press, Manchester.

Lyotard, J.-F. (1987) 'The sign of history', trans. G. Bennington, in D. Attridge, G. Bennington and R. Young (eds) (1987), pp. 163–80.

Lyotard, J.-F. (1988) *The Differend: Phrases in dispute*, trans. G. van den Abbeele, Manchester University Press, Manchester.

Lyotard, J.-F. (1989) *The Lyotard Reader*, ed. A. Benjamin, Blackwell, Oxford.

Lyotard, J.-F. (1990) *Heidegger and the Jews*, trans. A. Michel and M. Roberts, University of Minnesota Press, Minneapolis.

Lyotard, J.-F. (1993a) *Libidinal Economy*, trans. I.H. Grant, Athlone, London.

Lyotard, J.-F. (1993b) *Political Writings*, trans. B. Readings with K.P. Geiman, University College Press, London.

Lyotard, J.-F. and J.-L. Thébaud (1985) *Just Gaming*, trans. W. Godzich, Manchester University Press, Manchester.

McCannell, J.F. (1986) *Figuring Lacan: Criticism and the cultural unconscious*, Croom Helm, London.

McCarthy, T. (1978) *The Critical Theory of Jürgen Habermas*, MIT, Cambridge, MA.

McClintock, A. and Nixon, R. (1986) 'No names apart: The separation of word and history in Derrida's *Le Dernier Mot du Racisme*', *Critical Inquiry*, vol. 13, no. 1, pp. 140–54.

McGuirk, B.J. (ed.) (1994) *Redirections in Critical Theory: Truth, self, action, history*, Routledge, London.

Macherey, P. (1978) *A Theory of Literary Production*, trans. G. Wall, Routledge, London.

MacIntyre, A. (1970) *Marcuse*, Fontana, London.

MacIntyre, A. (1985) *After Virtue: A study in moral theory*, second edition with postscript, Duckworth, London.

MacIntyre, A. (1988) *Whose Justice? Which rationality?*, Notre Dame University Press, Notre Dame, Indiana.

Macksey, R. and Donato, E. (eds) (1972) *The Structuralist Controversy: The languages of criticism and the sciences of man*, Johns Hopkins University Press, Baltimore, MD.

MacNay, L. (1992) *Foucault and Feminism: Power, gender and the self*, Polity, Cambridge.

Madison, G.B. (ed.) (1993) *Working through Derrida*, Northwestern University Press, Evanston.

Mandel, E. (1975) *Late Capitalism*, trans. J. de Bres, Verso, London.

Marcuse, H. (1941) *Reason and Revolution: Hegel and the rise of social theory*, Oxford University Press, New York.

Marcuse, H. (1964) *One Dimensional Man*, Beacon, Boston, MA.

Marcuse, H. (1968) *Negations: Essays in critical theory*, trans. J.J. Shapiro, Allen Lane, London.

Marcuse, H. (1969) *An Essay on Liberation*, Penguin, Harmondsworth.

Marcuse, H. (1970) *Five Lectures: Psychoanalysis, politics and utopia*, trans. J.J. Shapiro and S.H. Weber, Allen Lane, London.

Marcuse, H. (1974) *Eros and Civilization: A philosophical inquiry into Freud*, Beacon, Boston, MA.

Marks, E. and Courtivron, I. de (eds) (1981) *New French Feminisms: An anthology*, Harvester Wheatsheaf, Hemel Hempstead.

Massumi, B. (1992) *A User's Guide to 'Capitalism and Schizophrenia': Deviations from Deleuze and Guattari*, MIT, Cambridge, MA.

Megill, A. (1985) *Prophets of Extremity: Nietzsche, Heidegger, Foucault, Derrida*, University of California Press, Berkeley.

Melville, S. (1986) *Philosophy Beside Itself: On deconstruction and modernism*, Manchester University Press, Manchester.

Merleau-Ponty, M. (1973) *Adventures of the Dialectic*, trans. J. Bien, Northwestern University Press, Evanston, IL.

Merquior, J.G. (1985) *Foucault*, Fontana, London.

Miller, J.H. (1963) 'The literary criticism of Georges Poulet', *Modern Language Notes*, vol. 78, no. 5, pp. 471–88.

Miller, J.H. (1966) 'The Geneva School: the criticism of Marcel Raymond, Albert Béguin, Georges Poulet, Jean Rousset, Jean-Pierre Richard, and Jean Starobinski', *Critical Quarterly*, vol. 8, no. 4, pp. 302–21.

Miller, J.H. (1970) 'Geneva or Paris: the recent work of Georges Poulet', *University of Toronto Quarterly*, vol. 39, no. 3, pp. 212–28.

Miller, J.H. (1974) 'Narrative and history', *English Literary History*, vol. 41, no. 3, pp. 455–73.

Miller, J.H. (1976) 'Ariadne's thread: repetition and the narrative line', *Critical Inquiry*, vol. 3, no. 1, pp. 57–77.

Miller, J.H. (1982) *Fiction and Repetition: Seven English novels*, Blackwell, Oxford.

Miller, J.H. (1987a) *The Ethics of Reading: Kant, de Man, Eliot, Trollope, James, Benjamin*, Columbia University Press, New York.

Miller, J.H. (1987b) 'Presidential address, 1986: The triumph of theory, the resistance to reading, and the question of the material base', *PMLA*, vol. 102, pp. 281–91.

Miller, J.H. (1990) *Versions of Pygmalion*, Harvard University Press, Cambridge, MA.

Miller, J.H. (1991) *Hawthorne and History: Defacing it*, Blackwell, Oxford.

Millett, K. (1971) *Sexual Politics*, Avon, New York

Mills, C.W. (1956) *The Power Elite*, Oxford University Press, New York.

Mills, C.W. (1963) *Power, Politics, and People: The collected essays of C. Wright Mills*, ed. I.L. Horowitz, Oxford University Press, New York.

Mills, S., Pearce, L., Spaull, S. and Millard, E. (1989) *Feminist Readings/Feminists Reading*, Harvester Wheatsheaf, Hemel Hempstead.

Mitchell, J. (1971) *Woman's Estate*, Penguin, Harmondsworth.

Mitchell, J. (1975) *Psychoanalysis and Feminism*, Penguin, Harmondsworth.

Mitchell, J. (1984) *Women: The Longest Revolution: Essays in feminism, literature and psychoanalysis*, Virago, London.

Mitchell, J. and Rose, J. (eds) (1982) *Feminine Sexuality: Jacques Lacan and the 'école freudienne'*, trans. J. Rose, Macmillan, London.

Mitchell, W.J.T. (ed.) *Against Theory: Literary studies and the new pragmatism*, University of Chicago Press, Chicago.

Mohanty, C.T. (1984) 'Under Western eyes: Feminist scholarship and colonial discourse', *Boundary 2*, vol. 13, no. 1, pp. 333–58.

Moi, T. (1985) *Sexual/Textual Politics: Feminist literary theory*, Methuen, London.

Moi, T. (ed.) (1987) *French Feminist Thought: A reader*, Blackwell, Oxford.

Montefiore, A. (ed.) (1983) *Philosophy in France Today*, Cambridge University Press, Cambridge.

Montefiore, J. (1987) *Feminism and Poetry: Language, experience, identity in women's writing*, Pandora, London.

Moraga, C. and Anzaldua, G. (eds) (1981) *This Bridge Called My Back: Writings of radical women of color*, Persephone Press, Watertown, MA.

Mouffe, C. (ed.) (1979) *Gramsci and Marxist Theory*, Routledge, London.

Mouffe, C. (1988) 'Hegemony and new political subjects: toward a new concept of democracy', in C. Nelson and L. Grossberg (eds) (1988), pp. 89–104.

Mulhern, F. (1992) 'Introduction' to *Contemporary Marxist Literary Criticism*, ed. F. Mulhern, Longman, Harlow, pp. 1–33.

Muller, J.P. and Richardson, N.J. (eds) (1988) *The Purloined Poe: Lacan, Derrida and psychoanalytic reading*, Johns Hopkins University Press, Baltimore, MD.

Mulvey, L. (1989) *Visual and Other Pleasures*, Macmillan, London.

Murray, D. (ed.) (1989) *Literary Theory and Poetry: Extending the canon*, Batsford, London.

Nelson, C. and Grossberg, L. (eds) (1988) *Marxism and the Interpretation of Culture*, University of Illinois Press, Urbana.

Norris, C. (1982) *Deconstruction: Theory and practice*, Methuen, London.

Norris, C. (1983) *The Deconstructive Turn: Essays in the rhetoric of philosophy*, Methuen, London.

Norris, C. (1985) *The Contest of Faculties: Philosophy and theory after deconstruction*, Methuen, London.

Norris, C. (1987) *Derrida*, Fontana, London.

Norris, C. (1988) *Paul de Man: Deconstruction and the critique of aesthetic ideology*, Routledge, London.

Norris, C. (1990) *What's Wrong with Postmodernism: Critical theory and the ends of philosophy*, Harvester Wheatsheaf, Hemel Hempstead.

Norris, C. (1991) *Spinoza and the Origins of Modern Critical Theory*, Blackwell, Oxford.

Nozick, R. (1980) *Anarchy, State and Utopia*, Blackwell, Oxford.

Nozick, R. (1981) *Philosophical Explanations*, Clarendon, Oxford.

Nozick, R. (1993) *The Nature of Rationality*, Princeton University Press, Princeton, NJ.

Nussbaum, M. (1990) *Love's Knowledge: Essays on philosophy and literature*, Oxford University Press, New York.

Nussbaum, M. (1992) 'Human functioning and social justice: in defense of Aristotelian essentialism', *Political Theory*, vol. 20, no. 2, pp. 202–46.

Nussbaum, M. and Sen, A. (eds) (1993) *The Quality of Life*, Clarendon, Oxford.

Oakley, A. (1972) *Sex, Gender and Society*, Temple Smith, London.

Oliver, K. (ed.) (1993) *Ethics, Politics and Difference in Julia Kristeva's Writing*, Routledge, New York.

Parker, A. (1981) 'Taking sides (on history): Derrida re-Marx', *Diacritics*, vol. 11, no. 2, pp. 57–73.

Parkinson, G.H.R. (ed.) (1982) *Marx and Marxisms*, Cambridge University Press, Cambridge.

Plant, R. (1991) *Modern Political Thought*, Blackwell, Oxford.

Plekhanov, G.V. (1957) *Unaddressed Letters and Art and Social Life*, Progress Publishers, Moscow.

Plekhanov, G.V. (1967) *Essays in the History of Materialism*, trans. R. Fox, Howard Fertig, New York.

Plekhanov, G.V. (1969) *Fundamental Problems of Marxism*, trans. J. Katzer, Wishart, London.

Poster, M. (1976) *Existential Marxism in Postwar France: Sartre to Althusser*, Princeton University Press, Princeton, NJ.

Poster, M. (1984) *Foucault, Marxism and History: Mode of production versus mode of information*, Polity, Cambridge.

Putnam, H. (1981) *Reason, Truth and History*, Cambridge University Press, Cambridge.

Putnam, H. (1988) *Representation and Reality*, MIT, Cambridge, MA.

Ragland-Sullivan, E. (1986) *Jacques Lacan and the Philosophy of Psychoanalysis*, University of Illinois Press, Urbana.

Rajchman, J. (1985) *Michel Foucault: The freedom of philosophy*, Columbia University Press, New York.

Rajchman, J. and West, C. (eds) (1985) *Post-Analytic Philosophy*, Columbia University Press, New York.

Rawls, J. (1971) *A Theory of Justice*, Harvard University Press, Cambridge, MA.

Rawls, J. (1985) 'Justice as fairness: political, not metaphysical', *Philosophy and Public Affairs*, vol. 14, no. 3, pp. 223–51.

Rawls, J. (1993) *Political Liberalism*, Columbia University Press, New York.

Reader, K. (1987) *Intellectuals and the Left in France*, Macmillan, London.

Readings, B. (1991) *Introducing Lyotard: Art and politics*, Routledge, New York.

Rich, A. (1976) *Of Woman Born: Motherhood as experience and institution*, Virago, London.

Rich, A. (1980a) 'Compulsory heterosexuality and lesbian existence', *Signs*, vol. 5, no. 4, pp. 631–60.

Rich, A. (1980b) *On Lies, Secrets, Silence: Selected prose, 1966–1978*, Virago, London.

Rieff, P. (1966) *The Triumph of the Therapeutic*, Harper & Row, New York.

Rieff, P. (1975) *Fellow Teachers*, Faber, London.

Rieff, P. (1979) *Freud: The mind of the moralist*, University of Chicago Press, Chicago.

Rorty, R. (1979) *Philosophy and the Mirror of Nature*, Princeton University Press, Princeton, NJ.

Rorty, R. (1982) *Consequences of Pragmatism: Essays 1972–1980*, University of Minnesota Press, Minneapolis.

Rorty, R. (1989) *Contingency, Irony, and Solidarity*, Cambridge University Press, Cambridge.

Rorty, R. (1991) *Objectivity, Relativism, and Truth: Philosophical papers*, volume 1, and *Essays on Heidegger and Others: Philosophical papers*, volume 2, Cambridge University Press, Cambridge.

Rorty, R. (1992) 'The intellectuals at the end of socialism', *Yale Review*, vol. 80, no. 2, pp. 1–16.

Rosaldo, M.Z. and Lamphere, L. (eds) (1974) *Woman, Culture and Society*, Stanford University Press, Stanford, CA.

Rose, G. (1978) *The Melancholy Science: An introduction to the thought of T.W. Adorno*, Macmillan, London.

Rose, G. (1984) *Dialectic of Nihilism: Post-structuralism and law*, Blackwell, Oxford.

Rose, G. (1992) *The Broken Middle: Out of our ancient society*, Blackwell, Oxford.

Rose, J. (1986) *Sexuality in the Field of Vision*, Verso, London.

Rose, J. (1993) *Why War?: Psychoanalysis, politics and the return to Melanie Klein*, Blackwell, Oxford.

Roszak, T. (1970) *The Making of a Counter-Culture: Reflections on the technocratic society and its youthful opposition*, Faber, London.

Rowbotham, S. (1974) *Women, Resistance and Revolution*, Vintage, New York.

Ryan, M. (1982) *Marxism and Deconstruction: A critical articulation*, Johns Hopkins University Press, Baltimore, MD.

Said, E.W. (1975) *Beginnings: Intention and method*, Basic Books, New York.

Said, E.W. (1978a) *Orientalism*, Routledge, London.

Said, E.W. (1978b) 'The problem of textuality: two exemplary positions', *Critical Inquiry*, vol. 4, pp. 673–714.

Said, E.W. (1984) *The World, the Text and the Critic*, Faber, London.

Said, E.W. (1993) *Culture and Imperialism*, Knopf, New York.

Sallis, J. (ed.) (1987) *Deconstruction and Philosophy*, Chicago University Press, Chicago.

Salusinsky, I. (1987) *Criticism and Society: Interviews with Jacques Derrida, Northrop Frye, Harold Bloom, Geoffrey Hartman, Frank Kermode, Edward Said, Barbara Johnson, Frank Lentricchia, and J. Hillis Miller*, Methuen, London.

Sandel, M. (1982) *Liberalism and the Limits of Justice*, Cambridge University Press, Cambridge.

Sargent, L. (ed.) (1981) *Women and Revolution: A discussion of the unhappy marriage of Marxism and feminism*, South End Press, Boston, MA.

Sarrup, M. (1992) *Jacques Lacan*, Harvester Wheatsheaf, Hemel Hempstead.

Sartre, J.-P. (1965) *What is Literature?*, trans. B. Frechtman, Harper & Row, New York.

Saussure, F. de (1974) *Course in General Linguistics*, trans. W. Baskin, ed. C. Bally and A. Sechehaye with A. Reidlinger, Fontana, London.

Sawicki, J. (1991) *Disciplining Foucault: Feminism, power and the body*, Routledge, New York.

Sayers, J., Evans, M. and Redcliff, N. (1987) *Engels Revisited: New feminist essays*, Tavistock, London.

Scholem, G. (1988) 'Walter Benjamin and his angel', in G. Smith (ed.) (1988), pp. 51–89.

Schoolman, M. (1980) *The Imaginary Witness: The critical theory of Herbert Marcuse*, Free Press, New York.

Schor, N. (1985) *Breaking the Chain: Women, theory, and French realist fiction*, Columbia University Press, New York.

Sellers, S. (ed.) (1988) *Writing Differences: Readings from the seminar of Hélène Cixous*, Open University Press, Milton Keynes.

Shiach, M. *Hélène Cixous: The politics of writing*, Routledge, London.

Sheridan, A. (1980) *Michel Foucault: The will to truth*, Tavistock, London.

Silverman, H.J. (ed.) (1989) *Derrida and Deconstruction*, Routledge, London.

Silverman, K. (1983) *The Subject of Semiotics*, Oxford University Press, New York.

Sinfield, A. (1992) *Faultlines: Cultural materialism and the politics of dissident reading*, Clarendon, Oxford.

Skinner, Q. (ed.) (1985) *The Return of Grand Theory in the Human Sciences*, Cambridge University Press, Cambridge.

Slater, P. (1977) *Origin and Significance of the Frankfurt School: A Marxist perspective*, Routledge, London.

Smart, B. (1983) *Foucault, Marxism and Critique*, Routledge, London.

Smith, B. (1980) *Towards a Black Feminist Criticism*, Out-and-Out Books, New York.

Smith, G. (ed.) (1988) *On Walter Benjamin: Critical essays and recollections*, MIT, Cambridge, MA.

Smith, J.H. and Kerrigan, W. (eds) (1983) *Interpreting Lacan*, Yale University Press, New Haven, CT.

Smith, J.H. and Kerrigan, W. (eds) (1984) *Taking Chances: Derrida, psychoanalysis and literature*, Johns Hopkins University Press, Baltimore, MD.

Spivak, G.C. (1987a) *In Other Worlds: Essays in cultural politics*, Methuen, London.

Spivak, G.C. (1987b) 'Speculation on reading Marx: After reading Derrida', in D. Attridge, G. Bennington and R. Young (eds) (1987), pp. 30–62.

Spivak, G.C. (1990a) 'Feminism and deconstruction, again: negotiating with unacknowledged masculinism', in T. Brennan (ed.) (1989), pp. 206–23.

Spivak, G.C. (1990b) *The Post-Colonial Critic: Interviews, strategies, dialogues*, ed. S. Harasym, Routledge, New York.

Spivak, G.C. (1993) *Outside in the Teaching Machine*, Routledge, New York.

Spivak, G.C. with Danius, S. and Jonsson, S. (1993) 'An interview with Gayatri Chakravorty Spivak', *Boundary 2*, vol. 20, no. 2, pp. 24–50.

Stallybrass, P. and White, A. (1986) *The Politics and Poetics of Transgression*, Methuen, London.

Still, J. and Worton, M. (eds) (1993) *Textuality and Sexuality: Reading theories and practices*, Manchester University Press, Manchester.

Sturrock, J. (ed.) (1979) *Structuralism and Since: From Lévi-Strauss to Derrida*, Oxford University Press, Oxford.

Tallack, D. (ed.) (1987) *Literary Theory at Work: Three texts*, Batsford, London.

Tallack, D. (1987) 'Women in the thirties' in H. Ickstadt, R. Kroes and B.C. Lee (eds), *The Thirties: Politics and culture in a time of broken dreams*, Free Press, Amsterdam, pp. 85–119.

Taylor, C. (1985) *Philosophical Papers*, Cambridge University Press, New York.

Taylor, C. (1986) 'Foucault on freedom and truth' in D.C. Hoy (ed.) (1986), pp. 69–102.

Taylor, C. (1989) 'Cross-purposes: The liberal–communitarian debate' in N.L. Rosenblum (ed.), *Liberalism and the Moral Life*, Harvard University Press, Cambridge, MA, 1989, pp. 159–83.

Taylor, C. (1989b) *Sources of the Self: The making of the modern identity*, Cambridge University Press, Cambridge.

Thompson, E.P. (1966) *The Making of the English Working Class*, Vintage, New York.

Thompson, E.P. (1978) *The Poverty of Theory and Other Essays*, Merlin, London.

Thompson, J. and Held, D. (eds) (1982) *Habermas: Critical debates*, MIT, Cambridge, MA.

Thoreau, H.D. (1980) *Walden or, Life in the Woods*, Signet, New York.

Timpanaro, S. (1975) *On Materialism*, trans. L. Garner, Verso, London.

Todorov, T. (1975) *The Fantastic: A structural approach to a literary genre*, trans. R. Howard, Cornell University Press, Ithaca, NY.

Tong, R. (1989) *Feminist Thought: A comprehensive introduction*, Unwin Hyman, London.

Trebilcot, J. (ed.) (1983) *Mothering: Essays in feminist theory*, Rowman & Allanheld, Totowa, NJ.

Trinh, Minh-ha T. (1989) *Woman, Native, Other: Writing, postcoloniality and feminism*, University of Indiana Press, Bloomington.

Turkle, S. (1978) *Psychoanalytic Politics: Jacques Lacan and Freud's French revolution*, Basic Books, New York.

Ulmer, G.L. (1985) *Applied Grammatology: Post(e)-edagogy from Jacques Derrida to Joseph Beuys*, Johns Hopkins University Press, Baltimore, MD.

Veeser, H.A. (ed.) (1989) *The New Historicism*, Routledge, New York.

Voloshinov, V.N. (1973) *Marxism and the Philosophy of Language*, trans. L. Matejka and I.R. Titunik, Seminar Press, New York.

Voloshinov, V.N. (1976) *Freudianism: A Marxist critique*, trans. I. Titunik, Academic Press, New York.

Wallach, J.R. (1992) 'Contemporary Aristotelianism', *Political Theory*, vol. 20, no. 4, pp. 613–41.

Walzer, M. (1983) *Spheres of Justice: A defense of pluralism and equality*, Basic Books, New York.

Walzer, M. (1990) 'The communitarian critique of liberalism', *Political Theory*, vol. 18, no. 1, pp. 6–23.

Waters, L. and Godzich, W. (eds) (1989) *Reading de Man Reading*, University of Minnesota Press, Minneapolis.

Weber, M. (1974) *From Max Weber: Essays in sociology*, ed. H.H. Gerth and C.W. Mills, Free Press, New York.

Weber, M. (1930) *The Protestant Ethic and the Spirit of Capitalism*, trans. T. Parsons, Allen & Unwin, London.

Weedon, C. (1987) *Feminist Practice and Poststructuralist Theory*, Blackwell, Oxford.

West, C. (1989) *The American Evasion of Philosophy: A genealogy of pragmatism*, Macmillan, London.

White, H. (1987) *The Content of the Form: Narrative discourse and historical representation*, Johns Hopkins University Press, Baltimore, MD.

White, H. (1973) *Metahistory: The historical imagination in nineteenth-century Europe*, Johns Hopkins University Press, Baltimore, MD.

White, H. (1978) *Topics of Discourse: Essays in cultural criticism*, Johns Hopkins University Press, Baltimore, MD.

White, S.K. (1988) *The Recent Work of Jürgen Habermas: Reason, justice and modernity*, Cambridge University Press, Cambridge.

Whitford, M. (1990) 'ReReading Irigaray' in T. Brennan (ed.) (1990), pp. 106–26.

Whitford, M. (1991) *Luce Irigaray: Philosophy in the feminine*, Routledge, London.

Williams, P. and Chrisman, L. (eds) (1993) *Colonial Discourse and Post-Colonial Theory: A reader*, Harvester Wheatsheaf, Hemel Hempstead.

Williams, R. (1963) *Culture and Society 1780–1950*, Penguin, Harmondsworth.

Williams, R. (1965) *The Long Revolution*, Penguin, London.

Williams, R. (1977) *Marxism and Literature*, Oxford University Press, Oxford.

Williams, R. (1980) *Problems in Materialism and Culture*, Verso, London.

Williams, R. (1981) *Politics and Letters: Interviews with 'New Left Review'*, Verso, London.

Wittig, M. (1975) *The Lesbian Body*, trans. D. LeVay, William Morrow, New York.

Wittig, M. (1992) *The Straight Mind and Other Essays*, Harvester Wheatsheaf, Hemel Hempstead.

Wolfe, S.J. and Penelope, J. (eds) (1993) *Sexual Practice/Textual Theory: Lesbian cultural criticism*, Blackwell, Oxford.

Wood, D. (ed.) (1992) *Derrida: A critical reader*, Blackwell, Oxford.

Worton, M. and Still, J. (eds) (1990) *Intertextuality: Theories and practices*, Manchester University Press, Manchester.

Wright, E. (1984) *Psychoanalytic Criticism: Theory in practice*, Methuen, London.

Yale French Studies (1981) *Feminist Readings: French Texts/American Contexts*, no. 62.

Young, I. (1981) 'Beyond the unhappy marriage: A critique of the dual systems theory' in L. Sargent (ed.) (1981), pp. 43–69.

Young, I. (1986) 'The ideal of community and the politics of difference', *Social Theory and Practice*, vol. 12, no. 1, pp. 2–25.
Young, R. (ed.) (1981) *Untying the Text: A post-structuralist reader*, Routledge, London.
Young, R. (1990) *White Mythologies: Writing, history and the West*, Routledge, London.

Acknowledgements

Grateful acknowledgement is made to the following sources for permission to reproduce material in this book previously published elsewhere. Every effort has been made to trace copyright holders, but if any have been inadvertently overlooked the publisher will be pleased to make the necessary arrangement at the first opportunity.

PART 1

1.1: Reprinted by permission of the estate of the author, the translator, Jonathan Cape, and Farrar, Straus & Giroux Inc., 1972.

1.2: © The University of Chicago Press, 1981.

1.3: *Revolution in Poetic Language*, Julia Kristeva, 1984, © Columbia University Press, New York. Reprinted with permission of the publisher.

1.4: From *Power/Knowledge* by Michel Foucault © 1972, 1975, 1976, 1977 by Michel Foucault. Reprinted by permission of Pantheon Books, a division of Random House Inc.

1.5: Paul de Man, 'The Resistance to Theory', *Yale French Studies*, 1982.

1.6: *The Ethics of Reading: Kant, de Man, Eliot, Trollope, James, Benjamin*, 1987, © Columbia University Press, New York. Reprinted with permission of the publisher.

PART 2

2.1: © The University of Chicago Press, 1979.

2.2: From *Eros and Civilisation* by Herbert Marcuse, © 1966 Beacon Press. Reprinted by permission of Beacon Press.

2.3: From *Sexual Politics* by Kate Millett, © 1970 by Kate Millett. Reprinted by permission of Georges Borchardt, Inc. for the author.

2.4: From *Ecrits* by Jacques Lacan, translated by A. Sheridan. Routledge, London, 1977.

2.5: *Breaking the Chain: Women, Theory and French Realist Fiction* by Naomi Schor, 1985, © Columbia University Press, New York. Reprinted with permission of the publisher.

2.6: © University of Minnesota Press and Athlone Press Ltd, 1984.

PART 3

3.1: © South End Press, Boston, MA, 1981.

3.2: © University of Minnesota Press and Manchester University Press, 1986.

3.3: Reprinted from *Outside in the Teaching Machine* (1993), by permission of the publisher, Routledge, New York.

3.4: *Woman, Native, Other: Writing, Postcoloniality and Feminism* by Trinh T. Minh-ha, Indiana University Press, 1989.

3.5: From *The Straight Mind* by Monique Wittig. © 1992 by Monique Wittig. Reprinted by permission of Beacon Press.

3.6: Reprinted by permission of the publishers from *In a Different Voice* by Carol Gilligan, Cambridge, MA: Harvard University Press, © 1982 by Carol Gilligan.

PART 4

4.1: From *Illuminations* by Walter Benjamin. © 1973, Jonathan Cape.

4.2: From *Prisms* by Theodor Adorno, translated by S. and S. Weber, The MIT Press, 1967.

4.3: © Verso, London, 1971.

4.4: © Oxford University Press, 1977. Reprinted from *Marxism and Literature* by Raymond Williams (1977) by permission of Oxford University Press.

4.5: Reprinted with permission from *The Political Unconscious: Narrative as a Socially Symbolic Act* by Fredric Jameson, Routledge, 1983.

4.6: © Verso, London, 1975.

4.7: © Verso, London, 1985.

PART 5

5.1: From *Objectivity, Relativism, and Truth: Philosophical Papers*, Volume 1, Cambridge University Press, 1991.

5.2: © Polity Press, 1985.

5.3: © Polity Press, 1992.

5.4: © Manchester University Press and University of Minnesota Press, 1983.

5.5: © Manchester University Press and University of Minnesota Press, 1984.

5.6: Reprinted with permission from *Je, tu, nous: Toward a Culture of Difference* by Luce Irigaray, translated by A. Martin, Routledge, New York, 1993.

5.7: © Sage Publications Inc., 1992.

Index